Moral Philosophy

AN INTRODUCTION

Second Edition

Paul F. Fink
Moorpark College

Dickenson Publishing Company, Inc.

Encino, California and Belmont, California

FOR MY BROTHERS,
KARL, DAVID, AND RICHARD;
BUT ESPECIALLY FOR KARL,
WHO DIED TOO SOON.

ISBN: 0-8221-0207-2

Printed in the United States of America
Printing (last digit): 9 8 7 6 5 4 3 2 1

Library of Congress Cataloging in Publication Data

Fink, Paul F.   comp.
   Moral philosophy.

   Bibliography
   1. Ethics — Addresses, essays, lectures.   2. Social ethics
— Addresses, essays, lectures.   I. Title.
BJ1012.F5   1977   170'.8   77-9291

Cover design by Preston J. Mitchell.

Contents

Preface to the Second Edition

This anthology is meant to be used in an introductory philosophy course, and its special emphasis is upon the problems and theories of morality. The selections have been chosen to present the student with a variety of arguments which lead one naturally into the consideration of important philosophical issues. By beginning with a brief survey of several contemporary moral issues, the student comes to appreciate the need for an ethical theory. Then, once he has begun to clarify his own moral principles, an analysis of the classical moral systems is undertaken. Finally, after the student has acquired some familiarity with the history of moral philosophy, he is introduced to a systematic discussion of three problems that often have been a source of puzzlement to moral philosophers. Clearly, however, the material of the text may be organized in other ways depending upon the purposes and preferences of the instructor.

This second edition includes a number of new essays, especially in Part One. Articles dealing with the subjects of abortion, euthanasia, and suicide serve to update that portion of the text which deals with topics of current interest and controversy. And articles by Kate Millett, Peter Kropotkin, Alexander B. Smith and Harriet Pollack, Thomas Hobbes, and Abraham Maslow strengthen other sections. For advice in these matters I am indebted to the following persons: Dr. Shane Andre, California State University, Long Beach; Prof. Howard Cohen, University of Massachusetts, Columbia Point; Prof. Walter D. Douglas, San Bernardino Valley College; Prof. Richard H. Lineback, Bowling Green State University; Prof. Barbara Mackinnon, University of San Francisco; Prof. Daniel Passell, Portland State University; Prof. Bruce B. Suttle, Parkland College, Champaign, Ill.; Prof. Joan Thureson, El Camino College; and Prof. James W. Woelfel, University of Kansas.

P. F. F.

"For no light matter is at stake; the question concerns the very manner in which human life is to be lived."—Plato, *Republic,* Book I, 352-D.

Introduction

That moral problems are a perennial feature of human existence would hardly seem a matter for dispute. Even the most light-hearted and cavalier of persons occasionally encounters a serious moral problem that cannot be easily sidestepped or ignored. It is true that we ordinarily live our lives in such a way that these occasions are uncommon. And we generally prefer to avoid the responsibility of making decisions that have an important bearing upon our own lives and those of other people. Yet each of us has experienced the frustration of moral bewilderment. And most of us, at some time or another, have resolved to face up to the task of defining ourselves by our choices and actions.

For some persons the problem of self-definition does not involve the consideration of perplexing philosophical issues. Such persons seem to be content simply to absorb and repeat the customary modes of behavior that normally are acquired from our social environment. Our family, church, school, and friends provide us with numerous ready-made principles that may be applied to the solution of the moral problems that we encounter. But, while the uncritical acceptance and application of conventional maxims does seem to provide us with a measure of guidance for the conduct of our daily lives, the more reflective person cannot be so easily satisfied.

The reflective person begins to experience vague feelings of doubt and dissatisfaction with the everyday morality of our society as soon as he becomes aware of its many ambiguities and contradictions. And furthermore, these feelings usually are reinforced rather than lessened by an extensive consideration of the conflicting values which characterize our times. For not only is there a wide disparity between what is preached and what is practiced, there are also widely divergent positions being preached. Hence, in order to maintain a constant adjustment to our many-faceted society, it seems necessary to become a moral chameleon—to change one's moral principles as rapidly as is necessary to conform to the standards and practices of our immediate surroundings. But the inconsistency and superficiality of this fluctuating kind of existence is neither possible nor appealing to anyone who is determined to achieve some kind of constancy and integrity of character. For such a person is not content to allow himself and his moral principles to become simply and totally a by-product of his social environment.

Besides being dissatisfied with the confusion of values within our society, the reflective person is likely to be further disturbed by a comparison of our values with those of other societies and ages. Even a cursory glance at the evidence from anthropology and history indicates that there have been widely divergent positions maintained in regard to the specific forms of conduct that are thought to be good or bad, right or wrong. And it often happens that an awareness of this fact produces an attitude of skepticism, since one is forced to a realization that the values he professes are no more than a reflection of the manners and mores of his own culture. Hence one's moral preferences seem to be the result of mere accident: if one had been born at another time or in another culture he would have become accustomed to believing and acting quite differently. Accordingly, it is disconcerting to think that one's moral views are determined by caprice, or that there may be no reason for rating one's own views any higher than those of other nations and other cultures.

The comparison of many moralities tends to evoke feelings of apprehension and disenchantment. But the loss of moral naiveté need not become self-destructive; cynicism about morality is not an inevitable consequence of disappointment with our conventional mores. Instead, one may resolve to turn his doubts into a more constructive and mature form of response. He may undertake a systematic analysis of the structure and foundations of morality with the intention of articulating a more sophisticated morality than that of custom. If conventional morality is confused and capricious, why not develop an ethics that is clear and consistent?

At this point, then, one perceives the need for an ethical theory. Such a theory would consist in a set of principles by means of which a person could clearly and consistently distinguish between right and wrong, identify his moral obligations, and regulate his conduct. Also, since the construction of an ethical theory is a philosophical task, one is expected to provide arguments which constitute a justification for his position. In philosophy it is not enough merely to enunciate a position; one also is expected to defend it. Though it is true that some philosophers have maintained that an intellectual defense of a system of moral principles is not possible, most philosophers have provided a rationale for their commitments. But before one can become involved with the problem of justifying his ethical theory, he must first have identified the moral principles which distinguish it.

Perhaps the most natural way to begin this identification of one's moral principles is to render explicit those maxims which have tended to guide the choices that he has made in the past. This approach is most natural because a person's first attempt at an ethical theory usually involves reconstructing and formalizing those principles that he already holds implicitly. To facilitate this phase of one's inquiry, time should be spent thinking through some moral issues and isolating the principles that he is inclined to use in working out a solution. Then, once one becomes clear about his *prima-facie* moral principles, he can proceed to determine their order of priority. For, what does one do if a situation occurs where his principles seem to conflict with one another? Suppose, for example, that one maintains that it is wrong to lie. Suppose that same person also believes that it is wrong to cause other people to experience anxiety and distress.

What should one do in the case where his telling the truth will inevitably produce unhappiness? Should he lie and thereby diminish the pain others would experience, or should he tell the truth no matter what may be the consequences? Which principle should be given priority? Is the principle that is to be given priority in this case always to be given priority in case it conflicts with any other moral principle? Is there any principle which is so important that it always should be given first priority? What is this first principle of morality?

Questions such as these normally arise in the attempt to institute some kind of hierarchical order among one's moral principles. However, even if these questions are answered, one has not nearly finished his moral philosophizing. For it is now necessary to engage in a sustained critical analysis of the position which has been reached. This cross-examination might be accomplished in a variety of ways—indeed, there is no single set pattern for philosophical analysis. Nevertheless, one result of this analysis is the clarification of the various meanings intended for the concepts and modes of speech that are used in articulating the position. And another result is the identification of a number of beliefs that may have been presupposed as a part of the general philosophical framework within which one's position was delineated. But what reasons are there for thinking that these presupposed beliefs are sound? Furthermore, what beliefs have other thinkers taken as a basis for their ethical theories?

Fortunately it is not necessary to think through all of the problems of moral philosophy by oneself. The history of philosophy offers us guidance since it provides numerous examples of alternative systems of morals. Philosophers often have thought it important to formulate an ethical theory that was both more definitive and more refined than the conventional morality of their age and their culture. Sometimes their systems have incorporated much that was traditional, but on other occasions they have departed extensively from the prevailing morality of their contemporaries. In any case, their efforts in thinking through the issues, presuppositions, and implications of morality stand as milestones in the history of moral philosophy. Certainly no one of these systems deserves to be regarded as the final and complete truth about ethics; but each of these philosophers has expressed insights and formulated arguments that it would be unwise to overlook or ignore. Presumably, therefore, one might expect to learn something from these thinkers that would prove to be applicable in his own efforts at philosophizing.

Eventually the persistent philosophy student will come to realize that the construction of an adequate ethical theory is something that cannot be simply and easily accomplished. For, the more carefully one considers the problems of moral philosophy, the more he will appreciate their interrelationships with problems that are treated in other disciplines such as theology, metaphysics, epistemology, and psychology. This is because philosophy cannot be done in little self-contained bits and pieces. Rather, the persistent thinker will find that each of his philosophical commitments is likely to involve some presuppositions and implications which lead naturally into other fields of investigation. Hence the construction and justification of an ethical theory eventually leads to the much larger task of developing an over-all philosophical outlook—a comprehensive philosophy of life. And this requires the formulation of commitments about a variety of topics with which philosophers deal.

Finally, in addition to being impressed by the great complexity of philosophy, the serious thinker may begin to appreciate the importance of philosophizing. Very often philosophic inquiry points up many shortcomings in the beliefs and practices to which we give assent in our everyday lives. An awareness of these shortcomings makes it imperative to remake our pre-philosophical views into a set of ideas and principles that will be able to stand up under the rigorous critical analysis that philosophy imposes. This process of philosophical self-appraisal and self-definition is an important aspect of our lives. Indeed it may be maintained that the degree of care we exhibit in undertaking this task is one measure of our integrity as rational human beings. Hence, each of us, if we are determined to assume this responsibility, must face up to this obligation to philosophize. Perhaps there is no better time to begin than now.

✿ PART ONE

SOME CONTEMPORARY
MORAL ISSUES

Abortion, Euthanasia, and *Suicide*

❀ INTRODUCTION

Philosophical inquiry into morality often begins with the attempt to resolve specific personal problems: Should I finish college? Should I major in business administration or art or social welfare? Should I marry? Should I have children? Should I cheat on my income tax forms? Should I join a social club? To make decisions concerning such matters is a commonplace of life. Yet to make these decisions responsibly and well is not altogether easy. For it is clear that these questions soon lead to even more puzzling and more complex questions such as: What is right? What values are truly superior? What goals are worthy of attainment? What obligations should I honor? What is the source of these obligations? What is the relationship between morality and custom, between morality and the civil law? These latter questions require answers in terms of general rules and basic principles, and it is for this reason that they are philosophical.

Of all the questions we encounter, the most serious, the most thought provoking, the most disturbing are questions that involve life and death issues. A few of us may be fortunate enough to go through life without being required to make momentous decisions concerning our own death or that of others. But most of us, sooner or later, will find it necessary to take a stand. And, assuming that we would prefer to be intelligent about the matter, how do we intend to decide? It is much easier to honestly and objectively consider the issues *now* when we are not caught up in the drama and agony of the situation than to wait until it is no longer possible to think carefully and clearly. At least it may be possible at this time to formulate some kind of orientation toward these problems which, when it becomes necessary, can be used to stabilize our impulses and calm our conflicting emotions. For the time and character of our own death, at least, is something which concerns us all.

In the articles which follow, the authors consider three life and death issues: abortion, euthanasia, and suicide. Though not all possible points of view are presented, widely varying positions are introduced and defended. In the attempt to analyze and appraise each position it is useful to notice the way in which a writer's particular social, political, or religious commitment affects his specific treatment of the issues involved. But it is especially important to consider those arguments which are designed to convince the reader who does not share the broader commitment of the author. Often it is only this latter kind of claim that provides the leverage needed to change our beliefs and attitudes. And, after all, the broadening and redefining of our own commitments are what we are primarily interested in.

❀ RICHARD STITH

1. A Secular Case Against Abortion on Demand

Richard Stith is a professor at Washington University.

The trouble with the debate over abortion laws is that it has really never begun. Both sides have from the start been blind to the possibility of a public discussion of moral values. They have instead seen values as a matter of private revelation or even taste, and *de gustibus non disputandum.* Thus political pressure rather than rational discussion of the issues has been characteristic of the recent legislative history of abortion reform. Not surprisingly, the "debate" has now culminated in pressure for abortion "on demand," rather than abortion only with a reasonable justification. Abortion "on demand" is abortion given to anyone on request, provided only that it be medically feasible. The "on demand" means that abortion is considered a value-neutral technical operation which does not need justification. The public legal world of shared values passes away to leave behind agreement only on what is an efficient abortion. Even continuous debate over precisely *what* might justify abortion would tend to unite us as a community, if not in agreement at least in the hope of convincing each other of our arguments. Abortion "on demand" leaves us with nothing to say to each other as citizens.

Yet abortion need not have been considered a merely private or religious matter. I believe that the "proponents" (if I may be permitted an abbreviation for "those who lobby for abortion 'on demand' ") have failed to see what is publicly at stake: respect for human life and for their fellow citizens. In giving some examples of what they do not see, I am not arguing for a specific kind of abortion law. I am only arguing that the whole matter is still worth debating, and therefore that reasonable men and women should oppose abortion "on demand."

Proponents often dismiss the charge of homicide by asserting that the fetus cannot be proven to be a person. But of course it cannot be proven not to be a person either. Moreover, we agree that it is a person, entitled to legal protection, as soon as it is born. So the proponents would have to argue that some drastic change, from non-person to person, must have taken place at birth or at some earlier moment, unless they wish also to advocate infanticide. Medical evidence shows no such sharp discontinuity in the development of the embryo. Indeed, science could hardly begin to explain these developmental processes if it did not assume that the child is actually emerging in them, rather than that the fetus is a sort of blind

Reprinted from Richard Stith, "A Secular Case Against Abortion on Demand," *Commonweal,* November, 1971.

growth which might by chance become a person. If the proponents wish to allege that the fetus is not a person before a certain point, the burden of proof is upon them. Let them make a convincing argument that there is a "metaphysical" difference between a fetus and an infant, in spite of physical similarity. For example, if they wish to make birth the decisive criterion of personhood, they must show some difference in kind between a premature infant and an infant in the womb at the same stage of development—or between a fetus destroyed within the uterus and a twin brother by chance viable upon ejection, whose life we try to save.

Why don't the proponents of abortion see the need to prove that the fetus is not a person in order to say that abortion is not killing? Ironically, the proponents themselves must be surreptitiously and perhaps unconsciously using a particular *theological* criterion of personhood. There just seems to be no secular reason why a being at an earlier stage of development should not be presumed to be the same individual as at a later stage, even if his appearance changes. Is the first sprout of an oak tree not the same plant as the fully developed tree? Only if they imagine that the person does not *grow*, but is somehow infused whole as a "soul" into a merely animal "body," could they consider the fetus different in kind from some later stage of human development.

Why does the proponents' theology postpone "ensoulment" to some time near birth? I suppose that most of us treat other human beings as persons because we somehow "see," or otherwise sense, their personhood. However, the unborn child is hidden from view—is neither readily seeable, nor even nameable (because its sex is unknown). Perhaps this hiddenness accounts in part for the proponents' abstract conception of the fetus as a "body" without a "soul," as mere matter without a form and direction.

(Not that this hiddenness would be a *reason*, as opposed to a *cause*, for considering the fetus non-human—just as distance and skin tone should not be allowed to obscure the humanity of the Vietnamese. More education might help in both cases.)

Even if we did not consider the unborn child a person, it is clearly "human life." ("It's not an Airedale," as a friend of mine has remarked.) All other human life receives legal protection. So far at least, we do not have minimum standards that life must meet. We protect the sick and the deformed from casual slaughter, athough it might be argued that they have a far less human future before them than does a healthy fetus. Indeed, we even provide protection for *dead* human bodies. It is illegal to dig up and destroy dead bodies. Cannibalism is not something done "on demand." Yet the fetus is disposed of in abortion as though it were cancer or excrement. If we safeguard the dignity of human flesh even in a dead body, a body without a future, how much more should we care for an unborn child, a child in whom a human future surges!

Sometimes the proponents will grant that if one begins with the value of the infant, one is logically forced to accord a similar value to the fetus. However, they argue, if one accords such a value to the fetus, then one is logically forced to accord it to the sperm and to the ovum, and then to the testes and to the ovaries, *ad infinitum*. Which supposedly goes to show that one shouldn't take logic too seriously. Yet the blindness in their argument is serious. To see no difference between an unfertilized and fertilized egg is to fail to distinguish *probability* from *potentiality*. The unfertilized ovum is incomplete. Its probability of development depends on the *chance* that another half will join it to determine its future form. The fertilized egg, however, contains *completely* its own genetic "map" for development. All it asks from its environment is, essentially, food rather than form. (The issue would be very different if the mother's body took an active part in shaping and organizing the fetus during pregnancy.) Unlike between a fetus and an infant, there is a qualitative difference between an unfertilized egg and a fertilized one. This difference might be summarized most succinctly in saying that the fertilized egg *grows*, while the unfertilized egg does not.

Bodies as Objects

The argument that every woman has a right to "control over her own body" seems likewise blind. This argument *begins* by viewing our bodies as "objects" to be controlled and by atomistically assuming that each object is separable from every other object. But we do not "control" our bodies. We *are* our bodies, and our bodies are constantly connected to the world by myriad needs and obligations. Insofar as we do not have a right to control over ourselves, because we are required to respond to the obligations of community life, we do not have a right to control over our bodies either. How else could we pay taxes, yield the right of way, or obey any other law if not with our bodies?

The law does, of course, prohibit assaults on a person's body. We do have a right to be "let alone," which includes a right to protection, rather than control, of our bodies. But if the mother's body is "let alone," she will give birth! It is abortion itself which is an intrusion upon the woman's body. Moreover, abortion is not even "private" in the sense that it is done by the woman alone against herself alone. Besides the unborn child, at least the doctor, the state, and the father are involved. Even if the woman were to have a right to mutilate her own body or the growing life within it, the doctor does not. He could be held liable if he were to cut off a woman's leg "on demand," without medical necessity. Likewise he ought to be held liable for destroying the unborn without a reason. Even if we were to consider the fetus to be part of the mother, surely it should have the same protection from mutilation as does a leg. The state is also involved in abortions, at least insofar as it prescribes technical medical procedures, provides financial assistance, and repeals previously existing abortion laws. (Thus abortion "on demand" may well be unconstitutional, because the state is engaged in deprival of life without "due process" of law.) Finally, especially the father (and perhaps also society) has a very strong interest in the unborn child. After all, the child is his as much as it is the mother's.

She has no right to kill it arbitrarily, anymore than a trustee can arbitrarily destroy that with which he has been entrusted.

Now, both the father and society are often unconscionably negligent in protecting their "interest." They "entrust" the bearing and rearing of the child solely to the mother and go on their merry ways. Yet they have the audacity to punish the mother for wanting the same freedom from the burdens of a child which they enjoy. No wonder proponents of abortion attack such a system as "unfair"! It is unfair. The father and society have been totally irresponsible in failing to aid and comfort the child and the mother, especially the unwed mother. But why not strive for equal responsibility rather than equal irresponsibility? Surely, "two wrongs don't make a right" is a most elementary moral principle. We should have, at least, tighter paternity laws, more part-time jobs so that husband and wife can share childbearing, and severe penalties for any discrimination against unwed mothers. State and private agencies should also encourage and assist couples to adopt children rather than to have their own. By adopting children, we would open our private worlds to share the distress of our sister-citizens. And by *wanting* to adopt children, we would miraculously help to stop both population growth and the growth of that ethos which considers children burdens to be avoided. But instead of asking for these reforms, around which we could begin to build a true community, most proponents seem to tolerate and even encourage paternal and social irresponsibility, as long as the woman is likewise not made responsible for the child. Only an ideal of universal irresponsibility can account for the proponents' extraordinary answer to the "fairness" question.

Again, I am not arguing against more liberal abortion laws. I am saying only that the fetus has a public value, primarily as organized and growing human life, and therefore that its destruction requires a public justification. Abortion "on demand" should not be permitted. We ought not to imitate New York. However, given the extreme hardships which sometimes surround pregnancy, we might wish to legalize abortions in certain circumstances. Nor do I argue that the courts or a panel of doctors ought to be the judge of whether a particular woman's case fits the approved circumstances. Perhaps the woman alone should judge whether her case fits. Once we agree that abortion requires a justification, specifying both the justifications and the persons we would trust as judges would be the difficult task of public dialogue.

The first step to dialogue would be to treat seriously the opinions of those who oppose abortion. Most proponents act as though abortion "on demand" were just another political issue, like electing a President or building a new road. They seem to assume that once all the lobbying and voting are over, we will all go quietly home and carry on as usual. But many Americans consider at least some forms of abortion to be murder. *Murder!* It is not just another political issue, but is an assault on their most fundamental moral convictions. Many proponents say they consider an abortion not to be an issue of conscience at all, but a matter of what is convenient for the individual. Indeed, since liberalized but still restrictive abortion laws could presumably permit all morally appropriate abortions, the *only* additional abortions permitted by an "on demand" clause would be those done merely for convenience. Even someone who thinks that all morality is purely a subjective matter must see the subjective difference in intensity, in unselfishness, and in centrality to conscience, between the positions of those who oppose and of those who favor abortion "on demand." Yet the opinions of those in opposition are not respected. These opinions are belittled as mere "private religious beliefs," in spite of the fact that they are publicly understandable, and have a longer sanction in public tradition than have those of the proponents.

Even if a majority of citizens did favor legalization, and I think it does not, convictions so deep as those of the opponents of abortion must be taken into account if they are not to be wholly alienated from the body politic. And the fact that no one who does not believe in abortion will be forced to engage in abortion (as yet) does not help. It is like telling someone in Nazi Germany, "Don't worry, your hands are clean. *You* don't have to guard the camps." In order to go on supporting a government which he thinks kills the innocent, a person must surely begin to lose whatever moral standards he has. A nation of amoral beasts may be the result—either that or revolt. At least one New York state senator refused to agree to any aspect of the new budget, as long as it contained money "to kill babies." Other citizens might begin a tax revolt, refusing to finance what they consider murder. For the same reason (murder), our government may already be losing its support among many good people, because of the war in Vietnam. But at least there the government offers "justifications," which can be discussed and refuted. Abortions "on demand" require no justification whatsoever, in the eyes of the proponents. They are considered merely "private affairs." How would we feel if President Nixon were to call the war his "private affair," and to refuse to discuss it? Our alienation and frustration would then perhaps be equivalent to that which the opponents of abortion must feel when abortion "on demand" is legalized. Yet these feelings are ignored by the proponents as they maneuver toward legislative success.

It is sometimes argued that the population explosion is a justification for encouraging as many abortions as possible. Now, I assume that the proponents do not contend that anything that cuts down on population is *per se* good, since surely they would not approve of famine, war, or disease. Most people who make this argument, I think, mean that we should not get *more* people. They are for preventing human life rather than killing it. I certainly agree with them about the need for birth control of some kind. But in this essay, I have argued that in the unborn child we've already *got* human life. It's too late to argue for birth control!

Some may be so concerned about the population explosion that they really do favor killing existing human life, in order to preserve the lives of the rest of us. They would favor killing the unborn because they are the least developed, and most easily disposed of, part of the human race. Such an argument is at least an honest one. But once we declare the unborn unworthy to live, would we necessarily stop there? Might we not eventually execute the deformed, the old, or the unintelligent?

The underlying assumption made by the proponents of abortion "on demand" appears to be this: dependency entails control. They seem to assume that if something is within our power, is dependent on us, then we have a right to total control over it, even to the point of destroying it. Now, the unborn child is clearly and inevitably totally dependent for nurture on its mother, so dependent that it cannot even be seen and grasped as a separate object. Therefore, the proponents can conclude that she has the right to destroy it. The same logic would make the proponents ignore the humanity of the destroyed unborn child. For if to be human is to have rights, and if to be dependent is to have no rights, then nothing which is dependent can be considered human. Humanity becomes characterized by individual independence of self-sufficiency. Indeed, the only argument which I have ever heard which sought to prove that the fetus is non-human is that it is not "self-sufficient" or "viable." I suspect that the proponents may think that since the unborn child cannot be independently seen and grasped, it simply does not exist, except perhaps subjectively.

Ordinary moral sensibility leads to a different conclusion. We generally feel that when someone is dependent on us, we are responsible for him. We do not thereby acquire rights over him. If anything, he acquires "rights" over us—not a right to just anything, but the right to be *cared* for, to be helped toward a healthy development. Dependency entails care, not control. Our arbitrary freedom is thus limited by having others depend on us. For example, a king ought to be far less free to follow his whims than are his subjects, insofar as they are dependent on him. Otherwise he is a tyrant. Precisely because the child is utterly dependent on the mother for its very existence, she has the greatest possible responsibility to care for it. And dependency does not make it less human. We are all dependent on others, although our dependency is not so focused as is the child's on its mother. And we, too have a kind of "right" to be cared for by those on whom we depend. A pregnant woman may not have a right to total control over the child, but both she and the child have a right to care from those on whom they depend, the father and society. Being cared for by others does not degrade our humanity, but elevates it. If the unborn child depends on us to recognize its very existence, it, too, is made no less human. To be held in memory or in anticipation, to be *believed* in by other men from whom he is partially or entirely hidden—that is one of the greatest honors a person can receive.

Care rather than control is, of course, possible only if we believe that the future is not wholly our invention. The ultimate issue is not whether we believe in abortion but whether we believe in pregnancy. If things and people are "pregnant," if they have "promise," if they "grow"

—in short, if they have *meaning*—then we have no right to impose our whims on them like tyrants. If we do interfere with them, we must at least have a justification. Such an attitude is no doubt difficult in a technological age bent on control of all things. Yet it is required not only for morality but for all understanding of nature. Hopefully the ecological issues are helping us realize that we cannot with impudence impose just any future on our natural environment. And if we can at least continue to believe that women can be pregnant, that they can carry the future within them, perhaps someday we may also see the "pregnancy," the meaning, of men and things.

🌸 JUDITH JARVIS THOMSON

2. *A Defense of Abortion*[1]

Judith Jarvis Thomson is a philosophy professor at the Massachusetts Institute of Technology.

Most opposition to abortion relies on the premise that the fetus is a human being, a person, from the moment of conception. The premise is argued for, but, as I think, not well. Take, for example, the most common argument. We are asked to notice that the development of a human being from conception through birth into childhood is continuous; then it is said that to draw a line, to choose a point in this development and say "before this point the thing is not a person, after this point it is a person" is to make an arbitrary choice, a choice for which in the nature of things no good reason can be given. It is concluded that the fetus is, or anyway that we had better say it is, a person from the moment of conception. But this conclusion does not follow. Similar things might be said about the development of an acorn into an oak tree, and it does not follow that acorns are oak trees, or that we had better say they are. Arguments of this form are sometimes called "slippery slope arguments"—the phrase is perhaps self-explanatory—and it is dismaying that opponents of abortion rely on them so heavily and uncritically.

I am inclined to agree, however, that the prospects for "drawing a line" in the development of the fetus look dim. I am inclined to think also that we shall probably have to agree that the fetus has already become a human person well before birth. Indeed, it comes as a surprise when one first learns how early in its life it begins to acquire human characteristics. By the tenth week, for example, it already has a face, arms and legs, fingers

Reprinted from Judith Jarvis Thomson, "A Defense of Abortion," *Philosophy and Public Affairs*, Vol. 1, No. 1, pp. 47–66. Copyright © 1971 by Princeton University Press. Reprinted by permission of Princeton University Press.

[1] I am very much indebted to James Thomson for discussion, criticism, and many helpful suggestions.

and toes; it has internal organs, and brain activity is detectable.[2] On the other hand, I think that the premise is false, that the fetus is not a person from the moment of conception. A newly fertilized ovum, a newly implanted clump of cells, is no more a person than an acorn is an oak tree. But I shall not discuss any of this. For it seems to me to be of great interest to ask what happens if, for the sake of argument, we allow the premise. How, precisely, are we supposed to get from there to the conclusion that abortion is morally impermissible? Opponents of abortion commonly spend most of their time establishing that the fetus is a person, and hardly any time explaining the step from there to the impermissibility of abortion. Perhaps they think the step too simple and obvious to require much comment. Or perhaps instead they are simply being economical in argument. Many of those who defend abortion rely on the premise that the fetus is not a person, but only a bit of tissue that will become a person at birth; and why pay out more arguments than you have to? Whatever the explanation, I suggest that the step they take is neither easy nor obvious, that it calls for closer examination than it is commonly given, and that when we do give it this closer examination we shall feel inclined to reject it.

I propose, then, that we grant that the fetus is a person from the moment of conception. How does the argument go from here? Something like this, I take it. Every person has a right to life. So the fetus has a right to life. No doubt the mother has a right to decide what shall happen in and to her body; everyone would grant that. But surely a person's right to life is stronger and more stringent than the mother's right to decide what happens in and to her body, and so outweighs it. So the fetus may not be killed; an abortion may not be performed.

It sounds plausible. But now let me ask you to imagine this. You wake up in the morning and find yourself back to back in bed with an unconscious violinist. A famous unconscious violinist. He has been found to have a fatal kidney ailment, and the Society of Music Lovers has canvassed all the available medical records and found that you alone have the right blood type to help. They have therefore kidnapped you, and last night the violinist's circulatory system was plugged into yours, so that your kidneys can be used to extract poisons from his blood as well as your own. The director of the hospital now tells you, "Look, we're sorry the Society of Music Lovers did this to you—we would never have permitted it if we had known. But still, they did it, and the violinist now is plugged into you. To unplug you would be to kill him. But never mind, it's only for nine months. By then he will have recovered from his ailment, and can safely be unplugged from you." Is it morally incumbent on you to accede to this

---

2Daniel Callahan, *Abortion: Law, Choice and Morality* (New York, 1970), p. 373. This book gives a fascinating survey of the available information on abortion. The Jewish tradition is surveyed in David M. Feldman, *Birth Control in Jewish Law* (New York, 1968), Part 5, the Catholic tradition in John T. Noonan, Jr., "An Almost Absolute Value in History," in *The Morality of Abortion*, ed. John T. Noonan, Jr. (Cambridge, Mass., 1970).

situation? No doubt it would be very nice of you if you did, a great kindness. But do you *have* to accede to it? What if it were not nine months, but nine years? Or longer still? What if the director of the hospital says, "Tough luck, I agree, but you've now got to stay in bed, with the violinist plugged into you, for the rest of your life. Because remember this. All persons have a right to life, and violinists are persons. Granted you have a right to decide what happens in and to your body, but a person's right to life outweighs your right to decide what happens in and to your body. So you cannot ever be unplugged from him." I imagine you would regard this as outrageous, which suggests that something really is wrong with that plausible-sounding argument I mentioned a moment ago.

In this case, of course, you were kidnapped; you didn't volunteer for the operation that plugged the violinist into your kidneys. Can those who oppose abortion on the ground I mentioned make an exception for a pregnancy due to rape? Certainly. They can say that persons have a right to life only if they didn't come into existence because of rape; or they can say that all persons have a right to life, but that some have less of a right to life than others, in particular, that those who came into existence because of rape have less. But these statements have a rather unpleasant sound. Surely the question of whether you have a right to life at all, or how much of it you have, shouldn't turn on the question of whether or not you are the product of a rape. And in fact the people who oppose abortion on the ground I mentioned do not make this distinction, and hence do not make an exception in case of rape.

Nor do they make an exception for a case in which the mother has to spend the nine months of her pregnancy in bed. They would agree that would be a great pity, and hard on the mother; but all the same, all persons have a right to life, the fetus is a person, and so on. I suspect, in fact, that they would not make an exception for a case in which, miraculously enough, the pregnancy went on for nine years, or even the rest of the mother's life.

Some won't even make an exception for a case in which continuation of the pregnancy is likely to shorten the mother's life; they regard abortion as impermissible even to save the mother's life. Such cases are nowadays very rare, and many opponents of abortion do not accept this extreme view. All the same, it is a good place to begin; a number of points of interest come out in respect to it.

1. Let us call the view that abortion is impermissible even to save the mother's life "the extreme view." I want to suggest first that it does not issue from the argument I mentioned earlier without the addition of some fairly powerful premises. Suppose a woman has become pregnant, and now learns that she has a cardiac condition such that she will die if she carries the baby to term. What may be done for her? The fetus, being a person, has a right to life, but as the mother is a person too, so has she a right to life. Presumably they have an equal right to life. How is it supposed to come out that an abortion may not be performed? If mother and child have an equal right to life, shouldn't we perhaps flip a coin? Or should we add to the

mother's right to life her right to decide what happens in and to her body, which everybody seems to be ready to grant—the sum of her rights now outweighing the fetus' right to life?

The most familiar argument here is the following. We are told that performing the abortion would be directly killing[3] the child, whereas doing nothing would not be killing the mother, but only letting her die. Moreover, in killing the child, one would be killing an innocent person, for the child has committed no crime, and is not aiming at his mother's death. And then there are a variety of ways in which this might be continued. (1) But as directly killing an innocent person is always and absolutely impermissible, an abortion may not be performed. Or, (2) as directly killing an innocent person is murder, and murder is always and absolutely impermissible, an abortion may not be performed.[4] Or, (3) as one's duty to refrain from directly killing an innocent person is more stringent than one's duty to keep a person from dying, an abortion may not be performed. Or, (4) if one's only options are directly killing an innocent person or letting a person die, one must prefer letting the person die, and thus an abortion may not be performed.[5]

Some people seem to have thought that these are not further premises which must be added if the conclusion is to be reached, but that they follow from the very fact that an innocent person has a right to life.[6] But this seems to me to be a mistake, and perhaps the simplest way to show this is to bring out that while we must certainly grant that innocent persons have a right to life, the theses in (1) through (4) are all false. Take (2), for ex-

---

[3]The term "direct" in the arguments I refer to is a technical one. Roughly, what is meant by "direct killing" is either killing as an end in itself, or killing as a means to some end, for example, the end of saving someone else's life. See note 6 . . . for an example of its use.

[4]Cf. *Encyclical Letter of Pope Pius XI on Christian Marriage,* St. Paul Editions (Boston, n.d.), p. 32: "however much we may pity the mother whose health and even life is gravely imperiled in the performance of the duty allotted to her by nature, nevertheless what could ever be a sufficient reason for excusing in any way the direct murder of the innocent? This is precisely what we are dealing with here." Noonan (*The Morality of Abortion,* p. 43) reads this as follows: "What cause can ever avail to excuse in any way the direct killing of the innocent? For it is a question of that."

[5]The thesis in (4) is in an interesting way weaker than those in (1), (2), and (3): they rule out abortion even in cases in which both mother *and* child will die if the abortion is not performed. By contrast, one who held the view expressed in (4) could consistently say that one needn't prefer letting two persons die to killing one.

[6]Cf. the following passage from Pius XII, *Address to the Italian Catholic Society of Midwives*: "The baby in the maternal breast has the right to life immediately from God.—Hence there is no man, no human authority, no science, no medical, eugenic, social, economic or moral 'indication' which can establish or grant a valid juridical ground for a direct deliberate disposition of an innocent human life, that is a disposition which looks to its destruction either as an end or as a means to another end perhaps in itself not illicit.—The baby, still not born, is a man in the same degree and for the same reason as the mother" (quoted in Noonan, *The Morality of Abortion,* p. 45).

ample. If directly killing an innocent person is murder, and thus is impermissible, then the mother's directly killing the innocent person inside her is murder, and thus is impermissible. But it cannot seriously be thought to be murder if the mother performs an abortion on herself to save her life. It cannot seriously be said that she *must* refrain, that she *must* sit passively by and wait for her death. Let us look again at the case of you and the violinist. There you are, in bed with the violinist, and the director of the hospital says to you, "It's all most distressing, and I deeply sympathize, but you see this is putting an additional strain on your kidneys, and you'll be dead within the month. But you *have* to stay where you are all the same. Because unplugging you would be directly killing an innocent violinist, and that's murder, and that's impermissible." If anything in the world is true, it is that you do not commit murder, you do not do what is impermissible, if you reach around to your back and unplug yourself from that violinist to save your life.

The main focus of attention in writings on abortion has been on what a third party may or may not do in answer to a request from a woman for an abortion. This is in a way understandable. Things being as they are, there isn't much a woman can safely do to abort herself. So the question asked is what a third party may do, and what the mother may do, if it is mentioned at all, is deduced, almost as an afterthought, from what it is concluded that third parties may do. But it seems to me that to treat the matter in this way is to refuse to grant to the mother that very status of person which is so firmly insisted on for the fetus. For we cannot simply read off what a person may do from what a third party may do. Suppose you find yourself trapped in a tiny house with a growing child. I mean a very tiny house, and a rapidly growing child—you are already up against the wall of the house and in a few minutes you'll be crushed to death. The child on the other hand won't be crushed to death; if nothing is done to stop him from growing he'll be hurt, but in the end he'll simply burst open the house and walk out a free man. Now I could well understand it if a bystander were to say, "There's nothing we can do for you. We cannot choose between your life and his, we cannot be the ones to decide who is to live, we cannot intervene." But it cannot be concluded that you too can do nothing, that you cannot attack it to save your life. However innocent the child may be, you do not have to wait passively while it crushes you to death. Perhaps a pregnant woman is vaguely felt to have the status of house, to which we don't allow the right of self-defense. But if the woman houses the child, it should be remembered that she is a person who houses it.

I should perhaps stop to say explicitly that I am not claiming that people have a right to do anything whatever to save their lives. I think, rather, that there are drastic limits to the right of self-defense. If someone threatens you with death unless you torture someone else to death, I think you have not the right, even to save your life, to do so. But the case under consideration here is very different. In our case there are only two people involved, one whose life is threatened, and one who threatens it. Both are innocent; the one who is threatened is not threatened because of any fault, the one who threatens does not threaten because of any fault. For this reason we may feel that we bystanders cannot intervene. But the person threatened can.

In sum, a woman surely can defend her life against the threat to it posed by the unborn child, even if doing so involves its death. And this shows not merely that the theses in (1) through (4) are false; it shows also that the extreme view of abortion is false, and so we need not canvass any other possible ways of arriving at it from the argument I mentioned at the outset.

2.   The extreme view could of course be weakened to say that while abortion is permissible to save the mother's life, it may not be performed by a third party, but only by the mother herself. But this cannot be right either. For what we have to keep in mind is that the mother and the unborn child are not like two tenants in a small house which has, by an unfortunate mistake, been rented to both: the mother *owns* the house. The fact that she does adds to the offensiveness of deducing that the mother can do nothing from the supposition that third parties can do nothing. But it does more than this: it casts a bright light on the supposition that third parties can do nothing. Certainly it lets us see that a third party who says "I cannot choose between you" is fooling himself if he thinks this is impartiality. If Jones has found and fastened on a certain coat, which he needs to keep him from freezing, but which Smith also needs to keep him from freezing, then it is not impartiality that says "I cannot choose between you" when Smith owns the coat. Women have said again and again "This body is *my* body!" and they have reason to feel angry, reason to feel that it has been like shouting into the wind. Smith, after all, is hardly likely to bless us if we say to him, "Of course it's your coat, anybody would grant that it is. But no one may choose between you and Jones who is to have it."

We should really ask what it is that says "no one may choose" in the face of the fact that the body that houses the child is the mother's body. It may be simply a failure to appreciate this fact. But it may be something more interesting, namely the sense that one has a right to refuse to lay hands on people, even where it would be just and fair to do so, even where justice seems to require that somebody do so. Thus justice might call for somebody to get Smith's coat back from Jones, and yet you have a right to refuse to be the one to lay hands on Jones, a right to refuse to do physical violence to him. This, I think, must be granted. But then what should be said is not "no one may choose," but only "*I* cannot choose," and indeed not even this, but "*I* will not *act*," leaving it open that somebody else can or should, and in particular that anyone in a position of authority, with the job of securing people's rights, both can and should. So this is no difficulty. I have not been arguing that any given third party must accede to the mother's request that he perform an abortion to save her life, but only that he may.

I suppose that in some views of human life the mother's body is only on loan to her, the loan not being one which gives her any prior claim to it. One who held this view might well think it impartiality to say "I cannot choose." But I shall simply ignore this possibility. My own view is that if a human being has any just, prior claim to anything at all, he has a just, prior claim to his own body. And perhaps this needn't be argued for here anyway, since, as I mentioned, the arguments against abortion we are look-ing at do grant that the woman has a right to decide what happens in and to her body.

But although they do grant it, I have tried to show that they do not take seriously what is done in granting it. I suggest the same thing will re-appear even more clearly when we turn away from cases in which the mother's life is at stake, and attend, as I propose we now do, to the vastly more common cases in which a woman wants an abortion for some less weighty reason than preserving her own life.

3. Where the mother's life is not at stake, the argument I men-tioned at the outset seems to have a much stronger pull. "Everyone has a right to life, so the unborn person has a right to life." And isn't the child's right to life weightier than anything other than the mother's own right to life, which she might put forward as ground for an abortion?

This argument treats the right to life as if it were unproblematic. It is not, and this seems to me to be precisely the source of the mistake.

For we should now, at long last, ask what it comes to, to have a right to life. In some views having a right to life includes having a right to be given at least the bare minimum one needs for continued life. But sup-pose that what in fact *is* the bare minimum a man needs for continued life is something he has no right at all to be given? If I am sick unto death, and the only thing that will save my life is the touch of Henry Fonda's cool hand on my fevered brow, then all the same, I have no right to be given the touch of Henry Fonda's cool hand on my fevered brow. It would be frightfully nice of him to fly in from the West Coast to provide it. It would be less nice, though no doubt well meant, if my friends flew out to the West Coast and carried Henry Fonda back with them. But I have no right at all against anybody that he should do this for me. Or again, to return to the story I told earlier, the fact that for continued life that violinist needs the continued use of your kidneys does not establish that he has a right to be given the continued use of your kidneys. He certainly has no right against you that *you* should give him continued use of your kidneys. For nobody has any right to use your kidneys unless you give him such a right; and nobody has the right against you that you shall give him this right—if you do allow him to go on using your kidneys, this is a kindness on your part, and not something he can claim from you as his due. Nor has he any right against anybody else that *they* should give him continued use of your kid-neys. Certainly he had no right against the Society of Music Lovers that they should plug him into you in the first place. And if you now start to unplug yourself, having learned that you will otherwise have to spend nine years in bed with him, there is nobody in the world who must try to pre-vent you, in order to see to it that he is given something he has a right to be given.

Some people are rather stricter about the right to life. In their view, it does not include the right to be given anything, but amounts to, and only to, the right not to be killed by anybody. But here a related difficulty arises. If everybody is to refrain from killing that violinist, then everybody must refrain from doing a great many different sorts of things. Everybody must refrain from slitting his throat, everybody must refrain from shooting him—and everybody must refrain from unplugging you from him. But does he have a right against everybody that they shall refrain from unplugging you from him? To refrain from doing this is to allow him to continue to use your kidneys. It could be argued that he has a right against us that *we* should allow him to continue to use your kidneys. That is, while he had no right against us that we should give him the use of your kidneys, it might be argued that he anyway has a right against us that we shall not now intervene and deprive him of the use of your kidneys. I shall come back to third-party interventions later. But certainly the violinist has no right against you that *you* shall allow him to continue to use your kidneys. As I said, if you do allow him to use them, it is a kindness on your part, and not something you owe him.

The difficulty I point to here is not peculiar to the right to life. It reappears in connection with all the other natural rights; and it is something which an adequate account of rights must deal with. For present purposes it is enough just to draw attention to it. But I would stress that I am not arguing that people do not have a right to life—quite to the contrary, it seems to me that the primary control we must place on the acceptability of an account of rights is that it should turn out in that account to be a truth that all persons have a right to life. I am arguing only that having a right to life does not guarantee having either a right to be given the use of or a right to be allowed continued use of another person's body—even if one needs it for life itself. So the right to life will not serve the opponents of abortion in the very simple and clear way in which they seem to have thought it would.

4. There is another way to bring out the difficulty. In the most ordinary sort of case, to deprive someone of what he has a right to is to treat him unjustly. Suppose a boy and his small brother are jointly given a box of chocolates for Christmas. If the older boy takes the box and refuses to give his brother any of the chocolates, he is unjust to him, for the brother has been given a right to half of them. But suppose that, having learned that otherwise it means nine years in bed with that violinist, you unplug yourself from him. You surely are not being unjust to him, for you gave him no right to use your kidneys, and no one else can have given him any such right. But we have to notice that in unplugging yourself, you are killing him; and violinists, like everybody else, have a right to life, and thus in the view we were considering just now, the right not to be killed. So here you do what he supposedly has a right you shall not do, but you do not act unjustly to him in doing it.

The emendation which may be made at this point is this: the right to life consists not in the right not to be killed, but rather in the right not to be killed unjustly. This runs a risk of circularity, but never mind: it would enable us to square the fact that the violinist has a right to life with the fact that you do not act unjustly toward him in unplugging yourself, thereby killing him. For if you do not kill him unjustly, you do not violate his right to life, and so it is no wonder you do him no injustice.

But if this emendation is accepted, the gap in the argument against abortion stares us plainly in the face: it is by no means enough to show that the fetus is a person, and to remind us that all persons have a right to life—we need to be shown also that killing the fetus violates its right to life, i.e., that abortion is unjust killing. And is it?

I suppose we may take it as a datum that in a case of pregnancy due to rape the mother has not given the unborn person a right to the use of her body for food and shelter. Indeed, in what pregnancy could it be supposed that the mother has given the unborn person such a right? It is not as if there were unborn persons drifting about the world, to whom a woman who wants a child says "I invite you in."

But it might be argued that there are other ways one can have acquired a right to the use of another person's body than by having been invited to use it by that person. Suppose a woman voluntarily indulges in intercourse, knowing of the chance it will issue in pregnancy, and then she does become pregnant; is she not in part responsible for the presence, in fact the very existence, of the unborn person inside her? No doubt she did not invite it in. But doesn't her partial responsibility for its being there itself give it a right to the use of her body?[7] If so, then her aborting it would be more like the boy's taking away the chocolates, and less like your un-plugging yourself from the violinist—doing so would be depriving it of what it does have a right to, and thus would be doing it an injustice.

And then, too, it might be asked whether or not she can kill it even to save her own life: If she voluntarily called it into existence, how can she now kill it, even in self-defense?

The first thing to be said about this is that it is something new. Opponents of abortion have been so concerned to make out the inde-pendence of the fetus, in order to establish that it has a right to life, just as its mother does, that they have tended to overlook the possible support they might gain from making out that the fetus is *dependent* on the mother, in order to establish that she has a special kind of responsibility for it, a responsibility that gives it rights against her which are not possessed by any independent person—such as an ailing violinist who is a stranger to her.

On the other hand, this argument would give the unborn person a right to its mother's body only if her pregnancy resulted from a voluntary act, undertaken in full knowledge of the chance a pregnancy might result from it. It would leave out entirely the unborn person whose existence is due to rape. Pending the availability of some further argument, then, we

---

[7]The need for a discussion of this argument was brought home to me by mem-bers of the Society for Ethical and Legal Philosophy, to whom this paper was originally presented.

would be left with the conclusion that unborn persons whose existence is due to rape have no right to the use of their mothers' bodies, and thus that aborting them is not depriving them of anything they have a right to and hence is not unjust killing.

And we should also notice that it is not at all plain that this argument really does go even as far as it purports to. For there are cases and cases, and the details make a difference. If the room is stuffy, and I therefore open a window to air it, and a burglar climbs in, it would be absurd to say, "Ah, now he can stay, she's given him a right to the use of her house —for she is partially responsible for his presence there, having voluntarily done what enabled him to get in, in full knowledge that there are such things as burglars, and that burglars burgle." It would be still more absurd to say this if I had had bars installed outside my windows, precisely to prevent burglars from getting in, and a burglar got in only because of a defect in the bars. It remains equally absurd if we imagine it is not a burglar who climbs in, but an innocent person who blunders or falls in. Again, suppose it were like this: people-seeds drift about in the air like pollen, and if you open your windows, one may drift in and take root in your carpets or upholstery. You don't want children, so you fix up your windows with fine mesh screens, the very best you can buy. As can happen, however, and on very, very rare occasions does happen, one of the screens is defective; and a seed drifts in and takes root. Does the person-plant who now develops have a right to the use of your house? Surely not—despite the fact that you voluntarily opened your windows, you knowingly kept carpets and upholstered funiture, and you knew that screens were sometimes defective. Someone may argue that you are responsible for its rooting, that it does have a right to your house, because after all you *could* have lived out your life with bare floors and furniture, or with sealed windows and doors. But this won't do—for by the same token anyone can avoid a pregnancy due to rape by having a hysterectomy, or anyway by never leaving home without a (reliable!) army.

It seems to me that the argument we are looking at can establish at most that there are *some* cases in which the unborn person has a right to the use of its mother's body, and therefore *some* cases in which abortion is unjust killing. There is room for much discussion and argument as to precisely which, if any. But I think we should sidestep this issue and leave it open, for at any rate the argument certainly does not establish that all abortion is unjust killing.

5. There is room for yet another argument here, however. We surely must all grant that there may be cases in which it would be morally indecent to detach a person from your body at the cost of his life. Suppose you learn that what the violinist needs is not nine years of your life, but only one hour: all you need do to save his life is to spend one hour in that bed with him. Suppose also that letting him use your kidneys for that one hour would not affect your health in the slightest. Admittedly you were kidnapped. Admittedly you did not give anyone permission to plug him

into you. Nevertheless it seems to me plain you *ought* to allow him to use your kidneys for that hour—it would be indecent to refuse.

Again, suppose pregnancy lasted only an hour, and constituted no threat to life or health. And suppose that a woman becomes pregnant as a result of rape. Admittedly she did not voluntarily do anything to bring about the existence of a child. Admittedly she did nothing at all which would give the unborn person a right to the use of her body. All the same it might well be said, as in the newly emended violinist story, that she *ought* to allow it to remain for that hour—that it would be indecent in her to refuse.

Now some people are inclined to use the term "right" in such a way that it follows from the fact that you ought to allow a person to use your body for the hour he needs, that he has a right to use your body for the hour he needs, even though he has not been given that right by any person or act. They may say that it follows also that if you refuse, you act unjustly toward him. This use of the term is perhaps so common that it cannot be called wrong; nevertheless it seems to me to be an unfortunate loosening of what we would do better to keep a tight rein on. Suppose that box of chocolates I mentioned earlier had not been given to both boys jointly, but was given only to the older boy. There he sits, stolidly eating his way through the box, his small brother watching enviously. Here we are likely to say "You ought not to be so mean. You ought to give your brother some of those chocolates." My own view is that it just does not follow from the truth of this that the brother has any right to any of the chocolates. If the boy refuses to give his brother any, he is greedy, stingy, callous—but not unjust. I suppose that the people I have in mind will say it does follow that the brother has a right to some of the chocolates, and thus that the boy does act unjustly if he refuses to give his brother any. But the effect of saying this is to obscure what we should keep distinct, namely the difference between the boy's refusal in this case and the boy's refusal in the earlier case, in which the box was given to both boys jointly, and in which the small brother thus had what was from any point of view clear title to half.

A further objection to so using the term "right" that from the fact that A ought to do a thing for B, it follows that B has a right against A that A do it for him, is that it is going to make the question of whether or not a man has a right to a thing turn on how easy it is to provide him with it; and this seems not merely unfortunate, but morally unacceptable. Take the case of Henry Fonda again. I said earlier that I had no right to the touch of his cool hand on my fevered brow, even though I needed it to save my life. I said it would be frightfully nice of him to fly in from the West Coast to provide me with it, but that I had no right against him that he should do so. But suppose he isn't on the West Coast. Suppose he has only to walk across the room, place a hand briefly on by brow—and lo, my life is saved. Then surely he ought to do it, it would be indecent to refuse. Is it to be said "Ah, well, it follows that in this case she has a right to the touch of his hand on her brow, and so it would be an injustice in him to refuse"? So that I have a right to it when it is easy for him to provide it, though no right when it's hard? It's rather a shocking idea that anyone's rights should fade away and disappear as it gets harder and harder to accord them to him.

So my own view is that even though you ought to let the violinist use your kidneys for the one hour he needs, we should not conclude that he has a right to do so—we would say that if you refuse, you are, like the boy who owns all the chocolates and will give none away, self-centered and callous, indecent in fact, but not unjust. And similarly, that even supposing a case in which a woman pregnant due to rape ought to allow the unborn person to use her body for the hour he needs, we should not conclude that he has a right to do so; we should conclude that she is self-centered, callous, indecent, but not unjust, if she refuses. The complaints are no less grave; they are just different. However, there is no need to insist on this point. If anyone does wish to deduce "he has a right" from "you ought," then all the same he must surely grant that there are cases in which it is not morally required of you that you allow that violinist to use your kidneys, and in which he does not have a right to use them, and in which you do not do him an injustice if you refuse. And so also for mother and unborn child. Except in such cases as the unborn person has a right to demand it—and we were leaving open the possibility that there may be such cases —nobody is morally *required* to make large sacrifices, of health, of all other interests and concerns, of all other duties and commitments, for nine years, or even for nine months, in order to keep another person alive.

6. We have in fact to distinguish between two kinds of Samaritan: the Good Samaritan and what we might call the Minimally Decent Samaritan. The story of the Good Samaritan, you will remember, goes like this:

> A certain man went down from Jerusalem to Jericho, and fell among thieves, which stripped him of his raiment, and wounded him, and departed, leaving him half dead.
>
> And by chance there came down a certain priest that way; and when he saw him, he passed by on the other side.
>
> And likewise a Levite, when he was at the place, came and looked on him, and passed by on the other side.
>
> But a certain Samaritan, as he journeyed, came where he was; and when he saw him he had compassion on him.
>
> And went to him, and bound up his wounds, pouring in oil and wine, and set him on his own beast, and brought him to an inn, and took care of him.
>
> And on the morrow, when he departed, he took out two pence, and gave them to the host, and said unto him, "Take care of him; and whatsoever thou spendest more, when I come again, I will repay thee."
>
> (Luke 10:30–35)

The Good Samaritan went out of his way, at some cost to himself, to help one in need of it. We are not told what the options were, that is, whether or not the priest and the Levite could have helped by doing less than the Good Samaritan did, but assuming they could have, then the fact they did nothing at all shows they were not even Minimally Decent Samaritans, not because they were not Samaritans, but because they were not even minimally decent.

These things are a matter of degree, of course, but there is a difference, and it comes out perhaps most clearly in the story of Kitty Genovese, who, as you will remember, was murdered while thirty-eight people watched or listened, and did nothing at all to help her. A Good Samaritan would have rushed out to give direct assistance against the murderer. Or perhaps we had better allow that it would have been a Splendid Samaritan who did this, on the ground that it would have involved a risk of death for himself. But the thirty-eight not only did not do this, they did not even trouble to pick up a phone to call the police. Minimally Decent Samaritanism would call for doing at least that, and their not having done it was monstrous.

After telling the story of the Good Samaritan, Jesus said "Go, and do thou likewise." Perhaps he meant that we are morally required to act as the Good Samaritan did. Perhaps he was urging people to do more than is morally required of them. At all events it seems plain that it was not morally required of any of the thirty-eight that he rush out to give direct assistance at the risk of his own life, and that it is not morally required of anyone that he give long stretches of his life—nine years or nine months —to sustaining the life of a person who has no special right (we were leaving open the possibility of this) to demand it.

Indeed, with one rather striking class of exceptions, no one in any country in the world is *legally* required to do anywhere near as much as this for anyone else. The class of exceptions is obvious. My main concern here is not the state of the law in respect to abortion, but it is worth drawing attention to the fact that in no state in this country is any man compelled by law to be even a Minimally Decent Samaritan to any person; there is no law under which charges could be brought against the thirty-eight who stood by while Kitty Genovese died. By contrast, in most states in this country women are compelled by law to be not merely Minimally Decent Samaritans, but Good Samaritans to unborn persons inside them. This doesn't by itself settle anything one way or the other, because it may well be argued that there should be laws in this country—as there are in many European countries—compelling at least Minimally Decent Samaritanism.[8] But it does show that there is a gross injustice in the existing state of the law. And it shows also that the groups currently working against liberalization of abortion laws, in fact working toward having it declared unconstitutional for a state to permit abortion, had better start working for the adoption of Good Samaritan laws generally, or earn the charge that they are acting in bad faith.

---

[8]For a discussion of the difficulties involved, and a survey of the European experience with such laws, see *The Good Samaritan and the Law,* ed. James M. Ratcliffe (New York, 1966).

I should think, myself, that Minimally Decent Samaritan laws would be one thing, Good Samaritan laws quite another, and in fact highly improper. But we are not here concerned with the law. What we should ask is not whether anybody should be compelled by law to be a Good Samaritan, but whether we must accede to a situation in which somebody is being compelled—by nature, perhaps—to be a Good Samaritan. We have, in other words, to look now at third-party interventions. I have been arguing that no person is morally required to make large sacrifices to sustain the life of another who has no right to demand them, and this even where the sacrifices do not include life itself; we are not morally required to be Good Samaritans or anyway Very Good Samaritans to one another. But what if a man cannot extricate himself from such a situation? What if he appeals to us to extricate him? It seems to me plain that there are cases in which we can, cases in which a Good Samaritan would extricate him. There you are, you were kidnapped, and nine years in bed with that violinist lie ahead of you. You have your own life to lead. You are sorry, but you simply cannot see giving up so much of your life to the sustaining of his. You cannot extricate yourself, and ask us to do so. I should have thought that— in light of his having no right to the use of your body—it was obvious that we do not have to accede to your being forced to give up so much. We can do what you ask. There is no injustice to the violinist in our doing so.

7. Following the lead of the opponents of abortion, I have throughout been speaking of the fetus merely as a person, and what I have been asking is whether or not the argument we began with, which proceeds only from the fetus' being a person, really does establish its conclusion. I have argued that it does not.

But of course there are arguments and arguments, and it may be said that I have simply fastened on the wrong one. It may be said that what is important is not merely the fact that the fetus is a person, but that it is a person for whom the woman has a special kind of responsibility issuing from the fact that she is its mother. And it might be argued that all by analogies are therefore irrelevant—for you do not have that special kind of responsibility for that violinist, Henry Fonda does not have that special kind of responsibility for me. And our attention might be drawn to the fact that men and women both *are* compelled by law to provide support for their children.

I have in effect dealt (briefly) with this argument in section 4 above; but a (still briefer) recapitulation now may be in order. Surely we do not have any such "special responsibility" for a person unless we have assumed it, explicitly or implicitly. If a set of parents do not try to prevent pregnancy, do not obtain an abortion, and then at the time of birth of the child do not put it out for adoption, but rather take it home with them, they have assumed responsibility for it, they have given it rights, and they cannot *now* withdraw support from it at the cost of its life because they now find it difficult to go on providing for it. But if they have taken all reasonable precautions against having a child, they do not simply by virtue of their biological relationship to the child who comes into existence have a special responsibility for it. They may wish to assume responsibility for it, or they may not wish to. And I am suggesting that if assuming responsibility for it would require large sacrifices, then they may refuse. A Good Samaritan would not refuse—or anyway, a Splendid Samaritan, if the sacrifices that had to be made were enormous. But then so would a Good Samaritan assume responsibility for that violinist; so would Henry Fonda, if he is a Good Samaritan, fly in from the West Coast and assume responsibility for me.

8. My argument will be found unsatisfactory on two counts by many of those who want to regard abortion as morally permissible. First, while I do argue that abortion is not impermissible, I do not argue that it is always permissible. There may well be cases in which carrying the child to term requires only Minimally Decent Samaritanism of the mother, and this is a standard we must not fall below. I am inclined to think it a merit of my account precisely that it does *not* give a general yes or a general no. It allows for and supports our sense that, for example, a sick and desperately frightened fourteen-year-old schoolgirl, pregnant due to rape, may *of course* choose abortion, and that any law which rules this out is an insane law. And it also allows for and supports our sense that in other cases resort to abortion is even positively indecent. It would be indecent in the woman to request an abortion, and indecent in a doctor to perform it, if she is in her seventh month, and wants the abortion just to avoid the nuisance of post-poning a trip abroad. The very fact that the arguments I have been drawing attention to treat all cases of abortion, or even all cases of abortion in which the mother's life is not at stake, as morally on a par ought to have made them suspect at the outset.

Secondly, while I am arguing for the permissibility of abortion in some cases, I am not arguing for the right to secure the death of the unborn child. It is easy to confuse these two things in.that up to a certain point in the life of the fetus it is not able to survive outside the mother's body; hence removing it from her body guarantees its death. But they are importantly different. I have argued that you are not morally required to spend nine months in bed, sustaining the life of that violinist; but to say this is by no means to say that if, when you unplug yourself, there is a miracle and he survives, you then have a right to turn round and slit his throat. You may detach yourself even if this costs him his life; you have no right to be guaranteed his death, by some other means, if unplugging yourself does not kill him. There are some people who will feel dissatisfied by this feature of my argument. A woman may be utterly devastated by the thought of a child, a bit of herself, put out for adoption and never seen or heard of again. She may therefore want not merely that the child be detached from her, but more, that it die. Some opponents of abortion are inclined to re-gard this as beneath contempt—thereby showing insensitivity to what is surely a powerful source of despair. All the same, I agree that the desire for the child's death is not one which anybody may gratify, should it turn out to be possible to detach the child alive.

At this place, however, it should be remembered that we have only been pretending throughout that the fetus is a human being from the moment of conception. A very early abortion is surely not the killing of a person, and so is not dealt with by anything I have said here.

✾ JOSEPH FLETCHER

3. The "Right" to Live and the "Right" to Die — A Protestant View

Joseph F. Fletcher III is a well known educator and clergyman. He holds the doctorate of literature from Ohio Wesleyan University and the doctorate of divinity from Episcopal Divinity School. Among his works are *Morals and Medicine* (1954), *Situation Ethics* (1966), and *The Ethics of Genetic Control* (1974).

. . . The history of jurisprudence and constitutional law reveals an interesting relation between human rights and human needs. At certain points in social development, liberals or radicals have demanded that society first recognize and then accept an obligation to meet certain needs that had thus far gone unacknowledged. After a hard struggle, such needs are finally recognized culturally and then given a legal status. The right to possess and bear arms might be an example out of our colonial history. A hundred years or more later, new needs come into view, but now their champions are met with resistance by conservatives and reactionaries, who deny the new needs indignantly in the name of the old rights. This was seen recently in the opposition to gun-control bills in the Congress by various sportsmen's lobbies.

In the 1964 presidential campaign Senator Barry Goldwater appealed to human rights ten times more often than President Johnson did. Some people speak piously of their right to bear children, when confronted by the population problem. They appeal to the right of free association, when civil-rights advocates point to the need of black schoolchildren for

Reprinted from Joseph Fletcher, "The 'Right' to Live and the 'Right' to Die—A Protestant View." This article first appeared in *The Humanist*, July/August 1974, and is reprinted by permission.

respect and acceptance. They assert their right to choose their own physicians, when the newly emerging "right to health" calls for group practice and neighborhood clinic care. And so it goes. The zealot, it is said, is one who, having lost sight of his goal, redoubles his efforts.

It was so with public education: bills to give schooling to all children were blocked by appeals to the rights of parental authority. Under the rubric of parental rights people can and do put their children in orphanages, and even though they only send them a Christmas card once a year they refuse to let them be adopted.

The legalism of so-called human rights can even twist a victory of a human need over a supposed human right into an ultimate defeat by another supposed right. For example, in 1967 the US Supreme Court struck down a Virginia law forbidding interracial marriages, saying that the "freedom to marry has long been recognized as one of the vital personal rights" of free men. Whereupon, now, a Catholic lawyer in Boston argues in an essay on ethics that people should be free to marry and produce babies if they choose to, because that is their right (natural and God-given, presumably), even if they know in advance that their children will be genetically or chromosomally defective. Such legalism speaks glibly of the right to marry whom we please, the right to have children as we may, and even a fetal monster's "right to be born"! In this way, we can see that the ethics of rights is indeed a monster morality.

The question is: Which comes first, rights or needs? Do rights define which needs are to be recognized, or is it the needs that validate the rights? I believe that needs have precedence over rights; that is my ethical stance. Therefore, to be candid and careful about this subject, I am not primarily concerned about any supposed right to live or supposed right to die; I am primarily concerned with human *need*—both of life and of death. This is my confession.

Now, then, let me move on to a fairly sharply focused examination of living and dying. What follows is an attempt in a Christian setting to face a serious and growing problem with Christian courage, and an effort to meet it with Christian conviction and faith. It is controversial, of course; that is, it is a *newthink* question, to be explored without the supports (or dangers) of consensus or conventional wisdom. And, in the future, no doubt some of our discussion of ethics and biology will appear to our descendants to be as grotesque as Henry VIII's theological discussions seem to us today.

If we believe that Jesus came so that men might have life and that they might have more abundant life, we should understand that this refers to spiritual or personal or human life—not to physical or biological life. Spiritual life is impossible without biological life to begin with, but, as we shall see, the two things are not by any means "coinherent." Whether they are related benignly or malignly depends on the case, on the situation. Vital processes sometimes undergird personality, and sometimes they undermine it. As in the balance of rights and needs, needs should come first, so in the balance of biological life and human life being a man or a person is of more value than simply being alive. Martyrs know this and heroes know it; I take it to be the meaning of the Cross.

The logic of what I am saying is that we should drop the classical sanctity-of-life ethic and embrace a quality-of-life ethic instead. That is, we should say that personal integrity is more important than biological survival. We are not vitalists, for whom the highest good is being alive. But to say this—to say that biological life is not sacrosanct and that there are more valuable things than being alive—is to make a break with established religion and medical piety. It is true that in a confused and contradictory way the tradition has allowed ranking that puts other things before being alive, in such matters as military service, capital punishment, heroism, sacrificial love, and self-defense. But in the realm of medical care the sanctity of life has had priority at all costs.

Doctors and nurses, as well as the general public, have insisted that when life can be preserved there are never any "trade-offs" allowed, to use the language of economists and value analysts. Life, it is supposed, is a self-validating good. The popular idea of life is that it is *intrinsically* good, which is just a form of the ethical legalism that finds good and evil to be inherent in things and acts, rather than extrinsic according to the variables of a situation. This denies the moral agent any decision-making role—except, of course, absolute obedience. In ethical language, vitalism is legalism; its rhetoric is grandiose talk about abstract and a priori "rights" rather than loving concern for human needs.

In an amazingly short time, fabulous biomedical gains have been made in neonatology, resuscitative treatment, artificial life-support systems, and organ replacement by means of transplanted tissue or implanted artificial substitutes. The question of human or medical initiatives in living and dying is therefore a success problem, not one of failure. Now we can preserve and prolong life beyond our grandfathers' rosiest dreams—so much so that we can at last see why prolonging life may paradoxically be prolonging dying. Along with the problem of how to save life comes the problem of when to stop it.

Thanatology is exploring in more realistic and contemporary terms the question of where we are to draw the line between prolonging living and prolonging dying. Whereas the so-called human vegetable (an unlovely piece of gallows humor) was once an infrequent problem in terminal wards of hospitals, it is now a common daily problem because of medical success. The loss of personal integrity now often occurs long before biological death. Death has changed its shape. The old Victorian deathbed scene of final farewells at home is replaced; death comes in hospitals, from chronic rather than from acute diseases, which are more apt to be metabolic than infectious or contagious. Patients do not *meet* death anymore; the end comes for them while comatose, betubed, aerated, glucosed, narcosed, sedated—not conscious, not even human anymore. Given this picture, it is no surprise that the white coat is losing some of its shine in patients' eyes, and that they begin to fear senility more than death.

Not only are the *conditions* of life and death changing; so are the *definitions* of life and death changing. The medical profession is at last accepting the ancient philosophical-theological idea that the *ratio,* man's rational faculty, is the core of human being, of humanness—not spontaneous organ function but cerebral function. When did Senator Robert Kennedy die? When the assassin's bullet smashed his midbrain, or eight hours later when the usual classical criteria said so—absence of pulse, heartbeat, breathing, pupillary light reflexes, and so on? What we call "mind" is what the brain *does*—its function or product. In the new view, death has ensued when brain function is lost irreversibly, no matter if heartbeat or blood circulation or breathing persist. The traditional criteria for the determination of death are subordinated and have been replaced by the concept of "brain death," as confirmed by retina and deoxygenation tests.

The essence of the new life-death concept, which favors *human* being rather than mere biological functioning, is caught up in a famous surgeon's remark, "When the brain is gone there's no point in keeping anything else going." This humane conception of life and death fits, for example, the urgencies of organ and tissue transplantation from cadavers in cases where the recipient's life would be lost if the replacement has to wait until all of the donor's functions have ceased spontaneously. This *quality-of-life* ethic is, you see, so much less selfish and egoistic, so much less stingy, so much more socially conscientious, and so much more adapted to saving *real* life, as well as being better adapted to respect for personal integrity.

There are, to be sure, four ethical questions at stake, and they are in turn related to a metaethical question about man: Who and what is he? Let me speak briefly to these questions in order.

1. The first ethical question is the one we have highlighted: Which do we prefer, quantity or quality of life? Ethics deals with the preferable, as science deals with the possible and probable. Do we prefer personal or human being, or do we favor biological life at any cost to personality and humanity? Can we any longer morally accept the principle that in medical care we are always obliged to prolong life as much as possible, either naturally or artificially? To say yes to this question is to embrace vitalism—that is, to assert as a value proposition that the quantity of life is more important than its quality. To say no is to embrace ethical humanism—that is, to assert that quality comes first and that being human is more important than being alive. The key question is: Which comes first, the *vita* or the *homo?* How do we answer?

2. The second ethical question is whether death may not sometimes be a friend, not always an enemy. After all, death is part of the natural order and likely to remain so for a long time in spite of the bizarre speculations of Alan Harrington and some of the cryonics investigators in the Soviet Union.

We are all under sentence of death. For those who like to believe in a creationist theology, *biological* death is even describable as a matter of the divine will—although St. Paul's declaration that death has lost its sting in Christ's resurrection might still be held to mean the end of *personal* death. How striking it is that those who profess faith in personal survival after biological death are often the ones who hang on most grimly and desperately to biological life in spite of the end of personal integrity.

3. The third ethical question is: May we humans assume any *initiative* in dying? Can we legitimate a stewardship of life and death as well as of health? We take the initiative and exert control over disease and injury, interfering with the natural processes of illness and accident. That "artificial" interference with nature is exactly what medicine is: a human intervention in what some religious believers would call God's establishment and what others would even call God's providence. Given such a simplistic theodicy, they would then argue that to prevent a conception or birth, or to hasten or contrive a death, is an impious invasion of the divine monopoly —that by special creation and special providence living and dying are in God's hands and that life is God's to give and only God's to take.

But this sacralistic theology, with its opposition to birth control and abortion and euthanasia, has at last run full tilt into humanistic medicine with its ethic of responsibility—its genetics, reproduction, contraception, prevention of defective births and unwanted children, as well as responsibility for the termination of subhuman life in posthuman beings. The heart of responsibility is response—response to human *need*. Birth control and death control go together. And to reject control and responsibility, to deny human beings the role of decision makers (H. Richard Niebuhr called it the role of "answerer") is to deny human beings their moral status. We become puppets, cease to be people. Fatalism and ethical absolutism are the religious forms of puppetry, and they are far and away more anti-human than scientific determinism could ever be.

The crucial business of ethics is decision making, not the adumbration of abstract principles. Moral absolutes and universal rights are excuses for not taking the risks of conscience. But as Soren Kierkegaard said, "To venture causes anxiety, but not to venture is to lose oneself." For moral understanding, go to the decision makers, not to the synthesizers or transcendentalizers or sermonizers. (A judge once asked an indigent man on trial if he had anybody to defend him, and the man replied, "Yes. God." The judge then very wisely said, "Okay, but don't you have anybody local?")

4. The fourth ethical question has to do with suicide and mercy killing. Right across the board, from orthodox Jews and Christians to humanists and atheists, there is a general agreement that in some situations we may let the dying patient go, that we are not morally obliged to "keep a patient going" in spite of his condition or regardless of the trade-offs involved (for example, financial ruin of the family or an unjust use of scarce medical resources—the problem of medical triage). But if this indirect or negative "good death" (euthanasia) is licit, why not a direct and positive action also? The end sought is the same. As Kant pointed out, if we will the end we will the means. The end (responding to human need) justifies

the means; the means do not justify the end. We may not betray love for law's sake, nor allow an alleged "right" to life to bypass a human need to die. We ought not to assign any intrinsic moral quality to the means we employ, as such and of themselves. If we were to do so, let us say, by condemning a toxic dose of analgesia or a neurosurgical lesion for a "human vegetable's" sake, we would be falling back into the legalistic thicket, supposing that our acts are or can be intrinsically right or wrong.

Situation ethics fits medical ethics because it is built on the *clinical* model. That is, situationists, like clinicians, are case-focused and empirical; they do not find the answers to right-wrong questions by consulting theories but by examining situations, just as physicians do for particular patients. They follow the line of milieu therapy in psychiatric medicine, field theory in psychology, and context-analysis in sociology. Situationists do not approach decisions with prefabricated a priori solutions, of the order of universal negatives, like "we must always maintain life" or "we may never interrupt a pregnancy" or "to end an innocent life is murder." These are the clichés of an irrelevant ideology.

Therefore, whether euthanasia, or good dying, is direct or indirect, it depends on the situation whether either would be right or wrong. Neither form is intrinsically or invariably good or evil. Sometimes mercy killing is right; sometimes "letting the patient go" is wrong. It depends. And this is the case with respect to the voluntary-involuntary distinction as well as the direct-indirect distinction. If patients *choose* their death, it is suicide, for voluntary euthanasia is a form of suicide. Involuntary euthanasia, direct or indirect, is a form of mercy killing—of shortening or hastening the process. The logic and semantics here quickly separate what William James called the tough-minded from the soft-minded—a difference that has nothing to do, by the way, with sensitivity and loving concern.

The metaethical question I have mentioned has to do with one's theory or doctrine or ideal of man. Who is a man? What is he? Who *are* we? What does it mean to be human? To be a person? What really is the *humanum* the theologians have always talked about?

It is no precious or merely academic question. It is faced thousands of times every day by physicians, nurses, and paramedical personnel as they deal with patients in terminal stages of illness and try to decide whether the patient is still a person or only a thing, a subject or an object. When has the time come to let the patient go? When is it time to help him to go? The philosophers and theologians have provided no guidelines to comfort or enlighten those in medical practice. No wonder they, as deadly serious decision makers, look upon clergy as not quite serious figures.

Can we supply the synthetic concepts of "human" and "man" and "person" with any operational terms? Would the agenda include cerebral-cortical functions? Self-awareness and self-control? Memory? A sense of futurity, of time? A capacity for interpersonal relationship? Love? A minimum IQ? Could we add a *desire* to live? What else? And in what preferential order would we rank them? This is serious ethical inquiry, and I am inclined to think that answers are more apt to be found in hospitals and scientific agencies than in universities and seminaries.

It is better, I believe, to explore these problems of ethics in a very contextual and concrete way. If a little boy is brought in from a sandlot cave-in after so much brain suffocation that the anoxia is irreparable, as happened recently in California and in Somerville, Massachusetts, would the medical staff be right to follow religious counsel and keep the body "going" in spite of his parents' plea to "let him go"? This is what happened in both cases. If an infant is brought in with pneumonia, and pediatrics finds that it is the victim of Tay-Sachs syndrome (inevitable loss of vision and hearing and almost continuous convulsions until death comes no later than the fourth year), should it be "saved" by penicillin and sent home? Or, if at birth it had been found to be macrocephalic or anencephalic, should it have been respirated? Whichever way you answer, why?

If a patient forty-two years old with kidney failure can only be rescued from uremic poisoning by artificial dialysis and if, after hearing what great inconveniences and loss of vocational hope it entails and that the most optimistic estimate is six or seven years of life, he says "No. The flame isn't worth the candle," and chooses to die, is he wrong? Should he be forced to go on the machine? I saw such a patient not long ago. A physician told me the other day of a fellow doctor brought in from a motor accident with a broken back, high up. Hardly able to speak, he asked his colleagues if it was a C-3 or C-4, and they said it was. He said, "Then don't hook me up" (to a respirator). And they didn't. Was he wrong? Were they? If a man with advanced tumorous metastases asked his physicians to transplant his liver, as yet unaffected (but remember that the liver is a single, not a paired organ), to his young wife who is dying in a hepatic coma from liver shutdown, with the hope that she might survive to live with their three children, should it be done?

Answering questions like these, in situational realism, will quickly help us to discover how we make our moral judgments, and with what presuppositions and generalizations.

I have one final point of some major importance to make. I might pose it in terms of a question put to me some time ago by two obstetricians, one in North Carolina and the other in Milwaukee. Why is it, they asked, that society tells them it's sometimes ethical to terminate life *in utero*, when there are medical and/or social indications, but that it is *never* right to do so *in terminus*? Why is fetal euthanasia all right, but not terminal euthanasia? It seems to me perfectly obvious that the same questions arise at both ends of the biological spectrum—the natal and the mortal: When is a life human? When does it become human? When does it cease to be human?

To speak of living and dying, therefore, and of human or medical initiative and stewardship, encompasses the abortion issue along with the euthanasia issue. They are ethically inseparable. It is troubling to see how progressive and generous and compassionate Catholics are on the social front, and how reactionary and cruel they are on the biological front. But at least Catholic teaching is far more logical than a lot of Protestant and popular opinion. It recognizes that to favor or oppose either euthanasia or abortion, as such, entails a similar stand on the other. The official Roman position is to condemn both, on such grounds as man's "right to life" or the claim that life is intrinsically untouchable, and to appeal to a *"fetal* right to live" as equally intrinsic.

As I said at the start, this logic results in a monster morality—both at birth and at death. Such rights are, of course, entirely metaphysical, religious-faith assertions that are nonempirical and neither verifiable nor falsifiable. They are not even in the order of true-false statements. But I believe that, when love and concern for human need is our ideal, rather than moral laws and rights, we then see that knowingly letting a monster be born into the world, or knowingly letting a man become a monster, is in any case not justifiable. . . .

✿ O. RUTH RUSSELL

4. *Moral and Legal Aspects of Euthanasia*

O. Ruth Russell is professor emeritus of psychology at Western Maryland College. She is the author of *Freedom to Die: Moral and Legal Aspects of Euthanasia.*

Present Law Regarding Euthanasia

Laws and court decisions regarding euthanasia vary from country to country. While no country has yet legalized euthanasia, in recent years in some non-English-speaking countries—Belgium, France, Germany, the Netherlands, and Italy, for instance—compassionate motive has been recognized in law as an extenuating circumstance in mercy killings and cases of assisted suicide, and punishment less than that for murder has been provided, especially when the action was taken at the request of the patient. The Swiss, in their revised Criminal Code of 1942, provided that punishment might be limited to imprisonment of three days or merely a fine. In Uruguay and Peru a person who aids or abets a suicide from an altruistic motive is exempt from penalty. The Code of Czechoslovakia seems to leave punishment in cases of merciful homicide to the determination of the judge. And a Japanese court in 1963 laid down six guiding principles for legal euthanasia.

Reprinted from O. Ruth Russell, "Moral and Legal Aspects of Euthanasia." This article first appeared in *The Humanist,* July/August 1974, and is reprinted by permission.

A case in Sweden in 1964 produced much discussion in medical and legal circles regarding passive euthanasia, when the Medicolegal Committee of the Swedish National Board of Health approved the action of a physician who stopped the intravenous support of an elderly comatose patient. The committee considered such action that might shorten the life of a dying patient "perfectly responsible and legitimate."

But motive has not been recognized in criminal law in the United States or in any other English-speaking country. Under present American law, any intentional shortening of another person's life is murder regardless of motive. And a physician's omission of any possible means to continue the body functioning of a patient may leave him open to a charge of negligence or nonfeasance. But the law on the books and the law applied in courts are clearly not the same. The fact that they are not illustrates that the law on the books is out of step with current concepts of mercy and justice, and this is the basis of the demand for new law.

Courts have seldom convicted a person in a case of mercy killing and, even in cases of conviction, judges have been very lenient in sentencing. The record is mostly one of failure to indict, acquittals on grounds of insanity, suspended sentences, and reprieves. It has been said by some authorities that rulings in this field are a conglomerate of common law, theological pronouncements, and ethical and moral considerations, and that juries have taken on the job of correcting the inequities of law and have in effect rewritten criminal law to give recognition to compassionate motive. But still laws have not been altered to conform to new needs and demands. The present state of affairs in law and in practice is, as Dr. Eliot Slater has said, "a patent absurdity."

I have found only seven legal actions against doctors for mercifully ending a life. In 1915, a Dr. Haiseldon of Chicago was cleared of having failed to save the life of a hopelessly deformed and defective newborn infant. Dr. Herman Sander of New Hampshire was acquitted of a murder charge in 1950 on the defense that the patient was virtually dead before he injected air into her veins, even though few persons questioned that he intentionally hastened her death as she had requested.

In 1957 Dr. John Bodkin Adams in England, even though he was the beneficiary of his patient's will, was acquitted of murder after having administered narcotics that apparently caused death. The judge held that a doctor who administers narcotics to relieve pain is not guilty of murder merely because the measures he takes incidentally shorten life. A Swedish court in 1964 refused to indict a doctor who stopped the intravenous feeding of an aged patient.

Most recently, Dr. Vincent A. Montemarano of New York was acquitted. The prosecution charged that he had injected a patient dying of cancer with a lethal dose.

It appears that only in the Netherlands has a court convicted a physician for mercifully ending a patient's life. There, in 1950, a fifty-year-old doctor received a one-year suspended sentence for giving sleeping pills and pain-killers to hasten the death of his brother, who was suffering from an incurable disease and who had asked that his life be ended. And in 1971 Dr. Gertruida Postma von Boven was charged with mercy killing when she reported that she had ended the life of her hopelessly ill mother, who had repeatedly begged that her life be ended. Under Dutch law this is a lesser charge than murder and carries a penalty of only up to twelve years. At the 1973 trial Dr. Postma said that her mother's "mental suffering became unbearable . . . [That] was most important to me. Now, after all these months, I am convinced I should have done it much earlier." Because of her admission, the court decided that it could do nothing but find her guilty, but it gave her only a one-week suspended sentence and a year's probation.

Dr. Postma's supporters considered even this minimum sentence a "defeat." And she said, "I don't think my action, based solely on the grounds of humanity, deserves any punishment, however light." She said she would consider appealing the case. Eighteen doctors from her community said they had practiced euthanasia at one time or another, and forty-five other doctors signed a letter in support of her.

In cases of mercy killing in which a parent, spouse, or other member of the family ended the life of a loved one in order to end hopeless suffering, judges and juries have shown great sympathy and an unwillingness to punish, even though the evidence showed clearly that the person had indeed violated criminal law. Exceptions are Roberts in Michigan in 1920 and Noxon in Massachusetts in 1943. Public response to an acquittal in such cases has usually been overwhelmingly favorable, giving further evidence that the law is not in accord with what many believe is humane and justifiable action.

Regarding the legality of terminating treatment and the patient's right to refuse treatment, court decisions have varied. United States courts in many cases have upheld the right of a competent adult patient to refuse medical treatment. (See the Martinez, Raasch, and Osborn cases.) In one of the most recent cases (Yetter, June 6, 1973, Court of Common Pleas, Northampton County, Pa.), Judge Alfred T. Williams, Jr., said, "In our opinion the constitutional right of privacy includes the right of a mature competent adult to refuse to accept medical recommendations that may prolong one's life and which, to a third person at least, appear to be in his best interests; in short, that the right of privacy includes a right to die with which the State should not interfere where there are no minor or unborn children and no clear and present danger to public health, welfare or morals."

Courts have ordered treatment of adults in cases in which the competence of the patient is questioned (Bettman and Heston cases), and also for patients who had voluntarily sought treatment but later changed their minds or became incompetent. There are also cases of court-ordered treatment of children over parental objection, based on the right of the state to protect "neglected" or dependent children.

However, courts have also held that the performance of medical procedures without the consent of the patient or his guardian constitutes assault and battery. It is for this reason that doctors and hospitals have sometimes applied to the courts for the appointment of a guardian in cases of patients who they claim are incompetent.

Some persons say that the exercise of the right to refuse treatment and the compliance of the doctor with the patient's request as testified to in the "living will" will take care of the problem of useless prolongation of life, but many legal authorities question this view. Some think it might serve as an effective defense for a doctor if he is sued by a member of the family for malpractice or charged with murder, but others think that courts may not recognize the "living will" under current law.

One writer has said that "the distinction between refusal of compulsory lifesaving treatment and euthanasia is all but illusory," and many agree with Glanville Williams, who has said that "there is no moral chasm between what may be called shortening life and accelerating death." It may be that Arthur Levisohn is right in saying that part of the problem pertaining to euthanasia is an inadequate public awareness of the need for legal clarification of the situation.

It is clear that current law and current application of law are vastly different. This encourages disrespect for law. It is a situation that should be remedied by bringing them into accord and in keeping with modern thinking regarding what is moral and humane. . . .

A RECOMMENDED SOLUTION

I submit that the best solution is to enact a comprehensive euthanasia law that would combine the best features of the bills proposed to date with other additions.

It is my view that a bill more comprehensive than any put forward to date is desirable—one that would provide for both active and passive euthanasia and that would meet a broad spectrum of needs and provide adequate safeguards for every case.

Many will protest that it would be impossible to get such a radical measure enacted and that it will be necessary to take one step at a time on the theory that "half a loaf is better than none." This may well be true. But it is also true that, when the British Voluntary Euthanasia Bill was being widely debated, one of the criticisms by both advocates and opponents was that it would not permit euthanasia for persons who could not speak for themselves, such as defective infants.

Furthermore, opponents have used the "wedge" argument, saying that a bill limited to voluntary euthanasia would be the opening wedge to other measures and be a "slippery slope" that would lead to Nazi-type compulsory euthanasia and the elimination of all "unwanted" persons. This is an unwarranted argument, but it persists; some of the fears might be alleviated if those who advocate euthanasia on the grounds of compassion were to "put all the cards on the table" at once and try to get a bill designed to meet the needs of those unable to make their wishes known, as well as of those who can make them known. However that may be, the total problem should be publicly discussed, openly and forthrightly.

It is not my intention to draft a proposed bill. Legal experts, with the collaboration of nurses, hospital chaplains, social workers, religious leaders, and others, can certainly draft a good, comprehensive bill if they have the will and determination to do so. It is desirable that efforts continue in individual states to draft and enact euthanasia legislation, but in order to have uniformity of law in all states it is urgent for a group such as the National Conference of Commissioners on Uniform State Laws to prepare a model euthanasia bill.

Other groups, such as the American Law Institute, the American Civil Liberties Union, the Russell Sage, Ford, and Rockefeller foundations, the Institute of Society, Ethics and Life Sciences, the Thanatology Foundation, the American Association of Retired Persons, and many church and civic groups, are concerned with these problems of life and death. They could no doubt be counted on to assist or give active leadership in the formulation and enactment of appropriate law—law that would safeguard both a person's right to live and his right to avoid unnecessary suffering and have euthanasia administered.

To initiate action, an appropriate national commission, such as the one on Health Science and Society proposed by Senator Walter Mondale, could study the matter with a view to drafting a model bill that could then be presented to the individual states for their consideration and action. In 1973, Congressman Tim Lee Carter introduced in the House of Representatives "A Bill To Establish a Commission on Medical Technology and the Dignity of Dying."

It is proposed that the bill be known as "A Euthanasia (good-death) Bill" and that it be divided into three parts as follows:

Part I. To provide for negative (passive) euthanasia, voluntary and nonvoluntary, as in the original 1973 Florida bill.

Part II. To provide for positive (active) euthanasia at the request of the patient, similar to the 1969 Idaho and British Voluntary Euthanasia bills and the 1973 Montana and Oregon bills, all of which make provision also for a person to make an advance declaration of his or her wishes in the event he or she is suffering from an irremediable condition as specified in the witnessed statement.

Part III. To provide for positive euthanasia at the request of the next of kin or legal guardian for those individuals who are unable to speak for themselves and have not made a prior declaration of their wishes. [Ed. note: This provision goes beyond the above Plea for Beneficent Euthanasia and would include severely defective infants.]

Since no personal liberty is absolute—as Justice Holmes said, freedom of speech does not embrace the right to cry "fire" falsely in a crowded theater—the freedom to choose euthanasia must be subject to some restrictions in order to protect the physician, the patient, and society, and to guard against foul play or a mistaken diagnosis.

The following provisions and safeguards should probably be among those included in a good euthanasia law.

1. Legislation would be permissive only, not mandatory or compulsory.

2. No secrecy of action for either passive or positive euthanasia would be permitted, and action taken would be officially recorded.

3. A written, witnessed, and notarized request for euthanasia would be made by the patient or, if he is not of testamentary capacity, by his next of kin or guardian. Such a declaration of one's wishes could be made in advance while in good health, as in making a will, indicating one's wish and requesting euthanasia in the event he became incapacitated in the future and legally incompetent; the documents should designate a surrogate and contingency surrogate to take action on the patient's behalf in such event. Such a request could be revoked at any time and it would have to be reaffirmed if the patient were capable of doing so before euthanasia could be administered.

4. Two or more physicians would certify that in their judgment the patient's condition is such that there is no reasonable chance of significant recovery and that the request for euthanasia is a bona fide one executed without pressure from relatives or others.

5. The application for euthanasia would be made only after consultation and agreement between the patient, or his legal guardian if he is incompetent, the attending physician, and at least one other physician who has certified that it is his judgment that the patient "qualifies" for euthanasia. In most cases, before an application would be made there would be consultation also with some other person or persons, such as a clergyman, hospital chaplain, nurse, psychologist, or social worker, and in practically all cases with at least some members of the family.

This idea of a "team approach" and also of an advisory panel is now being used in some hospitals to help physicians determine which patients will get the use of life-saving machines, blood for transfusions, or transplant organs that are in short supply. Such a panel or committee might be established in each hospital and be available for consultation if desired, especially when there are no relatives, but such a committee would not be empowered to make decisions regarding euthanasia, unless possibly in extreme circumstances as might be stipulated in the law.

6. The formal request for euthanasia accompanied by the "qualifying" statements of two doctors would be filed with the officer in the County Court House or other legally constituted authority whose duty it would be to deal with the application. If the official had any reason to suspect that the documents were not authentic or not properly completed, or if he suspected that there might have been coercion or foul play, he would immediately, in cooperation with the Board of Health or other appropriate

officials, direct an investigation and withhold the granting of a permit for euthanasia until such time as they were satisfied that the documents were legal and proper. A permit would then be issued for the kind of euthanasia requested in accordance with the waiting period provided for in the law and in accordance with the physician's recommendation. It may be desirable that a request for negative euthanasia be treated somewhat differently in most cases.

7.   A waiting period would be required in most cases to assure that a request for euthanasia by either the patient or his or her guardian had not been made in a moment of emotional distress. This period might vary depending on the severity of the suffering, the certainty of irremediability, and the nearness to death. The British bill stipulated a thirty-day waiting period; the Montana bill a fifteen-day period. Possibly, to prevent unnecessary hardship in some terminal cases, special provision might be made that would permit the request to be granted within as short a period as twenty-four hours.

This authorization of a permit would be comparable to the issuance of a marriage license, in that it would grant permission by the state for an authorized person to carry out the request of the applicant.

8.   The administration of euthanasia would be the responsibility of the patient's physician, a qualified nurse, or other medical or paramedical personnel specially designated to carry out the physician's instructions and the patient's wishes. If the patient so desired, the permit would allow the physician to provide the patient with the means to end his own life.

9.   The death certificate would indicate the kind of action taken.

10.   No physician, nurse, or other person would ever be required to administer euthanasia contrary to his conscience, judgment, religious beliefs, or will.

11.   It would be a criminal offense to willfully falsify, forge, conceal, destroy, or otherwise tamper with a declaration or request for euthanasia with intent to create a false impression of the wishes of the patient or his surrogate.

12.   A physician, nurse, or other specialist who performs an authorized act of euthanasia would not be guilty of any offense; this would apply to all forms of euthanasia.

13.   No insurance policy in force would be vitiated by the administration of negative euthanasia; and no policy that had been in force for a specified period would be vitiated by the administration of positive euthanasia.

14.   Any person knowing or suspicious of coercion or any malpractice or any pressure brought to bear on either the patient or his physician or physicians should immediately notify the license officer, who should immediately stay any action until an investigation and decision by his office could be made. This would apply especially to physicians who for reasons other than religion or conscience refuse to sign a qualifying statement either because of uncertainty regarding prognosis or judgment, or suspicion of foul play by anyone concerned.

15.   Each person who has reached the age of maturity should be encouraged to lodge with the appropriate office his or her desires pertaining to euthanasia, as well as his or her wishes pertaining to anatomical gifts and disposal of the body, and the whereabouts of the next of kin. He or she would then be issued a card to carry, indicating these wishes and authorizing action by appropriate persons, as is now possible for the transplantation of organs and tissues and for donation of one's body to a medical school.

Consideration should be given to the enactment of the euthanasia bill on a trial basis. This is a sound legislative procedure though not often used. Such a suggestion was made by Dean Claude L. Sowle in 1968 while he was professor of law at the University of Cincinnati. He proposed that whatever bill is passed should remain in effect only until a specified later session of the legislature, at which time it would have to be considered again after careful research had been made and the effects appraised.

In England, in a letter to *The Lancet* in 1962, T. H. Gillison also proposed that there be a "sort of pilot scheme" in which a few cities would be empowered to permit voluntary euthanasia for a trial run for, say, three years. During that period the advantages and shortcomings of the bill would be assessed. He thought such a scheme would tell more of the practicability of euthanasia than scores of debates. The proposal has merit and might well be considered by individual states.

THE CHALLENGE

In an age when men have devised the means to travel to the moon and back successfully and now seem on the verge of even being able to create human beings with characteristics of their own choosing, they can certainly, if they wish, devise a good euthanasia bill that would help to resolve many of the problems of senseless, cruel suffering of persons.

Professor Harry Kalven of the University of Chicago Law School has said that, if there were already a good law permitting euthanasia, no strong case could be made for changing it. But we do not now have such a law. One is urgently needed. Chief Justice Warren Burger has said, "The law always lags behind the most advanced thinking in every area. It must wait until the theologians and the moral leaders and events have created some common ground, some consensus."

It would seem that such common ground and consensus is fast developing regarding euthanasia. The right to choose death with dignity is an idea whose time has come.

Clearly new legislation is needed—legislation based on compassion, justice, common sense, and enlightened public opinion. To get such legislation, efforts must be energetic and persistent. Opposition is to be expected. It is not easy to break with custom or the inflexible stupidities of the past. The great Sir William Osler, addressing the Royal College of Physicians in London in 1906 on "The Growth of Truth," described the long years of physicians and the general public in order to obtain knowledge of the anatomy and functioning of the human body and the causes of disease. He said that opposition came chiefly from men who could not—not who would not—see the truth. But ultimately the fetters of dogma and authority get severed, and acceptance of new knowledge, new beliefs, and new laws finally comes. To illustrate resistance to change, he quoted lines that reputedly came to Henry Sidgwick in his sleep.

> We think so because all other people think so;
> Or because—or because after all, we do think so;
> Or because we were told so, and think we must think so;
> Or because we once thought so, and think we still think so;
> Or because, having thought so, we think we will think so.

This kind of thinking explains much of the opposition to euthanasia and the search for acceptable ways of avoiding useless suffering or a meaningless existence. It explains why Margaret Sanger sixty years ago was put in jail for championing the right to birth control.

It would seem that the time has come, and the need is urgent, for the enactment of a good euthanasia law that would permit intelligent control of death insofar as this is possible. Practices pertaining to the creation and termination of life would seem to be matters of conscience, to be decided chiefly by the individuals concerned or by the next of kin or guardians in cases of individuals who are not of testamentary capacity. As long as the exercise of the right to choose death does no harm to anyone else or to society, it would seem that society has no right to deny it.

It seems certain that it is only a matter of time until laws will be passed that will permit the administration of painless death when the only alternative is an agonizing or meaningless existence. It is a challenge to every citizen to hasten that day.

❀ BYRON L. SHERWIN

5. *Jewish Views on Euthanasia*

Byron L. Sherwin is an assistant professor of Jewish religious thought at Spertus College of Judaica in Chicago.

Many contemporary philosophers assume that moral judgments cannot be rationally or objectively justifiable, that there is no final truth in ethics any more than in physics. A similar claim was made by the medieval Jewish philosopher, Moses Maimonides, in the twelfth century. He rejected the theoretical possibility and therefore the actual attempts of

Reprinted from Byron L. Sherwin, "Jewish Views on Euthanasia." This article ancient and medieval philosophers to create a rational morality, to find in reason the grounds of obligation and the content of duty. Maimonides taught that morality cannot be derived from reason, that moral statements are neither true nor false.

Once one accepts the assumption that moral statements in themselves are bereft of truth value, one may choose the nihilistic alternative of moral chaos or one may seek a frame of reference within which to posit moral statements. In the latter alternative, the frame of reference serves as the basis for evaluating the truth value of the given statement. "Truth" becomes relative to the chosen framework. One commits oneself to the basic assumptions upon which the framework rests. These assumptions are *believed* but not *known* to be true, nor *can* they be known to be true. One makes one's moral decisions *as if* the assumptions upon which his frame of reference rests are true. Examples of such assumptions may be: (1) common sense will determine what is moral; (2) the reasonable man will know what is moral; (3) conscience can determine what is moral; (4) what is constitutional is morally correct; and so on.

In the approach sketched above, the statement "X is a morally valid position" would mean "in framework A, X is a morally valid position." The truth value of a given statement and the meaning of terms in a given proposition would be determined by the framework in which it or they are used. Certain questions may be essential in framework A but tangential or irrelevant to framework B. A given term may have one meaning in one framework but another meaning or no meaning in a second framework.

The present discussion will attempt to articulate the position of a specific frame of reference—Jewish ethics—regarding a particular moral problem—euthanasia. The sources drawn upon to elicit this position will be those of normative, historical Judaism. Before proceeding to formulate that position and taking into account what has already been stated, a number of preliminary points should be made.

The authenticity of a given position or the "meaningfulness" of a given term within Jewish ethics is determinable by whether or not there is precedent for that position within the classical texts of Judaica, by whether the terms used to express that position are operative and meaningful within the framework of normative Judaism. From this it would follow that a view of euthanasia held by an individual Jew or even by many Jews need not necessarily be one that is relevant to or representative of Jewish ethics as presently construed. Such a view may be "moral" and "meaningful" within a framework other than that of Jewish ethics, but unless it can claim authenticity on grounds of its consistency with precedent, the views of a single Jew or of many Jews on euthanasia remain irrelevant to the position of Jewish ethics on euthanasia.

It should be further noted that a characteristic of Jewish ethics or of the ethics of Judaism is to translate, whenever possible, abstract moral generalizations into particular legal obligations. Jewish ethics most clearly articulates itself in Jewish law. Therefore, to determine Judaism's position on euthanasia, one ought to consult Jewish legal literature.

Finally, one must remember that questions and terms often used in articulating a position on euthanasia in other frameworks may be irrelevant in Jewish ethics. Similarly, assumptions made and terms used within the framework of Jewish ethics may be irrelevant and meaningless in other frameworks. One such term, for example, crucial to discussion of euthanasia in Anglo-American legal and philosophical literature, has little or no operative meaning in Jewish ethics. The term "right" is not operative or meaningful in the framework of Jewish ethical or Jewish legal discourse. The question of whether or not an individual has the right to die is meaningless. In classical Hebrew, there is no term for "rights" as it is used in Anglo-American moral-legal terminology. The notion of rights in British and American jurisprudence is based upon historical and political circumstances that are peculiar to them but that remained irrelevant to developments in Jewish moral-legal literature.

Anglo-American jurisprudence, it may be claimed, revolves around questions of rights: What are my rights? What happens when there is a conflict of rights? Does A have the right to do X? Under what circumstances, if any, may B infringe upon my rights? What are C's penalties for infringing upon B's rights? And so on. Jewish law, on the other hand, revolves around the principle of religio-moral-legal obligation rather than the principle of rights. The basic question in Jewish law is not "What are my rights?" but "What are my obligations toward person A or in situation X?

In American law, for example, payment or nonpayment of a debt would be settled by determining the rights of the parties—for example, of the debtor or creditor to possession of money or objects borrowed, or of the debtor to bankruptcy wherein exercising a right might cancel a just and legal obligation. The problem in Jewish law is not one of rights but of obligations. The rabbinic court, guided by Jewish law, would force the debtor to pay his debt and thereby fulfill a commandment, a religio-moral-legal obligation. Consideration of the creditor's rights is not a determining factor in legal decision in Jewish law; the basic problem is determining the obligations of the debtor. Payment to the creditor is almost a secondary result of this determination. In this regard, Justice Moshe Silberg, of the Israeli Supreme Court, has written: "One may say, obviously with a grain of salt, that modern jurisprudence is not interested in obligations, it is only interested in rights, and the obligation of one who is indebted to pay is only the short expression of the claimant's right to coerce payment." (*Talmudic Law and the Modern State,* Burning Bush Press, New York, 1973)

The problem of euthanasia, when posed as the question of whether or not one has "the right to die," is as meaningless within the framework of Jewish legal terminology as the term "King of the United States" would be in American constitutional law. As valid and proper and necessary as it is to ask the question, in the framework of Anglo-American moral-legal discourse, of whether or not an individual has a right to die, it is improper, unnecessary, and meaningless to ask that same question in Jewish religio-moral-legal discourse. The problem of euthanasia, as all problems in Jewish law, may be properly articulated by asking, "What is person A obliged to do in situation X?" With specific regard to euthanasia, the following questions may be asked: What is an individual dying of a terminal disease obliged to do? What is he permitted to do? What is a physician treating a terminal patient obliged to do? What is he permitted to do? If the life of a terminal patient is ended by the patient himself or by someone else, is the killer a murderer? Are one's obligations different toward a terminal patient being kept alive artificially than they are toward one not being kept alive artificially? Is there any permissible alternative to euthanasia or death for the terminal patient? An attempt will now be made to respond to these questions from a consideration of euthanasia in the classical and contemporary literature of Judaism.

In contemporary literature on euthanasia in Judaism, one finds an unusual consensus among rabbinic authorities representing Orthodox, Conservative, and Reform approaches to Jewish law. The obvious reason for this rare phenomenon of consensus is the *apparently* clear and unequivocal position taken by the classical sources on the subject.

According to Jewish law, "a dying man is regarded as a living person in all respects." Active euthanasia—causing or accelerating his death in any way—is considered murder. Maimonides, in his classical legal code, wrote: "One who is in a dying condition is regarded as a living person in all respects. . . . He who touches him (thereby causing him to expire) is guilty of shedding blood. To what may he be compared? To a flickering flame, which is extinguished as soon as one touches it." According to another medieval source, even if the patient himself asks to be put out of his agony, one is forbidden to comply with his wishes. "If one suffers great agony and he says to another, 'You see I shall not live; kill me for I am unable to withstand this affliction,' one is enjoined not to touch the patient." (*Book of the Pious,* ed. Wistinetzki, Wahrmann, Frankfurt, 1924) The physician is especially enjoined from practicing euthanasia, even at the patient's request. Though he is exempt from criminal charges for unpremeditated murder, the physician who intentionally terminates the death of his patient may be criminally liable.

According to a later source, "Even if one has been dying for a long time, which causes agony to the patient and his family, it is still forbidden to accelerate his death." (Solomon Gunzfried, *Code of Jewish Law,* Hebrew publishing Co., 1927) Just as active involuntary euthanasia is generally forbidden in Jewish law, so is active voluntary euthanasia forbidden. A medieval text, for example, states, "Even when great suffering is visited upon an individual and he knows he will not survive very long, he is prohibited from killing himself." (*Book of the Pious*) The following Talmudic source is used by this and other later sources as a precedent in this regard: "The Romans took hold of Rabbi Hanania b. Teradion, wrapt him in a Torah scroll, placed bundles of branches around him and set them on fire. They then brought tufts of wool, which they had soaked in water, and placed them over his heart, so that he should not expire quickly. 'Open your mouth so that the fire may enter you and end your agony,' urged his students. The rabbi replied, 'No! Let only Him who gave me my life take it away. But no man should injure himself!' "

According to Jewish law, life is to be preserved, even at great cost. Each moment of human life is considered intrinsically sacred. Preserving life supersedes living the "good life." The sacredness of life and the uniqueness of the individual require every possible action to be taken to preserve life. Expressing this notion, for example, one text insists upon the rescue of an individual buried under a fallen building (*Shulhan Arukh, Orah Hayyim*). "Even if they find him so crushed he can live only for a short time, they continue to dig." According to a commentary on this passage, if the building fell on the Sabbath, one is *required* to violate the Sabbath even if it means granting him only "momentary life." Though active euthanasia is forbidden, passive euthanasia, in certain circumstances, is permitted by Jewish law. One is permitted, but not obliged, to remove any artificial means keeping a terminal patient alive because such activity is not considered a positive action (*Yoreh Deah*).

In the conclusion of the Talmudic account of the martyrdom of Hanania b. Teradion, the Roman executioner asks the rabbi whether he may remove the tufts of wool from over his heart that artificially prolong his life. The rabbi agrees to this and expires. Later sources interpret his actions as being nonsupportive of voluntary active euthanasia (that is, opening his mouth to let the fire enter) but supportive of voluntary and involuntary passive euthanasia (that is, removing the tufts of wool). (*Avodah Zara*) In other words, though prolonging natural life is always obligatory, artificially prolonging the life of a terminal patient is optional. One medieval source even goes so far as to prohibit any action that may prevent the patient's quick death and artificially lengthen his agony (*Book of the Pious*).

While a physician is enjoined not to actively cause a terminal patient's death, at least according to one Talmudic view, he is not obliged to tend the patient's illness (though he may reduce pain), thus providing the possibility for a quicker, easier death.*

One may argue the possibility of active euthanasia in Jewish law by combining related precedent with a form of argument characteristic of Jewish legal discourse. The relevant precedent is the only Talmudic text in which the term "euthanasia"—"an easy, good, or quick death"—occurs (Hebrew: *mitah yafa*). The form of argument is the inference *a fortiori* (Hebrew: *gal va-homer*, literally "the light and the weighty"). An example of this form of inference would be: "Here is a teetotaller who does not touch cider; he will certainly refuse whisky." The acceptability of applying this form of argument in Jewish legal discourse is stated in the Talmud (*Niddah* 19b).

---

*The problem, as expressed in classical literature, revolves around the question of whether the practice of medicine is by divine command (*mizvuh*) or by permission (*reshuth*).

On the basis of this discussion, it should be evident that the over-whelming consensus of the majority of Jewish religio-moral-legal literature on euthanasia is that active voluntary or involuntary euthanasia is prohibited and passive voluntary or involuntary euthanasia is permitted but by no means obligatory. At this point one may consider whether an alternative other than death is available to the terminal patient and whether that alternative may be justifiable according to Jewish law.

Recent advances in medical science provide a halakically acceptable possible alternative to euthanasia—that is, refrigeration. This alternative offers a chance to preserve life indefinitely through suspended animation. According to one reading of Jewish law, when there is a dilemma posed by certain death and a possibility of revival, we should choose the latter. If the situation is such that death is imminently certain but that there is a possibility that the patient may be revived if frozen, we are not prohibited from choosing the latter course of action (Azriel Rosenfeld, "Refrigeration, Resuscitation and Resurrection," *Tradition*, 7:2, 1967). This does not mean, however, that we are obliged to employ medical technology to prolong life indefinitely and artificially.

A final issue that bears discussion is whether active euthanasia, in any form, may be justifiable within the framework of Jewish law. If justifiable, such a view might be construed as a "minority opinion," since it challenges the weight of tradition and precedent. But Jewish law, like American constitutional law, makes provision for minority dissent within its broader framework. If legitimate and "valid" within the framework of a legal system, today's minority view may serve as tomorrow's majority view.

The term *mitah yafa* is used in the course of Talmudic discussion concerning the execution of criminals convicted of capital offenses. In one text, the verse "You should love your neighbor as yourself" (Leviticus 19:18) is interpreted to mean that the criminal is to be given a *mita yafa;* the pain usually inflicted by the variety of death sentence is to be reduced both in time and degree of affliction (*Sanhedrin* 45a, 52a). At this point, one may argue either (1) from one comparable case to another or (2) from the "weighty" to the "lighter" case.

1.   The terminal patient is compared by the Talmud to a criminal condemned to the death penalty, in that his case is hopeless (*Arakhin* 6b). From this equation one might argue that the terminal patient ought to be given at least the same consideration as a criminal about to be executed for having committed a capital offense.

2.   One may also argue that if a criminal, guilty of having committed a capital offense, is shown such consideration, how much more so should one innocent of any capital offense, one who is terminally ill.

Not only may one make a case for active euthanasia in Jewish law, one may also argue that in certain circumstances the killer is not to be considered a murderer. In order to consider an act as murder, according to Jewish law, two conditions must be satisfied: premeditation and malice (see Exodus 21:14). Rabbinic literature specifically exonerates a physician who kills his patient, even if he acted with willfulness, when malice is not also present. Though the medieval codes link premeditation with malice, there is no logical or psychological reason to do so. The rabbinic precedent may stand on its own. Thus under certain circumstances, according to this "minority" view, the physician may be legally (but not necessarily morally) blameless for practicing active euthanasia.

One specific case in which active euthanasia by patient, agent, or physician may be more justifiable than others, according to the literature, would be that in which the patient is terminally afflicted with a disease such as cancer.

Talmudic law distinguishes between a *goses,* that is, one terminally ill, and a *terefah* (literally, "torn"), that is, one terminally ill as the result of irreparable organic damage. Apparently, in the former case recovery is at least theoretically possible, whereas in the latter case recovery is altogether impossible. One who kills a *goses* is considered a murderer by the Talmud and the codes. But one who kills a *terefah* may not be guilty of murder (*Sanhedrin* 78a; *Mishneh Torah, Damages,* "Laws of Murderers" 2:8).

To sum up:

1. The dominant position in Jewish religio-moral-legal literature forbids active euthanasia of any kind but permits, while in no way requiring, passive euthanasia.

2. Because of recent scientific advances, refrigeration has become an option bypassing the problem of euthanasia. This alternative may be justified within the confines of Jewish law.

3. A limited, "minority" case may be made for active euthanasia within the framework of Jewish law.

❀ ST. THOMAS AQUINAS

6. *The Summa Theologica*

Thomas Aquinas (1224–1274) is regarded by the Catholic Church as a most eminent theologian and philosopher. He was born in Roccasecca, Italy, and was awarded a degree in theology at the age of 32. His writing consists of several long theological treatises as well as numerous disputations and commentaries on theological and philosophical topics. His greatest work is *The Summa Theologica.*

Reprinted from St. Thomas Aquinas, *The Summa Theologica,* tr. by the Fathers of the English Dominican Province, Paternoster Row, London, 1918. This passage is from Vol. II, Part I, Question 64, A5. Reprinted by permission of The Very Reverend Prior Provincial, St. Dominics Priory, London.

FIFTH ARTICLE.
WHETHER IT IS LAWFUL TO KILL ONESELF?

We proceed thus to the Fifth Article:—

Objection 1. It seems that it is lawful for a man to kill himself. For murder is a sin in so far as it is contrary to justice. But no man can do an injustice to himself, as is proved in *Ethic.* v. Therefore no man sins by killing himself.

Obj. 2. Further, It is lawful, for one who exercises public authority, to kill evildoers. Now he who exercises public authority is sometimes an evildoer. Therefore he may lawfully kill himself.

Obj. 3. Further, It is lawful for a man to suffer spontaneously a lesser danger that he may avoid a greater: thus it is lawful for a man to cut off a decayed limb even from himself, that he may save his whole body. Now sometimes a man by killing himself, avoids a greater evil, for example an unhappy life, or the shame of sin. Therefore a man may kill himself.

Obj. 4. Further, Samson killed himself, as related in Judges xvi., and yet he is numbered among the saints (Heb. xi). Therefore it is lawful for a man to kill himself.

Obj. 5. Further, It is related (2 Mach. xiv 42) that a certain Razias killed himself, *choosing to die nobly rather than to fall into the hands of the wicked, and to suffer abuses unbecoming his noble birth.* Now nothing that is done nobly and bravely is unlawful. Therefore suicide is not unlawful.

On the contrary, Augustine says (*De Civ. Dei* i.): *Hence it follows that the words 'Thou shalt not kill' refer to the killing of a man;—not another man; therefore, not even thyself. For he who kills himself, kills nothing else than a man.*

I answer that, It is altogether unlawful to kill oneself, for three reasons. First, because everything naturally loves itself, the result being that everything naturally keeps itself in *being,* and resists corruptions so far as it can. Wherefore suicide is contrary to the inclination of nature, and to charity whereby every man should love himself. Hence suicide is always a mortal sin, as being contrary to the natural law and to charity.

Secondly, because every part, as such, belongs to the whole. Now every man is part of the community, and so, as such, he belongs to the community. Hence by killing himself he injures the community, as the Philosopher declares (*Ethic.* v.).

Thirdly, because life is God's gift to man, and is subject to His power, Who kills and makes to live. Hence whoever takes his own life, sins against God, even as he who kills another's slave, sins against that slave's master, and as he who usurps to himself judgment of a matter not entrusted to him. For it belongs to God alone to pronounce sentence of death and life, according to Deut. xxxii. 39: *I will kill and I will make to live.*

Reply Obj. 1. Murder is a sin, not only because it is contrary to justice, but also because it is opposed to charity which a man should have towards himself: in this respect suicide is a sin in relation to oneself. In relation to the community and to God, it is sinful, by reason also of its opposition to justice.

Reply Obj. 2.   One who exercises public authority may lawfully put to death an evildoer, since he can pass judgment on him. But no man is judge of himself. Wherefore it is not lawful for one who exercises public authority to put himself to death for any sin whatever: although he may lawfully commit himself to the judgment of others.

Reply Obj. 3.   Man is made master of himself through his free-will: wherefore he can lawfully dispose of himself as to those matters which pertain to this life which is ruled by man's free-will. But the passage from this life to another and happier one is subject not to man's free-will but to the power of God. Hence it is not lawful for man to take his own life that he may pass to a happier life, nor that he may escape any unhappiness whatsoever of the present life, because the ultimate and most fearsome evil of this life is death, as the Philosopher states (*Ethic.* iii.). Therefore to bring death upon oneself in order to escape the other afflictions of this life, is to adopt a greater evil in order to avoid a lesser. In like manner it is unlawful to take one's own life on account of one's having committed a sin, both because by so doing one does oneself a very great injury, by depriving oneself of the time needful for repentance, and because it is not lawful to slay an evildoer except by the sentence of the public authority. Again it is unlawful for a woman to kill herself lest she be violated, because she ought not to commit on herself the very great sin of suicide, to avoid the lesser sin of another. For she commits no sin in being violated by force, provided she does not consent, since without consent of the mind there is no stain on the body, as the Blessed Lucy declared. Now it is evident that fornication and adultery are less grievous sins than taking a man's, especially one's own, life: since the latter is most grievous, because one injures oneself, to whom one owes the greatest love. Moreover it is most dangerous since no time is left wherein to expiate it by repentance. Again it is not lawful for anyone to take his own life for fear he should consent to sin, because evil must not be done that good may come (Rom. iii. 8) or that evil may be avoided, especially if the evil be of small account and an uncertain event, for it is uncertain whether one will at some future time consent to a sin, since God is able to deliver man from sin under any temptation whatever.

Reply Obj. 4.   As Augustine says (*De Civ. Dei* i.), *not even Samson is to be excused that he crushed himself together with his enemies under the ruins of the house, except the Holy Ghost, Who had wrought many wonders through him, had secretly commanded him to do this.* He assigns the same reason in the case of certain holy women, who at the time of persecution took their own lives, and who are commemorated by the Church.

Reply Obj. 5.   It belongs to fortitude that a man does not shrink from being slain by another, for the sake of the good of virtue, and that he may avoid sin. But that a man take his own life in order to avoid penal evils has indeed an appearance of fortitude (for which reason some, among whom was Razias, have killed themselves thinking to act from fortitude), yet it is not true fortitude, but rather a weakness of soul unable to bear penal evils, as the Philosopher (*Ethic.* iii.) and Augustine (*De Civ. Dei* i.) declare.

RICHARD B. BRANDT

7. *The Morality and Rationality of Suicide*

Richard B. Brandt is a professor at the University of Michigan. He has written extensively on topics that relate to value theory. His main works in this area are *Ethical Theory* (1959) and *Value and Obligation* (1961).

From the point of view of contemporary philosophy, suicide raises the following distinct questions: whether a person who commits suicide (assuming that there is suicide if and only if there is intentional termination of one's own life) is morally blameworthy, reprehensible, sinful in all circumstances; whether suicide is objectively right or wrong, and in what circumstances it is right or wrong, from a moral point of view; and whether, or in which circumstances, suicide is the best or the rational thing to do from the point of view of the agent's personal welfare.

The Moral Blameworthiness of Suicide

In former times the question of whether suicide is sinful was of great interest because the answer to it was considered relevant to how the agent would spend eternity. At present the practical issue is not as great, although a normal funeral service may be denied a person judged to have committed suicide sinfully. The chief practical issue now seems to be that persons may disapprove of a decedent for having committed suicide, and his friends or relatives may wish to defend his memory against moral charges.

The question of whether an act of suicide was sinful or morally blameworthy is not apt to arise unless it is already believed that the agent morally ought not to have done it: for instance, if he really had very poor reason for doing so, and his act foreseeably had catastrophic consequences for his wife and children. But, even if a given suicide is morally wrong, it

Reprinted from Richard B. Brandt, "The Morality and Rationality of Suicide." From *Handbook for the Study of Suicide,* edited by Seymour Perlin.

does not follow that it is morally reprehensible. For, while asserting that a given act of suicide was wrong, we may still think that the act was hardly morally blameworthy or sinful if, say, the agent was in a state of great emotional turmoil at the time. We might then say that, although what he did was wrong, his action is *excusable,* just as in the criminal law it may be decided that, although a person broke the law, he should not be punished because he was *not responsible,* that is, was temporarily insane, did what he did inadvertently, and so on.

The foregoing remarks assume that to be morally blameworthy (or sinful) on account of an act is one thing, and for the act to be wrong is another. But, if we say this, what after all does it *mean* to say that a person is morally blameworthy on account of an action? We cannot say there is agreement among philosophers on this matter, but I suggest the following account as being safe from serious objection: "X is morally blameworthy on account of an action *A*" may be taken to mean "X did *A,* and X would not have done *A* had not his character been in some respect below standard; and in view of this it is fitting or justified for X to have some disapproving attitudes including remorse toward himself, and for some other persons *Y* to have some disapproving attitudes toward X and to express them in behavior." Traditional thought would include God as one of the "other persons" who might have and express disapproving attitudes.

In case the foregoing definition does not seem obviously correct, it is worthwhile pointing out that it is usually thought that an agent is not blameworthy or sinful for an action unless it is a *reflection on him;* the definition brings this fact out and makes clear why.

If someone charges that a suicide was sinful, we may now properly ask, "What defect of character did it show?" Some writers have claimed that suicide is blameworthy because it is *cowardly,* and since being cowardly is generally conceded to be a defect of character, if an act of suicide is admitted to be both objectively wrong and also cowardly, the claim to blameworthiness might be warranted in terms of the above definition. Of course, many people would hesitate to call taking one's own life a cowardly act, and there will certainly be controversy about which acts are cowardly and which are not. But at least we can see part of what has to be done to make a charge of blameworthiness valid.

The most interesting question is the general one: which types of suicide in general are ones that, even if objectively wrong (in a sense to be explained below), are not sinful or blameworthy? Or, in other words, when is a suicide *morally excused* even if it is objectively wrong? We can at least identify some types that are morally excusable.

1. Suppose I *think* I am morally bound to commit suicide because I have a terminal illness and continued medical care will ruin my family financially. Suppose, however, that I am mistaken in this belief, and that suicide in such circumstances is not right. But surely I am not morally blameworthy; for I may be doing, out of a sense of duty to my family, what I would personally prefer not to do and is hard for me to do. What defect

of character might my action show? Suicide from a genuine sense of duty is not blameworthy, even when the moral conviction in question is mistaken.

2. Suppose that I commit suicide when I am temporarily of unsound mind, either in the sense of the M'Naghten rule that I do not know that what I am doing is wrong, or of the Durham rule that, owing to a mental defect, I am substantially unable to do what is right. Surely, any suicide in an unsound state of mind is morally excused.

3. Suppose I commit suicide when I could not be said to be temporarily of unsound mind, but simply because I am not myself. For instance, I may be in an extremely depressed mood. Now a person may be in a very depressed mood, and commit suicide on account of being in that mood, when there is nothing the matter with his character—or, in other words, his character is not in any relevant way below standard. What are other examples of being "not myself," of emotional states that might be responsible for a person's committing suicide, and that might render the suicide excusable even if wrong? Being frightened; being distraught; being in almost any highly emotional frame of mind (anger, frustration, disappointment in love); perhaps just being terribly fatigued.

So there are at least three types of suicide which can be morally excused even if they are objectively wrong. The main point is this: Mr. X may commit suicide and it may be conceded that he ought not to have done so, but it is another step to show that he is sinful, or morally blameworthy, for having done so. To make out that further point, it must be shown that his act is attributable to some substandard trait of character. So, Mrs. X after the suicide can concede that her husband ought not to have done what he did, but she can also point out that it is no reflection on his character. The distinction, unfortunately, is often overlooked. St. Thomas Aquinas, who recognizes the distinction in other places, seems blind to it in his discussion of suicide.

The Moral Reasons For and Against Suicide

Persons who say suicide is morally wrong must be asked which of two positions they are affirming: Are they saying that *every* act of suicide is wrong, *everything considered;* or are they merely saying that there is always *some* moral obligation—doubtless of serious weight—not to commit suicide, so that very often suicide is wrong, although it is possible that there are *countervailing considerations* which in particular situations make it right or even a moral duty? It is quite evident that the first position is absurd; only the second has a chance of being defensible.

In order to make clear what is wrong with the first view, we may begin with an example. Suppose an army pilot's single-seater plane goes out of control over a heavily populated area; he has the choice of staying in the plane and bringing it down where it will do little damage but at the cost of certain death for himself, and of bailing out and letting the plane fall where it will, very possibly killing a good many civilians. Suppose he chooses to do the former, and so, by our definition, commits suicide. Does anyone want to say that his action is morally wrong? Even Immanuel Kant, who opposed suicide in all circumstances, apparently would not wish to say that it is; he would, in fact, judge that this act is not one of suicide, for he says, "It is no suicide to risk one's life against one's enemies, and even to sacrifice it, in order to preserve one's duties toward oneself."[1] St. Thomas Aquinas, in his discussion of suicide, may seem to take the position that such an act would be wrong, for he says, "It is altogether unlawful to kill oneself," admitting as an exception only the case of being under special command of God. But I believe St. Thomas would, in fact, have concluded that the act is right because the basic intention of the pilot was to save the lives of civilians, and whether an act is right or wrong is a matter of basic intention.[2]

In general, we have to admit that there are things with some moral obligation to avoid which, on account of other morally relevant considerations, it is sometimes right or even morally obligatory to do. There may be some obligation to tell the truth on every occasion, but surely in many cases the consequences of telling the truth would be so dire that one is obligated to lie. The same goes for promises. There is some moral obligation to do what one has promised (with a few exceptions); but, if one can keep a trivial promise only at serious cost to another person (i.e., keep an appointment only by failing to give aid to someone injured in an accident), it is surely obligatory to break the promise.

The most that the moral critic of suicide could hold, then, is that there is *some* moral obligation not to do what one knows will cause one's death; but he surely cannot deny that circumstances exist in which there

[1]Immanuel Kant, *Lectures on Ethics*, New York: Harper Torchbook (1963), p. 150.

[2]See St. Thomas Aquinas, *Summa Theologica*, Second Part of the Second Part, Q. 64, Art. 5. In Article 7, he says: "Nothing hinders one act from having two effects, only one of which is intended, while the other is beside the intention. Now moral acts take their species according to what is intended, and not according to what is beside the intention, since this is accidental as explained above" (Q. 43, Art. 3: I–II, Q. 1, Art. 3, as 3). Mr. Norman St. John-Stevas, the most articulate contemporary defender of the Catholic view, writes as follows: "Christian thought allows certain exceptions to its general condemnation of suicide. That covered by a particular divine inspiration has already been noted. Another exception arises where suicide is the method imposed by the State for the execution of a just death penalty. A third exception is *altruistic* suicide, of which the best known example is Captain Oates. Such suicides are justified by invoking the principles of double effect. The act from which death results must be good or at least morally indifferent; some other good effect must result: The death must not be directly intended or the real means to the good effect: and a grave reason must exist for adopting the course of action" [*Life, Death and the Law*, Bloomington, Ind.: Indiana University Press (1961), pp. 250–51]. Presumably the Catholic doctrine is intended to allow suicide when this is required for meeting strong moral obligations; whether it can do so consistently depends partly on the interpretation given to "real means to the good effect." Readers interested in pursuing further the Catholic doctrine of double effect and its implications for our problem should read Philippa Foot, "The Problem of Abortion and the Doctrine of Double Effect," *The Oxford Review*, 5:5–15 (Trinity 1967).

are obligations to do things which, in fact, will result in one's death. If so, then in principle it would be possible to argue, for instance, that in order to meet my obligation to my family, it might be right for me to take my own life as the only way to avoid catastrophic hospital expenses in a terminal illness. Possibly the main point that critics of suicide on moral grounds would wish to make is that it is never right to take one's own life *for reasons of one's own personal welfare,* of any kind whatsoever. Some of the arguments used to support the immorality of suicide, however, are so framed that if they were supportable at all, they would prove that suicide is *never* moral.

One well-known type of argument against suicide may be classified as *theological.* St. Augustine and others urged that the Sixth Commandment ("Thou shalt not kill") prohibits suicide, and that we are bound to obey a divine commandment. To this reasoning one might first reply that it is arbitrary exegesis of the Sixth Commandment to assert that it was intended to prohibit suicide. The second reply is that if there is not some consideration which shows on the merits of the case that suicide is morally wrong, God had no business prohibiting it. It is true that some will object to this point, and I must refer them elsewhere for my detailed comments on the divine-will theory of morality.[3]

Another theological argument with wide support was accepted by John Locke, who wrote: ". . . Men being all the workmanship of one omnipotent and infinitely wise Maker; all the servants of one sovereign Master, sent into the world by His order and about His business; they are His property, whose workmanship they are made to last during His, not one another's pleasure. . . . Every one . . . is bound to preserve himself, and not to quit his station wilfully. . . ."[4] And Kant: "We have been placed in this world under certain conditions and for specific purposes. But a suicide opposes the purpose of his Creator; he arrives in the other world as one who has deserted his post; he must be looked upon as a rebel against God. So long as we remember the truth that it is God's intention to preserve life, we are bound to regulate our activities in conformity with it. This duty is upon us until the time comes when God expressly commands us to leave this life. Human beings are sentinels on earth and may not leave their posts until relieved by another beneficent hand."[5] Unfortunately, however, even if we grant that it is the duty of human beings to do what God commands or intends them to do, more argument is required to show that God does *not* permit human beings to quit this life when their own personal welfare would be maximized by so doing. How does one draw the requisite inference about the intentions of God? The difficulties and contradictions in

[3]R. B. Brandt, *Ethical Theory,* Englewood Cliffs, N.J.: Prentice-Hall (1959), pp. 61–82.

[4]John Locke, *Two Treatise of Government,* Ch. 2.

[5]Kant, *Lectures on Ethics,* p. 154.

arguments to reach such a conclusion are discussed at length and perspica-
ciously by David Hume in his essay "On Suicide," and in view of the un-
likelihood that readers will need to be persuaded about these, I shall merely
refer those interested to that essay.[6]

A second group of arguments may be classed as arguments *from
natural law*. St. Thomas says: "It is altogether unlawful to kill oneself, for
three reasons. First, because everything naturally loves itself, the result
being that everything naturally keeps itself in being, and resists corruptions
so far as it can. Wherefore suicide is contrary to the inclination of nature,
and to charity whereby every man should love himself. Hence suicide is
always a mortal sin, as being contrary to the natural law and to charity."[7]
Here St. Thomas ignores two obvious points. First, it is not obvious why a
human being is morally bound to do what he or she has some inclination
to do. (St. Thomas did not criticize chastity.) Second, while it is true that
most human beings do feel a strong urge to live, the human being who
commits suicide obviously feels a stronger inclination to do something else.
It is as natural for a human being to dislike, and to take steps to avoid,
say, great pain, as it is to cling to life.

A somewhat similar argument by Immanuel Kant may seem better.
In a famous passage Kant writes that the maxim of a person who commits
suicide is "From self-love I make it my principle to shorten my life if its
continuance threatens more evil than it promises pleasure. The only further
question to ask is whether this principle of self-love can become a universal
law of nature. It is then seen at once that a system of nature by whose law
the very same feeling whose function is to stimulate the furtherance of life
should actually destroy life would contradict itself and consequently could
not subsist as a system of nature. Hence this maxim cannot possibly hold
as a universal law of nature and is therefore entirely opposed to the supreme
principle of all duty."[8] What Kant finds contradictory is that the motive of
self-love (interest in one's own long-range welfare) should sometimes lead
one to struggle to preserve one's life, but at other times to end it. But where
is the contradiction? One's circumstances change, and, if the argument of
the following section in this chapter is correct, one sometimes maximizes
one's own long-range welfare by trying to stay alive, but at other times by
bringing about one's demise.

A third group of arguments, a form of which goes back at least to
Aristotle, has a more modern and convincing ring. These are arguments to
show that, in one way or another, a suicide necessarily does harm to other
persons, or to society at large. Aristotle says that the suicide treats the *state*

---

[6]This essay appears in collections of Hume's works.

[7]For an argument similar to Kant's, see also St. Thomas Aquinas, *Summa
Theologica*, II, II, Q. 64, Art. 5.

[8]Immanuel Kant, *The Fundamental Principles of the Metaphyic of Morals*,
trans. H. J. Paton, London: The Hutchinson Group (1948), Ch. 2.

unjustly.[9] Partly following Aristotle, St. Thomas says: "Every man is part of the community, and so, as such, he belongs to the community. Hence by killing himself he injures the community."[10] Blackstone held that a suicide is an offense against the king "who hath an interest in the preservation of all his subjects," perhaps following Judge Brown in 1563, who argued that suicide cost the king a subject—"he being the head has lost one of his mystical members."[11] The premise of such arguments is, as Hume pointed out, obviously mistaken in many instances. It is true that Freud would perhaps have injured society had he, instead of finishing his last book, committed suicide to escape the pain of throat cancer. But surely there have been many suicides whose demise was not a noticeable loss to society; an honest man could only say that in some instances society was better off without them.

It need not be denied that suicide is often injurious to other persons, especially the family of a suicide. Clearly it sometimes is. But, we should notice what this fact establishes. Suppose we admit, as generally would be done, that there is some obligation not to perform any action which will probably or certainly be injurious to other people, the strength of the obligation being dependent on various factors, notably the seriousness of the expected injury. Then there is *some* obligation not to commit suicide, when that act would probably or certainly be injurious to other people. But, as we have already seen, many cases of *some* obligation to do something nevertheless are *not* cases of a duty to do that thing, *everything considered.* So it could sometimes be morally justified to commit suicide, even if the act will harm someone. Must a man with a terminal illness undergo excruciating pain because his death will cause his wife sorrow— when she will be caused sorrow a month later anyway, when he is dead of natural causes? Moreover, to repeat, the fact that an individual has some obligation not to commit suicide when that act will probably injure other persons does not imply that, everything considered, it is wrong for him to do it, namely, that in all circumstances suicide *as such* is something there is some obligation to avoid.

Is there any sound argument, convincing to the modern mind, to establish that there is (or is not) *some moral obligation* to avoid suicide *as such,* an obligation, of course, which might be overridden by other obligations in some or many cases? (Captain Oates may have had a moral obligation not to commit suicide as such, but his obligation not to stand in the way of his comrades getting to safety might have been so strong that, everything considered, he was justified in leaving the polar camp and allowing himself to freeze to death.)

---

[9]Aristotle, *Nicomachaean Ethics,* Bk. 5, Ch. 10, p. 1138a.

[10]St. Thomas Aquinas, *Summa Theologica,* II, II, Q. 64, Art. 5.

[11]Sir William Blackstone, *Commentaries,* 4:189; Brown in Hales v. Petit, I Plow. 253, 75 E.R. 387 (C.B. 1563). Both cited by Norman St. John-Stevas, *Life, Death and the Law,* p. 235.

To present all the arguments necessary to answer this question convincingly would take a great deal of space. I shall, therefore, simply state one answer to it which seems plausible to some contemporary philosophers. Suppose it could be shown that it would maximize the long-run welfare of everybody affected if people were taught that there is a moral obligation to avoid suicide—so that people would be motivated to avoid suicide just because they thought it wrong (would have anticipatory guilt feelings at the very idea), and so that other people would be inclined to disapprove of persons who commit suicide unless there were some excuse (such as those mentioned in the first section). One might ask: how could it maximize utility to mold the conceptual and motivational structure of persons in this way? To which the answer might be: feeling in this way might make persons who are impulsively inclined to commit suicide in a bad mood, or a fit of anger or jealousy, take more time to deliberate; hence, some suicides that have bad effects generally might be prevented. In other words, it might be a good thing in its effects for people to feel about suicide in the way they feel about breach of promise or injuring others, just as it might be a good thing for people to feel a moral obligation not to smoke, or to wear seat belts. However, it might be that negative moral feelings about suicide as such would stand in the way of action by those persons whose welfare really is best served by suicide and whose suicide is the best thing for everybody concerned.

When a Decision to Commit Suicide is Rational From the Person's Point of View

The person who is contemplating suicide is obviously making a choice between future world-courses; the world-course that includes his demise, say, an hour from now, and several possible ones that contain his demise at a later point. One cannot have precise knowledge about many features of the latter group of world-courses, but it is certain that they will all end with death some (possibly short) finite time from now.

Why do I say the choice is between *world*-courses and not just a choice between future life-courses of the prospective suicide, the one shorter than the other? The reason is that one's suicide has some impact on the world (and one's continued life has some impact on the world), and that conditions in the rest of the world will often make a difference in one's evaluation of the possibilities. One *is* interested in things in the world other than just oneself and one's own happiness.

The basic question a person must answer, in order to determine which world-course is best or rational for him to choose, is which he *would* choose under conditions of optimal use of information, when *all* of his desires are taken into account. It is not just a question of what we prefer *now*, with some clarification of all the possibilities being considered. Our preferences change, and the preferences of tomorrow (assuming we can know something about them) are just as legitimately taken into account in deciding what to do now as the preferences of today. Since any reason that can be given today for weighting heavily today's preference can be given tomorrow for weighting heavily tomorrow's preference, the preferences of any time-stretch have a rational claim to an equal vote. Now the importance of that fact is this: we often know quite well that our desires, aversions, and preferences may change after a short while. When a person is in a state of despair—perhaps brought about by a rejection in love or discharge from a long-held position—nothing but the thing he cannot have seems desirable; everything else is turned to ashes. Yet we know quite well that the passage of time is likely to reverse all this; replacements may be found or other types of things that are available to us may begin to look attractive. So, if we were to act on the preferences of today alone, when the emotion of despair seems more than we can stand, we might find death preferable to life; but, if we allow for the preferences of the weeks and years ahead, when many goals will be enjoyable and attractive, we might find life much preferable to death. So, if a choice of what is best is to be determined by what we want not only now but later (and later desires on an equal basis with the present ones)—as it should be—then what is the best or preferable world-course will often be quite different from what it would be if the choice, or what is best for one, were fixed by one's desires and preferences now.

Of course, if one commits suicide there are no future desires or aversions that may be compared with present ones and that should be allowed an equal vote in deciding what is best. In that respect the course of action that results in death is different from any other course of action we may undertake. I do not wish to suggest the rosy possibility that it is often or always reasonable to believe that next week "I shall be more interested in living than I am today, if today I take a dim view of continued existence." On the contrary, when a person is seriously ill, for instance, he may have no reason to think that the preference-order will be reversed—it may be that tomorrow he will prefer death to life more strongly.

The argument is often used that one can never be *certain* what is going to happen, and hence one is never rationally justified in doing anything as drastic as committing suicide. But we always have to live by probabilities and make our estimates as best we can. As soon as it is clear beyond reasonable doubt not only that death is now preferable to life, but also that it will be every day from now until the end, the rational thing is to act promptly.

Let us not pursue the question of whether it is rational for a person with a painful terminal illness to commit suicide; it is. However, the issue seldom arises, and few terminally ill patients do commit suicide. With such patients matters usually get worse slowly so that no particular time seems to call for action. They are often so heavily sedated that it is impossible for the mental processes of decision leading to action to occur; or else they are incapacitated in a hospital and the very physical possibility of ending their lives is not available. Let us leave this grim topic and turn to a practically more important problem: whether it is rational for persons to commit suicide for some reason other than painful terminal physical illness. Most persons who commit suicide do so, apparently, because they face a nonphysical problem that depresses them beyond their ability to bear.

Among the problems that have been regarded as good and sufficient reasons for 'ending life, we find (in addition to serious illness) the following: some event that has made a person feel ashamed or lose his prestige and status; reduction from affluence to poverty; the loss of a limb or of physical beauty; the loss of sexual capacity; some event that makes it seem impossible to achieve things by which one sets store; loss of a loved one; disappointment in love; the infirmities of increasing age. It is not to be denied that such things can be serious blows to a person's prospects of happiness.

Whatever the nature of an individual's problem, there are various plain errors to be avoided—errors to which a person is especially prone when he is depressed—in deciding whether, everything considered, he prefers a world-course containing his early demise to one in which his life continues to its natural terminus. Let us forget for a moment the relevance to the decision of preferences that he may have tomorrow, and concentrate on some errors that may infect his preference as of today, and for which correction or allowance must be made.

In the first place, depression, like any severe emotional experience, tends to primitivize one's intellectual processes. It restricts the range of one's survey of the possibilities. One thing that a rational person would do is compare the world-course containing his suicide with his *best* alternative. But his best alternative is precisely a possibility he may overlook if, in a depressed mood, he thinks only of how badly off he is and cannot imagine any way of improving his situation. If a person is disappointed in love, it is possible to adopt a vigorous plan of action that carries a good chance of acquainting him with someone he likes at least as well; and if old age prevents a person from continuing the tennis game with his favorite partner, it is possible to learn some other game that provides the joys of competition without the physical demands.

Depression has another insidious influence on one's planning; it seriously affects one's judgment about probabilities. A person disappointed in love is very likely to take a dim view of himself, his prospects, and his attractiveness; he thinks that because he has been rejected by one person he will probably be rejected by anyone who looks desirable to him. In a less gloomy frame of mind he would make different estimates. Part of the reason for such gloomy probability estimates is that depression tends to repress one's memory of evidence that supports a nongloomy prediction. Thus, a rejected lover tends to forget any cases in which he has elicited enthusiastic response from ladies in relation to whom he has been the one who has done the rejecting. Thus his pessimistic self-image is based upon a highly selected, and pessimistically selected, set of data. Even when he is reminded of the data, moreover, he is apt to resist an optimistic inference.

Another kind of distortion of the look of future prospects is not a result of depression, but is quite normal. Events distant in the future feel small, just as objects distant in space look small. Their prospect does not have the effect on motivational processes that it would have if it were of an event in the immediate future. Psychologists call this the "goal-gradient" phenomenon; a rat, for instance, will run faster toward a perceived food box than a distant unseen one. In the case of a person who has suffered some misfortune, and whose situation now is an unpleasant one, this reduction of the motivational influence of events distant in time has the effect that present unpleasant states weigh far more heavily than probable future pleasant ones in any choice of world-courses.

If we are trying to determine whether we now prefer, or shall later prefer, the outcome of one world-course to that of another (and this is leaving aside the questions of the weight of the votes of preferences at a later date), we must take into account these and other infirmities of our "sensing" machinery. Since knowing that the machinery is out of order will not tell us what results it would give if it were working, the best recourse might be to refrain from making any decision in a stressful frame of mind. If decisions have to be made, one must recall past reactions, in a normal frame of mind, to outcomes like those under assessment. But many suicides seem to occur in moments of despair. What should be clear from the above is that a moment of despair, if one is seriously contemplating suicide, ought to be a moment of reassessment of one's goals and values, a reassessment which the individual must realize is very difficult to make objectively, because of the very quality of his depressed frame of mind.

A decision to commit suicide may in certain circumstances be a rational one. But a person who wants to act rationally must take into account the various possible "errors" and make appropriate rectification of his initial evaluations.

THE ROLE OF OTHER PERSONS

What is the moral obligation of other persons toward those who are contemplating suicide? The question of their moral blameworthiness may be ignored and what is rational for them to do from the point of view of personal welfare may be considered as being of secondary concern. Laws make it dangerous to aid or encourage a suicide. The risk of running afoul of the law may partly determine moral obligation, since moral obligation to do something may be reduced by the fact that it is personally dangerous.

The moral obligation of other persons toward one who is contemplating suicide is an instance of a general obligation to render aid to those in serious distress, at least when this can be done at no great cost to one's self. I do not think this general principle is seriously questioned by anyone, whatever his moral theory; so I feel free to assume it as a premise. Obviously the person contemplating suicide is in great distress of some sort; if he were not, he would not be seriously considering terminating his life.

How great a person's obligation is to one in distress depends on a number of factors. Obviously family and friends have special obligations to devote time to helping the prospective suicide—which others do not have. But anyone in this kind of distress has a moral claim on the time of any person who knows the situation (unless there are others more responsible who are already doing what should be done).

What is the obligation? It depends, of course, on the situation, and how much the second person knows about the situation. If the individual has decided to terminate his life if he can, and it is clear that he is right in this decision, then, if he needs help in executing the decision, there is a moral obligation to give him help. On this matter a patient's physician has a special obligation, from which any talk about the Hippocratic oath does not absolve him. It is true that there are some damages one cannot be' expected to absorb, and some risks which one cannot be expected to take, on account of the obligation to render aid.

On the other hand, if it is clear that the individual should not commit suicide, from the point of view of his own welfare, or if there is a presumption that he should not (when the only evidence is that a person is discovered unconscious, with the gas turned on), it would seem to be the individual's obligation to intervene, prevent the successful execution of the decision, and see to the availability of competent psychiatric advice and temporary hospitalization, if necessary, Whether one has a right to take such steps when a clearly sane person, after careful reflection over a period of time, comes to the conclusion that an end to his life is what is best for him and what he wants, is very doubtful, even when one thinks his conclusion a mistaken one; it would seem that a man's own considered decision about whether he wants to live must command respect, although one must concede that this could be debated.

The more interesting role in which a person may be cast, however, is that of adviser. It is often important to one who is contemplating suicide to go over his thinking with another, and to feel that a conclusion, one way or the other, has the support of a respected mind. One thing one can obviously do, in rendering the service of advice, is to discuss with the person the various types of issues discussed above, made more specific by the concrete circumstances of his case, and help him find whether, in view, say, of the damage his suicide would do to others, he has a moral obligation to refrain, and whether it is rational or best for him, from the point of view of his own welfare, to take this step or adopt some other plan instead.

To get a person to see what is the rational thing to do is no small job. Even to get a person, in a frame of mind when he is seriously contemplating (or perhaps has already unsuccessfully attempted) suicide, to recognize a plain truth of fact may be a major operation. If a man insists, "I am a complete failure," when it is obvious that by any reasonable standard he is far from that, it may be tremendously difficult to get him to see the fact. But there is another job beyond that of getting a person to see what is the rational thing to do; that is to help him *act* rationally, or *be* rational, when he has conceded what would be the rational thing.

How either of these tasks may be accomplished effectively may be discussed more competently by an experienced psychiatrist than by a philosopher. Loneliness and the absence of human affection are states which exacerbate any other problems; disappointment, reduction to poverty, and so forth, seem less impossible to bear in the presence of the affection of another. Hence simply to be a friend, or to find someone a friend, may be the largest contribution one can make either to helping a person be rational or see cleary what is rational for him to do; this service may make one who was contemplating suicide feel that there is a future for him which it is possible to face.

Suggested Readings

Aristotle, *Nichomachaen Ethics,* 1138 a7, trans. J.A.K. Thomson, Penguin Books, Baltimore, 1955.

Brandt, R. B., "The Morality of Abortion," *Monist,* 56, 1972.

Chesterton, G. K., "Euthanasia and Murder," *American Law Review,* 8, 1937.

Durkheim, E., *Suicide,* trans., J. A. Spaulding and G. Simpson, ed. G. Simpson, Free Press, New York, 1960.

Fletcher, J., *Morals and Medicine,* Beacon Press, Boston, 1960.

Hillman, J., *Suicide and the Soul,* Harper & Row, New York, 1973.

Kohl, M., *The Morality of Killing: Euthanasia, Abortion, and Transplants,* Humanities Press, New York, 1974.

Margolis, J., "Abortion," *Ethics,* 84, 1973.

Nagel, T., "Death," *Nous,* 4, 1971.

Pope Pius XI, *Casti Connubi,* Paulist Press, New York, 1941.

Sexual Relations

❊ INTRODUCTION

All societies have viewed marriage and sexual relations as of the utmost importance, not only for the individual, but also for the survival and well-being of the community. Thus every society has strongly defined and regulated the customs concerning them. Ordinarily these customs remain rather stable and for that reason they seldom occasion controversy. Nevertheless, our society now seems to be undergoing a period of extensive change in this area.[1] And these changes are of fundamental importance, since they profoundly affect our individual lives in addition to contributing towards the restructuring of our entire social organization.

There is little doubt that our society places an ever increasing emphasis upon sex. Indeed, we are so continuously bombarded by erotogenic stimuli that we often are unaware of the many ways in which they are used to affect our attitudes and influence our behavior. But during our more reflective moments we cannot fail to be struck by the manner in which our culture concentrates on the more superficial aspects of sex while ignoring the more complex and significant features of meaningful personal relationships. This tendency should not be too quickly dismissed, for not only is it an indication of the superficiality of most personal relationships, but it also may be symptomatic of the alienation and fragmentation which too often characterize the human psyche.

The essays which follow discuss of sex in its relationship with love, marriage, and social conventions. Widely divergent sexual codes are defended, and different sanctions are introduced to justify the positions that are proposed. It is interesting to notice the general philosophical perspective within which each view is framed and to begin thereby to consider some of the broader implications of one's personal principles. Though it may be difficult to assume an attitude of detachment and objectivity in considering the various factors that are so important a part of our individual lives, this is a necessary first step towards the development of a mature sexual code. And it becomes increasingly important to attain a proper perspective on sex so as to provide an inner immunity against those forces in our technocratic society which may seek to control our thoughts and actions by libidinal means.

Bertrand Russell, in a selection from his book *Marriage and Morals*,

---

[1]Cf. Pitirim Sorokin, *The American Sex Revolution* (Boston: Porter Sargent, 1956).

is concerned to distinguish clearly between sex and love. He also identifies many of the factors in society which tend to diminish our chances for the attainment of wholesome, loving relationships. Russell concludes by recommending companionate marriages. He believes that this reform would do much to promote human happiness and well-being.

Pope Pius XI reaffirms the Church's doctrine of the sacredness of marriage and sexual union. He insists that an acknowledgement of this supernatural sanction would decrease the levity with which contemporary secular society approaches the questions of marriage, birth control, divorce, and adultery. In opposition to prevailing attitudes and conventions Pius XI sets forth the "unalterable law of God" to reestablish the sanctity of human institutions and restore the dignity of the human soul. He calls upon the brethren of the Church to practice the eternal truths revealed in the Word of God and to resist the sinful tendencies exhibited in our ungodly age.

Donald Cantor provides extensive statistical data in support of his controversial position. He defends homosexuality, claiming that its practice is gradually gaining wider popular acceptance and that it is now morally imperative to accord it full social equality with heterosexuality.

Kate Millett discusses some of the social and political implications of sexuality. She shows how the domination of females by males is accomplished through the socialization of both sexes to rather clearly defined roles. These roles serve to establish and perpetuate numerous attitudes which contribute to the brutalization and exploitation of women as an inferior class. The elimination of this universal form of oppression will require a fundamental change in the character of the institutions of society.

❀ BERTRAND RUSSELL

8. Love, Sex and Trial Marriage

Bertrand Russell (1872–1970), British mathematician and philosopher, was born in Wales. Author of more than forty books and hundreds of articles, he distinguished himself as one of the greatest philosophers of the 20th century. Lord Russell received many honors for his work, including the Nobel Prize for Literature, in 1950. He devoted his last years to the organization of numerous social-action groups. Among the more important of these were: the Committee of 100, the Bertrand Russell Peace Foundation, the Who Killed Kennedy Committee, and the International War Crimes Tribunal.

The prevailing attitude of most communities towards love is curiously twofold: on the one hand, it is the chief theme of poetry, novels, and plays; on the other hand, it is completely ignored by most serious sociologists, and is not considered as one of the desiderata in schemes of economic or political reform. I do not think this attitude justifiable. I regard love as one of the most important things in human life, and I regard any system as bad which interferes unnecessarily with its free development.

Love, when the word is properly used, does not denote any and every relation between the sexes, but only one involving considerable emotion, and a relation which is psychological as well as physical. It may reach any degree of intensity. Such emotions as are expressed in *Tristan und Isolde* are in accordance with the experience of countless men and women. The power of giving artistic expression to the emotion of love is rare, but the emotion itself, at least in Europe, is not. It is much commoner in some societies than in others, and this depends, I think, not upon the nature of the people concerned but upon their conventions and institutions. In China it is rare, and appears in history as a characteristic of bad emperors who are misled by wicked concubines: traditional Chinese culture objected to all strong emotions, and considered that a man should in all circumstances preserve the empire of reason. In this it resembled the early eighteenth century. We, who have behind us the Romantic Movement, the French Revolution, and the Great War, are conscious that the part of reason in human life is not so dominant as was hoped in the reign of Queen Anne. And reason itself has turned traitor in creating the doctrine of psychoanalysis. The three main extra-rational activities in modern life are religion, war, and love; all these are extra-rational, but love is not anti-rational, that is to say, a reasonable man may reasonably rejoice in its existence. Owing to the causes that we have considered in earlier chapters, there is in the modern world a certain antagonism between religion and love. I do not think this antagonism is unavoidable; it is due only to the fact that the Christian religion, unlike some others, is rooted in asceticism.

In the modern world, however, love has another enemy more dangerous than religion, and that is the gospel of work and economic success. It is generally held, especially in America, that a man should not allow love to interfere with his career, and that if he does, he is silly. But in this as in all human matters a balance is necessary. It would be foolish, though in some cases it might be tragically heroic, to sacrifice career completely for love, but it is equally foolish and in no degree heroic to sacrifice love completely for career. Nevertheless this happens, and happens inevitably, in a society organized on the basis of a universal scramble for money. Consider the life of a typical business man of the present day, especially in America: from the time when he is first grown up he devotes all his best thoughts and all his best energies to financial success; everything else is merely unimportant recreation. In his youth he satisfies his physical needs from time to time with prostitutes: presently he marries, but his interests are totally different from his wife's, and he never becomes really intimate with her. He comes home late and tired from the office; he gets up in the morning before his wife is awake; he spends Sunday playing golf, because exercise is necessary to keep him fit for the money-making struggle. His wife's interests appear to him essentially feminine, and while he approves of them, he makes no attempt to share them. He has no time for illicit love any more than for love in marriage, though he may, of course, occasionally visit a prostitute when he is away from home on business. His wife probably remains sexually cold towards him, which is not to be wondered at, since he never has time to woo her. Subconsciously he is dissatisfied, but he does not know why. He drowns his dissatisfaction mainly in work, but also in other less desirable ways, for example, by the sadistic pleasure to be derived from watching prize-fights or persecuting radicals. His wife, who is equally unsatisfied, finds an outlet in second-rate culture, and in upholding virtue by harrying all those whose lives are generous and free. In this way the lack of sexual satisfaction both in husband and wife turns to hatred of mankind disguised as public spirit and a high moral standard. This unfortunate state of affairs is largely due to a wrong conception of our sexual needs. St. Paul apparently thought that the only thing needed in a marriage was opportunity for sexual intercourse, and this view has been on the whole encouraged by the teaching of Christian moralists. Their dislike of sex has blinded them to all the finer aspects of the sexual life, with the result that those who have suffered their teaching in youth go about the world blind to their own best potentialities. Love is something far more than desire for sexual intercourse; it is the principal means of escape from the loneliness which afflicts most men and women throughout the greater part of their lives. There is a deep-seated fear, in most people, of the cold world and the possible cruelty of the herd; there is a longing for affection, which is often concealed by roughness, boorishness or a bullying manner in men, and by nagging and scolding in women. Passionate mutual love while it lasts puts an end to this feeling; it breaks down the hard walls of the ego, producing a new being composed of two in one. Nature did not construct human beings to stand alone, since they cannot fulfil her biological purpose except with the help of another; and civilized people cannot fully satisfy their sexual instinct without love. The instinct is not completely satisfied unless a man's whole being, mental quite as much as physical, enters into the relation. Those who have never known the deep intimacy of the intense companionship of happy mutual love have missed the best thing that life has to give; unconsciously, if not consciously, they feel this, and the resulting disappointment inclines them towards envy, oppression and cruelty. To give due place to passionate love should be therefore a matter which concerns the sociologist, since, if they miss this experience, men and women cannot attain their full stature, and cannot feel towards the rest of the world that kind of generous warmth without which their social activities are pretty sure to be harmful.

Most men and women, given suitable conditions, will feel passionate love at some period of their lives. For the inexperienced, however, it is very difficult to distinguish passionate love from mere attraction; especially is this the case with well-brought-up girls, who have been taught that they could not possibly like to kiss a man unless they loved him. If a girl is expected to be a virgin when she marries, it will very often happen that she is trapped by a transient and trivial sex attraction, which a woman with sexual experience could easily distinguish from love. This has undoubtedly been a frequent cause of unhappy marriages. Even where mutual love exists, it may be poisoned by the belief of one or other that it is sinful. This belief may, of course, be well founded. Parnell, for example, undoubtedly sinned in committing adultery, since he thereby postponed the fulfilment of the hopes of Ireland for many years. But even where the sense of sin is unfounded, it will poison love just as much. If love is to bring all the good of which it is capable, it must be free, generous, unrestrained and wholehearted.

The sense of sin which a conventional education attaches to love, even to love within marriage, operates often subconsciously in men as well as in women, and in those whose conscious opinions are emancipated as well as in those who adhere to old traditions. The effects of this attitude are various; it often renders men brutal, clumsy and unsympathetic in their love-making, since they cannot bring themselves to speak about it so as to ascertain the woman's feelings, nor can they adequately value the gradual approaches to the final act which are essential to most women's enjoyment. Indeed they often fail to realize that a woman should experience enjoyment, and that if she does not, her lover is at fault. In women who have been conventionally educated there is often a certain pride in coldness, there is great physical reserve, and an unwillingness to allow easy physical intimacy. A skilful wooer can probably overcome these timidities, but a man who respects and admires them as the mark of a virtuous woman is not likely to overcome them, with the result that even after many years of marriage the relations of husband and wife remain constrained and more or less formal. In the days of our grandfathers, husbands never expected to see their wives naked, and their wives would have been horrified at such a suggestion. This attitude is still commoner than might be thought, and even among those who have advanced beyond this point, a good deal of the old restraint often remains.

There is another more psychological obstacle to the full development of love in the modern world, and that is the fear that many people feel of not preserving their individuality intact. This is a foolish and rather modern terror. Individuality is not an end in itself; it is something that must enter into fructifying contact with the world, and in so doing must lose its separateness. An individuality which is kept in a glass case withers, whereas one that is freely expended in human contacts becomes enriched. Love, children, and work are the great sources of fertilizing contact between the individual and the rest of the world. Of these love is usually chronologically the first. Moreover, it is essential to the best development of parental affection, since a child is apt to reproduce the characteristics of both parents, and if they do not love each other, each will only enjoy his own characteristics when they appear in the children, and will be pained by the characteristics of the other parent. Work is by no means always capable of bringing a man into fruitful contact with the outer world. Whether it does so or not depends upon the spirit in which it is undertaken. Work of which the motive is solely pecuniary cannot have this value, but only work which embodies some kind of devotion, whether to persons, to things, or merely to a vision. And love itself is worthless when it is merely possessive; it is then on a level with work which is merely pecuniary. In order to have the kind of value of which we are speaking, love must feel the ego of the beloved person as important as one's own ego, and must realize the other's feelings and wishes as though they were one's own. That is to say, there must be an instinctive and not merely conscious extension of egoistic feeling so as to embrace the other person as well. All this has been rendered difficult by our pugnacious competitive society, and by the foolish cult of personality derived partly from Protestantism and partly from the Romantic Movement.

Among modern emancipated people, love in the serious sense with which we are concerned is suffering a new danger. When people no longer feel any moral barrier against sexual intercourse on every occasion when even a trivial impulse inclines to it, they get into the habit of dissociating sex from serious emotion and from feelings of affection; they may even come to associate it with feelings of hatred. Of this sort of thing Aldous Huxley's novels afford the best illustration. His characters, like St. Paul, view sex intercourse merely as a physiological outlet; the higher values with which it is capable of being associated appear to be unknown to them. From such an attitude it is only a step to the revival of asceticism. Love has its own proper ideals and its own intrinsic moral standards. These are obscured both in Christian teaching and in the indiscriminate revolt against all sexual morality which has sprung up among considerable sections of the younger generation. Sex intercourse divorced from love is incapable of bringing any profound satisfaction to instinct. I am not saying that it should never occur, for to ensure this we should have to set up such rigid barriers that love also would become very difficult. What I am saying is that sex intercourse apart from love has little value, and is to be regarded primarily as experimentation with a view to love.

The claims of love to a recognized place in human life are, as we have seen, very great. But love is an anarchic force which, if it is left free, will not remain within any bounds set by law or custom. So long as children are not involved, this may not greatly matter. But as soon as children appear we are in a different region, where love is no longer autonomous but serves the biological purposes of the race. There has to be a social ethic connected with children, which may, where there is conflict, override the claims of passionate love. A wise ethic will, however, minimize this conflict to the uttermost, not only because love is good in itself, but also because it is good for children when their parents love each other. To secure as little interference with love as is compatible with the interests of children should be one of the main purposes of a wise sexual ethic. . . .

In a rational ethic, marriage would not count as such in the absence of children. A sterile marriage should be easily dissoluble, for it is through children alone that sexual relations become of importance to society, and worthy to be taken cognisance of by a legal institution. . . . In recent years, however, . . . neither men nor women invariably wait for marriage before experiencing sexual intercourse. In the case of men, provided their lapses were with prostitutes and decently concealed, they were comparatively easy to condone, but in the case of women other than professional prostitutes, the conventional moralists find what they call immorality much harder to put up with. Nevertheless, in America, in England, in Germany, in Scandinavia, a great change has taken place since the war. Very many girls of respectable families have ceased to think it worth while to preserve their "virtue," and young men, instead of finding an outlet with prostitutes, have had affairs with girls of the kind whom, if they were richer, they would wish to marry. It seems that this process has gone farther in the United States than it has in England, owing, I think, to Prohibition and automobiles. Owing to Prohibition, it has become *de rigueur* at any cheerful party for everybody to get more or less drunk. Owing to the fact that a very large percentage of girls possess cars of their own, it has become easy for them to escape with a lover from the eyes of parents and neighbours. The resulting state of affairs is described in Judge Lindsey's books.[1] The old accuse him of exaggeration, but the young do not. As far as a casual traveller can, I took pains to test his assertions by questioning young men. I did not find them inclined to deny anything that he said as to the facts. It seems to be the case throughout America that a very large percentage of girls who subsequently marry and become of the highest respectability have sex experience, often with several lovers. And even where complete relations do not occur, there is so much "petting" and "necking" that the absence of complete intercourse can only be viewed as a perversion.

I cannot say myself that I view the present state of affairs as satisfactory. It has certain undesirable features imposed upon it by conventional moralists, and until conventional morality is changed, I do not see how these undesirable features are to disappear. Bootlegged sex is in fact as inferior to what it might be as bootlegged alcohol. I do not think anybody can deny that there is enormously more drunkenness among young men, and still more among young women, in well-to-do America than there was before the introduction of Prohibition. In circumventing the law there is, of course, a certain spice and a certain pride of cleverness, and while the law about drink is being circumvented it is natural to circumvent the conventions about sex. Here, also, the sense of daring acts as an aphrodisiac. The consequence is that sex relations between young people tend to take the silliest possible form, being entered into not from affection but from bravado, and at times of intoxication. Sex, like liquor, has to be taken in forms which are concentrated and rather unpalatable, since these forms alone can escape the vigilance of the authorities. Sex relations as a dignified, rational, wholehearted activity in which the complete personality

---

[1] *The Revolt of Modern Youth*, 1925. *Companionate Marriage*, 1927.

cooperates, do not often, I think, occur in America outside marriage. To this extent the moralists have been successful. They have not prevented fornication; on the contrary, if anything, their opposition, by making it spicy, has made it more common. But they have succeeded in making it almost as undesirable as they say it is, just as they have succeeded in making much of the alcohol consumed as poisonous as they assert all alcohol to be. They have compelled young people to take sex neat, divorced from daily companionship, from a common work, and from all psychological intimacy. The more timid of the young do not go so far as complete sexual relations, but content themselves with producing prolonged states of sexual excitement without satisfaction, which are nervously debilitating, and calculated to make the full enjoyment of sex at a later date difficult or impossible. Another drawback to the type of sexual excitement which prevails among the young in America is that it involves either failure to work or loss of sleep, since it is necessarily connected with parties which continue into the small hours.

A graver matter, while official morality remains what it is, is the risk of occasional disaster. By ill luck it may happen that some one young person's doings come to the ears of some guardian of morality, who will proceed with a good conscience to a sadistic orgy of scandal. And since it is almost impossible for young people in America to acquire a sound knowledge of birth-control methods, unintended pregnancies are not infrequent. These are generally dealt with by procuring abortion, which is dangerous, painful, illegal, and by no means easy to keep secret. The complete gulf between the morals of the young and the morals of the old, which exists very commonly in present-day America, has another unfortunate result, namely that often there can be no real intimacy or friendship between parents and children, and that the parents are incapable of helping their children with advice or sympathy. When young people get into a difficulty, they cannot speak of it to their parents without producing an explosion—possibly scandal, certainly a hysterical upheaval. The relation of parent and child has thus ceased to be one performing any useful function after the child has reached adolescence. How much more civilized are the Trobriand Islanders, where a father will say to his daughter's lover: "You sleep with my child: very well, marry her."[2]

In spite of the drawbacks we have been considering, there are great advantages in the emancipation, however partial, of young people in America, as compared with their elders. They are freer from priggery, less inhibited, less enslaved to authority devoid of rational foundation. I think also that they are likely to prove less cruel, less brutal, and less violent than their seniors. For it has been characteristic of American life to take out in violence the anarchic impulses which could not find an outlet in sex. It may also be hoped that when the generation now young reaches middle age, it will not wholly forget its behaviour in youth, and will be tolerant of

[2]Malinowski, *The Sexual Life of Savages*, p. 73.

sexual experiments which at present are scarcely possible because of the need of secrecy.

The state of affairs in England is more or less similar to that in America, though not so developed owing to the absence of Prohibition and the paucity of motor-cars. There is also, I think, in England, and certainly on the Continent, very much less of the practice of sexual excitement without ultimate satisfaction. And respectable people in England, with some honourable exceptions, are on the whole less filled with persecuting zeal than corresponding people in America. Nevertheless, the difference between the two countries is only one of degree.

Judge Ben B. Lindsey, who was for many years in charge of the juvenile court at Denver, and in that position had unrivalled opportunities for ascertaining the facts, proposed a new institution which he calls "companionate marriage." Unfortunately he has lost his official position, for when it became known that he used it rather to promote the happiness of the young than to give them a consciousness of sin, the Ku Klux Klan and the Catholics combined to oust him. Companionate marriage is the proposal of a wise conservative. It is an attempt to introduce some stability into the sexual relations of the young, in place of the present promiscuity. He points out the obvious fact that what prevents the young from marrying is lack of money, and that money is required in marriage partly on account of children, but partly also because it is not the thing for the wife to earn her own living. His view is that young people should be able to enter upon a new kind of marriage, distinguished from ordinary marriage by three characteristics. First, that there should be for the time being no intention of having children, and that accordingly the best available birth-control information should be given to the young couple. Second, that so long as there are no children and the wife is not pregnant, divorce should be possible by mutual consent. And third, that in the event of divorce, the wife should not be entitled to alimony. He holds, and I think rightly, that if such an institution were established by law, a very great many young people, for example students at universities, would enter upon comparatively permanent partnerships, involving a common life, and free from the Dionysiac characteristics of their present sex relations. He brings evidence to bear that young students who are married do better work than such as are unmarried. It is indeed obvious that work and sex are more easily combined in a quasi-permanent relation than in the scramble and excitement of parties and alcoholic stimulation. There is no reason under the sun why it should be more expensive for two young people to live together than to live separately, and therefore the economic reasons which at present lead to postponement of marriage would no longer operate. I have not the faintest doubt that Judge Lindsey's plan, if embodied in the law, would have a very beneficent influence, and that this influence would be such as all might agree to be a gain from a moral point of view.

Nevertheless, Judge Lindsey's proposals were received with a howl of horror by all middle-aged persons and all newspapers throughout the length and breadth of America. It was said that he was attacking the sanctity of the home; it was said that in tolerating marriages not intended to lead at once to children he was opening the floodgates to legalized lust; it was said that he enormously exaggerated the prevalence of extra-marital sexual relations, that he was slandering pure American womanhood, and that most business men remained cheerfully continent up to the age of thirty or thirty-five. All these things were said, and I try to think that among those who said them were some who believed them. I listened to many invectives against Judge Lindsey, but I came away with the impression that the arguments which were regarded as decisive were two. First, that Judge Lindsey's proposals would not have been approved by Christ; and second, that they were not approved by even the more liberal of American divines. The second of these arguments appeared to be considered the more weighty, and indeed rightly, since the other is purely hypothetical, and incapable of being substantiated. I never heard any person advance any argument even pretending to show that Judge Lindsey's proposals would diminish human happiness. This consideration, indeed, I was forced to conclude, is thought wholly unimportant by those who uphold traditional morality.

For my part, while I am quite convinced that companionate marriage would be a step in the right direction, and would do a great deal of good, I do not think that it goes far enough. I think that all sex relations which do not involve children should be regarded as a purely private affair, and that if a man and a woman choose to live together without having children, that should be no one's business but their own. I should not hold it desirable that either a man or a woman should enter upon the serious business of a marriage intended to lead to children without having had previous sexual experience. There is a great mass of evidence to show that the first experience of sex should be with a person who has previous knowledge. The sexual act in human beings is not instinctive, and apparently never has been since it ceased to be performed *a tergo*. And apart from this argument, it seems absurd to ask people to enter upon a relation intended to be lifelong, without any previous knowledge as to their sexual compatibility. It is just as absurd as it would be if a man intending to buy a house were not allowed to view it until he had completed the purchase. The proper course, if the biological function of marriage were adequately recognized, would be to say that no marriage should be legally binding until the wife's first pregnancy. At present a marriage is null if sexual intercourse is impossible, but children, rather than sexual intercourse, are the true purpose of marriage, which should therefore be not regarded as consummated until such time as there is a prospect of children. This view depends, at least in part, upon that separation between procreation and mere sex which has been brought about by contraceptives. Contraceptives have altered the whole aspect of sex and marriage, and have made distinctions necessary which could formerly have been ignored. People may come together for sex alone, as occurs in prostitution, or for companion-

ship involving a sexual element, as in Judge Lindsey's companionate marriage, or, finally, for the purpose of rearing a family. These are all different,
and no morality can be adequate to modern circumstances which confounds
them in one indiscriminate total.

❀ POPE PIUS XI

9. The Sacredness of Love and Marriage

Pope Pius XI was born near Milan, Italy on May 31, 1857. After studying
at the Gregorian University in Rome, he became a professor at the
major seminary in Milan and was soon appointed to the staff of the
Ambrosian Library. He served the Church as Pontiff from 1922 until 1939.
His encyclical on Christian Marriage (Casti Connubii) was released
December 30, 1930.

When we consider the great excellence of chaste wedlock, Venerable
Brethren, it appears all the more regrettable that particularly in our day
we should witness this divine institution often scorned and on every side
degraded.

For now, alas, not secretly nor under cover, but openly, with all
sense of shame put aside, now by word again by writings, by theatrical
productions of every kind, by romantic fiction, by amorous and frivolous
novels, by cinematographs portraying in vivid scene, in addresses broadcast
by radio telephony, in short by all the inventions of modern science, the
sanctity of marriage is trampled upon and derided; divorce, adultery, all the
basest vices either are extolled or at least are depicted in such colors as to
appear to be free of all reproach and infamy. Books are not lacking which
dare to pronounce themselves as scientific but which in truth are merely
coated with a veneer of science in order that they may the more easily
insinuate their ideas. The doctrines defended in these are offered for sale
as the productions of modern genius, of that genius namely, which, anxious
only for truth, is considered to have *emancipated* itself from all those old-
fashioned and immature opinions of the ancients; and to the number of
these antiquated opinions they relegate the traditional doctrine of Christian marriage.

These thoughts are instilled into men of every class, rich and poor,
masters and workers, lettered and unlettered, married and single, the godly
and godless, old and young, but for these last, as easiest prey, the worst
snares are laid.

Reprinted from the Encyclical on "Christian Marriage," ("Casti Connubi"), in
Five Great Encyclicals (New York: The Paulist Press, 1939), by permission of The Paulist
Press.

Not all the sponsors of these new doctrines are carried to the extremes of unbridled lust; there are those who, striving as it were to ride a middle course, believe nevertheless that something should be conceded in our times as regards certain precepts of the divine and natural law. But these likewise, more or less wittingly, are emissaries of the great enemy who is ever seeking to sow cockle among the wheat. We, therefore, whom the Father has appointed over His field, We who are bound by Our most holy office to take care lest the good seed be choked by the weeds, believe it fitting to apply to Ourselves the most grave words of the Holy Ghost with which the Apostle Paul exhorted his beloved Timothy: "Be thou vigilant . . . Fulfill thy ministry . . . Preach the word, be instant in season, out of season, reprove, entreat, rebuke in all patience and doctrine."

And since, in order that the deceits of the enemy may be avoided, it is necessary first of all that they be laid bare; since much is to be gained by denouncing these fallacies for the sake of the unwary, even though We prefer not to name these iniquities "as becometh saints," Yet for the welfare of souls We cannot remain altogether silent.

To begin at the very source of these evils, their basic principle lies in this, that matrimony is repeatedly declared to be not instituted by the Author of nature nor raised by Christ the Lord to the dignity of a true sacrament, but invented by man. Some confidently assert that they have found no evidence for the existence of matrimony in nature or in her laws, but regard it merely as the means of producing life and gratifying in one way or another a vehement impulse; on the other hand, others recognize that certain beginnings or, as it were, seeds of true wedlock are found in the nature of man since, unless men were bound together by some form of permanent tie, the dignity of husband and wife or the natural end of propagating and rearing the offspring would not receive satisfactory provision. At the same time they maintain that in all beyond this germinal idea matrimony, through various concurrent causes, is invented solely by the mind of man, established solely by his will.

How grievously all these err and how shamelessly they leave the ways of honesty is already evident from what We have set forth here regarding the origin and nature of wedlock, its purposes and the good inherent in it. The evil of this teaching is plainly seen from the consequences which its advocates deduce from it, namely, that the laws, institutions and customs by which wedlock is governed, since they take their origin solely from the will of man, are subject entirely to him, hence can and must be founded, changed and abrogated according to human caprice and the shifting circumstances of human affairs; that the generative power which is grounded in nature itself is more sacred and has wider range than matrimony—hence it may be exercised both outside as well as within the confines of wedlock, and though the purpose of matrimony be set aside, as though to suggest that the license of a base fornicating woman should enjoy the same rights as the chaste motherhood of a lawfully wedded wife.

COMPANIONATE MARRIAGE

Armed with these principles, some men go so far as to concoct new species of unions, suited, as they say, to the present temper of men and the times, which various new forms of matrimony they presume to label "temporary," "experimental," and "companionate." These offer all the indulgence of matrimony and its rights without, however, the indissoluble bond, and without offspring, unless later the parties alter their cohabitation into a matrimony in the full sense of the law.

Indeed there are some who desire and insist that these practices be legitimized by the law or, at least, excused by their general acceptance among the people. They do not seem even to suspect that these proposals partake of nothing of the modern "culture" in which they glory so much, but are simply hateful abominations which beyond all question reduce our truly cultured nations to the barbarous standards of savage peoples.

BIRTH CONTROL

And now, Venerable Brethren, We shall explain in detail the evils opposed to each of the benefits of matrimony. First consideration is due to the offspring, which many have the boldness to call the disagreeable burden of matrimony and which they say is to be carefully avoided by married people not through virtuous continence (which Christian law permits in matrimony when both parties consent) but by frustrating the marriage act. Some justify this criminal abuse on the ground that they are weary of children and wish to gratify their desires without their consequent burden. Others say that they cannot on the one hand remain continent nor on the other can they have children because of the difficulties whether on the part of the mother or on the part of family circumstances.

But no reason, however grave, may be put forward by which anything intrinsically against nature may become conformable to nature and morally good. Since, therefore, the conjugal act is destined primarily by nature for the begetting of children, those who in exercising it deliberately frustrate its natural power and purpose sin against nature and commit a deed which is shameful and intrinsically vicious.

Small wonder, therefore, if Holy Writ bears witness that the Divine Majesty regards with greatest detestation this horrible crime and at times has punished it with death. As St. Augustine notes, "Intercourse even with one's legitimate wife is unlawful and wicked where the conception of the offspring is prevented. Onan, the son of Juda, did this and the Lord killed him for it."

DIVORCE

The advocates of the neopaganism of today have learned nothing from the sad state of affairs, but instead, day by day, more and more vehemently, they continue by legislation to attack the indissolubility of the marriage bond, proclaiming that the lawfulness of divorce must be recognized, and that the antiquated laws should give place to a new and more humane legislation. Many and varied are the grounds put forward for divorce, some arising from the wickedness and the guilt of the persons concerned, others arising from the circumstances of the case; the former they describe as subjective, the latter as objective; in a word, whatever might make married life hard or unpleasant. They strive to prove their contentions regarding these grounds for the divorce legislation they would bring about, by various arguments. Thus, in the first place, they maintain that it is for the good of either party that the one who is innocent should have the right to separate from the guilty, or that the guilty should be withdrawn from a union which is unpleasing to him and against his will. In the second place, they argue, the good of the child demands this, for either it will be deprived of a proper education or the natural fruits of it, and will too easily be affected by the discords and shortcomings of the parents, and drawn from the path of virtue. And thirdly the common good of society requires that these marriages should be completely dissolved, which are now incapable of producing their natural results, and that legal reparations should be allowed when crimes are to be feared as the result of the common habitation and intercourse of the parties. This last, they say must be admitted to avoid the crimes being committed purposely with a view to obtaining the desired sentence of divorce for which the judge can legally loose the marriage bond, as also to prevent people from coming before the courts when it is obvious from the state of the case that they are lying and perjuring themselves,—all of which brings the court and the lawful authority into contempt. Hence the civil laws, in their opinion, have to be reformed to meet these new requirements, to suit the changes of the times and the changes in men's opinions, civil institutions and customs. Each of these reasons is considered by them as conclusive, so that all taken together offer a clear proof of the necessity of granting divorce in certain cases.

Others, taking a step further, simply state that marriage, being a private contract, is, like other private contracts, to be left to the consent and good pleasure of both parties, and so can be dissolved for any reason whatsoever.

UNALTERABLE LAW OF GOD

Opposed to all these reckless opinions, Venerable Brethren, stands the unalterable law of God, fully confirmed by Christ, a law that can never be deprived of its force by the decrees of men, the ideas of a people or the will of any legislator: "What God hath joined together, let no man put asunder." And if any man, acting contrary to this law, shall have put asunder, his action is null and void, and the consequence remains, as Christ Himself has explicitly confirmed: "Everyone that putteth away his wife and marrieth another, committeth adultery: and he that marrieth her that is put away from her husband committeth adultery." Moreover, these words refer to every kind of marriage, even that which is natural and legitimate only; for, as has already been observed, that indissolubility by which the loosening of the bond is once and for all removed from the whim of the parties and from every secular power, is a property of every true marriage.

Let that solemn pronouncement of the Council of Trent be recalled to mind in which, under the stigma of anathema, it condemned these errors: "If anyone should say that on account of heresy or the hardships of cohabitation or a deliberate abuse of one party by the other the marriage tie may be loosened, let him be anathema"; and again: "If anyone should say that the Church errs in having taught or in teaching that, according to the teaching of the Gospel and the Apostles, the bond of marriage cannot be loosed because of the sin of adultery of either party; or that neither party, even though he be innocent, having given no cause for the sin of adultery, can contract another marriage during the lifetime of the other; and that he commits adultery who marries another after putting away his adulterous wife, and likewise that she commits adultery who puts away her husband and marries another: let him be anathema."

If, therefore, the Church has not erred and does not err in teaching this, and consequently it is certain that the bond of marriage cannot be loosed even on account of the sin of adultery, it is evident that all the other weaker excuses that can be, and are usually brought forward, are of no value whatsoever. And the objections brought against the firmness of the marriage bond are easily answered. For, in certain circumstances, imperfect separation of the parties is allowed, the bond not being severed. This separation, which the Church herself permits, and expressly mentions in her Canon Law in those canons which deal with the separation of the parties as to marital relationship and cohabitation, removes all the alleged inconveniences and dangers. It will be for the sacred law and, to some extent, also the civil law, in so far as civil matters are affected, to lay down the grounds, the conditions, the method and precautions to be taken in a case of this kind in order to safeguard the education of the children and the well-being of the family, and to remove all those evils which threaten the married persons, the children and the State. Now all those arguments that are brought forward to prove the indissolubility of the marriage tie, arguments which have already been touched upon, can equally be applied to excluding not only the necessity of divorce, but even the power to grant it; while for all the advantages that can be put forward for the former, there can be adduced as many disadvantages and evils which are a formidable menace to the whole of human society.

Adultery Forbidden

We may now consider another class of errors concerning conjugal faith. Every sin committed as regards the offspring becomes in some way a sin against conjugal faith, since both these blessings are essentially connected. However, We must mention briefly the sources of error and vice corresponding to those virtues which are demanded by conjugal faith, namely the chaste honor existing between man and wife, the due subjection of wife to husband, and the true love which binds both parties together.

It follows therefore that they are destroying mutual fidelity, who think that the ideas and morality of our present time concerning a certain harmful and false friendship with a third party can be countenanced, and who teach that a greater freedom of feeling and action in such external relations should be allowed to man and wife, particularly as many (so they consider) are possessed of an inborn sexual tendency which cannot be satisfied within the narrow limits of monogamous marriage. That rigid attitude which condemns all sensual affections and actions with a third party they imagine to be a narrowing of mind and heart, something obsolete, or an abject form of jealousy, and as a result they look upon whatever penal laws are passed by the State for the preserving of conjugal faith as void or to be abolished. Such unworthy and idle opinions are condemned by that noble instinct which is found in every chaste husband and wife, and even by the light of the testimony of nature alone—a testimony that is sanctioned and confirmed by the command of God: "Thou shalt not commit adultery," and the words of Christ: "Whosoever shall look on a woman to lust after her hath already committed adultery with her in his heart." The force of this divine precept can never be weakened by any merely human custom, bad example or pretext of human progress, for just as it is the one and the same "Jesus Christ, yesterday and today and the same forever," so it is the one and the same doctrine of Christ that abides and of which not one jot or tittle shall pass away till all is fulfilled.

The same false teachers who try to dim the luster of conjugal faith and purity do not scruple to do away with the honorable and trusting obedience which the woman owes to the man. Many of them even go further and assert that such a subjection of one party to the other is unworthy of human dignity, that the rights of husband and wife are equal; wherefore, they boldly proclaim, the emancipation of women has been or ought to be effected. This emancipation in their ideas must be threefold, in the ruling of the domestic society, in the administration of family affairs and in the rearing of the children. It must be social, economic, physiological:—physiological, that is to say, the woman is to be freed at her own good pleasure from the burdensome duties properly belonging to a wife as companion and mother (We have already said that this is not an emancipation but a crime); social, inasmuch as the wife being freed from the care of children and family, should, to the neglect of these, be able to follow her own bent and devote herself to business and even public affairs; finally economic, whereby the woman even without the knowledge and against the wish of her husband may be at liberty to conduct and administer her own affairs, giving her attention chiefly to these rather than to children, husband and family.

This, however, is not the true emancipation of woman, nor that rational and exalted liberty which belongs to the noble office of a Christian woman and wife; it is rather the debasing of the womanly character and the dignity of motherhood, and indeed of the whole family, as a result of which the husband suffers the loss of his wife, the children of their mother, and the home and the whole family of an ever watchful guardian. More than this, this false liberty and unnatural equality with the husband is to the detriment of the woman herself, for if the woman descends from her truly regal throne to which she has been raised within the walls of the home by means of the Gospel, she will soon be reduced to the old state of slavery (if not in appearance, certainly in reality) and become as amongst the pagans the mere instrument of man.

This equality of rights which is so much exaggerated and distorted, must indeed be recognized in those rights which belong to the dignity of the human soul and which are proper to the marriage contract and inseparably bound up with wedlock. In such things undoubtedly both parties enjoy the same rights and are bound by the same obligations; in other things there must be a certain inequality and due accommodation, which is demanded by the good of the family and the right ordering and unity and stability of home life.

As, however, the social and economic conditions of the married woman must in some way be altered on account of the changes in social intercourse, it is part of the office of the public authority to adapt the civil rights of the wife to modern needs and requirements, keeping in view what the natural disposition and temperament of the female sex, good morality, and the welfare of the family demands, and provided always that the essential order of the domestic society remain intact, founded as it is on something higher than human authority and wisdom, namely on the authority and wisdom of God, and so not changeable by public laws or at the pleasure of private individuals.

Mutual Love

These enemies of marriage go further, however, when they substitute for that true and solid love, which is the basis of conjugal happiness, a certain vague compatibility of temperament. This they call sympathy and assert that, since it is the only bond by which husband and wife are linked together, when it ceases the marriage is completely dissolved. What else is this than to build a house upon sand?—a house that in the words of Christ would forthwith be shaken and collapse, as soon as it was exposed to the waves of adversity "and the winds blew and they beat upon that house. And it fell: and great was the fall thereof." On the other hand, the house built upon a rock, that is to say on mutual conjugal chastity and strengthened by a deliberate and constant union of spirit, will not only never fall away but will never be shaken by adversity.

This conjugal faith, however, which is most aptly called by St. Augustine the "faith of chastity" blooms more freely, more beautifully and more nobly, when it is rooted in that more excellent soil, the love of husband and wife which pervades all the duties of married life and holds pride of place in Christian marriage. For matrimonial faith demands that husband and wife be joined in an especially holy and pure love, not as adulterers love each other, but as Christ loved the Church. This precept the Apostle laid down when he said: "Husbands, love your wives as Christ also loved the Church," that Church which of a truth He embraced with a boundless love not for the sake of His own advantage, but seeking only the good of His Spouse. The love, then, of which We are speaking is not that based on the passing lust of the moment nor does it consist in pleasing words only, but in the deep attachment of the heart which is expressed in action, since love is proved by deeds. This outward expression of love in the home demands not only mutual help but must go further; must have as its primary purpose that man and wife help each other day by day in forming and perfecting themselves in the interior life, so that through their partnership in life they may advance ever more and more in virtue, and above all that they may grow in true love towards God and their neighbor, on which indeed "dependeth the whole Law and the Prophets." For all men of every condition, in whatever honorable walk of life they may be, can and ought to imitate that most perfect example of holiness placed before man by God, namely Christ Our Lord, and by God's grace to arrive at the summit of perfection, as is proved by the example set us of many saints.

By this same love it is necessary that all the other rights and duties of the marriage state be regulated as the words of the Apostle: "Let the husband render the debt to the wife, and the wife also in like manner to the husband." Express not only a law of justice but of charity.

Domestic society being confirmed, therefore, by this bond of love, there should flourish in it that "order of love," as St. Augustine calls it. This order includes both the primacy of the husband with regard to the wife and children, the ready subjection of the wife and her willing obedience, which the Apostle commends in these words: "Let women be subject to their husbands as to the Lord, because the husband is the head of the wife, as Christ is the head of the Church."

This subjection, however, does not deny or take away the liberty which fully belongs to the woman both in view of her dignity as a human person, and in view of her most noble office as wife and mother and companion; nor does it bid her obey her husband's every request if not in harmony with right reason or with the dignity due to wife; nor, in fine, does it imply that the wife should be put on a level with those persons who in law are called minors, to whom it is not customary to allow free exercise of their rights on account of their lack of mature judgment, or of their ignorance of human affairs. But it forbids that exaggerated liberty which cares not for the good of the family; it forbids that in this body which is the family, the heart be separated from the head to the great detriment of the whole body and the proximate danger of ruin. For if the man is the head, the woman is the heart, and as he occupies the chief place in ruling, so she may and ought to claim for herself the chief place in love.

Again, this subjection of wife to husband in its degree and manner may vary according to the different conditions of persons, place and time. In fact, if the husband neglect his duty, it falls to the wife to take his place in directing the family. But the structure of the family and its fundamental law, established and confirmed by God, must always and everywhere be maintained intact. . . .

SACREDNESS OF MARRIAGE

Even by the light of reason alone and particularly if the ancient records of history are investigated, if the unwavering popular conscience is interrogated and the manners and institutions of all races examined, it is sufficiently obvious that there is a certain sacredness and religious character attaching even to the purely natural union of man and woman, "not something added by chance but innate, not imposed by men but involved in the nature of things," since it has "God for its author and has been even from the beginning a foreshadowing of the Incarnation of the Word of God." This sacredness of marriage which is intimately connected with religion and all that is holy, arises from the divine origin we have just mentioned, from its purpose which is the begetting and educating of children for God, and the binding of man and wife to God through Christian love and mutual support; and finally it arises from the very nature of wedlock, whose institution is to be sought for in the far-seeing Providence of God, whereby it is the means of transmitting life, thus making the parents the ministers, as it were, of the Divine Omnipotence. To this must be added that new element of dignity which comes from the sacrament, by which the Christian marriage is so ennobled and raised to such a level, that it appeared to the Apostle as a great sacrament, honorable in every way.

This religious character of marriage, its sublime signification of grace and the union between Christ and the Church, evidently requires that those about to marry should show a holy reverence towards it, and zealously endeavor to make their marriage approach as nearly as possible to the archetype of Christ and the Church.

In order, therefore, to restore due order in this matter of marriage, it is necessary that all should bear in mind what is the divine plan and strive to conform to it.

THE DIVINE PLAN

Wherefore, since the chief obstacle to this study is the power of unbridled lust, which indeed is the most potent cause of sinning against the sacred laws of matrimony, and since man cannot hold in check his passions, unless he first subject himself to God, this must be his primary endeavor, in accordance with the plan divinely ordained. For it is a sacred ordinance that whoever shall have first subjected himself to God will, by the aid of divine grace, be glad to subject to himself his own passions and concupiscence; while he who is a rebel against God will, to his sorrow, experience within himself the violent rebellion of his worst passions.

And how wisely this has been decreed, St. Augustine thus shows: "This indeed is fitting, that the lower be subject to the higher, so that he who would have subject to himself whatever is below him, should himself submit to whatever is above him. Acknowledge order, seek peace. Be thou subject to God, and thy flesh subject to thee. What more fitting! What more fair! Thou art subject to the higher and the lower is subject to thee. Do thou serve Him who made thee, so that that which was made for thee may serve thee. For we do not commend this order, namely, 'The flesh to thee and thou to God,' but 'Thou to God, and the flesh to thee.' If, however, thou despisest the subjection of thyself to God, thou shalt never bring about the subjection of the flesh to thyself. If thou dost not obey the Lord, thou shalt be tormented by thy servant." This right ordering on the part of God's wisdom is mentioned by the holy Doctor of the Gentiles, inspired by the Holy Ghost, for in speaking of those ancient philosophers who refused to adore and reverence Him whom they knew to be the Creator of the universe, he says: "Wherefore God gave them up to the desires of their heart, unto uncleanness, to dishonor their own bodies among themselves"; and again: "For this same God delivered them up to shameful affections." And St. James says: "God resisteth the proud and giveth grace to the humble," without which grace, as the same Doctor of the Gentiles reminds us, man cannot subdue the rebellion of his faith.

Consequently, as the onslaughts of these uncontrolled passions cannot in any way be lessened, unless the spirit first shows a humble compliance of duty and reverence towards its Maker, it is above all and before all needful that those who are joined in the bond of sacred wedlock should be wholly imbued with a profound and genuine sense of duty towards God, which will shape their whole lives, and fill their minds and wills with a very deep reverence for the majesty of God.

❀ DONALD J. CANTOR

10. The Homosexual Revolution

Donald J. Cantor is a practicing attorney in Hartford, Conn. He is a graduate of Harvard Law School and is a frequent contributor of articles on homosexuality, narcotics, and divorce to *The Atlantic Monthly* and other magazines.

Obscured by the Negro revolution, the homosexual is, almost unnoticed, pursuing and advancing his own revolutionary cause. Like the Negro, and like every other group that has fought to establish its rights, the

Reprinted from *The Humanist*, XXVII, Nos. 5 and 6 (September/December 1967). Used with the kind permission of the American Humanist Association.

homosexual first had to discover that he deserved rights, that what he had been told about himself was not true, that his intrinsic merit was the equal of his detractor's, that he need not feel guilt and inferiority by definition. The homosexual is achieving this sense of inner worth and is thus becoming able to withstand identification, in some instances even bear notoriety in service of his cause.

There was a time when homosexuality was thought to be a result of excessive debauchery, or a morbid predisposition activated by onanistic practices, or the placement of a male soul in a female body, or vice versa. Others postulated that homosexuality was a congenital abnormality, and some thought the explanation lay in the hormonal composition of the body. Thus, early theory, when coupled with theological condemnation ("Thou shalt not lie with mankind, as with womankind; it is abomination." *Leviticus* 18:22; "for even their women did change the natural use into that which is against nature . . . men with men working that which is unseemly. . . ." *Romans* 1:26, 1:27) made the homosexual easy to despise, for not only were his acts sinful but his condition was either freakish or degenerate or both.

The movement for homosexual rights could not, therefore, begin until at least one of these premises was challenged. Freud did just that. Freud maintained that all persons are born with a psychic sexual duality, the capacity to express *both* male and female characteristics. He traced the existence of homosexual tendencies to Oedipal trauma but did not identify such childhood difficulties as the exclusive cause. Today, the bulk of psychiatrists will point to the child's resolution of the Oedipus complex as crucial, but admit the existence of other childhood conflicts as possible causes. In short, most will concede that no one really knows what causes homosexuality.

But it was the late Dr. Kinsey's study of the sexual habits of the white American male and female which provided the impetus for the homosexual movement. Kinsey and his researchers concluded that one's sexual direction is conditioned by the effects of initial sexual experiences and the subsequent failure of cultural pressures to alter this direction. Kinsey considered homosexuality to be a capacity inherent in humans, not in some only, and not due to a failure to resolve infantile trauma. He wrote: "The homosexual has been a significant part of human sexual activity ever since the dawn of history, primarily because it is an expression of capacities that are basic in the human animal."

When Dr. Kinsey and his associates set forth their finding that 37 percent of the white American males have had at least one homosexual experience involving orgasm during their lives, they delivered a body blow to homosexual mythology from which it can never recover, for the stereotyped homosexual—the effeminate, mincing dandy—clearly was not one of every three males, and this meant that the great majority of persons who had expressed homosexual inclinations looked just like those who despised them. The inferior image, the crucial difference which had made the mythological homosexual ridiculous, and thus easily persecutable, was suddenly labeled false. Kinsey also attacked the old convenient notion of sexual categories, the idea that one was homosexual or heterosexual the way one was American or alien, and showed instead that sexual activity covered a broad spectrum, much of which was a mixture of homosexual and heterosexual, not clearly either. And thus was the purity of the heterosexual sullied. Kinsey forced society to see that, instead of having just heterosexuals and homosexuals, it had many active bisexuals, and many more who were potentially so.

Ten years later, in 1958, the Wolfenden Report was issued in London, and the homosexual movement was blessed with a champion of unimpeachable qualification and respectability.

This report by an English parliamentary committee would have been important solely because it recommended that private, adult, consensual homosexual acts be made lawful, but it was infinitely more important because of the caliber of its membership and because of its depth of research. The Wolfenden Report considered the varied arguments against making such acts lawful, i.e., that homosexuality deprives society of children, that homosexuality creates nervous, undependable persons, that homosexuality menaces the health of society, that homosexual behavior threatens the family, and that homosexuals may turn eventually to minors, and rebutted them all. This Report concluded that overpopulation, not underpopulation, was the social danger, that nervous homosexuals are so because of the present law not because of their homosexuality, that homosexuality is no threat to the social health, that homosexuality is no greater threat to the family than heterosexuality, and that, if anything, legalization of private, adult, consensual homosexual acts would decrease homosexual overtures to minors since these would remain unlawful.

The Wolfenden Report, however, served a greater function than the arguments and conclusions it advanced. It occasioned a great parliamentary debate, one which became a national and then an international education. Homosexuality, once a totally unmentionable subject, a contamination even to contemplate, became a topic people actually discussed and thought about and argued over—all without apparent injury.

Since the Wolfenden Report, more has happened to focus on and alleviate the troubles of the homosexual in the United States than in all the years prior.

In 1961, Illinois amended her criminal statutes and now does not make adult, private, consensual homosexual acts a crime.

Last year the criminal law of New York State came close to being similarly revised when a bill was presented to the legislature which would have made adult, private, consensual homosexual acts lawful, but this bill was amended on the floor of the legislature and such acts remain misdemeanors in New York State. But this last minute failure is of far less import than the fact that the attempt was made to liberalize New York law and that it nearly succeeded.

North Carolina amended its sodomy statute in 1965, eliminating a punishment of not less than five nor more than sixty years, and substituting in its place a fine or imprisonment "in the discretion of the court." The eradiction of the five year minimum sentence constitutes definite progress. Since the American Law Institute has drafted its Model Penal Code with this recommendation in it, in light of the influence of the Institute and the prestige of its members, there can be little doubt that like amendments will be offered in other states and probably again in New York.

But the true progress of the movement cannot be solely or even primarily gauged by statutory changes, although these changes are the primary goals. Much more crucial at this time are developments within the churches and within the homophile organizations themselves. The churches are important because homosexuality is mainly despised for reasons based upon the religious concept that homosexual acts are sinful. Thus, if the revolution of the homosexual is to succeed, it must reach the churches. This it is doing.

The Methodist Conference and the Congregational Union indicated support of the Wolfenden Report in 1958. In Philadelphia, during November of 1965, a special symposium met to discuss the homosexuality question in its various aspects, many different disciplines being represented. The reason, I was told, for the symposium being convened was that the United Presbyterian Church had felt the need to speak *to* the problem. (Churchmen, I have learned, never speak *of* or *about* a problem, but only *to* it.)

In Hartford, Connecticut, the Greater Hartford Council of Churches has for two years had a committee existent to study homosexuality and devise means by which the church can assist the homosexual, both as a group and as individuals. Great interest in this work has been manifested by other Councils of Churches throughout the United States. Denver has had an active Council of Churches. San Francisco, in 1964, formed the Council on Religion and the Homosexual, its purpose being "To promote a continuing dialogue between the religious community and homosexuals," and, in New York, the George W. Hency Foundation has, since 1948, offered assistance in many different forms to homosexuals in trouble. It has received backing from the Episcopal ministry, in particular, and now has a Connecticut branch which has broad Protestant support. In November, 1966, The National Council of Churches, Department of Ministry, meeting in White Plains, New York, discussed the relation of the church and the homosexual, and in August of 1966, The World Council of Churches, meeting in London, held a seminar on this question.

As to the homophile organizations themselves, they are not only existent and operative, but are becoming vocal and militant. Homophile organizations are no longer content to provide social comraderie and mutual reassurance; they are evolving into organs of protest, media for propaganda and active lobbyists. Their leaders do not shrink from publicity or shun public identification. The Homosexual Law Reform Society of America in Philadelphia has organized public demonstrations and distributed leaflets protesting the exclusion of homosexuals from the armed services. Mr. Clark Polak, Executive Secretary of the Homosexual Law Reform Society, has appeared on radio and television, at symposia, before service organizations, and has spoken to a great diversity of audiences to decry the injustice America inflicts on its homosexuals. When the Florida Legislature contemplated legislation deemed inimical to homosexuals, Richard Inman, President of Atheneum Society of America, Inc., now The Mattachine Society of Florida, Inc., not only propagandized and lobbied, but had articles sympathetic to his cause printed and distributed to all legislators. Homophile organizations have picketed the White House, Pentagon, State Department and the U.S. Civil Service Commission in Washington and the Philadelphia Navy Yard, among others. A survey taken by and of the Florida Mattachine Society indicated 82 percent of those questioned were in favor of public picketing by homosexuals, and sentiment in other homophile groups in the country appears similarly inclined.

This personal involvement of homosexuals in public advocacy of their view often accomplishes infinitely more than the propagation of those views. It serves the function of exposing the stereotype for the ridiculous nonsense it is. Every time a homosexual leader appears publicly, walks to his seat without swaying, dressed without frills, talking without a lisp, forcing his audience to the realization that they would not realize he was homosexual if he didn't tell them, a great stride is made. These leaders know this and thus seek constantly to address groups of all kinds. Nothing induces a man to feel tolerance more than seeing similarity between himself and the ones previously scorned. Difference is the root of prejudice, and prejudice dies as difference dissipates.

Those who administer the law give further evidence of this new feeling about homosexuality. Prosecutors, in deciding whether to prosecute and on what charge, and judges, in determining how to sentence, are good barometers of current social values. There is an unmistakable tendency today to allow homosexuals to plead guilty to lesser charges than those for which they were arrested and to sentence leniently, often with probation in place of incarceration. A study of the disposition of arrests for felonious homosexual acts in Los Angeles County, in March, 1966, the *U.C.L.A. Law Review*, showed that only .6 percent (3 defendants of 493) received ultimate felony dispositions. The remainder were all treated as misdemeanor offenders and the great majority received suspended sentences, probation or fines. John Gerassi, in his recently published book, *The Boys of Boise,* indicates that this trend is not restricted to the larger, supposedly more sophisticated metropolitan centers, but is a present fact of legal life in Boise, Idaho, as well.

There are other extremely important philosophical influences which are having and will continue to have their effect on the law and the relation of the law to the homosexual. One is the opinion that law should not legislate morality, but should rather confine its proscriptions to those areas where acts or omissions have demonstrably injurious social consequences. This is not, of course, a philosophical innovation; the same notion was quite eloquently advanced by John Stuart Mill in his essay *On Liberty,* and by others of note, but its adoption with specific reference to the question of homosexual acts by a Catholic body is of special importance.

When the Commission which produced the Wolfenden Report was created, it requested the view of many different committees representing churches, professions, and other organizations. The late Cardinal Griffin of Westminster commissioned *The Roman Catholic Advisory Committee on Prostitution and Homosexual Offenses and the Existing Law,* and the report of this body, while stating "all directly voluntary sexual pleasure outside of marriage is sinful," nonetheless also stated:

It is not the business of the State to intervene in the purely private sphere but to act solely as the defender of the common good. Morally evil things so far as they do not affect the common good are not the concern of the human legislator.

This singularly statesmanlike report went further, adding the following particularity.

Attempts by the State to enlarge its authority and invade the individual conscience, however high-minded, always fail and frequently do positive harm. The Volstead Act in the U.S.A. affords the best recent illustration of this principle. It should accordingly be stated clearly that penal sanctions are not justified for the purpose of attempting to restrain sins against sexual morality committed in private by responsible adults. They are, as later appears, at present employed for this purpose in this country and should be discontinued because:
(a) they are ineffectual;
(b) they are inequitable in this incidence;
(c) they involve severities disproportionate to the offense committed;
(d) they undoubtedly give scope for blackmail and other forms of corruption.

The position advanced by this Report gives a rationale for allowing private, adult, consensual homosexual acts to be lawful to those who regard those acts as morally odious, and therein lies its special significance and value. Now the one with moral objections can be approached, and often persuaded, to favor law reform on the fundamental basis of the need to separate theological morality from state power; the cause of the homosexual thus becomes identified with, and understandable to, all those groups whose history contains instances of persecution resulting from the joinder of morality and criminal law.

The second new philosophical position is that sexual acts should not be condemned morally simply because of their nature, but rather that sexual acts, like any acts, are moral or not depending upon the intentions behind them and the effects of them. In an address before the Missionary Society of the Berkeley Divinity School, on November 23, 1964, Dr. Alfred A. Gross, Executive Director of the George W. Hency Foundation, and long-time advocate of homosexual law reform, expounded this view as he has continued to do since.

And in the January, 1967, issue of *The Living Church,* a weekly magazine of the Episcopal Church, The Reverend R. W. Cromey, Vicar of St. Aidan's Church in San Francisco, calling for homosexual law reform as recommended by the Wolfenden Committee, stated:

I believe that the sex act is morally neutral. There is no sex act which in itself is sinful . . . I also believe that two people of the same sex can express love and deepen that love by sexual intercourse.

Acceptance of this view would necessarily lead to the law reform sought by the homosexual in light of the absence of any valid utilitarian reasons for the present restrictive laws.

The progress made by the homosexual toward equality has been assisted by a rash of plays (*The Toilet, A Taste of Honey, The Sign in Sidney Brustein's Window*), movies (*The Victim, Darling, The Leather Boys*), non-fiction books (*The Homosexual Revolution, In Defense of Homosexuality, The Homosexual in America*), and fiction by such established authors as Jean Genet, Gore Vidal and James Baldwin. In the law of obscene communication, the United States Supreme Court has facilitated the creation and distribution of literature dealing with homosexuality, and especially matter designed especially for homosexuals, by ruling that homosexual materials, including male nudes, are not ipso facto obscene. As the result of *Mishkin v. New York*, decided by the Supreme Court on March 21, 1966, material is obscene if the dominant theme of it taken as a whole appeals to the prurient interest in sex, not of the average man, but rather of the members of any special group—such as homosexuals—for which such material was designed and to which it was primarily disseminated.

The attitudes thus expressed should be contrasted, to be appreciated, with a 1922 Ohio case in which the judge referred to males who commit homosexual acts as "human degenerates" and "sexual perverts," or the 1938 Maine case in which the Maine Supreme Court had this to say:

The statute (sodomy) gives no definition of the crime but with due regard to the sentiments of decent humanity treats it as one not fit to be named, leaving the record undefiled by the details of different acts which may constitute the perversion.

Contrast it also with the older attitudes manifested in the sodomy statutes of the various states. In fourteen states the forbidden acts, which include acts between males and females as well as between persons of similar sex, are described as "abominable" or as both "abominable" and "detestable." (What does "detestable" add that "abominable" omits?) In seven states the acts are called "infamous." In ten states the phrases "crime against nature" or "against the order of nature" are used adjectivally; in three states "unnatural," "abnormal," or "perverted" are used. The depth and degree of antipathy which once characterized the public view of homosexual acts can be best appreciated when one recalls that no other crimes, including premeditated murder and rape, are so described.

It would be facile and utterly misleading to imply that the American homosexual is on the threshold of victory in his battle for equality. It is still painfully true that every state but Illinois condemns the private, adult, consensual acts of homosexuals as criminal, that in seven states life imprisonment is a possible sentence for such acts, and that in thirty-five other states the maximum penalty is at least ten years. When Sir Cyril Osborne, Conservative Member of Parliament, said during debate, "I am rather tired of democracy being made safe for the pimps, the prostitutes, the spivs, the pansies, and now, the queers," he may have spoken for a distinct minority in England (a recent Gallop Poll in England showed 60 percent of those polled favored homosexual law reform), but it is probable that he reflected the opinions of a larger percentage of Americans, though many would not be quite so intense about it.

John Gerassi tells us that only a decade ago a great number of Boiseans thought that homosexuals were communists. But the trend is clear. The opposition to homosexual law reform is progressively diminishing. The large amount of extortion and blackmail which has victimized the homosexual has reached public consciousness and created sympathy, and forced upon the public the realization that these anti-homosexuality laws, even when not strictly enforced, set the stage by their very existence for this extortion and blackmail. People are becoming aware that England is on the verge of making adult, private, consensual homosexual acts lawful, and wondering whether our oldest teacher has yet another lesson for us to learn.

There is a new sense of perspective alive in the land, born at Hiroshima, which has equipped men to appreciate the dimensions of real danger, and has made them less able to view alleged sexual dangers such as homosexuality quite as seriously as once was possible. There is a sense of reappraisal, an unwillingness in an age of incredible change to presume the rightness of doctrine simply because doctrine is and was. Fittingly, sexual mores are getting perhaps the most serious reappraisal, partially because of the pill and intrauterine device, but more, I think, because the sexual dogmas have had the greatest rigidity and least realism. Homosexuality therefore is benefitting, as part of the general field of sexuality, from this rising examination of the old rules governing intercourse out of marriage, abortion, censorship, and divorce.

There is also not a new, but an increased sense of the dignity of man and of man's right to dignity. The goals of the Negro are now national goals to an extent never before even approximated, not because he is Negro but because he is human. The homosexual is being gradually recognized as one seeking similar goals and deserving them.

Where a sexual act is done publicly, it is a nuisance and an invasion of the public's right to public propriety. It deserves punishment. Where a sexual act is committed with a minor, it is an invasion of the minor's right to privacy until he reaches the age of consent. It deserves punishment. Where a sexual act is done through force, duress, or fraud, or under any circumstances where consent is absent, it is an assault and deserves punishment. But where the act is private, between two consenting adults, where there is no victim, where nothing occurs but the physical expression of affection, it should not be punished.

Equality for the homosexual is an ethical imperative and the American people are beginning to realize this.

❀ KATE MILLETT

11. *Sexual Politics*

Katherine Murray Millett is a distinguished educator, author, and feminist. She was formerly an English professor at Bryn Mawr College and visiting professor at Sacramento State College. Among her writings are *Sexual Politics* (1970), *The Prostitution Papers* (1973), and *Flying* (1974).

In America, recent events have forced us to acknowledge at last that the relationship between the races is indeed a political one which involves the general control of one collectivity, defined by birth, over another collectivity, also defined by birth. Groups who rule by birthright are fast disappearing, yet there remains one ancient and universal scheme for the domination of one birth group by another—the scheme that prevails in the area of sex. The study of racism has convinced us that a truly political state of affairs operates between the races to perpetuate a series of oppressive circumstances. The subordinated group has inadequate redress through existing political institutions, and is deterred thereby from organizing into conventional political struggle and opposition.

Quite in the same manner, a disinterested examination of our system of sexual relationship must point out that the situation between the sexes now, and throughout history, is a case of that phenomenon Max Weber defined as *herrschaft*, a relationship of dominance and subordinance.[1] What goes largely unexamined, often even unacknowledged (yet is institutionalized nonetheless) in our social order, is the birthright priority whereby males rule females. Through this system a most ingenious form of "interior colonization" has been achieved. It is one which tends moreover to be sturdier than any form of segregation, and more rigorous than class stratification, more uniform, certainly more enduring. However muted its present appearance may be, sexual dominion obtains nevertheless as perhaps the most pervasive ideology of our culture and provides its most fundamental concept of power.

Reprinted from portions of chapter 2 of *Sexual Politics,* copyright © 1969, 1970 by Kate Millett. Reprinted by permission of Doubleday & Co., Inc. Footnotes have been renumbered.

[1]"Domination in the quite general sense of power, i.e. the possibility of imposing one's will upon the behavior of other persons, can emerge in the most diverse forms." In this central passage of *Wirtschaft und Gesellschaft* Weber is particularly interested in two such forms: control through social authority ("patriarchal, magisterial, or princely") and control through economic force. In patriarchy as in other forms of domination "that control over economic goods, i.e. economic power, is a frequent, often purposively willed, consequence of domination as well as one of its most important instruments." Quoted from Max Rheinstein's and Edward Shil's translation of portions of *Wirtschaft und Gesellschaft* entitled *Max Weber on Law in Economy and Society* (New York: Simon and Schuster, 1967), pp. 323–24.

This is so because our society, like all other historical civilizations, is a patriarchy.[2] The fact is evident at once if one recalls that the military, industry, technology, universities, science, political office, and finance—in short, every avenue of power within the society, including the coercive force of the police, is entirely in male hands. As the essence of politics is power, such realization cannot fail to carry impact. What lingers of supernatural authority, the Deity, "His" ministry, together with the ethics and values, the philosophy and art of our culture—its very civilization—as T. S. Eliot once observed, is of male manufacture.

If one takes patriarchal government to be the institution whereby that half of the populace which is female is controlled by that half which is male, the principles of patriarchy appear to be two fold: male shall dominate female, elder male shall dominate younger. However, just as with any human institution, there is frequently a distance between the real and the ideal; contradictions and exceptions do exist within the system. While patriarchy as an institution is a social constant so deeply entrenched as to run through all other political, social, or economic forms, whether of caste or class, feudality or bureaucracy, just as it pervades all major religions, it also exhibits great variety in history and locale. . . .

Hannah Arendt[3] has observed that government is upheld by power supported either through consent or imposed through violence. Conditioning to an ideology amounts to the former. Sexual politics obtains consent through the "socialization" of both sexes to basic patriarchal polities with regard to temperament, role, and status. As to status, a pervasive assent to the prejudice of male superiority guarantees superior status in the male, inferior in the female. The first item, temperament, involves the formation of human personality along stereotyped lines of sex category ("masculine" and "feminine"), based on the needs and values of the dominant group and dictated by what its members cherish in themselves and find convenient in subordinates: aggression, intelligence, force, and efficacy in the male; passivity, ignorance, docility, "virtue," and ineffectuality in the female. This is complemented by a second factor, sex role, which decrees a consonant and highly elaborate code of conduct, gesture and attitude for each sex. In terms of activity, sex role assigns domestic service and attendance upon infants to the female, the rest of human achievement, interest, and ambition to the male. The limited role allotted the female tends to arrest her at the level of biological experience. Therefore, nearly all that can be described as distinctly human rather than animal activity (in their own way animals also give birth and care for their young) is largely reserved for the male. Of course, status again follows from such an assignment. Were one to analyze

[2]No matriarchal societies are known to exist at present. Matrilineality, which may be, as some anthropologists have held, a residue or a transitional stage of matriarchy, does not constitute an exception to patriarchal rule, it simply channels the power held by males through female descent—, e.g. the Avunculate.

[3]Hannah Arendt, "Speculations on Violence," *The New York Review of Books*, Vol. XII No. 4, February 27, 1969, p. 24.

the three categories one might designate status as the political component, role as the sociological, and temperament as the psychological—yet their interdependence is unquestionable and they form a chain. Those awarded higher status tend to adopt roles of mastery, largely because they are first encouraged to develop temperaments of dominance. That this is true of caste and class as well is self-evident. . . .

Evidence from anthropology, religious and literary myth all attests to the politically expedient character of patriarchal convictions about women. One anthropologist refers to a consistent patriarchal strain of assumption that "woman's biological differences set her apart . . . she is essentially inferior," and since "human institutions grow from deep and primal anxieties and are shaped by irrational psychological mechanisms . . . socially organized attitudes toward women arise from basic tensions expressed by the male."[4] Under patriarchy the female did not herself develop the symbols by which she is described. As both the primitive and the civilized worlds are male worlds, the ideas which shaped culture in regard to the female were also of male design. The image of women as we know it is an image created by men and fashioned to suit their needs. These needs spring from a fear of the "otherness" of women. Yet this notion itself presupposes that patriarchy has already been established and the male has already set himself as the human norm, the subject and referent to which the female is "other" or alien. Whatever its origin, the function of the male's sexual antipathy is to provide a means of control over a subordinate group and a rationale which justifies the inferior station of those in a lower order, "explaining" the oppression of their lives.

The feeling that woman's sexual functions are impure is both worldwide and persistent. One sees evidence of it everywhere in literature, in myth, in primitive and civilized life. It is striking how the notion persists today. The event of menstruation, for example, is a largely clandestine affair, and the psycho-social effect of the stigma attached must have great effect on the female ego. There is a large anthropological literature on menstrual taboo; the practice of isolating offenders in huts at the edge of the village occurs throughout the primitive world. Contemporary slang denominates menstruation as "the curse." There is considerable evidence that such discomfort as women suffer during their period is often likely to be psychosomatic, rather than physiological, cultural rather than biological, in origin. That this may also be true to some extent of labor and delivery is attested to by the recent experiment with "painless childbirth." Patriarchal circumstances and beliefs seem to have the effect of poisoning the female's own sense of physical self until it often truly becomes the burden it is said to be.

Primitive peoples explain the phenomenon of the female's genitals in terms of a wound, sometimes reasoning that she was visited by a bird or

---

[4]H. R. Hays, *The Dangerous Sex, the Myth of Feminine Evil* (New York: Putnam, 1964). Much of my summary in this section is indebted to Hays's useful assessment of cultural notions about the female.

snake and mutilated into her present condition. Once she was wounded, now she bleeds. Contemporary slang for the vagina is "gash." The Freudian description of the female genitals is in terms of a "castrated" condition. The uneasiness and disgust female genitals arouse in patriarchal societies is attested to through religious, cultural, and literary proscription. In pre-literate groups fear is also a factor, as in the belief in a castrating *vagina dentata*. The penis, badge of the male's superior status in both preliterate and civilized patriarchies, is given the most crucial significance, the subject both of endless boasting and endless anxiety.

Nearly all patriarchies enforce taboos against women touching ritual objects (those of war or religion) or food. In ancient and preliterate societies women are generally not permitted to eat with men. Women eat apart today in a great number of cultures, chiefly those of the Near and Far East. Some of the inspiration of such custom appears to lie in fears of contamination, probably sexual in origin. In their function of domestic servants, females are forced to prepare food, yet at the same time may be liable to spread their contagion through it. A similar situation obtains with blacks in the United States. They are considered filthy and infectious, yet as domestics they are forced to prepare food for their queasy superiors. In both cases the dilemma is generally solved in a deplorably illogical fashion by segregat-ing the act of eating itself, while cooking is carried on out of sight by the very group who would infect the table. With an admirable consistency, some Hindu males do not permit their wives to touch their food at all. In nearly every patriarchal group it is expected that the dominant male will eat first or eat better, and even where the sexes feed togther, the male shall be served by the female. . . .[5]

Primitive society practices its misogyny in terms of taboo and mana which evolve into explanatory myth. In historical cultures, this is trans-formed into ethical, then literary, and in the modern period, scientific rationalizations for the sexual politic. Myth is, of course, a felicitous advance in the level of propaganda, since it so often bases its arguments on ethics or theories of origins. The two leading myths of Western culture are the classical tale of Pandora's box and the Biblical story of the Fall. In both cases earlier mana concepts of feminine evil have passed through a final literary phase to become highly influential ethical justifications of things as they are.

Pandora appears to be a discredited version of a Mediterranean fertility goddess, for in Hesiod's *Theogony* she wears a wreath of flowers and a sculptured diadem in which are carved all the creatures of land and sea.[6] Hesiod ascribes to her the introduction of sexuality which puts an end to the

---

[5]The luxury conditions of the "better" restaurant affords a quaint exception. There not only the cuisine but even the table service is conducted by males, at an expense commensurate with such an occasion.

[6]Wherever one stands in the long anthropologists' quarrel over patriarchal versus matriarchal theories of social origins, one can trace a demotion of fertility goddesses and their replacement by patriarchal deities at a certain period throughout ancient culture.

golden age when "the races of men had been living on earth free from all evils, free from laborious work, and free from all wearing sickness."[7] Pandora was the origin of "the damnable race of women—a plague which men must live with."[8] The introduction of what are seen to be the evils of the male human condition came through the introduction of the female and what is said to be her unique product, sexuality. In *Works and Days* Hesiod elaborates on Pandora and what she represents—a perilous temptation with "the mind of a bitch and a thievish nature," full of "the cruelty of desire and longings that wear out the body," "lies and cunning words and a deceitful soul," a snare sent by Zeus to be "the ruin of men."[9]

Patriarchy has God on its side. One of its most effective agents of control is the powerfully expeditious character of its doctrines as to the nature and origin of the female and the attribution to her alone of the dangers and evils it imputes to sexuality. The Greek example is interesting here: when it wishes to exalt sexuality it celebrates fertility through the phallus; when it wishes to denigrate sexuality, it cites Pandora. Patriarchal religion and ethics tend to lump the female and sex together as if the whole burden of the onus and stigma it attaches to sex were the fault of the female alone. Thereby sex, which is known to be unclean, sinful, and debilitating, pertains to the female, and the male identity is preserved as a human, rather than a sexual one.

The Pandora myth is one of two important Western archetypes which condemn the female through her sexuality and explain her position as her well-deserved punishment for the primal sin under whose unfortunate consequences the race yet labors. Ethics have entered the scene, replacing the simplicities of ritual, taboo, and mana. The more sophisticated vehicle of myth also provides official explanations of sexual history. In Hesiod's tale, Zeus, a rancorous and arbitrary father figure, in sending Epimetheus evil in the form of female genitalia, is actually chastising him for adult heterosexual knowledge and activity. In opening the vessel she brings (the vulva or hymen, Pandora's "box") the male satisfies his curiosity but sustains the discovery only by punishing himself at the hands of the father god with death and the assorted calamities of postlapsarian life. The patriarchal trait of male rivalry across age or status line, particularly those of powerful father and rival son, is present as well as the ubiquitous maligning of the female.

The myth of the Fall is a highly finished version of the same themes. As the central myth of the Judeo-Christian imagination and therefore of our immediate cultural heritage, it is well that we appraise and acknowledge

[7]Hesiod, *Works and Days*, translated by Richmond Lattimore (University of Michigan, 1959), p. 29.

[8]Hesiod, *Theogony*, translated by Norman O. Brown (Indianapolis, Liberal Arts Press, 1953), p. 70.

[9]Hesiod, *Works and Days*, phrases from lines 53–100. Some of the phrases are from Lattimore's translation, some from A. W. Mair's translation (Oxford, 1908).

the enormous power it still holds over us even in a rationalist era which has long ago given up literal belief in it while maintaining its emotional assent intact.[10] This mythic version of the female as the cause of human suffering, knowledge, and sin is still the foundation of sexual attitudes, for it represents the most crucial argument of the patriarchal tradition in the West.

The Israelites lived in a continual state of war with the fertility cults of their neighbors; these latter afforded sufficient attraction to be the source of constant defection, and the figure of Eve, like that of Pandora, has vestigial traces of a fertility goddess overthrown. There is some, probably unconscious, evidence of this in the Biblical account which announces, even before the narration of the fall has begun—"Adam called his wife's name Eve; because she was the mother of all living things." Due to the fact that the tale represents a compilation of different oral traditions, it provides two contradictory schemes for Eve's creation, one in which both sexes are created at the same time, and one in which Eve is fashioned later than Adam, an afterthought born from his rib, peremptory instance of the male's expropriation of the life force through a god who created the world without benefit of female assistance.

The tale of Adam and Eve is, among many other things, a narrative of how humanity invented sexual intercourse. Many such narratives exist in preliterate myth and folk tale. Most of them strike us now as delightfully funny stories of primal innocents who require a good deal of helpful instruction to figure it out. There are other major themes in the story: the loss of primeval simplicity, the arrival of death, and the first conscious experience of knowledge. All of them revolve about sex. Adam is forbidden to eat of the fruit of life or of the knowledge of good and evil, the warning states explicitly what should happen if he tastes of the latter: "in that day that thou eatest thereof thou shalt surely die." He eats but fails to die (at least in the story), from which one might infer that the serpent told the truth.

But at the moment when the pair eat of the forbidden tree they awake to their nakedness and feel shame. Sexuality is clearly involved, though the fable insists it is only tangential to a higher prohibition against disobeying orders in the matter of another and less controversial appetite—one for food. Róheim points out that the Hebrew verb for "eat" can also mean coitus. Everywhere in the Bible "knowing" is synonymous with sexuality, and clearly a product of contact with the phallus, here in the fable objectified as a snake. To blame the evils and sorrows of life—loss of Eden

[10]It is impossible to assess how deeply embedded in our consciousness is the Eden legend and how utterly its patterns are planted in our habits of thought. One comes across its tone and design in the most unlikely places, such as Antonioni's film *Blow-Up*, to name but one of many striking examples. The action of the film takes place in an idyllic garden, loaded with primal overtones largely sexual, where, prompted by a tempter with a phallic gun, the female again betrays the male to death. The photographer who witnesses the scene reacts as if he were being introduced both to the haggard knowledge of the primal scene and original sin at the same time.

and the rest—on sexuality, would all too logically implicate the male, and such implication is hardly the purpose of the story, designed as it is expressly in order to blame all this world's discomfort on the female. Therefore it is the female who is tempted first and "beguiled" by the penis, transformed into something else, a snake. Thus Adam has "beaten the rap" of sexual guilt, which appears to be why the sexual motive is so repressed in the Biblical account. Yet the very transparency of the serpent's universal phallic value shows how uneasy the mythic mind can be about its shifts. Accordingly, in her inferiority and vulnerability the woman takes and eats, simple carnal thing that she is, affected by flattery even in a reptile. Only after this does the male fall, and with him, humanity—for the fable has made him the racial type, whereas Eve is a mere sexual type and, according to tradition, either expendable or replaceable. And as the myth records the original sexual adventure, Adam was seduced by woman, who was seduced by a penis. "The woman whom thou gavest to be with me, she gave me of the fruit and I did eat" is the first man's defense. Seduced by the phallic snake, Eve is convicted for Adam's participation in sex.

Adam's curse is to toil in the "sweat of his brow," namely the labor the male associates with civilization. Eden was a fantasy world without either effort or activity, which the entrance of the female, and with her sexuality, has destroyed. Eve's sentence is far more political in nature and a brilliant "explanation" of her inferior status. "In sorrow thou shalt bring forth children. And thy desire shall be to thy husband. And he shall rule over thee." Again, as in the Pandora myth, a proprietary father figure is punishing his subjects for adult heterosexuality. It is easy to agree with Róheim's comment on the negative attitude the myth adopts toward sexuality: "Sexual maturity is regarded as a misfortune, something that has robbed mankind of happiness . . . the explanation of how death came into the world."[11]

What requires further emphasis is the responsibility of the female, a marginal creature, in bringing on this plague, and the justice of her suborned condition as dependent on her primary role in this original sin. The connection of woman, sex, and sin constitutes the fundamental pattern of western patriarchal thought thereafter.

The aspects of patriarchy already described have each an effect upon the psychology of both sexes. Their principal result is the interiorization of patriarchal ideology. Status, temperament, and role are all value systems with endless psychological ramifications for each sex. Patriarchal marriage and the family with its ranks and division of labor play a large part in enforcing them. The male's superior economic position, the female's inferior one have also grave implications. The large quantity of guilt attached to sexuality in patriarchy is overwhelmingly placed upon the female, who is, culturally speaking, held to be the culpable or the more culpable party in nearly any sexual liaison, whatever the extenuating circumstances. A ten-

---

[11]Géza Róheim, "Eden," *Psychoanalytic Review*, Vol. XXVII, New York,1940. See also Theodor Reik, *The Creation of Woman,* and the account given in Hays, *op. cit.*

dency toward the reification of the female makes her more often a sexual object than a person. This is particularly so when she is denied human rights through chattel status. Even where this has been partly amended the cumulative effect of religion and custom is still very powerful and has enormous psychological consequences. Woman is still denied sexual freedom and the biological control over her body through the cult of virginity, the double standard, the prescription against abortion, and in many places because contraception is physically or psychically unavailable to her.

The continual surveillance in which she is held tends to perpetuate the infantilization of women even in situations such as those of higher education. The female is continually obliged to seek survival or advancement through the approval of males as those who hold power. She may do this either through appeasement or through the exchange of her sexuality for support and status. As the history of patriarchal culture and the representations of herself within all levels of its cultural media, past and present, have a devastating effect upon her self image, she is customarily deprived of any but the most trivial sources of dignity or self-respect. In many patriarchies, language, as well as cultural tradition, reserve the human condition for the male. With the Indo-European langauges this is a nearly inescapable habit of mind, for despite all the customary pretense that "man" and "humanity" are terms which apply equally to both sexes, the fact is hardly obscured that in practice, general application favors the male far more often than the female as referent, or even sole referent, for such designations.[12]

When in any group of persons, the ego is subjected to such invidious versions of itself through social beliefs, ideology, and tradition, the effect is bound to be pernicious. This coupled with the persistent though frequently subtle denigration women encounter daily through personal contacts, the impressions gathered from the images and media about them, and the discrimination in matters of behavior, employment, and education which they endure, should make it no very special cause for surprise that women develop group characteristics common to those who suffer minority status and a marginal existence. A witty experiment by Philip Goldberg proves what everyone knows, that having internalized the disesteem in which they are held, women despise both themselves and each other.[13] This simple test consisted of asking women undergraduates to respond to the scholarship in an essay signed alternately by one John McKay and one Joan McKay. In making their assessments the students generally agreed that John was a remarkable thinker, Joan an unimpressive mind. Yet the articles were identical: the reaction was dependent on the sex of the supposed author.

[12]Languages outside the Indo-European group are instructive. Japanese, for example, has one word for man (otōko), another for woman (ōnna) and a third for human being (ningen). It would be as unthinkable to use the first to cover the third as it would be to use the second.

[13]Philip Goldberg, "Are Women Prejudiced Against Women?" *Transaction*, April 1968.

As women in patriarchy are for the most part marginal citizens when they are citizens at all, their situation is like that of other minorities, here defined not as dependent upon numerical size of the group, but on its status. "A minority group is any group of people who because of their physical or cultural characteristics, are singled out from others in the society in which they live for differential and unequal treatment."[14] Only a handful of sociologists have ever addressed themselves in any meaningful way to the minority status of women.[15] And psychology has yet to produce relevant studies on the subject of ego damage to the female which might bear comparison to the excellent work done on the effects of racism on the minds of blacks and colonials. The remarkably small amount of modern research devoted to the psychological and social effects of masculine supremacy on the female and on the culture in general attests to the widespread ignorance or unconcern of a conservative social science which takes patriarchy to be both the status quo and the state of nature.

What little literature the social sciences afford us in this context confirms the presence in women of the expected traits of minority status: group self-hatred and self-rejection, a contempt both for herself and for her fellows—the result of that continual, however subtle, reiteration of her inferiority which she eventually accepts as a fact.[16] Another index of minority status is the fierceness with which all minority group members are judged. The double standard is applied not only in cases of sexual conduct but other contexts as well. In the relatively rare instances of female crime too: in many American states a woman convicted of crime is awarded a longer sentence.[17] Generally an accused woman acquires a notoriety out of

[14]Louis Wirth, "Problems of Minority Groups," in *The Science of Men in the World Crisis*, ed. by Ralph Linton (New York, Appleton, 1945), p. 347. Wirth also stipulates that the group see itself as discriminated against. It is interesting that many women do not recognize themselves as discriminated against; no better proof could be found of the totality of their conditioning.

[15]The productive handful in question include the following:

Helen Mayer Hacker, "Women as a Minority Group," *Social Forces*, Vol. XXX, October 1951.

Gunnar Myrdal, *An American Dilemma*, Appendix 5 is a parallel of black minority status with women's minority status.

Everett C. Hughes, "Social Change and Status Protest: An Essay on the Marginal Man," *Phylon*, Vol. X, First Quarter, 1949.

Joseph K. Folsom, *"The Family and Democratic Society,"* 1943.

Godwin Watson, "Psychological Aspects of Sex Roles," *Social Psychology, Issues and Insights* (Philadelphia, Lippincott, 1966).

[16]My remarks on the minority status of women are summarized from all the articles listed, and I am particularly indebted to an accomplished critique of them in an unpublished draft by Professor Malene Dixon, fomerly of the University of Chicago's Department of Sociology and the Committee on Human Development, presently of McGill University.

[17]See The Commonwealth v. Daniels, 37 L.W. 2064, Pennsylvania Supreme Court, 7/1/68 (reversing 36 L.W. 2004).

proportion to her acts and due to sensational publicity she may be tried largely for her "sex life." But so effective is her conditioning toward passivity in patriarchy, woman is rarely extrovert enough in her maladjustment to enter upon criminality. Just as every minority member must either apologize for the excesses of a fellow or condemn him with a strident enthusiasm, women are characteristically harsh, ruthless and frightened in their censure of aberration among their numbers.

The gnawing suspicion which plagues any minority member, that the myths propagated about his inferiority might after all be true often reaches remarkable proportions in the personal insecurities of women. Some find their subordinate position so hard to bear that they repress and deny its existence. But a large number will recognize and admit their circumstances when they are properly phrased. Of two studies which asked women if they would have preferred to be born male, one found that one fourth of the sample admitted as much, and in another sample, one half.[18] When one inquires of children, who have not yet developed as serviceable techniques of evasion, what their choice might be, if they had one, the answers of female children in a large majority of cases clearly favor birth into the elite group, whereas boys overwhelmingly reject the option of being girls.[19] The phenomenon of parents' prenatal preference for male issue is too common to require much elaboration. In the light of the imminent possibility of parents actually choosing the sex of their child, such a tendency is becoming the cause of some concern in scientific circles.[20]

Comparisons such as Myrdal, Hacker, and Dixon draw between the ascribed attributes of blacks and women reveal that common opinion associates the same traits with both: inferior intelligence, an instinctual or sensual gratification, an emotional nature both primitive and childlike, an imagined prowess in or affinity for sexuality, a contentment with their own lot which is in accord with a proof of its appropriateness, a wily habit of deceit, and concealment of feeling. Both groups are forced to the same accommodational tactics: an ingratiating or supplicatory manner invented to please, a tendency to study those points at which the dominant group are subject to influence or corruption, and an assumed air of helplessness involving fraudulent appeals for direction through a show of ignorance.[21] It is ironic how misogynist literature has for centuries concentrated on just these traits, directing its fiercest enmity at feminine guile and corruption, and particularly that element of it which is sexual, or, as such sources would have it, "wanton."

18See Helen Hacker, *op. cit.*, and Carolyn Bird, *op. cit.*

19"One study of fourth graders showed ten times as many girls wishing they could have been boys, as boys who would have chosen to be girls," Watson, *op. cit.*, p. 477.

20Amitai Etzioni, "Sex Control, Science, and Society," *Science*, September 1968, pp. 1107–12.

21Myrdal, *op. cit.*, Hacker, *op. cit.*, Dixon, *op. cit.*

As with other marginal groups a certain handful of women are accorded higher status that they may perform a species of cultural policing over the rest. Hughes speaks of marginality as a case of status dilemma experienced by women, blacks, or second-generation Americans who have "come up" in the world but are often refused the rewards of their efforts on the grounds of their origins.[22] This is particularly the case with "new" or educated women. Such exceptions are generally obliged to make ritual, and often comic, statements of deference to justify their elevation. These characteristically take the form of pledges of "femininity," namely a delight in docility and a large appetite for masculine dominance. Politically, the most useful persons for such a role are entertainers and public sex objects. It is a common trait of minority status that a small percentage of the fortunate are permitted to entertain their rulers. (That they may entertain their fellow subjects in the process is less to the point.) Women entertain, please, gratify, satisfy and flatter men with their sexuality. In most minority groups athletes or intellectuals are allowed to emerge as "stars," identification with whom should content their less fortunate fellows. In the case of women both such eventualities are discouraged on the reasonable grounds that the most popular explanations of the female's inferior status ascribe it to her physical weakness or intellectual inferiority. Logically, exhibitions of physical courage or agility are indecorous, just as any display of serious intelligence tends to be out of place.

Perhaps partiarchy's greatest psychological weapon is simply its universality and longevity. A referent scarcely exists with which it might be contrasted or by which it might be confuted. While the same might be said of class, patriarchy has a still more tenacious or powerful hold through its successful habit of passing itself off as nature. Religion is also universal in human society and slavery was once nearly so; advocates of each were found of arguing in terms of fatality, or irrevocable human "instinct"—even "biological origins." When a system of power is thoroughly in command, it has scarcely need to speak itself aloud; when its workings are exposed and questioned, it becomes not only subject to discussion, but even to change.

22 Hughes, *op. cit.*

Suggested Readings

Atkinson, Ronald, *Sexual Morality,* Harcourt, Brace, New York, 1965.

Augustine, St., "On Marriage and Concupiscence," *Collected Works,* Vol. 15, Cima, New York, 1957.

Chesterton, G. K., *The Superstition of Divorce,* Lane, New York, 1920.

de Beauvoir, Simone, *The Second Sex,* Alfred A. Knopf, New York, 1953.

Heller, Agnes, "On the Future Relations Between the Sexes," *International Social Science Journal,* 21, 1969.

Mill, J. S., *The Subjection of Women,* Stokes, New York, 1911.

Morgan, Douglas, *Love: Plato, the Bible, and Freud,* Prentice-Hall, New York, 1964.

Rimmer, Robert H., *The Harrad Experiment,* Sherbourne Press, New York, 1966.

Russell, Bertrand, *Marriage and Morals,* Bantam Books, New York, 1959.

Westermarck, E., *The History of Human Marriage,* Macmillan and Co., London, 1921.

Civil Disobedience

❧ INTRODUCTION

Most persons at some time or another seriously consider performing acts of civil disobedience. I am not, of course, referring to situations where an individual deliberately, but secretly, breaks the civil law with the hope that he will not be apprehended. Rather, I am referring to an occasion when a person thinks that the law itself is wrong or immoral and that his breaking the law is therefore something honorable and right. In this case, then, there usually is no attempt made to keep his action secretive or to avoid apprehension by the civil authorities.

In recent years various student and civil rights groups have adopted civil disobedience as a means for achieving their goals. In 1960, for example, student sit-ins desegregated lunch counters in more than 150 cities within a year. These students were successful in calling national attention to a specific instance of racism and in remedying the injustice. Obviously, if the technique of civil disobedience worked so well in that case, there seemed to be no reason for thinking that it would not work in other areas where society was equally vulnerable to moral condemnation. Unfortunately, however, these other areas happened to be rather numerous. So the techniques of civil disobedience have been implemented in the treatment of a wide variety of issues ranging from the Vietnam War to gaining Black Studies courses in the college curricula. Now, in the 1970's, when strident voices call for militant action and revolution, it is imperative that the reflective student think seriously about this problem. It is important to formulate some general principles by which one can determine when civil disobedience is justified, and to provide a rationale for those principles.

Most people acknowledge that civil disobedience is sometimes justifiable. But how is one to decide exactly *when*? Where does one draw the line between the realm of private conscience and the authority of the state? How far should one go in allowing oneself to be coerced by the civil law? Under what circumstances does an individual have a right, or perhaps even an obligation, to subvert the social system? These troublesome questions are among those considered in the following articles.

The positions of classical liberalism and conservatism are stated by Thoreau and Plato, respectively. Both Hook and Audi introduce auxiliary factors to be considered, but their arguments presuppose the same democratic framework. Kropotkin, on the contrary, questions the very basis of an organized social system whether it be democratic or authoritarian. And finally, Smith and Pollack raise questions concerning the character of our civil law, arguing that its scope should be greatly delimited.

HENRY DAVID THOREAU

12. *The Case for Civil Disobedience*

Henry David Thoreau (1817–1862) was born at Concord, Massachusetts. He attended Harvard University where he impressed his acquaintances with his moral and intellectual integrity. A close friend of Ralph Waldo Emerson, he was an important spokesman for the position of the New England Transcendentalists. Thoreau's essay "Civil Disobedience" greatly influenced Gandhi in the development of his program for passive resistance to the British occupation of India.

I heartily accept the motto, "That government is best which governs least"; and I should like to see it acted up to more rapidly and systematically. Carried out, it finally amounts to this, which also I believe—"That government is best which governs not at all"; and when men are prepared for it, that will be the kind of government which they will have. Government is at best but an expedient; but most governments are usually, and all governments are sometimes, inexpedient. The objections which have been brought against a standing army, and they are many and weighty, and deserve to prevail, may also at last be brought against a standing government. The standing army is only an arm of the standing government. The government itself, which is only the mode which the people have chosen to execute their will, is equally liable to be abused and perverted before the people can act through it. Witness the present Mexican war, the work of comparatively a few individuals using the standing government as their tool; for, in the outset, the people would not have consented to this measure.

This American government—what is it but a tradition, though a recent one, endeavoring to transmit itself unimpaired to posterity, but each instant losing some of its integrity? It has not the vitality and force of a single living man; for a single man can bend it to his will. It is a sort of wooden gun to the people themselves. But it is not the less necessary for this; for the people must have some complicated machinery or other, and hear its din, to satisfy that idea of government which they have. . . .

But, to speak practically and as a citizen, unlike those who call themselves no-government men, I ask for, not at once no government, but *at once* a better government. Let every man make known what kind of government would command his respect, and that will be one step toward obtaining it.

After all, the practical reason why, when the power is once in the hands of the people, a majority are permitted, and for a long period continue, to rule is not because they are most likely to be in the right, nor because this seems fairest to the minority, but because they are physically the

Reprinted from the essay "Civil Disobedience," printed in 1849 in the first number of *Aesthetic Papers,* a literary journal.

strongest. But a government in which the majority rule in all cases cannot be based on justice, even as far as men understand it. Can there not be a government in which majorities do not virtually decide right and wrong, but conscience?—in which majorities decide only those questions to which the rule of expediency is applicable? Must the citizen ever for a moment, or in the least degree, resign his conscience to the legislator? Why has every man a conscience, then? I think that we should be men first, and subjects afterward. It is not desirable to cultivate a respect for the law, so much as for the right. The only obligation which I have a right to assume is to do at any time what I think right. It is truly enough said that a corporation has no conscience; but a corporation of conscientious men is a corporation *with* a conscience. Law never made men a whit more just; and, by means of their respect for it, even the well-disposed are daily made the agents of injustice. A common and natural result of an undue respect for law is, that you may see a file of soldiers, colonel, captain, corporal, privates, powder-monkeys, and all, marching in admirable order over hill and dale to the wars, against their wills, ay, against their common sense and consciences, which makes it very steep marching indeed, and produces a palpitation of the heart. They have no doubt that it is a damnable business in which they are concerned; they are all peaceably inclined. Now, what are they? Men at all? or small movable forts and magazines, at the service of some unscrupulous man in power? Visit the Navy Yard, and behold a marine, such a man as an American government can make, or such as it can make a man with its black arts—a mere shadow and reminiscence of humanity, a man laid out alive and standing, and already, as one may say, buried under arms with funeral accompaniments, though it may be.

> Not a drum was heard, not a funeral note,
> As his corpse to the rampart we hurried;
> Not a soldier discharged his farewell shot
> O'er the grave where our hero we buried.

The mass of men serve the state thus, not as men mainly, but as machines, with their bodies. They are the standing army, and the militia, jailers, constables, *posse comitatus,* etc. In most cases there is no free exercise whatever of the judgment or of the moral sense; but they put themselves on a level with wood and earth and stones; and wooden men can perhaps be manufactured that will serve the purpose as well. Such command no more respect than men of straw or a lump of dirt. They have the same sort of worth only as horses and dogs. Yet such as these even are commonly esteemed good citizens. Others—as most legislators, politicians, lawyers, ministers, and office-holders—serve the state chiefly with their heads; and, as they rarely make any moral distinctions, they are as likely to serve the devil, without *intending* it, as God. A very few—as heroes, patriots, martyrs, reformers in the great sense, and *men*—serve the state with their consciences also, and so necessarily resist it for the most part; and they are commonly treated as enemies by it. A wise man will only be useful as a man, and will not submit to be "clay," and "stop a hole to keep the wind away," but leave that office to his dust at least:

> I am too high-born to be propertied,
> To be a secondary at control,
> Or useful serving-man and instrument
> To any sovereign state throughout the world.

He who gives himself entirely to his fellow men appears to them useless and selfish; but he who gives himself partially to them is pronounced a benefactor and philanthropist.

How does it become a man to behave toward this American government today? I answer, that he cannot without disgrace be associated with it. I cannot for an instant recognize that political organization as *my* government which is the *slave's* government also.

All men recognize the right of revolution; that is, the right to refuse allegiance to, and to resist, the government, when its tyranny or its inefficiency are great and unendurable. But almost all say that such is not the case now. But such was the case, they think, in the Revolution of '75. If one were to tell me that this was a bad government because it taxed certain foreign commodities brought to its ports, it is most probable that I should not make an ado about it, for I can do without them. All machines have their friction; and possibly this does enough good to counterbalance the evil. At any rate, it is a great evil to make a stir about it. But when the friction comes to have its machine, and oppression and robbery are organized, I say, let us not have such a machine any longer. In other words, when a sixth of the population of a nation which has undertaken to be the refuge of liberty are slaves, and a whole country is unjustly overrun and conquered by a foreign army, and subjected to military law, I think that it is not too soon for honest men to rebel and revolutionize. What makes this duty the more urgent is the fact that the country so overrun is not our own, but ours is the invading army. . . .

Unjust laws exist: shall we be content to obey them, or shall we endeavor to amend them, and obey them until we have succeeded, or shall we transgress them at once? Men generally, under such a government as this, think that they ought to wait until they have persuaded the majority to alter them. They think that, if they should resist, the remedy would be worse than the evil. But it is the fault of the government itself that the remedy *is* worse than the evil. *It* makes it worse. Why is it not more apt to anticipate and provide for reform? Why does it not cherish its wise minority? Why does it cry and resist before it is hurt? Why does it not encourage its citizens to be on the alert to point out its faults, and *do* better than it would have them? Why does it always crucify Christ, and excommunicate Copernicus and Luther, and pronounce Washington and Franklin rebels?

One would think, that a deliberate and practical denial of its authority was the only offence never contemplated by government; else, why has it not assigned its definite, its suitable and proportionate, penalty?

If a man who has no property refuses but once to earn nine shillings for the State, he is put in prison for a period unlimited by any law that I know, and determined only by the discretion of those who placed him there; but if he should steal ninety times nine shillings from the State, he is soon permitted to go at large again.

If the injustice is part of the necessary friction of the machine of government, let it go, let it go: perchance it will wear smooth—certainly the machine will wear out. If the injustice has a spring, or a pulley, or a rope, or a crank, exclusively for itself, then perhaps you may consider whether the remedy will not be worse than the evil; but if it is of such a nature that it requires you to be the agent of injustice to another, then, I say, break the law. Let your life be a counter-friction to stop the machine. What I have to do is to see, at any rate, that I do not lend myself to the wrong which I condemn.

As for adopting the ways which the State has provided for remedying the evil, I know not of such ways. They take too much time, and a man's life will be gone. I have other affairs to attend to. I came into this world, not chiefly to make this a good place to live in, but to live in it, be it good or bad. A man has not everything to do, but something; and because he cannot do *everything*, it is not necessary that he should do *something* wrong. It is not my business to be petitioning the Governor or the Legislature any more than it is theirs to petition me; and if they should not hear my petition, what should I do then? But in this case the State has provided no way: its very Constitution is the evil. This may seem to be harsh and stubborn and unconciliatory; but it is to treat with the utmost kindness and consideration the only spirit that can appreciate or deserves it. So is all change for the better, like birth and death, which convulse the body. . . .

I meet this American government, or its representative, the State government, directly, and face to face, once a year—no more—in the person of its tax-gatherer; this is the only mode in which a man situated as I am necessarily meets it; and it then says distinctly, Recognize me; and the simplest, the most effectual, and, in the present posture of affairs, the indispensablest mode of treating with it on this head, of expressing your little satisfaction with and love for it, is to deny it then. My civil neighbor, the tax-gatherer, is the very man I have to deal with—for it is, after all, with men and not with parchment that I quarrel—and he has voluntarily chosen to be an agent of the government. How shall he ever know well what he is and does as an officer of the government, or as a man, until he is obliged to consider whether he shall treat me, his neighbor, for whom he has respect, as a neighbor and well-disposed man, or as a maniac and disturber of the peace, and see if he can get over this obstruction to his neighborliness without a ruder and more impetuous thought or speech corresponding with his action. I know this well, that if one thousand, if one hundred, if ten men whom I could name—if ten *honest* men only—ay, if *one* HONEST man, in this State of Massachusetts, *ceasing to hold slaves*, were actually to withdraw from this copartnership, and be locked up in the county jail therefor, it would be the abolition of slavery in America. For it matters not how small the beginning may seem to be: what is once well done is done forever. But we love better to talk about it: that we say is our mission. Reform keeps many scores of newspapers in its service, but not one man. If my esteemed neighbor, the State's ambassador, who will devote his days to the settlement of the question of human rights in the Council Chamber, instead of being threatened with the prisons of Carolina, were to sit down the prisoner of Massachusetts, that State which is so anxious to foist the sin of slavery upon her sister—though at present she can discover only an act of inhospitality to be the ground of a quarrel with her—the Legislature would not wholly waive the subject the following winter.

Under a government which imprisons any unjustly, the true place for a just man is also a prison. The proper place today, the only place which Massachusetts has provided for her freer and less desponding spirits, is in her prisons, to be put out and locked out of the State by her own act, as they have already put themselves out by their principles. It is there that the fugitive slave, and the Mexican prisoner on parole, and the Indian come to plead the wrongs of his race should find them; on that separate, but more free and honorable, ground, where the State places those who are not *with* her, but *against* her—the only house in a slave State in which a free man can abide with honor. If any think that there influence would be lost there, and their voices no longer afflict the ear of the State, that they would not be as an enemy within its walls, they do not know by how much truth is stronger than error, nor how much more eloquently and effectively he can combat injustice who has experienced a little in his own person. Cast your whole vote, not a strip of paper merely, but your whole influence. A minority is powerless while it conforms to the majority; it is not even a minority then; but it is irresistible when it clogs by its whole weight. If the alternative is to keep all just men in prison, or give up war and slavery, the State will not hesitate which to choose. If a thousand men were not to pay their tax bills this year, that would not be a violent and bloody measure, as it would be to pay them, and enable the State to commit violence and shed innocent blood. This is, in fact, the definition of a peaceable revolution, if any such is possible. If the tax-gatherer, or any other public officer, asks me, as one has done, "But what shall I do?" my answer is, "If you really wish to do anything, resign your office." When the subject has refused allegiance, and the officer has resigned his office, then the revolution is accomplished. But even suppose blood should flow. Is there not a sort of blood shed when the conscience is wounded? Through this wound a man's real manhood and immortality flow out, and he bleeds to an everlasting death. I see this blood flowing now. . . .

I have paid no poll-tax for six years. I was put into a jail once on this account, for one night; and, as I stood considering the walls of solid stone, two or three feet thick, the door of wood and iron, a foot thick, and the iron grating which strained the light, I could not help being struck with the foolishness of that institution which treated me as if I were mere flesh and blood and bones, to be locked up. I wondered that it should have concluded at length that this was the best use it could put me to, and had never thought to avail itself of my services in some way. I saw that, if there was a wall of stone between me and my townsmen, there was a still more difficult one to climb or break through before they could get to be as free as I was. I did not for a moment feel confined, and the walls seemed a great waste of stone and mortar. I felt as if I alone of all my townsmen had paid my tax. They plainly did not know how to treat me, but behaved like persons who are underbred. In every threat and in every compliment there was a blunder; for they thought that my chief desire was to stand the other side of that stone wall. I could not but smile to see how industriously they locked the door on my meditations, which followed them out again without let or hindrance, and *they* were really all that was dangerous. As they could not reach me, they had resolved to punish my body; just as boys, if they cannot come at some person against whom they have a spite, will abuse his dog. I saw that the State was half-witted, that it was timid as a lone woman with her silver spoons, and that it did not know its friends from its foes, and I lost all my remaining respect for it, and pitied it.

Thus the State never intentionally confronts a man's sense, intellectual or moral, but only his body, his senses. It is not armed with superior wit or honesty, but with superior physical strength. I was not born to be forced. I will breathe after my own fashion. Let us see who is the strongest. What force has a multitude? They only can force me who obey a higher law than I. They force me to become like themselves. I do not hear of *men* being *forced* to live this way or that by masses of men. What sort of life were that to live? When I meet a government which says to me, "Your money or your life," why should I be in haste to give it my money? It may be in a great strait, and not know what to do: I cannot help that. It must help itself; do as I do. It is not worth the while to snivel about it. I am not responsible for the successful working of the machinery of society. I am not the son of the engineer. I perceive that, when an acorn and a chestnut fall side by side, the one does not remain inert to make way for the other, but both obey their own laws, and spring and grow and flourish as best they can, till one, perchance, overshadows and destroys the other. If a plant cannot live according to its nature, it dies; and so a man. . . .

I do not wish to quarrel with any man or nation. I do not wish to split hairs, to make fine distinctions, or set myself up as better than my neighbors. I seek rather, I may say, even an excuse for conforming to the laws of the land. I am but too ready to conform to them. Indeed, I have reason to suspect myself on this head; and each year, as the tax-gatherer comes round, I find myself disposed to review the acts and position of the general and State governments, and the spirit of the people, to discover a pretext for conformity.

We must affect our country as our parents,
And if at any time we alienate
Our love or industry from doing it honor,
We must respect effects and teach the soul
Matter of conscience and religion,
And not desire of rule or benefit.

I believe that the State will soon be able to take all my work of this sort out of my hands, and then I shall be no better a patriot than my fellow-countrymen. Seen from a lower point of view, the Constitution, with all its faults, is very good; the law and the courts are very respectable; even this State and this American government are, in many respects, very admirable, and rare things, to be thankful for, such as a great many have described them; but seen from a point of view a little higher, they are what I have described them; seen from a higher still, and the highest, who shall say what they are, or that they are worth looking at or thinking of at all? . . .

The authority of government, even such as I am willing to submit to—for I will cheerfully obey those who know and can do better than I, and in many things even those who neither know nor can do so well—is still an impure one: to be strictly just, it must have the sanction and consent of the governed. It can have no pure right over my person and property but what I concede to it. The progress from an absolute to a limited monarchy, to a democracy, is a progress toward a true respect for the individual. Even the Chinese philosopher was wise enough to regard the individual as the basis of the empire. Is a democracy, such as we know it, the last improvement possible in government? Is it not possible to take a step further towards recognizing and organizing the rights of man? There will never be a really free and enlightened State until the State comes to recognize the individual as a higher and independent power, from which all its own power and authority are derived, and treats him accordingly. I please myself with imagining a State at last which can afford to be just to all men, and to treat the individual with respect as a neighbor; which even would not think it inconsistent with its own repose if a few were to live aloof from it, not meddling with it, nor embraced by it, who fulfilled all the duties of neighbors and fellow men. A State which bore this kind of fruit, and suffered it to drop off as fast as it ripened, would prepare the way for a still more perfect and glorious State, which also I have imagined, but not yet anywhere seen.

✿ PLATO

13. Reasons for Obeying the Law

Plato was born in Athens in 428 B.C., the son of aristocratic parents. At the age of twenty he became the friend and pupil of Socrates. After Socrates' death Plato wrote the following dialogue which is supposed to relate a discussion between Crito and Socrates, who was in prison awaiting the death penalty. Plato also wrote a number of additional dialogues dealing with a variety of philosophical subjects. He was especially concerned with metaphysical, ethical, and political questions.

PERSONS OF THE DIALOGUE:

Socrates.
Crito.

Scene: The Prison of Socrates.

Soc.   Why have you come at this hour, Crito? it must be quite early?
Crito.   Yes, certainly.
Soc.   What is the exact time?
Cr.   The dawn is breaking.
Soc.   I wonder the keeper of the prison would let you in.
Cr.   He knows me because I often come, Socrates; moreover, I have done him a kindness.
Soc.   And are you only just come?
Cr.   No, I came some time ago.
Soc.   Then why did you sit and say nothing, instead of awakening me at once?
Cr.   Why, indeed, Socrates, I myself would rather not have all this sleeplessness and sorrow. But I have been wondering at your peaceful slumbers, and that was the reason why I did not awaken you, because I wanted you to be out of pain. I have always thought you happy in the calmness of your temperament; but never did I see the like of the easy, cheerful way in which you bear this calamity.
Soc.   Why, Crito, when a man has reached my age he ought not to be repining at the prospect of death.
Cr.   And yet other old men find themselves in similar misfortunes, and age does not prevent them from repining.

From the *Crito* in Vol. I of *The Dialogues of Plato* trans. Benjamin Jowett (New York: Scribner, Armstrong, and Co., 1873).

Soc. That may be. But you have not told me why you come at this early hour.

Cr. I come to bring you a message which is sad and painful; not as I believe, to yourself, but to all of us who are your friends, and saddest of all to me.

Soc. What! I suppose that the ship has come from Delos, on the arrival of which I am to die?

Cr. No, the ship has not actually arrived, but she will probably be here today, as persons who have come from Sunium tell me that they left her there; and therefore tomorrow, Socrates, will be the last day of your life.

Soc. Very well, Crito; if such is the will of God, I am willing; but my belief is that there will be a delay of a day.

Cr. Why do you say this?

Soc. I will tell you. I am to die on the day after the arrival of the ship?

Cr. Yes; that is what the authorities say.

Soc. But I do not think that the ship will be here until tomorrow; this I gather from a vision which I had last night, or rather only just now, when you fortunately allowed me to sleep.

Cr. And what was the nature of the vision?

Soc. There came to me the likeness of a woman, fair and comely, clothed in white raiment, who called to me and said: O Socrates,—

"The third day hence, to Phthia shalt thou go."

Cr. What a singular dream, Socrates!

Soc. There can be no doubt about the meaning, Crito, I think.

Cr. Yes: the meaning is only too clear. But, O! my beloved Socrates, let me entreat you once more to take my advice and escape. For if you die I shall not only lose a friend who can never be replaced, but there is another evil: people who do not know you and me will believe that I might have saved you if I had been willing to give money, but that I did not care. Now, can there be a worse disgrace than this—that I should be thought to value money more than the life of a friend? For the many will not be persuaded that I wanted you to escape, and that you refused.

Soc. But why, my dear Crito, should we care about the opinion of the many? Good men, and they are the only persons who are worth considering, will think of these things truly as they happened.

Cr. But do you see, Socrates, that the opinion of the many must be regarded, as is evident in your own case, because they can do the very greatest evil to any one who has lost their good opinion.

Soc. I only wish, Crito, that they could; for then they could also do the greatest good, and that would be well. But the truth is, that they can do neither good nor evil: they cannot make a man wise or make him foolish; and whatever they do is the result of chance.

Cr. Well, I will not dispute about that; but please to tell me, Socrates, whether you are not acting out of regard to me and your other friends: are you not afraid that if you escape hence we may get into trouble with the informers for having stolen you away, and lose either the whole or a great part of our property; or that even a worse evil may happen to us? Now, if this is your fear, be at ease; for in order to save you, we ought surely to run this, or even a greater risk; be persuaded, then, and do as I say.

Soc. Yes, Crito, that is one fear which you mention, but by no means the only one.

Cr. Fear not. There are persons who at no great cost are willing to save you and bring you out of prison; and as for the informers, you may observe that they are far from being exorbitant in their demands; a little money will satisfy them. My means, which, as I am sure, are ample, are at your service, and if you have a scruple about spending all mine, here are strangers who will give you the use of theirs; and one of them, Simmias the Theban, has brought a sum of money for this very purpose; and Cebes and many others are willing to spend their money too. I say therefore, do not on that account hesitate about making your escape, and do not say, as you did in the court, that you will have a difficulty in knowing what to do with yourself if you escape. For men will love you in other places to which you may go, and not in Athens only; there are friends of mine in Thessaly, if you like to go to them, who will value and protect you, and no Thessalian will give you any trouble. Nor can I think that you are justified, Socrates, in betraying your own life when you might be saved; this is playing into the hands of your enemies and destroyers; and moreover I should say that you were betraying your children; for you might bring them up and educate them; instead of which you go away and leave them, and they will have to take their chance; and if they do not meet with the usual fate of orphans, there will be small thanks to you. No man should bring children into the world who is unwilling to persevere to the end in their nurture and education. But you are choosing the easier part, as I think, not the better and manlier, which would rather have become one who professes virtue in all his actions, like yourself. And indeed, I am ashamed not only of you, but of us who are your friends, when I reflect that this entire business of yours will be attributed to our want of courage. The trial need never have come on, or might have been brought to another issue; and the end of all, which is the crowning absurdity, will seem to have been permitted by us, through cowardice and baseness, who might have saved you, as you might have saved yourself, if we had been good for anything (for there was no difficulty in escaping); and we did not see how disgraceful, Socrates, and also miserable all this will be to us as well as to you. Make your mind up then, or rather have your mind already made up, for the time of deliberation is over, and there is only one thing to be done, which must be done, if at all, this very night, and which any delay will render all but impossible; I beseech you therefore, Socrates, to be persuaded by me, and to do as I say.

Soc. Dear Crito, your zeal is invaluable, if a right one; but if wrong, the greater the zeal the greater the evil; and therefore we ought to consider whether these things shall be done or not. For I am and always have been one of those natures who must be guided by reason, whatever the reason may be which upon reflection appears to me to be the best; and now that this fortune has come upon me, I cannot put away the reasons which I have before given: the principles which I have hitherto honored and revered I still honor, and unless we can find other and better principles on the instant, I am certain not to agree with you; no, not even if the power of the multitude could inflict many more imprisonments, confiscations, deaths, frightening us like children with hobgoblin terrors But what will be the fairest way of considering the question? Shall I return to your old argument about the opinions of men? some of which are to be regarded, and others, as we were saying, are not to be regarded. Now were we right in maintaining this before I was condemned? And has the argument which was once good now proved to be talk for the sake of talking; in fact an amusement only, and altogether vanity? That is what I want to consider with your help, Crito: whether, under my present circumstances, the argument appears to be in any way different or not; and is to be allowed by me or disallowed. That argument, which, as I believe, is maintained by many who assume to be authorities, was to the effect, as I was saying, that the opinions of some men are to be regarded, and of other men not to be regarded. Now you, Crito, are a disinterested person who are not going to die tomorrow—at least, there is no human probability of this, and you are therefore not liable to be deceived by the circumstances in which you are placed. Tell me then, whether I am right in saying that some opinions, and the opinions of some men only, are to be valued, and other opinions, and the opinions of other men, are not to be valued. I ask you whether I was right in maintaining this?

Cr. Certainly.

Soc. The good are to be regarded, and not the bad?

Cr. Yes.

Soc. And the opinions of the wise are good, and the opinions of the unwise are evil?

Cr. Certainly.

Soc. And what was said about another matter? Was the disciple in gymnastics supposed to attend to the praise and blame and opinion of every man, or of one man only—his physician or trainer, whoever that was?

Cr. Of one man only.

Soc. And he ought to fear the censure and welcome the praise of that one only, and not of the many?

Cr. That is clear.

Soc. And he ought to live and train, and eat and drink in the way which seems good to his single master who has understanding, rather than according to the opinion of all other men put together?

Cr. True.

Soc. And if he disobeys and disregards the opinion and approval of the one, and regards the opinion of the many who have no understanding, will he not suffer evil?

Cr. Certainly he will.

Soc. And what will the evil be, whither tending and what affecting, in the disobedient person?

Cr. Clearly, affecting the body; that is what is destroyed by the evil.

Soc. Very good; and is not this true, Crito, of other things which we need not separately enumerate? In the matter of just and unjust, fair and foul, good and evil, which are the subjects of our present consultation, ought we to follow the opinion of the many and to fear them; or the opinion of the one man who has understanding, and whom we ought to fear and reverence more than all the rest of the world: and whom deserting we shall destroy and injure that principle in us which may be assumed to be improved by justice and deteriorated by injustice; is there not such a principle?

Cr. Certainly there is, Socrates.

Soc. Take a parallel instance: if, acting under the advice of men who have no understanding, we destroy that which is improvable by health and deteriorated by disease—when that has been destroyed, I say, would life be worth having? And that is—the body?

Cr. Yes.

Soc. Could we live, having an evil and corrupted body?

Cr. Certainly not.

Soc. And will life be worth having, if that higher part of man be depraved, which is improved by justice and deteriorated by injustice? Do we suppose that principle, whatever it may be in man, which has to do with justice and injustice, to be inferior to the body?

Cr. Certainly not.

Soc. More honored, then?

Cr. Far more honored.

Soc. Then, my friend, we must not regard what the many say of us: but what he, the one man who has understanding of just and unjust, will say, and what the truth will say. And therefore you begin in error when you suggest that we should regard the opinion of the many about just and unjust, good and evil, honorable and dishonorable. Well, some one will say, "But the many can kill us."

Cr. Yes, Socrates; that will clearly be the answer.

Soc. That is true: but still I find with surprise that the old argument is, as I conceive, unshaken as ever. And I should like to know whether I may say the same of another proposition—that not life, but a good life, is to be chiefly valued?

Cr. Yes, that also remains.

Soc. And a good life is equivalent to a just and honorable one—that holds also?

Cr. Yes, that holds.

Soc. From these premises I proceed to argue the question whether I ought or ought not to try and escape without the consent of the Athenians: and if I am clearly right in escaping, then I will make the attempt; but if not, I will abstain. The other considerations which you mention, of money and loss of character and the duty of educating children, are, as I fear, only the doctrines of the multitude, who would be as ready to call people to life, if they were able, as they are to put them to death—and with as little reason. But now, since the argument has thus far prevailed, the only question which remains to be considered is, whether we shall do rightly either in escaping or in suffering others to aid in our escape and paying them in money and thanks, or whether we shall not do rightly; and if the latter, then death or any other calamity which may ensue on my remaining here must not be allowed to enter into the calculation.

Cr. I think that you are right, Socrates; how then shall we proceed?

Soc. Let us consider the matter together, and do you either refute me if you can, and I will be convinced; or else cease, my dear friend, from repeating to me that I ought to escape against the wishes of the Athenians: for I am extremely desirous to be persuaded by you, but not against my own better judgment. And now please to consider my first position, and do your best to answer me.

Cr. I will do my best.

Soc. Are we to say that we are never intentionally to do wrong, or that in one way we ought and in another way we ought not to do wrong, or is doing wrong always evil and dishonorable, as I was just now saying, and as has been already acknowledged by us? Are all our former admissions which were made within a few days to be thrown away? And have we, at our age, been earnestly discoursing with one another all our life long only to discover that we are no better than children? Or are we to rest assured, in spite of the opinion of the many, and in spite of consequences whether better or worse, of the truth of what was then said, that injustice is always an evil and dishonor to him who acts unjustly? Shall we affirm that?

Cr. Yes.

Soc. Then we must do no wrong?

Cr. Certainly not.

Soc. Nor when injured injure in return, as the many imagine; for we must injure no one at all?

Cr. Clearly not.

Soc. Again, Crito, may we do evil?

Cr. Surely not, Socrates.

Soc. And what of doing evil in return for evil, which is the morality of the many—is that just or not?

Cr. Not just.

Soc. For doing evil to another is the same as injuring him?

Cr. Very true.

Soc. Then we ought not to retaliate or render evil for evil to any one, whatever evil we may have suffered from him. But I would have you consider, Crito, whether you really mean what you are saying. For this opinion has never been held, and never will be held, by any considerable number of persons; and those who are agreed and those who are not agreed upon this point have no common ground, and can only despise one another when they see how widely they differ. Tell me, then, whether you agree with and assent to my first principle, that neither injury nor retaliation nor warding off evil by evil is ever right. And shall that be the premise of our argument? Or do you decline and dissent from this? For this has been of old and is still my opinion; but, if you are of another opinion, let me hear what you have to say. If, however, you remain of the same mind as formerly, I will proceed to the next step.

Cr. You may proceed, for I have not changed my mind.

Soc. Then I will proceed to the next step, which may be put in the form of a question: Ought a man to do what he admits to be right, or ought he to betray the right?

Cr. He ought to do what he thinks right.

Soc. But if this is true, what is the application? In leaving the prison against the will of the Athenians, do I wrong any? or rather do I not wrong those whom I ought least to wrong? Do I not desert the principles which were acknowledged by us to be just? What do you say?

Cr. I cannot tell, Socrates; for I do not know.

Soc. Then consider the matter in this way: Imagine that I am about to play truant (you may call the proceeding by any name which you like), and the laws and the government come and interrogate me: "Tell us, Socrates," they say; "what are you about? are you going by an act of yours to overturn us—the laws and the whole state, as far as in you lies? Do you imagine that a state can subsist and not be overthrown, in which the decisions of law have no power, but are set aside and overthrown by individuals?" What will be our answer, Crito, to these and the like words? Any one, and especially a clever rhetorician, will have a good deal to urge about the evil of setting aside the law which requires a sentence to be carried out; and we might reply, "Yes; but the state has injured us and given an unjust sentence." Suppose I say that?

Cr. Very good, Socrates.

Soc. "And was that our agreement with you?" the law would say; "or were you to abide by the sentence of the state?" And if I were to express astonishment at their saying this, the law would probably add: "Answer, Socrates, instead of opening your eyes: you are in the habit of asking and answering questions. Tell us what complaint you have to make against us which justifies you in attempting to destroy us and the state? In the first place did we not bring you into existence? Your father married your mother by our aid and begat you. Say whether you have any objection to urge against those of us who regulate marriage?" None, I should reply. "Or against those of us who regulate the system of nurture and education of children in which you were trained? Were not the laws, who have the charge of this, right in commanding your father to train you in music and gymnastic?" Right, I should reply. "Well then, since you were brought into the world and nurtured and educated by us, can you deny in the first place that you are our child and slave, as your fathers were before you? And if this is true you are not on equal terms with us; nor can you think that you have a right to do to us what we are doing to you. Would you have any right to strike or revile or do any other evil to a father or to your master, if you had one, when you have been struck or reviled by him, or received some other evil at his hands?—you would not say this? And because we think right to destroy you, do you think that you have any right to destroy us in return, and your country as far as in you lies? And will you, O professor of true virtue, say that you are justified in this? Has a philosopher like you failed to discover that our country is more to be valued and higher and holier far than mother or father or any ancestor, and more to be regarded in the eyes of the gods and of men of understanding? also to be soothed, and gently and reverently entreated when angry, even more than a father, and if not persuaded, obeyed? And when we are punished by her, whether with imprisonment or stripes, the punishment is to be endured in silence; and if she leads us to wounds or death in battle, thither we follow as is right; neither may any one yield or retreat or leave his rank, but whether in battle or in a court of law, or in any other place, he must do what his city and his country order him; or he must change their view of what is just: and if he may do no violence to his father or mother, much less may he do violence to his country." What answer shall we make to this, Crito? Do the laws speak truly, or do they not?

Cr. I think that they do.

Soc. Then the laws will say: "Consider, Socrates, if this is true, that in your present attempt you are going to do us wrong. For, after having brought you into the world, and nurtured and educated you, and given you and every other citizen a share in every good that we had to give, we further proclaim and give the right to every Athenian, that if he does not like us when he has come of age and has seen the ways of the city, and made our acquaintance, he may go where he pleases and take his goods with him; and none of us laws will forbid him or interfere with him. Any of you who does not like us and the city, and who wants to go to a colony or to any other city, may go where he likes, and take his goods with him. But he who has experience of the manner in which we order justice and administer the state, and still remains, has entered into an implied contract that he will do as we command him. And he who disobeys us is, as we maintain, thrice wrong: first, because in disobeying us he is disobeying his parents; secondly, because we are the authors of his education; thirdly, because he has made an agreement with us that he will duly obey our commands; and he neither obeys them nor convinces us that our commands are wrong; and we do not rudely impose them, but give him the alternative of obeying or convincing us; that is what we offer, and he does neither. These are the sort of accusations to which, as we were saying, you, Socrates, will be exposed if you accomplish your intentions; you, above all other Athenians."

Suppose I ask, why is this? they will justly retort upon me that I above all other men have acknowledged the agreement. "There is clear proof," they will say, "Socrates, that we and the city were not displeasing to you. Of all Athenians you have been the most constant resident in the city, which, as you never leave, you may be supposed to love. For you never went out of the city either to see the games, except once when you went to the Isthmus, or to any other place unless when you were on military service; nor did you travel as other men do. Nor had you any curiosity to know other states or their laws: your affections did not go beyond us and our state; we were your special favorites, and you acquiesced in our government of you; and this is the state in which you begat your children, which is a proof of your satisfaction. Moreover, you might, if you had liked, have fixed the penalty at banishment in the course of the trial—the state which refuses to let you go now would have let you go then. But you pretended that you preferred death to exile, and that you were not grieved at death. And now you have forgotten these fine sentiments, and pay no respect to us the laws, of whom you are the destroyer; and are doing what only a miserable slave would do, running away and turning your back upon the compacts and agreements which you made as a citizen. And first of all answer this very question: Are we right in saying that you agreed to be governed according to us in deed, and not in word only? Is that true or not? How shall we answer that, Crito? Must we not agree?

Cr. There is no help, Socrates.

Soc. Then will they not say: "You, Socrates, are breaking the covenants and agreements which you made with us at your leisure, not in any haste or under any compulsion or deception, but having had seventy years to think of them, during which time you were at liberty to leave the city, if we were not to your mind, or if our covenants appeared to you to be unfair. You had your choice, and might have gone either to Lacedaemon or Crete, which you often praise for their good government, or to some other Hellenic or foreign state. Whereas you above all other Athenians, seemed to be so fond of the state, or, in other words, of us her laws (for who would like a state that has no laws), that you never stirred out of her: the halt, the blind, the maimed were not more stationary in her than you were. And now you run away and forsake your agreements. Not so, Socrates, if you will take our advice; do not make youself ridiculous by escaping out of the city.

"For just consider, if you transgress and err in this sort of way, what good will you do, either to yourself or to your friends? That your friends will be driven into exile and deprived of citizenship, or will lose their property, is tolerably certain; and you yourself, if you fly to one of the neighboring cities, as, for example, Thebes or Megara, both of which are well-governed cities, will come to them as an enemy, Socrates, and their government will be against you, and all patriotic citizens will cast an evil eye upon you as a subverter of the laws, and you will confirm in the minds of the judges the justice of their own condemnation of you. For he who is a corrupter of the laws is more than likely to be corrupter of the young and foolish portion of mankind. Will you then flee from well-ordered cities and virtuous men? and is existence worth having on these terms? Or will you go to them without shame, and talk to them, Socrates? And what will you say to them? What you say here about virtue and justice and institutions and laws being the best things among men? Would that be decent of you? Surely not. But if you go away from well-governed states to Crito's friends in Thessaly, where there is great disorder and license, they will be charmed to have the tale of your escape from prison, set off with ludicrous particulars of the manner in which you were wrapped in a goatskin or some other disguise, and metamorphosed as the fashion of runaways is—that is very likely; but will there be no one to remind you that in your old age you violated the most sacred laws from a miserable desire of a little more life. Perhaps not, if you keep them in a good temper; but if they are out of temper you will hear many degrading things; you will live, but how?— as the flatterer of all men, and the servant of all men; and doing what?— eating and drinking in Thessaly, having gone abroad in order that you may get a dinner. And where will be your fine sentiments about justice and virtue then? Say that you wish to live for the sake of your children, that you may bring them up and educate them—will you take them into Thessaly and deprive them of Athenian citizenship? Is that the benefit which you would confer upon them? Or are you under the impression that they will be better cared for and educated here if you are still alive, although absent from them; for that your friends will take care of them? Do you fancy that if you are an inhabitant of Thessaly they will take care of them, and if you are an inhabitant of the other world they will not take care of them? Nay; but if they who call themselves friends are truly friends, they surely will.

"Listen, then, Socrates, to us who have brought you up. Think not of life and children first, and of justice afterwards, but of justice first, that you may be justified before the princes of the world below. For neither will you nor any that belong to you be happier or holier or juster in this life, or happier in another, if you do as Crito bids. Now you depart in innocence, a sufferer and not a doer of evil; a victim, not of the laws, but of men. But if you go forth, returning evil for evil, and injury for injury, breaking the covenants and agreements which you have made with us, and wronging those whom you ought least to wrong, that is to say, yourself, your friends, your country, and us, we shall be angry with you while you live, and our brethren, the laws in the world below, will receive you as an enemy; for they will know that you have done your best to destroy us. Listen, then, to us and not to Crito."

This is the voice which I seem to hear murmuring in my ears, like the sound of the flute in the ears of the mystic; that voice, I say, is humming in my ears, and prevents me from hearing any other. And I know that anything more which you may say will be vain. Yet speak, if you have anything to say.

Cr. I have nothing to say, Socrates.

Soc. Then let me follow the intimations of the will of God.

❀ SIDNEY HOOK

14. Social Protest and Civil Obedience

Sidney Hook is professor of philosophy and chairman of the Department of Philosophy at New York University. Past president of the American Philosophical Association, he has written a number of important books. Among these are: *Reason, Social Myths and Democracy* (1940), *From Hegel to Marx* (1950), *Marx and the Marxists: The Ambiguous Legacy* (1955), *Political Power and Personal Freedom* (1959), *Paradoxes of Freedom* (1962), and *Religion in a Free Society* (1967).

In times of moral crisis what has been accepted as commonplace truth sometimes appears questionable and problematic. We have all been nurtured in the humanistic belief that in a democracy, citizens are free to disagree with a law but that so long as it remains in force, they have a *prima facie* obligation to obey it. The belief is justified on the ground that this procedure enables us to escape the twin evils of tyranny and anarchy. Tyranny is avoided by virtue of the freedom and power of dissent to win the uncoerced consent of the community. Anarchy is avoided by reliance on due process, the recognition that there is a right way to correct a wrong, and a wrong way to secure a right. To the extent that anything is demonstrable in human affairs, we have held that democracy as a political system is not viable if members systematically refused to obey laws whose wisdom or morality they dispute.

Nonetheless, during the past decade of tension and turmoil in American life there has developed a mass phenomenon of civil disobedience even among those who profess devotion to democratic ideals and institutions. This phenomenon has assumed a character similar to a tidal wave which has not yet reached its crest. It has swept from the field of race relations to the campuses of some universities, subtly altering the connotation of the term "academic." It is being systematically developed as an instrument of influencing foreign policy. It is leaving its mark on popular culture. I am told it is not only a theme of comic books but that children in our more sophisticated families no longer resort to tantrums in defying parental discipline—they go limp!

More seriously, in the wake of civil disobedience there has occasionally developed *uncivil* disobedience, sometimes as a natural psychological development, and often because of the failure of law enforcement agencies especially in the South to respect and defend legitimate expressions of social protest. The line between civil and uncivil disobedience is not only an uncertain and wavering one in practice, it has become so in theory. A recent prophet of the philosophy of the absurd in recommending

Reprinted from *The Humanist*, XXVII, Nos. 5 and 6 (September/December 1967). Used with the kind permission of the American Humanist Association.

civil disobedience as a form of creative disorder in a democracy cited
Shay's Rebellion as an illustration. This Rebellion was uncivil to the point
of bloodshed. Indeed, some of the techniques of protesting American involvement in Vietnam have departed so far from traditional ways of civil
disobedience as to make it likely that they are inspired by the same confusion between civil and uncivil disobedience.

All this has made focal the perennial problems of the nature and
limits of the citizen's obligation to obey the law, of the relation between the
authority of conscience and the authority of the state, of the rights and
duties of a democratic moral man in an immoral democratic society. The
classical writings on these questions have acquired a burning relevance to
the political condition of man today. I propose briefly to clarify some of
these problems.

To begin with I wish to stress the point that there is no problem
concerning "social protest" as such in a democracy. Our Bill of Rights was
adopted not only to make protest possible but to encourage it. The political
logic, they very ethos of any democracy that professes to rest, no matter how
indirectly, upon freely given consent *requires* that social protest be permitted—and not only permitted but *protected* from interference by those
opposed to the protest, which means protected by agencies of law enforcement.

Not social protest but *illegal* social protest constitutes our problem.
It raises the question: "When, if ever, is illegal protest justified in a democratic society?" It is of the first importance to bear in mind that we are
raising the question as principled democrats and humanists in a democratic society. To urge that illegal social protests, motivated by exalted
ideals, are sanctified in a democratic society by precedents like the Boston
Tea Party, is a lapse into political illiteracy. Such actions occurred in
societies in which those affected by unjust laws had no power peacefully to
change them.

Further, many actions dubbed civilly disobedient by local authorities, strictly speaking, are not such at all. An action launched in violation of
a local law or ordinance, and undertaken to test it, on the ground that the
law itself violates state or federal law, or launched in violation of a state
law in the sincerely held belief that the state law outrages the Constitution,
the supreme law of the land, is not civilly disobedient. In large measure
the original sympathy with which the original sit-ins were received, especially the Freedom Rides, marches and demonstrations that flouted local
Southern laws, was due to the conviction that they were constitutionally
justified, in accordance with the heritage of freedom, enshrined in the
Amendments and enjoyed in other regions of the country. Practically everything the marchers did was sanctioned by the phrase of the First Amendment which upholds "the right of the people peaceably to assemble and to
petition the Government for a redress of grievances." Actions of this kind
may be wise or unwise, timely or untimely, but they are not civilly disobedient.

They become civilly disobedient when they are in deliberate violation of laws that have been sustained by the highest legislative and judicial bodies of the nation, e.g., income tax laws, conscription laws, laws forbidding segregation in education, and discrimination in public accommodations and employment. Another class of examples consists of illegal social protest against local and state laws that clearly do not conflict with Federal Law.

Once we grasp the proper issue, the question is asked with deceptive clarity: "Are we under an obligation in a democratic community always to obey an unjust law?" To this question Abraham Lincoln is supposed to have made the classic answer in an eloquent address on "The Perpetuation of Our Political Institution," calling for absolute and religious obedience until the unjust law is repealed.

I said that this question is asked with deceptive clarity because Lincoln, judging by his other writings and the pragmatic cast of his basic philosophy, could never have subscribed to this absolutism or meant what he seemed literally to have said. Not only are we under no moral obligation *always* to obey unjust laws, we are under no moral obligation *always* to obey a just law. One can put it more strongly sometimes it may be necessary in the interests of the greater good to violate a just or sensible law. A man who refused to violate a sensible traffic law if it were necessary to do so to avoid a probably fatal accident would be a moral idiot. There are other values in the world besides legality or even justice, and sometimes they may be of overriding concern and weight. Everyone can imagine some situation in which the violation of some existing law is the lesser moral evil, but this does not invalidate recognition of our obligation to obey just laws.

There is a difference between disobeying a law which one approves of in general but whose application in a specific case seems wrong, and disobeying a law in protest against the injustice of the law itself. In the latter case the disobedience is open and public; in the former, not. But if the grounds of disobedience in both cases are moral considerations, there is only a difference in degree between them. The rejection, therefore, of legal absolutism, or the fetishism of legality—that one is never justified in violating any law in any circumstances—is a matter of common sense.

The implications drawn from this moral commonplace by some ritualistic liberals are clearly absurd. For they have substituted for the absolutism of law, something very close to the absolutism of individual conscience. Properly rejecting the view that the law, no matter how unjust, must be obeyed in all circumstances, they have taken the view that the law is to be obeyed only when the individual deems it just or when it does not outrage his conscience. Fantastic comparisons are made between those who do not act on the dictates of their conscience and those who accepted and obeyed Hitler's laws. These comparisons completely disregard the systems of law involved, the presence of alternatives of action, the differences in the behavior commanded, in degrees of complicity of guilt, in the moral costs and personal consequences of compliance and other relevant matters.

It is commendable to recognize the primacy of morality to law but unless we recognize the centrality of intelligence to morality, we stumble with blind self-righteousness into moral disaster. Because, Kant to the contrary notwithstanding, it is not wrong sometimes to lie to save a human life; because it is not wrong sometimes to kill in defense to save many from being killed, it does not follow that the moral principles: "Do not lie!" "Do not kill!" are invalid. When more than one valid principle bears on a problem of moral experience, the very fact of their conflict means that not all of them can hold unqualifiedly. One of them must be denied. The point is that such negation or violation entails upon us the obligation of justifying it and moral justification is a matter of reasons not of conscience. The burden of proof rests on the person violating the rules. Normally, we don't have to justify telling the truth. We do have to justify *not* telling the truth. Similarly, with respect to the moral obligation of a democrat who breaches his political obligation to obey the laws of a democratic community, the resort to conscience is not enough. There must always be reasonable justification.

This is all the more true because just as we can, if challenged, give powerful reasons for the moral principle of truth-telling, so we can offer logically coercive grounds for the obligation of a democrat to obey the laws of a democracy. The grounds are many and they can be amplified beyond the passing mention we give here. It is a matter of fairness, of social utility, of peace, or ordered progress, of redeeming an implicit commitment.

There is one point, however, which has a particular relevance to the claims of those who counterpose to legal absolutism, the absolutism of conscience. There is the empirically observable tendency for public disobedience to law to spread from those who occupy high moral ground to those who dwell on low ground with consequent growth of disorder and insecurity.

Conscience by itself is not the measure of high or low moral ground. This is the work of reason. Where it functions properly the democratic process permits this resort to reason. If the man of conscience loses in the court of reason, why should he assume that the decision or the law is mistaken rather than the deliverances of his conscience?

The voice of conscience may sound loud and clear. But it may conflict at times not only with the law but with another man's conscience. Every conscientious objector to a law knows that at least one man's conscience is wrong, viz., the conscience of the man who asserts that *his* conscience tells him that he must not tolerate conscientious objectors. From this if he is reasonable he should conclude that when he hears the voice of conscience, he is hearing not the voice of God, but the voice of a finite, limited man in this time and in this place, and that conscience is neither a special nor an infallible organ of apprehending moral truth, that conscience without conscientiousness, conscience which does not cap the process of critical reflective morality, is likely to be prejudice masquerading as a First Principle or a Mandate from Heaven.

The mark of an enlightened democracy is, as far as is possible with its security, to respect the religious commitment of a citizen who believes, on grounds of conscience or any other ground, that his relation to God involves duties superior to those arising from any human relation. It, therefore, exempts him from his duty as a citizen to protect his country. However, the mark of the genuine conscientious objector in a democracy is to respect the democratic process. He does not use his exemption as a political weapon to coerce where he has failed to convince or persuade. Having failed to influence national policy by rational means within the law, in the political processes open to him in a free society, he cannot justifiably try to defeat that policy by resorting to obstructive techniques outside the law and still remain a democrat.

It is one thing on grounds of conscience or religion to plead exemption from the duty of serving one's country when drafted. It is quite another to adopt harassing techniques to prevent others from volunteering or responding to the call of duty. It is one thing to oppose American involvement in Vietnam by teach-ins, petitions, electoral activity. It is quite another to attempt to stop troop trains: to take possession of the premises of draft boards where policies are not made; to urge recruits to sabotage their assignments and feign illness to win discharge. The first class of actions fall within the sphere of legitimate social protest; the second class are implicitly insurrectionary since it is directed against the authority of a democratic government which it seeks to overthrow not by argument and discussion but by resistance—albeit passive resistance.

Nonetheless since we have rejected legal absolutism we must face the possibility that in protest on ethical grounds individuals may refuse to obey some law which they regard as uncommonly immoral or uncommonly foolish. If they profess to be democrats, their behavior must scrupulously respect the following conditions:

First, it must be non-violent—peaceful not only in form but in actuality. After all, the protesters are seeking to dramatize a great evil that the community allegedly has been unable to overcome because of complacency or moral weakness. Therefore, they must avoid the guilt of imposing hardship or harm on others who in the nature of the case can hardly be responsible for the situation under protest. Passive resistance should not be utilized merely as a safer or more effective strategy than active resistance of imposing their wills on others.

Secondly, resort to civil disobedience is never morally legitimate where other methods of remedying the evil complained of are available. Existing grievance procedures should be used. No grievance procedures were available to the southern Negroes. The Courts often shared the prejudices of the community and offered no relief, not even minimal protection. But such procedures *are* available in the areas of industry and education. For example, where charges against students are being heard such procedures may result in the dismissal of the charges, not the students. Or the faculty on appeal may decide to suspend the rules rather than the students. To jump the gun to civil disobedience in bypassing these procedures is tell-tale evidence that those who are calling the shots are after other game than preserving the rights of students.

Thirdly, those who resort to civil disobedience are duty bound to accept the legal sanctions and punishments imposed by the laws. Attempts to evade and escape them involve not only a betrayal of the community, but they erode the moral foundations of civil disobedience itself. Socrates' argument in the *Crito* is valid only on democratic premises. The rationale of the protesters is the hope that the pain and hurt and indignity they voluntarily accept will stir their fellow citizens to compassion, open their minds to second thoughts, and move them to undertake the necessary healing action. When, however, we observe the heroics of defiance being followed by the dialectics of legal evasion, we question the sincerity of the action.

Fourth, civil disobedience is unjustified if a major moral issue is not clearly at stake. Differences about negotiable details that can easily be settled with a little patience should not be fanned into a blaze of illegal opposition.

Fifth, where intelligent men of good will and character differ on large and complex moral issues, discussion and agitation are more appropriate than civilly disobedient action. Those who feel strongly about animal rights and regard the consumption of animal flesh as food as morally evil would have a just cause for civil disobedience if *their* freedom to obtain other food was threatened. They would have no moral right to resort to similar action to prevent their fellow-citizens from consuming meat. Similarly, with fluoridation.

Sixth, where civil disobedience is undertaken, there must be some rhyme and reason in the time, place, and targets selected. If one is convinced, as I am not, that the Board of Education of New York City is remiss in its policy of desegregation, what is the point of dumping garbage on bridges to produce traffic jams that seriously discomfort commuters who have not the remotest connection with educational policies in New York. Such action can only obstruct the progress of desegregation in the communities of Long Island. Gandhi, who inspired the civil disobedience movement in the 20th Century, was a better tactician than many who invoke his name but ignore his teachings. When he organized his campaign of civil disobedience against the Salt Tax, he marched with his followers to the sea to make salt. He did not hold up food trains or tie up traffic.

Finally, there is such a thing as historical timing. Democrats who resort to civil disobedience must ask themselves whether the cumulative consequences of their action may in the existing climate of opinion undermine the peace and order on which the effective exercise of other human rights depend. This is a cost which one may be willing to pay but which must be taken into the reckoning.

These observations in the eyes of some defenders of the philosophy of civil disobedience are far from persuasive. They regard them as evading the political realities. The political realities, it is asserted, do not provide meaningful channels for the legitimate expression of dissent. The "Establishment" is too powerful or indifferent to be moved. Administrations are voted into office that are not bound by their election pledges. The right to form minority parties is hampered by unconstitutional voting laws. What does even "the right of the people to present petitions for the redress of grievances" amount to if it does not carry with it the right to have those petitions paid attention to, at least to have them read, if not acted upon?

No, the opposing argument runs on. Genuine progress does not come by enactment of laws, by appeals to the good will or conscience of one's fellow citizens, but only by obstructions which interfere with the functioning of the system itself, by actions whose nuisance value is so high that the Establishment finds it easier to be decent and yield to demands than to be obdurate and oppose them. The time comes, as one student leader of the civilly disobedient Berkeley students advised, "when it is necessary for you to throw your bodies upon the wheels and gears and levers and bring the machine to a grinding halt." When one objects that such obstruction, as a principle of political action, is almost sure to produce chaos, and that it is unnecessary and undesirable in a democracy, the retort is made: "Amen, if only this were a democracy, how glad we would be to stop!"

It is characteristic of those who argue this way to define the presence or absence of the democratic process by whether or not *they* get their political way, and not by the presence or absence of democratic institutional processes. The rules of the game exist to enable them to win and if they lose that's sufficient proof the game is rigged and dishonest. The sincerity with which the position is held is no evidence whatsoever of its coherence. The right to petition does not carry with it the right to be heard if that means influence on those to whom it is addressed. What would they do if they received incompatible petitions from two different and hostile groups of petitioning citizens? The right of petition gives one a chance to persuade and the persuasion must rest on the power of words, on the effective appeal to emotion, sympathy, reason and logic. Petitions are weapons of criticism, and their failure does not justify appeal to other kinds of weapons.

It is quite true that some local election laws do hamper minority groups in the organization of political parties; but there is always the right of appeal to the Courts. Even if this fails there is a possibility of influencing other political parties. It is difficult but so long as one is free to publish and speak, it can be done. If a group is unsuccessful in moving a majority by the weapons of criticism, in a democracy it may resort to peaceful measures of obstruction, provided it is willing to accept punishment for its obstructionist behavior. But these objections are usually a preface to some form of elitism or moral snobbery which is incompatible with the very grounds given in defending the right of civil disobedience on the part of democrats in a democracy.

All of the seven considerations listed above are cautionary, not categorical. We have ruled out only two positions—blind obedience to any and all laws in a democracy, and unreflective violation of laws at the behest of individual consciences. Between these two obviously unacceptable extremes, there is a spectrum of views which shade into each other. Intelligent persons can differ on their application to specific situations. These differences will reflect different assessments of the historical mood of a culture, of the proper timing of protest and acquiescence, and of what the most desirable emphasis and direction of our teaching should be in order to extend "the blessing of liberty" as we preserve "domestic tranquillity."

Without essaying the role of a prophet, here is my reading of the needs of the present. It seems to me that the Civil Rights Acts of 1964 and the Voting Acts of 1965 mark a watershed in the history of social and civil protest in the U.S. Upon their enforcement a great many things we hold dear depend, especially those causes in behalf of which in the last decade so many movements of social protest were launched. We must recall that it was the emasculation of the 15th Amendment in the South which kept the Southern Negro in a state of virtual peonage. The prospect of enforcement of the new civil rights legislation is a function of many factors—most notably the law-abiding behavior of the hitherto recalcitrant elements in the southern white communities. Their *uncivil,* violent disobedience has proved unavailing. We need not fear this so much as that they will adopt the strategies and techniques of the civil disobedience itself in their opposition to long-delayed and decent legislation to make the ideals of American democracy a greater reality.

On the other hand, I think the movement of civil disobedience, as distinct from legal protest, in regions of the country in which Negroes have made slow but substantial advances are not likely to make new gains commensurate with the risks. Those risks are that what is begun as civil disobedience will be perverted by extremists into uncivil disobedience, and alienate large numbers who have firmly supported the cause of freedom.

One of the unintended consequences of the two World Wars is that in many ways they strengthened the position of the Negroes and all other minorities in American political life. We do not need another, a third World War, to continue the process of liberation. We can do it in peace— without war and without civil war. The Civil Rights and Voting Acts of 1964 and 1965 are far in advance of the actual situation in the country where discrimination is so rife. Our present task is to bring home and reinforce popular consciousness of the fact that those who violate their provisions are violating the highest law of the land, and that their actions are outside the law. Therefore, our goal must *now* be to build up and strengthen a mood of respect for the law, for civil obedience to laws, even by those who deem them unwise or who opposed them in the past. Our hope is that those who abide by the law may learn not only to tolerate them but, in time, as their fruits develop, to accept them. To have the positive law on the side of right and justice is to have a powerful weapon that makes for voluntary compliance—but only if the *reasonableness* of the *prima facie* obligation to obey the law is recognized.

✿ PETER KROPOTKIN

15. *Revolt Against All Laws*

Peter Kropotkin (1842–1921) was a Russian anarchist and revolutionary. After his escape from prison in Russia, he lived as an exile in London. Most of his writings consist of defenses of anarchism.

I

"When ignorance reigns in society and disorder in the minds of men, laws are multiplied, legislation is expected to do everything, and each fresh law being a fresh miscalculation, men are continually led to demand from it what can proceed only from themselves, from their own education and their own morality." It is no revolutionist who says this, nor even a reformer. It is the jurist, Dalloy, author of the Collection of French law known as "Repertoire de la Legislation." And yet, though these lines were written by a man who was himself a maker and admirer of law, they perfectly represent the abnormal condition of our society.

In existing States a fresh law is looked upon as a remedy for evil. Instead of themselves altering what is bad, people begin by demanding a *law* to alter it. If the road between two villages is impassable, the peasant says:—"There should be a law about parish roads." If a park-keeper takes advantage of the want of spirit in those who follow him with servile observance and insults one of them, the insulted man says "There should be a law to enjoin more politeness upon park-keepers." If there is stagnation in agriculture or commerce, the husbandman, cattle-breeder, or corn speculator argues, "It is protective legislation that we require." Down to the old clothesman there is not one who does not demand a law to protect his own little trade. If the employer lowers wages or increases the hours of labour, the politician in embryo exclaims, "We must have a law to put all that to rights," instead of telling the workers that there are other, and much more effectual means of settling these things straight; namely, recovering from the employer the wealth of which he has been despoiling the workmen for generations. In short, a law everywhere and for everything! A law about fashions, a law about mad dogs, a law about virtue, a law to put a stop to all the vices and all the evils which result from human indolence and cowardice.

We are so perverted by an education which from infancy seeks to kill in us the spirit of revolt, and to develop that of submission to authority; we are so perverted by this existence under the ferule of a law, which regulates every event in life—our birth, our education, our development, our love, our friendship—that, if this state of things continues, we shall lose

Selected from *Law and Authority*, Reeves, London, 1866. Chapters have been renumbered.

all initiative, all habit of thinking for ourselves. Our society seems no longer able to understand that it is possible to exist otherwise than under the reign of Law, elaborated by a representative government and administered by a handful of rulers; and even when it has gone so far as to emancipate itself from the thraldom, its first care has been to reconstitute it immediately. "The Year I. of Liberty" has never lasted more than a day, for after proclaiming it men put themselves the very next morning under the yoke of Law and Authority.

Indeed, for some thousands of years, those who govern us have done nothing but ring the changes upon "Respect for law, obedience to authority." This is the moral atmosphere in which parents bring up their children, and school only serves to confirm the impression. Cleverly assorted scraps of spurious science are inculcated upon the children to prove necessity of law; obedience to the law is made a religion; moral goodness and the law of the masters are fused into one and the same divinity. The historical hero of the schoolroom is the man who obeys the law, and defends it against rebels.

Later, when we enter upon public life, society and literature, impressing us day by day and hour by hour, as the water drop hollows the stone, continue to inculcate the same prejudice. Books of history, of political science, of social economy are stuffed with this respect for law; even the physical sciences have been pressed into the service by introducing artificial modes of expression, borrowed from theology and arbitrary power, into knowledge which is purely the result of observation. Thus our intelligence is successfully befogged, and always to maintain our respect for law. The same work is done by newspapers. They have not an article which does not preach respect for law, even where the third page proves every day to demonstrate the imbecility of that law, and shows how it is dragged through every variety of mud and filth by those charged with its administration. Servility before the law has become a virtue, and I doubt if there was ever even a revolutionist who did not begin in his youth as the defender of law against what are generally called "abuses," although these last are inevitable consequences of the law itself.

Art pipes in unison with would-be science. The hero of the sculptor, the painter, the musician, shields Law beneath his buckler, and with flashing eyes and distended nostrils stands ever ready to strike down the man who would lay hands upon her. Temples are raised to her; revolutionists themselves hesitate to touch the high priests consecrated to her service, and when revolution is about to sweep away some ancient institution, it is still by law that it endeavours to sanctify the deed.

The confused mass of rules of conduct called Law, which has been bequeathed to us by slavery, serfdom, feudalism, and royalty, has taken the place of those stone monsters before whom human victims used to be immolated, and whom slavish savages dared not even touch lest they should be slain by the thunderbolts of heaven.

This new worship has been established with especial success since the rise to supreme power of the middle class—since the great French Revolution. Under the ancient *regime,* men spoke little of laws; unless, indeed, it were, with Montesquieu, Rousseau and Voltaire, to oppose them to royal caprice: obedience to the good pleasure of the king and his lackeys was compulsory on pain of hanging or imprisonment. But during and after the revolutions when the lawyers rose to power, they did their best to strengthen the principle upon which their ascendancy depended. The middle class at once accepted as a dyke to dam up the popular torrent. The priestly crew hastened to sanctify it, to save their bark from foundering amid the breakers. Finally the people received it as an improvement upon the arbitrary authority and violence of the past.

To understand this, we must transport ourselves in imagination into the eighteenth century. Our hearts must have ached at the story of the atrocities committed by the all-powerful nobles of that time upon the men and women of the people, before we can understand what must have been the magic influence upon the peasant's mind of the words, "Equality before the law, obedience to the law without distinction of birth or fortune." He, who until then, had been treated more cruelly than a beast, he who had never had any rights, he who had never obtained justice against the most revolting actions on the part of a noble, unless in revenge he killed him and was hanged—he saw himself recognised by this maxim, at least in theory, at least with regard to his personal rights, as the equal of his lord. Whatever this law might be, it promised to affect lord and peasant alike; it proclaimed the equality of rich and poor before the judge. The promise was a lie, and to-day we know it; but at that period it was an advance, a homage to justice, as hypocrisy is a homage rendered to truth. This is the reason that when the saviours of the menaced middle class (the Robespierres and the Dantons) took their stand upon the writings of the Rousseaus and the Voltaires, and proclaimed "respect for law, the same for every man," the people accepted the compromise; for their revolutionary impetus had already spent its force in the contest with a foe whose ranks drew closer day by day, they bowed their neck beneath the yoke of law to save themselves from the arbitrary power of their lords.

The Middle Class has ever since continued to make the most of this maxim, which with another principle, that of representative government, sums up the whole philosophy of the bourgeois age, the XIX. century. It has preached this doctrine in its schools, it has propagated it in its writings, it has moulded its art and science to the same purpose, it has thrust its beliefs into every hole and corner—like a pious Englishwoman, who slips tracts under the door—and it has done all this so successfully that to-day we behold the issue in the detestable fact, that, at the very moment when the spirit of turbulent criticism is reawakening, men who long for freedom begin the attempt to obtain it by entreating their masters to be kind enough to protect them by modifying the laws which these masters themselves have created!

But times and tempers are changed since a hundred years ago. Rebels are everywhere to be found, who no longer wish to obey the law without knowing whence it comes, what are its uses, and whither arises the obligation to submit to it, and the reverence with which it is encompassed. The rebels of our day are criticising the very foundations of Society, which have hitherto been held sacred, and first and foremost amongst them that fetish, law. Just for this reason the upheaval which is at hand is no meet insurrection, it is a *Revolution*.

The critics analyse the sources of law, and find there, either a god, product of the terrors of the savage, and stupid, paltry and malicious as the priests who vouch for its supernatural origin, or else, bloodshed, conquest by fire and sword. They study the characteristics of law, and instead of perpetual growth corresponding to that of the human race, they find its distinctive trait to be immobility, a tendency to crystallise what should be modified and developed day by day. They ask how law has been maintained, and in its service they see the atrocities of Byzantinism, the cruelties of the Inquisition, the tortures of the Middle Ages, living flesh torn by the lash of the executioner, chains, clubs, axes, the gloomy dungeons of prisons, agony, curses and tears. In our own days they see, as before, the axe, the cord, the rifle, the prison; on the one hand, the brutalized prisoner, reduced to the condition of a caged beast by the debasement of his whole moral being, and on the other, the judge, stripped of every feeling which does honour to human nature, living like a visionary in a world of legal fictions, revelling in the infliction of imprisonment and death, without even suspecting, in the cold malignity of his madness, the abyss of degradation into which he has himself fallen before the eyes of those whom he condemns.

They see a race of law-makers legislating without knowing what their laws are about; to-day voting a law on the sanitation of towns, without the faintest notion of hygiene, to-morrow making regulations for the armament of troops, without so much as understanding a gun; making laws about teaching and education without ever having given a lesson of any sort, or even an honest education to their own children; legislating at random in all directions, but never forgetting the penalties to be meted out to ragamuffins, the prison and the galleys, which are to be the portion of men a thousand times less immoral than these legislators themselves.

Finally, they see the gaoler on the way to lose all human feeling, the detective trained as a blood-hound, the police spy despising himself; "informing," metamorphosed into a virtue; corruption, erected into a system; all the vices, all the evil qualities of mankind countenanced and cultivated to insure the triumph of law.

All this we see, and therefore, instead of inanely repeating the old formula, "Respect the law," we say, "Despise law and all its attributes!" In place of the cowardly phrase "Obey the law," our cry is "Revolt against all laws!"

Only compare the misdeeds accomplished in the name of each law, with the good it has been able to effect, and weigh carefully both good and evil, and you will see if we are right.

II

Relatively speaking, law is a product of modern times. For ages and ages mankind lived without any written law, even that graved in symbols upon the entrance stones of a temple. During that period, human relations were simply regulated by customs, habits and usages, made sacred by constant repetition, and acquired by each person in childhood, exactly as he learned how to obtain his food by hunting, cattle-rearing, or agriculture.

All human societies have passed through this primitive phase, and to this day a large proportion of mankind have no written law. Every tribe has its own manners and customs; customary law, as the jurists say. It has social habits, and that suffices to maintain cordial relations between the inhabitant of the village, the members of the tribe or community. Even amongst ourselves—the "civilised" nations—when we leave large towns, and go into the country, we see that there the mutual relations of the inhabitants are still regulated according to ancient and generally accepted customs, and not according to the written law of the legislators. The peasants of Russia, Italy and Spain, and even of a large part of France and England, have no conception of written law. It only meddles with their lives to regulate their relations with the State. As to relations between themselves, though these are sometimes very complex, they are simply regulated according to ancient custom. Formerly, this was the case with mankind in general.

Two distinctly marked currents of custom are revealed by analysis of the usages of primitive people.

As man does not live in a solitary state, habits and feelings develop within him which are useful for the preservation of society and the propagation of the race. Without social feelings and usages, life in common would have been absolutely impossible. It is not law which has established them; they are anterior to all law. Neither is it religion which has ordained them; they are anterior to all religions. They are found amongst all animals living in society. They are spontaneously developed by the very nature of things, like those habits in animals which men call instinct. They spring from a process of evolution, which is useful, and, indeed, necessary, to keep society together in the struggle it is forced to maintain for existence. Savages end by no longer eating one another, because they find it in the long run more advantageous to devote themselves to some sort of cultivation, than to enjoy the pleasure of feasting upon the flesh of an aged relative once a year. Many travellers have depicted the manners of absolutely independent tribes, where laws and chiefs are unknown, but where the members of the tribe have given up stabbing one another in every dispute, because the habit of living in society has ended by developing certain feelings of fraternity and oneness of interest, and they prefer appealing to a third person to settle their differences. The hospitality of primitive peoples, respect for human life, the sense of reciprocal obligation, compassion for the weak, courage, extending even to the sacrifice of self for others, which is first learnt for the sake of children and friends, and later, for that of members of the same community—all these qualities are developed in man anterior to all law, independently of all religion, as in the case of the social animals. Such feelings and practices are the inevitable results of social life. Without being, as say priests and metaphysicians, inherent in man, such qualities are the consequence of life in common.

But side by side with these customs, necessary to the life of societies and the preservation of the race, other desires, other passions, and therefore other habits and customs, are evolved in human association. The desire to dominate others and impose one's own will upon them; the desire to seize upon the products of the labour of a neighbouring tribe; the desire to surround oneself with comforts without producing anything, whilst slaves provide their master with the means of procuring every sort of pleasure and luxury—these selfish, personal desires give rise to another current of habits and customs. The priest and the warrior, the charlatan who makes a profit out of superstition, and after freeing himself from the fear of the devil, cultivates it in others; and the bully, who procures the invasion and pillage of his neighbours, that he may return laden with booty, and followed by slaves; these two, hand in hand, have succeeded in imposing upon primitive society customs advantageous to both of them, but tending to perpetuate their domination of the masses. Profiting by the indolence, the fears, the inertia of the crowd, and thanks to the continual repetition of the same acts, they have permanently established customs which have become a solid basis for their own domination.

For this purpose, they would have made use, in the first place, of that tendency to run in a groove, so highly developed in mankind. In children and all savages it attains striking proportions, and it may also be observed in animals. Man, when he is at all superstitious, is always afraid to introduce any sort of change into existing conditions; he generally venerates what is ancient. "Our fathers did so and so; they got on pretty well; they brought you up; they were not unhappy; do the same!" the old say to the young, every time the latter wish to alter things. The unknown frightens them, they prefer to cling to the past, even when that past represents poverty, oppression and slavery. It may even be said that the more miserable a man is, the more he dreads every sort of change, lest it may make him more wretched still. Some ray of hope, a few scraps of comfort, must penetrate his gloomy abode before he can begin to desire better things, to criticise the old ways of living, and prepare to imperil them for the sake of bringing about a change. So long as he is not imbued with hope, so long as he is not freed from the tutelage of those who utilise his superstition and his fears, he prefers remaining in his former position. If the young desire any change, the old raise a cry of alarm against the innovators. Some savages would rather die than transgress the customs of their country, because they have been told from childhood that the least infraction of established routine would bring ill-luck, and ruin the whole tribe. Even in the present day, what numbers of politicians, economists, and would-be revolutionists act under the same impression, and cling to a vanishing past. How many care only to seek for precedents. How many fiery innovators are mere copyists of bygone revolutions.

The spirit of routine, originating in superstition, indolence, and cowardice, has in all times been the mainstay of oppression. In primitive human societies, it was cleverly turned to account by priests and military chiefs. They perpetuated customs useful only to themselves, and succeeded in imposing them on the whole tribe. So long as this conservative spirit could be exploited so as to assure the chief in his encroachments upon individual liberty, so long as the only inequalities between men were the work of nature, and these were not increased a hundred-fold by the concentration of power and wealth, there was no need for law, and the formidable paraphernalia of tribunals and ever-agumenting penalties to enforce it.

But as society became more and more divided into two hostile classes, one seeking to establish its domination, the other struggling to escape, the strife began. Now the conqueror was in a hurry to secure the results of his actions in a permanent form, he tried to place them beyond question, to make them holy and venerable by every means in his power. Law made its appearance under the sanction of the priest, and the warrior's club was placed at its service. Its office was to render immutable such customs as were to the advantage of the dominant minority. Military authority undertook to ensure obedience. This new function was a fresh guarantee to the power of the warrior; now he had not only mere brute force at his service; he was the defender of law.

If law, however, presented nothing but a collection of prescriptions serviceable to rulers, it would find some difficulty in insuring acceptance and obedience. Well, the legislators confounded in one code the two currents of custom, of which we have just been speaking, the maxims which represent principles of morality and social union wrought out as a result of life in common, and the mandates, which are meant to ensure external existence to inequality. Customs, absolutely essential to the very being of society, are, in the code, cleverly intermingled with usages imposed by the ruling caste, and both claim equal respect from the crowd. "Do not kill," says the code, and hastens to add, "And pay tithes to the priest." "Do not steal," says the code, and immediately after, "He who refuses to pay taxes, shall have his hand struck off."

Such was law; and it has maintained its two-fold character to this day. Its origin is the desire of the ruling class to give permanence to customs imposed by themselves for their own advantage. Its character is the skilful comingling of customs useful to society, customs which have no need of law to insure respect, with other customs useful only to rulers, injurious to the mass of the people, and maintained only by the fear of punishment.

Like individual capital, which was born of fraud and violence, and developed under the auspices of authority, law has no title to the respect of men. Born of violence and superstition, and established in the interests of consumer, priest and rich exploiter, it must be utterly destroyed on the day when the people desire to break their chains. . . .

III

The millions of laws which exist for the regulation of humanity, appear upon investigation to be divided into three principal categories— protection of property, protection of persons, protection of government. And by analysing each of these three categories, we arrive at the same logical and necessary conclusion: *the usefulness and hurtfulness of law.*

Socialists know what is meant by protection of property. Laws on property are not made to guarantee either to the individual or to society the enjoyment of the produce of their own labour. On the contrary, they are made to rob the producer of a part of what he has created, and to secure to certain other people that portion of the produce which they have stolen either from the producer or from society as a whole. When, for example, the law establishes Mr. So-and-So's right to a house, it is not establishing his right to a cottage he has built for himself, or to a house he has erected with the help of some of his friends. In that case no one would have disputed his right. On the contrary, the law is establishing his right to a house which is *not* the product of his labour; first of all, because he has had it built for him by others to whom he has not paid the full value of their work; and next because that house represents a social value, which he could not have produced for himself. The law is establishing his right to what belongs to everybody in general and to nobody in particular. The same house built in the midst of Siberia would not have the value it possesses in a large town, and, as we know, that value arises from the labour of something like fifty generations of men who have built the town, beautified it, supplied it with water and gas, fine promenades, colleges, theatres, shops, railways and roads leading in all directions. Thus, by recognising the right of Mr. So-and-So to a particular house in Paris, London or Rouen, the law is unjustly appropriating to him a certain portion of the produce of the labour of mankind in general. And it is precisely because this appropriation and all other forms of property, bearing the same character, are a crying injustice, that a whole arsenal of laws, and a whole army of soldiers, policemen and judges are needed to maintain it against the good sense and just feeling inherent in humanity.

Well, half our laws, the civil code in each country serves no other purpose than to maintain this appropriation, this monopoly for the benefit of certain individuals, against the whole of mankind. Three-fourths of the causes decided by the tribunals are nothing but quarrels between monopolists—two robbers disputing over their booty. And a great many of our criminal laws have the same object in view, their end being to keep the workman in a subordinate position towards his employer, and thus afford security for exploitation.

As for guaranteeing the product of his labour to the producer, there are no laws which even attempt such a thing. It is so simple and natural, so much a part of the manners and customs of mankind, that law has not given it so much as a thought. Open brigandage, sword in hand, is no feature of our age. Neither does one workman ever come and dispute the produce of his labour with another. If they have a misunderstanding they settle it by calling in a third person, without having recourse to law. The only person who exacts from another what that other has produced, is the proprietor, who comes in and deducts the lion's share. As for humanity in general, it everywhere respects the right of each to what he has created, without the interposition of any special laws.

As all the laws about property, which make up thick volumes of codes, and are the delight of our lawyers, have no other object than to protect the unjust appropriation of human labour by certain monopolists, there is no reason for their existence, and, of the day of the Revolution, social revolutionists are thoroughly determined to put an end to them. Indeed, a bonfire might be made with perfect justice of all laws bearing upon the so called "rights of property," all title-deeds, all registers, in a word, of all that is in any way connected with an institution which will soon be looked upon as a blot in the history of humanity, as humiliating as the slavery and serfdom of past ages.

The remarks just made upon laws concerning property are quite as applicable to the second category of laws; those for the maintenance of government, *i.e.*, Constitutional Law.

It again is a complete arsenal of laws, decrees, ordinances, orders in council, and what not, all serving to protect the diverse forms of representative government, delegated or usurped, beneath which humanity is writhing. We know very well—Anarchists have often enough pointed out in their perpetual criticism of the various forms of government—that the mission of all governments, monarchical, constitutional, or republican, is to protect and maintain by force the privileges of the classes in possession, the aristocracy, clergy and traders. A good third of our laws—and each country possesses some tens of thousands of them—the fundamental laws on taxes, excise duties, the organization of ministerial departments and their offices, of the army, the police, the Church, etc., have no other end than to maintain, patch up, and develop the administrative machine. And this machine in its turn serves almost entirely to protect the privileges of the possessing classes. Analyse all these laws, observe them in action day by day, and you will discover that not one is worth preserving.

About such laws there can be no two opinions. Not only Anarchists, but more or less revolutionary radicals also, are agreed that the only use to be made of laws concerning the organization of government is to fling them into the fire.

The third category of law still remains to be considered, that relating to the protection of the person and the detection and prevention of "crime." This is the most important, because most prejudices attach to it; because, if law enjoys a certain amount of consideration, it is in consequence of the belief that this species of law is absolutely indispensable to the maintenance of security in our societies. These are laws developed from the nucleus of customs useful to human communities, which have been turned to account by rulers to sanctify their own domination. The authority of the chiefs of tribes, of rich families in towns, and of the king, depended upon their judicial functions, and even down to the present day, whenever the necessity of government is spoken of, its function as supreme judge is the thing implied. "Without a government men would tear one another to pieces," argues the village orator. "The ultimate end of all government is to secure twelve honest jurymen to every accused person," said Burke.

Well, in spite of all the prejudices existing on this subject, it is quite time that Anarchists should boldly declare this category of laws as useless and injurious as the preceding ones.

First of all, as to so-called "crimes"—assaults upon persons—it is well-known that two-thirds, and often as many as three-fourths, of such "crimes" are instigated by the desire to obtain possession of someone's wealth. This immense class of so-called "crimes and misdemeanours" will disappear on the day on which private property ceases to exist. "But," it will be said, "there will always be brutes who will attempt the lives of their fellow-citizens, who will lay their hands to a knife in every quarrel, and revenge the slightest offence by murder, if there are no laws to restrain and punishments to withhold them." This refrain is repeated every time the right of society *to punish* is called in question.

Yet there is one fact upon this head which at the present time is thoroughly established; the severity of punishment does not diminish the amount of crime. Hang, and, if you like, quarter murderers, and the number of murders will not decrease by one. On the other hand, abolish the penalty of death, and there will not be one murder more; there will be fewer. Statistics prove it. But if the harvest is good, and bread cheap, and the weather fine, the number of murders immediately decreases. This again is proved by statistics. The amount of crime always augments and diminishes in proportion to the price of provisions and the state of the weather. Not that all murderers are actuated by hunger. That is not the case. But when the harvest is good, and provisions are at an obtainable price, and when the sun shines, men, lighter hearted and less miserable than usual, do not give way to gloomy passions, do not from trivial motives, plunge a knife into the bosom of a fellow creature.

Moreover, it is also a well-known fact that the fear of punishment has never stopped a single murderer. He who kills his neighbour from revenge or misery does not reason much about consequences; and there have been few murderers who were not firmly convinced that they should escape prosecution.

Without speaking of a society in which a man will receive a better education, in which the development of all his faculties, and the possibility of exercising them, will procure him so many enjoyments, that he will not seek to poison them by remorse—without speaking of the society of the future—even in our society, even with those sad products of misery, whom we see to-day in the public-houses of great cities—on the day when no punishment is inflicted upon murderers, the number of murders will not augment by a single case; and it is extremely probable that it will be, on the contrary, diminished by all those cases which are due at present to habitual criminals, who have been brutalised in prisons.

We are continually being told of the benefits conferred by law, and the beneficial effect of penalties, but have the speakers ever attempted to strike a balance between the benefits attributed to laws and penalties, and the degrading effect of these penalties upon humanity? Only calculate all the evil passions awakened in mankind by the atrocious punishments formerly inflicted in our streets! Man is the cruellest animal upon earth; and who has pampered and developed the cruel instincts unknown, even amongst monkeys, if it is not the king, the judge, and the priest, armed with law, who caused flesh to be torn off in strips, boiling pitch to be poured into wounds, limbs to be dislocated, bones to be crushed, men to be sawn asunder to maintain their authority? Only estimate the torrent of depravity let loose in human society by the "informing" which is countenanced by judges, and paid in hard cash by governments, under pretext of assisting in the discovery of "crime." Only go into the gaols and study what man becomes when he is deprived of freedom and shut up with other depraved beings, steeped in the vice and corruption which oozes from the very walls of our existing prisons. Only remember that the more these prisons are reformed, the more detestable they become; our model penitentiaries are a hundred-fold more abominable than the dungeons of the middle ages. Finally, consider what corruption, depravity of mind, is kept up amongst men by idea of obedience, the very essence of law; of chastisement; of authority having the right to punish, to judge irrespective of our conscience and the esteem of our friends; of the necessity for executioners, gaolers and informers—in a word, by all the attributes of law and authority. Consider all this, and you will assuredly agree with us in saying that a law inflicting penalties is an abomination which should cease to exist.

Peoples without political organisation, and therefore less depraved than ourselves, have perfectly understood that the man who is called "criminal" is simply unfortunate; that the remedy is not to flog him, to chain him up, or to kill him on the scaffold or in prison, but to relieve him by the most brotherly care, by treatment based on equality, by the usages of life amongst honest men. In the next revolution we hope that this cry will go forth:

"Burn the guillotines; demolish the prisons; drive away the judges, policemen and informers—the impurest race upon the face of the earth; treat as a brother the man who has been led by passion to do ill to his fellow; above all take from the ignoble products of middle-class idleness the possibility of displaying their vices in attractive colours; and be sure that but few crimes will mar our society."

The main supports of crime are idleness, law and authority; laws about property, laws about government, laws about penalties and misdemeanours; and authority, which takes upon itself to manufacture these laws and to apply them.

No more laws! No more judges! Liberty, equality, and practical human sympathy are the only effectual barriers we can oppose to the anti-social instincts of certain amongst us.

   ✿ ALEXANDER B. SMITH
      HARRIET POLLACK

16. *Should We Legislate Morals?*

Alexander B. Smith is a professor of sociology at the John Jay College of Criminal Justice of the City University of New York. Harriet Pollack is an assistant professor of government at the same college.

Few people would dispute that crime probably heads today's list of troubles besetting our urban population. City-dwellers are afraid of being mugged, robbed, raped, or murdered. In addition, they are disgusted: by the blatant soliciting from prostitutes; by gay bars; by seedy pornography shops; by openly sold heroin and marijuana; and by crooked cops. The response on the part of our law enforcement agencies has been to attempt better surveillance of high crime areas in order to protect people against assault and robbery, and to mount campaigns to clean up the downtown neighborhoods where pimps, female and male prostitutes, bookies, pornographers, et al., assemble.

Whatever the merits and feasibility of increased police patrols to handle street crime, there is at least no doubt that citizens need to be protected against thieves and murderers. There is a real question, however, whether campaigns against gamblers, prostitutes, and dope pushers are not actually counter-productive in terms of producing a decent, stable society.

Despite the attractiveness of the notion of a "clean" Times Square or Loop as morally pure as the more genteel sections of New York City or Chicago, are there hidden social costs to such clean-ups that society may not care to pay? Is there some relationship between the use of the criminal justice system to police our morals and its failure to protect our persons? Is how to handle prostitutes and pornographers the problem, or is it the larger question of whether morals offenses should be considered as crimes? Will a fresh look at the penal code be more fruitful in the long run than arguing over whether displaced prostitutes or pornographers will be likely to go to the suburbs if hounded out of the inner cities?

Conceptually, our penal code prohibits two kinds of acts: those that are *malum in se* (evil in themselves) and those that are *malum prohibitum* (evil because prohibited). *Malum in se* acts (murder, rape, arson,

Selected from "Crimes Without Victims," in *Saturday Review*, 54, December 4, 1971, pp. 27–29.

assault) are true crimes in the sense that no society can tolerate such conduct and survive. But a large part of our penal code is concerned with acts that are not universally considered evil, but that we, at this moment in time, for a variety of reasons, have labeled as sufficiently undesirable to be punished by the criminal justice system. In New York State, for example, gambling is prohibited by law, and the police, courts, and jails are expected to deal with numbers runners, bookies, and the like. At the same time, the state itself not only permits gambling at the race tracks and runs a lottery based on the outcome of the horse races, but has set up OTB, a corporation for handling off-track bets, from which the state expects to derive revenue. Nevada, among other states, licenses and taxes casinos and similar gambling establishments. Clearly, nothing in gambling per se is inconsistent with a viable society; yet the resources of our criminal justice system are diverted to the enforcement of anti-gambling laws.

Our attitudes toward drug use are equally inconsistent: We forbid the use of marijuana and heroin; yet we tolerate the limited use of amphetamines and barbiturates, and we encourage, through ubiquitous advertising, the indiscriminate sale of pills for every conceivable purpose, physiological and psychological. Hundreds of sections of the criminal law are concerned with acts that are criminal mainly because society at large says they are: homosexual activity between consenting adults, prostitution, gambling, possession of obscene and pornographic materials, to name a few. The enforcement of these laws takes the lion's share of our criminal justice resources. For every murderer arrested and prosecuted, literally dozens of gamblers, prostitutes, dope pushers, and derelicts crowd our courts' dockets. If we took the numbers runners, the kids smoking pot, and the winos out of the criminal justice system, we would substantially reduce the burden on the courts and the police. If we permitted the sale of heroin on a controlled prescription basis (as the British do, and as we do with other dangerous drugs), we would probably eliminate well over half of the cases going through our criminal courts. Myths to the contrary, there is no scientific evidence that the use of heroin, in and of itself, causes criminal conduct. By cutting off all legal access to heroin, however, we have driven the price so high that experienced observers estimate that more than half the crimes in New York City are committed by addicts seekings drugs or the money for drugs. The greater part of the social evil incident to the use of heroin, thus, comes not from its use, but from the laws that make it impossible to obtain the drug legally. This is not to say, of course, that the use of heroin is not harmful to the addict. It is only that our penal code has extended that harm from the user himself to those who are victimized by his crime. In short, the net effect of our drug laws is highly counter-productive in that they create more anti-social conduct than they prevent.

Morals laws that do not reflect contemporary mores or that cannot be enforced should be removed from the penal code through legislative action, because, at best, they undermine respect for the law, and, at worst, as in the case of our drug laws, they exacerbate a tragic situation. Admittedly, such a deliberate legislative policy would fly in the face of all historical American experience. As Morris Ernst once remarked, Americans do not repeal morals legislation; they simply allow such laws to fall into desuetude. Sunday blue laws are a classic example of this process. The New York State Sunday Closing Law currently on the books has in the past been read to forbid movie, stage, and radio performances on Sunday. Of course, this interpretation is archaic at present; the courts have simply stopped interpreting this law in so restrictive a manner. The police also have become so unconcerned with enforcing it that they ignore violations. In 1970, the New York City police commissioner, recognizing that no one any longer cared about the Sunday Closing Law, announced that his men would not even attempt to enforce it. Such forthrightness on the part of an administrative official is unusual; most laws go unenforced by default rather than by deliberate policy.

More important, despite the commissioner's candor and despite the inutility of this law, the legislature has not bothered to repeal it. The reasons are obvious: Any such attempt would lead to an outcry by small but militant minority groups who would convert a simple act of legislative housekeeping into a debate over morality. No legislator wants to be cast in the role of the defender of immorality, even in the case of a custom widely accepted and practiced by a good part of his constituency. It is much easier, and politically more sensible, simply to sweep the issue under the rug by ignoring it.

Unfortunately, we can no longer afford the luxury of waiting for administrative action (or inaction) to catch up with public morality. Possibly because we live in an era that has seen great changes in public mores in a relatively short time, we have too many laws that the police are attempting to enforce and the courts to handle that large segments of the public simply will not obey. Gambling laws are an obvious example, as are those forbidding prostitution, homosexual acts between adults, and possession of pornographic materials. The most troublesome morals laws, however, are those forbidding the possession and sale of marijuana, heroin, LSD, and other similar drugs.

There is something very frightening to most people in advocating repeal of morals laws. It is as though, by advocating repeal, the conduct that heretofore has been forbidden is being endorsed. Nothing could be further from the truth. In repealing morals laws, the legislature is not proposing that people become immoral; it is simply declaring that the criminal sanction will no longer be used to enforce a particular mode of conduct. Most human conduct, after all, is regulated by non-legal institutions: the home, the school, the church, the family, the peer group. Most husbands work hard and support their wives and children because they respond to cultural demands, not because they could be put in jail for non-support if they failed to do so. The unpalatable truth is that passing a law does not mean that it will be obeyed or that it can be enforced. Conversely, the repeal of a law does not necessarily mean an increase in undesirable conduct.

Prohibition is probably tłe most clear-cut example of the effect of enacting and then repealing a morals law. The Eighteenth Amendment had virtually no effect in reducing per capita alcohol consumption in this country, and its repeal did not increase either the amount of drinking or the problems of alcoholism. The only effect the Eighteenth Amendment had was to create a flourishing bootlegging industry, and it was this spin-off—the rise in serious crime due to an unenforceable law—that constituted one of the principal reasons for repeal.

We are in a similar position today. Our gambling and drug laws particularly have created a situation in which an enormous organized crime industry thrives on satisfying a consumer demand that cannot be met legitimately. Worse yet, the effort to cope with the crime wave resulting from our unenforceable drug and gambling laws is destroying our criminal justice system and rendering it incapable of dealing with criminals who violate laws that might, under better circumstances, be reasonably enforceable.

While the chances for legislative modification of morals laws are still poor, there are signs that public opinion is beginning to recognize the need for change, especially in the areas of gambling and consensual adult sex practices. Proposed repeal of drug laws (even those relating to marijuana) has aroused far more anxiety, and there are still virtually no prominent public figures willing to openly advocate the legalization of heroin. There is probably some risk in repealing the ban on heroin. Many policemen, among others, believe that if the ban were lifted, a substantial number of people (especially youngsters), eager to try forbidden fruit, would be hooked into an addiction that would last the rest of their lives. Removing heroin from the penal code does not, however, mean permitting its sale in every candy store. As with many other pharmaceuticals, distribution could be regulated by prescription. But more than that, almost everyone familiar with the drug scene (especially the police) agrees that the present law has not deterred anyone who doesn't want to be deterred. It is easy to get heroin in New York City today, despite the law and the entire criminal justice system arrayed in support of the law. Apparently, those who are not using heroin are abstaining voluntarily, in which case repeal carries minimal risks.

Not only are morals laws frequently counter-productive in terms of their causing more crime than they prevent, but their enforcement is particularly dangerous to civil liberties since crimes resulting from their violation have no victims. The prostitute's client has not been forcibly seduced; the housewife who bets a quarter on the numbers has not been robbed; the dope user has harmed only himself. Because there is no victims available to testify for the state, the burden of producing enough evidence for the prosecution rests entirely on the police. It is this need for evidence to make morals offense violations "stick" that traditionally has produced the greatest number of civil liberties violations by the police. Prostitutes, for example, are frequently victims of entrapment by plainclothesmen. If their customers will not testify, who besides the plainclothesmen can? And what better way of establishing a case than by offering an obviously willing girl a little "encouragement"? Official police records indicate that an incredible number of gamblers and drug pushers "drop" gambling slips and narcotics at the mere approach of a policeman. This so-called dropsie evidence is frequently a euphemism for an illegal search. The amount of dropsie evidence has increased markedly since 1961 when the Supreme Court in *Mapp* v. *Ohio* banned the use of overtly, illegally seized evidence in state courts.

Such violations of civil liberties occur not because the police prefer to act illegally, but because it is difficult to build a legitimate case where there is no real victim. At the Supreme Court level, it is noteworthy that most of the decisions censuring police conduct deal with state and local enforcement procedures rather than federal ones. This is not because FBI agents are inherently more civil libertarian or cognizant of legalities than local policemen. It is because they deal with different kinds of wrongdoings. In such crimes as kidnapping, bank robbery, or counterfeiting, there are real victims, and federal agents can build their cases in an ethical, professional manner: obtaining statements from victims, interviewing eyewitnesses, obtaining fingerprints, weapons, contraband, etc. Local police, in dealing with pimps, numbers runners, and dope pushers, are not afforded this luxury. They must make a case the best way they can, and frequently this involves illegal snooping, searching, and arrests.

The enforcement of morals laws not only involves the police in violations of civil liberties but is the source of most of the corruption within police departments. All police departments are plagued with a small number of rogues who join forces with the criminals they are supposed to apprehend and participate in burglaries, extortion, etc. This kind of corruption is relatively rare and usually not difficult to eliminate. Seldom does it extend to the top administrative levels. The most common type of police corruption is the pay-offs policemen receive (and pass along to their superior officers) from criminals involved with drugs, gambling, or prostitution. This sort of graft is almost impossible to eradicate, partly because the illegal activities involved are so profitable and the pay-offs so lucrative, and partly because the activities themselves do not seem terribly immoral to the police, possibly because the crimes have no real victims. Such corruption spreads, moreover, throughout entire departments, from the patrolman on the beat through top administrators and sometimes even to the commissioner, mayor, or other elected officials. Periodic exposés reveal a pattern that has varied little from the pattern laid bare at the turn of the century by Lincoln Steffens in *The Shame of the Cities;* however, the waves of reform following such exposés lead to little more than temporary remissions. No way has yet been found to eliminate this kind of corruption as long as the public wants to gamble, take illegal drugs, frequent prostitutes, etc., and as long as immense profits can be earned by criminals meeting these desires.

Perhaps the most important benefit that would result from the elimination of morals offenses from the penal code would be the relief of the criminal justice system. Prison riots, inordinately delayed trials, crimes committed by defendants out on bail, a clamor for preventive detention— all testify to the dangerously strained conditions of our criminal justice institutions. No one knows how much time is spent by the police, prosecutors, and courts in processing morals defendants, but it has been estimated that as little as 10 per cent of the courtroom hours available in our criminal courts are now devoted to the processing of serious crimes. If we were free to devote the remaining 90 per cent of our courtroom hours to the handling of dangerous offenders or serious crimes of property, we would be able to overcome most of the shortcomings of our present criminal justice system. With fewer offenders to concern them, police work could be more thorough and legitimate. The decongestion of court calendars would reduce the pressure for plea bargaining, as would, incidentally, more carefully prepared cases based on legally gathered evidence. The burden on probation and parole officers would also be lessened, and if the likelihood of arrest were greater due to better police work, then prison sentences might be more likely to act as a deterrent.

At the moment, proposals to repeal morals legislation are neither popular nor acceptable. Such proposals are attacked from both ends of the morality spectrum. On the one hand, guardians of public order are outraged at the prospect of "legalizing" gambling, drug sales, and sexual soliciting. "How would you feel if it were your sixteen-year-old daughter who became hooked on heroin?" "Terrible. But thousands are hooked now, and if she does become hooked, at least she will not have to steal, prostitute herself, victimize other people, or die of an overdose." The response in the imaginary colloquy is correct, but probably unconvincing to those who look at the printed word of the law as an amulet to ward off evil. The police, on the whole, do not favor the repeal of morals laws, in part because they see repeal as an admission of their limited role in society, i.e., that they can enforce only those laws the general public is willing to obey. Such an admission is not only ego-bruising but a distinct handicap in the annual race for their share of the public budget.

On the other hand, many people are making a good living out of dope peddling, gambling, etc., and they are not likely to give up their livelihood without a struggle. What the ties of the underworld to elected and appointed officials are, no one really knows, but they exist, and organized crime is certainly capable of exerting pressure behind the scenes to discourage unfavorable legislation.

One can only hope that the uncommitted majority will come to realize the price we pay in corruption, the denial of civil liberties, and the overburdening of our criminal justice system for the luxury of using our penal code to enforce our currently fashionable behavior preferences. We need courage enough to admit that certain kinds of behavior cannot be controlled through the punitive sanction, and faith enough to believe that cultural pressure (or innate decency) will suffice to keep us from mass dissipation and self-destruction. And we need political leaders with guts enough to get up and say so.

Suggested Readings

Bedau, Hugo (ed.), *Civil Disobedience,* Western Pub. Co., Pegasus Books, New York, 1969.

Mayer, Peter (ed.), *The Pacifist Conscience,* Henry Regnery, Chicago, 1966.

Ramsey, Paul, *War and the Christian Conscience,* Duke University Press, Durham, 1961.

Wasserstrom, Richard, "The Relevance of Nuremberg," *Philosophy and Public Affairs,* Vol. 1, 1971.

Wasserstrom, Richard, *War and Morality,* Wadsworth, Belmont, Calif., 1971.

SOME MODELS FOR AN ETHICAL THEORY

Ancient Traditions In Ethics

❀ INTRODUCTION

Controversies generated by an attempt to resolve specific moral problems tend to create an awareness of the diversity of moral choice. And this awareness, in turn, often fosters a curiosity concerning the moral principles of those persons who chose differently from oneself. Not only is one likely to wonder about the moral principles of his friends and fellow classmates, but he may be motivated to explore the history of philosophy in an effort to discover something about the positions of various moral philosophers.

Of course there is no guarantee that a study of the history of moral philosophy will provide definite answers to the specific questions that originally stimulated this inquiry. On the contrary, moral philosophers have not been concerned primarily with providing wise solutions to particular practical problems. Instead they have been interested in more fundamental issues; they have directed their attention towards the identification, analysis, and defense of the beliefs and principles which are *presupposed* in resolving specific issues. Thus their work has been mainly theoretical, and it has resulted in the production of a number of systems of thought especially designed to provide both a framework and a rationale for moral choice.

Since the history of moral philosophy has been so richly endowed by the ancient Greeks, there may be no better place to begin our inquiry than with an investigation of the position of Plato, one of the first Greek thinkers to formulate an ethical theory. But Plato is not an easy philosopher to understand, partly because his position is presented in the form of dialogues rather than as a systematic treatise. In these dialogues Socrates is the central figure; he is portrayed by Plato as engaging in lengthy debates with various philosophers and politicians. During the course of these debates numerous views are considered, and in this way Plato develops a framework for the statement of his own position. An understanding, then, of this position requires an awareness of those doctrines which serve to distinguish the views of Plato's opponents, i.e.:

1 "Justice" Reduced to "Power" This doctrine is often popularly expressed by the statement "Might makes right." The implications of this contention are obvious. There are no objective canons of justice. Instead, those individuals or groups that are in a position of superior power are able to define the standards of justice in such a way as to serve their own interests. The weak must simply submit or attempt to maneuver themselves into a position of power so that they too will have something to say about what will be thought to be "just."

2 Psychological Egoism   The proponent of psychological egoism maintains that all the actions of men are motivated by the desire to benefit themselves. This position does not involve the denial that many actions *appear at first glance* to be done for reasons other than self-interest. But, nevertheless, the psychological egoist would maintain that if one probes a little more carefully into the *fundamental* motive in these cases, he will discover that it is selfish. The importance of this position, it is commonly claimed, is that it rules out the possibility of altruistic action. Hence any ethical theory which obliges one to act alturistically is requiring the impossible.

3 Hedonism   A philosopher who thinks that only pleasure is intrinsically worthwhile, is called a "hedonist" (after the Greek "hedone," meaning pleasure). The hedonist does not deny that we ordinarily regard many things as worthwhile. But he would insist that the value of these things is derived solely from the pleasure that is obtained from them. Pleasure, then, is thought to be the only thing that is valuable in and of itself. All other things are desirable only to the extent that they produce pleasure or forestall pain.

4 Ethical Relativism   An ethical relativist is a philosopher who maintains that ethical principles are, *in some sense,* relative. Two varieties of ethical relativism customarily have been proposed. Some have maintained that ethical principles are relative to particular societies, or cultures. Each society has its own conventions, and these conventions serve to define what is right *for that society only.* Alternatively, others have maintained a more extreme variety of relativism. They claim that ethical principles are relative to the individual. Each person, then, must ultimately determine his own principles, and there are no absolute, or objective, standards that can be used to decide which person is more nearly right.

Plato, in the selection which follows, explicitly considers and rejects some of the above doctrines, and he eventually develops positions which are quite opposed to the others. Some of these new positions provide an introduction for Aristotle's ethics, which was strongly influenced by the thinking of Socrates and Plato. Nevertheless, because Aristotle extensively revises their positions and adds new doctrines, his own ethical theory is distinct from theirs. In place of Plato's absolute Idea of Good, Aristotle presents happiness as the *summum bonum.* His task therefore is to define happiness and to describe how it is properly attained.

The positions of Epicurus and Epictetus represent markedly divergent views concerning the nature of man and the manner in which one ought to live. Epicurus defends the doctrine of hedonism and formulates a number of rules one should follow in discriminating among pleasures and pains. Epictetus attacks hedonism and proposes a "right-will" as the goal at which one should aim. The cultivation of a "right-will" requires determination and self-discipline while its attainment yields freedom and blessedness—qualities that are beyond the grasp of those who seek pleasure.

The final selection in this chapter is representative of a tradition in ethics which has its roots in Judaism and Christianity. This tradition, which allies morality with religion, has had a profound effect upon Western culture. Fundamental to this position is the belief that our most important moral obligations stem from divine imperatives revealed originally to Moses and the ancient Hebrew prophets and later amplified by the teachings of Jesus. Saint Augustine, an early Christian writer, defends this tradition and contrasts it with the views of earlier philosophers. He emphasizes the importance of one's belief in God and the futility of all attempts to develop a secular moral philosophy.

❀ PLATO

17. *Justice and the Idea of Good*

Plato (428–347 B.C.), was the son of aristocratic Athenian parents. At the age of twenty he became the friend and pupil of Socrates. Most of the remaining sixty years of his life was spent in intellectual pursuits. During this time he founded the Academy and was engaged in teaching and writing. The *Republic* is one of his major works.

[The entire dialogue is supposed to have been narrated by Socrates the day after it actually took place. In Book I Socrates describes his discussions with Cephalus, Polemarchus, and Thrasymachus. The primary concern is with Thrasymachus's two contentions that "justice is the interest of the stronger" and that "injustice is more profitable than justice." Socrates makes a preliminary attempt at refuting these contentions. But the issue remains unsettled and provides the point of departure for Book II, which is where the following selections begin.—Editor]

With these words I was thinking that I had made an end of the discussion; but the end, in truth, proved to be only a beginning. For Glaucon, who is always the most pugnacious of men, was dissatisfied at Thrasymachus's retirement; he wanted to have the battle out. So he said to me: Socrates, do you wish really to persuade us, or only to seem to have persuaded us, that to be just is always better than to be unjust?

I should wish really to persuade you, I replied, if I could.

Then you certainly have not succeeded. Let me ask you now: How would you arrange goods—are there not some which we welcome for their

From Books II, IV, VI, VII, and IX of the *Republic,* trans. Benjamin Jowett (New York and London: The Colonial Press, 1901).

I wish, he said, that you would hear me as well as him, and then

own sakes, and independently of their consequences, as, for example, harmless pleasures and enjoyments, which delight us at the time, although nothing follows from them?

I agree in thinking that there is such a class, I replied.

Is there not also a second class of goods, such as knowledge, sight, health, which are desirable not only in themselves, but also for their results?

Certainly, I said.

And would you not recognize a third class, such as gymnastic, and the care of the sick, and the physician's art; also the various ways of money-making—these do us good but we regard them as disagreeable; and no one would choose them for their own sakes, but only for the sake of some reward or result which flows from them?

There is, I said, this third class also. But why do you ask?

Because I want to know in which of the three classes you would place justice?

In the highest class, I replied—among those goods which he who would be happy desires both for their own sake and for the sake of their results.

Then the many are of another mind; they think that justice is to be reckoned in the troublesome class, among goods which are to be pursued for the sake of rewards and of reputation, but in themselves are disagreeable and rather to be avoided.

I know, I said, that this is their manner of thinking, and that this was the thesis which Thrasymachus was maintaining just now, when he censured justice and praised injustice. But I am too stupid to be convinced by him.

I wish, he said, that you would hear me as well as him, and then I shall see whether you and I agree. For Thrasymachus seems to me, like a snake, to have been charmed by your voice sooner than he ought to have been; but to my mind the nature of justice and injustice has not yet been made clear. Setting aside their rewards and results, I want to know what they are in themselves, and how they inwardly work in the soul. If you please, then, I will revive the argument of Thrasymachus. And first I will speak of the nature and origin of justice according to the common view of them. Secondly, I will show that all men who practise justice do so against their will, of necessity, but not as a good. And thirdly, I will argue that there is reason in this view, for the life of the unjust is after all better far than the life of the just—if what they say is true, Socrates, since I myself am not of their opinion. But still I acknowledge that I am perplexed when I hear the voices of Thrasymachus and myriads of others dinning in my ears; and, on the other hand, I have never yet heard the superiority of justice to injustice maintained by anyone in a satisfactory way. I want to hear justice praised in respect of itself; then I shall be satisfied, and you are the person from whom I think that I am most likely to hear this; and therefore I will praise the unjust life of the utmost of my power, and my manner of speaking will indicate the manner in which I desire to hear you too praising justice and censuring injustice. Will you say whether you approve of my proposal?

Indeed I do; nor can I imagine any theme about which a man of sense would oftener wish to converse.

I am delighted, he replied, to hear you say so, and shall begin by speaking, as I proposed, of the nature and origin of justice.

They say that to do injustice is, by nature, good; to suffer injustice, evil; but that the evil is greater than the good. And so when men have both done and suffered injustice and have had experience of both, not being able to avoid the one and obtain the other, they think that they had better agree among themselves to have neither; hence there arise laws and mutual covenants; and that which is ordained by law is termed by them lawful and just. This they affirm to be the origin and nature of justice; it is a mean or compromise, between the best of all, which is to do injustice and not be punished, and the worst of all, which is to suffer injustice without the power of retaliation; and justice, being at a middle point between the two, is tolerated not as a good, but as the lesser evil, and honored by reason of the inability of men to do injustice. For no man who is worthy to be called a man would ever submit to such an agreement if he were able to resist; he would be mad if he did. Such is the received account, Socrates, of the nature and origin of justice.

Now that those who practise justice do so involuntarily and because they have not the power to be unjust will best appear if we imagine something of this kind: having given both to the just and the unjust power to do what they will, let us watch and see whither desire will lead them; then we shall discover in the very act the just and unjust man to be proceeding along the same road, following their interest, which all natures deem to be their good, and are only diverted into the path of justice by the force of law. The liberty which we are supposing may be most completely given to them in the form of such a power as is said to have been possessed by Gyges, the ancestor of Crœsus the Lydian. According to the tradition, Gyges was a shepherd in the service of the King of Lydia; there was a great storm, and an earthquake made an opening in the earth at the place where he was feeding his flock. Amazed at the sight, he descended into the opening, where, among other marvels, he beheld a hollow brazen horse, having doors, at which he, stooping and looking in, saw a dead body of stature, as appeared to him, more than human and having nothing on but a gold ring; this he took from the finger of the dead and reascended. Now the shepherds met together, according to custom, that they might send their monthly report about the flocks to the King; into their assembly he came having the ring on his finger, and as he was sitting among them he chanced to turn the collet of the ring inside his hand, when instantly he became invisible to the rest of the company and they began to speak of him as if he were no longer present. He was astonished at this, and again touching the ring he turned the collet outward and reappeared; he made several trials of the ring, and always with the same result—when he turned the collet inward he became invisible, when outward he reappeared. Whereupon he contrived to be chosen one of the messengers who were sent to the court; where as soon as he arrived he seduced the Queen, and with her help conspired against the King and slew him and took the kingdom. Suppose now that there were two such magic rings, and the just put on one of them and the unjust the other; no man can be imagined to be of such an iron nature that he would stand fast in justice. No man would keep his hands off what was not his own when he could safely take what he liked out of the market, or go into houses and lie with anyone at his pleasure, or kill or release from prison whom he would, and in all respects be like a god among men. Then the actions of the just would be as the actions of the unjust; they would both come at last to the same point. And this we may truly affirm to be a great proof that a man is just, not willingly or because he thinks that justice is any good to him individually, but of necessity, for wherever anyone thinks that he can safely be unjust, there he is unjust. For all men believe in their hearts that injustice is far more profitable to the individual than justice, and he who argues as I have been supposing, will say that they are right. If you could imagine anyone obtaining this power of becoming invisible, and never doing any wrong or touching what was another's, he would be thought by the lookers-on to be a most wretched idiot, although they would praise him to one another's faces, and keep up appearances with one another from a fear that they too might suffer injustice. Enough of this.

Now, if we are to form a real judgment of the life of the just and unjust, we must isolate them; there is no other way; and how is the isolation to be effected? I answer: Let the unjust man be entirely unjust, and the just man entirely just; nothing is to be taken away from either of them, and both are to be perfectly furnished for the work of their respective lives. First, let the unjust be like other distinguished masters of craft; like the skilful pilot or physician, who knows intuitively his own powers and keeps within their limits, and who, if he fails at any point, is able to recover himself. So let the unjust make his unjust attempts in the right way, and lie hidden if he means to be great in his injustice (he who is found out is nobody): for the highest reach of injustice is, to be deemed just when you are not. Therefore I say that in the perfectly unjust man we must assume the most perfect injustice; there is to be no deduction, but we must allow him, while doing the most unjust acts, to have acquired the greatest reputation for justice. If he have taken a false step he must be able to recover himself; he must be one who can speak with effect, if any of his deeds come to light, and who can force his way where force is required by his courage and strength, and command of money and friends. And at his side let us place the just man in his nobleness and simplicity, wishing, as Æschylus says, to be and not to seem good. There must be no seeming, for if he seem to be just he will be honored and rewarded, and then we shall not know whether he is just for the sake of justice or for the sake of honor and rewards; therefore, let him be clothed in justice only, and have no other covering; and he must be imagined in a state of life the opposite of the former. Let him be the best of men, and let him be thought the worst; then he will have been put to the proof; and we shall see whether he will be affected by the fear of infamy and its consequences. And let him continue thus to the hour of death; being just and seeming to be unjust. When both have reached the uttermost extreme, the one of justice and the other of injustice, let judgment be given which of them is the happier of the two.

Heavens! my dear Glaucon, I said, how energetically you polish them up for the decision, first one and then the other, as if they were two statues.

I do my best, he said. And now that we know what they are like there is no difficulty in tracing out the sort of life which awaits either of them. . . .

[Here Adeimantus, the brother of Glaucon, takes up the argument.]

. . . Knowing all this, Socrates, how can a man who has any superiority of mind or person or rank or wealth, be willing to honor justice; or indeed to refrain from laughing when he hears justice praised? And even if there should be someone who is able to disprove the truth of my words, and who is satisfied that justice is best, still he is not angry with the unjust, but is very ready to forgive them, because he also knows that men are not just of their own free will; unless, peradventure, there be someone whom the divinity within him may have inspired with a hatred of injustice, or who has attained knowledge of the truth—but no other man. He only blames injustice, who, owing to cowardice or age or some weakness, has not the power of being unjust. And this is proved by the fact that when he obtains the power, he immediately becomes unjust as far as he can be.

The cause of all this, Socrates, was indicated by us at the beginning of the argument, when my brother and I told you how astonished we were to find that of all the professing panegyrists of justice—beginning with the ancient heroes of whom any memorial has been preserved to us, and ending with the men of our own time—no one has ever blamed injustice or praised justice except with a view of the glories, honors, and benefits which flow from them. No one has ever adequately described either in verse or prose the true essential nature of either of them abiding in the soul, and invisible to any human or divine eye; or shown that of all the things of a man's soul which he has within him, justice is the greatest good, and injustice the greatest evil. Had this been the universal strain, had you sought to persuade us of this from our youth upward, we should not have been on the watch to keep one another from doing wrong, but everyone would have been his own watchman, because afraid, if he did wrong, of harboring in himself the greatest of evils. I dare say that Thrasymachus and others would seriously hold the language which I have been merely repeating, and words even stronger than these about justice and injustice, grossly, as I conceive, perverting their true nature. But I speak in this vehement manner, as I must frankly confess to you, because I want to hear from you the opposite side;

and I would ask you to show not only the superiority which justice has over injustice, but what effect they have on the possessor of them which makes the one to be a good and the other an evil to him. And please, as Glaucon requested of you, to exclude reputations; for unless you take away from each of them his true reputation and add on the false, we shall say that you do not praise justice, but the appearance of it; we shall think that you are only exhorting us to keep injustice dark, and that you really agree with Thrasymachus in thinking that justice is another's good and the interest of the stronger, and that injustice is a man's own profit and interest, though injurious to the weaker. Now as you have admitted that justice is one of that highest class of goods which are desired, indeed, for their results, but in a far greater degree for their own sakes—like sight or hearing or knowledge or health, or any other real and natural and not merely conventional good—I would ask you in your praise of justice to regard one point only: I mean the essential good and evil which justice and injustice work in the possessors of them. Let others praise justice and censure injustice, magnifying the rewards and honors of the one and abusing the other; that is a manner of arguing which, coming from them, I am ready to tolerate, but from you who have spent your whole life in the consideration of this question, unless I hear the contrary from your own lips, I expect something better. And therefore, I say, not only prove to us that justice is better than injustice, but show what they either of them do to the possessor of them, which makes the one to be a good and the other an evil, whether seen or unseen by gods and men.

I had always admired the genius of Glaucon and Adeimantus, but on hearing these words I was quite delighted, and said: Sons of an illustrious father, that was not a bad beginning of the elegiac verses which the admirer of Glaucon made in honor of you after you had distinguished yourselves at the battle of Megara:

"Sons of Ariston," he sang, "divine offspring of an illustrious hero."

The epithet is very appropriate, for there is something truly divine in being able to argue as you have done for the superiority of injustice, and remaining unconvinced by your own arguments. And I do believe that you are not convinced—this I infer from your general character, for had I judged only from your speeches I should have mistrusted you. But now, the greater my confidence in you, the greater is my difficulty in knowing what to say. For I am in a strait between two; on the one hand I feel that I am unequal to the task; and my inability is brought home to me by the fact that you were not satisfied with the answer which I made to Thrasymachus, proving, as I thought, the superiority which justice has over injustice. And yet I cannot refuse to help, while breath and speech remain to me; I am afraid that there would be an impiety in being present when justice is evil spoken of and not lifting up a hand in her defence. And therefore I had best give such help as I can.

Glaucon and the rest entreated me by all means not to let the question drop, but to proceed in the investigation. They wanted to arrive at the truth, first, about the nature of justice and injustice, and secondly, about their relative advantages. I told them, what I really thought, that the inquiry would be of a serious nature, and would require very good eyes. Seeing then, I said, that we are no great wits, I think that we had better adopt a method which I may illustrate thus; suppose that a short-sighted person had been asked by someone to read small letters from a distance; and it occurred to someone else that they might be found in another place which was larger and in which the letters were larger—if they were the same and he could read the larger letters first, and then proceed to the lesser—this would have been thought a rare piece of good-fortune.

Very true, said Adeimantus; but how does the illustration apply to our inquiry?

I will tell you, I replied; justice, which is the subject of our inquiry, is, as you know, sometimes spoken of as the virtue of an individual, and sometimes as the virtue of a State.

True, he replied.

And is not a State larger than an individual?

It is.

Then in the larger the quantity of justice is likely to be larger and more easily discernible. I propose therefore that we inquire into the nature of justice and injustice, first as they appear in the State, and secondly in the individual, proceeding from the greater to the lesser and comparing them.

That, he said, is an excellent proposal. . . .

[At this point Socrates delivers a lengthy statement of his views concerning an ideal society. In describing this ideal, perfectly just society he maintains that its three chief elements—the deliberative and governing, the administrative, and the productive—are to be kept distinct. He insists that social harmony will result only if this pattern of differentiation is maintained so as to enable each part to perform its proper function in the proper way. Now he is prepared to return to the problem of virtue and justice as they appear in the individual.]

We will not, I said, be over-positive as yet; but if, on trial, this conception of justice be verified in the individual as well as in the State, there will be no longer any room for doubt; if it be not verified, we must have a fresh inquiry. First let us complete the old investigation, which we began, as you remember, under the impression that, if we could previously examine justice on the larger scale, there would be less difficulty in discerning her in the individual. That larger example appeared to be the State, and accordingly we constructed as good a one as we could, knowing well that in the good State justice would be found. Let the discovery which we made be now applied to the individual—if they agree, we shall be satisfied; or, if there be a difference in the individual, we will come back to the State and have another trial of the theory. The friction of the two when rubbed together may possibly strike a light in which justice will shine forth, and the vision which is then revealed we will fix in our souls.

That will be in regular course; let us do as you say.

I proceeded to ask: When two things, a greater and less, are called by the same name, are they like or unlike in so far as they are called the same?

Like, he replied.

The just man then, if we regard the idea of justice only, will be like the just State?

He will.

And a State was thought by us to be just when the three classes in the State severally did their own business; and also thought to be temperate and valiant and wise by reason of certain other affections and qualities of these same classes?

True, he said.

And so of the individual; we may assume that he has the same three principles in his own soul which are found in the State; and he may be rightly described in the same terms, because he is affected in the same manner?

Certainly, he said.

Once more, then, O my friend, we have alighted upon an easy question—whether the soul has these three principles or not?

An easy question! Nay, rather, Socrates, the proverb holds that hard is the good.

Very true, I said; and I do not think that the method which we are employing is at all adequate to the accurate solution of this question; the true method is another and a longer one. Still we may arrive at a solution not below the level of the previous inquiry.

May we not be satisfied with that? he said; under the circumstances, I am quite content.

I, too, I replied, shall be extremely well satisfied.

Then faint not in pursuing the speculation, he said.

Must we not acknowledge, I said, that in each of us there are the same principles and habits which there are in the State; and that from the individual they pass into the State?—how else can they come there? Take the quality of passion or spirit; it would be ridiculous to imagine that this quality, when found in States, is not derived from the individuals who are supposed to possess it, e.g., the Thracians, Scythians, and in general the Northern nations; and the same may be said of the love of knowledge, which is the special characteristic of our part of the world, or of the love of money, which may, with equal truth, be attributed to the Phœnicians and Egyptians.

Exactly so, he said.

There is no difficulty in understanding this.

None whatever.

But the question is not quite so easy when we proceed to ask whether these principles are three or one; whether, that is to say, we learn with one part of our nature, are angry with another, and with a third part desire the satisfaction of our natural appetites; or whether the whole soul comes into play in each sort of action—to determine that is the difficulty. . . .

[Socrates proceeds to demonstrate that reason, spirit, and desire are different, and they cannot be reduced to one.]

And so, after much tossing, we have reached land, and are fairly agreed that the same principles which exist in the State exist also in the individual, and that they are three in number.

Exactly.

Must we not then infer that the individual is wise in the same way, and in virtue of the same quality which makes the State wise?

Certainly.

Also that the same quality which constitutes courage in the State constitutes courage in the individual, and that both the State and the individual bear the same relation to all the other virtues?

Assuredly.

And the individual will be acknowledged by us to be just in the same way in which the State is just?

That follows of course.

We cannot but remember that the justice of the State consisted in each of the three classes doing the work of its own class?

We are not very likely to have forgotten, he said.

We must recollect that the individual in whom the several qualities of his nature do their own work will be just, and will do his own work?

Yes, he said, we must remember that too.

And ought not the rational principle, which is wise, and has the care of the whole soul, to rule, and the passionate or spirited principle to be the subject and ally?

Certainly. . . .

And these two, thus nurtured and educated, and having learned truly to know their own functions, will rule over the concupiscent, which in each of us is the largest part of the soul and by nature most insatiable of gain; over this they will keep guard, lest, waxing great and strong with the fulness of bodily pleasures, as they are termed, the concupiscent soul, no longer confined to her own sphere, should attempt to enslave and rule those who are not her natural-born subjects, and overturn the whole life of man?

Very true, he said.

Both together will they not be the best defenders of the whole soul and the whole body against attacks from without; the one counselling, and the other fighting under his leader, and courageously executing his commands and counsels?

True.

And he is to be deemed courageous whose spirit retains in pleasure and in pain the commands of reason about what he ought or ought not to fear?

Right, he replied.

And him we call wise who has in him that little part which rules, and which proclaims these commands; that part too being supposed to have a knowledge of what is for the interest of each of the three parts and of the whole?

Assuredly.

And would you not say that he is temperate who has these same elements in friendly harmony, in whom the one ruling principle of reason, and the two subject ones of spirit and desire, are equally agreed that reason ought to rule, and do not rebel?

Certainly, he said, that is the true account of temperance whether in the State or individual.

And surely, I said, we have explained again and again how and by virtue of what quality a man will be just.

That is very certain.

And is justice dimmer in the individual, and is her form different, or is she the same which we found her to be in the State?

There is no difference, in my opinion, he said.

Because, if any doubt is still lingering in our minds, a few common-place instances will satisfy us of the truth of what I am saying.

What sort of instances do you mean?

If the case is put to us, must we not admit that the just State, or the man who is trained in the principles of such a State, will be less likely than the unjust to make away with a deposit of gold or silver? Would anyone deny this?

No one, he replied.

Will the just man or citizen ever be guilty of sacrilege or theft, or treachery either to his friends or to his country?

Never.

Neither will he ever break faith where there have been oaths or agreements.

Impossible.

No one will be less likely to commit adultery, or to dishonor his father and mother, or to fail in his religious duties?

No one.

And the reason is that each part of him is doing its own business, whether in ruling or being ruled?

Exactly so.

Are you satisfied, then, that the quality which makes such men and such States is justice, or do you hope to discover some other?

Not I, indeed. . . .

But in reality justice was such as we were describing, being concerned, however, not with the outward man, but with the inward, which is the true self and concernment of man: for the just man does not permit the several elements within him to interfere with one another, or any of them to do the work of others—he sets in order his own inner life, and is his own master and his own law, and at peace with himself; and when he has bound together the three principles within him, which may be compared to the higher, lower, and middle notes of the scale, and the intermediate intervals—when he has bound all these together, and is no longer many, but has become one entirely temperate and perfectly adjusted nature, then he proceeds to act, if he has to act, whether in a matter of property, or in the treatment of the body, or in some affair of politics or private business; always thinking and calling that which preserves and cooperates with this harmonious condition just and good action, and the knowledge which presides over it wisdom, and that which at any time impairs this condition he will call unjust action, and the opinion which presides over it ignorance.

You have said the exact truth, Socrates.

Very good; and if we were to affirm that we had discovered the just man and the just State, and the nature of justice in each of them, we should not be telling a falsehood?

Most certainly not.

May we say so, then?

Let us say so.

And now, I said, injustice has to be considered.

Clearly.

Must not injustice be a strife which arises among the three principles—a meddlesomeness, and interference, and rising up of a part of the soul against the whole, an assertion of unlawful authority, which is made by a rebellious subject against a true prince, of whom he is the natural vassal—what is all this confusion and delusion but injustice, and intemperance, and cowardice, and ignorance, and every form of vice?

Exactly so.

And if the nature of justice and injustice be known, then the meaning of acting unjustly and being unjust, or, again, of acting justly, will also be perfectly clear?

What do you mean? he said.

Why, I said, they are like disease and health; being in the soul just what disease and health are in the body.

How so? he said.

Why, I said, that which is healthy causes health, and that which is unhealthy causes disease.

Yes.

And just actions cause justice, and unjust actions cause injustice?

That is certain.

And the creation of health is the institution of a natural order and government of one by another in the parts of the body; and the creation of disease is the production of a state of things at variance with this natural order?

True.

And is not the creation of justice the institution of a natural order and government of one by another in the parts of the soul, and the creation of injustice the production of a state of things at variance with the natural order?

Exactly so, he said.

Then virtue is the health, and beauty, and well-being of the soul, and vice the disease, and weakness, and deformity, of the same?

True.

And do not good practices lead to virtue, and evil practices to vice?

Assuredly.

Still our old question of the comparative advantage of justice and injustice has not been answered: Which is the more profitable, to be just and act justly and practise virtue, whether seen or unseen of gods and men, or to be unjust and act unjustly, if only unpunished and unreformed?

In my judgment, Socrates, the question has now become ridiculous.
. . .

From what point of view, then, and on what ground can we say that a man is profited by injustice or intemperance or other baseness, which will make him a worse man, even though he acquire money or power by his wickedness?

From no point of view at all.

What shall he profit, if his injustice be undetected and unpunished? He who is undetected only gets worse, whereas he who is detected and punished has the brutal part of his nature silenced and humanized; the gentler element in him is liberated, and his whole soul is perfected and ennobled by the acquirement of justice and temperance and wisdom, more than the body ever is by receiving gifts of beauty, strength, and health, in proportion as the soul is more honorable than the body.

Certainly, he said.

To this nobler purpose the man of understanding will devote the energies of his life. And in the first place, he will honor studies which impress these qualities on his soul, and will disregard others?

Clearly, he said.

In the next place, he will regulate his bodily habit and training, and so far will he be from yielding to brutal and irrational pleasures, that he will regard even health as quite a secondary matter; his first object will be not that he may be fair or strong or well, unless he is likely thereby to gain temperance, but he will always desire so to attemper the body as to preserve the harmony of the soul?

Certainly he will, if he has true music in him.

And in the acquisition of wealth there is a principle of order and harmony which he will also observe; he will not allow himself to be dazzled by the foolish applause of the world, and heap up riches to his own infinite harm?

Certainly not, he said.

He will look at the city which is within him, and take heed that no disorder occur in it, such as might arise either from superfluity or from want; and upon this principle he will regulate his property and gain or spend according to his means.

Very true.

And, for the same reason, he will gladly accept and enjoy such honors as he deems likely to make him a better man; but those, whether private or public, which are likely to disorder his life, he will avoid?

Then, if that is his motive, he will not be a statesman.

By the dog of Egypt, he will! in the city which is his own he certainly will, though in the land of his birth perhaps not, unless he have a divine call.

I understand; you mean that he will be a ruler in the city of which we are the founders, and which exists in idea only; for I do not believe that there is such a one anywhere on earth?

In heaven, I replied, there is laid up a pattern of it, methinks, which he who desires may behold, and beholding, may set his own house in order. But whether such a one exists, or ever will exist in fact, is no matter; for he will live after the manner of that city, having nothing to do with any other.

I think so, he said. . . .

[Socrates has just intimated that there is some sort of *pattern* which one might behold—a pattern which might be used as a model for the purpose of organizing one's life. In addition he indicates that knowledge of this ideal conception would serve to clarify the virtues of justice, courage, wisdom, and temperance. Hence it is important to push his inquiry still further in order to identify this conception and to explain how it might be known.]

We were saying, if I am not mistaken, that he who wanted to see them in their perfect beauty must take a longer and more circuitous way, at the end of which they would appear; but that we could add on a popular exposition of them on a level with the discussion which had preceded. And you replied that such an exposition would be enough for you, and so the inquiry was continued in what to me seemed to be a very inaccurate manner; whether you were satisfied or not, it is for you to say.

Yes, he said, I thought and the others thought that you gave us a fair measure of truth.

But, my friend, I said, a measure of such things which in any degree falls short of the whole truth is not fair measure; for nothing imperfect is the measure of anything, although persons are too apt to be contented and think that they need search no further.

Not an uncommon case when people are indolent.

Yes, I said; and there cannot be any worse fault in a guardian of the State and of the laws.

True.

The guardian then, I said, must be required to take the longer circuit, and toil at learning as well as at gymnastics, or he will never reach the highest knowledge of all which, as we were just now saying, is his proper calling.

What, he said, is there a knowledge still higher than this—higher than justice and the other virtues?

Yes, I said, there is. And of the virtues too we must behold not the outline merely, as at present—nothing short of the most finished picture should satisfy us. When little things are elaborated with an infinity of pains, in order that they may appear in their full beauty and utmost clearness, how ridiculous that we should not think the highest truths worthy of attaining the highest accuracy!

A right noble thought; but do you suppose that we shall refrain from asking you what is this highest knowledge?

Nay, I said, ask if you will; but I am certain that you have heard the answer many times, and now you either do not understand me or, as I rather think, you are disposed to be troublesome; for you have often been told that the idea of good is the highest knowledge, and that all other things become useful and advantageous only by their use of this. You can hardly be ignorant that of this I was about to speak, concerning which, as you have often heard me say, we know so little; and without which, any other knowledge or possession of any kind will profit us nothing. Do you think that the possession of all other things is of any value if we do not possess the good? or the knowledge of all other things if we have no knowledge of beauty and goodness?

Assuredly not. . . .

There can be no doubt about the numerous difficulties in which this question is involved.

There can be none. . . .

Still, I must implore you, Socrates, said Glaucon, not to turn away just as you are reaching the goal; if you will only give such an explanation of the good as you have already given of justice and temperance and the other virtues, we shall be satisfied. . . .

Yes, I said, but I must first come to an understanding with you, and remind you of what I have mentioned in the course of this discussion, and at many other times.

What?

The old story, that there is many a beautiful and many a good, and so of other things which we describe and define; to all of them the term "many" is implied.

True, he said.

And there is an absolute beauty and an absolute good, and of other things to which the term "many" is applied there is an absolute; for they may be brought under a single idea, which is called the essence of each.

Very true.

The many, as we say, are seen but not known, and the ideas are known but not seen. . . .

And now, I said, let me show in a figure how far our nature is enlightened or unenlightened: Behold! human beings living in an underground den, which has a mouth open toward the light and reaching all along the den; here they have been from their childhood, and have their legs and necks chained so that they cannot move, and can only see before them, being prevented by the chains from turning round their heads. Above and behind them a fire is blazing at a distance, and between the fire and the prisoners there is a raised way; and you will see, if you look, a low wall built along the way, like the screen which marionette-players have in front of them, over which they show the puppets.

I see.

And do you see, I said, men passing along the wall carrying all sorts of vessels, and statues and figures of animals made of wood and stone and various materials, which appear over the wall? Some of them are talking, others silent.

You have shown me a strange image, and they are strange prisoners.

Like ourselves, I replied; and they see only their own shadows, or the shadows of one another, which the fire throws on the opposite wall of the cave?

True, he said; how could they see anything but the shadows if they were never allowed to move their heads?

And of the objects which are being carried in like manner they would only see the shadows?

Yes, he said.

And if they were able to converse with one another, would they not suppose that they were naming what was actually before them?

Very true.

And suppose further that the prison had an echo which came from the other side, would they not be sure to fancy when one of the passers-by spoke that the voice which they heard came from the passing shadow?

No question, he replied.

To them, I said, the truth would be literally nothing but the shadows of the images.

That is certain.

And now look again, and see what will naturally follow if the prisoners are released and disabused of their error. At first, when any of them is liberated and compelled suddenly to stand up and turn his neck round and walk and look toward the light, he will suffer sharp pains; the glare will distress him, and he will be unable to see the realities of which in his former state he had seen the shadows; and then conceive someone saying to him, that what he saw before was an illusion, but that now, when he is approaching nearer to being and his eye is turned toward more real existence, he has a clearer vision—what will be his reply? And you may further imagine that his instructor is pointing to the objects as they pass and requiring him to name them—will he not be perplexed? Will he not fancy that the shadows which he formerly saw are truer than the objects which are now shown to him?

Far truer.

And if he is compelled to look straight at the light, will he not have a pain in his eyes which will make him turn away to take refuge in the objects of vision which he can see, and which he will conceive to be in reality clearer than the things which are now being shown to him?

True, he said.

And suppose once more, that he is reluctantly dragged up a steep and rugged ascent, and held fast until he is forced into the presence of the sun himself, is he not likely to be pained and irritated? When he approaches the light his eyes will be dazzled, and he will not be able to see anything at all of what are now called realities.

Not all in a moment, he said.

He will require to grow accustomed to the sight of the upper world. And first he will see the shadows best, next the reflections of men and other objects in the water, and then the objects themselves; then he will gaze upon the light of the moon and the stars and the spangled heaven; and he will see the sky and the stars by night better than the sun or the light of the sun by day?

Certainly.

Last of all he will be able to see the sun, and not mere reflections of him in the water, but he will see him in his own proper place, and not in another; and he will contemplate him as he is.

Certainly.

He will then proceed to argue that this is he who gives the season and the years, and is the guardian of all that is in the visible world, and in a certain way the cause of all things which he and his fellows have been accustomed to behold?

Clearly, he said, he would first see the sun and then reason about him.

And when he remembered his old habitation, and the wisdom of the den and his fellow-prisoners, do you not suppose that he would felicitate himself on the change, and pity him?

Certainly, he would.

And if they were in the habit of conferring honors among themselves on those who were quickest to observe the passing shadows and to remark which of them went before, and which followed after, and which were together; and who were therefore best able to draw conclusions as to the future, do you think that he would care for such honors and glories, or envy the possessors of them? Would he not say with Homer,

"Better to be the poor servant of a poor master,"

and to endure anything, rather than think as they do and live after their manner?

Yes, he said, I think that he would rather suffer anything than entertain these false notions and live in this miserable manner.

Imagine once more, I said, such a one coming suddenly out of the sun to be replaced in his old situation; would he not be certain to have his eyes full of darkness?

To be sure, he said.

And if there were a contest, and he had to compete in measuring the shadows with the prisoners who had never moved out of the den, while his sight was still weak, and before his eyes had become steady (and the time which would be needed to acquire this new habit of sight might be very considerable), would he not be ridiculous? Men would say of him that up he went and down he came without his eyes; and that it was better not even to think of ascending; and if anyone tried to loose another and lead him up to the light, let them only catch the offender, and they would put him to death.

No question, he said.

This entire allegory, I said, you may now append, dear Glaucon, to the previous argument; the prison-house is the world of sight, the light of the fire is the sun, and you will not misapprehend me if you interpret the journey upward to be the ascent of the soul into the intellectual world according to my poor belief, which, at your desire, I have expressed—whether rightly or wrongly, God knows. But, whether true or false, my opinion is that in the world of knowledge the idea of good appears last of all, and is seen only with an effort; and, when seen, is also inferred to be the universal author of all things beautiful and right, parent of light and of the lord of light in this visible world, and the immediate source of reason and truth in the intellectual; and that this is the power upon which he who would act rationally either in public or private life must have his eye fixed.

I agree, he said, as far as I am able to understand you.

❀ ARISTOTLE

18. Happiness, Wisdom, and the Golden Mean

Aristotle (384–322 B.C.) entered Plato's Academy at the age of eighteen and remained there until Plato's death twenty years later. In 343 B.C. he became a tutor to King Philip's thirteen-year-old son, later known as Alexander the Great. At the age of forty-nine Aristotle returned to Athens where he founded the Lyceum and wrote voluminously. The *Nicomachean Ethics* is the first of his two major treatises on ethical theory. It takes its name from Nicomachus, Aristotle's son, who was probably responsible for editing it.

From Books I, II, and X of *Ethica Nicomachea*, in *The Works of Aristotle Translated into English*, Vol IX, trans. W. D. Ross (Oxford: Oxford University Press, 1915). Reprinted by permission of the Clarendon Press, Oxford. Footnotes omitted.

Book I

Every art and every inquiry, and similarly every action and pursuit, is thought to aim at some good; and for this reason the good has rightly been declared to be that at which all things aim. But a certain difference is found among ends; some are activities, others are products apart from the activities that produce them. Where there are ends apart from the actions, it is the nature of the products to be better than the activities. Now, as there are many actions, arts, and sciences, their ends also are many; the end of the medical art is health, that of shipbuilding a vessel, that of strategy victory, that of economics wealth. But where such arts fall under a single capacity—as bridle-making and the other arts concerned with the equipment of horses fall under the art of riding, and this and every military action under strategy, in the same way other arts fall under yet others—in all of these the ends of the master arts are to be preferred to all the subordinate ends; for it is for the sake of the former that the latter are pursued. It makes no difference whether the activities themselves are the ends of the actions, or something else apart from the activities, as in the case of the sciences just mentioned.

If, then, there is some end of the things we do, which we desire for its own sake (everything else being desired for the sake of this), and if we do not choose everything for the sake of something else (for at that rate the process would go on to infinity, so that our desire would be empty and vain), clearly this must be the good and the chief good. Will not the knowledge of it, then, have a great influence on life? Shall we not, like archers who have a mark to aim at, be more likely to hit upon what is right? If so, we must try, in outline at least, to determine what it is, and of which of the sciences or capacities it is the object. It would seem to belong to the most authoritative art and that which is most truly the master art. And politics appears to be of this nature; for it is this that ordains which of the sciences should be studied in a state, and which each class of citizens should learn and up to what point they should learn them; and we see even the most highly esteemed of capacities to fall under this, e.g., strategy, economics, rhetoric; now, since politics uses the rest of the sciences, and since, again, it legislates as to what we are to do and what we are to abstain from, the end of this science must include those of the others, so that this end must be the good for man. For even if the end is the same for a single man and for a state, that of the state seems at all events something greater and more complete whether to attain or to preserve; though it is worth while to attain the end merely for one man, it is finer and more godlike to attain it for a nation or for city-states. These, then, are the ends at which our inquiry aims, since it is political science, in one sense of that term.

Our discussion will be adequate if it has as much clearness as the subject-matter admits of, for precision is not to be sought for alike in all discussions, any more than in all the products of the crafts. Now fine and just actions, which political science investigates, admit of much variety and fluctuation of opinion, so that they may be thought to exist only by convention, and not by nature. And goods also give rise to a similar fluctuation because they bring harm to many people; for before now men have been undone by reason of their wealth, and others by reason of their courage. We must be content, then, in speaking of such subjects and with such premises to indicate the truth roughly and in outline, and in speaking about things which are only for the most part true and with premises of the same kind to reach conclusions that are no better. In the same spirit, therefore, should each type of statement be *received;* for it is the mark of an educated man to look for precision in each class of things just so far as the nature of the subject admits; it is evidently equally foolish to accept probable reasoning from a mathematician and to demand from a rhetorician scientific proofs.

Now each man judges well the things he knows, and of these he is a good judge. And so the man who has been educated in a subject is a good judge of that subject, and the man who has received an all-round education is a good judge in general. Hence a young man is not a proper hearer of lectures on political science; for he is inexperienced in the actions that occur in life, but its discussions start from these and are about these; and, further, since he tends to follow his passions, his study will be vain and unprofitable, because the end aimed at is not knowledge but action. And it makes no difference whether he is young in years or youthful in character; the defect does not depend on time, but on his living, and pursuing each successive object, as passion directs. For to such persons, as to the incontinent, knowledge brings no profit; but to those who desire and act in accordance with a rational principle knowledge about such matters will be of great benefit.

These remarks about the student, the sort of treatment to be expected, and the purpose of the inquiry, may be taken as our preface.

Let us resume our inquiry and state, in view of the fact that all knowledge and every pursuit aims at some good, what it is that we say political science aims at and what is the highest of all goods achievable by action. Verbally there is very general agreement; for both the general run of men and people of superior refinement say that it is happiness, and identify living well and doing well with being happy; but with regard to what happiness is they differ, and the many do not give the same account as the wise. For the former think it is some plain and obvious thing, like pleasure, wealth, or honour; they differ, however, from one another—and often even the same man identifies it with different things, with health when he is ill, with wealth when he is poor; but, conscious of their ignorance, they admire those who proclaim some great ideal that is above their comprehension. Now some thought that apart from these many goods there is another which is self-subsistent and causes the goodness of all these as well. To examine all the opinions that have been held were perhaps somewhat fruitless; enough to examine those that are most prevalent or that seem to be arguable. . . .

Let us, however, resume our discussion from the point at which we digressed. To judge from the lives that men lead, most men, and men of the most vulgar type, seem (not without some ground) to identify the good, or

happiness, with pleasure; which is the reason why they love the life of enjoyment. For there are, we may say, three prominent types of life—that just
mentioned, the political, and thirdly the contemplative life. Now the mass
of mankind are evidently quite slavish in their tastes, preferring a life suitable to beasts, but they get some ground for their view from the fact that
many of those in high places share the tastes of Sardanapallus. A consideration of the prominent types of life shows that people of superior refinement
and of active disposition identify happiness with honour; for this is, roughly
speaking, the end of the political life. But it seems too superficial to be what
we are looking for, since it is thought to depend on those who bestow honour
rather than on him who receives it, but the good we divine to be something
proper to a man and not easily taken from him. Further, men seem to pursue
honour in order that they may be assured of their goodness; at least it is by
men of practical wisdom that they seek to be honoured, and among those
who know them, and on the ground of their virtue; clearly, then, according
to them, at any rate, virtue is better. And perhaps one might even suppose
this to be, rather than honour, the end of the political life. But even this
appears somewhat incomplete; for possession of virtue seems actually compatible with being asleep, or with lifelong inactivity, and, further, with the
greatest sufferings and misfortunes; but a man who was living so no one
would call happy, unless he were maintaining a thesis at all costs. But
enough of this; for the subject has been sufficiently treated even in the current discussions. Third comes the contemplative life, which we shall consider
later.

The life of money-making is one undertaken under compulsion, and
wealth is evidently not the good we are seeking; for it is merely useful and
for the sake of something else. And so one might rather take the aforenamed
objects to be ends; for they are loved for themselves. But it is evident that
not even these are ends; yet many arguments have been thrown away in support of them. Let us leave this subject, then. . . .

Let us again return to the good we are seeking, and ask what it can
be. It seems different in different actions and arts; it is different in medicine,
in strategy, and in the other arts likewise. What then is the good of each?
Surely that for whose sake everything else is done. In medicine this is health,
in strategy victory, in architecture a house, in any other sphere something
else, and in every action and pursuit the end; for it is for the sake of this that
all men do whatever else they do. Therefore, if there is an end for all that we
do, this will be the good achievable by action, and if there are more than
one, these will be the goods achievable by action.

So the argument has by a different course reached the same point;
but we must try to state this even more clearly. Since there are evidently
more than one end, and we choose some of these (e.g., wealth, flutes, and in
general instruments) for the sake of something else, clearly not all ends are
final ends; but the chief good is evidently something final. Therefore, if
there is only one final end, this will be what we are seeking, and if there are

more than one, the most final of these will be what we are seeking. Now we call that which is in itself worthy of pursuit more final than that which is worthy of pursuit for the sake of something else, and that which is never desirable for the sake of something else more final than the things that are desirable both in themselves and for the sake of that other thing, and therefore we call final without qualification that which is always desirable in itself and never for the sake of something else.

Now such a thing happiness, above all else, is held to be; for this we choose always for itself and never for the sake of something else, but honour, pleasure, reason, and every virtue we choose indeed for themselves (for if nothing resulted from them we should still choose each of them), but we choose them also for the sake of happiness, judging that by means of them we shall be happy. Happiness, on the other hand, no one chooses for the sake of these, nor, in general, for anything other than itself. . . .

Presumably, however, to say that happiness is the chief good seems a platitude, and a clearer account of what it is is still desired. This might perhaps be given, if we could first ascertain the function of man. For just as for a flute-player, a sculptor, or any artist, and, in general, for all things that have a function or activity, the good and the "well" is thought to reside in the function, so would it seem to be for man, if he has a function. Have the carpenter, then, and the tanner certain functions or activities, and has man none? Is he born without a function? Or as eye, hand, foot, and in general each of the parts evidently has a function, may one lay it down that man similarly has a function apart from all these? What then can this be? Life seems to be common even to plants, but we are seeking what is peculiar to man. Let us exclude, therefore, the life of nutrition and growth. Next there would be a life of perception, but *it* also seems to be common even to the horse, the ox, and every animal. There remains, then, an active life of the element that has a rational principle; of this, one part has such a principle in the sense of being obedient to one, the other in the sense of possessing one and exercising thought. And, as "life of the rational element" also has two meanings, we must state that life in the sense of activity is what we mean; for this seems to be the more proper sense of the term. Now if the function of man is an activity of soul which follows or implies a rational principle, and if we say "a so-and-so" and "a good so-and-so" have a function which is the same in kind, e.g., a lyre-player and a good lyre-player, and so without qualification in all cases, eminence in respect of goodness being added to the name of the function (for the function of a lyre-player is to play the lyre, and that of a good lyre-player is to do so well): if this is the case, [and we state the function of man to be a certain kind of life, and this to be an activity or actions of the soul implying a rational principle, and the function of a good man to be the good and noble performance of these, and if any action is well performed when it is performed in accordance with the appropriate excellence: if this is the case,] human good turns out to be activity of soul in accordance with virtue, and if there are more than one virtue, in accordance with the best and most complete.

But we must add "in a complete life." For one swallow does not make a summer, nor does one day; and so too one day, or a short time, does not make a man blessed and happy. . . .

Since happiness is an activity of soul in accordance with perfect virtue, we must consider the nature of virtue; for perhaps we shall thus see better the nature of happiness. The true student of politics, too, is thought to have studied virtue above all things; for he wishes to make his fellow citizens good and obedient to the laws. As an example of this we have the lawgivers of the Cretans and the Spartans, and any others of the kind that there may have been. And if this inquiry belongs to political science, clearly the pursuit of it will be in accordance with our original plan. But clearly the virtue we must study is human virtue; for the good we were seeking was human good and the happiness human happiness. By human virtue we mean not that of the body but that of the soul; and happiness also we call an activity of soul. But if this is so, clearly the student of politics must know somehow the facts about soul, as the man who is to heal the eyes or the body as a whole must know about the eyes or the body; and all the more since politics is more prized and better than medicine; but even among doctors the best educated spend much labour on acquiring knowledge of the body. The student of politics, then, must study the soul, and must study it with these objects in view, and do so just to the extent which is sufficient for the questions we are discussing; for further precision is perhaps something more laborious than our purposes require.

Some things are said about it, adequately enough, even in the discussions outside our school, and we must use these; e.g., that one element in the soul is irrational and one has a rational principle. Whether these are separated as the parts of the body or of anything divisible are, or are distinct by definition but by nature inseparable, like convex and concave in the circumference of a circle, does not affect the present question.

Of the irrational element one division seems to be widely distributed, and vegetative in its nature, I mean that which causes nutrition and growth; for it is this kind of power of the soul that one must assign to all nurslings and to embryos, and this same power to full-grown creatures; this is more reasonable than to assign some different power to them. Now the excellence of this seems to be common to all species and not specifically human; for this part or faculty seems to function most in sleep, while goodness and badness are least manifest in sleep (whence comes the saying that the happy are no better off than the wretched for half their lives; and this happens naturally enough, since sleep is an inactivity of the soul in that respect in which it is called good or bad), unless perhaps to a small extent some of the movements actually penetrate to the soul, and in this respect the dreams of good men are better than those of ordinary people. Enough of this subject, however; let us leave the nutritive faculty alone, since it has by its nature no share in human excellence.

There seems to be also another irrational element in the soul—one which in a sense, however, shares in a rational principle. For we praise the rational principle of the continent man and of the incontinent, and the part of their soul that has such a principle, since it urges them aright and towards the best objects; but there is found in them also another element naturally opposed to the rational principle, which fights against and resists that principle. For exactly as paralysed limbs when we intend to move them to the right turn on the contrary to the left, so is it with the soul; the impulses of incontinent people move in contrary directions. But while in the body we see that which moves astray, in the soul we do not. No doubt, however, we must none the less suppose that in the soul too there is something contrary to the rational principle, resisting and opposing it. In what sense it is distinct from the other elements does not concern us. Now even this seems to have a share in a rational principle, as we said; at any rate in the continent man it obeys the rational principle—and presumably in the temperate and brave man it is still more obedient; for in him it speaks, on all matters, with the same voice as the rational principle.

Therefore the irrational element also appears to be twofold. For the vegetative element in no way shares in a rational principle, but the appetitive and in general the desiring element in a sense shares in it, in so far as it listens to and obeys it; this is the sense in which we speak of "taking account" of one's father or one's friends, not that in which we speak of "accounting" for a mathematical property. That the irrational element is in some sense persuaded by a rational principle is indicated also by the giving of advice and by all reproof and exhortation. And if this element also must be said to have a rational principle, that which has a rational principle (as well as that which has not) will be twofold, one subdivision having it in the strict sense and in itself, and the other having a tendency to obey as one does one's father.

Virtue too is distinguished into kinds in accordance with this difference; for we say that some of the virtues are intellectual and others moral, philosophic wisdom and understanding and practical wisdom being intellectual, liberality and temperance moral. For in speaking about a man's character we do not say that he is wise or has understanding but that he is good-tempered or temperate; yet we praise the wise man also with respect to his state of mind; and of states of mind we call those which merit praise virtues.

Book II

Virtue, then, being of two kinds, intellectual and moral, intellectual virtue in the main owes both its birth and its growth to teaching (for which reason it requires experience and time), while moral virtue comes about as a result of habit, whence also its name (ἠθική) is one that is formed by a slight variation from the word ἔθος (habit). From this it is also plain that none of the moral virtues arises in us by nature; for nothing that exists by nature can form a habit contrary to its nature. For instance the stone which by nature moves downwards cannot be habituated to move upwards, not even if one tries to train it by throwing it up ten thousand times; nor can fire be habituated to move downwards, nor can anything else that by nature behaves in one way be trained to behave in another. Neither by nature, then, nor contrary to nature do the virtues arise in us; rather we are adapted by nature to receive them, and are made perfect by habit. . . .

Again, it is from the same causes and by the same means that every virtue is both produced and destroyed, and similarly every art; for it is from playing the lyre that both good and bad lyre-players are produced. And the corresponding statement is true of builders and of all the rest; men will be good or bad builders as a result of building well or badly. For if this were not so, there would have been no need of a teacher, but all men would have been born good or bad at their craft. This, then, is the case with the virtues also; by doing the acts that we do in our transactions with other men we become just or unjust, and by doing the acts that we do in the presence of danger, and being habituated to feel fear or confidence, we become brave or cowardly. The same is true of appetites and feelings of anger; some men become temperate and good-tempered, others self-indulgent and irascible, by behaving in one way or the other in the appropriate circumstances. Thus, in one word, states of character arise out of like activities. This is why the activities we exhibit must be of a certain kind; it is because the states of character correspond to the differences between these. It makes no small difference, then, whether we form habits of one kind or of another from our very youth; it makes a very great difference, or rather *all* the difference. . . .

We must, however, not only describe virtue as a state of character, but also say what sort of state it is. We may remark, then, that every virtue or excellence both brings into good condition the thing of which it is the excellence and makes the work of that thing be done well; e.g., the excellence of the eye makes both the eye and its work good; for it is by the excellence of the eye that we see well. Similarly the excellence of the horse makes a horse both good in itself and good at running and at carrying its rider and at awaiting the attack of the enemy. Therefore, if this is true in every case, the virtue of man also will be the state of character which makes a man good and which makes him do his own work well.

How this is to happen we have stated already, but it will be made plain also by the following consideration of the specific nature of virtue. In everything that is continuous and divisible it is possible to take more, less, or an equal amount, and that either in terms of the thing itself or relatively to us; and the equal is an intermediate between excess and defect. By the intermediate in the object I mean that which is equidistant from each of the extremes, which is one and the same for all men; by the intermediate relatively to us that which is neither too much nor too little—and this is not one, nor the same for all. For instance, if ten is many and two is few, six is the intermediate, taken in terms of the object; for it exceeds and is exceeded by an equal amount; this is intermediate according to arithmetical proportion. But the intermediate relatively to us is not to be taken so; if ten pounds are too much for a particular person to eat and two too little, it does not follow that the trainer will order six pounds; for this also is perhaps too much for the person who is to take it, or too little—too little for Milo, too much for the beginner in athletic exercises. The same is true of running and wrestling. Thus a master of any art avoids excess and defect, but seeks the intermediate and chooses this—the intermediate not in the object but relatively to us. . . .

Virtue, then, is a state of character concerned with choice, lying in a mean, i.e., the mean relative to us, this being determined by a rational principle, and by that principle by which the man of practical wisdom would determine it. Now it is a mean between two vices, that which depends on excess and that which depends on defect; and again it is a mean because the vices respectively fall short of or exceed what is right in both passions and actions, while virtue both finds and chooses that which is intermediate. Hence in respect of its substance and the definition which states its essence virtue is a mean, with regard to what is best and right an extreme.

But not every action nor every passion admits of a mean; for some have names that already imply badness, e.g., spite, shamelessness, envy, and in the case of actions adultery, theft, murder; for all of these and suchlike things imply by their names that they are themselves bad, and not the excesses or deficiencies of them. It is not possible, then, ever to be right with regard to them; one must always be wrong. Nor does goodness or badness with regard to such things depend on committing adultery with the right woman, at the right time, and in the right way, but simply to do any of them is to go wrong. It would be equally absurd, then, to expect that in unjust, cowardly, and voluptuous action there should be a mean, an excess, and a deficiency; for at that rate there would be a mean of excess and of deficiency, an excess of excess, and a deficiency of deficiency. But as there is no excess and deficiency of temperance and courage because what is intermediate is in a sense an extreme, so too of the actions we have mentioned there is no mean nor any excess and deficiency, but however they are done they are wrong; for in general there is neither a mean of excess and deficiency, nor excess and deficiency of a mean.

We must, however, not only make this general statement, but also apply it to the individual facts. For among statements about conduct those which are general apply more widely, but those which are particular are more genuine, since conduct has to do with individual cases, and our statements must harmonize with the facts in these cases. We may take these cases from our table. With regard to feelings of fear and confidence courage is the mean; of the people who exceed, he who exceeds in fearlessness has no name (many of the states have no name), while the man who exceeds in confidence is rash, and he who exceeds in fear and falls short in confidence is a coward. With regard to pleasures and pains—not all of them, and not so much with regard to the pains—the mean is temperance, the excess self-indulgence. Persons deficient with regard to the pleasures are not often found; hence such persons also have received no name. But let us call them "insensible."

With regard to giving and taking of money the mean is liberality, the excess and the defect prodigality and meanness. In these actions people exceed and fall short in contrary ways; the prodigal exceeds in spending and falls short in taking, while the mean man exceeds in taking and falls short in spending. (At present we are giving a mere outline or summary, and are satisfied with this; later these states will be more exactly determined.) With regard to money there are also other dispositions—a mean, magnificence (for the magnificent man differs from the liberal man; the former deals with large sums, the latter with small ones), an excess, tastelessness and vulgarity, and a deficiency, niggardliness; these differ from the states opposed to liberality, and the mode of their difference will be stated later.

With regard to honour and dishonour the mean is proper pride, the excess is known as a sort of "empty vanity," and the deficiency is undue humility; and as we said liberality was related to magnificence, differing from it by dealing with small sums, so there is a state similarly related to proper pride, being concerned with small honours while that is concerned with great. For it is possible to desire honour as one ought, and more than one ought, and less, and the man who exceeds in his desires is called ambitious, the man who falls short unambitious, while the intermediate person has no name. The dispositions also are nameless, except that that of the ambitious man is called ambition. Hence the people who are at the extremes lay claim to the middle place; and we ourselves sometimes call the intermediate person ambitious and sometimes unambitious, and sometimes praise the ambitious man and sometimes the unambitious. The reason of our doing this will be stated in what follows; but now let us speak of the remaining states according to the method which has been indicated.

With regard to anger also there is an excess, a deficiency, and a mean. Although they can scarcely be said to have names, yet since we call the intermediate person good-tempered let us call the mean good temper; of the persons at the extremes let the one who exceeds be called irascible, and his vice irascibility, and the man who falls short an inirascible sort of person, and the deficiency inirascibility.

There are also three other means, which have a certain likeness to one another, but differ from one another: for they are all concerned with intercourse in words and actions, but differ in that one is concerned with truth in this sphere, the other two with pleasantness; and of this one kind is exhibited in giving amusement, the other in all the circumstances of life. We must therefore speak of these too, that we may the better see that in all things the mean is praiseworthy, and the extremes neither praiseworthy nor right, but worthy of blame. Now most of these states also have no names, but we must try, as in the other cases, to invent names ourselves so that we may be clear and easy to follow. With regard to truth, then, the intermediate is a truthful sort of person and the mean may be called truthfulness, while the pretence which exaggerates is boastfulness and the person characterized by it a boaster, and that which understates is mock modesty and the person characterized by it mock-modest. With regard to pleasantness in the giving of amusement the intermediate person is ready-witted and the disposition ready wit, the excess is buffoonery and the person characterized by it a buffoon, while the man who falls short is a sort of boor and his state is boorishness. With regard to the remaining kind of pleasantness, that which is exhibited in life in general, the man who is pleasant in the right way is friendly and the mean is friendliness, while the man who exceeds is an obsequious person if he has no end in view, a flatterer if he is aiming at his own advantage, and the man who falls short and is unpleasant in all circumstances is a quarrelsome and surly sort of person. . . .

Book X

If happiness is activity in accordance with virtue, it is reasonable that it should be in accordance with the highest virtue; and this will be that of the best thing in us. Whether it be reason or something else that is this element which is thought to be our natural ruler and guide and to take thought of things noble and divine, whether it be itself also divine or only the most divine element in us, the activity of this in accordance with its proper virtue will be perfect happiness. That this activity is contemplative we have already said.

Now this would seem to be in agreement both with what we said before and with the truth. For, firstly, this activity is the best (since not only is reason the best thing in us, but the objects of reason are the best of knowable objects); and, secondly, it is the most continuous, since we can contemplate truth more continuously than we can *do* anything. And we think happiness has pleasure mingled with it, but the activity of philosophic wisdom is admittedly the pleasantest of virtuous activities; at all events the pursuit of it is thought to offer pleasures marvellous for their purity and their enduringness, and it is to be expected that those who know will pass their time more pleasantly than those who inquire. And the self-sufficiency that is spoken of must belong most to the contemplative activity. For while a philosopher, as well as a just man or one possessing any other virtue, needs the necessaries of life, when they are sufficiently equipped with things of that sort the just man needs people towards whom and with whom he shall act justly, and the temperate man, the brave man, and each of the others is in the same case, but the philosopher, even when by himself, can contemplate truth, and the better the wiser he is; he can perhaps do so better if he has fellow-workers, but still he is the most self-sufficient. And this activity alone would seem to be loved for its own sake; for nothing arises from it apart from the contemplating, while from practical activities we gain more or less apart from the action. . . .

But such a life would be too high for man; for it is not in so far as he is man that he will live so, but in so far as something divine is present in him; and by so much as this is superior to our composite nature is its activity superior to that which is the exercise of the other kind of virtue. If reason is divine, then, in comparison with man, the life according to it is divine in comparison with human life. But we must not follow those who advise us, being men, to think of human things, and, being mortal, of mortal things, but must, so far as we can, make ourselves immortal, and strain every nerve to live in accordance with the best thing in us; for even if it be small in bulk, much more does it in power and worth surpass everything. This would seem, too, to be each man himself, since it is the authoritative and better part of him. It would be strange, then, if he were to choose not the life of his self but that of something else. And what we said before will apply now; that which is proper to each thing is by nature best and most pleasant for each thing; for man, therefore, the life according to reason is best and pleasantest, since reason more than anything else *is* man. This life therefore is also the happiest. . . .

❀ EPICURUS

19. *Critical Hedonism*

Epicurus (341–270 B.C.) was born and educated on the island of Samos in the Aegean Sea. In 306 B.C. he moved to Athens where he taught until his death. He founded the famous "Garden of Epicurus," which ranked among the great schools of antiquity—along with Plato's Academy, Aristotle's Lyceum, and Zeno's Stoa Poikile. Although Epicurus is believed to have been a profilic writer, only a few letters and fragments of his writings are extant. A more complete statement of his philosophy is provided by the works of his disciples, the most distinguished of whom was the Roman, Lucretius Carus.

EPICURUS TO HERODOTUS

For those who are unable, Herodotus, to work in detail through all that I have written about nature, or to peruse the larger books which I have composed, I have already prepared at sufficient length an epitome of the whole system, that they may keep adequately in mind at least the most general principles in each department, in order that as occasion arises they may be able to assist themselves on the most important points, in so far as they undertake the study of nature. But those also who have made considerable progress in the survey of the main principles ought to bear in mind the scheme of the whole system set forth in its essentials. For we have frequent need of the general view, but not so often of the detailed exposition. Indeed it is necessary to go back on the main principles, and constantly to fix in one's memory enough to give one the most essential comprehension of the truth. And in fact the accurate knowledge of details

From the two letters, "Epicurus to Herodotus" and "Epicurus to Menoeceus," in *Epicurus: The Extant Remains,* trans. Cyril Bailey (Oxford: Clarendon Press, 1926). Reprinted by permission of the Clarendon Press, Oxford.

will be fully discovered, if the general principles in the various departments are thoroughly grasped and borne in mind; for even in the case of one fully initiated the most essential feature in all accurate knowledge is the capacity to make a rapid use of observation and mental apprehension, and [this can be done if everything] is summed up in elementary principles and formulae. For it is not possible for any one to abbreviate the complete course through the whole system, if he cannot embrace in his own mind by means of short formulae all that might be set out with accuracy in detail. Wherefore since the method I have described is valuable to all those who are accustomed to the investigation of nature, I who urge upon others the constant occupation in the investigation of nature, and find my own peace chiefly in a life so occupied, have composed for you another epitome on these lines, summing up the first principles of the whole doctrine. . . .

Having made these points clear, we must now consider things imperceptible to the senses. First of all, that nothing is created out of that which does not exist: for if it were, everything would be created out of everything with no need of seeds. And again, if that which disappears were destroyed into that which did not exist, all things would have perished, since that into which they were dissolved would not exist. Furthermore, the universe always was such as it is now, and always will be the same. For there is nothing into which it changes: for outside the universe there is nothing which could come into it and bring about the change.

Moreover, the universe is (bodies and space): for that bodies exist, sense itself witnesses in the experience of all men, and in accordance with the evidence of sense we must of necessity judge of the imperceptible by reasoning, as I have already said. And if there were not that which we term void and place and intangible existence, bodies would have nowhere to exist and nothing through which to move, as they are seen to move. And besides these two nothing can even be thought of either by conception or on the analogy of things conceivable such as could be grasped as whole existences and not spoken of as the accidents or properties of such existences. Furthermore, among bodies some are compounds, and others those of which compounds are formed. And these latter are indivisible and unalterable (if, that is, all things are not to be destroyed into the non-existent, but something permanent is to remain behind at the dissolution of compounds): they are completely solid in nature, and can by no means be dissolved in any part. So it must needs be that the first-beginnings are indivisible corporeal existences.

Moreover, the universe is boundless. For that which is bounded has an extreme point: and the extreme point is seen against something else. So that as it has no extreme point, it has no limit; and as it has no limit, it must be boundless and not bounded. Furthermore, the infinite is boundless both in the number of the bodies and in the extent of the void. For if on the one hand the void were boundless, and the bodies limited in number, the bodies could not stay anywhere, but would be carried about and scattered through the infinite void, not having other bodies to support them and keep them in place by means of collisions. But if, on the other hand, the void were limited, the infinite bodies would not have room wherein to take their place.

Besides this the indivisible and solid bodies, out of which too the compounds are created and into which they are dissolved, have an incomprehensible number of varieties in shape: for it is not possible that such great varieties of things should arise from the same (atomic) shapes, if they are limited in number. And so in each shape the atoms are quite infinite in number, but their differences of shape are not quite infinite, but only incomprehensible in number.

And the atoms move continuously for all time, some of them [falling straight down, others swerving, and others recoiling from their collisions. And of the latter, some are borne on] separating to a long distance from one another, while others again recoil and recoil, whenever they chance to be checked by the interlacing with others, or else shut in by atoms interlaced around them. For on the one hand the nature of the void which separates each atom by itself brings this about, as it is not able to afford resistance, and on the other hand the hardness which belongs to the atoms makes them recoil after collision to as great a distance as the interlacing permits separation after the collision. And these motions have no beginning, since the atoms and the void are the cause.

These brief sayings, if all these points are borne in mind, afford a sufficient outline for our understanding of the nature of existing things.

Furthermore, there are infinite worlds both like and unlike this world of ours. For the atoms being infinite in number, as was proved already, are borne on far out into space. For those atoms, which are of such nature that a world could be created out of them or made by them, have not been used up either on one world or on a limited number of worlds, nor again on all the worlds which are alike, or on those which are different from these. So that there nowhere exists an obstacle to the infinite number of the worlds. . . .

Moreover, we must suppose that the atoms do not possess any of the qualities belonging to perceptible things, except shape, weight, and size, and all that necessarily goes with shape. For every quality changes; but the atoms do not change at all, since there must needs be something which remains solid and indissoluble at the dissolution of compounds, which can cause changes; not changes into the non-existent or from the non-existent, but changes effected by the shifting of position of some particles, and by the addition or departure of others. For this reason it is essential that the bodies which shift their position should be imperishable and should not possess the nature of what changes, but parts and configuration of their own. For thus much must needs remain constant. For even in things perceptible to us which change their shape by the withdrawal of matter it is seen that shape remains to them, whereas the qualities do not remain in the changing object, in the way in which shape is left behind, but are lost from the entire body. Now these particles which are left behind are sufficient to cause the differences in compound bodies, since it is essential that some things should be left behind and not be destroyed into the non-existent. . . .

Next, referring always to the sensations and the feelings [for in this way you will obtain the most trustworthy ground of belief], you must consider that the soul is a body of fine particles distributed throughout the whole structure, and most resembling wind with a certain admixture of heat, and in some respects like to one of these and in some to the other. There is also the part which is many degrees more advanced even than these in fineness of composition, and for this reason is more capable of feeling in harmony with the rest of the structure as well. Now all this is made manifest by the activities of the soul and the feelings and the readiness of its movements and its processes of thought and by what we lose at the moment of death. Further, you must grasp that the soul possesses the chief cause of sensation: yet it could not have acquired sensation, unless it were in some way enclosed by the rest of the structure. And this in its turn having afforded the soul this cause of sensation acquires itself too a share in this contingent capacity from the soul. Yet it does not acquire all the capacities which the soul possesses: and therefore when the soul is released from the body, the body no longer has sensation. For it never possessed this power in itself, but used to afford opportunity for it to another existence, brought into being at the same time with itself: and this existence, owing to the power now consummated within itself as a result of motion, used spontaneously to produce for itself the capacity of sensation and then to communicate it to the body as well, in virtue of its contact and correspondence of movement, as I have already said. Therefore, so long as the soul remains in the body, even though some other part of the body be lost, it will never lose sensation; nay more, whatever portions of the soul may perish too, when that which enclosed it is removed either in whole or in part, if the soul continues to exist at all, it will retain sensation. On the other hand the rest of the structure, though it continues to exist either as a whole or in part, does not retain sensation, if it has once lost that sum of atoms, however small it be, which together goes to produce the nature of the soul. Moreover, if the whole structure is dissolved, the soul is dispersed and no longer has the same powers nor performs its movements, so that it does not possess sensation either. For it is impossible to imagine it with sensation, if it is not in this organism and cannot effect these movements, when what encloses and surrounds it is no longer the same as the surroundings in which it now exists and performs these movements. Furthermore, we must clearly comprehend as well, that the incorporeal in the general acceptation of the term is applied to that which could be thought of as such as an independent existence. Now it is impossible to conceive the incorporeal as a separate existence, except the void: and the void can neither act nor be acted upon, but only provides opportunity of motion through itself to bodies. So that those who say that the soul is incorporeal are talking idly. For it would not be able to act or be acted on in any respect, if it were of this nature. But as it is, both these occurrences are clearly distinguished in respect of the soul. Now if one refers all these reasonings about the soul to the standards of feeling and sensation and remembers what was said at the outset, he will see that they are sufficiently embraced in these general formulae to enable him to work out with certainty on this basis the details of the system as well. . . .

Furthermore, the motions of the heavenly bodies and their turnings and eclipses and risings and settings, and kindred phenomena to these, must not be thought to be due to any being who controls and ordains or has ordained them and at the same time enjoys perfect bliss together with immortality (for trouble and care and anger and kindness are not consistent with a life of blessedness, but these things come to pass where there is weakness and fear and dependence on neighbours). Nor again must we believe that they, which are but fire agglomerated in a mass, possess blessedness, and voluntarily take upon themselves these movements. But we must preserve their full majestic significance in all expressions which we apply to such conceptions, in order that there may not arise out of them opinions contrary to this notion of majesty. Otherwise this very contradiction will cause the greatest disturbance in men's souls. Therefore we must believe that it is due to the original inclusion of matter in such agglomerations during the birth-process of the world that this law of regular succession is also brought about. . . .

And besides all these matters in general we must grasp this point, that the principal disturbance in the minds of men arises because they think that these celestial bodies are blessed and immortal, and yet have wills and actions and motives inconsistent with these attributes; and because they are always expecting or imagining some everlasting misery, such as is depicted in legends, or even fear the loss of feeling in death as though it would concern them themselves; and, again, because they are brought to this pass not by reasoned opinion, but rather by some irrational presentiment, and therefore, as they do not know the limits of pain, they suffer a disturbance equally great or even more extensive than if they had reached this belief by opinion. But peace of mind is being delivered from all this, and having a constant memory of the general and most essential principles.

Wherefore we must pay attention to internal feelings and to external sensations in general and in particular, according as the subject is general or particular, and to every immediate intuition in accordance with each of the standards of judgement. For if we pay attention to these, we shall rightly trace the causes whence arose our mental disturbance and fear, and, by learning the true causes of celestial phenomena and all other occurrences that come to pass from time to time, we shall free ourselves from all which produces the utmost fear in other men.

Here, Herodotus, in my treatise on the chief points concerning the nature of the general principles, abridged so that my account would be easy to grasp with accuracy. I think that, even if one were unable to proceed to all the detailed particulars of the system, he would from this obtain an unrivalled strength compared with other men. For indeed he will clear up for himself many of the detailed points by reference to our general system, and these very principles, if he stores them in his mind, will constantly aid him. For such is their character that even those who are at present engaged in working out the details to a considerable degree, or even completely, will be able to carry out the greater part of their investigations into the nature of the whole by conducting their analysis in reference to such a survey as this. And as for all who are not fully among those on the way to being perfected, some of them can from this summary obtain a hasty view of the most important matters without oral instruction so as to secure peace of mind.

EPICURUS TO MENOECEUS

Let no one when young delay to study philosophy, nor when he is old grow weary of his study. For no one can come too early or too late to secure the health of his soul. And the man who says that the age for philosophy has either not yet come or has gone by is like the man who says that the age for happiness is not yet come to him, or has passed away. Wherefore both when young and old a man must study philosophy, that as he grows old he may be young in blessings through the grateful recollection of what has been, and that in youth he may be old as well, since he will know no fear of what is to come. We must then meditate on the things that make our happiness, seeing that when that is with us we have all, but when it is absent we do all to win it.

The things which I used unceasingly to commend to you, these do and practice, considering them to be the first principles of the good life. First of all believe that god is a being immortal and blessed, even as the common idea of a god is engraved on men's minds, and do not assign to him anything alien to his immortality or ill-suited to his blessedness: but believe about him everything that can uphold his blessedness and immortality. For gods there are, since the knowledge of them is by clear vision. But they are not such as the many believe them to be: for indeed they do not consistently represent them as they believe them to be. And the impious man is not he who denies the gods of the many, but he who attaches to the gods the beliefs of the many. For the statements of the many about the gods are not conceptions derived from sensation, but false suppositions, according to which the greatest misfortunes befall the wicked and the greatest blessings [the good] by the gift of the gods. For men being accustomed always to their own virtues welcome those like themselves, but regard all that is not of their nature as alien.

Become accustomed to the belief that death is nothing to us. For all good and evil consists in sensation, but death is deprivation of sensation. And therefore a right understanding that death is nothing to us makes the mortality of life enjoyable, not because it adds to it an infinite span of time, but because it takes away the craving for immortality. For there is nothing terrible in life for the man who has truly comprehended that there is nothing terrible in not living. So that the man speaks but idly who says that he fears death not because it will be painful when it comes, but because it is painful in anticipation. For that which gives no trouble when it comes, is but an empty pain in anticipation. So death, the most terrifying of ills, is nothing to us, since so long as we exist, death is not with us; but when death comes, then we do not exist. It does not then concern either the living or the dead, since for the former it is not, and the latter are no more.

But the many at one moment shun death as the greatest of evils, at another [yearn for it] as a respite from the [evils] in life. [But the wise man neither seeks to escape life] nor fears the cessation of life, for neither does life offend him nor does the absence of life seem to be any evil. And just as with food he does not seek simply the larger share and nothing else, but rather the most pleasant, so he seeks to enjoy not the longest period of time, but the most pleasant.

And he who counsels the young man to live well, but the old man to make a good end, is foolish, not merely because of the desirability of life, but also because it is the same training which teaches to live well and to die well. Yet much worse still is the man who says it is good not to be born, but "once born make haste to pass the gates of Death." For if he says this from conviction why does he not pass away out of life? For it is open to him to do so, if he had firmly made up his mind to this. But if he speaks in jest, his words are idle among men who cannot receive them.

We must then bear in mind that the future is neither ours, nor yet wholly not ours, so that we may not altogether expect it as sure to come, nor abandon hope of it, as if it will certainly not come.

We must consider that of desires some are natural, others vain, and of the natural some are necessary and others merely natural; and of the necessary some are necessary for happiness, others for the repose of the body, and others for very life. The right understanding of these facts enables us to refer all choice and avoidance to the health of the body and [the soul's] freedom from disturbance, since this is the aim of the life of blessedness. For it is to obtain this end that we always act, namely, to avoid pain and fear. And when this is once secured for us, all the tempest of the soul is dispersed, since the living creature has not to wander as though in search of something that is missing, and to look for some other thing by which he can fulfil the good of the soul and the good of the body. For it is then that we have need of pleasure, when we feel pain owing to the absence of pleasure; [but when we do not feel pain,] we no longer need pleasure. And for this cause we call pleasure the beginning and end of the blessed life. For we recognize pleasure as the first good innate in us, and from pleasure we begin every act of choice and avoidance, and to pleasure we return again, using the feeling as the standard by which we judge every good.

And since pleasure is the first good and natural to us, for this very reason we do not choose every pleasure, but sometimes we pass over many pleasures, when greater discomfort accrues to us as the result of them: and similarly we think many pains better than pleasures, since a greater pleasure comes to us when we have endured pains for a long time. Every pleasure then because of its natural kinship to us is good, yet not every pleasure is to be chosen: even as every pain also is an evil, yet not all are always of a nature to be avoided. Yet by a scale of comparison and by the consideration of advantages and disadvantages we must form our judgement on all these matters. For the good on certain occasions we treat as bad, and conversely the bad as good.

And again independence of desire we think a great good—not that we may at all times enjoy but a few things, but that, if we do not possess many, we may enjoy the few in the genuine persuasion that those have the sweetest pleasure in luxury who least need it, and that all that is natural is easy to be obtained, but that which is superfluous is hard. And so plain savours bring us a pleasure equal to a luxurious diet, when all the pain due to want is removed; and bread and water produce the highest pleasure, when one who needs them puts them to his lips. To grow accustomed therefore to simple and not luxurious diet gives us health to the full, and makes a man alert for the needful employments of life, and when after long intervals we approach luxuries disposes us better towards them, and fits us to be fearless of fortune.

When, therefore, we maintain that pleasure is the end, we do not mean the pleasures of profligates and those that consist in sensuality, as is supposed by some who are either ignorant or disagree with us or do not understand, but freedom from pain in the body and from trouble in the mind. For it is not continuous drinkings and revellings, nor the satisfaction of lusts, nor the enjoyment of fish and other luxuries of the wealthy table, which produce a pleasant life, but sober reasoning, searching out the motives for all choice and avoidance, and banishing mere opinions, to which are due the greatest disturbance of the spirit.

Of all this the beginning and the greatest good is prudence. Wherefore prudence is a more precious thing even than philosophy: for from prudence are sprung all the other virtues, and it teaches us that it is not possible to live pleasantly without living prudently and honourably and justly, [nor, again, to live a life of prudence, honour, and justice] without living pleasantly. For the virtues are by nature bound up with the pleasant life, and the pleasant life is inseparable from them. For indeed who, think you, is a better man than he who holds reverent opinions concerning the gods, and is at all times free from fear of death, and has reasoned out the end ordained by nature? He understands that the limit of good things is easy to fulfil and easy to attain, whereas the course of ills is either short in time or slight in pain: he laughs at [destiny], whom some have introduced as the mistress of all things. [He thinks that with us lies the chief power in determining events, some of which happen by necessity] and some by chance, and some are within our control; for while necessity cannot be called to account, he sees that chance is inconstant, but that which is in our control is subject to no master, and to it are naturally attached praise and blame. For, indeed, it were better to follow the myths about the gods than to become a slave to the destiny of the natural philosophers: for the former suggests a hope of placating the gods by worship, whereas the latter involves a necessity which knows no placation. As to chance, he does not regard it as a god as most men do (for in a god's acts there is no disorder), nor as an uncertain cause [of all things]: for he does not believe that good and evil are given by chance to man for the framing of a blessed life, but that opportunities for great good and great evil are afforded by it. He therefore thinks it better to be unfortunate in reasonable action than to prosper in unreason. For it is better in a man's actions that what is well chosen [should fail, rather than that what is ill chosen] should be successful owing to chance.

Meditate therefore on these things and things akin to them night and day by yourself, and with a companion like to yourself, and never shall you be disturbed waking or asleep, but you shall live like a god among men. For a man who lives among immortal blessings is not like to a mortal being.

EPICTETUS

20. *Stoicism*

Epictetus is thought to have been born in the Greek city of Hierapolis, in Phrygia, about A.D. 50. It is reported that as a child he was sold into slavery. In keeping with Roman practice, Epictetus was allowed to attend the lectures of a teacher of the Stoic philosophy which had developed from the school of Zeno (336–264 B.C.). After the death of his master he gained his freedom and became a teacher of philosophy. Although nothing has been preserved of the original writings of Epictetus, a disciple named Arrian transcribed and edited his ideas in eight volumes.

The Discourses of Epictetus

Arrian to Lucius Gellius, with wishes for his happiness

I neither wrote these Discourses of Epictetus in the way in which a man might write such things; nor did I make them public myself, inasmuch as I declare that I did not even write them. But whatever I heard him say, the same I attempted to write down in his own words as nearly as possible, for the purpose of preserving them as memorials to myself afterward of the thoughts and the freedom of speech of Epictetus. Accordingly

From *The Discourses of Epictetus* and *The Encheiridion, or Manual,* trans. George Long (New York: William L. Allison Co., 1899). Footnotes omitted.

the Discourses are naturally such as a man would address without preparation to another, not such as a man would write with the view of others reading them. Now, being such, I do not know how they fell into the hands of the public, without either my consent or my knowledge. But it concerns me little if I shall be considered incompetent to write; and it concerns Epictetus not at all if any man shall despise his words; for at the time when he uttered them, it was plain that he had no other purpose than to move the minds of his hearers to the best things. If, indeed, these Discourses should produce this effect, they will have, I think, the result which the words of philosophers ought to have. But if they shall not, let those who read them know that, when Epictetus delivered them, the hearer could not avoid being affected in the way that Epictetus wished him to be. But if the Discourses themselves, as they are written, do not effect this result, it may be that the fault is mine, or, it may be, that the thing is unavoidable. . . .

How a Man Should Proceed from the Principle of God Being the Father of All Men to the Rest

If a man should be able to assent to this doctrine as he ought, that we are all sprung from God in an especial manner, and that God is the father both of men and of gods, I suppose that he would never have any ignoble or mean thoughts about himself. But if Cæsar (the Emperor) should adopt you, no one could endure your arrogance; and if you know that you are the son of Zeus, will you not be elated? Yet we do not so; but since these two things are mingled in the generation of man, body in common with the animals, and reason and intelligence in common with the gods, many incline to this kinship, which is miserable and mortal; and some few to that which is divine and happy. Since then it is of necessity that every man uses everything according to the opinion which he has about it, those, the few, who think that they are formed for fidelity and modesty and a sure use of appearances have no mean or ignoble thoughts about themselves; but with the many it is quite the contrary. For they say, What am I? A poor, miserable man, with my wretched bit of flesh. Wretched, indeed; but you possess something better than your bit of flesh. Why then do you neglect that which is better, and why do you attach yourself to this?

Through this kinship with the flesh, some of us inclining to it become like wolves, faithless and treacherous and mischievous: some become like lions, savage and untamed; but the greater part of us become foxes and other worse animals. For what else is a slanderer and a malignant man than a fox, or some other more wretched and meaner animal? See then and take care that you do not become some one of these miserable things.

That the Deity Oversees All Things

When a person asked him how a man could be convinced that all his actions are under the inspection of God, he answered, Do you not think that all things are united in one? I do, the person replied. Well, do you not think that earthly things have a natural agreement and union with heavenly things? I do. And how else so regularly as if by God's command, when He bids the plants to flower, do they flower? when He bids them to send forth shoots, do they shoot? when He bids them to produce fruit, how else do they produce fruit? when He bids the fruit to ripen, does it ripen? when again He bids them to cast down the fruits, how else do they cast them down? and when to shed the leaves, do they shed the leaves? and when He bids them to fold themselves up and to remain quiet and rest, how else do they remain quiet and rest? And how else at the growth and the wane of the moon, and at the approach and recession of the sun, are so great an alteration and change to the contrary seen in earthly things? But are plants and our bodies so bound up and united with the whole, and are not our souls much more? and our souls so bound up and in contact with God as parts of Him and portions of Him; and does not God perceive every motion of these parts as being His own motion connate with Himself? Now are you able to think of the divine administration, and about all things divine, and at the same time also about human affairs, and to be moved by ten thousand things at the same time in your senses and in your understanding, and to assent to some, and to dissent from others, and again as to some things to suspend your judgment; and do you retain in your soul so many impressions from so many and various things, and being moved by them, do you fall upon notions similar to those first impressed, and do you retain numerous arts and the memories of ten thousand things; and is not God able to oversee all things, and to be present with all, and to receive from all a certain communication? And is the sun able to illuminate so large a part of the All, and to leave so little not illuminated, that part only which is occupied by the earth's shadow; and He who made the sun itself and makes it go round, being a small part of Himself compared with the whole, cannot He perceive all things?

But I cannot, the man may reply, comprehend all these things at once. But who tells you that you have equal power with Zeus? . . .

What Is the Nature of the Good?

God is beneficial. But the Good also is beneficial. It is consistent then that where the nature of God is, there also the nature of the good should be. What then is the nature of God? Flesh? Certainly not. An estate in land? By no means. Fame? No. Is it intelligence, knowledge, right reason? Yes. Herein then simply seek the nature of the good; for I suppose that you do not seek it in a plant. No. Do you seek it in an irrational animal? No. If then you seek it in a rational animal, why do you still seek it anywhere except in the superiority of rational over irrational animals? Now plants have not even the power of using appearances, and for this reason you do not apply the term good to them. The good then requires the use of appearances. Does it require this use only? For if you say that it requires this use only, say that the good, and that happiness and unhappiness are in irrational animals also. But you do not say this, and you do right; for if they possess even in the highest degree the use of appearances, yet they have not the faculty of understanding the use of appearances; and there is good reason for this, for they exist for the purpose of serving others, and they exercise no superiority. For the ass, I suppose, does not exist for any superiority over others. No; but because we had need of a back which is able to bear something; and in truth we had need also of his being able to walk, and for this reason he received also the faculty of making use of appearances, for otherwise he would not have been able to walk. And here then the matter stopped. For if he had also received the faculty of comprehending the use of appearances, it is plain that consistently with reason he would not then have been subjected to us, nor would he have done us these services, but he would have been equal to us and like to us.

Will you not then seek the nature of good in the rational animal? for if it is not there, you will not choose to say that it exists in any other thing (plant or animal). What then? are not plants and animals also the works of God? They are; but they are not superior things, nor yet parts of the gods. But you are a superior thing; you are a portion separated from the deity; you have in yourself a certain portion of him. Why then are you ignorant of your own noble descent? Why do you not know whence you came? will you not remember when you are eating, who you are who eat and whom you feed? When you are in conjunction with a woman, will you not remember who you are who do this thing? When you are in social intercourse, when you are exercising yourself, when you are engaged in discussion, know you not that you are nourishing a god, that you are exercising a god? Wretch, you are carrying about a god with you, and you know it not. Do you think that I mean some god of silver or of gold, and external? You carry him within yourself, and you perceive not that you are polluting him by impure thoughts and dirty deeds. And if an image of God were present, you would not dare to do any of the things which you are doing: but when God himself is present within and sees all and hears all, you are not ashamed of thinking such things and doing such things, ignorant as you are of your own nature and subject to the anger of God. . . .

Of the Things Which Are in Our Power, and Not in Our Power

Of all the faculties (except that which I shall soon mention), you will find not one which is capable of contemplating itself; and, consequently, not capable either of approving or disapproving. How far does the grammatic art possess the contemplating power? As far as forming a judgment about what is written and spoken. And how far music? As far as judging about melody. Does either of them then contemplate itself? By no means. But when you must write something to your friend, grammar will tell you what words you must write; but whether you should write or not, grammar will not tell you. And so it is with music as to musical sounds; but whether you should sing at the present time and play on the lute, or do neither, music will not tell you. What faculty then will tell you? That which contemplates both itself and all other things. And what is this faculty? The rational faculty; for this is the only faculty that we have received which examines itself, what it is, and what power it has, and what is the value of this gift, and examines all other faculties: for what else is there which tells us that golden things are beautiful, for they do not say so themselves? Evidently it is the faculty which is capable of judging of appearances. What else judges of music, grammar, and the other faculties, proves their uses and points out the occasions for using them? Nothing else.

As then it was fit to be so, that which is best of all and supreme over all is the only thing which the gods have placed in our power, the right use of appearances; but all other things they have not placed in our power. Was it because they did not choose? I indeed think that, if they had been able, they would have put these other things also in our power, but they certainly could not. For as we exist on the earth, and are bound to such a body and to such companions, how was it possible for us not to be hindered as to these things by externals?

But what says Zeus? Epictetus, if it were possible, I would have made both your little body and your little property free and not exposed to hindrance. But now be not ignorant of this: this body is not yours, but it is clay finely tempered. And since I was not able to do for you what I have mentioned, I have given you a small portion of us, this faculty of pursuing an object and avoiding it, and the faculty of desire and aversion, and, in a word, the faculty of using the appearances of things; and if you will take care of this faculty and consider it your only possession, you will never be hindered, never meet with impediments; you will not lament, you will not blame, you will not flatter any person.

Well, do these seem to you small matters? I hope not. Be content with them then and pray to the gods. But now when it is in our power to look after one thing, and to attach ourselves to it, we prefer to look after many things, and to be bound to many things, to the body and to property, and to brother and to friend, and to child and to slave. Since then we are bound to many things, we are depressed by them and dragged down. For this reason, when the weather is not fit for sailing, we sit down and torment ourselves, and continually look out to see what wind is blowing. It is north. What is that to us? When will the west wind blow? When it shall choose, my good man, or when it shall please Æolus; for God has not made you the manager of the winds, but Æolus. What then? We must make the best use that we can of the things which are in our power, and use the rest according to their nature. What is their nature then? As God may please. . . .

On the Power of Speaking

. . . Man, be neither ungrateful for these gifts nor yet forget the things which are superior to them. But indeed for the power of seeing and hearing, and indeed for life itself, and for the things which contribute to support it, for the fruits which are dry, and for wine and oil give thanks to God: but remember that he has given you something else better than all these, I mean the power of using them, proving them and estimating the value of each. For what is that which gives information about each of these powers, what each of them is worth? Is it each faculty itself? Did you ever hear the faculty of vision saying anything about itself? or the faculty of hearing? or wheat, or barley, or a horse or a dog? No; but they are appointed as ministers and slaves to serve the faculty which has the power of making use of the appearances of things. . . .

What then? it (the will) says, if the fact is so, can that which ministers be superior to that to which it ministers, can the horse be superior to the rider, or the dog to the huntsman, or the instrument to the musician, or the servants to the king? What is that which makes use of the rest? The will. What takes care of all? The will. What destroys the whole man, at one time by hunger, at another time by hanging, and at another time by a precipice? The will. Then is anything stronger in men than this? and how is it possible that the things which are subject to restraint are stronger than that which is not? What things are naturally formed to hinder the faculty of vision? Both will and things which do not depend on the faculty of the will. It is the same with the faculty of hearing, with the faculty of speaking in like manner. But what has a natural power of hindering the will? Nothing which is independent of the will; but only the will itself, when it is perverted. Therefore this (the will) is alone vice or alone virtue. . . .

What then? Does any man despise the other faculties? I hope not. Does any man say that there is no use or excellence in the speaking faculty? I hope not. That would be foolish, impious, ungrateful toward God. But a man renders to each thing its due value. For there is some use even in an ass, but not so much as in an ox: there is also use in a dog, but not so much as in a slave: there is also some use in a slave, but not so much as in citizens: there is also some use in citizens, but not so much as in magistrates. Not indeed because some things are superior, must we undervalue the use which other things have. There is a certain value in the power of speaking, but it is not so great as the power of the will. When then I speak thus, let no man think that I ask you to neglect the power of speaking, for neither do I ask you to neglect the eyes, nor the ears nor the hands nor the feet, nor clothing nor shoes. But if you ask me what then is the most excellent of all things, what must I say? I cannot say the power of speaking, but the power of the will, when it is right. For it is this which uses the other (the power of speaking), and all the other faculties both small and great. For when this faculty of the will is set right, a man who is not good becomes good: but when it fails, a man becomes bad. It is through this that we are unfortunate, that we are fortunate, that we blame one another, are pleased with one another.

How a Man on Every Occasion Can Maintain His Proper Character

To the rational animal only is the irrational intolerable; but that which is rational is tolerable. Blows are not naturally intolerable. How is that? See how the Lacedæmonians endure whipping when they have learned that whipping is consistent with reason. To hang yourself is not intolerable. When then you have the opinion that it is rational, you go and hang yourself. In short, if we observe, we shall find that the animal man is pained by nothing so much as by that which is irrational; and, on the contrary, attracted to nothing so much as to that which is rational.

But the rational and the irrational appear such in a different way to different persons, just as the good and the bad, the profitable and the unprofitable. For this reason, particularly, we need discipline, in order to learn how to adapt the preconception of the rational and the irrational to the several things conformably to nature. But in order to determine the rational and the irrational, we use not only the estimates of external things, but we consider also what is appropriate to each person. For to one man it is consistent with reason to hold a chamber pot for another, and to look to this only, that if he does not hold it, he will receive stripes, and he will not receive his food: but if he shall hold the pot, he will not suffer anything hard or disagreeable. But to another man not only does the holding of a chamber pot appear intolerable for himself, but intolerable also for him to allow another to do this office for him. If then you ask me whether you should hold the chamber pot or not, I shall say to you that the receiving of food is worth more than the not receiving of it, and the being scourged is a greater indignity than not being scourged; so that if you measure your interests by these things, go and hold the chamber pot. "But this," you say, "would not be worthy of me." Well, then, it is you who must introduce this consideration into the inquiry, not I; for it is you who know yourself, how much you are worth to yourself, and at what price you sell yourself; for men sell themselves at various prices. . . .

Some person asked, How then shall every man among us perceive what is suitable to his character? How, he replied, does the bull alone, when the lion has attacked, discover his own powers and put himself forward in defense of the whole herd? It is plain that with the powers the perception of having them is immediately conjoined; and, therefore, whoever of us has such powers will not be ignorant of them. Now a bull is not made suddenly, nor a brave man; but we must discipline ourselves in the winter for the summer campaign, and not rashly run upon that which does not concern us.

Only consider at what price you sell your own will; if for no other reason, at least for this, that you sell it not for a small sum. But that which is great and superior perhaps belongs to Socrates and such as are like him. Why then, if we are naturally such, are not a very great number of us like him? Is it true then that all horses become swift, that all dogs are skilled in tracking footprints? What, then, since I am naturally dull, shall I, for this reason, take no pains? I hope not. Epictetus is not superior to Socrates; but if he is not inferior, this is enough for me; for I shall never be a Milo, and yet I do not neglect my body; nor shall I be a Crœsus, and yet I do not neglect my property; nor, in a word, do we neglect looking after anything because we despair of reaching the highest degree.

How We May Discover the Duties of Life from Names

Consider who you are. In the first place, you are a man; and this is one who has nothing superior to the faculty of the will, but all other things subjected to it; and the faculty itself he possesses unenslaved and free from subjection. Consider then from what things you have been separated by reason. You have been separated from wild beasts: you have been separated from domestic animals. Further, you are a citizen of the world, and a part of it, not one of the subservient (serving), but one of the principal (ruling) parts, for you are capable of comprehending the divine administration and of considering the connection of things. What then does the character of a citizen promise (profess)? To hold nothing as profitable to himself; to deliberate about nothing as if he were detached from the community, but to act as the hand or foot would do, if they had reason and understood the constitution of nature, for they would never put themselves in motion nor desire anything otherwise than with reference to the whole. Therefore the philosophers say well, that if the good man had foreknowledge of what would happen, he would cooperate toward his own sickness and death and mutilation, since he knows that these things are assigned to him according to the universal arrangement, and that the whole is superior to the part, and the state to the citizen. But now because we do not know the future, it is our duty to stick to the things which are in their nature more suitable for our choice, for we were made among other things for this.

After this remember that you are a son. What does this character promise? To consider that everything which is the son's belongs to the father, to obey him in all things, never to blame him to another, nor to say or do anything which does him injury, to yield to him in all things and give way, cooperating with him as far as you can. After this know that you are a brother also, and that to this character it is due to make concessions; to be easily persuaded, to speak good of your brother, never to claim in opposition to him any of the things which are independent of the will, but readily to give them up, that you may have the larger share in what is dependent on the will. For see what a thing it is, in place of a lettuce, if it should so happen, or a seat, to gain for yourself goodness of disposition. How great is the advantage.

Next to this, if you are senator of any state, remember that you are a senator: if a youth, that you are a youth: if an old man, that you are an old man; for each of such names, if it comes to be examined, marks out the proper duties. . . .

What the Beginning of Philosophy Is

The beginning of philosophy, to him at least who enters on it in the right way and by the door, is a consciousness of his own weakness and inability about necessary things. For we come into the world with no natural notion of a right-angled triangle, or of a diesis (a quarter tone), or of a half tone; but we learn each of these things by a certain transmission according to art; and for this reason those who do not know them, do not think that they know them. But as to good and evil, and beautiful and ugly, and becoming and unbecoming, and happiness and misfortune, and proper and improper, and what we ought to do and what we ought not to do, who ever came into the world without having an innate idea of them? Wherefore we all use these names and we endeavor to fit the preconceptions to the several cases (things) thus: he has done well, he has not done well; he has done as he ought, not as he ought; he has been unfortunate, he has been fortunate; he is unjust, he is just: who does not use these names? who among us defers the use of them till he has learned them, as he defers the use of the words about lines (geometrical figures) or sounds? And the cause of this is that we come into the world already taught as it were by nature some things on this matter. . . .

In What a Man Ought to Be Exercised Who Has Made Proficiency; and That We Neglect the Chief Things

There are three things (topics) in which a man ought to exercise himself who would be wise and good. The first concerns the desires and the aversions, that a man may not fail to get what he desires, and that he may not fall into that which he does not desire. The second concerns the movements (toward an object) and the movements from an object, and generally in doing what a man ought to do, that he may act according to order, to reason, and not carelessly. The third thing concerns freedom from deception and rashness in judgment, and generally it concerns the assents. Of these topics the chief and the most urgent is that which relates to the affects (perturbations); for an affect is produced in no other way than by a failing to obtain that which a man desires or a falling into that which a man would wish to avoid. This is that which brings in perturbations, disorders, bad fortune, misfortunes, sorrows, lamentations and envy; that which makes men envious and jealous; and by these causes we are unable even to listen to the precepts of reason. The second topic concerns the duties of a man; for I ought not to be free from affects like a statue, but I ought to maintain the relations natural and acquired, as a pious man, as a son, as a father, as a citizen.

The third topic is that which immediately concerns those who are making proficiency, that which concerns the security of the other two, so that not even in sleep any appearance unexamined may surprise us, nor in intoxication, nor in melancholy. This, it may be said, is above our power. But the present philosophers neglecting the first topic and the second (the affects and duties), employ themselves on the third, using sophistical arguments, making conclusions from questioning, employing hypotheses, lying. For a man must, as it is said, when employed on these matters, take care that he is not deceived. Who must? The wise and good man. This then is all that is wanting to you. . . .

About Freedom

He is free who lives as he wishes to live; who is neither subject to compulsion nor to hindrance, nor to force; whose movements to action are not impeded, whose desires attain their purpose, and who does not fall into that which he would avoid. Who then chooses to live in error? No man.

Who chooses to live deceived, liable to mistake, unjust, unrestrained, discontented, mean? No man. Not one then of the bad lies as he wishes; nor is he then free. And who chooses to live in sorrow, fear, envy, pity, desiring and failing in his desires, attempting to avoid something and falling into it? Not one. Do we then find any of the bad free from sorrow, free from fear, who does not fall into that which he would avoid, and does not obtain that which he wishes? Not one; nor then do we find any bad man free.

If then a man who has been twice consul should hear this, if you add. But you are a wise man; this is nothing to you: he will pardon you. But if you tell him the truth, and say, You differ not at all from those who have been thrice sold as to being yourself not a slave, what else ought you to expect than blows? For he says, What, I a slave, I whose father was free, whose mother was free, I whom no man can purchase: I am also of senatorial rank, and a friend of Caesar, and I have been a consul, and I own many slaves. In the first place, most excellent senatorial man, perhaps your father also was a slave in the same kind of servitude, and your mother, and your grandfather and all your ancestors in an ascending series. But even if they were as free as it is possible, what is this to you? What if they were of a noble nature, and you of a mean nature; if they were fearless, and you a coward; if they had the power of self-restraint, and you are not able to exercise it.

And what, you may say, has this to do with being a slave? Does it seem to you to be nothing to do a thing unwillingly, with compulsion, with groans, has this nothing to do with being a slave? It is something, you say: but who is able to compel me, except the lord of all, Caesar? Then even you yourself have admitted that you have one master. But that he is the common master of all, as you say, let not this console you at all: but know that you are a slave in a great family. So also the people of Nicopolis are used to exclaim, By the fortune of Caesar, we are free.

However, if you please, let us not speak of Caesar at present. But tell me this: did you never love any person, a young girl, or slave, or free? What then is this with respect to being a slave or free? Were you never commanded by the person beloved to do something which you did not wish to do? have you never flattered your little slave? have you never kissed her feet? And yet if any man compelled you to kiss Caesar's feet, you would think it an insult and excessive tyranny. What else then is slavery? Did you never go out by night to some place whither you did not wish to go, did you not expend what you did not wish to expend, did you not utter words with sighs and groans, did you not submit to abuse and to be excluded? . . .

Well then let us recapitulate the things which have been agreed on. The man who is not under restraint is free, to whom things are exactly in that state in which he wishes them to be; but he who can be restrained or compelled or hindered, or thrown into any circumstances against his will, is a slave. But who is free from restraint? He who desires nothing that belongs to (is in the power of) others. And what are the things which belong to others? Those which are not in our power either to have or not to have, or to have of a certain kind or in a certain manner. Therefore the body belongs to another, the parts of the body belong to another, possession (property) belongs to another. If then you are attached to any of these things as your own, you will pay the penalty which it is proper for him to pay who desires what belongs to another. This road leads to freedom, this is the only way of escaping from slavery, to be able to say at last with all your soul:

> Lead me, O Zeus, and thou O destiny,
> The way that I am bid by you to go.

That We Ought Not to Be Disturbed by Any News

When anything shall be reported to you which is of a nature to disturb, have this principle in readiness, that the news is about nothing which is within the power of your will. Can any man report to you that you have formed a bad opinion, or had a bad desire? By no means. But perhaps he will report that some person is dead. What then is that to you? He may report that some person speaks ill of you. What then is that to you? Or that your father is planning something or other. Against whom? Against your will? How can he? But is it against your poor body, against your little property? You are quite safe: it is not against you. But the judge declares that you have committed an act of impiety. And did not the judges make the same declaration against Socrates? Does it concern you that the judge has made this declaration? No. Why then do you trouble yourself any longer about it? Your father has a certain duty, and if he shall not fulfill it, he loses the character of a father, of a man of natural affection, of gentleness. Do not wish him to lose anything else on this account. For never does a man do wrong in one thing, and suffer in another. On the other side it is your duty to make your defense firmly, modestly, without anger: but if you do not, you also lose the character of a son, of a man of modest behavior, of generous character. Well then, is the judge free from danger? No; but he also is in equal danger. Why then are you still afraid of his decision? What have you to do with that which is another man's evil? It is your own evil to make a bad defense: be on your guard against this only. But to be condemned or not to be condemned, as that is the act of another person, so it is the evil of another person. A certain person threatens you. Me? No. He blames you. Let him see how he manages his own affairs. He is going to condemn you unjustly. He is a wretched man.

Against Those Who on Account of Sickness Go Away Home

I am sick here, said one of the pupils, and I wish to return home. At home, I suppose, you were free from sickness. Do you not consider whether you are doing anything here which may be useful to the exercise of your will, that it may be corrected? For if you are doing nothing toward this end, it was to no purpose that you came. Go away. Look after your affairs at home. . . .

The Encheiridion, or Manual

I

Of things some are in our power, and others are not. In our power are opinion, movement toward a thing, desire, aversion (turning from a thing); and in a word, whatever are our own acts: not in our power are the body, property, reputation, offices (magisterial power), and in a word whatever are not our own acts. And the things in our power are by nature free, not subject to restraint nor hindrance: but the things not in our power are weak, slavish, subject to restraint, in the power of others. Remember then that if you think the things which are by nature slavish to be free, and the things which are in the power of others to be your own, you will be hindered, you will lament, you will be disturbed, you will blame both gods and men: but if you think that only which is your own to be your own, and you think that what is another's, as it really is, belongs to another, no man will ever compel you, no man will hinder you, you will never blame any man, you will accuse no man, you will do nothing involuntarily (against my will), no man will harm you, you will have no enemy, for you will not suffer any harm.

If then you desire (aim at) such great things, remember that you must not (attempt to) lay hold of them with a small effort; but you must leave alone some things entirely, and postpone others for the present. But if you wish for these things also (such great things), and power (office) and wealth, perhaps you will not gain even these very things (power and wealth) because you aim also at those former things (such great things): certainly you will fail in those things through which alone happiness and freedom are secured. Straightway then practice saying to every harsh appearance, You are an appearance, and in no manner what you appear to be. Then examine it by the rules which you possess, and by this first and chiefly, whether it relates to the things which are in our power or to the things which are not in our power: and if it relates to anything which is not in our power, be ready to say, that it does not concern you.

II

Remember that desire contains in it the profession (hope) of obtaining that which you desire; and the profession (hope) in aversion (turning from a thing) is that you will not fall into that which you attempt to avoid; and he who fails in his desire is unfortunate; and he who falls into that which he would avoid is unhappy. If then you attempt to avoid only the things contrary to nature which are within your power, you will not be involved in any of the things which you would avoid. But if you attempt to avoid disease or death or poverty, you will be unhappy. Take away then aversion from all things which are not in our power, and transfer it to the things contrary to nature which are in our power. But destroy desire completely for the present. For if you desire anything which is not in our power, you must be unfortunate: but of the things in our power, and which it would be good to desire, nothing yet is before you. But employ only the power of moving toward an object and retiring from it; and these powers indeed only slightly and with exceptions and with remission. . . .

V

Men are disturbed not by the things which happen, but by the opinions about the things: for example, death is nothing terrible, for if it were, it would have seemed so to Socrates; for the opinion about death, that it is terrible, is the terrible thing. When then we are impeded or disturbed or grieved, let us never blame others, but ourselves, that is, our opinions. It is the act of an ill-instructed man to blame others for his own bad condition; it is the act of one who has begun to be instructed, to lay the blame on himself; and of one whose instruction is completed, neither to blame another, nor himself. . . .

VIII

Seek not that the things which happen should happen as you wish; but wish the things which happen to be as they are, and you will have a tranquil flow of life.

IX

Disease is an impediment to the body, but not to the will, unless the will itself chooses. Lameness is an impediment to the leg, but not to the will. And add this reflection on the occasion of everything that happens; for you will find it an impediment to something else, but not to yourself. . . .

XVI

When you see a person weeping in sorrow either when a child goes abroad or when he is dead, or when the man has lost his property, take care that the appearance do not hurry you away with it, as if he were suffering in external things. But straightway make a distinction in your own mind, and be in readiness to say, it is not that which has happened that afflicts this man, for it does not afflict another, but it is the opinion about this thing which afflicts the man. So far as words then do not be unwilling to show him sympathy, and even if it happens so, to lament with him. But take care that you do not lament internally also.

XVII

Remember that thou art an actor in a play of such a kind as the teacher (author) may choose; if short, of a short one; if long, of a long one: if he wishes you to act the part of a poor man, see that you act the part naturally; if the part of a lame man, of a magistrate, of a private person (do the same). For this is your duty, to act well the part that is given to you; but to select the part, belongs to another. . . .

XXXIV

If you have received the impression of any pleasure, guard yourself against being carried away by it; but let the thing wait for you, and allow yourself a certain delay on your own part. Then think of both times, of the time when you will enjoy the pleasure, and of the time after the enjoyment of the pleasure when you will repent and will reproach yourself. And set against these things how you will rejoice if you have abstained from the pleasure, and how you will commend yourself. But if it seem to you seasonable to undertake (do) the thing, take care that the charm of it, and the pleasure, and the attraction of it shall not conquer you: but set on the other side the consideration how much better it is to be conscious that you have gained this victory.

CX

A man should choose (pursue) not every pleasure, but the pleasure which leads to goodness.

CXI

It is the part of a wise man to resist pleasures, but of a foolish man to be a slave to them.

CXII

Pleasure, like a kind of bait, is thrown before (in front of) everything which is really bad, and easily allures greedy souls.

CXIII

Choose rather to punish your appetites than to be punished through them.

CXIV

No man is free who is not master of himself.

CXV

The vine bears three bunches of grapes: the first is that of pleasure, the second of drunkenness, the third of violence.

CXVI

Over your wine do not talk much to display your learning; for you will utter bilious stuff.

🌼 THE HOLY SCRIPTURES

SAINT AUGUSTINE

21. The Judaeo-Christian Tradition

The Judaeo-Christian tradition is represented by selections from three sources. Part One is from the books of Genesis and Exodus, Part Two is from the Gospel of Matthew, and Part Three is from the writings of Saint Augustine. Aurelius Augustine (A.D. 354–430) was born at Thagaste, in North Africa. His career as a teacher of rhetoric took him to Italy, where he eventually was converted to Christianity. He entered the priesthood in 391 and within four years he became Bishop of Hippo. He used his knowledge of Greek philosophy and his talent as a writer in the service of the Church. Today he is recognized as the foremost Christian theologian in the ancient world.

Part One*

Genesis, Chapter One

In the beginning God created the heaven and the earth.

2 And the earth was without form, and void; and darkness *was* upon the face of the deep. And the Spirit of God moved upon the face of the waters.

3 And God said, Let there be light: and there was light.

4 And God saw the light, that *it was* good: and God divided the light from the darkness.

5 And God called the light Day, and the darkness he called Night. And the evening and the morning were the first day.

6 ¶ And God said, Let there be a firmament in the midst of the waters, and let it divide the waters from the waters.

7 And God made the firmament, and divided the waters which *were* under the firmament from the waters which *were* above the firmament: and it was so.

8 And God called the firmament Heaven. And the evening and the morning were the second day.

9 ¶ And God said, Let the waters under the heaven be gathered together unto one place, and let the dry *land* appear: and it was so.

10 And God called the dry *land* Earth; and the gathering together of the waters called the seas: and God saw that *it was* good.

11 And God said, Let the earth bring forth grass, the herb yielding seed, *and* the fruit tree yielding fruit after his kind, whose seed *is* in itself, upon the earth: and it was so.

*Part One of this selection is from *Genesis*, Chapters 1–3, and *Exodus*, Chapters 19–24. This is the King James translation.

12 And the earth brought forth grass, *and* herb yielding seed after his kind, and the tree yielding fruit, whose seed *was* in itself, after his kind: and God saw that *it was* good.

13 And the evening and the morning were the third day.

14 ¶ And God said, Let there be lights in the firmament of the heaven to divide the day from the night; and let them be for signs, and for seasons, and for days, and years:

15 And let them be for lights in the firmament of the heaven to give light upon the earth: and it was so.

16 And God made two great lights; the greater light to rule the day, and the lesser light to rule the night: *he made* the stars also.

17 And God set them in the firmament of the heaven to give light upon the earth,

18 And to rule over the day and over the night, and to divide the light from the darkness: and God saw that *it was* good.

19 And the evening and the morning were the fourth day.

20 And God said, Let the waters bring forth abundantly the moving creature that hath life, and fowl *that* may fly above the earth in the open firmament of heaven.

21 And God created great whales, and every living creature that moveth, which the waters brought forth abundantly, after their kind, and every winged fowl after his kind: and God saw that *it was* good.

22 And God blessed them, saying, Be fruitful, and multiply, and fill the waters in the seas, and let fowl multiply in the earth.

23 And the evening and the morning were the fifth day.

24 ¶ And God said, Let the earth bring forth the living creature after his kind, cattle, and creeping thing, and beast of the earth after his kind: and it was so.

25 And God made the beast of the earth after his kind, and cattle after their kind, and every thing that creepeth upon the earth after his kind: and God saw that *it was* good.

26 ¶ And God said, Let us make man in our image, after our likeness: and let them have dominion over the fish of the sea, and over the fowl of the air, and over the cattle, and over all the earth, and over every creeping thing that creepeth upon the earth.

27 So God created man in his *own* image, in the image of God created he him; male and female created he them.

28 And God blessed them, and God said unto them, Be fruitful, and multiply, and replenish the earth, and subdue it: and have dominion over the fish of the sea, and over the fowl of the air, and over every living thing that moveth upon the earth. . . .

Genesis, Chapter Two

. . . 8 ¶ And the Lord God planted a garden eastward in Eden; and there he put the man whom he had formed.

9 And out of the ground made the Lord God to grow every tree

that is pleasant to the sight, and good for food; the tree of life also in the midst of the garden, and the tree of knowledge of good and evil. . . .

15 And the LORD God took the man, and put him into the garden of Eden to dress it and to keep it.

16 And the LORD God commanded the man, saying, Of every tree of the garden thou mayest freely eat:

17 But of the tree of the knowledge of good and evil, thou shalt not eat of it: for in the day that thou eatest thereof thou shalt surely die.

18 ¶ And the LORD God said, *It is* not good that the man should be alone; I will make him a help meet for him.

19 And out of the ground the LORD God formed every beast of the field, and every fowl of the air; and brought *them* unto Adam to see what he would call them: and whatsoever Adam called every living creature, that *was* the name thereof.

20 And Adam gave names to all cattle, and to the fowl of the air, and to every beast of the field; but for Adam there was not found a help meet for him.

21 And the LORD God caused a deep sleep to fall upon Adam, and he slept; and he took one of his ribs, and closed up the flesh instead thereof.

22 And the rib, which the LORD God had taken from the man, made he a woman, and brought her unto the man.

23 And Adam said, This *is* now bone of my bones, and flesh of my flesh: she shall be called Woman, because she was taken out of man.

24 Therefore shall a man leave his father and his mother, and shall cleave unto his wife: and they shall be one flesh.

25 And they were both naked, the man and his wife, and were not ashamed.

Genesis, Chapter Three

Now the serpent was more subtile than any beast of the field which the LORD God had made. And he said unto the woman, Yea, hath God said, Ye shall not eat of every tree of the garden?

2 And the woman said unto the serpent, We may eat of the fruit of the trees of the garden:

3 But of the fruit of the tree which *is* in the midst of the garden, God hath said, Ye shall not eat of it, neither shall ye touch it, lest ye die.

4 And the serpent said unto the woman, Ye shall not surely die:

5 For God doth know that in the day ye eat thereof, then your eyes shall be opened, and ye shall be as gods, knowing good and evil.

6 And when the woman saw that the tree *was* good for food, and that it *was* pleasant to the eyes, and a tree to be desired to make *one* wise, she took of the fruit thereof, and did eat, and gave also unto her husband with her; and he did eat.

7 And the eyes of them both were opened, and they knew that they *were* naked; and they sewed fig leaves together, and made themselves aprons.

8 And they heard the voice of the LORD God walking in the garden in the cool of the day: and Adam and his wife hid themselves from the presence of the LORD God amongst the trees of the garden.

9 And the LORD God called unto Adam, and said unto him, Where *art* thou?

10 And he said, I heard thy voice in the garden, and I was afraid, because I *was* naked; and I hid myself.

11 And he said, Who told thee that thou *wast* naked? Hast thou eaten of the tree, whereof I commanded thee that thou shouldest not eat?

12 And the man said, The woman whom thou gavest *to be* with me, she gave me of the tree, and I did eat.

13 And the LORD God said unto the woman, What *is* this *that* thou hast done? And the woman said, The serpent beguiled me, and I did eat.

14 And the LORD God said unto the serpent, Because thou hast done this, thou *art* cursed above all cattle, and above every beast of the field; upon thy belly shalt thou go, and dust shalt thou eat all the days of thy life:

15 And I will put enmity between thee and the woman, and between thy seed and her seed; it shall bruise thy head, and thou shalt bruise his heel.

16 Unto the woman he said, I will greatly multiply thy sorrow and thy conception; in sorrow thou shalt bring forth children; and thy desire *shall be* to thy husband, and he shall rule over thee.

17 And unto Adam he said, Because thou hast hearkened unto the voice of thy wife, and hast eaten of the tree, of which I commanded thee, saying, Thou shalt not eat of it: cursed *is* the ground for thy sake; in sorrow shalt thou eat *of* it all the days of thy life;

18 Thorns also and thistles shall it bring forth to thee; and thou shalt eat the herb of the field:

19 In the sweat of thy face shalt thou eat bread, till thou return unto the ground; for out of it wast thou taken: for dust thou *art,* and unto dust shalt thou return.

20 And Adam called his wife's name Eve; because she was the mother of all living.

21 Unto Adam also and to his wife did the LORD God make coats of skins, and clothed them.

22 ¶ And the LORD God said, Behold, the man is become as one of us, to know good and evil: and now, lest he put forth his hand, and take also of the tree of life, and eat, and live for ever:

23 Therefore the LORD God sent him forth from the garden of Eden, to till the ground from whence he was taken.

24 So he drove out the man: and he placed at the east of the garden of Eden cherubim, and a flaming sword which turned every way, to keep the way of the tree of life. . . .

Exodus, Chapter Nineteen

In the third month, when the children of Israel were gone forth out of the land of Egypt, the same day came they *into* the wilderness of Sinai.

2 For they were departed from Rephidim, and were come *to* the desert of Sinai, and had pitched in the wilderness; and there Israel camped before the mount.

3 And Moses went up unto God, and the LORD called unto him out of the mountain, saying, Thus shalt thou say to the house of Jacob, and tell the children of Israel;

4 Ye have seen what I did unto the Egyptians, and *how* I bare you on eagles' wings, and brought you unto myself.

5 Now therefore, if ye will obey my voice indeed, and keep my covenant, then ye shall be a peculiar treasure unto me above all people: for all the earth *is* mine:

6 And ye shall be unto me a kingdom of priests, and a holy nation. These *are the* words which thou shalt speak unto the children of Israel.

7 ¶ And Moses came and called for the elders of the people, and laid before their faces all these words which the LORD commanded him.

8 And all the people answered together, and said, All that the LORD hath spoken we will do. And Moses returned the words of the people unto the LORD.

9 And the LORD said unto Moses, Lo, I come unto thee in a thick cloud, that the people may hear when I speak with thee, and believe thee for ever. And Moses told the words of the people unto the LORD.

10 ¶ And the LORD said unto Moses, Go unto the people, and sanctify them to day and to morrow, and let them wash their clothes,

11 And be ready against the third day: for the third day the LORD will come down in the sight of all the people upon mount Sinai.

12 And thou shalt set bounds unto the people round about, saying, Take heed to yourselves, *that ye* go *not* up into the mount, or touch the border of it: whosoever toucheth the mount shall be surely put to death:

13 There shall not a hand touch it, but he shall surely be stoned, or shot through; whether *it be* beast or man, it shall not live: when the trumpet soundeth long, they shall come up to the mount.

14 ¶ And Moses went down from the mount unto the people, and sanctified the people; and they washed their clothes.

15 And he said unto the people, Be ready against the third day: come not at *your* wives.

16 ¶ And it came to pass on the third day in the morning, that there were thunders and lightnings, and a thick cloud upon the mount, and the voice of the trumpet exceeding loud; so that all the people that *was* in the camp trembled.

17 And Moses brought forth the people out of the camp to meet with God; and they stood at the nether part of the mount.

18 And mount Sinai was altogether on a smoke, because the LORD descended upon it in fire: and the smoke thereof ascended as the smoke of a furnace, and the whole mount quaked greatly.

19 And when the voice of the trumpet sounded long, and waxed louder and louder, Moses spake, and God answered him by a voice.

20 And the LORD came down upon mount Sinai, on the top of the mount: and the LORD called Moses *up* to the top of the mount; and Moses went up.

21 And the LORD said unto Moses, Go down, charge the people, lest they break through unto the LORD to gaze, and many of them perish.

22 And let the priests also, which come near to the LORD, sanctify themselves, lest the LORD break forth upon them.

23 And Moses said unto the LORD, The people cannot come up to mount Sinai: for thou chargedst us, saying, Set bounds about the mount, and sanctify it

24 And the LORD said unto him, Away, get thee down, and thou shalt come up, thou, and Aaron with thee: but let not the priests and the people break through to come up unto the LORD, lest he break forth upon them.

25 So Moses went down unto the people, and spake unto them.

Exodus, Chapter Twenty

And God spake all these words, saying,

2 I *am* the LORD thy God, which have brought thee out of the land of Egypt, out of the house of bondage.

3 Thou shalt have no other gods before me.

4 Thou shalt not make unto thee any graven image, or any likeness *of any thing* that *is* in heaven above, or that *is* in the earth beneath, or that *is* in the water under the earth:

5 Thou shalt not bow down thyself to them, nor serve them: for I the LORD thy God *am* a jealous God, visiting the iniquity of the fathers upon the children unto the third and fourth *generation* of them that hate me;

6 And shewing mercy unto thousands of them that love me, and keep my commandments.

7 Thou shalt not take the name of the LORD thy God in vain: for the LORD will not hold him guiltless that taketh his name in vain.

8 Remember the sabbath day, to keep it holy.

9 Six days shalt thou labour, and do all thy work:

10 But the seventh day *is* the sabbath of the LORD thy God: *in it* thou shalt not do any work, thou, nor thy son, nor thy daughter, thy manservant, nor thy maidservant, nor thy cattle, nor thy stranger that *is* within thy gates:

11 For *in* six days the LORD made heaven and earth, the sea, and all that in them *is,* and rested the seventh day: wherefore the LORD blessed the sabbath day, and hallowed it.

12 ¶ Honour thy father and thy mother: that thy days may be long upon the land which the Lord thy God giveth thee.

13 Thou shalt not kill.

14 Thou shalt not commit adultery

15 Thou shalt not steal.

16 Thou shalt not bear false witness against thy neighbour.

17 Thou shalt not covet thy neighbour's house, thou shalt not covet thy neighbour's wife, nor his manservant, nor his maidservant, nor his ox, nor his ass, nor any thing that *is* thy neighbour's.

18 ¶ And all the people saw the thunderings, and the lightnings, and the noise of the trumpet, and the mountain smoking: and when the people saw *it*, they removed, and stood afar off.

19 And they said unto Moses, Speak thou with us, and we will hear: but let not God speak with us, lest we die.

20 And Moses said unto the people, Fear not: for God is come to prove you, and that his fear may be before your faces, that ye sin not.

21 And the people stood afar off, and Moses drew near unto the thick darkness where God *was*.

22 ¶ And the Lord said unto Moses, Thus thou shalt say unto the children of Israel, Ye have seen that I have talked with you from heaven.

23 Ye shall not make with me gods of silver, neither shall ye make unto you gods of gold.

24 ¶ An altar of earth thou shalt make unto me, and shalt sacrifice thereon thy burnt offerings, and thy peace offerings, thy sheep, and thine oxen: in all places where I record my name I will come unto thee, and I will bless thee.

25 And if thou wilt make me an altar of stone, thou shalt not build it of hewn stone: for if thou lift up thy tool upon it, thou hast polluted it.

26 Neither shalt thou go up by steps unto mine altar, that thy nakedness be not discovered thereon.

Exodus, Chapter Twenty-one

Now these *are* the judgments which thou shalt set before them.

2 If thou buy a Hebrew servant, six years he shall serve: and in the seventh he shall go out free for nothing.

3 If he came in by himself, he shall go out by himself: if he were married, then his wife shall go out with him.

4 If his master have given him a wife, and she have borne him sons or daughters; the wife and her children shall be her master's, and he shall go out by himself.

5 And if the servant shall plainly say, I love my master, my wife, and my children; I will not go out free:

6 Then his master shall bring him unto the judges; he shall also bring him to the door, or unto the door post; and his master shall bore his ear through with an awl; and he shall serve him for ever.

7 ¶ And if a man sell his daughter to be a maidservant, she shall not go out as the menservants do.

8 If she please not her master, who hath betrothed her to himself, then shall he let her be redeemed: to sell her unto a strange nation he shall have no power, seeing he hath dealt deceitfully with her.

9 And if he have betrothed her unto his son, he shall deal with her after the manner of daughters.

10 If he take him another *wife,* her food, her raiment, and her duty of marriage, shall he not diminish.

11 And if he do not these three unto her, then shall she go out free without money.

12 ¶ He that smiteth a man, so that he die, shall be surely put to death.

13 And if a man lie not in wait, but God deliver *him* into his hand; then I will appoint thee a place whither he shall flee.

14 But if a man come presumptuously upon his neighbour, to slay him with guile; thou shalt take him from mine altar, that he may die.

15 ¶ And he that smiteth his father, or his mother, shall be surely put to death.

16 ¶ And he that stealeth a man, and selleth him, or if he be found in his hand, he shall surely be put to death.

17 ¶ And he that curseth his father, or his mother, shall surely be put to death.

18 ¶ And if men strive together, and one smite another with a stone, or with *his* fist, and he die not, but keepeth *his* bed:

19 If he rise again, and walk abroad upon his staff, then shall he that smote *him* be quit: only he shall pay *for* the loss of his time, and shall cause *him* to be thoroughly healed.

20 ¶ And if a man smite his servant, or his maid, with a rod, and he die under his hand; he shall be surely punished.

21 Notwithstanding, if he continue a day or two, he shall not be punished: for he *is* his money.

22 ¶ If men strive, and hurt a woman with child, so that her fruit depart *from her,* and yet no mischief follow: he shall be surely punished, according as the woman's husband will lay upon him; and he shall pay as the judges *determine.*

23 And if *any* mischief follow, then thou shalt give life for life,

24 Eye for eye, tooth for tooth, hand for hand, foot for foot,

25 Burning for burning, wound for wound, stripe for stripe.

26 ¶ And if a man smite the eye of his servant, or the eye of his maid, that it perish; he shall let him go free for his eye's sake.

27 And if he smite out his manservant's tooth, or his maidservant's tooth; he shall let him go free for his tooth's sake.

28 ¶ If an ox gore a man or a woman, that they die: then the ox shall be surely stoned, and his flesh shall not be eaten; but the owner of the ox *shall be* quit.

29 But if the ox were wont to push with his horn in time past, and it hath been testified to his owner, and he hath not kept him in, but that he hath killed a man or a woman; the ox shall be stoned, and his owner also shall be put to death.

30 If there be laid on him a sum of money, then he shall give for the ransom of his life whatsoever is laid upon him.

31 Whether he have gored a son, or have gored a daughter, according to this judgment shall it be done unto him.

32 If the ox shall push a manservant or a maidservant; he shall give unto their master thirty shekels of silver, and the ox shall be stoned.

33 ¶ And if a man shall open a pit, or if a man shall dig a pit, and not cover it, and an ox or an ass fall therein;

34 The owner of the pit shall make *it* good, *and* give money unto the owner of them; and the dead *beast* shall be his.

35 ¶ And if one man's ox hurt another's, that he die; then they shall sell the live ox, and divide the money of it; and the dead *ox* also they shall divide.

36 Or if it be known that the ox hath used to push in time past, and his owner hath not kept him in; he shall surely pay ox for ox; and the dead shall be his own.

Exodus, Chapter Twenty-two

If a man shall steal an ox, or a sheep, and kill it, or sell it; he shall restore five oxen for an ox, and four sheep for a sheep.

2 ¶ If a thief be found breaking up, and be smitten that he die, *there shall* no blood *be shed* for him.

3 If the sun be risen upon him, *there shall be* blood *shed* for him; *for* he should make full restitution: if he have nothing, then he shall be sold for his theft.

4 If the theft be certainly found in his hand alive, whether it be ox, or ass, or sheep; he shall restore double.

5 ¶ If a man shall cause a field or vineyard to be eaten, and shall put in his beast, and shall feed in another man's field; of the best of his own field, and of the best of his own vineyard, shall he make restitution.

6 ¶ If fire break out, and catch in thorns, so that the stacks of corn, or the standing corn, or the field, be consumed *therewith;* he that kindled the fire shall surely make restitution.

7 ¶ If a man shall deliver unto his neighbour money or stuff to keep, and it be stolen out of the man's house; if the thief be found, let him pay double.

8 If the thief be not found, then the master of the house shall be brought unto the judges, *to see* whether he have put his hand unto his neighbour's goods.

9 For all manner of trespass, *whether it be* for ox, for ass, for sheep, for raiment, *or* for any manner of lost thing, which *another* challengeth to

be his, the cause of both parties shall come before the judges; *and* whom the judges shall condemn, he shall pay double unto his neighbour.

10 If a man deliver unto his neighbour an ass, or an ox, or a sheep, or any beast, to keep; and it die, or be hurt, or driven away, no man seeing *it:*

11 *Then* shall an oath of the Lord be between them both, that he hath not put his hand unto his neighbour's goods; and the owner of it shall accept *thereof,* and he shall not make *it* good.

12 And if it be stolen from him, he shall make restitution unto the owner thereof.

13 If it be torn in pieces, *then* let him bring it *for* witness, *and* he shall not make good that which was torn.

14 ¶ And if a man borrow *aught* of his neighbour, and it be hurt, or die, the owner thereof *being* not with it, he shall surely make *it* good.

15 *But* if the owner thereof *be* with it, he shall not make *it* good: if it *be* a hired *thing,* it came for his hire.

16 ¶ And if a man entice a maid that is not betrothed, and lie with her, he shall surely endow her to be his wife.

17 If her father utterly refuse to give her unto him, he shall pay money according to the dowry of virgins.

18 ¶ Thou shalt not suffer a witch to live

19 ¶ Whosoever lieth with a beast shall surely be put to death.

20 ¶ He that sacrificeth unto *any* god, save unto the Lord only, he shall be utterly destroyed.

21 ¶ Thou shalt neither vex a stranger, nor oppress him: for ye were strangers in the land of Egypt.

22 ¶ Ye shall not afflict any widow, or fatherless child.

23 If thou afflict them in any wise, and they cry at all unto me, I will surely hear their cry;

24 And my wrath shall wax hot, and I will kill you with the sword; and your wives shall be widows, and your children fatherless.

25 ¶ If thou lend money to *any of* my people *that is* poor by thee, thou shalt not be to him as a usurer, neither shalt thou lay upon him usury.

26 If thou at all take thy neighbour's raiment to pledge, thou shalt deliver it unto him by that the sun goeth down:

27 For that *is* his covering only, it *is* his raiment for his skin: wherein shall he sleep? and it shall come to pass, when he crieth unto me, that I will hear; for I *am* gracious.

28 ¶ Thou shalt not revile the gods, nor curse the ruler of thy people.

29 ¶ Thou shalt not delay *to offer* the first of thy ripe fruits, and of thy liquors: the firstborn of thy sons shalt thou give unto me.

30 Likewise shalt thou do with thine oxen, *and* with thy sheep: seven days it shall be with his dam; on the eighth day thou shalt give it me.

31 ¶ And ye shall be holy men unto me: neither shall ye eat *any* flesh *that is* torn of beasts in the field; ye shall cast it to the dogs.

Exodus, Chapter Twenty-three

Thou shalt not raise a false report: put not thine hand with the wicked to be an unrighteous witness.

2 ¶ Thou shalt not follow a multitude to *do* evil; neither shalt thou speak in a cause to decline after many to wrest *judgment:*

3 ¶ Neither shalt thou countenance a poor man in his cause.

4 ¶ If thou meet thine enemy's ox or his ass going astray, thou shalt surely bring it back to him again.

5 If thou see the ass of him that hateth thee lying under his burden, and wouldest forbear to help him, thou shalt surely help with him.

6 Thou shalt not wrest the judgment of thy poor in his cause.

7 Keep thee far from a false matter; and the innocent and righteous slay thou not: for I will not justify the wicked.

8 ¶ And thou shalt take no gift: for the gift blindeth the wise, and perverteth the words of the righteous.

9 ¶ Also thou shalt not oppress a stranger: for ye know the heart of a stranger, seeing ye were strangers in the land of Egypt.

10 And six years thou shalt sow thy land, and shalt gather in the fruits thereof:

11 But the seventh *year* thou shalt let it rest and lie still; that the poor of thy people may eat: and what they leave the beasts of the field shall eat. In like manner thou shalt deal with thy vineyard, *and* with thy olive-yard.

12 Six days thou shalt do thy work, and on the seventh day thou shalt rest: that thine ox and thine ass may rest, and the son of thy hand-maid, and the stranger, may be refreshed.

13 And in all *things* that I have said unto you be circumspect: and make no mention of the name of other gods, neither let it be heard out of thy mouth.

14 ¶ Three times thou shalt keep a feast unto me in the year.

15 Thou shalt keep the feast of unleavened bread: (thou shalt eat unleavened bread seven days, as I commanded thee, in the time appointed of the month Abib; for in it thou camest out from Egypt: and none shall appear before me empty:)

16 And the feast of harvest, the firstfruits of thy labours, which thou hast sown in the field: and the feast of ingathering, *which is* in the end of the year, when thou hast gathered in thy labours out of the field.

17 Three times in the year all thy males shall appear before the Lord GOD.

18 Thou shalt not offer the blood of my sacrifice with leavened bread; neither shall the fat of my sacrifice remain until the morning.

19 The first of the firstfruits of thy land thou shalt bring into the house of the LORD thy God. Thou shalt not seethe a kid in his mother's milk.

20 ¶ Behold, I send an Angel before thee, to keep thee in the way, and to bring thee into the place which I have prepared.

21 Beware of him, and obey his voice, provoke him not; for he will not pardon your transgressions: for my name *is* in him.

22 But if thou shalt indeed obey his voice, and do all that I speak; then I will be an enemy unto thine enemies, and an adversary unto thine adversaries.

23 For mine Angel shall go before thee, and bring thee in unto the Amorites, and the Hittites, and the Perizzites, and the Canaanites, the Hivites, and the Jebusites; and I will cut them off.

24 Thou shalt not bow down to their gods, nor serve them, nor do after their works: but thou shalt utterly overthrow them, and quite break down their images.

25 And ye shall serve the LORD your God, and he shall bless thy bread, and thy water; and I will take sickness away from the midst of thee.

26 ¶ There shall nothing cast their young, nor be barren, in thy land: the number of thy days I will fulfil.

27 I will send my fear before thee, and will destroy all the people to whom thou shalt come; and I will make all thine enemies turn their backs unto thee.

28 And I will send hornets before thee, which shall drive out the Hivite, the Canaanite, and the Hittite, from before thee.

29 I will not drive them out from before thee in one year; lest the land become desolate, and the beast of the field multiply against thee.

30 By little and little I will drive them out from before thee, until thou be increased, and inherit the land.

31 And I will set thy bounds from the Red sea even unto the sea of the Philistines, and from the desert unto the river: for I will deliver the inhabitants of the land into your hand; and thou shalt drive them out before thee.

32 Thou shalt make no covenant with them, nor with their gods.

33 They shall not dwell in thy land, lest they make thee sin against me: for if thou serve their gods, it will surely be a snare unto thee.

Exodus, Chapter Twenty-four

And he said unto Moses, Come up unto the LORD, thou, and Aaron, Nadab, and Abihu, and seventy of the elders of Israel; and worship ye afar off.

2 And Moses alone shall come near the LORD: but they shall not come nigh; neither shall the people go up with him.

3 ¶ And Moses came and told the people all the words of the LORD, and all the judgments: and all the people answered with one voice, and said, All the words which the LORD hath said will we do. . . .

Part Two*

The Sermon on the Mount

And seeing the multitudes, he went up into a mountain: and when he was set, his disciples came unto him: and he opened his mouth, and taught them, saying,

"Blessed are the poor in spirit:
For theirs is the kingdom of heaven.

Blessed are they that mourn:
For they shall be comforted.

Blessed are the meek:
For they shall inherit the earth.

Blessed are they which do hunger and thirst after righteousness:
For they shall be filled.

Blessed are the merciful:
For they shall obtain mercy.

Blessed are the pure in heart:
For they shall see God.

Blessed are the peacemakers:
For they shall be called the children of God.

Blessed are they which are persecuted for righteousness' sake:
For theirs is the kingdom of heaven.

Blessed are ye, when men shall revile you, and persecute you, and
shall say all manner of evil against you falsely, for my sake.

Rejoice, and be exceeding glad: for great is your reward in heaven: for
so persecuted they the prophets which were before you.

"Ye are the salt of the earth: but if the salt have lost his savour, wherewith shall it be salted? it is thenceforth good for nothing, but to be cast out, and to be trodden under foot of men.

"Ye are the light of the world. A city that is set on a hill cannot be hid. Neither do men light a candle, and put it under a bushel, but on a candlestick; and it giveth light unto all that are in the house. Let your light so shine before men, that they may see your good works, and glorify your Father which is in heaven.

"Think not that I am come to destroy the law, or the prophets: I am not come to destroy, but to fulfil. For verily I say unto you, 'Till heaven and earth pass, one jot or one tittle shall in no wise pass from the law, till all be fulfilled.' Whosoever therefore shall break one of these least commandments, and shall teach men so, he shall be called the least in the kingdom of heaven: but whosoever shall do and teach them, the same shall be called great in the kingdom of heaven. For I say unto you, 'Except your

*Part Two of this selection is from the Gospel of Matthew, in *The Bible Designed to Be Read As Literature*, Ernest Sutherland Bates, ed. (New York: Simon and Schuster, 1936). By permission of Simon and Schuster, Inc.

righteousness shall exceed the righteousness of the scribes and Pharisees, ye shall in no case enter into the kingdom of heaven.'

"Ye have heard that it was said by them of old time, 'Thou shalt not kill'; and whosoever shall kill shall be in danger of the judgment. But I say unto you, 'Whosoever is angry with his brother without a cause shall be in danger of the judgment: and whosoever shall say to his brother, "Raca," shall be in danger of the council: but whosoever shall say, "Thou fool," shall be in danger of hell fire.' Therefore if thou bring thy gift to the altar, and there rememberest that thy brother hath ought against thee; leave there thy gift before the altar, and go thy way; first be reconciled to thy brother, and then come and offer thy gift. Agree with thine adversary quickly, while thou art in the way with him; lest at any time the adversary deliver thee to the judge, and the judge deliver thee to the officer, and thou be cast into prison. Verily I say unto thee, 'Thou shalt by no means come out thence, till thou hast paid the uttermost farthing.'

"Ye have heard that it was said by them of old time, 'Thou shalt not commit adultery.' But I say unto you, 'Whosoever looketh on a woman to lust after her hath committed adultery with her already in his heart. And if thy right eye offend thee, pluck it out, and cast it from thee: for it is profitable for thee that one of thy members should perish, and not that thy whole body should be cast into hell. And if thy right hand offend thee, cut it off, and cast it from thee: for it is profitable for thee that one of thy members should perish, and not that thy whole body should be cast into hell.' It hath been said, 'Whosoever shall put away his wife, let him give her a writing of divorcement.' But I say unto you, 'Whosoever shall put away his wife, saving for the cause of fornication, causeth her to commit adultery: and whosoever shall marry her that is divorced committeth adultery.'

"Again, ye have heard that it hath been said by them of old time, 'Thou shalt not forswear thyself, but shalt perform unto the Lord thine oaths.' But I say unto you, 'Swear not at all; neither by heaven; for it is God's throne: nor by the earth; for it is his footstool: neither by Jerusalem; for it is the city of the great King. Neither shalt thou swear by thy head, because thou canst not make one hair white or black. But let your communication be, "Yea, yea"; "Nay, nay": for whatsoever is more than these cometh of evil.'

"Ye have heard that it hath been said, 'An eye for an eye, and a tooth for a tooth.' But I say unto you, 'Resist not evil: but whosoever shall smite thee on thy right cheek, turn to him the other also. And if any man will sue thee at the law, and take away thy coat, let him have thy cloak also. And whosoever shall compel thee to go a mile, go with him twain. Give to him that asketh thee, and from him that would borrow of thee turn not thou away.'

"Ye have heard that it hath been said, 'Thou shalt love thy neighbour, and hate thine enemy.' But I say unto you, 'Love your enemies, bless them that curse you, do good to them that hate you, and pray for them which despitefully use you, and persecute you; that ye may be the children of your Father which is in heaven: for he maketh his sun to rise on the evil and on the good, and sendeth rain on the just and on the unjust.' For if ye love them which love you, what reward have ye? do not even the publicans the same? And if ye salute your brethren only, what do ye more than others? do not even the publicans so? Be ye therefore perfect, even as your Father which is in heaven is perfect.

"Take heed that ye do not your alms before men, to be seen of them: otherwise ye have no reward of your Father which is in heaven. Therefore when thou doest thine alms, do not sound a trumpet before thee, as the hypocrites do in the synagogues and in the streets, that they may have glory of men. Verily I say unto you, 'They have their reward.' But when thou doest alms, let not thy left hand know what thy right hand doeth: that thine alms may be in secret: and thy Father which seeth in secret himself shall reward thee openly.

"And when thou prayest, thou shalt not be as the hypocrites are: for they love to pray standing in the synagogues and in the corners of the streets, that they may be seen of men. Verily I say unto you, 'They have their reward.' But thou, when thou prayest, enter into thy closet, and when thou hast shut thy door, pray to thy Father which is in secret; and thy Father which seeth in secret shall reward thee openly. But when ye pray, use not vain repetitions, as the heathen do: for they think that they shall be heard for their much speaking. Be not ye therefore like unto them: for your Father knoweth what things ye have need of, before ye ask him. After this manner therefore pray ye:

> " 'Our Father which art in heaven,
> Hallowed be thy name.
> Thy Kingdom come.
> Thy will be done
> In earth, as it is in heaven.
>
> Give us this day
> Our daily bread.
> And forgive us our debts,
> As we forgive our debtors.
> And lead us not into temptation,
> But deliver us from evil:
>
> For thine is the kingdom,
> And the power,
> And the glory,
> For ever, Amen.'

"For if ye forgive men their trespasses, your heavenly Father will also forgive you: but if ye forgive not men their trespasses, neither will your Father forgive your trespasses.

"Moreover when ye fast, be not, as the hypocrites, of a sad countenance: for they disfigure their faces, that they may appear unto men to fast. Verily I say unto you, 'They have their reward.' But thou, when thou fastest, anoint thine head, and wash thy face; that thou appear not unto men to fast, but unto thy Father which is in secret: and thy Father, which seeth in secret shall reward thee openly.

"Lay not up for yourselves treasures upon earth,
Where moth and rust doth corrupt,
And where thieves break through and steal:

But lay up for yourselves treasures in heaven,
Where neither moth nor rust doth corrupt,
And where thieves do not break through nor steal.

For where your treasure is, there will your heart be also.

"The light of the body is the eye: if therefore thine eye be single, thy whole body shall be full of light. But if thine eye be evil, thy whole body shall be full of darkness. If therefore the light that is in thee be darkness, how great is that darkness!

"No man can serve two masters: for either he will hate the one, and love the other; or else he will hold to the one, and despise the other. Ye cannot serve God and Mammon.

"Therefore I say unto you, 'Take no thought for your life, what ye shall eat, or what ye shall drink; nor yet for your body, what ye shall put on.' Is not the life more than meat, and the body than raiment? Behold the fowls of the air: for they sow not, neither do they reap, nor gather into barns; yet your heavenly Father feedeth them. Are ye not much better than they? Which of you by taking thought can add one cubit unto his stature? And why take ye thought for raiment? Consider the lilies of the field, how they grow; they toil not, neither do they spin: and yet I say unto you that even Solomon in all his glory was not arrayed like one of these.

"Wherefore, if God so clothe the grass of the field, which today is, and to-morrow is cast into the oven, shall he not much more clothe you, O ye of little faith? Therefore take no thought, saying, 'What shall we eat?' or, 'What shall we drink?' or, 'Wherewithal shall we be clothed?' (For after all these things do the Gentiles seek): for your heavenly Father knoweth that ye have need of all these things. But seek ye first the kingdom of God, and his righteousness; and all these things shall be added unto you. Take therefore no thought for the morrow: for the morrow shall take thought for the things of itself. Sufficient unto the day is the evil thereof.

"Judge not, that ye be not judged. For with what judgment ye judge, ye shall be judged: and with what measure ye mete, it shall be measured to you again. And why beholdest thou the mote that is in thy brother's eye, but considerest not the beam that is in thine own eye? Or how wilt thou say to thy brother, 'Let me pull out the mote out of thine eye'; and, behold, a beam is in thine own eye? Thou hypocrite, first cast out the beam out of thine own eye; and then shalt thou see clearly to cast out the mote out of thy brother's eye.

"Give not that which is holy unto the dogs,
Neither cast ye your pearls before swine,
Lest they trample them under their feet,
And turn again and rend you.

Ask, and it shall be given you;
Seek, and ye shall find;
Knock, and it shall be opened unto you:

For every one that asketh receiveth;
And he that seeketh findeth;
And to him that knocketh it shall be opened.

Or what man is there of you, whom if his son ask bread, will he give him a stone? Or if he ask a fish, will he give him a serpent? If ye then, being evil, know how to give good gifts unto your children, how much more shall your Father which is in heaven give good things to them that ask him? Therefore all things whatsoever ye would that men should do to you, do ye even so to them: for this is the law and the prophets.

"Enter ye in at the strait gate: for wide is the gate, and broad is the way, that leadeth to destruction, and many there be which go in thereat: because strait is the gate, and narrow is the way, which leadeth unto life, and few there be that find it.

"Beware of false prophets, which come to you in sheep's clothing, but inwardly they are ravening wolves. Ye shall know them by their fruits. Do men gather grapes of thorns, or figs of thistles? Even so every good tree bringeth forth good fruit; but a corrupt tree bringeth forth evil fruit. A good tree cannot bring forth evil fruit, neither can a corrupt tree bring forth good fruit. Every tree that bringeth not forth good fruit is hewn down, and cast into the fire. Wherefore by their fruits ye shall know them.

"Not every one that saith unto me, 'Lord, Lord,' shall enter into the kingdom of heaven; but he that doeth the will of my Father which is in heaven. Many will say to me in that day, 'Lord, Lord, have we not prophesied in thy name? and in thy name have cast out devils? and in thy name done many wonderful works?' And then will I profess unto them, 'I never knew you: depart from me, ye that work iniquity.'

"Therefore whosoever heareth these sayings of mine, and doeth them, I will liken him unto a wise man, which built his house upon a rock: and the rain descended, and the floods came and the winds blew, and beat upon that house; and it fell not: for it was founded upon a rock. And every one that heareth these sayings of mine, and doeth them not, shall be likened unto a foolish man, which built his house upon the sand: and the rain descended, and the floods came, and the winds blew, and beat upon that house; and it fell: and great was the fall of it."

And it came to pass, when Jesus had ended these sayings, the people were astonished at his doctrine: for he taught them as one having authority, and not as the scribes.

PART THREE*

1. That the World Is Neither Without Beginning, Nor Yet Created by a New Decree of God, by Which He Afterwards Willed What He Had Not Before Willed

Of all visible things, the world is the greatest; of all invisible, the greatest is God. But, that the world is, we see; that God is, we believe. That God made the world, we can believe from no one more safely than from God Himself. But where have we heard Him? Nowhere more distinctly than in the Holy Scriptures, where His prophet said, "In the beginning God created the heavens and the earth." Was the prophet present when God made the heavens and the earth? No; but the wisdom of God, by whom all things were made, was there, and wisdom insinuates itself into holy souls, and makes them the friends of God and His prophets, and noiselessly informs them of His works. They are taught also by the angels of God, who always behold the face of the Father, and announce His will to whom it befits. Of these prophets was he who said and wrote, "In the beginning God created the heavens and the earth." And so fit a witness was he of God, that the same Spirit of God, who revealed these things to him, enabled him also so long before to predict that our faith also would be forthcoming.

2. That the Disobedience of the First Man Would Have Plunged All Men into the Endless Misery of the Second Death, Had Not the Grace of God Rescued Many.

We have already stated in the preceding books that God, desiring not only that the human race might be able by their similarity of nature to associate with one another, but also that they might be bound together in harmony and peace by the ties of relationship, was pleased to derive all men from one individual, and created man with such a nature that the members of the race should not have died, had not the two first (of whom the one was created out of nothing, and the other out of him) merited this by their disobedience; for by them so great a sin was committed, that by it the human nature was altered for the worse, and was transmitted also to their posterity, liable to sin and subject to death. And the kingdom of death so reigned over men, that the deserved penalty of sin would have hurled all headlong even into the second death, of which there is no end, had not the undeserved grace of God saved some therefrom. And thus it has come to pass, that though there are very many and great nations all over the earth, whose rites and customs, speech, arms, and dress, are distinguished by marked differences, yet there are no more than two kinds of human society, which we may justly call two cities, according to the language of our Scriptures.

*Part Three of this selection is from Augustine's *City of God*, Vols. 1 and 2, Books 11, 14, 15, and 19, trans. the Rev. Marcus Dods (Edinburgh: T & T Clark, 1871), and the *Enchiridion*, Chapter 9 (Edinburgh: T & T Clark, 1873). The sections have been renumbered and some of the footnotes have been omitted.

The one consists of those who wish to live after the flesh, the other of those who wish to live after the spirit; and when they severally achieve what they wish, they live in peace, each after their kind.

3. Of Carnal Life, Which is to Be Understood Not Only of Living in Bodily Indulgence, but also of Living in the Vices of the Inner Man

First, we must see what it is to live after the flesh, and what to live after the spirit. For any one who either does not recollect, or does not sufficiently weigh, the language of sacred Scripture, may, on first hearing what we have said, suppose that the Epicurean philosophers live after the flesh, because they place man's highest good in bodily pleasure; and that those others do so who have been of opinion that in some form or other bodily good is man's supreme good; and that the mass of men do so who, without dogmatizing or philosophizing on the subject, are so prone to lust that they cannot delight in any pleasure save such as they receive from bodily sensations: and he may suppose that the Stoics, who place the supreme good of men in the soul, live after the spirit; for what is man's soul, if not spirit? But in the sense of the divine Scripture both are proved to live after the flesh. For by flesh it means not only the body of a terrestrial and mortal animal, as when it says, "All flesh is not the same flesh, but there is one kind of flesh of men, another flesh of beasts, another of fishes, another of birds,"[1] but it uses this word in many other significations; and among these various usages, a frequent one is to use flesh for man himself, the nature of man taking the part for the whole, as in the words, "By the deeds of the law there shall no flesh be justified";[2] for what does he mean here by "no flesh" but "no man"? And this, indeed, he shortly after says more plainly: "No man shall be justified by the law";[3] and in the Epistle to the Galatians, "Knowing that a man is not justified by the works of the law." And so we understand the words, "And the Word was made flesh,"[4]—that is, man, which some not accepting in its right sense, have supposed that Christ had not a human soul.[5] For as the whole is used for the part in the words of Mary Magdalene in the Gospel, "They have taken away my Lord, and I know not where they have laid Him,"[6] by which she meant only the flesh of Christ, which she supposed had been taken from the tomb where it had been buried, so the part is used for the whole, flesh being named, while man is referred to, as in the quotations above cited.

Since, then, Scripture uses the word flesh in many ways, which there is not time to collect and investigate, if we are to ascertain what it is to live after the flesh (which is certainly evil, though the nature of flesh is not itself evil), we must carefully examine that passage of the epistle which the Apostle Paul wrote to the Galatians, in which he says, "Now the works of the flesh are manifest, which are these: adultery, fornication, uncleanness,

[1]Cor. xv. 39.   [2]Rom. iii. 20.
[3]Gal. iii. 11.   [4]John i. 14.
[5]The Apollinarians.   [6]John xx. 13.

lasciviousness, idolatry, witchcraft, hatred, variance, emulations, wrath, strife, seditions, heresies, envyings, murders, drunkenness, revellings, and such like: of the which I tell you before, as I have also told you in time past, that they which do such things shall not inherit the kingdom of God."[7] This whole passage of the apostolic epistle being considered, so far as it bears on the matter in hand, will be sufficient to answer the question, what it is to live after the flesh. For among the works of the flesh which he said were manifest, and which he cited for condemnation, we find not only those which concern the pleasure of the flesh, as fornications, uncleanness, lasciviousness, drunkenness, revellings, but also those which, though they be remote from fleshly pleasure, reveal the vices of the soul. For who does not see that idolatries, witchcrafts, hatreds, variance, emulations, wrath, strife, heresies, evnyings, are vices rather of the soul than of the flesh? For it is quite possible for a man to abstain from fleshly pleasures for the sake of idolatry or some heretical error; and yet, even when he does so, he is proved by this apostolic authority to be living after the flesh; and in abstaining from fleshly pleasure, he is proved to be practising damnable works of the flesh. Who that has enmity has it not in his soul? or who would say to his enemy, or to the man he thinks his enemy, You have a bad flesh towards me, and not rather, You have a bad spirit towards me? In fine, if any one heard of what I may call "carnalities," he would not fail to attribute them to the carnal part of man; so no one doubts that "animosities" belong to the soul of man. Why then does the doctor of the Gentiles in faith and verity call all these and similar things works of the flesh, unless because, by that mode of speech whereby the part is used for the whole, he means us to understand by the word flesh the man himself?

4. That Sin Is Caused Not by the Flesh, But by the Soul, and That the Corruption Contracted from Sin Is Not Sin, But Sin's Punishment

But if any one says that the flesh is the cause of all vices and ill conduct, inasmuch as the soul lives wickedly only because it is moved by the flesh, it is certain he has not carefully considered the whole nature of man. For "the corruptible body, indeed, weigheth down the soul."[8] Whence, too, the apostle, speaking of this corruptible body, of which he had shortly before said, "though our outward man perish,"[9] says, "We know that if our earthly house of this tabernacle were dissolved, we have a building of God, an house not made with hands, eternal in the heavens. For in this we groan, earnestly desiring to be clothed upon with our house which is from heaven: if so be that being clothed we shall not be found naked. For we that are in this tabernacle do groan, being burdened: not for that we would be unclothed, but clothed upon, that mortality might be swallowed up in life."[10] We are then burdened with this corruptible body; but knowing that the cause of this burdensomeness is not the nature and substance of the body,

---

[7]Gal. v. 19–21.
[9]2 Cor. iv. 16.

[8]Wisd. ix. 15.
[10]2 Cor. v. 1–4.

but its corruption, we do not desire to be deprived of the body, but to be clothed with its immortality. For then, also, there will be a body, but it shall no longer be a burden, being no longer corruptible. At present, then, "the corruptible body presseth down the soul, and the earthly tabernacle weigheth down the mind that museth upon many things," nevertheless they are in error who suppose that all the evils of the soul proceed from the body.

Virgil, indeed, seems to express the sentiments of Plato in the beautiful lines, where he says,—

> "A fiery strength inspires their lives,
> An essence that from heaven derives,
> Though clogged in part by limbs of clay,
> And the dull 'vesture of decay'; "[11]

but though he goes on to mention the four most common mental emotions, —desire, fear, joy, sorrow,—with the intention of showing that the body is the origin of all sins and vices, saying,—

> "Hence wild desires and grovelling fears,
> And human laughter, human tears,
> Immured in dungeon-seeming night,
> They look abroad, yet see no light,"[12]

yet we believe quite otherwise. For the corruption of the body, which weighs down the soul, is not the cause but the punishment of the first sin; and it was not the corruptible flesh that made the soul sinful, but the sinful soul that made the flesh corruptible. And though from this corruption of the flesh there arise certain incitements to vice, and indeed vicious desires, yet we must not attribute to the flesh all the vices of a wicked life. . . .

5. Of the Nature of the Two Cities, the Earthly and the Heavenly

Accordingly, two cities have been formed by two loves: the earthly by the love of self, even to the contempt of God; the heavenly by the love of God, even to the contempt of self. The former, in a word, glories in itself, the latter in the Lord. For the one seeks glory from men; but the greatest glory of the other is God, the witness of conscience. The one lifts up its head in its own glory; the other says to its God, "Thou art my glory, and the lifter up of mine head."[13] In the one, the princes and the nations it subdues are ruled by the love of ruling; in the other, the princes and the subjects serve one another in love, the latter obeying, while the former take thought for all. The one delights in its own strength, represented in the persons of its rulers; the other says to its God, "I will love Thee, O Lord, my strength."[14] And therefore the wise men of the one city, living according to man, have sought for profit to their own bodies or souls, or both, and those who have known God "glorified Him not as God, neither were thankful, but became vain in their imaginations, and their foolish heart was darkened; professing themselves to be wise,"—that is, glorying in their own wisdom,

---

[11]*Æneid*, vi. 730–32.   [12]*Ibid.* 733, 734.
[13]Ps. iii. 3.   [14]Ps. xviii. 1.

and being possessed by pride,—"they became fools, and changed the glory of the incorruptible God into an image made like to corruptible man, and to birds, and four-footed beasts, and creeping things." For they were either leaders or followers of the people in adoring images, "and worshipped and served the creature more than the Creator, who is blessed for ever."[15] But in the other city there is no human wisdom, but only godliness, which offers due worship to the true God, and looks for its reward in the society of the saints, of holy angels as well as holy men, "that God may be all in all."[16]

6. What the Christians Believe Regarding the Supreme Good and Evil, in Opposition to the Philosophers, Who Have Maintained That the Supreme Good Is in Themselves

If, then, we be asked what the city of God has to say upon these points, and, in the first place, what its opinion regarding the supreme good and evil is, it will reply that life eternal is the supreme good, death eternal the supreme evil, and that to obtain the one and escape the other we must live rightly. And thus it is written, "The just lives by faith,"[17] for we do not as yet see our good, and must therefore live by faith; neither have we in ourselves power to live rightly, but can do so only if He who has given us faith to believe in His help do help us when we believe and pray. As for those who have supposed that the sovereign good and evil are to be found in this life, and have placed it either in the soul or the body, or in both, or, to speak more explicitly, either in pleasure or in virtue, or in both; in repose or in virtue, or in both; in pleasure and repose, or in virtue, or in all combined; in the primary objects of nature, or in virtue, or in both,—all these have, with a marvellous shallowness, sought to find their blessedness in this life and in themselves. Contempt has been poured upon such ideas by the Truth, saying by the prophet, "The Lord knoweth the thoughts of men" (or, as the Apostle Paul cites the passage, "The Lord knoweth the thoughts of the *wise*") "that they are vain."[18] . . .

In fine, virtue itself, which is not among the primary objects of nature, but succeeds to them as the result of learning, though it holds the highest place among human good things, what is its occupation save to wage perpetual war with vices,—not those that are outside of us, but within; not other men's, but our own,—a war which is waged especially by that virtue which the Greeks call σωφροσύνη, and we temperance,[19] and which bridles carnal lusts, and prevents them from winning the consent of the spirit to wicked deeds? For we must not fancy that there is no vice in us, when, as the apostle says, "The flesh lusteth against the spirit;"[20] for to this vice there is a contrary virtue, when, as the same writer says, "The spirit lusteth against the flesh." "For these two," he says, "are contrary one to the other, so that you cannot do the things which you would." But what is it we wish

153 Rom. i. 21–25.
17 Hab. ii. 4.
19 Cicero, *Tusc. Quæst.* iii. 8.

164.1 Cor. xv. 28.
18 Ps. xciv. 11, and 1 Cor. iii. 20.
20 Gal. v. 17.

to do when we seek to attain the supreme good, unless that the flesh should cease to lust against the spirit, and that there be no vice in us against which the spirit may lust? And as we cannot attain to this in the present life, however ardently we desire it, let us by God's help accomplish at least this, to preserve the soul from succumbing and yielding to the flesh that lusts against it, and to refuse our consent to the perpetration of sin. Far be it from us, then, to fancy that while we are still engaged in this intestine war, we have already found the happiness which we seek to reach by victory. And who is there so wise that he has no conflict at all to maintain against his vices?

What shall I say of that virtue which is called prudence? Is not all its vigilance spent in the discernment of good from evil things, so that no mistake may be admitted about what we should desire and what avoid? And thus it is itself a proof that we are in the midst of evils, or that evils are in us; for it teaches us that it is an evil to consent to sin, and a good to refuse this consent. And yet this evil, to which prudence teaches and temperance enables us not to consent, is removed from this life neither by prudence nor by temperance. And justice, whose office it is to render to every man his due, whereby there is in man himself a certain just order of nature, so that the soul is subjected to God, and the flesh to the soul, and consequently both soul and flesh to God,—does not this virtue demonstrate that it is as yet rather labouring towards its end than resting in its finished work? For the soul is so much the less subjected to God as it is less occupied with the thought of God; and the flesh is so much the less subjected to the spirit as it lusts more vehemently against the spirit. So long, therefore, as we are beset by this weakness, this plague, this disease, how shall we dare to say that we are safe? and if not safe, then how can we be already enjoying our beatitude? Then that virtue which goes by the name of fortitude is the plainest proof of the ills of life, for it is these ills which it is compelled to bear patiently. And this holds good, no matter though the ripest wisdom co-exists with it. And I am at a loss to understand how the Stoic philosophers can presume to say that these are no ills, though at the same time they allow the wise man to commit suicide and pass out of this life if they become so grievous that he cannot or ought not to endure them. But such is the stupid pride of these men who fancy that the supreme good can be found in this life, and that they can become happy by their own resources, that their wise man, or at least the man whom they fancifully depict as such, is always happy, even though he become blind, deaf, dumb, mutilated, racked with pains, or suffer any conceivable calamity such as may compel him to make away with himself; and they are not ashamed to call the life that is beset with these evils happy. O happy life, which seeks the aid of death to end it! If it is happy, let the wise man remain in it; but if these ills drive him out of it, in what sense is it happy? Or how can they say that these are not evils which conquer the virtue of fortitude, and force it not only to yield, but so to rave that it in one breath calls life happy and recommends it to be given

21Rom. viii. 24.

up? For who is so blind as not to see that if it were happy it would not be fled from? And if they say we should flee from it on account of the infirmities that beset it, why then do they not lower their pride and acknowledge that it is miserable? . . .

The wise man, I admit, ought to bear death with patience, but when it is inflicted by another. If, then, as these men maintain, he is obliged to inflict it on himself, certainly it must be owned that the ills which compel him to this are not only evils, but intolerable evils. The life, then, which is either subject to accidents, or environed with evils so considerable and greivous, could never have been called happy, if the men who give it this name had condescended to yield to the truth, and to be conquered by valid arguments, when they inquired after the happy life, as they yield to unhappiness, and are overcome by overwhelming evils, when they put themselves to death, and if they had not fancied that the supreme good was to be found in this mortal life; for the very virtues of this life, which are certainly its best and most useful possessions, are all the more telling proofs of its miseries in proportion as they are helpful against the violence of its dangers, toils, and woes. For if these are true virtues,—and such cannot exist save in those who have true piety,—they do not profess to be able to deliver the men who possess them from all miseries; for true virtues tell no such lies, but they profess that by the hope of the future world this life, which is miserably involved in the many and great evils of this world, is happy as it is also safe. For if not yet safe, how could it be happy? And therefore the Apostle Paul, speaking not of men without prudence, temperance, fortitude, and justice, but of those whose lives were regulated by true piety, and whose virtues were therefore true, says, "For we are saved by hope: now hope which is seen is not hope; for what a man seeth, why doth he yet hope for? But if we hope for that we see not, then do we with patience wait for it."[21] As, therefore, we are saved, so we are made happy by hope. And as we do not as yet possess a present, but look for a future salvation, so is it with our happiness, and this "with patience;" for we are encompassed with evils, which we ought patiently to endure, until we come to the ineffable enjoyment of unmixed good; for there shall be no longer anything to endure. Salvation, such as it shall be in the world to come, shall itself be our final happiness. And this happiness these philosophers refuse to believe in, because they do not see it, and attempt to fabricate for themselves a happiness in this life, based upon a virtue which is as deceitful as it is proud.

7. That the Saints Are in This Life Blessed in Hope

Since, then, the supreme good of the city of God is perfect and eternal peace, not such as mortals pass into and out of by birth and death, but the peace of freedom from all evil, in which the immortals ever abide, who can deny that that future life is most blessed, or that, in comparison with it, this life which now we live is most wretched, be it filled with all blessings of body and soul and external things? And yet, if any man uses this life with a reference to that other which he ardently loves and confidently hopes for, he may well be called even now blessed, though not in reality so much as in hope. But the actual possession of the happiness of this life, without the hope of what is beyond, is but a false happiness and profound misery. For the true blessings of the soul are not now enjoyed; for that is no true wisdom which does not direct all its prudent observations, manly actions, virtuous self-restraint, and just arrangements, to that end in which God shall be all and all in a secure eternity and perfect peace.

8. *What We Are to Believe. In Regard to Nature It Is Not Necessary for the Christian to Know More Than That the Goodness of the Creator Is the Cause of All Things*

When, then, the question is asked what we are to believe in regard to religion, it is not necessary to probe into the nature of things, as was done by those whom the Greeks call *physici;* nor need we be in alarm lest the Christian should be ignorant of the force and number of the elements,—the motion, and order, and eclipses of the heavenly bodies; the form of the heavens; the species and the natures of animals, plants, stones, fountains, rivers, mountains; about chronology and distances; the signs of coming storms; and a thousand other things which those philosophers either have found out, or think they have found out. For even these men themselves, endowed though they are with so much genius, burning with zeal, abounding in leisure, tracking some things by the aid of human conjecture, searching into others with the aids of history and experience, have not found out all things; and even their boasted discoveries are oftener mere guesses than certain knowledge. It is enough for the Christian to believe that the only cause of all created things, whether heavenly or earthly, whether visible or invisible, is the goodness of the Creator, the one true God; and that nothing exists but Himself that does not derive its existence from Him; and that He is the Trinity—to wit, the Father, and the Son begotten of the Father, and the Holy Spirit proceeding from the same Father, but one and the same Spirit of Father and Son.

9. *That Where There Is No True Religion There Are No True Virtues*

For though the soul may seem to rule the body admirably, and the reason the vices, if the soul and reason do not themselves obey God, as God has commanded them to serve Him, they have no proper authority over the body and the vices. For what kind of mistress of the body and the vices can that mind be which is ignorant of the true God, and which, instead of being subject to His authority, is prostituted to the corrupting influences of the most vicious demons? It is for this reason that the virtues which it seems to itself to possess, and by which it restrains the body and the vices that it may obtain and keep what it desires, are rather vices than virtues so long as there is no reference to God in the matter. For although some suppose that virtues which have a reference only to themselves, and are desired only on their own account, are yet true and genuine virtues, the fact is that even then they are inflated with pride, and are therefore to be reckoned vices rather than virtues. For as that which gives life to the flesh is not derived from flesh, but is above it, so that which gives blessed life to man is not derived from man, but is something above him; and what I say of man is true of every celestial power and virtue whatsoever.

Suggested Readings

PLATO

Jaeger, W. W., *Paideia, the Ideals of Greek Culture,* Vol. III, Blackwell and Mott, Oxford, 1944.

Lodge, R. C., *Plato's Theory of Ethics,* Paul, Trench, Trubner, London, 1928.

Nettleship, R. L., *Lectures on the Republic of Plato,* Macmillan and Co., London, 1937.

Plato, *The Dialogues of Plato,* tr. B. Jowett, Oxford University Press, New York, 1892.

Taylor, A. E., *Plato, the Man and His Works,* Methuen, London, 1926.

ARISTOTLE

Aristotle, "Nichomachean Ethics," from *The Works of Aristotle,* tr. W. D. Ross, Vol. IX, The Clarendon Press, Oxford, 1925.

Case, T., "Aristotle," *Encyclopaedia Britannica,* Vol. II, 1910.

Mure, G. R. G., *Aristotle,* Benn, London, 1932.

Randall, J. H., *Aristotle,* Columbia University Press, New York, 1960.

Stewart, J. A., *Notes on the Nichomachean Ethics,* The Clarendon Press, Oxford, 1892.

EPICURIUS

Bailey, C., *The Greek Atomists and Epicurius,* the Clarendon Press, Oxford, 1928.

Hicks, R. D., *Stoic and Epicurean,* Charles Scribner's Sons, New York, 1910.

Laertius, Diogenes, *Lives and Opinions of Eminent Philosophers,* tr. R. D. Hicks, Harvard University Press, Cambridge, 1925.

Murray, G., *Five Stages of Greek Religion,* The Clarendon Press, Oxford, 1925.

Zeller, E., *Stoics, Epicureans and Sceptics,* Longmans, Green, London, 1892.

EPICTETUS

Arnold, E. V., *Roman Stoicism,* Cambridge University Press, New York, 1911.

Beuan, E., *Stoics and Sceptics,* The Clarendon Press, Oxford, 1913.

Laertius, Diogenes, *Lives and Opinions of Eminent Philosophers,* tr. R. D. Hicks, Harvard University Press, Cambridge, 1925.

Zeller, E., *Stoics, Epicureans and Sceptics,* Longmans, Green, London, 1892.

St. Augustine

Bourke, V. J., *Augustine's Quest of Wisdom,* Bruce, Milwaukee, 1945.

Brown, P. R. L., *Augustine of Hippo; A Biography,* University of California Press, Berkeley, 1967.

Cochrane, C. N., *Christianity and Classical Culture,* The Clarendon Press, Oxford, 1940.

Warfield, B., *Studies in Tertullian and Augustine,* Oxford University Press, New York, 1931.

Modern Approaches to Ethical Theory

✿ INTRODUCTION

The philosophers in the preceding section adopted significantly different positions in regard to morality. But in spite of the diversity of their ethical theories, the overall pattern of their thinking remains essentially the same. For example, each author identified a single good as the highest good. Plato claimed that is was the Idea (or Form) of Good; Aristotle, happiness; Epicurus, pleasure; Epictetus, a right-will; St. Augustine, salvation. Furthermore each philosopher delineated a number of virtues and vices and formulated a set of rules for the conduct of one's life. In this way each sought to describe a particular life-style, and to contrast it with alternative, less desirable modes of existence. And finally, each thinker provides a theoretical framework for his ethical theory by showing its connection with broader views concerning the nature of the universe and man.

All of the philosophers whose views are presented in this section were strongly influenced by both the Graeco-Roman and the Judaeo-Christian traditions in ethics. But none of these thinkers was content simply to reformulate and defend the positions of earlier philosophers. Instead, their efforts produced ethical theories that represent both distinctive and important developments in moral philosophy.

Thomas Hobbes, a tough-minded secular philosopher, defends a system of ethics that contrasts sharply with the religious outlook of St. Augustine. Adopting the principles and temper of seventeenth-century science, he formulates an ethics that is this worldly and deterministic. Self-preservation and self-enhancement emerge as the ultimate ends of human conduct, and individuals are able to obtain these goals only by organizing themselves together in some form of stable society.

Utilitarianism, the ethical theory of Bentham and Mill, is clearly in the tradition of Epicurus. But Bentham and, especially, Mill revise the aristocratic self-centered hedonism of Epicurus into a democratic and humane social ethic. This is accomplished by requiring a careful consideration of the consequences that one's actions have for the lives of other persons. Thus one must temper his own pleasure or happiness with a consideration for the welfare of all others who are affected by his actions. Only those acts, then, which have maximum social utility are to be commended and performed.

One important feature of Utilitarianism is its reduction of the entire realm of morality to one fundamental principle. This principle, the Greatest

Happiness Principle, constitutes an ultimate criterion for judging the rightness or wrongness of human conduct. It thereby satisfies the demand for a single reference point to be used in resolving moral problems. Both Bentham and Mill expected that a careful and extensive use of this principle would produce fundamental changes in our entire social system.

Kant too wanted to systematize morality and to diminish its relativity and subjectivity. Hence he formulated a basic principle, the categorical imperative, which requires individuals to be both consistent and objective in making moral judgments. Kant presents this principle as a necessary, self-imposed maxim to be endorsed by each rational person who aspires to act morally.

In providing an introduction for the categorical imperative, Kant develops an approach to ethics that is quite opposed to both the hedonism and the teleological modes of justification that characterize Utilitarianism. Whereas Utilitarianism directs our attention to the long-range consequences of our actions, Kant advises us to consider the motive of the person performing the act. In fact, for Kant, this motive emerges as the crucial factor in the establishment of moral worth. Accordingly, one must always inquire concerning the actor's intentions. Is this person acting out of a sincere determination to do what is right? Or does he have ulterior motives? Only if the former is true does one deserve moral praise. And this moral praise is warranted even if it should happen that things do not turn out so well as one had intended.

The final philosopher in this section, Friedrich Nietzsche, adopts a striking position in regard to ethical theory. He explicitly rejects all attempts to reduce morality to a "basic principle" or a "final system" which might be universally acknowledged and practiced. Instead he proposes a transvaluation of all earlier moral systems. As a necessary first step in this transvaluation he calls upon the person of superior intellect and feeling to reject many of the conventional values of Western civilization. The purpose of this rejection is not to give reign to moral anarchy or to provide a rationalization for the aggressive behavior of the neurotic nay-sayer, the destructive personality. Rather it is to purge morality of the many superstitions and taboos which are symptomatic of psychic illness. This, in turn, may make possible a new, higher, and more noble morality—a morality that emphasizes intellectual integrity, mental and physical health, spiritual wholesomeness, and aesthetic sensitivity.

✾ THOMAS HOBBES

22. *Morality Derived from Causation, Power, and Self-Interest*

Thomas Hobbes (1588–1679) was born in Malmesbury, England. Because his parents were poor and uneducated, his uncle provided the financial assistance needed to send him to Oxford University. After graduation in 1608, Hobbes became the tutor of the young son of the Cavendish family. This appointment provided him with sufficient time to travel, study, and write. His writings distinguished him as the first philosopher to apply the basic assumptions of seventeenth-century science to psychology, ethics, and political philosophy.

OF SENSE

Concerning the thoughts of man, I will consider them first singly, and afterwards in train, or dependence upon one another. Singly, they are every one a *representation* or *appearance,* of some quality, or other accident of a body without us, which is commonly called an *object.* Which object worketh on the eyes, ears, and other parts of a man's body; and by diversity of working, produceth diversity of appearances.

The original of them all, is that which we call SENSE, for there is no conception in a man's mind, which hath not at first, totally, or by parts, been begotten upon the organs of sense. The rest are derived from that original.

To know the natural cause of sense, is not very necessary to the business now in hand; and I have elsewhere written of the same at large. Nevertheless, to fill each part of my present method, I will briefly deliver the same in this place.

The cause of sense, is the external body, or object, which presseth the organ proper to each sense, either immediately, as in the taste and touch; or mediately, as in seeing, hearing, and smelling; which pressure, by the mediation of the nerves, and other strings and membranes of the body, continued inwards to the brain and heart, causeth there a resistance, or counter-pressure, or endeavour of the heart to deliver itself, which endeavour, because *outward,* seemeth to be some matter without. And this *seeming,* or *fancy,* is that which men call *sense;* and consisteth, as to the eye, in a *light,* or *colour* figured; to the ear, in a *sound;* to the nostril, in an *odour;* to the tongue and palate, in a *savour;* and to the rest of the body, in *heat, cold, hardness, softness,* and such other qualities as we discern by *feeling.*

Selected from chapters 1, 2, 6, 10, 13, and 14 of the *Leviathan* as it appears in *The English Works of Thomas Hobbes,* Vol. III, collected and edited by Sir William Molesworth, published by John Bohn, London, 1839.

All which qualities, called *sensible,* are in the object, that causeth them, but so many several motions of the matter, by which it presseth our organs diversely. Neither in us that are pressed, are they any thing else, but divers motions; for motion produceth nothing but motion. But their appearance to us is fancy, the same waking, that dreaming. And as pressing, rubbing, or striking the eye, makes us fancy a light; and pressing the ear, produceth a din; so do the bodies also we see, or hear, produce the same by their strong, though unobserved action. For if those colours and sounds were in the bodies, or objects that cause them, they could not be severed from them, as by glasses, and in echoes by reflection, we see they are; where we know the thing we see is in one place, the appearance in another. And though at some certain distance, the real and very object seem invested with the fancy it begets in us; yet still the object is one thing, the image or fancy is another. So that sense, in all cases, is nothing else but original fancy, caused, as I have said, by the pressure, that is, by the motion, of external things upon our eyes, ears, and other organs thereunto ordained. . . .

OF IMAGINATION

That when a thing lies still, unless somewhat else stir it, it will lie still for ever, is a truth that no man doubts of. But that when a thing is in motion, it will eternally be in motion, unless somewhat else stay it, though the reason be the same, namely, that nothing can change itself, is not so easily assented to. For men measure, not only other men, but all other things, by themselves; and because they find themselves subject after motion to pain, and lassitude, think every thing else grows weary of motion, and seeks repose of its own accord; little considering, whether it be not some other motion, wherein that desire of rest they find in themselves, consisteth. From hence it is, that the schools say, heavy bodies fall downwards, out of an appetite to rest, and to conserve their nature in that place which is most proper for them; ascribing appetite, and knowledge of what is good for their conservation, which is more than man has, to things inanimate, absurdly.

When a body is once in motion, it moveth, unless something else hinder it, eternally; and whatsoever hindreth it, cannot in an instant, but in time, and by degrees, quite extinguish it; and as we see in the water, though the wind cease, the waves give not over rolling for a long time after: so also it happeneth in that motion, which is made in the internal parts of a man, then, when he sees, dreams, &c. For after the object is removed, or the eye shut, we still retain an image of the thing seen, though more obscure than when we see it. And this is it, the Latins call *imagination,* from the image made in seeing; and apply the same, though improperly, to all the other senses. But the Greeks call it *fancy;* which signifies *appearance,* and is as proper to one sense, as to another. IMAGINATION therefore is nothing but *decaying sense;* and is found in men, and many other living creatures, as well sleeping, as waking.

The decay of sense in men waking, is not the decay of the motion made in sense; but an obscuring of it, in such manner as the light of the sun obscureth the light of the stars; which stars do no less exercise their virtue, by which they are visible, in the day than in the night. But because amongst many strokes, which our eyes, ears, and other organs receive from external bodies, the predominant only is sensible; therefore, the light of the sun being predominant, we are not affected with the action of the stars. And any object being removed from our eyes, though the impression it made in us remain, yet other objects more present succeeding, and working on us, the imagination of the past is obscured, and made weak, as the voice of a man is in the noise of the day. From whence it followeth, that the longer the time is, after the sight or sense of any object, the weaker is the imagination. For the continual change of man's body destroys in time the parts which in sense were moved: so that distance of time, and of place, hath one and the same effect in us. For as at a great distance of place, that which we look at appears dim, and without distinction of the smaller parts; and as voices grow weak, and inarticulate; so also, after great distance of time, our imagination of the past is weak; and we lose, for example, of cities we have seen, many particular streets, and of actions, many particular circumstances. This *decaying sense,* when we would express the thing itself, I mean *fancy* itself, we call *imagination,* as I said before: but when we would express the decay, and signify that the sense is fading, old, and past, it is called *memory.* So that imagination and memory are but one thing, which for divers considerations hath divers names. . . .

Of the Interior Beginings of Voluntary Motions

There be in animals, two sorts of *motions* peculiar to them: one called *vital;* begun in generation, and continued without interruption through their whole life; such as are the *course* of the *blood,* the *pulse,* the *breathing,* the *concoction, nutrition, excretion,* &c. to which motions there needs no help of imagination: the other is *animal motion,* otherwise called *voluntary motion;* as to go, to *speak,* to *move* any of our limbs, in such manner as is first fancied in our minds. That sense is motion in the organs and interior parts of man's body, caused by the action of the things we see, hear, &c.; and that fancy is but the relics of the same motion, remaining after the sense, has been already said in the first and second chapters. And because *going, speaking,* and the like voluntary motions, depend always upon a precedent thought of *whither, which way,* and *what;* it is evident, that the imagination is the first internal beginning of all voluntary motion. And although unstudied men do not conceive any motion at all to be there, where the thing moved is invisible; or the space it is moved in is, for the shortness of it, insensible; yet that doth not hinder, but that such motions are. For let a space be never so little, that which is moved over a greater space, whereof that little one is part, must first be moved over that.

These small beginnings of motion, within the body of man, before they appear in walking, speaking, striking, and other visible actions, are commonly called ENDEAVOUR.

This endeavour, when it is toward something which causes it, is called APPETITE, or DESIRE; the latter, being the general name; and the other oftentimes restrained to signify the desire of food, namely *hunger* and *thirst.* And when the endeavour is fromward something, it is generally called AVERSION. These words, *appetite* and *aversion,* we have from the Latins; and they both of them signify the motions, one of approaching, the other of retiring. . . .

Of appetites and aversions, some are born with men; as appetite of food, appetite of excretion, and exoneration, which may also and more properly be called aversions, from somewhat they feel in their bodies; and some other appetites, not many. The rest, which are appetites of particular things, proceed from experience, and trial of their effects upon themselves or other men. For of things we know not at all, or believe not to be, we can have no further desire, than to taste and try. But aversion we have for things, not only which we know have hurt us, but also that we do not know whether they will hurt us, or not.

Those things which we neither desire, nor hate, we are said to *contemn;* CONTEMPT being nothing else but an immobility, or contumacy of the heart, in resisting the action of certain things; and proceeding from that the heart is already moved otherwise, by other more potent objects; or from want of experience of them.

And because the constitution of a man's body is in continual mutation, it is impossible that all the same things should always cause in him the same appetites, and aversions: much less can all men consent, in the desire of almost any one and the same object.

But whatsoever is the object of any man's appetite or desire, that is it which he for his part calleth *good:* and the object of his hate and aversion, *evil;* and of his contempt, *vile* and *inconsiderable.* For these words of good, evil, and contemptible, are ever used with relation to the person that useth them: there being nothing simply and absolutely so; nor any common rule of good and evil, to be taken from the nature of the objects themselves; but from the person of the man, where there is no commonwealth; or, in a commonwealth, from the person that representeth it; or from an arbitrator or judge, whom men disagreeing shall by consent set up, and make his sentence the rule thereof. . . .

When in the mind of man, appetites, and aversions, hopes, and fears, concerning one and the same thing, arise alternately; and divers good and evil consequences of the doing, or omitting the thing propounded, come successively into our thoughts; so that sometimes we have an appetite to it; sometimes an aversion from it; sometimes hope to be able to do it; sometimes despair, or fear to attempt it; the whole sum of desires, aversions, hopes and fears continued till the thing be either done, or thought impossible, is that we call DELIBERATION.

Therefore of things past, there is no *deliberation;* because manifestly impossible to be changed: nor of things known to be impossible, or thought so; because men know, or think such deliberation vain. But of things impossible, which we think possible, we may deliberate; not knowing it is in vain. And it is called *deliberation;* because it is a putting an end to the *liberty* we had of doing, or omitting, according to our own appetite, or aversion.

This alternate succession of appetites, aversions, hopes and fears, is no less in other living creatures than in man: and therefore beasts also deliberate.

Every *deliberation* is then said to *end,* when that whereof they deliberate, is either done, or thought impossible; because till then we retain the liberty of doing, or omitting; according to our appetite, or aversion.

In *deliberation,* the last appetite, or aversion, immediately adhering to the action, or to the omission thereof, is that we call the WILL; the act, not the faculty, of *willing.* And beasts that have *deliberation,* must necessarily also have *will.* The definition of the *will,* given commonly by the Schools, that it is a *rational appetite,* is not good. For if it were, then could there be no voluntary act against reason. For a *voluntary act* is that, which proceedeth from the *will,* and no other. But if instead of a rational appetite, we shall say an appetite resulting from a precedent deliberation, then the definition is the same that I have given here. *Will* therefore *is the last appetite in deliberating.* And though we say in common discourse, a man had a will once to do a thing, that nevertheless he forbore to do; yet that is properly but an inclination, which makes no action voluntary; because the action depends not of it, but of the last inclination, or appetite. For if the interventient appetites, make any action voluntary; then by the same reason all intervenient aversions, should make the same action involuntary; and so one and the same action, should be both voluntary and involuntary.

By this it is manifest, that not only actions that have their beginning from covetousness, ambition, lust, or other appetites to the thing propounded; but also those that have their beginning from aversion, or fear of those consequences that follow the omission, are *voluntary actions.* . . .

And because in deliberation, the appetites, and aversions, are raised by foresight of the good and evil consequences, and sequels of the action whereof we deliberate; the good or evil effect thereof dependeth on the foresight of a long chain of consequences, of which very seldom any man is able to see to the end. But for so far as a man seeth, if the good in those consequences be greater than the evil, the whole chain is that which writers call *apparent,* or *seeming good.* And contrarily, when the evil exceedeth the good, the whole is *apparent, or seeming evil:* so that he who hath by experience, or reason, the greatest and surest prospect of consequences, deliberates best himself; and is able when he will, to give the best counsel unto others.

Continual success in obtaining those things which a man from time to time desireth, that is to say, continual prospering, is that men call FELICITY; I mean the felicity of this life. For there is no such thing as perpetual tranquillity of mind, while we live here; because life itself is but motion, and can never be without desire, nor without fear, no more than without sense. . . .

OF POWER

The power *of a man,* to take it universally, is his present means; to obtain some future apparent good; and is either *original* or *instrumental.*

Natural power, is the eminence of the faculties of body, or mind: as extraordinary strength, form, prudence, arts, eloquence, liberality, nobility. *Instrumental* are those powers, which acquired by these, or by fortune, are means and instruments to acquire more: as riches, reputation, friends, and the secret working of God, which men call good luck. For the nature of power, is in this point, like to fame, increasing as it proceeds; or like the motion of heavy bodies, which the further they go, make still the more haste.

The greatest of human powers, is that which is compounded of the powers of most men, united by consent, in one person, natural, or civil, that has the use of all their powers depending on his will; such as is the power of a common-wealth: or depending on the wills of each particular; such as is the power of a faction or of divers factions leagued. Therefore to have servants, is power; to have friends, is power: for they are strengths united.

Also riches joined with liberality, is power; because it procureth friends, and servants: without liberality, not so; because in this case they defend not; but expose men to envy, as a prey.

Reputation of power, is power; because it draweth with it the adherence of those that need protection.

So is reputation of love of a man's country, called popularity, for the same reason.

Also, what quality soever maketh a man beloved, or feared of many; or the reputation of such quality, is power; because it is a means to have the assistance, and service of many.

Good success is power; because it maketh reputation of wisdom, or good fortune; which makes men either fear him, or rely on him.

Affability of men already in power, is increase of power; because it gaineth love.

Reputation of prudence in the conduct of peace or war, is power; because to prudent men, we commit the government of ourselves, more willingly than to others.

Nobility is power, not in all places, but only in those common-wealths, where it has privileges: for in such privileges, consisteth their power.

Eloquence is power, because it is seeming prudence.

Form is power; because being a promise of good, it recommendeth men to the favour of women and strangers.

The sciences, are small power; because not eminent; and therefore, not acknowledged in any man; nor are at all, but in a few, and in them, but of a few things. For science is of that nature, as none can understand it to be, but such as in a good measure have attained it.

Arts of public use, as fortification, making of engines, and other instruments of war; because they confer to defence, and victory, are power: . . .

OF THE NATURAL CONDITION OF MANKIND AS CONCERNING THEIR FELICITY, AND MISERY

Nature hath made men so equal, in the faculties of the body, and mind; as that though there be found one man sometimes manifestly stronger in body; or of quicker mind than another; yet when all is reckoned together, the difference between man, and man, is not so considerable, as that one man can thereupon claim to himself any benefit, to which another may not pretend, as well as he. For as to the strength of body, the weakest has strength enough to kill the strongest, either by secret machination, or by confederacy with others, that are in the same danger with himself.

And as to the faculties of the mind, setting aside the arts grounded upon words, and especially that skill of proceeding upon general, and infallible rules, called science; which very few have, and but in few things; as being not a native faculty, born with us; nor attained, as prudence, while we look after somewhat else, I find yet a greater equality amongst men, than that of strength. For prudence, is but experience; which equal time, equally bestows on all men, in those things they equally apply themselves unto. That which may perhaps make such equality incredible, is but a vain conceit of one's own wisdom, which almost all men think they have in a greater degree, than the vulgar; that is, than all men but themselves, and a few others, whom by fame, or for concurring with themselves, they approve. For such is the nature of men, that howsoever they may acknowledge many others to be more witty, or more eloquent, or more learned; yet they will hardly believe there be many so wise as themselves; for they see their own wit at hand, and other men's at a distance. But this proveth rather that men are in that point equal, than unequal. For there is not ordinarily a greater sign of the equal distribution of any thing, than that every man is contented with his share.

From this equality of ability, ariseth equality of hope in the attaining of our ends. And therefore if any two men desire the same thing, which nevertheless they cannot both enjoy, they become enemies; and in the way to their end, which is principally their own conservation, and sometimes their delectation only, endeavour to destroy, or subdue one another. And from hence it comes to pass, that where an invader hath no more to fear, than another man's single power; if one plant, sow, build, or possess a convenient seat, others may probably be expected to come prepared with forces united, to dispossess, and deprive him, not only of the fruit of his labour, but also of his life, or liberty. And the invader again is in the like danger of another.

And from this diffidence of one another, there is no way for any man to secure himself, so reasonable, as anticipation; that is, by force, or wiles, to master the persons of all men he can, so long, till he see no other power great enough to endanger him: and this is no more than his own conservation requireth, and is generally allowed. Also because there be some, that taking pleasure in contemplating their own power in the acts of conquest, which they pursue farther than their security requires; if others, that otherwise would be glad to be at ease within modest bounds, should not by invasion increase their power, they would not be able, long time, by standing only on their defence, to subsist. And by consequence, such augmentation of dominion over men being necessary to a man's conservation, it ought to be allowed him.

Again, men have no pleasure, but on the contrary a great deal of grief, in keeping company, where there is no power able to over-awe them all. For every man looketh that his companion should value him, at the same rate he sets upon himself: and upon all signs of contempt, or undervaluing, naturally endeavours, as far as he dares, (which amongst them that have no common power to keep them in quiet, is far enough to make them destroy each other), to extort a greater value from his contemners, by damage; and from others, by the example.

So that in the nature of man, we find three principal causes of quarrel. First, competition; secondly, diffidence; thirdly, glory.

The first, maketh men invade for gain; the second, for safety; and the third, for reputation. The first use violence, to make themselves masters of other men's persons, wives, children, and cattle; the second, to defend them; the third, for trifles, as a word, a smile, a different opinion, and any other sign of undervalue, either direct in their persons, or by reflection in their kindred, their friends, their nation, their profession, or their name.

Hereby it is manifest, that during the time men live without a common power to keep them all in awe, they are in that condition which is called war; and such a war, as is of every man, against every man. For WAR, consisteth not in battle only, or the act of fighting; but in a tract of time, wherein the will to contend by battle is sufficiently known: and therefore the notion of *time,* is to be considered in the nature of war; as it is in the nature of weather. For as the nature of foul weather, lieth not in a shower or two of rain; but in an inclination thereto of many days together: so the nature of war, consisteth not in actual fighting; but in the known disposition thereto, during all the time there is no assurance to the contrary. All other time is PEACE.

Whatsoever therefore is consequent to a time of war, where every man is enemy to every man; the same is consequent to the time, wherein men live without other security, than what their own strength, and their own invention shall furnish them withal. In such condition, there is no place for industry; because the fruit thereof is uncertain: and consequently no culture of the earth; no navigation, nor use of the commodities that may be imported by sea; no commodious building; no instruments of moving, and removing, such things as require much force; no knowledge of the face of the earth; no account of time; no arts; no letters; no society; and which is worst of all, continual fear, and danger of violent death; and the life of man, solitary, poor, nasty, brutish, and short.

It may seem strange to some man, that has not well weighed these things; that nature should thus dissociate, and render men apt to invade, and destroy one another: and he may therefore, not trusting to this inference, made from the passions, desire perhaps to have the same confirmed by experience. Let him therefore consider with himself, when taking a journey, he arms himself, and seeks to go well accompanied; when going to sleep, he locks his doors; when even in his house he locks his chests; and this when he knows there be laws, and public officers, armed, to revenge all injuries shall be done him; what opinion he has of his fellow-subjects, when he rides armed; of his fellow citizens, when he locks his doors; and of his children, and servants, when he locks his chests. Does he not there as much accuse mankind by his actions, as I do by my words? But neither of us accuse man's nature in it. The desires, and other passions of man, are in themselves no sin. No more are the actions, that proceed from those passions, till they know a law that forbids them: which till laws be made they cannot know: nor can any law be made, till they have agreed upon the person that shall make it.

It may peradventure be thought, there was never such a time, nor condition of war as this; and I believe it was never generally so, over all the world: but there are many places, where they live so now. For the savage people in many places of America, except the government of small families, the concord whereof dependeth on natural lust, have no government at all; and live at this day in that brutish manner, as I said before. Howsoever, it may be perceived what manner of life there would be, where there were no common power to fear, by the manner of life, which men that have formerly lived under a peaceful government, use to degenerate into, in a civil war.

But though there had never been any time, wherein particular men were in a condition of war one against another; yet in all times, kings, and persons of sovereign authority, because of their independency, are in continual jealousies, and in the state and posture of gladiators; having their weapons pointing, and their eyes fixed on one another; that is, their forts, garrisons, and guns upon the frontiers of their kingdoms; and continual spies upon their neighbours; which is a posture of war. But because they uphold thereby, the industry of their subjects; there does not follow from it, that misery, which accompanies the liberty of particular men.

To this war of every man, against every man, this also is consequent; that nothing can be unjust. The notions of right and wrong, justice and injustice have there no place. Where there is no common power, there is no law: where no law, no injustice. Force, and fraud, are in war the two cardinal virtues. Justice, and injustice are none of the faculties neither of the body, nor mind. If they were, they might be in a man that were alone in the world, as well as his senses, and passions. They are qualities, that relate to men in society, not in solitude. It is consequent also to the same condition, that there be no propriety, no dominion, no *mine* and *thine* distinct; but only that to be every man's, that he can get; and for so long, as he can keep it. And thus much for the ill condition, which man by mere nature is actually placed in; though with a possibility to come out of it, consisting partly in the passions, partly in his reason.

The passions that incline men to peace, are fear of death; desire of such things as are necessary to commodius living; and a hope by their industry to obtain them. And reason suggesteth convenient articles of peace, upon which men may be drawn to agreement. These articles, are they, which otherwise are called the Laws of Nature. . . .

Of the First and Second Natural Laws

The right of nature, which writers commonly call *jus naturale,* is the liberty each man hath, to use his own power, as he will himself, for the preservation of his own nature; that is to say, of his own life; and consequently, of doing any thing, which in his own judgment, and reason, he shall conceive to be the aptest means thereunto.

By LIBERTY, is understood, according to the proper signification of the word, the absence of external impediments: which impediments, may oft take away part of a man's power to do what he would; but cannot hinder him from using the power left him, according as his judgment, and reason shall dictate to him.

A LAW OF NATURE, *lex naturalis,* is a precept or general rule, found out by reason, by which a man is forbidden to do that, which is destructive of his life, or taketh away the means of preserving the same; and to omit that, by which he thinketh it may be best preserved. For though they that speak of this subject, use to confound *jus,* and *lex, right* and *law:* yet they ought to be distinguished; because RIGHT, consisteth in liberty to do, or to forbear; whereas LAW, determineth, and bindeth to one of them: so that law, and right, differ as much, as obligation, and liberty; which in one and the same matter are inconsistent.

And because the condition of man, as hath been declared in the precedent chapter, is a condition of war of every one against every one; in which case every one is governed by his own reason; and there is nothing he can make use of, that may not be a help unto him, in preserving his life against his enemies; it followeth, that in such a condition, every man has a right to every thing; even to one another's body. And therefore, as long as this natural right of every man to every thing endureth, there can be no security to any man, how strong or wise soever he be, of living out the time, which nature ordinarily alloweth men to live. And consequently it is a precept, or general rule of reason, *that every man, ought to endeavour peace, as far as he has hope of obtaining it; and when he cannot obtain it, that he may seek, and use, all helps, and advantages of war.* The first branch of which rule, containeth the first, and fundamental law of nature; which is, *to seek peace, and follow it.* The second, the sum of the right of nature; which is *by all means we can, to defend ourselves.*

From this fundamental law of nature, by which men are commanded to endeavour peace, is derived this second law; *that a man be willing, when others are so too, as far-forth, as for peace, and defence of himself he shall think it necessary, to lay down this right to all things; and be contented with so much liberty against other men, as he would allow other men against himself.* For as long as every man holdeth this right, of doing any thing he liketh; so long are all men in the condition of war. But if other men will not lay down their right, as well as he; then there is no reason for any one, to divest himself of his: for that were to expose himself to prey, which no man is bound to, rather than to dispose himself to peace. . . .

To *lay down* a man's *right* to any thing, is to *divest* himself of the *liberty,* of hindering another of the benefit of his own right to the same. For he that renounceth, or passeth away his right, giveth not to any other man a right which he had not before; because there is nothing to which every man had not right by nature: but only standeth out of his way, that he may enjoy his own original right, without hindrance from him; not without hindrance from another. So that the effect which redoundeth to one man, by another man's defect of right, is but so much diminution of impediments to the use of his own right original.

Right is laid aside, either by simply renouncing it; or by transferring it to another. By *simply* RENOUNCING; when he cares not to whom the benefit thereof redoundeth. By TRANSFERRING; when he intendeth the benefit thereof to some certain person, or persons. And when a man hath in either manner abandoned, or granted away his right; then is he said to be OBLIGED, or BOUND, not to hinder those, to whom such right is granted, or abandoned, from the benefit of it: and that he *ought,* and it is his DUTY, not to make void that voluntary act of his own: and that such hindrance is INJUSTICE, and INJURY, as being *sine jure;* the right being before renounced, or transferred. So that *injury,* or *injustice,* in the controversies of the world, is somewhat like to that, which in the disputations of scholars is called *absurdity.* For as it is there called an absurdity, to contradict what one maintained in the beginning: so in the world, it is called injustice, and injury, voluntarily to undo that, which from the beginning he had voluntarily done. The way by which a man either simply renounceth, or transferreth his right, is a declaration, or signification, by some voluntary and sufficient sign, or signs, that he doth so renounce, or transfer; or hath so renounced, or transferred the same, to him that accepteth it. And these signs are either words only, or actions only; or, as it happeneth most often, both words, and actions. And the same are the BONDS, by which men are bound, and obliged: bonds, that have their strength, not from their own nature, for nothing is more easily broken than a man's word, but from fear of some evil consequence upon the rupture.

Whensoever a man transferreth his right, or renounceth it; it is either in consideration of some right reciprocally transferred to himself; or for some other good he hopeth for thereby. For it is a voluntary act: and of the voluntary acts of every man, the object is some *good to himself.* And therefore there be some rights, which no man can be understood by any words, or other signs, to have abandoned, or transferred. As first a man cannot lay down the right of resisting them, that assault him by force, to take away his life; because he cannot be understood to aim thereby, at any good to himself. The same may be said of wounds, and chains, and imprisonment; both because there is no benefit consequent to such patience; as there is to the patience of suffering another to be wounded, or imprisoned: as also because a man cannot tell, when he seeth men proceed against him by violence, whether they intend his death or not. And lastly the motive, and end for which this renouncing, and transferring of right is introduced, is nothing else but the security of a man's person, in his life, and in the means of so preserving life, as not to be weary of it. And therefore if a man by words, or other signs, seem to despoil himself of the end, for which those signs were intended; he is not to be understood as if he meant it, or that it was his will; but that he was ignorant of how such words and actions were to be interpreted. . . .

✤ JEREMY BENTHAM
JOHN STUART MILL

23. *Utilitarianism*

Jeremy Bentham (1748–1832) was a leading figure in founding the English Utilitarian school of thought. In addition to his writings on ethics and political philosophy, he is known for numerous legal and political reforms which he steadfastly advocated.

John Stuart Mill (1806–1873) was the major British philosopher of his period. He wrote extensively on a variety of topics including logic, epistemology, politics, ethics, and religion. In ethics he was primarily concerned with defending the position that had been propounded by his father (James Mill) and Jeremy Bentham.

PART ONE*

Of the Principle of Utility

I. Nature has placed mankind under the governance of two sovereign masters, *pain* and *pleasure*. It is for them alone to point out what we ought to do, as well as to determine what we shall do. On the one hand the standard of right and wrong, on the other the chain of causes and effects, are fastened to their throne. They govern us in all we do, in all we say, in all we think: every effort we can make to throw off our subjection, will serve but to demonstrate and confirm it. In words a man may pretend to abjure their empire: but in reality he will remain subject to it all the while. The *principle of utility* recognises this subjection, and assumes it for the foundation of that system, the object of which is to rear the fabric of felicity by the hands of reason and of law. Systems which attempt to question it, deal in sounds instead of sense, in caprice instead of reason, in darkness instead of light.

But enough of metaphor and declamation: it is not by such means that moral science is to be improved.

II. The principle of utility is the foundation of the present work: it will be proper therefore at the outset to give an explicit and determinate account of what is meant by it. By the principle of utility is meant that principle which approves or disapproves of every action whatsoever, according to the tendency which it appears to have to augment or diminish the happiness of the party whose interest is in question: or, what is the same thing in other words, to promote or to oppose that happiness. I say of every action whatsoever; and therefore not only of every action of a private individual, but of every measure of government.

III. By utility is meant that property in any object, whereby it tends to produce benefit, advantage, pleasure, good, or happiness, (all this in the present case comes to the same thing) or (what comes again to the same thing) to prevent the happening of mischief, pain, evil, or unhappiness to the party whose interest is considered: if that party be the community in general, then the happiness of the community: if a particular individual, then the happiness of that individual.

IV. The interest of the community is one of the most general expressions that can occur in the phraseology of morals: no wonder that the meaning of it is often lost. When it has a meaning, it is this. The community is a fictitious *body*, composed of the individual persons who are considered as constituting as it were its *members*. The interest of the community then is, what?—the sum of the interests of the several members who compose it.

V. It is in vain to talk of the interest of the community, without understanding what is the interest of the individual. A thing is said to promote the interest, or to be *for* the interest, of an individual, when it

---

*Part One is selected from Chapters 1 and 4 of Bentham's *An Introduction to the Principles of Morals and Legislation* (London: Oxford at the Clarendon Press, 1907).

tends to add to the sum total of his pleasures: or, what comes to the same thing, to diminish the sum total of his pains.

VI. An action then may be said to be conformable to the principle of utility, or, for shortness sake, to utility, (meaning with respect to the community at large) when the tendency it has to augment the happiness of the community is greater than any it has to diminish it.

VII. A measure of government (which is but a particular kind of action, performed by a particular person or persons) may be said to be conformable to or dictated by the principle of utility, when in like manner the tendency which it has to augment the happiness of the community is greater than any which it has to diminish it.

VIII. When an action, or in particular a measure of government, is supposed by a man to be conformable to the principle of utility, it may be convenient, for the purposes of discourse, to imagine a kind of law or dictate, called a law or dictate of utility: and to speak of the action in question, as being conformable to such law or dictate.

IX. A man may be said to be a partizan of the principle of utility, when the approbation or disapprobation he annexes to any action, or to any measure, is determined by and proportioned to the tendency which he conceives it to have to augment or to diminish the happiness of the community: or in other words, to its conformity or unconformity to the laws or dictates of utility.

X. Of an action that is conformable to the principle of utility one may always say either that it is one that ought to be done, or at least that it is not one that ought not to be done. One may say also, that it is right it should be done; at least that it is not wrong it should be done: that it is a right action; at least that it is not a wrong action. When thus interpreted, the words *ought,* and *right* and *wrong,* and others of that stamp, have a meaning: when otherwise, they have none.

XI. Has the rectitude of this principle been ever formally contested? It should seem that it had, by those who have not known what they have been meaning. Is it susceptible of any direct proof? it should seem not: for that which is used to prove every thing else, cannot itself be proved: a chain of proofs must have their commencement somewhere. To give such proof is as impossible as it is needless.

XII. Not that there is or ever has been that human creature breathing, however stupid or perverse, who has not on many, perhaps on most occasions of his life, deferred to it. By the natural constitution of the human frame, on most occasions of their lives men in general embrace this principle, without thinking of it: if not for the ordering of their own actions, yet for the trying of their own actions, as well as of those of other men. There have been, at the same time, not many, perhaps, even of the most intelligent, who have been disposed to embrace it purely and without reserve. There are even few who have not taken some occasion or other to quarrel with it, either on account of their not understanding always how to apply it, or on account of some prejudice or other which they were afraid to examine into, or could not bear to part with. For such is the stuff that man is made of: in principle and in practice, in a right track and in a wrong one, the rarest of all human qualities is consistency. . . .

Value of a Lot of Pleasure or Pain, How to Be Measured

I. Pleasures then, and the avoidance of pains, are the *ends* which the legislator has in view: it behoves him therefore to understand their *value*. Pleasures and pains are the *instruments* he has to work with: it behoves him therefore to understand their force, which is again, in other words, their value.

II. To a person considered *by himself,* the value of a pleasure or pain considered *by itself,* will be greater or less, according to the four following circumstances[1]:

1. Its *intensity.*
2. Its *duration.*
3. Its *certainty* or *uncertainty.*
4. Its *propinquity* or *remoteness.*

III. These are the circumstances which are to be considered in estimating a pleasure or pain considered each of them by itself. But when the value of any pleasure or pain is considered for the purpose of estimating the tendency or any *act* by which it is produced, there are two other circumstances to be taken into the account; these are,

5. Its *fecundity,* or the chance it has of being followed by sensations of the *same* kind: that is, pleasures, if it be a pleasure: pains, if it be a pain.

6. Its *purity,* or the chance it has of *not* being followed by sensations of the *opposite* kind: that is, pains, if it be a pleasure: pleasures, if it be a pain.

These two last, however, are in strictness scarcely to be deemed properties of the pleasure or the pain itself; they are not, therefore, in strictness to be taken into the account of the value of that pleasure or that pain. They are in strictness to be deemed properties only of the act, or other event, by which such pleasure or pain has been produced; and accordingly are only to be taken into the account of the tendency of such act or such event.

IV. To a *number* of persons, with reference to each of whom the

---

[1]These circumstances have since been denominated *elements* or *dimensions* of *value* in a pleasure or a pain.

Not long after the publication of the first edition, the following memoriter verses were framed, in the view of lodging more effectually, in the memory, these points, on which the whole fabric of morals and legislation may be seen to rest.

> Intense, long, certain, speedy, fruitful, pure—
> Such marks in *pleasures* and in *pains* endure.
> Such pleasures seek if *private* be thy end:
> If it be *public,* wide let them *extend.*
> Such *pains* avoid, whichever be thy view:
> If pains *must* come, let them *extend* to few.

value of a pleasure or a pain is considered, it will be greater or less, according to seven circumstances: to wit, the six preceding ones; *viz.*

1. Its *intensity.*
2. Its *duration.*
3. Its *certainty* or *uncertainty.*
4. Its *propinquity* or *remoteness.*
5. Its *fecundity.*
6. Its *purity.*

And one other; to wit:

7. Its *extent;* that is, the number of persons to whom it *extends;* or (in other words) who are affected by it.

V. To take an exact account then of the general tendency of any act, by which the interests of a community are affected, proceed as follows. Begin with any one person of those whose interests seem most immediately to be affected by it: and take an account,

1. Of the value of each distinguishable *pleasure* which appears to be produced by it in the *first* instance.

2. Of the value of each *pain* which appears to be produced by it in the *first* instance.

3. Of the value of each pleasure which appears to be produced by it *after* the first. This constitutes the *fecundity* of the first *pleasure* and the *impurity* of the first *pain.*

4. Of the value of each *pain* which appears to be produced by it after the first. This constitutes the *fecundity* of the first *pain,* and the *impurity* of the first pleasure.

5. Sum up all the values of all the *pleasures* on the one side, and those of all the pains on the other. The balance, if it be on the side of pleasure, will give the *good* tendency of the act upon the whole, with respect to the interests of that *individual* person; if on the side of pain, the *bad* tendency of it upon the whole.

6. Take an account of the *number* of persons whose interests appear to be concerned; and repeat the above process with respect to each. *Sum up* the numbers expressive of the degrees of *good* tendency, which the act has, with respect to each individual, in regard to whom the tendency of it is *good* upon the whole: do this again with respect to each individual, in regard to whom the tendency of it is *good* upon the whole: do this again with respect to each individual, in regard to whom the tendency of it is *bad* upon the whole. Take the *balance;* which, if on the side of *pleasure,* will give the general *good tendency* of the act, with respect to the total number or community of individuals concerned; if on the side of pain, the general *evil tendency,* with respect to the same community.

VI. It is not to be expected that this process should be strictly pursued previously to every moral judgment, or to every legislative or judicial operation. It may, however, be always kept in view: and as near as the process actually pursued on these occasions approaches to it, so near will such process approach to the character of an exact one.

VII. The same process is alike applicable to pleasure and pain, in whatever shape they appear: and by whatever denomination they are distinguished: to pleasure, whether it be called *good* (which is properly the cause or instrument of pleasure) or *profit* (which is distant pleasure, or the cause or instrument of distant pleasure,) or *convenience*, or *advantage, benefit, emolument, happiness,* and so forth: to pain, whether it be called *evil*, (which corresponds to *good*) or *mischief*, or *inconvenience*, or *disadvantage*, or *loss,* or *unhappiness,* and so forth.

VIII. Nor is this a novel and unwarranted, any more than it is a useless theory. In all this there is nothing but what the practice of mankind, wheresoever they have a clear view of their own interest, is perfectly conformable to. . . .

PART TWO*

What Utilitarianism Is

A passing remark is all that needs be given to the ignorant blunder of supposing that those who stand up for utility as the test of right and wrong, use the term in that restricted and merely colloquial sense in which utility is opposed to pleasure. An apology is due to the philosophical opponents of utilitarianism, for even the momentary appearance of confounding them with any one capable of so absurd a misconception; which is the more extraordinary, inasmuch as the contrary accusation, of referring everything to pleasure, and that too in its grossest form, is another of the common charges against utilitarianism: and, as has been pointedly remarked by an able writer, the same sort of persons, and often the very same persons, denounce the theory "as impracticably dry when the word utility precedes the word pleasure, and as too practicably voluptuous when the word pleasure precedes the word utility." Those who know anything about the matter are aware that every writer, from Epicurus to Bentham, who maintained the theory of utility, meant by it, not something to be contradistinguished from pleasure, but pleasure itself, together with exemption from pain; and instead of opposing the useful to the agreeable or the ornamental, have always declared that the useful means these, among other things. Yet the common herd, including the herd of writers, not only in newspapers and periodicals, but in books of weight and pretension, are perpetually falling into this shallow mistake. Having caught up the word utilitarian, while knowing nothing whatever about it but its sound, they habitually express by it the rejection, or the neglect, of pleasure in some of its forms; of beauty, of ornament, or of amusement. Nor is the term thus ignorantly misapplied solely in disparagement, but occasionally in compliment; as though it implied superiority to frivolity and the mere pleasures of the moment. And this perverted use is the only one in which the word is popularly known, and

*Part Two is from Mill's *Utilitarianism* (London: J. M. Dent & Sons, Ltd., 1910). Some footnotes have been omitted.

the one from which the new generation are acquiring their sole notion of its meaning. Those who introduced the word, but who had for many years discontinued it as a distinctive appellation, may well feel themselves called upon to resume it, if by doing so they can hope to contribute anything towards rescuing it from this utter degradation.

The creed which accepts as the foundation of morals, Utility, or the Greatest Happiness Principle, holds that actions are right in proportion as they tend to promote happiness, wrong as they tend to produce the reverse of happiness. By happiness is intended pleasure, and the absence of pain; by unhappiness, pain, and the privation of pleasure. To give a clear view of the moral standard set up by the theory, much more requires to be said; in particular, what things it includes in the ideas of pain and pleasure; and to what extent this is left an open question. But these supplementary explanations do not affect the theory of life on which this theory of morality is grounded—namely, that pleasure, and freedom from pain, are the only things desirable as ends; and that all desirable things (which are as numerous in the utilitarian as in any other scheme) are desirable either for the pleasure inherent in themselves, or as means to the promotion of pleasure and the prevention of pain.

Now, such a theory of life excites in many minds, and among them in some of the most estimable in feeling and purpose, inveterate dislike. To suppose that life has (as they express it) no higher end than pleasure— no better and nobler object of desire and pursuit—they designate as utterly mean and grovelling; as a doctrine worthy only of swine, to whom the followers of Epicurus were, at a very early period, contemptuously likened; and modern holders of the doctrine are occasionally made the subject of equally polite comparisons by its German, French, and English assailants.

When thus attacked, the Epicureans have always answered, that it is not they, but their accusers, who represent human nature in a degrading light; since the accusation supposes human beings to be capable of no pleasures except those of which swine are capable. If this supposition were true, the charge could not be gainsaid, but would then be no longer an imputation; for if the sources of pleasure were precisely the same to human beings and to swine, the rule of life which is good enough for the one would be good enough for the other. The comparison of the Epicurean life to that of beasts is felt as degrading, precisely because a beast's pleasures do not satisfy a human being's conceptions of happiness. Human beings have faculties more elevated than the animal appetites, and when once made conscious of them, do not regard anything as happiness which does not include their gratification. I do not, indeed, consider the Epicureans to have been by any means faultless in drawing out their scheme of consequences from the utilitarian principle. To do this in any sufficient manner, many Stoic, as well as Christian elements require to be included. But there is no known Epicurean theory of life which does not assign to the pleasures of the intellect, of the feelings and imagination, and of the moral sentiments, a much higher value as pleasures than to those of mere sensation. It must be admitted, however, that utilitarian writers in general have placed the superiority of mental over bodily pleasures chiefly in the greater permanency, safety, uncostliness, etc., of the former—that is, in their circumstantial advantages rather than in their intrinsic nature. And on all these points utilitarians have fully proved their case; but they might have taken the other, and, as it may be called, higher ground, with entire consistency. It is quite compatible with the principle of utility to recognise the fact, that some *kinds* of pleasure are more desirable and more valuable than others. It would be absurd that while, in estimating all other things, quality is considered as well as quantity, the estimation of pleasures should be supposed to depend on quantity alone.

If I am asked, what I mean by difference of quality in pleasures, or what makes one pleasure more valuable than another, merely as a pleasure, except its being greater in amount, there is but one possible answer. Of two pleasures, if there be one to which all or almost all who have experience of both give a decided preference, irrespective of any feeling of moral obligation to prefer it, that is the more desirable pleasure. If one of the two is, by those who are competently acquainted with both, placed so far above the other that they prefer it, even though knowing it to be attended with a greater amount of discontent, and would not resign it for any quantity of the other pleasure which their nature is capable of, we are justified in ascribing to the preferred enjoyment a superiority in quality, so far outweighing quantity as to render it, in comparison, of small account.

Now it is an unquestionable fact that those who are equally acquainted with, and equally capable of appreciating and enjoying, both, do give a most marked preference to the manner of existence which employs their higher faculties. Few human creatures would consent to be changed into any of the lower animals, for a promise of the fullest allowance of a beast's pleasures; no intelligent human being would consent to be a fool, no instructed person would be an ignoramus, no person of feeling and conscience would be selfish and base, even though they should be persuaded that the fool, the dunce, or the rascal is better satisfied with his lot than they are with theirs. They would not resign what they possess more than he for the most complete satisfaction of all the desires which they have in common with him. If they ever fancy they would, it is only in cases of unhappiness so extreme, that to escape from it they would exchange their lot for almost any other, however undesirable in their own eyes. A being of higher faculties requires more to make him happy, is capable probably of more acute suffering, and certainly accessible to it at more points, than one of an inferior type; but in spite of these liabilities, he can never really wish to sink into what he feels to be a lower grade of existence. We may give what explanation we please of this unwillingness; we may attribute it to pride, a name which is given indiscriminately to some of the most and to some of the least estimable feelings of which mankind are capable: we may refer it to the love of liberty and personal independence, an appeal to which was with the Stoics one of the most effective means for the inculcation of it; to the love of power, or to the love of excitement, both of which do really enter into and contribute to it: but its most appropriate appellation is a sense of dignity, which all human beings possess in one form or other, and in some, though by no means in exact, proportion to their higher faculties, and which is so essential a part of the happiness of those in whom it is strong, that nothing which conflicts with it could be, otherwise than momentarily, an object of desire to them. Whoever supposes that this preference takes place at a sacrifice of happiness—that the superior being, in anything like equal circumstances, is not happier than the inferior—confounds the two very different ideas, of happiness, and content. It is indisputable that the being whose capacities of enjoyment are low, has the greatest chance of having them fully satisfied; and a highly endowed being will always feel that any happiness which he can look for, as the world is constituted, is imperfect. But he can learn to bear its imperfections, if they are at all bearable; and they will not make him envy the being who is indeed un-conscious of the imperfections, but only because he feels not at all the good which those imperfections qualify. It is better to be a human being dis-satisfied than a pig satisfied; better to be Socrates dissatisfied than a fool satisfied. And if the fool, or the pig, are of a different opinion, it is because they only know their own side of the question. The other party to the comparison knows both sides.

It may be objected, that many who are capable of the higher plea-sures, occasionally, under the influence of temptation, postpone them to the lower. But this is quite compatible with a full appreciation of the intrinsic superiority of the higher. Men often, from infirmity of character, make their election for the nearer good, though they know it to be the less valuable; and this no less when the choice is between two bodily pleasures, than when it is between bodily and mental. They pursue sensual indulgences to the injury of health, though perfectly aware that health is the greater good. It may be further objected, that many who begin with youthful enthusiasm for everything noble, as they advance in years sink into indolence and selfishness. But I do not believe that those who undergo this very com-mon change, voluntarily choose the lower description of pleasures in preference to the higher. I do believe that before they devote themselves exclusively to the one, they have already become incapable of the other. Capacity for the nobler feelings is in most natures a very tender plant, easily killed, not only by hostile influences, but by mere want of sustenance; and in the majority of young persons it speedily dies away if the occupations to which their position in life has devoted them, and the society into which it has thrown them, are not favourable to keeping that higher capacity in exercise. Men lose their high aspirations as they lose their intellectual tastes, because they have not time or opportunity for indulging them; and they addict themselves to inferior pleasures, not because they deliberately prefer them, but because they are either the only ones to which they have access, or the only ones which they are any longer capable of enjoying. It may be questioned whether any one who has remained equally susceptible to both classes of pleasures, ever knowingly and calmly preferred the lower; though many, in all ages, have broken down in an ineffectual attempt to combine both.

From this verdict of the only competent judges, I apprehend there can be no appeal. On a question which is the best worth having of two pleasures, or which of two modes of existence is the most grateful to the feelings, apart from its moral attributes and from its consequences, the judgment of those who are qualified by knowledge of both, or, if they differ, that of the majority among them, must be admitted as final. And there needs be the less hesitation to accept this judgment respecting the quality of pleasures, since there is no other tribunal to be referred to even on the question of quantity. What means are there of determining which is the acutest of two pains, or the intensest of two pleasurable sensations, except the general suffrage of those who are familiar with both? Neither pains nor pleasures are homogeneous, and pain is always heterogeneous with pleasure. What is there to decide whether a particular pleasure is worth purchasing at the cost of a particular pain, except the feelings and judgment of the experienced? When, therefore, those feelings and judgment declare the pleasures derived from the higher faculties to be preferable *in kind,* apart from the question of intensity, to those of which the animal nature, disjoined from the higher faculties, is susceptible, they are entitled on this subject to the same regard.

I have dwelt on this point, as being a necessary part of a perfectly just conception of Utility or Happiness, considered as the directive rule of human conduct. But it is by no means an indispensable condition to the acceptance of the utilitarian standard; for that standard is not the agent's own greatest happiness, but the greatest amount of happiness altogether; and if it may possibly be doubted whether a noble character is always the happier for its nobleness, there can be no doubt that it makes other people happier, and that the world in general is immensely a gainer by it. Utilitarianism, therefore, could only attain its end by the general cultivation of nobleness of character, even if each individual were only benefited by the nobleness of others, and his own, so far as happiness is concerned, were a sheer deduction from the benefit. But the bare enunciation of such an absurdity as this last, renders refutation superfluous.

According to the Greatest Happiness Principle, as above explained, the ultimate end, with reference to and for the sake of which all other things are desirable (whether we are considering our own good or that of other people), is an existence exempt as far as possible from pain, and as rich as possible in enjoyments, both in point of quantity and quality; the test of quality, and the rule for measuring it against quantity, being the preference felt by those who in their opportunities of experience, to which must be added their habits of self-consciousness and self-observation, are best furnished with the means of comparison. This, being, according to the utilitarian opinion, the end of human action, is necessarily also the standard of morality; which may accordingly be defined, the rules and precepts for human conduct, by the observance of which an existence such as has been described might be, to the greatest extent possible, secured to all mankind; and not to them only, but, so far as the nature of things admits, to the whole sentient creation. . . .

The objectors perhaps may doubt whether human beings, if taught to consider happiness as the end of life, would be satisfied with such a moderate share of it. But great numbers of mankind have been satisfied with much less. The main constituents of a satisfied life appear to be two, either of which by itself is often found sufficient for the purpose: tranquillity, and excitement. With much tranquillity, many find that they can be content with very little pleasure: with much excitement, many can reconcile themselves to a considerable quantity of pain. There is assuredly no inherent impossibility in enabling even the mass of mankind to unite both; since the two are so far from being incompatible that they are in natural alliance, the prolongation of either being a preparation for, and exciting a wish for, the other. It is only those in whom indolence amounts to a vice, that do not desire excitement after an interval of repose: it is only those in whom the need of excitement is a disease, that feel the tranquillity which follows excitement dull and insipid, instead of pleasurable in direct proportion to the excitement which preceded it. When people who are tolerably fortunate in their outward lot do not find in life sufficient enjoyment to make it valuable to them, the cause generally is, caring for nobody but themselves. To those who have neither public nor private affections, the excitements of life are much curtailed, and in any case dwindle in value as the time approaches when all selfish interests must be terminated by death: while those who leave after them objects of personal affection, and especially those who have also cultivated a fellow-feeling with the collective interests of mankind, retain as lively an interest in life on the eve of death as in the vigour of youth and health. Next to selfishness, the principal cause which makes life unsatisfactory is want of mental cultivation. A cultivated mind— I do not mean that of a philosopher, but any mind to which the fountains of knowledge have been opened, and which has been taught, in any tolerable degree, to exercise its faculties—finds sources of inexhaustible interest in all that surrounds it; in the objects of nature, the achievements of art, the imaginations of poetry, the incidents of history, the ways of mankind, past and present, and their prospects in the future. It is possible, indeed, to become indifferent to all this, and that too without having exhausted a thousandth part of it; but only when one has had from the beginning no moral or human interest in these things, and has sought in them only the gratification of curiosity.

Now there is absolutely no reason in the nature of things why an amount of mental culture sufficient to give an intelligent interest in these objects of contemplation, should not be the inheritance of every one born in a civilised country. As little is there an inherent necessity that any human being should be a selfish egotist, devoid of every feeling or care but those which centre in his own miserable individuality. Something far superior to this is sufficiently common even now, to give ample earnest of what the human species may be made. Genuine private affections, and a sincere interest in the public good, are possible, though in unequal degrees, to every rightly brought up human being. In a world in which there is so much to interest, so much to enjoy, and so much also to correct and improve, every one who has this moderate amount of moral and intellectual requisites is capable of an existence which may be called enviable; and unless such a person, through bad laws, or subjection to the will of others, is denied the liberty to use the sources of happiness within his reach, he will not fail to find this enviable existence, if he escape the positive evils of life, the great sources of physical and mental suffering—such as indigence, disease, and the unkindness, worthlessness, or premature loss of objects of affection. The main stress of the problem lies, therefore, in the contest with these calamities, from which it is a rare good fortune entirely to escape; which, as things now are, cannot be obviated, and often cannot be in any material degree mitigated. Yet no one whose opinion deserves a moment's consideration can doubt that most of the great positive evils of the world are in themselves removable, and will, if human affairs continue to improve, be in the end reduced within narrow limits. Poverty, in any sense implying suffering, may be completely extinguished by the wisdom of society, combined with the good sense and providence of individuals. Even that most intractable of enemies, disease, may be indefinitely reduced in dimensions by good physical and moral education, and proper control of noxious influences; while the progress of science holds out a promise for the future of still more direct conquests over this detestable foe. And every advance in that direction relieves us from some, not only of the chances which cut short our own lives, but, what concerns us still more, which deprive us of those in whom our happiness is wrapt up. As for vicissitudes of fortune, and other disappointments connected with worldly circumstances, these are principally the effect either of gross imprudence, of ill-regulated desires, or of bad or imperfect social institutions. All the grand sources, in short, of human suffering are in a great degree, many of them almost entirely, conquerable by human care and effort; and though their removal is grievously slow— though a long succession of generations will perish in the breach before the conquest is completed, and this world becomes all that, if will and knowledge were not wanting, it might easily be made—yet every mind sufficiently intelligent and generous to bear a part, however small and unconspicuous, in the endeavour, will draw a noble enjoyment from the contest itself, which he would not for any bribe in the form of selfish indulgence consent to be without. . . .

The objectors to utilitarianism cannot always be charged with representing it in a discreditable light. On the contrary, those among them who entertain anything like a just idea of its disinterested character, sometimes find fault with its standard as being too high for humanity. They say it is exacting too much to require that people shall always act from the inducement of promoting the general interests of society. But this is to mistake the very meaning of a standard of morals, and confound the rule of action with the motive of it. It is the business of ethics to tell us what are our duties, or by what test we may know them; but no system of ethics requires that the sole motive of all we do shall be a feeling of duty; on the contrary, ninety-nine hundredths of all our actions are done from other motives, and rightly so done, if the rule of duty does not condemn them. It is the more unjust to utilitarianism that this particular misapprehension should be made a ground of objection to it, inasmuch as utilitarian moralists have gone beyond almost all others in affirming that the motive has nothing to do with the morality of the action, though much with the worth of the agent. He who saves a fellow creature from drowning does what is morally right, whether his motive be duty, or the hope of being paid for his trouble; he who betrays the friend that trusts him, is guilty of a crime, even if his object be to serve another friend to whom he is under greater obligations. But to speak only of actions done from the motive of duty, and in direct obedience to principle: it is a misapprehension of the utilitarian mode of thought, to conceive it as implying that people should fix their minds upon so wide a generality as the world, or society at large. The great majority of good actions are intended not for the benefit of the world, but for that of individuals, of which the good of the world is made up; and the thoughts of the most virtuous man need not on these occasions travel beyond the particular persons concerned, except so far as is necessary to assure himself that in benefiting them he is not violating the rights, that is, the legitimate and unauthorised expectations, of any one else. The multiplication of happiness is, according to the utilitarian ethics, the object of virtue: the occasions on which any person (except one in a thousand) has it in his power to do this on an extended scale, in other words to be a public benefactor, are but exceptional; and on these occasions alone is he called on to consider public utility; in every other case, private utility, the interest or happiness of some few persons, is all he has to attend to. Those alone the influence of whose actions extends to society in general, need concern themselves habitually about so large an object. In the case of abstinences indeed—of things which people forbear to do from moral considerations, though the consequences in the particular case might be beneficial—it would be unworthy of an intelligent agent not to be consciously aware that the action is of a class which, if practised generally, would be generally injurious, and that this is the ground of the obligation to abstain from it. The amount of regard for the public interest implied in this recognition, is no greater than is demanded by every system of morals, for they all enjoin to abstain from whatever is manifestly pernicious to society. . . .

Of the Ultimate Sanction of the Principle of Utility

The question is often asked, and properly so, in regard to any supposed moral standard—What is its sanction? what are the motives to obey it? or more specifically, what is the source of its obligation? whence does it derive its binding force? It is a necessary part of moral philosophy to provide the answer to this question; which, though frequently assuming the shape of an objection to the utilitarian morality, as if it had some special applicability to that above others, really arises in regard to all standards. It arises, in fact, whenever a person is called on to *adopt* a standard, or refer morality to any basis on which he has not been accustomed to rest it. For the customary morality, that which education and opinion have consecrated, is the only one which presents itself to the mind with the feeling of being *in itself* obligatory; and when a person is asked to believe that this morality *derives* its obligation from some general principle round which custom has not thrown the same halo, the assertion is to him a paradox; the supposed corollaries seem to have a more binding force than the original theorem; the superstructure seems to stand better without, than with, what is represented as its foundation. He says to himself, I feel that I am bound not to rob or murder, betray or deceive; but why am I bound to promote the general happiness? If my own happiness lies in something else, why may I not give that the preference?

If the view adopted by the utilitarian philosophy of the nature of the moral sense be correct, this difficulty will always present itself, until the influences which form moral character have taken the same hold of the principle which they have taken of some of the consequences—until, by the improvement of education, the feeling of unity with our fellow-creatures shall be (what it cannot be denied that Christ intended it to be) as deeply rooted in our character, and to our own consciousness as completely a part of our nature, as the horror of crime is in an ordinarily well brought up young person. In the meantime, however, the difficulty has no peculiar application to the doctrine of utility, but is inherent in every attempt to analyse morality and reduce it to principles; which, unless the principle is already in men's minds invested with as much sacredness as any of its applications, always seems to divest them of a part of their sanctity.

The principle of utility either has, or there is no reason why it might not have, all the sanctions which belong to any other system of morals. Those sanctions are either external or internal. Of the external sanctions it is not necessary to speak at any length. They are, the hope of favour and the fear of displeasure, from our fellow-creatures or from the Ruler of the Universe, along with whatever we may have of sympathy or affection for them, or of love and awe of Him, inclining us to do his will independently of selfish consequences. There is evidently no reason why all these motives for observance should not attach themselves to the utilitarian morality, as completely and as powerfully as to any other. Indeed, those of them which refer to our fellow-creatures are sure to do so, in proportion to the amount of general intelligence; for whether there be any other ground of moral obligation than the general happiness or not, men do desire happiness; and however imperfect may be their own practice, they desire and commend all conduct in others towards themselves, by which they think their happiness is promoted. With regard to the religious motive, if men believe, as most profess to do, in the goodness of God, those who think that conduciveness to the general happiness is the essence, or even only the criterion of good, must necessarily believe that it is also that which God approves. The whole force therefore of external reward and punishment, whether physical or moral, and whether proceeding from God or from our fellow men, together with all that the capacities of human nature admit of disinterested devotion to either, become available to enforce the utilitarian morality, in proportion as the morality is recognised; and the more powerfully, the more the appliances of education and general cultivation are bent to the purpose.

So far as to external sanctions. The internal sanction of duty, whatever our standard of duty may be, is one and the same—a feeling in our own mind; a pain, more or less intense, attendant on violation of duty, which in properly cultivated moral natures rises, in the more serious cases, into shrinking from it as an impossibility. This feeling, when disinterested, and connecting itself with the pure idea of duty, and not with some particular form of it, or with any of the merely accessory circumstances, is the essence of Conscience; though in that complex pheomenon as it actually exists, the simple fact is in general all encrusted over with collateral associations, derived from sympathy, from love, and still more from fear; from all the forms of religious feeling; from the recollections of childhood and of all our past life; from self-esteem, desire of the esteem of others, and occasionally even self-abasement. This extreme complication is, I apprehend, the origin of the sort of mystical character which, by a tendency of the human mind of which there are many other examples, is apt to be attributed to the idea of moral obligation, and which leads people to believe that the idea cannot possibly attach itself to any other objects than those which, by a supposed mysterious law, are found in our present experience to excite it. Its binding force, however, consists in the existence of a mass of feeling which must be broken through in order to do what violates our standard of right, and which, if we do nevertheless violate that standard, will probably have to be encountered afterwards in the form of remorse. Whatever theory we have of the nature or origin of conscience, this is what essentially constitutes it.

The ultimate sanction, therefore, of all morality (external motives apart) being a subjective feeling in our own minds, I see nothing embarrassing to those whose standard is utility, in the question, what is the sanction of that particular standard? We may answer, the same as of all other moral standards—the conscientious feelings of mankind. Undoubtedly this sanction has no binding efficacy on those who do not possess the feelings it appeals to; but neither will these persons be more obedient to any other moral principle than to the utilitarian one. On them morality of any kind has no hold but through the external sanctions. Meanwhile the feelings exist, a fact in human nature, the reality of which, and the great power with which they are capable of acting on those in whom they have been duly cultivated, are proved by experience. No reason has ever been shown why they may not be cultivated to as great intensity in connection with the utilitarian, as with any other rule of morals. . . .

It is not necessary, for the present purpose, to decide whether the feeling of duty is innate or implanted. Assuming it to be innate, it is an open question to what objects it naturally attaches itself; for the philosophic supporters of that theory are now agreed that the intuitive percepion is of principles of morality and not of the details. If there be anything innate in the matter, I see no reason why the feeling which is innate should not be that of regard to the pleasures and pains of others. If there is any principle of morals which is intuitively obligatory, I should say it must be that. If so, the intuitive ethics would coincide with the utilitarian, and there would be no further quarrel between them. Even as it is, the intuitive moralists, though they believe that there are other intuitive moral obligations, do already believe this to be one; for they unanimously hold that a large *portion* of morality turns upon the consideration due to the interests of our fellow-creatures. Therefore, if the belief in the transcendental origin of moral obligation gives any additional efficacy to the internal sanction, it appears to me that the utilitarian principle has already the benefit of it.

On the other hand, if, as is my own belief, the moral feelings are not innate, but acquired, they are not for that reason the less natural. It is natural to man to speak, to reason, to build cities, to cultivate the ground, though these are acquired faculties. The moral feelings are not indeed a part of our nature, in the sense of being in any perceptible degree present in all of us; but this, unhappily, is a fact admitted by those who believe the most strenuously in their transcendental origin. Like the other acquired capacities above referred to, the moral faculty, if not a part of our nature, is a natural outgrowth from it; capable, like them, in a certain small degree, of springing up spontaneously; and susceptible of being brought by cultivation to a high degree of development. Unhappily it is also susceptible, by a sufficient use of the external sanctions and of the force of early impressions, of being cultivated in almost any direction: so that there is hardly anything so absurd or so mischievous that it may not, by means of these influences, be made to act on the human mind with all the authority of conscience. To doubt that the same potency might be given by the same means to the principle of utility, even if it had no foundation in human nature, would be flying in the face of all experience.

But moral associations which are wholly of artificial creation, when intellectual culture goes on, yield by degrees to the dissolving force of analysis: and if the feeling of duty, when associated with utility, would appear equally arbitrary; if there were no leading department of our nature, no powerful class of sentiments, with which that association would harmonise, which would make us feel it congenial, and incline us not only to foster it in others (for which we have abundant interested motives), but also to cherish it in ourselves; if there were not, in short, a natural basis of sentiment for utilitarian morality, it might well happen that this association also, even after it had been implanted by education, might be analysed away.

But there *is* this basis of powerful natural sentiment; and this it is which, when once the general happiness is recognised as the ethical standard, will constitute the strength of the utilitarian morality. This firm foundation is that of the social feelings of mankind; the desire to be in unity with our fellow creatures, which is already a powerful principle in human nature, and happily one of those which tend to become stronger, even without express inculcation, from the influences of advancing civilisation. . . .

Neither is it necessary to the feeling which constitutes the binding force of the utilitarian morality on those who recognise it, to wait for those social influences which would make its obligation felt by mankind at large. In the comparatively early state of human advancement in which we now live, a person cannot indeed feel that entireness of sympathy with all others, which would make any real discordance in the general direction of their conduct in life impossible; but already a person in whom the social feeling is at all developed, cannot bring himself to think of the rest of his fellow-creatures as struggling rivals with him for the means of happiness, whom he must desire to see defeated in their object in order that he may succeed in his. The deeply rooted conception which every individual even now has of himself as a social being, tends to make him feel it one of his natural wants that there should be harmony between his feelings and aims and those of his fellow-creatures. If differences of opinion and of mental culture make it impossible for him to share many of their actual feelings—perhaps make him denounce and defy those feelings—he still needs to be conscious that his real aim and theirs do not conflict; that he is not opposing himself to what they really wish for, namely their own good, but is, on the contrary, promoting it. This feeling in most individuals is much inferior in strength to their selfish feelings, and is often wanting altogether. But to those who have it, it possesses all the characters of a natural feeling. It does not present itself to their minds as a superstition of education, or a law despotically imposed by the power of society, but as an attribute which it would not be well for them to be without. This conviction is the ultimate sanction of the greatest happiness morality. This it is which makes any mind, of well-developed feelings, work with, and not against, the outward motives to care for others, afforded by what I have called the external sanctions; and when those sanctions are wanting, or act in an opposite direction, constitutes in itself a powerful internal binding force, in proportion to the sensitiveness and thoughtfulness of the character; since few but those whose mind is a moral blank, could bear to lay out their course of life on the plan of paying no regard to others except so far as their own private interest compels.

❁ IMMANUEL KANT

24. Good Will, Duty, and the Categorical Imperative

Immanuel Kant (1724–1804) is one of the most important thinkers in the history of Western philosophy. His most revolutionary philosophical work, the *Critique of Pure Reason,* is a classic in the fields of epistemology and metaphysics. Kant taught at the University of Königsberg in East Prussia. Although his writing style is rather formidable, he has exerted an important influence upon many subsequent schools of thought.

FIRST SECTION

Transition from the Common Rational Knowledge of Morality to the Philosophical

Nothing can possibly be conceived in the world, or even out of it, which can be called good, without qualification, except a Good Will. Intelligence, wit, judgment, and the other *talents* of the mind, however they may be named, or courage, resolution, perseverance, as qualities of temperament, are undoubtedly good and desirable in many respects; but these gifts of nature may also become extremely bad and mischievous if the will which is to make use of them, and which, therefore, constitutes what is called *character,* is not good. It is the same with the *gifts of fortune.* Power, riches, honour, even health, and the general well-being and contentment with one's condition which is called *happiness,* inspire pride, and often presumption, if there is not a good will to correct the influence of these on the mind, and with this also to rectify the whole principle of acting, and adapt it to its end. The sight of a being who is not adorned with a single feature of a pure and good will, enjoying unbroken prosperity, can never give pleasure to an impartial rational spectator. Thus a good will appears to constitute the indispensable condition even of being worthy of happiness.

There are even some qualities which are of service to this good will itself, and may facilitate its action, yet which have no intrinsic unconditional value, but always presuppose a good will, and this qualifies the esteem that we justly have for them, and does not permit us to regard them as absolutely good. Moderation in the affections and passions, self-control, and calm deliberation are not only good in many respects, but even seem to constitute part of the intrinsic worth of the person; but they are far from deserving to be called good without qualification, although they have been so unconditionally praised by the ancients. For without the principles of a

From *Fundamental Principles of the Metaphysics of Morals,* by Immanuel Kant, Sections 1 and 2. Translated by T. K. Abbott (1898). Original footnotes have been omitted.

good will, they may become extremely bad; and the coolness of a villain not only makes him far more dangerous, but also directly makes him more abominable in our eyes than he would have been without it.

A good will is good not because of what it performs or effects, not by its aptness for the attainment of some proposed end, but simply by virtue of the volition, that is, it is good in itself, and considered by itself is to be esteemed much higher than all that can be brought about by it in favour of any inclination, nay, even of the sum-total of all inclinations. Even if it should happen that,. owing to special disfavour of fortune, or the niggardly provision of a step-motherly nature, this will should wholly lack power to accomplish its purpose, if with its greatest efforts it should yet achieve nothing, and there should remain only the good will (not, to be sure, a mere wish, but the summoning of all means in our power), then, like a jewel, it would still shine by its own light, as a thing which has its whole value in itself. Its usefulness or fruitlessness can neither add to nor take away anything from this value. It would be, as it were, only the setting to enable us to handle it the more conveniently in common commerce, or to attract to it the attention of those who are not yet connoisseurs, but not to recommend it to true connoisseurs, or to determine its value.

There is, however, something so strange in this idea of the absolute value of the mere will, in which no account is taken of its utility, that notwithstanding the thorough assent of even common reason to the idea, yet a suspicion must arise that it may perhaps really be the product of mere high-flown fancy, and that we may have misunderstood the purpose of nature in assigning reason as the governor of our will. Therefore we will examine this idea from this point of view.

In the physical constitution of an organized being, that is, a being adapted suitably to the purposes of life, we assume it as a fundamental principle that no organ for any purpose will be found but what is also the fittest and best adapted for that purpose. Now in a being which has reason and a will, if the proper object of nature were its *conservation,* its *welfare,* in a word, its *happiness,* then nature would have hit upon a very bad arrangement in selecting the reason of the creature to carry out this purpose. For all the actions which the creature has to perform with a view to this purpose, and the whole rule of its conduct, would be far more surely prescribed to it by instinct, and that end would have been attained thereby much more certainly than it ever can be by reason. Should reason have been communicated to this favoured creature over and above, it must only have served it to contemplate the happy constitution of its nature, to admire it, to congratulate itself thereon, and to feel thankful for it to the beneficent cause, but not that it should subject its desires to that weak and delusive guidance, and meddle bunglingly with the purpose of nature. In a word, nature would have taken care that reason should not break forth into *practical exercise,* nor have the presumption, with its weak insight, to think out for itself the plan of happiness, and of the means of attaining it. Nature would not only have taken on herself the choice of the ends, but also of the means, and with wise foresight would have entrusted both to instinct.

And, in fact, we find that the more a cultivated reason applies itself with deliberate purpose to the enjoyment of life and happiness, so much the more does the man fail of true satisfaction. And from this circumstance there arises in many, if they are candid enough to confess it, a certain degree of *misology*, that is, hatred of reason, especially in the case of those who are most experienced in the use of it, because after calculating all the advantages they derive, I do not say from the invention of all the arts of common luxury, but even from the sciences (which seem to them to be after all only a luxury of the understanding), they find that they have, in fact, only brought more trouble on their shoulders, rather than gained in happiness; and they end by envying, rather than despising, the more common stamp of men who keep closer to the guidance of mere instinct, and do not allow their reason much influence on their conduct. And this we must admit, that the judgment of those who would very much lower the lofty eulogies of the advantages which reason gives us in regard to the happiness and satisfaction of life, or who would even reduce them below zero, is by no means morose or ungrateful to the goodness with which the world is governed, but that there lies at the root of these judgments the idea that our existence has a different and far nobler end, for which, and not for happiness, reason is properly intended, and which must, therefore, be regarded as the supreme condition to which the private ends of man must, for the most part, be postponed.

For as reason is not competent to guide the will with certainty in regard to its objects and the satisfaction of all our wants (which it to some extent even multiplies), this being an end to which an implanted instinct would have led with much greater certainty; and since, nevertheless, reason is imparted to us as a practical faculty, *i.e.* as one which is to have influence on the *will,* therefore, admitting that nature generally in the distribution of her capacities has adapted the means to the end, its true destination must be to produce a *will,* not merely good as a *means* to something else, but *good in itself,* for which reason was absolutely necessary. This will then, though not indeed the sole and complete good, must be the supreme good and the condition of every other, even of the desire of happiness. Under these circumstances, there is nothing inconsistent with the wisdom of nature in the fact that the cultivation of the reason, which is requisite for the first and unconditional purpose, does in many ways interfere, at least in this life, with the attainment of the second, which is always conditional, namely, happiness. Nay, it may even reduce it to nothing, without nature thereby failing of her purpose. For reason recognizes the establishment of a good will as its highest practical destination, and in attaining this purpose is capable only of a satisfaction of its own proper kind, namely, that from the attainment of an end, which end again is determined by reason only, notwithstanding that this may involve many a disappointment to the ends of inclination.

We have then to develop the notion of a will which deserves to be highly esteemed for itself, and is good without a view to anything further, a notion which exists already in the sound natural understanding, requiring rather to be cleared up than to be taught, and which in estimating the value of our actions always takes the first place, and constitutes the condition of all the rest. In order to do this, we will take the notion of duty, which includes that of a good will, although implying certain subjective restrictions and hindrances. These, however, far from concealing it, or rendering it unrecognizable, rather bring it out by contrast, and make it shine forth so much the brighter.

I omit here all actions which are already recognized as inconsistent with duty, although they may be useful for this or that purpose, for with these the question whether they are done *from duty* cannot arise at all, since they even conflict with it. I also set aside those actions which really conform to duty, but to which men have *no* direct *inclination,* performing them because they are impelled thereto by some other inclination. For in this case we can readily distinguish whether the action which agrees with duty is done *from duty,* or from a selfish view. It is much harder to make this distinction when the action accords with duty, and the subject has besides a *direct* inclination to it. For example, it is always a matter of duty that a dealer should not overcharge an inexperienced purchaser; and wherever there is much commerce the prudent tradesman does not overcharge, but keeps a fixed price for everyone, so that a child buys of him as well as any other. Men are thus *honestly* served; but this is not enough to make us believe that the tradesman has so acted from duty and from principles of honesty: his own advantage required it; it is out of the question in this case to suppose that he might besides have a direct inclination in favour of the buyers, so that, as it were, from love he should give no advantage to one over another. Accordingly the action was done neither from duty nor from direct inclination, but merely with a selfish view.

On the other hand, it is a duty to maintain one's life; and, in addition, everyone has also a direct inclination to do so. But on this account the often anxious care which most men take for it has no intrinsic worth, and their maxim has no moral import. They preserve their life *as duty requires,* no doubt, but not *because duty requires.* On the other hand, if adversity and hopeless sorrow have completely taken away the relish for life; if the unfortunate one, strong in mind, indignant at his fate rather than desponding or dejected, wishes for death, and yet preserves his life without loving it—not from inclination or fear, but from duty—then his maxim has a moral worth.

To be beneficent when we can is a duty; and besides this, there are many minds so sympathetically constituted that, without any other motive of vanity or self-interest, they find a pleasure in spreading joy around them, and can take delight in the satisfaction of others so far as it is their own work. But I maintain that in such a case an action of this kind, however proper, however amiable it may be, has nevertheless no true moral worth, but is on a level with other inclinations, *e.g.* the inclination to honour, which, if it is happily directed to that which is in fact of public utility and accordant with duty, and consequently honourable, deserves praise and encouragement, but not esteem. For the maxim lacks the moral import, namely, that such actions be done *from duty,* not from inclination. Put the case that the mind of that philanthropist was clouded by sorrow of his own, extinguishing all sympathy with the lot of others, and that while he still has the power to benefit others in distress, he is not touched by their trouble because he is absorbed with his own; and now suppose that he tears himself out of this dead insensibility, and performs the action without any inclination to it, but simply from duty, then first has his action its genuine moral worth. Further still; if nature has put little sympathy in the heart of this or that man; if he, supposed to be an upright man, is by temperament cold and indifferent to the sufferings of others, perhaps because in respect of his own he is provided with the special gift of patience and fortitude, and supposes, or even requires, that others should have the same—and such a man would certainly not be the meanest product of nature—but if nature had not specially framed him for a philanthropist, would he not still find in himself a source from whence to give himself a far higher worth than that of a good-natured temperament could be? Unquestionably. It is just in this that the moral worth of the character is brought out which is incomparably the highest of all, namely, that he is beneficent, not from inclination, but from duty. . . .

The second[1] proposition is: That an action done from duty derives its moral worth, *not from the purpose* which is to be attained by it, but from the maxim by which it is determined, and therefore does not depend on the realization of the object of the action, but merely on the *principle of volition* by which the action has taken place, without regard to any object of desire. It is clear from what precedes that the purposes which we may have in view in our actions, or their effects regarded as ends and springs of the will, cannot give to actions any unconditional or moral worth. In what, then, can their worth lie, if it is not to consist in the will and in reference to its expected effect? It cannot lie anywhere but in the *principle of the will* without regard to the ends which can be attained by the action. For the will stands between its *à priori* principle, which is formal, and its *à posteriori* spring, which is material, as between two roads, and as it must be determined by something, it follows that it must be determined by the formal principle of volition when an action is done from duty, in which case every material principle has been withdrawn from it.

The third proposition, which is a consequence of the two preceding, I would express thus: *Duty is the necessity of acting from respect for the law.* I may have *inclination* for an object as the effect of my proposed action, but I cannot have *respect* for it, just for this reason, that it is an effect and not an energy of will. Similarly, I cannot have respect for in-

---

[1][The first proposition was that to have moral worth an action must be done from duty.]

clination, whether my own or another's; I can at most, if my own, approve it; if another's, sometimes even love it; *i.e.* look on it as favourable to my own interest. It is only what is connected with my will as a principle, by no means as an effect—what does not subserve my inclination, but over-powers it, or at least in case of choice excludes it from its calculation—in other words, simply the law of itself, which can be an object of respect, and hence a command. Now an action done from duty must wholly exclude the influence of inclination, and with it every object of the will, so that nothing remains which can determine the will except objectively the *law,* and subjectively *pure respect* for this practical law, and consequently the maxim[1] that I should follow this law even to the thwarting of all my in-clinations.

Thus the moral worth of an action does not lie in the effect ex-pected from it, nor in any principle of action which requires to borrow its motive from this expected effect. For all these effects—agreeableness of one's condition, and even the promotion of the happiness of others—could have been also brought about by other causes, so that for this there would have been no need of the will of a rational being; whereas it is in this alone that the supreme and unconditional good can be found. The pre-eminent good which we call moral can therefore consist in nothing else than *the conception of law* in itself, *which certainly is only possible in a rational being,* in so far as this conception, and not the expected effect, determines the will. This is a good which is already present in the person who acts ac-cordingly, and we have not to wait for it to appear first in the result.

But what sort of law can that be, the conception of which must determine the will, even without paying any regard to the effect expected from it, in order that this will may be called good absolutely and without qualification? As I have deprived the will of every impulse which could arise to it from obedience to any law, there remains nothing but the universal conformity of its actions to law in general, which alone is to serve the will as a principle, *i.e.* I am never to act otherwise than *so that I could also will that my maxim should become a universal law.* Here, now, it is the simple conformity to law in general, without assuming any particular law applica-ble to certain actions, that serves the will as its principle, and must so serve it, if duty is not to be a vain delusion and a chimerical notion. The common reason of men in its practical judgments perfectly coincides with this and always has in view the principle here suggested. Let the question be, for example: May I when in distress make a promise with the intention not to keep it? I readily distinguish here between the two significations which the question may have: Whether it is prudent, or whether it is right, to make a false promise? The former may undoubtedly often be the case. I see clearly indeed that it is not enough to extricate myself from a present difficulty by means of this subterfuge, but it must be well considered whether there may not hereafter spring from this lie much greater inconvenience than that from which I now free myself, and as, with all my supposed *cunning,* the conse-quences cannot be so easily foreseen but that credit once lost may be much more injurious to me than any mischief which I seek to avoid at present, it should be considered whether it would not be more *prudent* to act herein according to a universal maxim, and to make it a habit to promise nothing except with the intention of keeping it. But it is soon clear to me that such a maxim will still only be based on the fear of consequences. Now it is a wholly different thing to be truthful from duty, and to be so from apprehension of injurious consequences. In the first case, the very notion of the action already implies a law for me; in the second case, I must first look about elsewhere to see what results may be combined with it which would affect myself. For to deviate from the principle of duty is beyond all doubt wicked; but to be unfaithful to my maxim of prudence may often be very advantageous to me, although to abide by it is certainly safer. The shortest way, however, and an unerring one, to discover the answer to this question whether a lying promise is consistent with duty, is to ask myself, Should I be content that my maxim (to extricate myself from difficulty by a false promise) should hold good as a universal law, for myself as well as for others? and should I be able to say to myself, "Every one may make a deceitful promise when he finds himself in a difficulty from which he cannot otherwise extricate himself"? Then I presently become aware that while I can will the lie, I can by no means will that lying should be a universal law. For with such a law there would be no promises at all, since it would be in vain to allege my intention in regard to my future actions to those who would not believe this allegation, or if they over-hastily did so, would pay me back in my own coin. Hence my maxim, as soon as it should be made a universal law, would necessarily destroy itself.

I do not, therefore, need any far-reaching penetration to discern what I have to do in order that my will may be morally good. Inexperienced in the course of the world, incapable of being prepared for all its contingencies, I only ask myself: Canst thou also will that thy maxim should be a universal law? If not, then it must be rejected, and that not because of a disadvantage accruing from it to myself or even to others, but because it cannot enter as a principle into a possible universal legislation, and reason extorts from me immediate respect for such legislation. I do not indeed as yet *discern* on what this respect is based (this the philosopher may inquire), but at least I understand this, that it is an estimation of the worth which far outweighs all worth of what is recommended by inclination, and that the necessity of acting from *pure* respect for the practical law is what constitutes duty, to which every other motive must give place, because it is the condition of a will being good *in itself*, and the worth of such a will is above everything. . . .

Second Section

Transition from Popular Moral Philosophy to the Metaphysic of Morals

. . . From what has been said, it is clear that all moral conceptions have their seat and origin completely *à priori* in the reason, and that, moreover, in the commonest reason just as truly as in that which is in the highest degree speculative; that they cannot be obtained by abstraction from any empirical, and therefore merely contingent knowledge; that it is just this purity of their origin that makes them worthy to serve as our supreme practical principle, and that just in proportion as we add anything empirical, we detract from their genuine influence, and from the absolute value of actions; that it is not only of the greatest necessity, in a purely speculative point of view, but is also of the greatest practical importance, to derive these notions and laws from pure reason, to present them pure and unmixed, and even to determine the compass of this practical or pure rational knowledge, *i.e.* to determine the whole faculty of pure practical reason; and, in doing so, we must not make its principles dependent on the particular nature of human reason, though in speculative philosophy this may be permitted, or may even at times be necessary; but since moral laws ought to hold good for every rational creature, we must derive them from the general concept of a rational being. . . .

Everything in nature works according to laws. Rational beings alone have the faculty of acting according *to the conception* of laws, that is according to principles, *i.e.* have a *will.* Since the deduction of actions from principles requires *reason,* the will is nothing but practical reason. If reason infallibly determines the will, then the actions of such a being which are recognized as objectively necessary are subjectively necessary also, *i.e.* the will is a faculty to choose *that only* which reason independent on inclination recognizes as practically necessary, *i.e.* as good. But if reason of itself does not sufficiently determine the will, if the latter is subject also to subjective conditions (particular impulses) which do not always coincide with the objective conditions; in a word, if the will does not *in itself* completely accord with reason (which is actually the case with men), then the actions which objectively are recognized as necessary are subjectively contingent, and the determination of such a will according to objective laws is *obligation,* that is to say, the relation of the objective laws to a will that is not thoroughly good is conceived as the determination of the will of a rational being by principles of reason, but which the will from its nature does not of necessity follow.

The conception of an objective principle, in so far as it is obligatory for a will, is called a command (of reason), and the formula of the command is called an Imperative. . . .

Now all *imperatives* command either *hypothetically* or *categorically.* The former represent the practical necessity of a possible action as means to something else that is willed (or at least which one might possibly will). The categorical imperative would be that which represented an action as necessary of itself without reference to another end, *i.e.,* as objectively necessary.

Since every practical law represents a possible action as good, and on this account, for a subject who is practically determinable by reason, necessary, all imperatives are formulae determining an action which is necessary according to the principle of a will good in some respects. If now the action is good only as a means *to something else,* then the imperative is *hypothetical;* if it is conceived as good *in itself* and consequently as being necessarily the principle of a will which of itself conforms to reason, then it is *categorical.* . . .

When I conceive a hypothetical imperative, in general I do not know beforehand what it will contain until I am given the condition. But when I conceive a categorical imperative, I know at once what it contains. For as the imperative contains besides the law only the necessity that the maxims[1] shall conform to this law, while the law contains no conditions restricting it, there remains nothing but the general statement that the maxim of the action should conform to a universal law, and it is this conformity alone that the imperative properly represents as necessary.

There is therefore but one categorical imperative, namely, this: *Act only on that maxim whereby thou canst at the same time will that it should become a universal law.*

Now if all imperatives of duty can be deduced from this one imperative as from their principle, then, although it should remain undecided whether what is called duty is not merely a vain notion, yet at least we shall be able to show what we understand by it and what this notion means.

Since the universality of the law according to which effects are produced constitutes what is properly called *nature* in the most general sense (as to form), that is the existence of things so far as it is determined by general laws, the imperative of duty may be expressed thus: *Act as if the maxim of thy action were to become by thy will a universal law of nature.*

We will now enumerate a few duties, adopting the usual division of them into duties to ourselves and to others, and into perfect and imperfect duties.

1. A man reduced to despair by a series of misfortunes feels wearied of life, but is still so far in possession of his reason that he can ask himself whether it would not be contrary to his duty to himself to take his own life. Now he inquires whether the maxim of his action could become a universal law of nature. His maxim is: From self-love I adopt it as a principle to shorten my life when its longer duration is likely to bring more evil than satisfaction. It is asked then simply whether this principle founded on self-love can become a universal law of nature. Now we see at once that a system of nature of which it should be a law to destroy life by means of the very feeling whose special nature it is to impel to the improvement of life would contradict itself, and therefore could not exist as a system of nature; hence that maxim cannot possibly exist as a universal law of nature, and consequently would be wholly inconsistent with the supreme principle of all duty.

2. Another finds himself forced by necessity to borrow money. He knows that he will not be able to repay it, but sees also that nothing will be lent to him, unless he promises stoutly to repay it in a definite time. He desires to make this promise, but he has still so much conscience as to ask himself: Is it not unlawful and inconsistent with duty to get out of a difficulty in this way? Suppose, however, that he resolves to do so, then the

maxim of his action would be expressed thus: When I think myself in want of money, I will borrow money and promise to repay it, although I know that I never can do so. Now this principle of self-love or of one's own advantage may perhaps be consistent with my whole future welfare; but the question now is, Is it right? I change then the suggestion of self-love into a universal law, and state the question thus: How would it be if my maxim were a universal law? Then I see at once that it could never hold as a universal law of nature, but would necessarily contradict itself. For supposing it to be a universal law that everyone when he thinks himself in a difficulty should be able to promise whatever he pleases, with the purpose of not keeping his promise, the promise itself would become impossible, as well as the end that one might have in view in it, since no one would consider that anything was promised to him, but would ridicule all such statements as vain pretences.

3. A third finds in himself a talent which with the help of some culture might make him a useful man in many respects. But he finds himself in comfortable circumstances, and prefers to indulge in pleasure rather than to take pains in enlarging and improving his happy natural capacities. He asks, however, whether his maxim of neglect of his natural gifts, besides agreeing with his inclination to indulgence, agrees also with what is called duty. He sees then that a system of nature could indeed subsist with such a universal law although men (like the South Sea islanders) should let their talents rest, and resolve to devote their lives merely to idleness, amusement, and propagation of their species—in a word, to enjoyment; but he cannot possibly *will* that this should be a universal law of nature, or be implanted in us as such by a natural instinct. For, as a rational being, he necessarily wills that his faculties be developed, since they serve him, and have been given him, for all sorts of possible purposes.

4. A fourth, who is in prosperity, while he sees that others have to contend with great wretchedness and that he could help them, thinks: What concern is it of mine? Let everyone be as happy as Heaven pleases, or as he can make himself; I will take nothing from him nor even envy him, only I do not wish to contribute anything to his welfare or to his assistance in distress! Now no doubt if such a mode of thinking were a universal law, the human race might very well subsist, and doubtless even better than in a state in which everyone talks of sympathy and good-will, or even takes care occasionally to put it into practice, but, on the other side, also cheats when he can, betrays the rights of men, or otherwise violates them. But although it is possible that a universal law of nature might exist in accordance with that maxim, it is impossible to *will* that such a principle should have the universal validity of a law of nature. For a will which resolved this would contradict itself, inasmuch as many cases might occur in which one would have need of the love and sympathy of others, and in which, by such a law of nature, sprung from his own will, he would deprive himself of all hope of the aid he desires.

These are a few of the many actual duties, or at least what we regard as such, which obviously fall into two classes on the one principle that we have laid down. We must be *able to will* that a maxim of our action should be a universal law. This is the canon of the moral appreciation of the action generally. Some actions are of such a character that their maxim cannot without contradiction be even *conceived* as a universal law of nature, far from it being possible that we should *will* that it should be so. In others this intrinsic impossibility is not found, but still it is impossible to *will* that their maxim should be raised to the universality of a law of nature, since such a will would contradict itself. It is easily seen that the former violate strict or rigorous (inflexible) duty; the latter only laxer (meritorious) duty. Thus it has been completely shown by these examples how all duties depend as regards the nature of the obligation (not the object of the action) on the same principle. . . .

We have thus established at least this much, that if duty is a conception which is to have any import and real legislative authority for our actions, it can only be expressed in categorical, and not at all in hypothetical imperatives. We have also, which is of great importance, exhibited clearly and definitely for every practical application the content of the categorical imperative, which must contain the principle of all duty if there is such a thing at all. We have not yet, however, advanced so far as to prove à *priori* that there actually is such an imperative, that there is a practical law which commands absolutely of itself, and without any other impulse, and that the following of this law is duty. . . .

Here then we see philosophy brought to a critical position, since it has to be firmly fixed, notwithstanding that it has nothing to support it in heaven or earth. Here it must show its purity as absolute director of its own laws, not the herald of those which are whispered to it by an implanted sense or who knows what tutelary nature. Although these may be better than nothing, yet they can never afford principles dictated by reason, which must have their source wholly à *priori* and thence their commanding authority, expecting everything from the supremacy of the law and the due respect for it nothing from inclination, or else condemning the man to self-contempt and inward abhorrence. . . .

Now I say: man and generally any rational being *exists* as an end in himself, *not merely as a means* to be arbitrarily used by this or that will, but in all his actions, whether they concern himself or other rational beings, must be always regarded at the same time as an end. All objects of the inclinations have only a conditional worth; for if the inclinations and the wants founded on them did not exist, then their object would be without value. But the inclinations themselves being sources of want are so far from having an absolute worth for which they should be desired, that, on the contrary, it must be the universal wish of every rational being to be wholly free from them. Thus the worth of any object which is *to be acquired* by our action is always conditional. Beings whose existence depends not on our will but on nature's, have nevertheless, if they are rational beings, only a relative value as means, and are therefore called *things*; rational beings, on the contrary, are called *persons*, because their very nature points them out as ends in themselves, that is as something which must not be used merely as means, and so far therefore restricts freedom of action (and is an object of respect). These, therefore, are not merely subjective ends whose existence has a worth *for us* as an effect of our action, but *objective ends*, that is things whose existence is an end in itself: an end moreover for which no other can be substituted, which they should subserve *merely* as means, for otherwise nothing whatever would possess *absolute worth*; but if all worth were conditioned and therefore contingent, then there would be no supreme practical principle of reason whatever.

If then there is a supreme practical principle or, in respect of the human will, a categorical imperative, it must be one which, being drawn from the conception of that which is necessarily an end for everyone because it is *an end in itself*, constitutes an *objective* principle of will, and can therefore serve as a universal practical law. The foundation of this principle is: *rational nature exists as an end in itself*. Man necessarily conceives his own existence as being so: so far then this is a *subjective* principle of human actions. But every other rational being regards its existence similarly, just on the same rational principle that holds for me[1]: so that it is at the same time an objective principle, from which as a supreme practical law all laws of the will must be capable of being deduced. Accordingly the practical imperative will be as follows: *So act as to treat humanity, whether in thine own person or in that of any other, in every case as an end withal, never as means only*. . . . Looking back now on all previous attempts to discover the principle of morality, we need not wonder why they all failed. It was seen that man was bound to laws by duty, but it was not observed that the laws to which he is subject are *only those of his own giving*, though at the same time they are *universal*, and that he is only bound to act in conformity with his own will; a will, however, which is designed by nature to give universal laws. For when one has conceived man only as subject to a law (no matter what), then this law required some interest, either by way of attraction or constraint, since it did not originate as a law from *his own* will, but this will was according to a law obliged by *something else* to act in a certain manner. Now by this necessary consequence all the labour spent in finding a supreme principle of *duty* was irrevocably lost. For men never elicited duty, but only a necessity of acting from a certain interest. Whether this interest was private or otherwise, in any case the imperative must be conditional, and could not by any means be capable of being a moral command. I will therefore call this the principle of *Autonomy* of the will, in contrast with every other which I accordingly reckon as *Heteronomy*.

The conception of every rational being as one which must consider itself as giving in all the maxims of its will universal laws, so as to judge itself and its actions from this point of view—this conception leads to another which depends on it and is very fruitful, namely, that of a *kingdom of ends*.

By a *kingdom* I understand the union of different rational beings in a system by common laws. Now since it is by laws that ends are determined as regards their universal validity, hence, if we abstract from the personal differences of rational beings, and likewise from all the content of their private ends, we shall be able to conceive all ends combined in a systematic whole (including both rational beings as ends in themselves, and also the special ends which each may propose to himself), that is to say, we can conceive a kingdom of ends, which on the preceding principles is possible.

For all rational beings come under the *law* that each of them must treat itself and all others *never merely as means*, but in every case *at the same time as ends in themselves*. Hence results a systematic union of rational beings by common objective laws, *i.e.*, a kingdom which may be called a kingdom of ends, since what these laws have in view is just the relation of these beings to one another as ends and means. It is certainly only an ideal.

A rational being belongs as a *member* to the kingdom of ends when, although giving universal laws in it, he is also himself subject to these laws. He belongs to it *as sovereign* when, while giving laws, he is not subject to the will of any other.

A rational being must always regard himself as giving laws either as member or as sovereign in a kingdom of ends which is rendered possible by the freedom of will. He cannot, however, maintain the latter position merely by the maxims of his will, but only in case he is a completely independent being without wants and with unrestricted power adequate to his will.

Morality consists then in the reference of all action to the legislation which alone can render a kingdom of ends possible. This legislation must be capable of existing in every rational being, and of emanating from his will, so that the principle of this will is, never to act on any maxim which could not without contradiction be also a universal law, and accordingly always so to act *that the will could at the same time regard itself as giving in its maxims universal laws*. If now the maxims of rational beings are not by their own nature coincident with this objective principle, then the necessity of acting on it is called practical necessitation, i.e. *duty*. Duty does not apply to the sovereign in the kingdom of ends, but it does to every member of it and to all in the same degree.

The practical necessity of acting on this principle, *i.e.* duty, does not rest at all on feelings, impulses, or inclinations, but solely on the relation of rational beings to one another, a relation in which the will of a rational being must always be regarded as *legislative*, since otherwise it could not be conceived as *an end in itself*. Reason then refers every maxim of the will, regarding it as legislating universally, to every other will and also to every action towards oneself; and this not on account of any other practical motive or any future advantage, but from the idea of the *dignity of* a rational being, obeying no law but that which he himself also gives.

In the kingdom of ends everything has either Value or Dignity. Whatever has a value can be replaced by something else which is *equivalent*; whatever, on the other hand, is above all value, and therefore admits of no equivalent, has a dignity.

Whatever has reference to the general inclinations and wants of mankind has a *market value*; whatever, without presupposing a want, corresponds to a certain taste, that is to a satisfaction in the mere purposeless play of our faculties, has a *fancy value*; but that which constitutes the condition under which alone anything can be an end in itself, this has not merely a relative worth, *i.e.* value, but an intrinsic worth, that is *dignity*.

Now morality is the condition under which alone a rational being can be an end in himself, since by this alone it is possible that he should be a legislating member in the kingdom of ends. Thus morality, and humanity as capable of it, is that which alone has dignity. Skill and diligence in labour have a market value; wit, lively imagination, and humour, have fancy value; on the other hand, fidelity to promises, benevolence from principle (not from instinct), have an intrinsic worth. Neither nature nor art contains anything which in default of these it could put in their place, for their worth consists not in the effects which spring from them, not in the use and advantage which they secure, but in the disposition of mind, that is, the maxims of the will which are ready to manifest themselves in such actions, even though they should not have the desired effect. These actions also need no recommendation from any subjective taste or sentiment, that they may be looked on with immediate favour and satisfaction: they need no immediate propension or feeling for them; they exhibit the will that performs them as an object of an immediate respect, and nothing but reason is required to *impose* them on the will; not to *flatter* it into them, which, in the case of duties, would be a contradiction. This estimation therefore shows that the worth of such a disposition is dignity, and places it infinitely above all value, with which it cannot for a moment be brought into comparison or competition without as it were violating its sanctity.

What then is it which justifies virtue or the morally good disposition, in making such lofty claims? It is nothing less than the privilege it secures to the rational being of participating in the giving of universal laws, by which it qualifies him to be a member of a possible kingdom of ends, a privilege to which he was already destined by his own nature as being an end in himself, and on that account legislating in the kingdom of ends; free as regards all laws of physical nature, and obeying those only which he himself gives, and by which his maxims can belong to a system of universal law, to which at the same time he submits himself. For nothing has any worth except what the law assigns it. Now the legislation itself which assigns the worth of everything must for that very reason possess dignity, that is an unconditional incomparable worth; and the word *respect* alone supplies a becoming expression for the esteem which a rational being must have for it. *Autonomy* then is the basis of the dignity of human and of every rational nature.

FRIEDRICH NIETZSCHE

25. *The New Morality*

Friedrich Nietzsche (1844–1900) was born in the Prussian city of Röcken. His home life and early education were entirely in keeping with the family tradition of piety, for both his parents were descendants of theologians. On the strength of his exceptional academic ability he was appointed Professor of Philology at the University of Basel of Switzerland at the age of twenty-four. Because of poor health he retired ten years later and for the remainder of his active life he traveled, studied, and wrote. Despite sickness and loneliness he produced a succession of brilliant books until 1889, when a violent seizure, followed by insanity, terminated his work.

A Prelude in Rhyme[1]

Invitation.

Venture, comrades, I implore you,
On the fare I set before you,
You will like it more to-morrow,
Better still the following day:
If yet more you're then requiring,
Old success I'll find inspiring,
And fresh courage thence will borrow
Novel dainties to display.

Foresight.

In yonder region travelling, take good care!
An hast thou wit, then be thou doubly ware!
They'll smile and lure thee; then thy limbs they'll tear:
Fanatics' country this where wits are rare!

Interpretation.

If I explain my wisdom, surely
'Tis but entangled more securely,
I can't expound myself aright:
But he that's boldly up and doing,
His own unaided course pursuing,
Upon my image casts more light!

Reprinted from Vols. 9–13 and 15–17 of Friedrich Nietzsche, *The Complete Works of Friedrich Nietzsche,* Oscar Levy, ed. (London: T. N. Foulis, 1909–1910; New York: Russell & Russell, 1964). Reprinted by permission of Russell & Russell, Publishers.

[1]From *Joyful Wisdom.*

Excelsior.

"How shall I reach the top?" No time
For thus reflecting! Start to climb!

Narrow Souls.

Narrow souls hate I like the devil,
Souls wherein grows nor good nor evil.

The Sage Speaks.

Strange to the crowd, yet useful to the crowd,
I still pursue my path, now sun, now cloud,
But always pass above the crowd!

Star Morality.

Foredoomed to spaces vast and far,
What matters darkness to the star?

Roll calmly on, let time go by,
Let sorrows pass thee—nations die!

Compassion would but dim the light
That distant worlds will gladly sight.

To thee one law—be pure and bright!

PREFACE[2]

This book belongs to the very few. Maybe not one of them is yet
alive; unless he be of those who understand my Zarathustra. How *can* I
confound myself with those who to-day already find a hearing?—Only the
day after to-morrow belongs to me. Some are born posthumously.

I am only too well aware of the conditions under which a man
understands me, and then *necessarily* understands. He must be intellectually
upright to the point of hardness, in order even to endure my seriousness
and my passion. He must be used to living on mountain-tops,—and to
feeling the wretched gabble of politics and national egotism *beneath* him.
He must have become indifferent; he must never inquire whether truth is
profitable or whether it may prove fatal. . . . Possessing from strength a
predilection for questions for which no one has enough courage nowadays;
the courage for the *forbidden;* his predestination must be the labyrinth.
The experience of seven solitudes. New ears for new music. New eyes for
the most remote things. A new conscience for truths which hitherto have remained dumb. And the will to economy on a large scale: to husband his
strength and his enthusiasm. . . . He must honour himself, he must love
himself; he must be absolutely free with regard to himself. . . . Very well
then! Such men alone are my readers, my proper readers, my preordained
readers: of what account are the rest?—the rest are simply—humanity.—
One must be superior to humanity in power, in loftiness of soul,—in contempt. . . .

[2]From *The Antichrist.*

343. What our Cheerfulness Signifies[3]

The most important of more recent events—that "God is dead," that the belief in the Christian God has become unworthy of belief—already begins to cast its first shadows over Europe. To the few at least whose eye, whose *suspecting* glance, is strong enough and subtle enough for this drama, some sun seems to have set, some old, profound confidence seems to have changed into doubt: our old world must seem to them daily more darksome, distrustful, strange and "old." In the main, however, one may say that the event itself is far too great, too remote, too much beyond most people's power of apprehension, for one to suppose that so much as the report of it could have *reached* them; not to speak of many who already knew *what* had really taken place, and what must all collapse now that his belief had been undermined,—because so much was built upon it, so much rested on it, and had become one with it: for example, our entire European morality. This lengthy, vast and uninterrupted process of crumbling, destruction, ruin and overthrow which is now imminent: who has realised it sufficiently to-day to have to stand up as the teacher and herald of such a tremendous logic of terror, as to the prophet of a period of gloom and eclipse, the like of which has probably never taken place on earth before? . . . Even we, the born riddle-readers, who wait as it were on the mountains posted 'twixt to-day and to-morrow, and engirt by their contradiction, we, the firstlings and premature children of the coming century, into whose sight especially the shadows which must forthwith envelop Europe *should* already have come—how is it that even we, without genuine sympathy for this period of gloom, contemplate its advent without any *personal* solicitude or fear? Are we still, perhaps, too much under the *immediate effects* of the event—and are these effects, especially as regards *ourselves,* perhaps the reverse of what was to be expected—not at all sad and depressing, but rather like a new and indescribable variety of light, happiness, relief, enlivenment, enouragement, and dawning day? . . . In fact, we philosophers and "free spirits" feel ourselves irradiated as by a new dawn by the report that the "old God is dead"; our hearts overflow with gratitude, astonishment, presentiment and expectation. At last the horizon seems open once more, granting even that it is not bright; our ships can at last put out to sea in face of every danger; every hazard is again permitted to the discerner; the sea, *our* sea, again lies open before us; perhaps never before did such an "open sea" exist.—

347. Believers and Their Need of Belief

How much *faith* a person requires in order to flourish, how much "fixed opinion" he requires which he does not wish to have shaken, because he *holds* himself thereby—is a measure of his power (or more plainly speaking, of his weakness). Most people in old Europe, as it seems to me, still need Christianity at present, and on that account it still finds belief.

[3]Sections 343, 347, 345, and 380 are from *Joyful Wisdom.*

For such is man: a theological dogma might be refuted to him a thousand times,—provided, however, that he had need of it, he would again and again accept it as "true,"—according to the famous "proof of power" of which the Bible speaks. Some have still need of metaphysics; but also the impatient *longing for certainty* which at present discharges itself in scientific, positivist fashion among large numbers of the people, the longing by all means to get at something stable (while on account of the warmth of the longing the establishing of the certainty is more leisurely and negligently undertaken): even this is still the longing for a hold, a support; in short, the *instinct of weakness,* which, while not actually creating religions, metaphysics, and convictions of all kinds, nevertheless—preserves them. In fact, around all these positivist systems there fume the vapours of a certain pessimistic gloom, something of weariness, fatalism, disillusionment, and fear of new disillusionment—or else manifest animosity, ill-humour, anarchic exasperation, and whatever there is of symptom or masquerade of the feeling of weakness. . . .

Belief is always most desired, most pressingly needed where there is a lack of will: for the will, as emotion of command, is the distinguishing characteristic of sovereignty and power. That is to say, the less a person knows how to command, the more urgent is his desire for one who commands, who commands sternly,—a God, a prince, a caste, a physician, a confessor, a dogma, a party conscience. From whence perhaps it could be inferred that the two world-religions, Buddhism and Christianity, might well have had the cause of their rise, and especially of their rapid extension, in an extraordinary *malady of the will.* And in truth it has been so: both religions lighted upon a longing, monstrously exaggerated by malady of the will, for an imperative, a "Thou-shalt," a longing going the length of despair; both religions were teachers of fanaticism in times of slackness of will-power, and thereby offered to innumerable persons a support, a new possibility of exercising will, an enjoyment in willing. For in fact fanaticism is the sole "volitional strength" to which the weak and irresolute can be excited, as a sort of hypnotising of the entire sensory-intellectual system, in favour of the over-abundant nutrition (hypertrophy) of a particular point of view and a particular sentiment, which then dominates—the Christian calls it his *faith.* When a man arrives at the fundamental conviction that he *requires* to be commanded, he becomes "a believer." Reversely, one could imagine a delight and a power of self-determining, and a *freedom* of will whereby a spirit could bid farewell to every belief, to every wish for certainty, accustomed as it would be to support itself on slender cords and possibilities, and to dance even on the verge of abyss. Such a spirit would be the *free spirit par excellence.*

345

. . . How is it that I have not yet met with any one, not even in books, . . . who knew morality as a problem, and this problem as *his own* personal need, affliction, pleasure and passion? It is obvious that up to the present morality has not been a problem at all; it has rather been the very ground on which people have met, after all distrust, dissension, and contradiction, the hallowed place of peace, where thinkers could obtain rest even from themselves, could recover breath and revive. I see no one who has ventured to *criticise* the estimates of moral worth. I miss in this connection even the attempts of scientific curiosity, and the fastidious, groping imagination of psychologists and historians, which easily anticipates a problem and catches it on the wing, without rightly knowing what it catches. With difficulty I have discovered some scanty data for the purpose of furnishing a *history of the origin* of these feelings and estimates of value (which is something different from a criticism of them, and also something different from a history of ethical systems). In an individual case, I have done everything to encourage the inclination and talent for this kind of history—in vain, as it would seem to me at present. There is little to be learned from those historians of morality (especially Englishmen): they themselves are usually, quite unsuspiciously, under the influence of a definite morality, and act unwittingly as its armour-bearers and followers—perhaps still repeating sincerely the popular superstition of Christian Europe, that the characteristic of moral action consists in abnegation, self-denial, self-sacrifice, or in fellow-feeling and fellow-suffering. The usual error in their premises is their insistence on a certain *consensus* among human beings, at least among civilised human beings, with regard to certain propositions of morality, and from thence they conclude that these propositions are absolutely binding even upon you and me; or reversely, they come to the conclusion that *no* morality at all is binding, after the truth has dawned upon them that to different peoples moral valuations are *necessarily* different: both of which conclusions are equally childish follies. The error of the more subtle amongst them is that they discover and criticise the probably foolish opinions of a people about its own morality, or the opinions of mankind about human morality generally; they treat accordingly of its origin, its religious sanctions, the superstition of free will, and such matters; and they think that just by so doing they have criticised the morality itself. But the worth of a precept, "Thou shalt," is still fundamentally different from and independent of such opinions about it, and must be distinguished from the weeds of error with which it has perhaps been overgrown: just as the worth of a medicine to a sick person is altogether independent of the question whether he has a scientific opinion about medicine, or merely thinks about it as an old wife would do. A morality could even have grown *out of* an error: but with this knowledge the problem of its worth would not even be touched.—Thus, no one has hitherto tested the *value* of that most celebrated of all medicines, called morality: for which purpose it is first of all necessary for one—*to call it in question*. Well, that is just our work.—

380. "THE WANDERER" SPEAKS

In order for once to get a glimpse of our European morality from a distance, in order to compare it with other earlier or future moralities, one must do as the traveller who wants to know the height of the towers of a city: for that purpose he *leaves* the city. "Thoughts concerning moral prejudices," if they are not to be prejudices concerning prejudices, presuppose a position *outside of* morality, some sort of world beyond good and evil, to which one must ascend, climb, or fly—and in the given case at any rate, a position beyond *our* good and evil, an emancipation from all "Europe," understood as a sum of inviolable valuations which have become part and parcel of our flesh and blood. That one *wants* in fact to get outside, or aloft, is perhaps a sort of madness, a peculiarly unreasonable "thou must"—for even we thinkers have our idiosyncrasies of "unfree will"—: the question is whether one *can* really get there. That may depend on manifold conditions: in the main it is a question of how light or how heavy we are, the problem of our "specific gravity." One must be *very light* in order to impel one's will to knowledge to such a distance, and as it were beyond one's age, in order to create eyes for oneself for the survey of millenniums, and a pure heaven in these eyes besides! One must have freed oneself from many things by which we Europeans of to-day are oppressed, hindered, held down, and made heavy. The man of such a "Beyond," who wants to get even in sight of the highest standards of worth of his age, must first of all "surmount" this age in himself—it is the test of his power—and consequently not only his age, but also his past aversion and opposition *to* his age, his suffering *caused by* his age, his unseasonableness, his Romanticism. . . .

260[4]

In a tour through the many finer and coarser moralities which have hitherto prevailed or still prevail on the earth, I found certain traits recurring regularly together and connected with one another, until finally two primary types revealed themselves to me, and a radical distinction was brought to light. There is *master-morality* and *slave-morality*;—I would at once add, however, that in all higher and mixed civilisations, there are also attempts at the reconciliation of the two moralities; but one finds still oftener the confusion and mutual misunderstanding of them, indeed, sometimes their close juxtaposition—even in the same man, within one soul. The distinctions of moral values have either originated in a ruling caste, pleasantly conscious of being different from the ruled—or among the ruled class, the slaves and dependents of all sorts. In the first case, when it is the rulers who determine the conception "good," it is the exalted, proud disposition which is regarded as the distinguishing feature, and that which determines the order of rank. The noble type of man separates from himself the beings in whom the opposite of this exalted, proud disposition displays itself: he despises them. Let it at once be noted that in this first kind of morality the antithesis "good" and "bad" means practically the same as "noble" and "despicable"; —the antithesis "good" and "*evil*" is of a different origin. The cowardly, the

[4]From *Beyond Good and Evil.*

timid, the insignificant, and those thinking merely of narrow utility are despised; moreover, also, the distrustful, with their constrained glances, the self-abasing, the dog-like kind of men who let themselves be abused, the mendicant flatterers, and above all the liars:—it is a fundamental belief of all aristocrats that the common people are untruthful. "We truthful ones"—the nobility in ancient Greece called themselves. It is obvious that everywhere the designations of moral value were at first applied to *men*, and were only derivatively and at a later period applied to *actions*; it is a gross mistake, therefore, when historians of morals start with questions like, "Why have sympathetic actions been praised?" The noble type of man regards *himself* as a determiner of values; he does not require to be approved of; he passes the judgment: "What is injurious to me is injurious in itself"; he knows that it is he himself only who confers honour on things; he is a *creator of values*. He honours whatever he recognises in himself: such morality is self-glorification. In the foreground there is the feeling of plenitude, of power, which seeks to overflow, the happiness of high tension, the consciousness of a wealth which would fain give and bestow:—the noble man also helps the unfortunate, but not—or scarcely—out of pity, but rather from an impulse generated by the superabundance of power. The noble man honours in himself the powerful one, him also who has power over himself, who knows how to speak and how to keep silence, who takes pleasure in subjecting himself to severity and hardness, and has reverence for all that is severe and hard. "Wotan placed a hard heart in my breast," says an old Scandinavian Saga: it is thus rightly expressed from the soul of a proud Viking. Such a type of man is even proud of *not* being made for sympathy; the hero of the Saga therefore adds warningly: "He who has not a hard heart when young, will never have one." The noble and brave who think thus are the furthest removed from the morality which sees precisely in sympathy, or in acting for the good of others, or in *désintéressement*, the characteristic of the moral. . . .

It is otherwise with the second type of morality, *slave-morality*. Supposing that the abused, the oppressed, the suffering, the unemancipated, the weary, and those uncertain of themselves, should moralise, what will be the common element in their moral estimates? Probably a pessimistic suspicion with regard to the entire situation of man will find expression, perhaps a condemnation of man, together with his situation. The slave has an unfavourable eye for the virtues of the powerful; he has a scepticism and distrust, a *refinement* of distrust of everything "good" that is there honoured—he would fain persuade himself that the very happiness there is not genuine. On the other hand, *those* qualities which serve to alleviate the existence of sufferers are brought into prominence and flooded with light; it is here that sympathy, the kind, helping hand, the warm heart, patience, diligence, humility, and friendliness attain to honour; for here these are the most useful qualities, and almost the only means of supporting the burden of existence. Slave-morality is essentially the morality of utility. Here is the seat of the origin of the famous antithesis "good" and "*evil*":—power and dangerousness are assumed to reside in the evil, a certain dreadfulness, subtlety, and strength, which do not admit of being despised. According to slave-morality, therefore, the "evil" man arouses fear; according to master-morality, it is precisely the "good" man who arouses fear and seeks to arouse it, while the bad man is regarded as the despicable being. The contrast attains its maximum when, in accordance with the logical consequences of slave-morality, a shade of depreciation—it may be slight and well-intentioned—at last attaches itself even to the "good" man of this morality; because, according to the servile mode of thought, the good man must in any case be the *safe* man: he is good-natured, easily deceived, perhaps a little stupid, *un bonhomme*. . . .

10[5]

The revolt of the slaves in morals begins in the very principle of *resentment* becoming creative and giving birth to values—a resentment experienced by creatures who, deprived as they are of the proper outlet of action, are forced to find their compensation in an imaginary revenge. While every aristocratic morality springs from a triumphant affirmation of its own demands, the slave morality says "no" from the very outset to what is "outside itself," "different from itself," and "not itself": and this "no" is its creative deed. This volte-face of the valuing standpoint—this *inevitable* gravitation to the objective instead of back to the subjective—is typical of "resentment": the slave-morality requires as the condition of its existence an external and objective world, to employ physiological terminology, it requires objective stimuli to be capable of action at all—its action is fundamentally a reaction. The contrary is the case when we come to the aristocrat's system of values: it acts and grows spontaneously, it merely seeks its antithesis in order to pronounce a more grateful and exultant "yes" to its own self;—its negative conception, "low," "vulgar," "bad," is merely a pale late-born foil in comparison with its positive and fundamental conception (saturated as it is with life and passion), of "we aristocrats, we good ones, we beautiful ones, we happy ones." . . .

4[6]

I will formulate a principle. All naturalism in morality—that is to say, every sound morality is ruled by a life instinct,—any one of the laws of life is fulfilled by the definite canon "thou shalt," "thou shalt not," and any sort of obstacle or hostile element in the road of life is thus cleared away. Conversely, the morality which is antagonistic to nature—that is to say, almost every morality that has been taught, honoured and preached hitherto, is directed precisely against the life-instincts,—it is a condemnation, now secret, now blatant and impudent, of these very instincts. Inasmuch as it says "God sees into the heart of man," it says Nay to the profoundest and most superior desires of life and takes God as the enemy of life. The saint in

[5]From *Geneology of Morals*.
[6]From *Twilight of the Idols*.

whom God is well pleased, is the ideal eunuch. Life terminates where the "Kingdom of God" begins.

5[7]

We must not deck out and adorn Christianity: it has waged a deadly war upon this *higher* type of man, it has set a ban upon all the fundamental instincts of this type, and has distilled evil and the devil himself out of these instincts:—the strong man as the typical pariah, the villain. Christianity has sided with everything weak, low, and botched; it has made an ideal out of *antagonism* towards all the self-preservative instincts of strong life: it has corrupted even the reason of the strongest intellects, by teaching that the highest values of intellectuality are sinful, misleading and full of temptations. The most lamentable example of this was the corruption of Pascal, who believed in the perversion of his reason through original sin, whereas it had only been perverted by his Christianity.

7

Christianity is called the religion of *pity.*—Pity is opposed to the tonic passions which enhance the energy of the feeling of life: its action is depressing. A man loses power when he pities. By means of pity the drain on strength which suffering itself already introduces into the world is multiplied a thousandfold. Through pity, suffering itself becomes infectious; in certain circumstances it may lead to a total loss of life and vital energy, which is absurdly out of proportion to the magnitude of the cause. . . .

8[8]

. . . The unmasking of Christian morality is an event which is unequalled in history, it is a real catastrophe. The man who throws light upon it is a *force majeure*, a fatality; he breaks the history of man into two. Time is reckoned up before him and after him. The lightning flash of truth struck precisely that which theretofore had stood highest: he who understands what was destroyed by that flash should look to see whether he still holds anything in his hands. Everything which until then was called truth, has been revealed as the most detrimental, most spiteful, and most subterranean form of life; the holy pretext, which was the "improvement" of man, has been recognised as a ruse for draining life of its energy and of its blood.

. . . The man who unmasks morality has also unmasked the worthlessness of the values in which men either believe or have believed; he no longer sees anything to be revered in the most venerable man—even in the types of men that have been pronounced holy; all he can see in them is the

---

[7]Sections 5 and 7 are from *The Antichrist*.
[8]From *Ecce Homo*.

most fatal kind of abortions, fatal, *because they fascinate.* The concept "God" was invented as the opposite of the concept life—everything detrimental, poisonous, and slanderous, and all deadly hostility to life, was bound together in one horrible unit in Him. The concepts "beyond" and "true world" were invented in order to depreciate the only world that exists —in order that no goal or aim, no sense or task, might be left to earthly reality. The concepts "soul," "spirit," and last of all the concept "immortal soul," were invented in order to throw contempt on the body, in order to make it sick and "holy," in order to cultivate an attitude of appalling levity towards all things in life which deserve to be treated seriously, *i.e.* the questions of nutrition and habitation, of intellectual diet, the treatment of the sick, cleanliness, and weather. Instead of health, we find the "salvation of the soul"—that is to say, a *folie circulaire* fluctuating between convulsions and penitence and the hysteria of redemption. The concept "sin," together with the torture instrument appertaining to it, which is the concept "free will," was invented in order to confuse and muddle our instincts, and to render the mistrust of them man's second nature! In the concepts "disinterestedness" and "self-denial," the actual signs of decadence are to be found. The allurement of that which is detrimental, the inability to discover one's own advantage and self-destruction, are made into absolute qualities, into the "duty," the "holiness," and the "divinity" of man. Finally—to keep the worst to the last—by the notion of the *good* man, all that is favoured which is weak, ill, botched, and sick-in-itself, which *ought to be wiped out.* The law of selection is thwarted, an ideal is made out of opposition to the proud, well-constituted man, to him who says yea to life, to him who is certain of the future, and who guarantees the future—this man is henceforth called the *evil* one. And all this was believed in as *morality!—Ecrasez l'infâme!*

9[9]

It is upon this theological instinct that I wage war. I find traces of it everywhere. Whoever has the blood of theologians in his veins, stands from the start in a false and dishonest position to all things. The pathos which grows out of this state, is called *Faith:* that is to say, to shut one's eyes once and for all, in order not to suffer at the sight of incurable falsity. People convert this faulty view of all things into a moral, a virtue, a thing of holiness. They endow their distorted vision with a good conscience,—they claim that no *other* point of view is any longer of value, once theirs has been made sacrosanct with the names "God," "Salvation," "Eternity." I unearthed the instinct of the theologian everywhere: it is the most universal, and actually the most subterranean form of falsity on earth. That which a theologian considers true, *must* of necessity be false: this furnishes almost the criterion of truth. It is his most profound self-preservative instinct which forbids reality ever to attain to honour in any way, or even to raise its voice.

9From *The Antichrist.*

Whithersoever the influence of the theologian extends, *valuations* are topsy-turvy, and the concepts "true" and "false" have necessarily changed places: that which is most deleterious to life, is here called "true," that which enhances it, elevates it, says Yea to it, justifies it and renders it triumphant, is called "false." . . .

319. As Interpreters of our Experiences[10]

One form of honesty has always been lacking among founders of religions and their kin:—they have never made their experiences a matter of the intellectual conscience. "What did I really experience? What then took place in me and around me? Was my understanding clear enough? Was my will directly opposed to all deception of the senses, and courageous in its defence against fantastic notions?"—None of them ever asked these questions, nor to this day do any of the good religious people ask them. They have rather a thirst for things which are *contrary to reason,* and they don't want to have too much difficulty in satisfying this thirst,—so they experience "miracles" and "regenerations," and hear the voices of angels! But we who are different, who are thirsty for reason, want to look as carefully into our experiences, as in the case of a scientific experiment, hour by hour, day by day! We ourselves want to be our own experiments, and our own subjects of experiment.

283. Pioneers

I greet all the signs indicating that a more manly and warlike age is commencing, which will, above all, bring heroism again into honour! For it has to prepare the way for a yet higher age, and gather the force which the latter will one day require,—the age which will carry heroism into knowledge, and *wage war* for the sake of ideas and their consequences. For that end many brave pioneers are now needed, who, however, cannot originate out of nothing,—and just as little out of the sand and slime of present-day civilisation and the culture of great cities: men silent, solitary and resolute, who know how to be content and persistent in invisible activity: men who with innate disposition seek in all things that which is *to be overcome* in them: men to whom cheerfulness, patience, simplicity, and contempt of the great vanities belong just as much as do magnanimity in victory and indulgence to the trivial vanities of all the vanquished: men with an acute and independent judgment regarding all victors, and concerning the part which chance has played in the winning of victory and fame: men with their own holidays, their own work-days, and their own periods of mourning; accustomed to command with perfect assurance, and equally ready, if need be, to obey, proud in the one case as in the other, equally serving their own interests: men more imperilled, more productive, more happy! For believe me!—the secret of realising the largest productivity and the greatest enjoy-

[10]Sections 319, 283, and 301 are from *Joyful Wisdom.*

ment of existence is *to live in danger!* Build your cities on the slope of Vesuvius! Send your ships into unexplored seas! Live in war with your equals and with yourselves! Be robbers and spoilers, ye knowing ones, as long as ye cannot be rulers and possessors! The time will soon pass when you can be satisfied to live like timorous deer concealed in the forests. Knowledge will finally stretch out her hand for that which belongs to her:—she means to *rule* and *possess*, and you with her!

301.   ILLUSION OF THE CONTEMPLATIVE

Higher men are distinguished from lower, by seeing and hearing immensely more, and in a thoughtful manner—and it is precisely this that distinguishes man from the animal, and the higher animal from the lower. The world always becomes fuller for him who grows up into the full stature of humanity; there are always more interesting fishing-hooks, thrown out to him; the number of his stimuli is continually on the increase, and similarly the varieties of his pleasure and pain,—the higher man becomes always at the same time happier and unhappier. An *illusion*, however, is his constant accompaniment all along: he thinks he is placed as a *spectator* and *auditor* before the great pantomime and concert of life; he calls his nature a *contemplative nature*, and thereby overlooks the fact that he himself is also a real creator, and continuous poet of life,—that he no doubt differs greatly from the *actor* in this drama, the so-called practical man, but differs still more from a mere onlooker or spectator *before* the stage. There is certainly *vis contemplativa*, and re-examination of his work peculiar to him as poet, but at the same time, and first and foremost, he has the *vis creativa*, which the practical man or doer *lacks*, whatever appearance and current belief may say to the contrary. It is we, we who think and feel, that actually and unceasingly *make* something which does not yet exist: the whole eternally increasing world of valuations, colours, weights, perspectives, gradations, affirmations and negations. This composition of ours is continually learnt, practised, and translated into flesh and actuality, and even into the commonplace, by the so-called practical men (our actors, as we have said). Whatever has *value* in the present world, has it not in itself, by its nature,—nature is always worthless:—but a value was once given to it, bestowed upon it, and it was *we* who gave and bestowed! We only have created the world *which is of any account to man!*—But it is precisely this knowledge that we lack, and when we get hold of it for a moment we have forgotten it the next: we misunderstand our highest power, we contemplative men, and estimate ourselves at too low a rate,—we are neither as *proud nor as happy* as we might be.

212[11]

It is always more obvious to me that the philosopher, as a man *indispensable* for the morrow and the day after the morrow, has ever found himself, and *has been obliged* to find himself, in contradiction to the day in

---

[11]Sections 212, 44, and 43 are from *Beyond Good and Evil.*

which he lives; his enemy has always been the ideal of his day. Hitherto all those extraordinary furtherers of humanity whom one calls philosophers— who rarely regarded themselves as lovers of wisdom, but rather as disagreeable fools and dangerous interrogators—have found their mission, their hard, involuntary, imperative mission (in the end however the greatness of their mission), in being the bad conscience of their age. In putting the vivisector's knife to the breast of the very *virtues of their age*, they have betrayed their own secret; it has been for the sake of a *new* greatness of man, a new untrodden path to his aggrandisement. They have always disclosed how much hypocrisy, indolence, self-indulgence, and self-neglect, how much falsehood was concealed under the most venerated types of contemporary morality, how much virtue was *outlived;* they have always said: "We must remove hence to where *you* are least at home." In face of a world of "modern ideas," which would like to confine every one in a corner, in a "specialty," a philosopher, if there could be philosophers nowadays, would be compelled to place the greatness of man, the conception of "greatness," precisely in his comprehensiveness and multifariousness, in his all-roundness; he would even determine worth and rank according to the amount and variety of that which a man could hear and take upon himself, according to the *extent* to which a man could stretch his responsibility. Nowadays the taste and virtue of the age weaken and attenuate the will; nothing is so adapted to the spirit of the age as weakness of will. . . .

44

Need I say expressly after all this that they will be free, *very* free spirits, these philosophers of the future—as certainly also they will not be merely free spirits, but something more, higher, greater, and fundamentally different, which does not wish to be misunderstood and mistaken? But while I say this, I feel under *obligation* almost as much to them as to ourselves (we free spirits who are their heralds and forerunners) to sweep away from ourselves conjointly a stupid old prejudice and misunderstanding, which, like a fog, has too long made the conception of "free spirit" obscure. In every country of Europe, and the same in America, there is at present something which makes an abuse of this name: a very narrow, prepossessed, enchained class of spirits, who desire almost the opposite of what our intentions and instincts prompt—not to mention that in respect to the *new* philosophers who are appearing, they must still more be closed windows and bolted doors. Briefly and regrettably, they belong to the *levellers*, these wrongly named "free spirits"—as glib-tongued and scribe-fingered slaves of the democratic taste and its "modern ideas": all of them men without solitude, without personal solitude, blunt honest fellows to whom neither courage nor honourable conduct ought to be denied; only, they are not free, and are ludicrously superficial, especially in their innate partiality for seeing the cause of almost *all* human misery and failure in the old forms in which society has hitherto existed—a notion which happily inverts the truth entirely! What they would fain attain with all their strength, is the universal, green-meadow happiness of the herd, together with security, safety, comfort, and alleviation of life for every one; their two most frequently chanted songs and doctrines are called "Equality of Rights" and "Sympathy with all Sufferers"—and suffering itself is looked upon by them as something which must be *done away with*. We opposite ones, however, who have opened our eye and conscience to the question how and where the plant "man" has hitherto grown most vigorously, believe that this has always taken place under the opposite conditions, that for this end the dangerousness of his situation had to be increased enormously, his inventive faculty and dissembling power (his "spirit") had to develop into subtlety and daring under long oppression and compulsion, and his Will to Life had to be increased to the unconditioned Will to Power. . . .

What wonder that we "free spirits" are not exactly the most communicative spirits? that we do not wish to betray in every respect *what* a spirit can free itself from, and *where* perhaps it will then be driven? And as to the import of the dangerous formula, "Beyond Good and Evil," with which we at least avoid confusion, we *are* something else than *"libres-penseurs," "liberi pensatori,"* "free-thinkers," and whatever these honest advocates of "modern ideas" like to call themselves. Having been at home, or at least guests, in many realms of the spirit; having escaped again and again from the gloomy, agreeable nooks in which preferences and prejudices, youth, origin, the accident of men and books, or even the weariness of travel seemed to confine us; full of malice against the seductions of dependency which lie concealed in honours, money, positions, or exaltation of the senses; grateful even for distress and the vicissitudes of illness, because they always free us from some rule, and its "prejudice,' grateful to the God, devil, sheep, and worm in us; inquisitive to a fault, investigators to the point of cruelty, with unhesitating fingers for the intangible, with teeth and stomachs for the most indigestible, ready for any business that requires sagacity and acute senses, ready for every adventure, owing to an excess of "free will"; with anterior and posterior souls, into the ultimate intentions of which it is difficult to pry, with foregrounds and backgrounds to the end of which no foot may run; hidden ones under the mantles of light, appropriators although we resemble heirs and spendthrifts, arrangers and collectors from morning till night, misers of our wealth and our full-crammed drawers, economical in learning and forgetting, inventive in scheming; sometimes proud of tables of categories, sometimes pedants, sometimes night-owls of work even in full day; yea, if necessary, even scarecrows—and it is necessary nowadays, that is to say, inasmuch as we are the born, sworn, jealous friends of *solitude*, of our own profoundest midnight and mid-day solitude:—such kind of men are we, we free spirits! And perhaps *ye* are also something of the same kind, ye coming ones, ye *new* philosophers?

43

Will they be new friends of "truth," these coming philosophers? Very probably, for all philosophers hitherto have loved their truths. But assuredly they will not be dogmatists. It must be contrary to their pride, and also contrary to their taste, that their truth should still be truth for every one—that which has hitherto been the secret wish and ultimate purpose of all dogmatic efforts. "My opinion is *my* opinion: another person has not easily a right to it"—such a philosopher of the future will say, perhaps. One must renounce the bad taste of wishing to agree with many people. "Good" is no longer good when one's neighbour takes it into his mouth. And how could there be a "common good"! The expression contradicts itself; that which can be common is always of small value. In the end things must be as they are and have always been—the great things remain for the great, the abysses for the profound, the delicacies and thrills for the refined, and, to sum up shortly, everything rare for the rare.

382. GREAT HEALTHINESS[12]

We, the new, the nameless, the hard-to-understand, we firstings of a yet untried future—we require for a new end also a new means, namely, a new healthiness, stronger, sharper, tougher, bolder and merrier than any healthiness hitherto. He whose soul longs to experience the whole range of hitherto recognised values and desirabilities, and to circumnavigate all the coasts of this ideal "Mediterranean Sea," who, from the adventures of his most personal experience, wants to know how it feels to be a conqueror, and discoverer of the ideal—as likewise how it is with the artist, the saint, the legislator, the sage, the scholar, the devotee, the prophet, and the godly Nonconformist of the old style:—requires one thing above all for that purpose, *great healthiness*—such healthiness as one not only possesses, but also constantly acquires and must acquire, because one continually sacrifies it again, and must sacrifice it!—And now, after having been long on the way in this fashion, we Argonauts of the ideal, who are more courageous perhaps than prudent, and often enough shipwrecked and brought to grief, nevertheless, as said above, healthier than people would like to admit, dangerously healthy, always healthy again,—it would seem, as if in recompense for it all, that we have a still undiscovered country before us, the boundaries of which no one has yet seen, a beyond to all countries and corners of the ideal known hitherto, a world so over-rich in the beautiful, the strange, the questionable, the frightful, and the divine, that our curiosity as well as our thirst for possession thereof, have got out of hand—alas! that nothing will now any longer satisfy us! How could we still be content with *the man of the present day* after such peeps, and with such a craving in our conscience and consciousness? What a pity; but it is unavoidable that we should look on the worthiest aims and hopes of the man of the present day with ill-concealed amusement, and perhaps should no longer look at them. . . .

1009[13]

The standpoint from which my values are determined: is abundance or desire active? . . . Is one a mere spectator, or is one's own shoulder at the

---

[12]From *Joyful Wisdom.*   [13]From *Will to Power.*

wheel—is one looking away or is one turning aside? . . . Is one acting spontaneously, as the result of accumulated strength, or is one merely reacting to a goad or to a stimulus? . . . Is one simply acting as the result of a paucity of elements, or of such an overwhelming dominion over a host of elements that this power enlists the latter into its service if it requires them? . . . Is one a *problem* one's self or is one a *solution* already? . . . Is one *perfect* through the smallness of the task, or *imperfect* owing to the extraordinary character of the aim? . . . Is one genuine or only an *actor;* is one genuine as an actor, or only the bad copy of an actor? is one a representative or the creature represented? Is one a personality or merely a rendezvous of personalities? . . . Is one ill from a disease or from surplus health? Does one lead as a shepherd, or as an "exception" (third alternative: as a fugitive)? Is one in need of dignity, or can one play the clown? Is one in search of resistance, or is one evading it? Is one imperfect owing to one's precocity or to one's tardiness? Is it one's nature to say yea, or no, or is one a peacock's tail of garish parts? Is one proud enough not to feel ashamed even of one's vanity? . . .

290. One Thing is Needful[14]

To "give style" to one's character—that is a grand and a rare art! He who surveys all that his nature presents in its strength and in its weakness, and then fashions it into an ingenious plan, until everything appears artistic and rational, and even the weaknesses enchant the eye—exercises that admirable art. Here there has been a great amount of second nature added, there a portion of first nature has been taken away:—in both cases with long exercise and daily labour at the task. Here the ugly, which does not permit of being taken away, has been concealed, there it has been re-interpreted into the sublime. Much of the vague, which refuses to take form, has been reserved and utilised for the perspectives:—it is meant to give a hint of the remote and immeasurable. In the end, when the work has been completed, it is revealed how it was the constraint of the same taste that organised and fashioned it in whole or in part: whether the taste was good or bad is of less importance than one thinks,—it is sufficient that it was *a taste!*—It will be the strong imperious natures which experience their most refined joy in such constraint, in such confinement and perfection under their own law; the passion of their violent volition lessens at the sight of all disciplined nature, all conquered and ministering nature: even when they have palaces to build and gardens to lay out, it is not to their taste to allow nature to be free.—It is the reverse with weak characters who have not power over themselves, and *hate* the restriction of style: they feel that if this repugnant constraint were laid upon them, they would necessarily become *vulgarised* under it: they become slaves as soon as they serve, they hate service. Such intellects—they may be intellects of the first rank—are always concerned with fashioning or interpreting themselves and their surroundings as *free* nature—wild, arbi-

14From *Joyful Wisdom.*

trary, fantastic, confused and surprising: and it is well for them to do so, because only in this manner can they please themselves! . . .

227[15]

Honesty, granting that it is the virtue from which we cannot rid ourselves, we free spirits—well, we will labour at it with all our perversity and love, and not tire of "perfecting" ourselves in *our* virtue, which alone remains: may its glance some day overspread like a gilded, blue, mocking twilight this aging civilisation with its dull gloomy seriousness! And if, nevertheless, our honesty should one day grow weary, and sigh, and stretch its limbs, and find us too hard, and would fain have it pleasanter, easier, and gentler, like an agreeable vice, let us remain *hard*, we latest Stoics, and let us send to its help whatever devilry we have in us:—our disgust at the clumsy and undefined, our *"nitimur in vetitum,"* our love of adventure, our sharpened and fastidious curiosity, our most subtle, disguised, intellectual Will to Power and universal conquest, which rambles and roves avidiously around all the realms of the future—. . .

556. THE FOUR VIRTUES[16]

Honest towards ourselves, and to all and everything friendly to us; brave in the face of our enemy; generous towards the vanquished; polite at all times: such do the four cardinal virtues wish us to be.

344[17]

. . . The question whether *truth* is necessary, must not merely be affirmed beforehand, but must be affirmed to such an extent that the principle, belief, or conviction finds expression, that "there is *nothing more necessary* than truth, and in comparison with it everything else has only a secondary value."—This absolute will to truth: what is it? Is it the will *not to allow ourselves to be deceived?* Is it the will *not to deceive?* For the will to truth could also be interpreted in this fashion, provided one includes under the generalisation, "I will not deceive," the special case, "I will not deceive myself." But why not deceive? Why not allow oneself to be deceived?—Let it be noted that the reasons for the former eventuality belong to a category quite different from those for the latter: one does not want to be deceived oneself, under the supposition that it is injurious, dangerous, or fatal to be deceived,—in this sense science would be a prolonged process of caution, foresight and utility; against which, however, one might reasonably make objections. What? is not-wishing-to-be-deceived really less injurious, less dangerous, less fatal? What do you know of the

[15]From *Beyond Good and Evil.*
[16]From *Dawn of Day.*
[17]From *Joyful Wisdom.*

character of existence in all its phases to be able to decide whether the greater advantage is on the side of absolute distrust, or of absolute trustfulness? In case, however, of both being necessary, much trusting *and* much distrusting, whence then should science derive the absolute belief, the conviction on which it rests, that truth is more important than anything else, even than every other conviction? This conviction could not have arisen if truth *and* untruth had both continually proved themselves to be useful: as is the case. Thus—the belief in science, which now undeniably exists, cannot have had its origin in such a utilitarian calculation, but rather *in spite of* the fact of the inutility and dangerousness of the "Will to truth," of "truth at all costs," being continually demonstrated. "At all costs": alas, we understand that sufficiently well, after having sacrificed and slaughtered one belief after another at this altar!—Consequently, "Will to truth" does *not* imply, "I will not allow myself to be deceived," but—there is no other alternative—"I will not deceive, not even myself": *and thus we have reached the realm of morality.* For, let one just ask oneself fairly: "Why wilt thou not deceive?" especially if it should seem—and it does seem—as if life were laid out with a view to appearance, I mean, with a view to error, deceit, dissimulation, delusion, self-delusion. . . .

230[18]

. . . *Counter to this* propensity for appearance, for simplification, for a disguise, for a cloak, in short, for an outside—for every outside is a cloak—there operates the sublime tendency of the man of knowledge, which takes, and *insists* on taking things profoundly, variously, and thoroughly; as a kind of cruelty of the intellectual conscience and taste, which every courageous thinker will acknowledge in himself, provided, as it ought to be, that he has sharpened and hardened his eye sufficiently long for introspection, and is accustomed to severe discipline and even severe words. He will say: "There is something cruel in the tendency of my spirit": let the virtuous and amiable try to convince him that it is not so! In fact, it would sound nicer, if, instead of our cruelty, perhaps our "extravagant honesty" were talked about, whispered about and glorified—we free, *very* free spirits—and some day perhaps *such* will actually be our—posthumous glory! Meanwhile—for there is plenty of time until then—we should be least inclined to deck ourselves out in such florid and fringed moral verbiage; our whole former work has just made us sick of this taste and its sprightly exuberance. They are beautiful, glistening, jingling, festive words: honesty, love of truth, love of wisdom, sacrifice for knowledge, heroism of the truthful—there is something in them that makes one's heart swell with pride. But we anchorites and marmots have long ago persuaded ourselves in all the secrecy of an anchorite's conscience, that this worthy parade of verbiage also belongs to the old false adornment, frippery, and gold-dust of

[18]From *Beyond Good and Evil.*

unconscious human vanity, and that even under such flattering colour and repainting, the terrible original text *homo natura* must again be recognised. In effect, to translate man back again into nature; to master the many vain and visionary interpretations and subordinate meanings which have hitherto been scratched and daubed over the eternal original text, *homo natura;* to bring it about that man shall henceforth stand before man as he now, hardened by the discipline of science, stands before the *other* forms of nature, with fearless Œdipus-eyes, and stopped Ulysses-ears, deaf to the enticements of old metaphysical bird-catchers, who have piped to him far too long: "Thou are more! thou are higher! thou hast a different origin!"— this may be a strange and foolish task, but that it is a *task,* who can deny! ...

POSTSCRIPT[19]

When Zarathustra had spoken these words, he paused, like one who had not said his last word; and long did he balance the staff doubtfully in his hand. At last he spake thus—and his voice had changed:

I now go alone, my disciples! Ye also now go away, and alone! So will I have it.

Verily, I advise you: depart from me, and guard yourselves against Zarathustra! And better still: be ashamed of him! Perhaps he hath deceived you.

The man of knowledge must be able not only to love his enemies, but also to hate his friends.

One requiteth a teacher badly if one remain merely a scholar. And why will ye not pluck at my wreath?

Ye venerate me; but what if your veneration should some day collapse? Take heed lest a statue crush you!

Ye say, ye believe in Zarathustra? But of what account is Zarathustra! Ye are my believers: but of what account are all believers!

Ye had not yet sought yourselves: then did ye find me. So do all believers; therefore all belief is of so little account.

Now do I bid you lose me and find yourselves; and only when ye have all denied me, will I return unto you.

Verily, with other eyes, my brethren, shall I then seek my lost ones; with another love shall I then love you.

And once again shall ye have become friends unto me, and children of one hope: then will I be with you for the third time, to celebrate the great noontide with you.

And it is the great noontide, when man is in the middle of his course between animal and Superman, and celebrateth his advance to the evening as his highest hope: for it is the advance to a new morning. ...

Thus Spake Zarathustra.

[19]From *Thus Spake Zarathustra.*

Suggested Readings

HOBBES

Catlin, G. E. G., *Thomas Hobbes as Philosopher, Publicist and Man of Letters,* Blackwell, Oxford, 1922.

Gooch, G. P., *Hobbes,* Milford, London, 1940.

Stephen, L., *Hobbes,* Macmillan and Co., London, 1904.

Taylor, A. E., *Thomas Hobbes,* Constable, London, 1908.

Watkins, J., *Hobbes' System of Ideas,* Hutchinson, London, 1965.

BENTHAM AND MILL

Broad, C. D., *Five Types of Ethical Theory,* Harcourt, Brace, New York, 1930.

Cowling, Maurice, *Mill and Liberalism,* Cambridge University Press, New York, 1963.

Moore, G. E., *Ethics,* Chapters I and II, Henry Holt, New York, 1912.

Plamenatz, J., *The English Utilitarians,* Blackwell, Oxford, 1944.

Stephen, L., *The English Utilitarians,* Pitman's, New York, 1900.

KANT

Broad, C. D., *Five Types of Ethical Theory,* Chapter 5, Harcourt, Brace, New York, 1930.

Kant, I., *Critique of Practical Reason,* tr. L. W. Beck, Liberal Arts Press, New York, 1956.

Paton, H. J., *The Categorical Imperative,* University of Chicago Press, Chicago, 1948.

Scott, J. W., *Kant on the Moral Life,* The Macmillan Co., New York, 1924.

NIETZSCHE

Brinton, C. C., *Nietzsche,* Harper & Row, New York, 1965.

Danto, A. C., *Nietzsche as Philosopher,* The Macmillan Co., New York, 1965.

Kaufmann, W. A., *Nietzsche: Philosopher, Psychologist, Antichrist,* Princeton University Press, Princeton, 1950.

Morgan, G. A., *What Nietzsche Means,* Harvard University Press, Cambridge, 1943.

Salter, W. M., *Nietzsche as Philosopher,* Henry Holt, New York, 1917.

PART THREE

CHALLENGES TO
ETHICAL THEORY

Determinism

❀ INTRODUCTION

Thus far we have considered the positions of a number of moral philosophers. But a review of these positions is not likely to terminate philosophic inquiry. For philosophical perplexity about morality may occur at different levels, and a thorough analysis at one level is likely to bring to light questions and problems that are even more profoundly philosophical than those which occasioned the analysis in the first place. Thus the attempt to construct an ethical theory ineluctably raises additional problems—problems which are the result of questioning some of the basic presuppositions of ethical theorists. Three such challenges to ethical theory will be presented in this final part, beginning with the so-called problem of "free-will vs. determinism."

The reason that the problem of free-will is repeatedly encountered in moral philosophy is not difficult to detect. Most moral philosophizing seems to presuppose that human thoughts and actions are not completely determined by factors over which the individual has no control. It is assumed, therefore, that we generally are faced with various alternatives when we are about to act, and that it makes sense to hold people responsible for choosing one alternative rather than another. But occasionally we have doubts about this so-called "free-will" that we uncritically suppose ourselves and others to possess. At these times we may be tempted to call the legitimacy of this presupposition into question. Perhaps this conception, like others in our everyday common-sense thinking, is a mere rationalization. If so, what would be the overall implications for ethics?

Determinism can be considered from a variety of perspectives. William James, writing as a psychologist and a pragmatist, is concerned with tracing the psychological effects which result from assuming the respective positions of the determinist and the free-willist. He then argues in favor of free-will, claiming that this position has better practical consequences for the individual. Ledger Wood, on the other hand, attempts to refute James' position and claims that scientific evidence substantiates the position of determinism.

John Hospers discusses an additional complication which must be considered in working out an adequate solution to the problem of free-will. He shows how our behavior often is affected by unconscious motives and how the deep-seated forces of our unconscious have been molded by factors over which we have very little control. Hence, in light of psychoanalytic theory, free-will is attainable only to a limited degree, and then only for the psychologically well-adjusted individual.

In the final essay of this section the existentialist Simone de Beauvoir takes a fundamentally different approach to the problem of freedom. She attempts a phenomenological analysis of the role which freedom assumes in our lives. This analysis does not seek to demonstrate the possibility of free-will. Rather it is conducted in order to describe the phenomena of willing, and to elucidate their various implications for our psyche. Willing is something that we cannot avoid, so it is the manner of our willing that is important to consider. Furthermore, the manner of our willing is to be understood as an expression of our inward state of being. DeBeauvoir claims that to attain the state of "ethical freedom" a continuous struggle is required, and this struggle necessarily gives birth to anguish and uncertainty. Nevertheless our authenticity as human beings cannot be won in any other way. Hence we must resolve to face up to the full responsibility of our choices.

WILLIAM JAMES

26. *The Case for Free-Will*

William James (1842–1910) was born in New York City. In 1870 he graduated from Harvard University Medical School, and shortly after began a teaching career. He eventually distinguished himself as a leading American psychologist and philosopher. As a philosopher he played an important role in establishing pragmatism, an influential twentieth-century movement. Some of his major works were: *The Principles of Psychology* (1890), *The Varieties of Religious Experience* (1902), and *Pragmatism* (1907).

A common opinion prevails that the juice has ages ago been pressed out of the free-will controversy, and that no new champion can do more than warm up stale arguments which every one has heard. This is a radical mistake. I know of no subject less worn out, or in which inventive genius has a better chance of breaking open new ground,—not, perhaps, of forcing a conclusion or of coercing assent, but of deepening our sense of what the issue between the two parties really is, of what the ideas of fate and of free-will imply. . . .

If I can make . . . the necessarily implied corollaries of determinism clearer to you than they have been made before, I shall have made it possible for you to decide for or against that doctrine with a better understanding of what you are about. And if you prefer not to decide at all, but to remain doubters, you will at least see more plainly what the subject of

From the essay "The Dilemma of Determination," in *The Will To Believe* (New York: Longmans, Green & Co., 1897). Footnotes have been omitted.

your hesitation is. I thus disclaim openly on the threshold all pretension to prove to you that the freedom of the will is true. The most I hope is to induce some of you to follow my own example in assuming it true, and acting as if it were true. If it be true, it seems to me that this is involved in the strict logic of the case. Its truth ought not to be forced willy-nilly down our indifferent throats. It ought to be freely espoused by men who can equally well turn their backs upon it. In other words, our first act of freedom, if we are free, ought in all inward propriety to be to affirm that we are free. This should exclude, it seems to me, from the free-will side of the question all hope of a coercive demonstration,—a demonstration which I, for one, am perfectly contented to go without.

With thus much understood at the outset, we can advance. But not without one more point understood as well. The arguments I am about to urge all proceed on two suppositions: first, when we make theories about the world and discuss them with one another, we do so in order to attain a conception of things which shall give us subjective satisfaction; and, second, if there be two conceptions, and the one seems to us, on the whole, more rational than the other, we are entitled to suppose that the more rational one is the truer of the two. I hope that you are all willing to make these suppositions with me; for I am afraid that if there be any of you here who are not, they will find little edification in the rest of what I have to say. I cannot stop to argue the point; but I myself believe that all the magnificent achievements of mathematical and physical science—our doctrines of evolution, of uniformity of law, and the rest—proceed from our indomitable desire to cast the world into a more rational shape in our minds than the shape into which it is thrown there by the crude order of our experience. The world has shown itself, to a great extent, plastic to this demand of ours for rationality. How much farther it will show itself plastic no one can say. Our only means of finding out is to try; and I, for one, feel as free to try conceptions of moral as of mechanical or of logical rationality. If a certain formula for expressing the nature of the world violates my moral demand, I shall feel as free to throw it overboard, or at least to doubt it, as if it disappointed my demand for uniformity of sequence, for example; the one demand being, so far as I can see, quite as subjective and emotional as the other is. The principle of causality, for example,—what is it but a postulate, an empty name covering simply a demand that the sequence of events shall some day manifest a deeper kind of belonging of one thing with another than the mere arbitrary juxtaposition which now phenomenally appears? It is as much an altar to an unknown god as the one that Saint Paul found at Athens. All our scientific and philosophic ideals are altars to unknown gods. Uniformity is as much so as is free-will. If this be admitted, we can debate on even terms. But if any one pretends that while freedom and variety are, in the first instance, subjective demands, necessity and uniformity are something altogether different, I do not see how we can debate at all.

To begin, then, I must suppose you acquainted with all the usual arguments on the subject. I cannot stop to take up the old proofs from causation, from statistics, from the certainty with which we can foretell one another's conduct, from the fixity of character, and all the rest. But there are two *words* which usually encumber these classical arguments, and which we must immediately dispose of if we are to make any progress. One is the eulogistic word *freedom*, and the other is the opprobrious word *chance*. The word "chance" I wish to keep, but I wish to get rid of the word "freedom." Its eulogistic associations have so far overshadowed all the rest of its meaning that both parties claim the sole right to use it, and determinists to-day insist that they alone are freedom's champions. Old-fashioned determinism was what we may call *hard* determinism. It did not shrink from such words as fatality, bondage of the will, necessitation, and the like. Nowadays, we have a *soft* determinism which abhors harsh words, and, repudiating fatality, necessity, and even predetermination, says that its real name is freedom; for freedom is only necessity understood, and bondage to the highest is identical with true freedom. . . .

Now, all this is a quagmire of evasion under which the real issue of fact has been entirely smothered. Freedom in all these senses presents simply no problem at all. No matter what the soft determinist mean by it, —whether he mean the acting without external constraint; whether he mean the acting rightly, or whether he mean the acquiescing in the law of the whole,—who cannot answer him that sometimes we are free and sometimes we are not? But there *is* a problem, an issue of fact and not of words, an issue of the most momentous importance, which is often decided without discussion in one sentence,—nay, in one clause of a sentence,—by those very writers who spin out whole chapters in their efforts to show what "true" freedom is; and that is the question of determinism, about which we are to talk to-night.

Fortunately, no ambiguities hang about this word or about its opposite, indeterminism. Both designate an outward way in which things may happen, and their cold and mathematical sound has no sentimental associations that can bribe our partiality either way in advance. Now, evidence of an external kind to decide between determinism and indeterminism is, as I intimated a while back, strictly impossible to find. Let us look at the difference between them and see for ourselves. What does determinism profess?

It professes that those parts of the universe already laid down absolutely appoint and decree what the other parts shall be. The future has no ambiguous possibilities hidden in its womb: the part we call the present is compatible with only one totality. Any other future complement than the one fixed from eternity is impossible. The whole is in each and every part, and welds it with the rest into an absolute unity, an iron block, in which there can be no equivocation or shadow of turning.

> With earth's first clay they did the last man knead,
> And there of the last harvest sowed the seed.

And the first morning of creation wrote
What the last dawn of reckoning shall read.

Indeterminism, on the contrary, says that the parts have a certain amount of loose play on one another, so that the laying down of one of them does not necessarily determine what the others shall be. It admits that possibilities may be in excess of actualities, and that things not yet revealed to our knowledge may really in themselves be ambiguous. Of two alternative futures which we conceive, both may now be really possible; and the one becomes impossible only at the very moment when the other excludes it by becoming real itself. Indeterminism thus denies the world to be one unbending unit of fact. It says there is a certain ultimate pluralism in it; and, so saying, it corroborates our ordinary unsophisticated view of things. To that view, actualities seem to float in a wider sea of possibilities from out of which they are chosen; and, *somewhere*, indeterminism says, such possibilities exist, and form a part of truth.

Determinism, on the contrary, says they exist *nowhere*, and that necessity on the one hand and impossibility on the other are the sole categories of the real. Possibilities that fail to get realized are, for determinism, pure illusions: they never were possibilities at all. There is nothing inchoate, it says, about this universe of ours, all that was or is or shall be actual in it having been from eternity virtually there. The cloud of alternatives our minds escort this mass of actuality withal is a cloud of sheer deceptions, to which "impossibilities" is the only name that rightfully belongs.

The issue, it will be seen, is a perfectly sharp one, which no eulogistic terminology can smear over or wipe out. The truth *must* lie with one side or the other, and its lying with one side makes the other false.

The question relates solely to the existence of possibilities, in the strict sense of the term, as things that may, but need not, be. Both sides admit that a volition, for instance, has occurred. The indeterminists say another volition might have occurred in its place: the determinists swear that nothing could possibly have occurred in its place. Now, can science be called in to tell us which of these two point-blank contradicters of each other is right? Science professes to draw no conclusions but such as are based on matters of fact, things that have actually happened; but how can any amount of assurance that something actually happened give us the least grain of information as to whether another thing might or might not have happened in its place? Only facts can be proved by other facts. With things that are possibilities and not facts, facts have no concern. If we have no other evidence than the evidence of existing facts, the possibility-question must remain a mystery never to be cleared up.

And the truth is that facts practically have hardly anything to do with making us either determinists or indeterminists. Sure enough, we make a flourish of quoting facts this way or that; and if we are determinists, we talk about the infallibility with which we can predict one another's conduct; while if we are indeterminists, we lay great stress on the fact that it it just because we cannot foretell one another's conduct, either in war or statecraft or in any of the great and small intrigues and businesses of men, that life is so intensely anxious and hazardous a game. But who does not see the wretched insufficiency of this so-called objective testimony on both sides? What fills up the gaps in our minds is something not objective, not external. What divides us into possibility men and anti-possibility men is different faiths or postulates,—postulates of rationality. To this man the world seems more rational with possibilities in it,—to that man more rational with possibilities excluded; and talk as we will about having to yield to evidence, what makes us monists or pluralists, determinists or indeterminists, is at bottom always some sentiment like this.

The stronghold of the deterministic sentiment is the antipathy to the idea of chance. As soon as we begin to talk indeterminism to our friends, we find a number of them shaking their heads. This notion of alternative possibility, they say, this admission that any one of several things may come to pass, is, after all, only a roundabout name for chance; and chance is something the notion of which no sane mind can for an instant tolerate in the world. What is it, they ask, but barefaced crazy unreason, the negation of intelligibility and law? And if the slightest particle of it exist anywhere, what is to prevent the whole fabric from falling together, the stars from going out, and chaos from recommencing her topsy-turvy reign?

Remarks of this sort about chance will put an end to discussion as quickly as anything one can find. I have already told you that "chance" was a word I wished to keep and use. Let us then examine exactly what it means, and see whether it ought to be such a terrible bugbear to us. I fancy that squeezing the thistle boldly will rob it of its sting.

The sting of the word "chance" seems to lie in the assumption that it means something positive, and that if anything happens by chance, it must needs be something of an intrinsically irrational and preposterous sort. Now, chance means nothing of the kind. It is a purely negative and relative term, giving us no information about that of which it is predicated, except that it happens to be disconnected with something else,—not controlled, secured, or necessitated by other things in advance of its own actual presence. As this point is the most [subtle] one of the whole lecture, and at the same time the point on which all the rest hinges, I beg you to pay particular attention to it. What I say is that it tells us nothing about what a thing may be in itself to call it "chance." It may be a bad thing, it may be a good thing. It may be lucidity, transparency, fitness incarnate, matching the whole system of other things, when it has once befallen, in an unimaginably perfect way. All you mean by calling it "chance" is that this is not guaranteed, that it may also fall out otherwise. For the system of other things has no positive hold on the chance-thing. Its origin is in a certain fashion negative: it escapes, and says, Hands off! coming, when it comes, as a free gift, or not at all.

This negativeness, however, and this opacity of the chance-thing when thus considered *ab extra,* or from the point of view of previous things or distant things, do not preclude its having any amount of positiveness and luminosity from within, and at its own place and moment. All that its chance-character asserts about it is that there is something in it really of its own, something that is not the unconditional property of the whole. If the whole wants this property, the whole must wait till it can get it, if it be a matter of chance. That the universe may actually be a sort of joint-stock society of this sort, in which the sharers have both limited liabilities and limited powers, is of course a simple and conceivable notion.

Nevertheless, many persons talk as if the minutest dose of discon-nectedness of one part with another, the smallest modicum of independence, the faintest tremor of ambiguity about the future, for example, would ruin everything, and turn this goodly universe into a sort of insane sand-heap or nulliverse, no universe at all. Since future human volitions are as a mat-ter of fact the only ambiguous things we are tempted to believe in, let us stop for a moment to make ourselves sure whether their independent and accidental character need be fraught with such direful consequences to the universe as these.

What is meant by saying that my choice of which way to walk home after the lecture is ambiguous and matter of chance as far as the present moment is concerned? It means that both Divinity Avenue and Oxford Street are called; but that only one, and that one *either* one, shall be chosen. Now, I ask you seriously to suppose that this ambiguity of my choice is real; and then to make the impossible hypothesis that the choice is made twice over, and each time falls on a different street. In other words, imagine that I first walk through Divinity Avenue, and then imagine that the powers governing the universe annihilate ten minutes of time with all that it contained, and set me back at the door of this hall just as I was before the choice was made. Imagine then that, everything else being the same, I now make a different choice and traverse Oxford Street. You, as passive spectators, look on and see the two alternative universes,—one of them with me walking through Divinity Avenue in it, the other with the same me walking through Oxford Street. Now, if you are determinists you believe one of these universes to have been from eternity impossible: you believe it to have been impossible because of the intrinsic irrationality or acciden-tality somewhere involved in it. But looking outwardly at these universes, can you say which is the impossible and accidental one, and which the ra-tional and necessary one? I doubt if the most ironclad determinist among you could have the slightest glimmer of light on this point. In other words, either universe *after the fact* and once there would, to our means of obser-vation and understanding, appear just as rational as the other. There would be absolutely no criterion by which we might judge one necessary and the other matter of chance. Suppose now we relieve the gods of their hypothet-ical task and assume my choice, once made, to be made forever. I go through Divinity Avenue for good and all. If, as good determinists, you now begin to affirm, what all good determinists punctually do affirm, that in the nature of things I *couldn't* have gone through Oxford Street,—had I done so it would have been chance, irrationality, insanity, a horrid gap in nature,—I simply call your attention to this, that your affirmation is what the Germans call a *Machtspruch,* a mere conception fulminated as a dogma and based on no insight into details. Before my choice, either street seemed as natural to you as to me. Had I happened to take Oxford Street, Divinity Avenue would have figured in your philosophy as the gap in nature; and you would have so proclaimed it with the best deterministic conscience in the world.

But what a hollow outcry, then, is this against a chance which, if it were present to us, we could by no character whatever distinguish from a rational necessity! I have taken the most trivial of examples, but no possible example could lead to any different result. For what are the alternatives which, in point of fact, offer themselves to human volition? What are those futures that now seem matters of chance? Are they not one and all like the Divinity Avenue and Oxford Street of our example? Are they not all of them *kinds* of things already here and based in the existing frame of nature? Is any one ever tempted to produce an *absolute* accident, something utterly irrelevant to the rest of the world? Do not all the motives that assail us, all the futures that offer themselves to our choice, spring equally from the soil of the past; and would not either one of them, whether realized through chance or through necessity, the moment it was realized, seem to us to fit that past, and in the completest and most continuous manner to interdigitate with the phenomena already there?

The more one thinks of the matter, the more one wonders that so empty and gratuitous a hubbub as this outcry against chance should have found so great an echo in the hearts of men. It is a word which tells us absolutely nothing about what chances, or about the *modus operandi* of the chancing; and the use of it as a war-cry shows only a temper of intellectual absolutism, a demand that the world shall be a solid block, subject to one control,—which temper, which demand, the world may not be bound to gratify at all. In every outwardly verifiable and practical respect, a world in which the alternatives that now actually distract *your* choice were decided by pure chance would be by *me* absolutely undistinguished from the world in which I now live. I am, therefore, entirely willing to call it, so far as your choices go, a world of chance for me. To *yourselves,* it is true, those very acts of choice, which to me are so blind, opaque, and external, are the opposites of this, for you are within them and effect them. To you they appear as decisions; and decisions, for him who makes them, are altogether peculiar psychic facts. Self-luminous and self-justifying at the living moment at which they occur, they appeal to no outside moment to put its stamp upon them or make them continuous with the rest of nature. Themselves it is rather who seem to make nature continuous; and in their strange and intense function of granting consent to one possibility and withholding it from another, to transform an equivocal and double future into an inalterable and simple past.

But with the psychology of the matter we have no concern this evening. The quarrel which determinism has with chance fortunately has nothing to do with this or that psychological detail. It is a quarrel altogether

metaphysical. Determinism denies the ambiguity of future volitions, because it affirms that nothing future can be ambiguous. But we have said
enough to meet the issue. Indeterminate future volitions *do* mean chance.
Let us not fear to shout it from the house-tops if need be; for we now know
that the idea of chance is, at bottom, exactly the same thing as the idea of
gift,—the one simply being a disparaging, and the other a eulogistic, name
for anything on which we have no effective *claim*. And whether the world
be the better or the worse for having either chances or gifts in it will depend altogether on *what* these uncertain and unclaimable things turn out
to be.

And this at last brings us within sight of our subject. We have seen
what determinism means: we have seen that indeterminism is rightly described as meaning chance; and we have seen that chance, the very name
of which we are urged to shrink from as from a metaphysical pestilence,
means only the negative fact that no part of the world, however big, can
claim to control absolutely the destinies of the whole. But although, in discussing the word "chance," I may at moments have seemed to be arguing
for its real existence, I have not meant to do so yet. We have not yet ascertained whether this be a world of chance or no; at most, we have agreed
that it seems so. And I now repeat what I said at the outset, that, from any
strict theoretical point of view, the question is insoluble. To deepen our
theoretic sense of the *difference* between a world with chances in it and a
deterministic world is the most I can hope to do; and this I may now at
last begin upon, after all our tedious clearing of the way.

I wish first of all to show you just what the notion that this is a
deterministic world implies. The implications I call your attention to are
all bound up with the fact that it is a world in which we constantly have
to make what I shall, with your permission, call judgments of regret. Hardly
an hour passes in which we do not wish that something might be otherwise;
and happy indeed are those of us whose hearts have never echoed the wish
of Omar Khayam—

> That we might clasp, ere closed, the book of fate,
>   And make the writer on a fairer leaf
> Inscribe our names, or quite obliterate.
>
> Ah! Love, could you and I with fate conspire
> To mend this sorry scheme of things entire,
>   Would we not shatter it to bits, and then
> Remould it nearer to the heart's desire?

Now, it is undeniable that most of these regrets are foolish, and
quite on a par in point of philosophic value with the criticisms on the universe of that friend of our infancy, the hero of the fable The Atheist and
the Acorn,—

> Fool! had that bought a pumpkin bore,
> Thy whimsies would have worked no more,

etc. Even from the point of view of our own ends, we should probably make a botch of remodeling the universe. How much more then from the point of view of ends we cannot see! Wise men therefore regret as little as they can. But still some regrets are pretty obstinate and hard to stifle,—regrets for acts of wanton cruelty or treachery, for example, whether performed by others or by ourselves. Hardly any one can remain *entirely* optimistic after reading the confession of the murderer at Brockton the other day: how, to get rid of the wife whose continued existence bored him, he inveigled her into a desert spot, shot her four times, and then, as she lay on the ground and said to him, "You didn't do it on purpose, did you, dear?" replied, "No, I didn't do it on purpose," as he raised a rock and smashed her skull. Such an occurrence, with the mild sentence and self-satisfaction of the prisoner, is a field for a crop of regrets, which one need not take up in detail. We feel that, although a perfect mechanical fit to the rest of the universe, it is a bad moral fit, and that something else would really have been better in its place.

But for the deterministic philosophy the murder, the sentence, and the prisoner's optimism were all necessary from eternity; and nothing else for a moment had a ghost of a chance of being put into their place. To admit such a chance, the determinists tell us, would be to make a suicide of reason; so we must steel our hearts against the thought. And here our plot thickens, for we see the first of those difficult implications of determinism and monism which it is my purpose to make you feel. If this Brockton murder was called for by the rest of the universe, if it had to come at its preappointed hour, and if nothing else would have been consistent with the sense of the whole, what are we to think of the universe? Are we stubbornly to stick to our judgment of regret, and say, though it *couldn't* be, yet it *would* have been a better universe with something different from this Brockton murder in it? That, of course, seems the natural and spontaneous thing for us to do; and yet it is nothing short of deliberately espousing a kind of pessimism. The judgment of regret calls the murder bad. Calling a thing bad means, if it mean anything at all, that the thing ought not to be, that something else ought to be in its stead. Determinism, in denying that anything else can be in its stead, virtually defines the universe as a place in which what ought to be is impossible,—in other words, as an organism whose constitution is afflicted with an incurable taint, an irremediable flaw. The pessimism of a Schopenhauer says no more than this,—that the murder is a symptom; and that it is a vicious symptom because it belongs to a vicious whole, which can express its nature no otherwise than by bringing forth just such a symptom as that at this particular spot. Regret for the murder must transform itself, if we are determinists and wise, into a larger regret. It is absurd to regret the murder alone. Other things being what they are, *it* could not be different. What we should regret is that whole frame of things of which the murder is one member. I see no escape whatever from this pessimistic conclusion, if, being determinists, our judgment of regret is to be allowed to stand at all. . . .

But this brings us right back, after such a long détour, to the question of indeterminism and to the conclusion of all I came here to say to-night. For the only consistent way of representing a pluralism and a world whose parts may affect one another through their conduct being either good or bad is the indeterministic way. What interest, zest, or excitement can there be in achieving the right way, unless we are enabled to feel that the wrong way is also a possible and a natural way,—nay, more, a menacing and an imminent way? And what sense can there be in condemning our-selves for taking the wrong way, unless we need have done nothing of the sort, unless the right way was open to us as well? I cannot understand the willingness to act, no matter how we feel, without the belief that acts are really good and bad. I cannot understand the belief that an act is bad, without regret at its happening. I cannot understand regret without the admission of real, genuine possibilities in the world. Only *then* is it other than a mockery to feel, after we have failed to do our best, that an irrepar-able opportunity is gone from the universe, the loss of which it must for-ever after mourn.

If you insist that this is all superstition, that possibilty is in the eye of science and reason impossibility, and that if I act badly 't is that the uni-verse was foredoomed to suffer this defect, you fall right back into the dilemma, the labyrinth, of pessimism . . . from out of whose toils we have just wound our way.

Now, we are of course free to fall back, if we please. For my own part, though, whatever difficulties may beset the philosophy of objective right and wrong, and the indeterminism it seems to imply, determinism, with its alternative of pessimism . . . , contains difficulties that are greater still. But you will remember that I expressly repudiated awhile ago the pretension to offer any arguments which could be coercive in a so-called scientific fashion in this matter. And I consequently find myself, at the end of this long talk, obliged to state my conclusions in an altogether personal way. This personal method of appeal seems to be among the very condi-tions of the problem; and the most any one can do is to confess as candidly as he can the grounds for the faith that is in him, and leave his example to work on others as it may.

Let me, then, without circumlocution say just this. The world is enigmatical enough in all conscience, whatever theory we may take up to-ward it. The indeterminism I defend, the free-will theory of popular sense based on the judgment of regret, represents that world as vulnerable, and liable to be injured by certain of its parts if they act wrong. And it repre-sents their acting wrong as a matter of possibility or accident, neither in-evitable nor yet to be infallibly warded off. In all this, it is a theory devoid either of transparency or of stability. It gives us a pluralistic, restless uni-verse, in which no single point of view can ever take in the whole scene; and to a mind possessed of the love of unity at any cost, it will, no doubt, remain forever inacceptable. A friend with such a mind once told me that the thought of my universe made him sick, like the sight of the horrible motion of a mass of maggots in their carrion bed.

But while I freely admit that the pluralism and the restlessness are repugnant and irrational in a certain way, I find that every alternative to them is irrational in a deeper way. The indeterminism with its maggots, if you please to speak so about it, offends only the native absolutism of my intellect,—an absolutism which, after all, perhaps, deserves to be snubbed and kept in check. But the determinism with its necessary carrion, to continue the figure of speech, and with no possible maggots to eat the latter up, violates my sense of moral reality through and through. When, for example, I imagine such carrion as the Brockton murder, I cannot conceive it as an act by which the universe, as a whole, logically and necessarily expresses its nature without shrinking from complicity with such a whole. And I deliberately refuse to keep on terms of loyalty with the universe by saying blankly that the murder, since it does flow from the nature of the whole, is not carrion. There are *some* instinctive reactions which I, for one, will not tamper with. . . .

But now you will bring up your final doubt. Does not the admission of such an unguaranteed chance or freedom preclude utterly the notion of a Providence governing the world? Does it not leave the fate of the universe at the mercy of the chance-possibilities, and so far insecure? Does it not, in short, deny the craving of our nature for an ultimate peace behind all tempests, for a blue zenith above all clouds?

To this my answer must be very brief. The belief in free-will is not in the least incompatible with the belief in Providence, provided you do not restrict the Providence to fulminating nothing but *fatal* decrees. If you allow him to provide possibilities as well as actualities to the universe, and to carry on his own thinking in those two categories just as we do ours, chances may be there, uncontrolled even by him, and the course of the universe be really ambiguous; and yet the end of all things may be just what he intended it to be from all eternity.

An analogy will make the meaning of this clear. Suppose two men before a chessboard,—the one a novice, the other an expert player of the game. The expert intends to beat. But he cannot foresee exactly what any one actual move of his adversary may be. He knows, however, all the *possible* moves of the latter; and he knows in advance how to meet each of them by a move of his own which leads in the direction of victory. And the victory infallibly arrives, after no matter how devious a course, in the one predestined form of check-mate to the novice's king.

Let now the novice stand for us finite free agents, and the expert for the infinite mind in which the universe lies. Suppose the latter to be thinking out his universe before he actually creates it. Suppose him to say, I will lead things to a certain end, but I will not *now* decide on all the steps thereto. At various points, ambiguous possibilities shall be left open, *either* of which, at a given instant, may become actual. But whichever branch of these bifurcations become real, I know what I shall do at the *next* bifurcation to keep things from drifting away from the final result I intend.

The creator's plan of the universe would thus be left blank as to many of its actual details, but all possibilities would be marked down. The realization of some of these would be left absolutely to chance; that is, would only be determined when the moment of realization came. Other possibilities would be *contingently* determined; that is, their decision would have to wait till it was seen how the matters of absolute chance fell out. But the rest of the plan, including its final upshot, would be rigorously determined once for all. So the creator himself would not need to know *all* the details of actuality until they came; and at any time his own view of the world would be a view partly of facts and partly of possibilities, exactly as ours is now. Of one thing, however, he might be certain; and that is that his world was safe, and that no matter how much it might zig-zag he could surely bring it home at last.

Now, it is entirely immaterial, in this scheme, whether the creator leave the absolute chance-possibilities to be decided by himself, each when its proper moment arrives, or whether, on the contrary, he alienate this power from himself, and leave the decision out and out to finite creatures such as we men are. The great point is that the possibilities are really *here*. Whether it be we who solve them, or he working through us, at those soul-trying moments when fate's scales seem to quiver, and good snatches the victory from evil or shrinks nerveless from the fight, is of small account, so long as we admit that the issue is decided nowhere else than *here* and *now*. *That* is what gives the palpitating reality to our moral life and makes it tingle . . . with so strange and elaborate an excitement. This reality, this excitement, are what the determinisms, hard and soft alike, suppress by their denial that *anything* is decided here and now, and their dogma that all things were foredoomed and settled long ago. If it be so, may you and I then have been foredoomed to the error of continuing to believe in liberty. It is fortunate for the winding up of controversy that in every discussion with determinism this *argumentum ad hominem* can be its adversary's last word.

✿ LEDGER WOOD

27. *The Case Against Free-Will*

Ledger Wood (1901–   ) has been a philosophy professor at Princeton University since 1927. He has written articles for a number of journals and has published books on the theory of knowledge and the history of philosophy. These works are: *Analysis of Knowledge* (1941), and *History of Philosophy* which was written by Frank Thilly and then revised by Ledger Wood in 1952.

Reprinted from Ledger Wood, "The Free-Will Controversy," *Philosophy*, XVI (1941) 386–397. Used with the kind permission of the editor of *Philosophy* and the author.

Few philosophical controversies have been waged with greater acrimony than the controversy between the libertarians and the determinists; the vigour with which both sides of the question have been espoused is due not only to the metaphysical importance of the issue—which is indeed considerable—but more especially to its moral and religious implications. No other philosophical issues, with the exception of those pertaining to God and the immortality of the soul, are of greater ethical and theological moment. So thoroughly has the question been debated that further consideration of it may seem futile. Has not the evidence been so completely canvassed on both sides of the controversy that further discussion will be a fruitless reiteration of long familiar arguments? The free-will problem is considered by many contemporary thinkers an admittedly unsolved but completely outmoded problem to which they respond with impatience or complete indifference. This attitude toward the problem is quite indefensible since the question of the freedom of the will is one of those perennially significant philosophical issues which takes on new meaning in every age and is particularly significant in the context of contemporary science and philosophy. Recent psychology, in large measure through the influence of Freud, has achieved a more penetrating analysis of human motivation by bringing to the fore certain hitherto obscure factors which are operative in volition. The psychology of the subconscious by filling in apparent gaps in the psychological causation of volition has furthered the case for determinism. Furthermore, behaviouristic psychology by subjecting all human behaviour, including so-called volitional acts, to a mechanistic formula bears directly on the free-will issue and like the Freudian psychology seems to strengthen the deterministic position. Recent developments in the physical sciences are not without their significance for the free-will issue; the principle of indeterminacy in quantum mechanics has been eagerly seized upon by the libertarians in the belief that it affords a physical foundation for their position. Finally, in philosophy proper the progress of philosophical analysis and of the philosophical theory of meaning renders possible a more exact statement of the free-will issue and permits a more just appraisal of the traditional arguments on both sides of the free-will controversy than has hitherto been possible. The concepts of determinacy, indeterminacy, compulsion, choice, etc., are elucidated by analysis in accordance with the theory of meaning of recent positivism and radical empiricism. It is for these reasons that a contemporary re-examination of the free-will issue is not only legitimate but most imperative.

The question of the freedom of the will, reduced to its barest essentials, is simply this: *Are all human acts of will causally produced by antecedent conditions or are at least some volitional actions exempt from causal determination?* The determinist insists that all actions, even the most carefully planned and deliberate, can be causally explained and that if we knew enough about a man's hereditary traits and the environmental influences which have moulded his character, we could predict just how he would behave under any specified set of circumstances. The free-willist or libertarian, on the other hand, asserts that there are at least some human actions of the volitional type in which the individual by the exercise of his will-power, acts independently of conditioning factors—that he, so to speak, "lifts himself up by his boot-straps."

The freedom of caprice (the traditional *liberum arbitrium*) when precisely defined means that some, and perhaps all, volitional acts are causally indeterminate, that is to say, are not conjoined in any uniform way with antecedent conditions. The uniform antecedents of free acts are, on this view, undiscoverable for the simple reason that they do not exist. Free-acts are the products of pure chance and, therefore, remain unexplained because they are inherently inexplicable; they are, in the strict sense of the word, miracles—a miracle being defined as any occurrence which cannot be brought within the compass of natural law. The freedom of chance, conceived in this extreme fashion, would, if it existed, utterly disrupt social intercourse, for, no one could possibly anticipate when another, or even himself, might act freely, or in other words, miraculously. Perhaps the closest approximation to a capricious free-will is to be found in a lunatic—but even his acts are not genuinely free, since a psychiatrist can, at least ideally, explain and even predict them. The maniac's actions, however strange they may seem when judged by the sane man's standards of normal behaviour, are psychologically explicable; they conform to certain uniform patterns of abnormal psychology, which, in turn, are assimilable to the laws of general psychology. The free-willist—however much he may seek to disguise the fact—introduces an element of indeterminacy into human behaviour; he admits an effect, namely, the volitional action, without a sufficient and adequate natural cause. The free-will of man, according to the extreme defenders of the free-will doctrine, swoops down from above and injects into the volitional situation an arbitrary, capricious, and incalculable factor.

I propose to give a brief résumé of the free-will controversy, examining first the arguments for the freedom of the will and then stating the case for determinism. Although the position taken throughout the present paper is avowedly deterministic, the attempt will be made to state with fairness the case for and against both of the rival positions and on the basis of these arguments, to give a just appraisal of the two positions. The strength of the deterministic position will be found to lie not only in the positive evidence which may be adduced to support it, but also in its easy ability to meet the arguments advanced by the free-willists.

Arguments for the Freedom of the Will

The arguments of the free-willist are for the most part humanistic and non-scientific in character and may be conveniently considered under the following heads:

    (1) the introspective or psychological argument,
    (2) the moral and religious arguments,
    (3) the argument from physical indeterminacy.

(1) *The Introspective or Psychological Argument*

Most advocates of the free-will doctrine believe that the mind is directly aware of its freedom in the very act of making a decision, and thus that freedom is an immediate datum of our introspective awareness. "I feel myself free, *therefore*, I am free," runs the simplest and perhaps the most compelling of the arguments for freedom. In the elaboration of his argument, the free-willist offers a detailed description of what, in his opinion, is introspectively observable whenever the self makes a free choice. Suppose I find myself forced to choose between conflicting and incompatible lines of action. At such a time, I stand, so to speak, at the moral cross-roads, I deliberate, and finally by some mysterious and inexplicable power of mind, I decide to go one way rather than the other. Deliberative decision, if this description is correct, is analysable into these three constituents: (a) the envisaging of two or more incompatible courses of action, (b) the review of considerations favourable and unfavourable to each of the conflicting possibilities of action, and (c) the choice among the alternative possibilities.

Deliberative, or so-called "moral" decisions, are fairly numerous in the lives of all of us and are made on the most trivial occasions, as well as on matters of grave import. The university undergraduate's resolution of the conflict between his desire to see the latest cinema at the local playhouse and his felt obligation to devote the evening to his studies, trivial and inconsequential as it may seem, is the *type* of all moral decisions and differs in no essential respect from such a momentous decision as his choice of a life career. Each of these decisions to the extent that it is truly deliberative involves (a) the imaginative contemplation of alternative actions, (b) the weighing of considerations *for* and *against* the several alternatives involving, perhaps, an appeal to ideals and values approved by the moral agent, and finally (c) the choice between the several possibilities of action. At the moment of making the actual decision, the mind experiences a *feeling* of self-assertion and of independence of determining influences both external and internal. The libertarian rests his case for free-will on the authenticity of this subjective feeling of freedom.

The phenomenon of decision after deliberation is an indubitable *fact* which determinist and free-willist alike must acknowledge, but the real issue is whether this fact warrants the *construction* which the free-willist puts upon it. The determinist, replying to the introspective argument, urges that the *feeling* of freedom is nothing but a sense of relief following upon earlier tension and indecision. After conflict and uncertainty, the pent-up energies of the mind—or rather of the underlying neural processes—are released and this process is accompanied by an inner sense of power. Thus the feeling of freedom or of voluntary control over one's actions is a mere subjective illusion which cannot be considered evidence for psychological indeterminacy.

Besides the direct appeal to the sense of freedom, there is a psychological argument which *infers* freedom from the mind's ability to resolve an equilibrium of opposing motives. The allegedly "prerogative" or "critical" instance of free-will, is that in which the will makes a choice between two or more actions which are equally attractive, or equally objectionable. If, after a careful weighing of all the considerations *for* and *against* each of the alternative actions, the mind finds the rival claimants exactly equal, a decision is possible, argues the libertarian, only by a free act of will. We weigh the motives against one another, find the scale balanced, and then, in the words of William James, . . . "we feel, in deciding as if we ourselves by our wilful act inclined the beam."[1] This argument from the equilibrium of motives is indeed plausible, but the determinist has a ready reply. *If* the motives really had been exactly equal and opposite, then the mind would have remained indefinitely in a state of suspended judgment and consequent inaction or would, in Hamlet fashion, have oscillated between the two incompatibles, never able to yield to one or to the other. The analogy of the balanced scale would lead one to expect the will under these circumstances to do just this. Indeed, there are undoubtedly some pathological minds which are in a perpetual tug-of-war between conflicting tendencies of action and whose wills, as a consequence, are completely paralysed. But in normal minds the "motives" on the one side or the other become momentarily stronger because of some new external factor injected into the situation or because of the inner reorganization of forces and then action immediately ensues. Often the decision is determined by accidental and contingent circumstances—a literal flip of the coin—or perhaps one allows one's action to be decided by a chance idea or impulse, that is to say, by a "mental flip of the coin." In any case the fact that a decision is actually made testifies to the eventual inequality of the opposing forces. Under no circumstances is it necessary to resort to a mysterious, inner force of will to "incline the beam" one way rather than the other.

Still another introspective fact cited by the libertarian in support of his doctrine is that the moral agent is in retrospect convinced that he might, *if he had chosen,* have followed a course of action different from that which he actually pursued. The belief that there are genuine alternatives of action and that the choice between them is indeterminate is usually stronger in prospect and in retrospect than at the time of actual decision. The alternatives exist in prospect as imaginatively envisaged possibilities of action and in retrospect as the memory of the state of affairs before the agent had, so to speak, "made up his mind." Especially in retrospect does the agent recall his earlier decision with remorse and repentance, dwelling sorrowfully upon rejected possibilities of action which now loom up as opportunities missed. How frequently one hears the lament: "I regret that decision; I should, and I could, have acted otherwise." Now the contemplation of supposed alternatives of action along with the sentiment of regret produces the illusion of indeterminate choice between alternatives, but a careful analysis of the import of the retrospective judgment, "I could have acted otherwise than I did," will, I believe, disclose it to be an empirically meaningless statement.

[1] *The Principles of Psychology*, vol. ii, p. 534.

If I decided in favour of this alternative, rather than that, it can only mean that the circumstances being what they were, and I in the frame of mind I was at the time, no other eventuation was really possible. My statement that I could have acted differently expresses only my memory of an earlier state of suspense, indecision, and uncertainty, intensified by my present remorse and the firm determination that if, in the future, I am faced with a similar choice, I shall profit by my earlier mistake. There is, however, in the deliberate situation no evidence of genuine alternatives of action, or the indeterminacy of my choice between them.

(2) The Moral and Religious Arguments

The moral argument assumes a variety of forms, but they all agree in their attempt to infer volitional freedom of the moral agent from some feature of the moral situation. The most characteristic feature of moral action is that it seems to be directed toward the realization of an ideal or the fulfilment of an obligation. But argues the free-willist, it is of the very nature of an ideal or an obligation that it shall be *freely* embraced; the acceptance or rejection of a moral ideal and the acknowledgement of an obligation as binding can only be accounted for on the assumption of the agent's free choice. The very existence of moral ideals, norms, or standards which, though *coercive* or not *compulsive,* testifies to the freedom of the agent who acknowledges them. Thus did Kant in his famous formula: "I ought, therefore I can" directly infer the agent's freedom from his recognition of moral obligation.

The moral argument is so loose in its logic that unable to put one's finger on its fallacy one is tempted to resort to the logicians' "catch-all," and call it a *non sequitur.* A moral agent's adoption of a moral ideal or recognition of a moral obligation simply does *not* imply that he possesses a free-will in the sense of psychological indeterminacy. An adequate critique of the moral argument would require a detailed psychological account of the genesis of moral ideals and duties without recourse to freedom of the libertarian sort and I am convinced that such an account is forthcoming. The emergence of ideals in the mind of an individual moral agent along with the feeling that such ideals are coercive is largely non-volitional and even when it rises to the volitional level and represents a choice between competing ideals, there is even then no reason for abandoning psychological determinism. The moral argument for freedom is found, on close examination, to be the psychological argument in disguise and like it, is introspectively false; there is no indication of volitional freedom either in the original adoption of moral standards nor in subsequent moral decisions in accordance with those standards once they have been embraced.

The moral argument for freedom has sometimes been stated from the point of view not of the moral agent but of the moral critic who passes judgment on the action of another or even upon his own actions. A judgment of praise or blame, of approval or condemnation, so the argument runs, imputes freedom to the agent whose action is judged. When I praise your unselfish and benevolent acts, I imply that you could, if you had chosen, have been cruel and selfish instead. Condemnation of another's conduct seems even more surely to suggest that he acted willingly, or rather "wilfully." Otherwise, would it not be in order to pity rather than condemn the wrong-doer? Should we not say with condescension, "Poor misguided fool, he can't help what he does, he is simply that kind of man"? Instead, we reprove his action and by so doing implicitly acknowledge that he is a free moral agent. A novel variant of this argument is contained in William James's essay "The Dilemma of Determinism." The determinist, so James argues, finds himself in a curious logical predicament whenever he utters a judgment of regret. If I, a determinist, pass an adverse judgment on my own or another's actions, I thereby acknowledge that they ought not to have been, that others ought to have been performed in their place. But how can I meaningfully make such a statement if these particular actions, and no others, were possible?[2] "What sense can there be in condemning ourselves for taking the wrong way, unless the right way was open to us as well?"[3] James advanced the moral argument, not as an absolute *proof* of freedom (he admits that it is not intellectually coercive), but rather as a belief to be *freely* embraced. As a pragmatically effective, moral fiction, freedom has much to be said in its favour: the belief in freedom no doubt fosters moral earnestness, whereas the belief in determinism may, at least in certain persons, induce moral lassitude. Most defenders of the free-will doctrine do not, however, share James's cautious restraint; they advance the moral argument as a conclusive proof of an indeterminate free-will. The fallacy again can only be described as a *non sequitur*. Moral appraisal has nothing to do with the freedom of the will; the mere fact that *I* approve certain of *your* actions because I consider them good and condemn others as wrong may give some indication of *my* moral make-up, but it proves nothing whatsoever regarding the freedom of *your* will. Your moral acts, even though completely determined, may be judged in accordance with prevailing standards to be laudable or repre-hensible. I praise your good conduct and condemn your bad conduct even though both are inexorably determined and—the determinist would add—I too am determined to judge them as I do. Hence the freedom of a moral agent cannot possibly be inferred from the judgments of approbation and disapprobation passed upon him by a moral critic.

The determinist finds no difficulty in assimilating to his determin-istic scheme the facts of moral approval and disapproval. Moral valuation is not the detached and disinterested judgment of a moral critic, but is an instrumentality for the social propagation of norms of conduct. Morality is essentially a social phenomenon; society has gradually evolved its patterns

[2]William James, *The Will to Believe and Other Essays in Popular Philosophy*, p. 163.

[3]*Ibid.*, p. 175.

of social behaviour which it imposes upon its individual members by means of various sanctions including the favourable or adverse judgments which members of society pass upon one another. Judgments of moral valuation rest upon the socially constituted norms of action and are the media through which these norms are communicated from individual to individual. I reprove your unsocial or antisocial behaviour in the belief that my adverse judgment may influence you to desist therefrom. When I pass a moral judgment on another, far from implying his free-will, I tacitly assume that my judgment of him, in so far as he takes cognizance of it, operates as a determining influence on his conduct. Thus moral criticism when interpreted naturalistically harmonizes with the theory of moral determinism.

Another moral argument, closely paralleling the argument from obligation, stresses the concept of moral responsibility. The free-willist considers freedom a *sine qua non* of responsibility; his argument runs: "Without freedom, there can be no responsibility, but there *must* be responsibility, hence man is free." There are *two* ways of attacking this argument: (1) we may pertinently ask: "But *why* must there be responsibility?", or, (2) we may challenge the underlying assumption of the argument, namely, that freedom is an indispensable condition of responsibility. The first criticism is a rejection of the minor and usually tacit premise of the free-willist's argument, the conviction, namely, that there must be responsibility. The conviction prevalent among moralists that responsibility, obligation, etc., because they are morally significant must actually exist, would seem to be the outcome of a curiously perverse ontological argument. Whatever is morally useful and significant must actually exist. But why must it? What assurance have we that reality is constituted so as to satisfy the insistent demands of our moral nature? Even if responsibility could be shown to be an indispensable adjunct of genuine morality, this would not suffice to guarantee its factuality. There is only one way of establishing the fact of responsibility, and that is by exhibiting actual instances of morally responsible actions. The concept of moral responsibility no doubt admits of precise empirical definition and exemplification; there is a real distinction between responsible and irresponsible actions. But when responsibility is analysed in this empirical and positivistic fashion, it will be found in no wise to imply volitional freedom. A careful analysis of responsible actions will show them to be if anything no more indeterminate than non-responsible and irresponsible actions. And this brings us to the second criticism of the argument from responsibility: *viz.*, the failure to establish the alleged implication of the concept of freedom by the concept of responsibility. The concepts of freedom and responsibility are by no means indissolubly connected; on the contrary, the freedom of indeterminacy, far from guaranteeing responsibility, would, if it existed, actually be prejudicial to it. If freedom is the complete divorce of the will from antecedent conditions, including my moral character, I cannot then be held accountable for my actions. A will which descends upon me like "a bolt from the blue" is not *my* will and it is manifestly unfair to take me to task for its caprices.

Closely allied with—perhaps in the last analysis indistinguishable from—the moral argument is the *religious* argument for free-will. The free-will dogma is deeply rooted in the Hebraic-Christian theology. The essential connection between freedom and responsibility to God is the real theme of the Book of *Genesis*: Man's freedom is necessary to insure what William James has aptly referred to as man's "forensic responsibility before God."[4] Were man not free, he could not be held accountable for his action, but he *must* be held accountable, therefore, man is free. The Hebraic doctrine of the freedom of the will arises from a paternalistic conception of the relation between God and man. On this view, moral principles are the command-ments of God to which man yields as does the child to parental authority. But, just as a recalcitrant child may defy his father, so man may, at his own peril, rebel against the divine moral code. The principles of morality are authoritative in that they emanate from God, but they are not compulsive since man may or may not choose to conform to them. The paternalism of the Hebraic conception of God is embodied in the myth of creation. God created Adam and endowed him with a will, free to choose between good and evil. Adam yielded to temptation and his original sin has been trans-mitted to all his descendants. The story of the fall of man is a highly sym-bolic expression of the theological doctrine that man is accountable for his actions only on the assumption that they are free. Incidentally, the ascription of a free-will to man, absolves God from any responsibility for the sins of mankind and thus affords an easy solution to one of the most perplexing of theological problems, the problem of evil.

The religious argument may be dismissed quite summarily by re-jecting outright the conception of God as a task-master who maintains dis-cipline over humanity by conferring upon him a freedom which shall insure his responsibility and justify his punishment. If the Hebraic con-ception of an austere and vengeful God be renounced, the religious argu-ment for freedom loses all force; it then reduces to the simple moral argument from responsibility to freedom, the fallacies of which have already been exposed. The determinist by his rejection of this particular concep-tion of divinity is not necessarily committed to atheism. Determinism and theology in certain of its forms are entirely compatible; thus the theological doctrine of predestination, though of course very different in its emphasis from physical and psychological determinism of the naturalistic sort, is by no means inconsistent with the latter. There is then no strictly theological argument proof for freedom and theological considerations can at best serve to reinforce the moral argument for freedom.

(3) *The Argument from Physical Indeterminacy*

Free-willists have recently derived not a little encouragement from the advent of the principle of physical indeterminacy which even if it does not suffice to demonstrate freedom of the will, at least seems to remove a

---

[4]*The Principles of Psychology*, vol. ii, p. 349.

serious obstacle to its acceptance. If there is a real indeterminacy at the subatomic level of quantum mechanics, this affords at least the *possibility* of the physiological and ultimately of the psychological indeterminacy which constitutes the freedom of the will. Recent quantum theory seems on the surface to afford a physical basis for a volitional indeterminacy much as the swerve of the atoms invoked by the ancient Epicureans seemed to justify their free-will doctrine. But the contemporary argument is defective and in very much the same respects as its historic prototype.

Against the modern version of the indeterminacy argument, it may be urged in the first place that the physical theory of indeterminacy merely expresses an observational difficulty encountered in the attempt to determine both the position and the velocity of an electron and that consequently it posits a methodological and not the physical or ontological indeterminacy which is requisite for the purposes of the free-will doctrine. But secondly, even supposing that the indeterminacy principle is physical and not merely methodological, it has not been shown that this subatomic indeterminacy manifests itself in the behaviour of ordinary mass-objects and in particular that it is exemplified in just those neural processes which are supposedly the basis of the act of free-will. The psychophysical correlation of a neural indeterminacy with its psychological counterpart, could be effected only by the introspective observation of the volitional indeterminacy along with the underlying physical indeterminacy, and thus the evidence of introspection is an essential link in the argument from physical indeterminacy. The physical theory of indeterminacy is at the present time far from demonstrating the existence of or giving a complete picture of the *modus operandi* of a free-will and thus the freedom of indeterminacy remains, even on the background of physical indeterminacy, a more speculative possibility.

The Case for Determinism

Whereas the evidence for the free-will doctrine is largely humanistic and moralistic, the case for determinism is an appeal to scientific evidence; the determinist finds that the sciences of *physiology, psychology,* and *sociology* afford evidence that human behaviour is no exception to the causal uniformity of nature.

(1) Physiological Evidence

The more we know about the physiological and neural processes which go on inside the human organism, even when it reacts to the most complicated of stimuli, the more evident it becomes that there is no break in the continuous chain of causation. Physiology gives us a reasonably clear picture of the mechanism of human behaviour. The behaviourists, the most recent recruits to the cause of determinism, have with infinite patience applied the objective method of the physiologists to human conduct; they have described in the minutest detail the mechanism of reflexes and the manner of their conditioning. There seems to remain no missing link in the causal chain from stimulus to ultimate response—even when that response is long "delayed." Delayed responses are mediated by very complex neural processes which on their subjective side are called conflict, indecision, and deliberation, but they are no exception to the behaviouristic formula.

(2) Psychological Evidence

While the deterministic thesis receives its most obvious support from physiology and behaviouristic psychology, introspective psychology makes its contribution also. An unbiased introspective examination of volition supports the theory of psychological determinism. The more carefully I scrutinize my decisions, the more clearly do I discern the motives which determine them. If one's powers of introspection were sufficiently developed, one could presumably after any decision discover the exact psychological influences which rendered that particular decision inevitable. Doubtless for a complete explanation of certain decisions it is necessary in addition to the conscious antecedents of the volitional act to recover the more recondite sub-conscious and unconscious influences; the extensive researches of the Freudians into the submerged factors in human motivation provide the explanation of otherwise inexplicable mental acts and therefore tend to supply the missing links in the chain of psychic causation. Indeed, the existence of consciously inexplicable conscious events was one of the most compelling reasons for the original positing of an unconscious or subconscious mind. It remains true, however, that a fairly complete account of the psychological causation of volitional decisions is possible even without recourse to an unconscious mind.

Perhaps the best classical statement of the case for psychological determinism was given by David Hume. Hume, whose introspective subtlety has rarely been surpassed, commits himself unequivocally to psychological determinism in his assertion that "There is a great uniformity among the actions of men. . . . *The same motives always produce the same actions.*"[5] Every historian, as Hume points out, appeals to this principle in judging the accuracy of historical documents; he asks himself whether the reported actions conform to what is known of human nature. And we might add, the same criterion is appealed to even in the evaluation of works of fiction. The novelist or the playwright gives a portrayal of his characters; he places them in definite situations, and then describes how they act. If his account of their behaviour under these precisely defined circumstances violates any of the recognized laws of human motivation, his literary and dramatic artistry is to that extent defective. Thus the principle of psychological determinism serves as a recognized canon on historical, literary, and dramatic criticism, and while this does not "prove" the correctness of psychological determinism, it does afford confirmation of it from an unsuspected quarter.

[5] *Enquiry Concerning Human Understanding*, section viii.

(3) Sociological Evidence

The social sciences yield abundant evidence for a deterministic view of human behaviour. The fact that the conduct of large aggregates of individuals is expressible in terms of statistical law, although it is by no means a conclusive proof of individual determinism, certainly points in that direction. I may not be able to predict how you as an individual will behave in any specified circumstances, but I can formulate a statistical law applicable to a large group of individuals of which you are a member. It is difficult to reconcile the possibility of the laws of groups or mass action with individual free-will.

The conclusion reached as a result of the survey of the arguments on both sides of the free-will controversy is that the strength of the deterministic position lies not only in the overwhelming array of psychological, physiological, and sociological evidence for the uniformity of human behaviour, but also in its ability to meet the psychological, moral, and religious "proofs" of free-will. Accordingly, we seem fully justified in concluding that a capricious free-will, that is to say, a will capable of acting independently of antecedent conditions, psychological or physiological, is a philosophical absurdity.

❀ JOHN HOSPERS

28. Free-Will and Psychoanalysis

John Hospers (1918–   ) has taught philosophy at Brooklyn College and at California State College at Los Angeles. He is presently the Director of the School of Philosophy at the University of Southern California. Some of his books are: *Meaning and Truth in the Arts* (1946), *Introduction to Philosophical Analysis* (1953), *Human Conduct* (1962), and *Readings in Introductory Philosophical Analysis* (1968).

> O Thou, who didst with pitfall and with gin
> Beset the Road I was to wander in,
>   Thou will not with Predestined Evil round
> Enmesh, and then impute my Fall to Sin!
>   —Edward FitzGerald, *The Rubaiyat of Omar Khayyam.*

. . . It is extremely common for nonprofessional philosophers and iconoclasts to deny that human freedom exists, but at the same time to have no clear idea of what it is that they are denying to exist. The first thing that needs to be said about the free-will issue is that any meaningful term

The essay appearing here is the abridged version in *Readings in Ethical Theory,* Wilfrid Sellars and John Hospers eds. (New York: Appleton-Century-Crofts, 1952). Originally published in *Philosophy and Phenomenological Research,* X (March 1950). Reprinted by permission of the author and *Philosophy and Phenomenological Research.*

must have a meaningful opposite: if it is meaningful to assert that people are not free, it must be equally meaningful to assert that people *are* free, whether this latter assertion is in fact true or not. Whether it is true, of course, will depend on the meaning that is given the weasel-word "free." For example, if freedom is made dependent on indeterminism, it may well be that human freedom is nonexistent. But there seem to be no good grounds for asserting such a dependence, especially since lack of causation is the furthest thing from people's minds when they call an act free. Doubt-less there are other senses that can be given to the word "free"—such as "able to do anything we want to do"—in which no human beings are free. But the first essential point about which the denier of freedom must be clear is *what* it is that he is denying. If one knows what it is like for people not to be free, one must know what it *would* be like for them to *be* free.

Philosophers have advanced numerous senses of "free" in which countless acts performed by human beings can truly be called free acts. The most common conception of a free act is that according to which an act is free if and only if it is a *voluntary* act. But the word "voluntary" does not always carry the same meaning. Sometimes to call an act voluntary means that we can do the act *if* we choose to do it: in other words, that it is physi-cally and psychologically possible for us to do it, so that the occurrence of the act follows upon the decision to do it. (One's decision to raise his arm is in fact followed by the actual raising of his arm, unless he is a paralytic; one's decision to pluck the moon from the sky is not followed by the actual event.) Sometimes a voluntary act is conceived (as by Moore[1] as an act which would not have occurred if, just beforehand, the agent had chosen not to perform it. But these senses are different from the sense in which a voluntary act is an act resulting from *deliberation,* or perhaps merely from *choice.* For example, there are many acts which we could have avoided, if we had chosen to do so, but which we nevertheless did not *choose* to perform, much less *deliberate* about them. The act of raising one's leg in the process of taking a step while out for a walk, is one which a person could have avoided by choosing to, but which, after one has learned to walk, takes place automatically or semi-automatically through habit, and thus is not the result of choice. (One may have chosen to take the walk, but not to take this or that step while walking.) Such acts are free in Moore's sense but are not free in the sense of being deliberate. Moreover, there are classes of acts of the same general character which are not even covered by Moore's sense: sudden outbursts of feeling, in some cases at least, could not have been avoided by an immediately preceding volition, so that if these are to be included under the heading of voluntary acts, the proviso that the act could have been avoided by an immediately preceding volition must be amended to read "could have been avoided by a volition or series of voli-tions by the agent *at some time in the past"*—such as the adoption of a dif-ferent set of habits in the agent's earlier and more formative years.

[1]*Ethics,* pp. 15–16.

(Sometimes we call *persons*, rather than their acts, free. Stebbing, for example, declares that one should never call acts free, but only the doers of the acts.[2] But the two do not seem irreconcilable: can we not speak of a *person* as free *with respect to a certain act* (never just free in general) if that *act* is free—whatever we may then go on to mean by saying that an act is free? Any statement about a free act can then be translated into a statement about the doer of the act.)

Now, no matter in which of the above ways we may come to define "voluntary," there are still acts which are voluntary *but which we would be very unlikely to think of as free*. Thus, when a person submits to the command of an armed bandit, he may do so voluntarily in every one of the above senses: he may do so as a result of choice, even of deliberation, and he could have avoided doing it by willing not to—he could, instead, have refused and been shot. The man who reveals a state secret under torture does the same: he could have refused and endured more torture. Yet such acts, and persons in respect of such acts, are not generally called free. We say that they were performed *under compulsion*, and if an act is performed under compulsion we do not call it free. We say, "He wasn't free because he was forced to do as he did," though of course his act was voluntary.

This much departure from the identification of free acts with voluntary acts almost everyone would admit. Sometimes, however, it would be added that this is all the departure that can be admitted. According to Schlick, for example,

> Freedom means the opposite of compulsion; a man is *free* if he does not act under *compulsion*, and he is compelled or unfree when he is hindered from without in the realization of his natural desires. Hence he is unfree when he is locked up, or chained, or when someone forces him at the point of a gun to do what otherwise he would not do. This is quite clear, and everyone will admit that the everyday or legal notion of the lack of freedom is thus correctly interpreted, and that a man will be considered quite free . . . if no such external compulsion is exerted upon him.[3]

Schlick adds that the entire vexed free-will controversy in philosophy is so much wasted ink and paper, because compulsion has been confused with causality and necessity with uniformity. If the question is asked whether every event is caused, the answer is doubtless yes; but if it is whether every event is compelled, the answer is clearly no. Free acts are uncompelled acts, not uncaused acts. Again, when it is said that some state of affairs (such as water flowing downhill) is necessary, if "necessary" means "compelled," the answer is no; if it means merely that it always happens that way, the answer is yes: universality of application is confused with compulsion. And this, according to Schlick, is the end of the matter.

Schlick's analysis is indeed clarifying and helpful to those who have fallen victim to the confusions he exposes—and this probably includes most

[2]*Philosophy and the Physicists*, p. 212.
[3]*The Problems of Ethics*, Rynin translation, p. 150.

persons in their philosophical growing-pains. But *is* this the end of the matter? Is it true that all acts, though caused, are free as long as they are not compelled in the sense which he specifies? May it not be that, while the identification of "free" with "uncompelled" is acceptable, the area of compelled acts is vastly greater than he or most other philosophers have ever suspected? (Moore is more cautious in this respect than Schlick; while for Moore an act is free if it is voluntary in the sense specified above, he thinks there may be another sense in which human beings, and human acts, are not free at all.[4]) We remember statements about human beings being pawns of their early environment, victims of conditions beyond their control, the result of causal influences stemming from their parents, and the like, and we ponder and ask, "Still, are we really free?" Is there not something in what generations of sages have said about man being fettered? Is there not perhaps something too facile, too sleight-of-hand, in Schlick's cutting of the Gordian knot? For example, when a metropolitan newspaper headlines an article with the words "Boy Killer Is Doomed Long before He Is Born,"[5] and then goes on to describe how a twelve-year-old boy has been sentenced to prison for the murder of a girl, and how his parental background includes records of drunkenness, divorce, social maladjustment, and paresis, are we still to say that his act, though voluntary and assuredly *not* done at the point of a gun, is free? The boy has early displayed a tendency toward sadistic activity to hide an underlying masochism and "prove that he's a man"; being coddled by his mother only worsens this tendency, until, spurned by a girl is his attempt on her, he kills her—not simply in a fit of anger, but calculatingly, deliberately. Is he free in respect of his criminal act, or for that matter in most of the acts of his life? Surely to ask this question is to answer it in the negative. Perhaps I have taken an extreme case; but it is only to show the superficiality of the Schlick analysis the more clearly. Though not everyone has criminotic tendencies, everyone has been moulded by influences which in large measure at least determine his present behavior; he is literally the product of these influences, stemming from periods prior to his "years of discretion," giving him a host of character traits that he cannot change now even if he would. So obviously does what a man is depend upon how a man comes to be, that it is small wonder that philosophers and sages have considered man far indeed from being the master of his fate. It is not at if man's will were standing high and serene above the flux of events that have molded him; it is itself caught up in this flux, itself carried along on the current. An act is free when it is determined by the man's character, say moralists; but what if the most decisive aspects of his character were already irrevocably acquired before he could do anything to mold them? What if even the degree of will power available to him in shaping his habits and disciplining himself now to overcome the influence of his early environment is a factor over which he has no control? What are we to say

4*Ethics*, Chapter 6, pp. 217 ff.
5*New York Post*, Tuesday, May 18, 1948, p. 4.

of this kind of "freedom?" Is it not rather like the freedom of the machine to stamp labels on cans when it has been devised for just that purpose? Some machines can do so more efficiently than others, but only because they have been better constructed.

It is not my purpose here to establish this thesis in general, but only in one specific respect which has received comparatively little attention, namely, the field referred to by psychiatrists as that of unconscious motivation. In what follows I shall restrict my attention to it because it illustrates as clearly as anything the points I wish to make.

Let me try to summarize very briefly the psychoanalytic doctrine on this point.[6] The conscious life of the human being, including the conscious decisions and volitions, is merely a mouthpiece for the unconscious—not directly for the enactment of unconscious drives, but of the compromise between unconscious drives and unconscious reproaches. There is a Big Three behind the scenes which the automaton called the conscious personality carries out: the id, an "eternal gimme," presents its wish and demands its immediate satisfaction; the super-ego says no to the wish immediately upon presentation, and the unconscious ego, the mediator between the two, tries to keep peace by means of compromise.[7]

To go into examples of the functioning of these three "bosses" would be endless; psychoanalytic case books supply hundreds of them. The important point for us to see in the present context is that *it is the unconscious that determines what the conscious impulse and the conscious action shall be.* Hamlet, for example, had a strong Oedipus wish, which was violently counteracted by super-ego reproaches; these early wishes were vividly revived in an unusual adult situation in which his uncle usurped the coveted position from Hamlet's father and won his mother besides. This situation evoked strong strictures on the part of Hamlet's super-ego, and it was this that was responsible for his notorious delay in killing his uncle. A dozen times Hamlet could have killed Claudius easily; but every time Hamlet "decided" not to: a free choice, moralists would say—but no, listen to the super-ego: "What you feel such hatred toward your uncle for, what you are plotting to kill him for, is precisely the crime which you yourself desire to commit: to kill your father and replace him in the affections of your mother. Your fate and your uncle's are bound up together." This paralyzes Hamlet into inaction. Consciously all he knows is that he is unable to act;

---

[6] I am aware that the theory presented below is not accepted by all practicing psychoanalysts. Many non-Freudians would disagree with the conclusions presented below. But I do not believe that this fact affects my argument, as long as the concept of unconscious motivation is accepted. I am aware, too, that much of the language employed in the following descriptions is animistic and metaphorical; but as long as I am presenting a view I would prefer to "go the whole hog" and present it in its most dramatic form. The theory can in any case be made clearest by the use of such language, just as atomic theory can often be made clearest to students with the use of models.

[7] This view is very clearly developed in Edmund Bergler, *Divorce Won't Help,* especially Chapter I.

this conscious inability he rationalizes, giving a different excuse each time.[8]

We have always been conscious of the fact that we are not masters of our fate in every respect—that there are many things which we cannot do, that nature is more powerful than we are, that we cannot disobey laws without danger of reprisals, etc. We have become "officially" conscious, too, though in our private lives we must long have been aware of it, that we are not free with respect to the emotions that we feel—whom we love or hate, what types we admire, and the like. More lately still we have been reminded that there are unconscious motivations for our basic attractions and repulsions, our compulsive actions or inabilities to act. But what is not welcome news is that our very acts of volition, and the entire train of deliberations leading up to them, are but façades for the expression of unconscious wishes, or rather, unconscious compromises and defenses.

A man is faced by a choice: shall he kill another person or not? Moralists would say, here is a free choice—the result of deliberation, an action consciously entered into. And yet, though the agent himself does not know it, and has no awareness of the forces that are at work within him, his choice is already determined for him: his conscious will is only an instrument, a slave, in the hands of a deep unconscious motivation which determines his action. If he has a great deal of what the analyst calls "free-floating guilt," he will not; but if the guilt is such as to demand immediate absorption in the form of self-damaging behavior, this accumulated guilt will have to be discharged in some criminal action. The man himself does not know what the inner clockwork is; he is like the hands on the clock, thinking they move freely over the face of the clock.

A woman has married and divorced several husbands. Now she is faced with a choice for the next marriage: shall she marry Mr. A, or Mr. B, or nobody at all? She may take considerable time to "decide" this question, and her decision may appear as a final triumph of her free will. Let us assume that A is a normal, well-adjusted, kind, and generous man, while B is a leech, an impostor, one who will become entangled constantly in quarrels with her. If she belongs to a certain classifiable psychological type, she will inevitably choose B, and she will do so even if her previous husbands have resembled B, so that one would think that she "had learned from experience." Consciously, she will of course "give the matter due consideration," etc., etc. To the psychoanalyst all this is irrelevant chaff in the wind—only a camouflage for the inner workings about which she knows nothing consciously. If she is of a certain kind of masochistic strain, as exhibited in her previous set of symptoms, she *must* choose B: her super-ego, always out to maximize the torment in the situation, seeing what dazzling possibilities for self-damaging behavior are promised by the choice of B, compels her

---

[8]See *The Basic Writings of Sigmund Freud* (Modern Library), p. 310 (in *The Interpretation of Dreams*). Cf. also the essay by Ernest Jones, "A Psycho-analytical Study of Hamlet."

to make the choice she does, and even to conceal the real basis of the choice behind an elaborate facade of rationalizations.

A man is addicted to gambling. In the service of his addiction he loses all his money, spends what belongs to his wife, even sells his property and neglects his children. For a time perhaps he stops; then, inevitably, he takes it up again. The man does not know that he is a victim rather than an agent; or, if he sometimes senses that he is in the throes of something-he-knows-not-what, he will have no inkling of its character and will soon relapse into the illusion that he (his conscious self) is freely deciding the course of his own actions. What he does not know, of course, is that he is still taking out on his mother the original lesion to his infantile narcissism, getting back at her for her fancied refusal of his infantile wishes—and this be rejecting everything identified with her, namely education, discipline, logic, common sense, training. At the roulette wheel, almost alone among adult activities, chance—the opposite of all these things—rules supreme; and his addiction represents his continued and emphatic reiteration of his rejection of Mother and all she represents to his unconscious.

This pseudo-aggression of his is of course masochistic in its effects. In the long run he always loses; he can never quit while he is winning. And far from playing in order to win, rather one can say that his losing is a *sine qua non* of his psychic equilibrium (as it was for example with Dostoyevsky): guilt demands punishment, and in the ego's "deal" with the super-ego the super-ego has granted satisfaction of infantile wishes in return for the self-damaging conditions obtaining. Winning would upset the neurotic equilibrium.[9]

A man has wash-compulsion. He must be constantly washing his hands—he uses up perhaps 400 towels a day. Asked why he does this, he says, "I need to, my hands are dirty"; and if it is pointed out to him that they are not really dirty, he says "They feel dirty anyway, I feel better when I wash them." So once again he washes them. He "freely decides" every time; he feels that he must wash them, he deliberates for a moment perhaps, but always ends by washing them. What he does not see, of course, are the invisible wires inside him pulling him inevitably to do the thing he does: the infantile id-wish concerns preoccupation with dirt, the super-ego charges him with this, and the terrified ego must respond, "No, I don't like dirt, see how clean I like to be, look how I wash my hands!"

Let us see what further "free acts" the same patient engages in (this is an actual case history): he is taken to a concentration camp, and given the worst of treatment by the Nazi guards. In the camp he no longer chooses to be clean, does not even try to be—on the contrary, his choice is now to wallow in filth as much as he can. All he is aware of now is a dis-

[9]See Edmund Bergler's article on the pathological gambler in *Diseases of the Nervous System* (1943). Also "Suppositions about the Mechanism of Criminosis," *Journal of Criminal Psychopathology* (1944) and "Clinical Contributions to the Psychogenesis of Alcohol Addiction," *Quarterly Journal of Studies on Alcohol*, 5:434 (194).

inclination to be clean, and every time he must choose he chooses not to be. Behind the scenes, however, another drama is being enacted: the super-ego, perceiving that enough torment is being administered from the outside, can afford to cease pressing its charges in this quarter—the outside world is doing the torturing now, so the super-ego is relieved of the responsibility. Thus the ego is relieved of the agony of constantly making terrified replies in the form of washing to prove that the super-ego is wrong. The defense no longer being needed, the person slides back into what is his natural predilection anyway, for filth. This becomes too much even for the Nazi guards: they take hold of him one day, saying "We'll teach you how to be clean!" drag him into the snow, and pour bucket after bucket of icy water over him until he freezes to death. Such is the end-result of an original id-wish, caught in the machinations of a destroying super-ego.

Let us take, finally, a less colorful, more everyday example. A student at a university, possessing wealth, charm, and all that is usually considered essential to popularity, begins to develop the following personality-pattern: although well taught in the graces of social conversation, he always makes a *faux pas* somewhere, and always in the worst possible situation; to his friends he makes cutting remarks which hurt deeply—and always apparently aimed in such a way as to hurt the most: a remark that would not hurt A but would hurt B he invariably makes to B rather than to A, and so on. None of this is conscious. Ordinarily he is considerate of people, but he contrives always (unconsciously) to impose on just those friends who would resent it most, and at just the times when he should know that he should not impose: at 3 o'clock in the morning, without forewarning, he phones a friend in a near-by city demanding to stay at his apartment for the weekend; naturally the friend is offended, but the person himself is not aware that he has provoked the grievance ("common sense" suffers a temporary eclipse when the neurotic pattern sets in, and one's intelligence, far from being of help in such a situation, is used in the interest of the neurosis), and when the friend is cool to him the next time they meet, he wonders why and feels unjustly treated. Aggressive behavior on his part invites resentment and aggression in turn, but all that he consciously sees is others' behavior towards him—and he considers himself the innocent victim of an unjustified "persecution."

Each of these acts is, from the moralist's point of view, free: he chose to phone his friend at 3 a.m.; he chose to make the cutting remark that he did, etc. What he does not know is that an ineradicable masochistic pattern has set in. His unconscious is far more shrewd and clever than is his conscious intellect; it sees with uncanny accuracy just what kind of behavior will damage him most, and unerringly forces him into that behavior. Consciously, the student "doesn't know why he did it"—he gives different "reasons" at different times, but they are all, once again, rationalizations cloaking the unconscious mechanism which propels him willy-nilly into actions that his "common sense" eschews.

The more of this sort of thing one observes, the more he can see what the psychoanalyst means when he talks about *the illusion of freedom*. And the more of a psychiatrist one becomes, the more he is overcome with a sense of what an illusion this free-will can be. In some kinds of cases most of us can see it already: it takes no psychiatrist to look at the epileptic and sigh with sadness at the thought that soon this person before you will be as one possessed, not the same thoughtful intelligent person you knew. But people are not aware of this in other contexts, for example when they express surprise at how a person whom they have been so good to could treat them so badly. Let us suppose that you help a person financially or morally or in some other way, so that he is in your debt; suppose further that he is one of the many neurotics who unconsciously identify kindness with weakness and aggression with strength, then he will unconsciously take your kindness to him as weakness and use it as the occasion for enacting some aggression against you. He can't help it, he may regret it himself later; still, he will be driven to do it. If we gain a little knowledge of psychiatry, we can look at him with pity, that a person otherwise so worthy should be so unreliable— but we will exercise realism too, and be aware that there are some types of people that you cannot be good to in "free" acts of their conscious volition, they will use your own goodness against you.

Sometimes the persons themselves will become dimly aware that "something behind the scenes" is determining their behavior. The divorcee will sometimes view herself with detachment, as if she were some machine (and indeed the psychoanalyst does call her a "repeating-machine"): "I know I'm caught in a net, that I'll fall in love with this guy and marry him and the whole ridiculous merry-go-round will start all over again."

We talk about free will, and we say, for example, the person is free to do so-and-so if he can do so *if* he wants to—and we forget that his wanting to is itself caught up in the stream of determinism, that unconscious forces drive him into the wanting or not wanting to do the thing in question. The analogy of the puppet whose motions are manipulated from behind by invisible wires, or better still, by springs inside, is a telling one at almost every point.

And the glaring fact is that it all started so early, before we knew what was happening. The personality-structure is inelastic after the age of five, and comparatively so in most cases after the age of three. Whether one acquires a neurosis or not is determined by that age—and just as involuntarily as if it had been a curse of God. If, for example, a masochistic pattern was set up, under pressure of hyper-narcissism combined with real or fancied infantile deprivation, then the masochistic snowball was on its course downhill long before we or anybody else know what was happening, and long before anyone could do anything about it. To speak of human beings as "puppets" in such a context is no idle metaphor, but a stark rendering of a literal fact: only the psychiatrist knows what puppets people really are; and it is no wonder that the protestations of philosophers that "the act which is the result of a volition, a deliberation, a conscious decision, is free" leave these persons, to speak mildly, somewhat cold.

But, one may object, all the states thus far described have been abnormal, neurotic ones. The well-adjusted (normal) person at least is free.

Leaving aside the question of how clearly and on what grounds one can distinguish the neurotic from the normal, let me use an illustration of a proclivity that everyone would call normal, namely, the decision of a man to support his wife and possibly a family, and consider briefly its genesis, according to psychoanalytic accounts.[10]

Every baby comes into the world with a full-fledged case of megalomania—interested only in himself, acting as is believing that he is the center of the universe and that others are present only to fulfill his wishes, and furious when his own wants are not satisfied immediately no matter for what reason. Gratitude, even for all the time and worry and care expended on him by the mother, is an emotion entirely foreign to the infant, and as he grows older it is inculcated in him only with the greatest difficulty; his natural tendency is to assume that everything that happens to him is due to himself, except for denials and frustrations, which are due to the "cruel, denying" outer world, in particular the mother; and that he owes nothing to anyone, is dependent on no one. This omnipotence-complex, or illusion of non-dependence, has been called the "autarchic fiction." Such a conception of the world is actually fostered in the child by the conduct of adults, who automatically attempt to fulfill the infant's every wish concerning nourishment, sleep, and attention. The child misconceives causality and sees in these wish-fulfillments not the results of maternal kindness and love, but simply the result of his own omnipotence.

This fiction of omnipotence is gradually destroyed by experience, and its destruction is probably the deepest disappointment of the early years of life. First of all, the infant discovers that he is the victim of organic urges and necessities: hunger, defecation, urination. More important, he discovers that the maternal breast, which he has not previously distinguished from his own body (he has not needed to, since it was available when he wanted it), is not a part of himself after all, but of another creature upon whom he is dependent. He is forced to recognize this, e.g., when he wants nourishment and it is at the moment not present; even a small delay is most damaging to the "autarchic fiction." Most painful of all is the experience of weaning, probably the greatest tragedy in every baby's life, when his dependence is most cruelly emphasized; it is a frustrating experience because what he wants is no longer there at all; and if he has been able to some extent to preserve the illusion of non-dependence heretofore, he is not able to do so now—it is plain that the source of his nourishment is not dependent on him, but he on it. The shattering of the autarchic fiction is a great disillusionment to every child, a tremendous blow to his ego which he will, in one way or another, spend the rest of his life trying to repair. How does he do this?

First of all, his reaction to frustration is anger and fury; and he responds by kicking, biting, etc., the only ways he knows. But he is motorically helpless, and these measures are ineffective, and only serve to emphasize his dependence the more. Moreover, against such responses of the child the parental reaction is one of prohibition, often involving deprivation of attention and affection. Generally the child soon learns that this form of rebellion is profitless, and brings him more harm than good. He wants to respond to frustration with violent aggression, and at the same time learns that he will be punished for such aggression, and that in any case the latter is ineffectual. What face-saving solution does he find? Since he must "face facts," since he must in any case "conform" if he is to have any peace at all, he tries to make it seem as if he himself is the source of the commands and prohibitions: the *external* prohibitive force is *internalized*—and here we have the origin of conscience. By making the prohibitive agency seem to come from within himself, the child can "save face"—as if saying, "The prohibition comes from within me, not from outside, so I'm not subservient to external rule, I'm only obeying rules I've set up myself," thus to some extent saving the autarchic fiction, and at the same time avoiding unpleasant consequences directed against himself by complying with parental commands.

Moreover, the boy[11] has unconsciously never forgiven the mother for his dependence on her in early life, for nourishment and all other things. It has upset his illusion of non-dependence. These feelings have been repressed and are not remembered; but they are acted out in later life in many ways —e.g., in the constant deprecation man has for woman's duties such as cooking and housework of all sorts ("All she does is stay home and get together a few meals, and she calls that work"), and especially in the man's identification with the mother in his sex experiences with women. By identifying with someone one cancels out in effect the person with whom he identifies—replacing that person, unconsciously denying his existence, and the man, identifying with his early mother, playing the active rôle in "giving" to his wife as his mother has "given" to him, is in effect the denial of his mother's existence, a fact which is narcissistically embarrassing to his ego because it is chiefly responsible for shattering his autarchic fiction. In supporting his wife, he can unconsciously deny that his mother gave to him, and that he was dependent on her giving. Why is it that the husband plays the provider, and wants his wife to be dependent on no one else, although twenty years before he was nothing but a parasitic baby? This is a face-saving device on his part: he can act out the reasoning "See, I'm not the parasitic baby, on the contrary I'm the provider, the giver." His playing the provider is a constant face-saving device, to deny his early dependence which is so embarrassing to his ego. It is no wonder that men generally dislike to be reminded of their babyhood, when they were dependent on woman.

[11]The girl's development after this point is somewhat different. Society demands more aggressiveness of the adult male, hence there are more super-ego strictures on tendencies toward passivity in the male; accordingly his defenses must be stronger.

Thus we have here a perfectly normal adult reaction which is unconsciously motivated. The man "chooses" to support a family—and his choice is as unconsciously motivated as anything could be. (I have described here only the "normal" state of affairs, uncomplicated by the well-nigh infinite number of variations that occur in actual practice.)

Now, what of the notion of responsibility? What happens to it on our analysis?

Let us begin with an example, not a fictitious one. A woman and her two-year-old baby are riding on a train to Montreal in mid-winter. The child is ill. The woman wants badly to get to her destination. She is, unknown to herself, the victim of a neurotic conflict whose nature is irrelevant here except for the fact that it forces her to behave aggressively toward the child, partly to spite her husband whom she despises and who loves the child, but chiefly to ward off super-ego charges of masochistic attachment. Consciously she loves the child, and when she says this she says it sincerely, but she must behave aggressively toward it nevertheless, just as many children love their mothers but are nasty to them most of the time in neurotic pseudo-aggression. The child becomes more ill as the train approaches Montreal; the heating system of the train is not working, and the conductor pleads with the woman to get off the train at the next town and get the child to a hospital at once. The woman refuses. Soon after, the child's condition worsens, and the mother does all she can to keep it alive, without, however, leaving the train, for she declares that it is absolutely necessary that she reach her destination. But before she gets there the child is dead. After that, of course, the mother grieves, blames herself, weeps hysterically, and joins the church to gain surcease from the guilt that constantly overwhelms her when she thinks of how her aggressive behavior has killed her child.

Was she responsible for her deed? In ordinary life, after making a mistake, we say, "Chalk it up to experience." Here we should say, "Chalk it up to the neurosis." *She* could not help it if her neurosis forced her to act this way—she didn't even know what was going on behind the scenes, her conscious self merely acted out its assigned part. This is far more true than is generally realized: criminal actions in general are not actions for which their agents are responsible; the agents are passive, not active—they are victims of a neurotic conflict. Their very hyper-activity is unconsciously determined.

To say this is, of course, not to say that we should not punish criminals. Clearly, for our own protection, we must remove them from our midst so that they can no longer molest and endanger organized society. And, of course, if we use the word "responsible" in such a way that justly to hold someone responsible for a deed is by definition identical with being justified in punishing him, then we can and do hold people responsible. But this is like the sense of "free" in which free acts are voluntary ones. It does not go deep enough. In a deeper sense we cannot hold the person responsible:

we can hold his neurosis responsible, but *he is not responsible for his neurosis,* particularly since the age at which its onset was inevitable was an age before he could even speak.

The neurosis is responsible—but isn't the neurosis a part of *him?* We have been speaking all the time as if the person and his unconscious were two separate beings; but isn't he one personality, including conscious and unconscious departments together?

I do not wish to deny this. But it hardly helps us here; for what people want when they talk about freedom, and what they hold to when they champion it, is the idea that the *conscious* will is the master of their destiny. "I am the master of my fate, I am the captain of my soul"—and they surely mean their conscious selves, the self that they can recognize and search and introspect. Between an unconscious that willy-nilly determines your actions, and an external force which pushes you, there is little if anything to choose. The unconscious is just *as if* it were an outside force; and indeed, psychiatrists will assert that the inner Hitler (your super-ego) can torment you far more than any external Hitler can. Thus the kind of freedom that people want, the only kind they will settle for, is precisely the kind that psychiatry says that they cannot have.

Heretofore it was pretty generally thought that, while we could not rightly blame a person for the color of his eyes or the morality of his parents, or even for what he did at the age of three, or to a large extent what impulses he had and whom he fell in love with, one *could* do so for other of his adult activities, particularly the acts he performed voluntarily and with premeditation. Later this attitude was shaken. Many voluntary acts came to be recognized, at least in some circles, as compelled by the unconscious. Some philosophers recognized this too—Ayer[12] talks about the kleptomaniac being unfree, and about a person being unfree when another person exerts a habitual ascendancy over his personality. But this is as far as he goes. The usual examples, such as the kleptomaniac and the schizophrenic, apparently satisfy most philosophers, and with these exceptions removed, the rest of mankind is permitted to wander in the vast and alluring fields of freedom and responsibility. So far, the inroads upon freedom left the vast majority of humanity untouched; they began to hit home when psychiatrists began to realize, though philosophers did not, that the domination of the conscious by the unconscious extended, not merely to a few exceptional individuals, but to all human beings, that the "big three behind the scenes" are not respecters of persons, and dominate us all, even including that *sanctum sanctorum* of freedom, our conscious will. To be sure, the domination by the unconscious in the case of "normal" individuals is somewhat more benevolent than the tyranny and despotism exercised in neurotic cases, and therefore the former have evoked less comment; but the principle

---

12A. J. Ayer, "Freedom and Necessity," *Polemic* (September–October 1946), pp. 40–43.

remains in all cases the same: the unconscious is the master of every fate and the captain of every soul.

We speak of a machine turning out good products most of the time but every once in a while it turns out a "lemon." We do not, of course, hold the product responsible for this, but the machine, and via the machine, its maker. Is it silly to extend to inanimate objects the idea of responsibility? Of course. But is it any less so to employ the notion in speaking of human creatures? Are not the two kinds of cases analogous in countless important ways? Occasionally a child turns out badly too, even when his environment and training are the same as that of his brothers and sisters who turn out "all right." He is the "bad penny." His acts of rebellion against parental discipline in adult life (such as the case of the gambler, already cited) are traceable to early experiences of real or fancied denial of infantile wishes. Sometimes the denial has been real, though many denials are absolutely necessary if the child is to grow up to observe the common decencies of civilized life; sometimes, if the child has an unusual quantity of narcissism, every event that occurs is interpreted by him as a denial of his wishes, and nothing a parent could do, even granting every humanly possible wish, would help. In any event, the later neurosis can be attributed to this. Can the person himself be held responsible? Hardly. If he engages in activities which are a menace to society, he must be put into prison, of course, but responsibility is another matter. The time when the events occurred which rendered his neurotic behavior inevitable was a time long before he was capable of thought and decision. As an adult, he is a victim of a world he never made—only this world is inside him.

What about the children who turn out "all right?" All we can say is that "it's just lucky for them" that what happened to their unfortunate brother didn't happen to them; *through no virtue of their own* they are not doomed to the life of unconscious guilt, expiation, conscious depression, terrified ego-gestures for the appeasement of a tyrannical super-ego, that he is. The machine turned them out with a minimum of damage. But if the brother cannot be blamed for his evils, neither can they be praised for their good; unless, of course, we should blame people for what is not their fault, and praise them for lucky accidents.

We all agree that machines turn out "lemons," we all agree that nature turns out misfits in the realm of biology—the blind, the crippled, the diseased; but we hesitate to include the realm of the personality, for here, it seems, is the last retreat of our dignity as human beings. Our ego can endure anything but this; this island at least must remain above the encroaching flood. But may not precisely the same analysis be made here also? Nature turns out psychological "lemons" too, in far greater quantities than any other kind; and indeed all of us are "lemons" in some respect or other, the difference being one of degree. Some of us are lucky enough not to have a gambling-neurosis or criminotic tendencies or masochistic mother-attachment or overdimensional repetition-compulsion to make our lives miserable, but most of our actions, those usually considered the most important, are unconsciously dominated just the same. And, if a neurosis may be likened to a curse of God, let those of us, the elect, who are enabled to enjoy a measure of life's happiness without the hell-fire of neurotic guilt, take this, not as our own achievement, but simply for what it is—a gift of God.

Let us, however, quit metaphysics and put the situation schematically in the form of a deductive argument.

1. An occurrence over which we had no control is something we cannot be held responsible for.

2. Events E, occurring during our babyhood, were events over which we had no control.

3. Therefore events E were events which we cannot be held responsible for.

4. But if there is something we cannot be held responsible for, neither can we be held responsible for something that inevitably results from it.

5. Events E have as inevitable consequence Neurosis N, which in turn has as inevitable consequence Behavior B.

6. Since N is the inevitable consequence of E and B is the inevitable consequence of N, B is the inevitable consequence of E.

7. Hence, not being responsible for E, we cannot be responsible for B.

In Samuel Butler's Utopian satire *Erewhon* there occurs the following passage, in which a judge is passing sentence on a prisoner:

> It is all very well for you to say that you came of unhealthy parents, and had a severe accident in your childhood which permanently undermined your constitution; excuses such as these are the ordinary refuge of the criminal; but they cannot for one moment be listened to by the ear of justice. I am not here to enter upon curious metaphysical questions as to the origin of this or that—questions to which there would be no end were their introduction once tolerated, and which would result in throwing the only guilt on the tissues of the primordial cell, or on the elementary gases. There is no question of how you came to be wicked, but only this—namely, are you wicked or not? This has been decided in the affirmative, neither can I hesitate for a single moment to say that it has been decided justly. You are a bad and dangerous person, and stand branded in the eyes of your fellow countrymen with one of the most heinous known offenses.[13]

As moralists read this passage, they may perhaps nod with approval. But the joke is on them. The sting comes when we realize what the crime is for which the prisoner is being sentenced: namely, consumption. The defendant is reminded that during the previous year he was sentenced for aggravated bronchitis, and is warned that he should profit from experience in the future. Butler is employing here his familiar method of presenting some human tendency (in this case, holding people responsible for what isn't their fault) to a ridiculous extreme and thereby reducing it to absurdity.

Assuming the main conclusions of this paper to be true, is there any room left for freedom?

This, of course, all depends on what we mean by "freedom." In the senses suggested at the beginning of this paper, there are countless free acts, and unfree ones as well. When "free" means "uncompelled," and only external compulsion is admitted, again there are countless free acts. But now we have extended the notion of compulsion to include determination by unconscious forces. With this sense in mind, our question is, "With the concept of compulsion thus extended, and in the light of present psychoanalytic knowledge, is there any freedom left in human behavior?"

If practicing psychoanalysts were asked this question, there is little doubt that their answer would be along the following lines: they would say that they were not accustomed to using the term "free" at all, but that if they had to suggest a criterion for distinguishing the free from the unfree, they would say that a person's freedom is present *in inverse proportion to his neuroticism;* in other words, the more his acts are determined by a *malevolent* unconscious, the less free he is. Thus they would speak of *degrees* of freedom. They would say that as a person is cured of his neurosis he becomes more free—free to realize capabilities that were blocked by the neurotic affliction. The psychologically well-adjusted individual is in this sense comparatively the most free. Indeed, those who are cured of mental disorders are sometimes said to have *regained their freedom:* they are freed from the tyranny of a malevolent unconscious which formerly exerted as much of a domination over them as if they had been the abject slaves of a cruel dictator.

But suppose one says that a person is free only to the extent that his acts are *not unconsciously determined at all,* be they unconscious benevolent *or* malevolent? If this is the criterion, psychoanalysts would say, most human behavior cannot be called free at all: our impulses and volitions having to do with our basic attitudes toward life, whether we are optimists or pessimists, tough-minded or tender-minded, whether our tempers are quick or slow, whether we are "naturally self-seeking" or "naturally benevolent" (and *all the acts consequent upon these things*), what things annoy us, whether we take to blondes or brunettes, old or young, whether we become philosophers or artists or businessmen—all this has its basis in the unconscious. If people generally call most acts free, it is not because they believe that compelled acts should be called free, it is rather through not knowing how large a proportion of our acts actually are compelled. Only the comparatively "vanilla-flavored" aspects of our lives—such as our behavior toward people who don't really matter to us—are exempted from this rule.

These, I think, are the two principal criteria for distinguishing freedom from the lack of it which we might set up on the basis of psychoanalytic knowledge. Conceivably we might set up others. In every case, of course, it remains trivially true that "it all depends on how we choose to use the word." The facts are what they are, regardless of what words we choose for labeling them. But if we choose to label them in a way which is not in accord with what human beings, however vaguely, have long had in mind in applying these labels, as we would be doing if we labeled as "free" many acts which we know as much about as we now do through modern psychoanalytic methods, then we shall only be manipulating words to mislead our fellow creatures.

❀ SIMONE DE BEAUVOIR

29. *An Existentialist View of Freedom*

Simone de Beauvoir (1908–   ) is an important French novelist, dramatist, and philosopher. Through both her literary and philosophical writings she has distinguished herself as a leading proponent of French existentialism. Her main philosophical work, *The Ethics of Ambiguity*, published in 1948, is an exposition of a moral philosophy which complements that of Jean-Paul Sartre. In 1954 she won the Prix Goncourt for *The Mandarins*.

. . . As for us, whatever the case may be, we believe in freedom. Is it true that this belief must lead us to despair? Must we grant this curious paradox: that from the moment a man recognizes himself as free, he is prohibited from wishing for anything?

On the contrary, it appears to us that by turning toward this freedom we are going to discover a principle of action whose range will be universal. The characteristic feature of all ethics is to consider human life as a game that can be won or lost and to teach man the means of winning. Now, we have seen that the original scheme of man is ambiguous: he wants to be, and to the extent that he coincides with this wish, he fails. All the plans in which this will to be is actualized are condemned; and the ends circumscribed by these plans remain mirages. Human transcendence is vainly engulfed in those miscarried attempts. But man also wills himself to be a disclosure of being, and if he coincides with this wish, he wins, for the fact is that the world becomes present by his presence in it. But the disclosure implies a perpetual tension to keep being at a certain distance, to tear oneself from the world, and to assert oneself as a freedom. To wish for the disclosure of the world and to assert oneself as freedom are one and the same movement. Freedom is the source from which all significations and all values spring. It is the original condition of all justification of existence. The man who seeks to justify his life must want freedom itself absolutely

Reprinted from *The Ethics of Ambiguity*, trans. Bernard Fretchman, Philosophical Library, Inc., New York, 1948. By permission of the Philosophical Library.

and above everything else. At the same time that it requires the realization of concrete ends, of particular projects, it requires itself universally. It is not a ready-made value which offers itself from the outside to my abstract adherence, but it appears (not on the plane of facility, but on the moral plane) as a cause of itself. It is necessarily summoned up by the values which it sets up and through which it sets itself up. It can not establish a denial of itself, for in denying itself, it would deny the possibility of any foundation. To will oneself moral and to will oneself free are one and the same decision. . . .

Now, Sartre declares that every man is free, that there is no way of his not being free. When he wants to escape his destiny, he is still freely fleeing it. Does not this presence of a so to speak natural freedom contradict the notion of ethical freedom? What meaning can there be in the words *to will oneself* free, since at the beginning we *are* free? It is contradictory to set freedom up as something conquered if at first it is something given.

This objection would mean something only if freedom were a thing or a quality naturally attached to a thing. Then, in effect, one would either have it or not have it. But the fact is that it merges with the very movement of this ambiguous reality which is called existence and which *is* only by making itself be; to such an extent that it is precisely only by having to be conquered that it gives itself. To will oneself free is to effect the transition from nature to morality by establishing a genuine freedom on the original upsurge of our existence.

Every man is originally free, in the sense that he spontaneously casts himself into the world. But if we consider this spontaneity in its facticity, it appears to us only as a pure contingency, an upsurging as stupid as the clinamen of the Epicurean atom which turned up at any moment whatsoever from any direction whatsoever. And it was quite necessary for the atom to arrive somewhere. But its movement was not justified by this result which had not been chosen. It remained absurd. Thus, human spontaneity always projects itself toward something. The psychoanalyst discovers a meaning even in abortive acts and attacks of hysteria. But in order for this meaning to justify the transcendence which discloses it, it must itself be founded, which it will never be if I do not choose to found it myself. Now, I can evade this choice. We have said that it would be contradictory deliberately to will oneself not free. But one can choose not to will himself free. In laziness, heedlessness, capriciousness, cowardice, impatience, one contests the meaning of the project at the very moment that one defines it. The spontaneity of the subject is then merely a vain living palpitation, its movement toward the object is a flight, and itself is an absence. To convert the absence into presence, to convert my flight into will, I must assume my project positively. It is not a matter of retiring into the completely inner and, moreover, abstract movement of a given spontaneity, but of adhering to the concrete and particular movement by which this spontaneity defines itself by thrusting itself toward an end. It is through this end that it sets up that my spontaneity confirms itself by reflecting upon itself. Then, by a single movement, my will, establishing the content of the act, is legitimized by it. I realize my escape toward the other as a freedom when, assuming the presence of the object, I thereby assume myself before it as a presence. But this justification requires a constant tension. My project is never founded; it founds itself. To avoid the anguish of this permanent choice, one may attempt to flee into the object itself, to engulf one's own presence in it. In the servitude of the serious, the original spontaneity strives to deny itself. It strives in vain, and meanwhile it then fails to fulfill itself as moral freedom.

We have just described only the subjective and formal aspect of this freedom. But we also ought to ask ourselves whether one can will oneself free in any matter, whatsoever it may be. It must first be observed that this will is developed in the course of time. It is in time that the goal is pursued and that freedom confirms itself. And this assumes that it is realized as a unity in the unfolding of time. One escapes the absurdity of the clinamen only by escaping the absurdity of the pure moment. An existence would be unable to found itself if moment by moment it crumbled into nothingness. That is why no moral question presents itself to the child as long as he is still incapable of recognizing himself in the past or seeing himself in the future. It is only when the moments of his life begin to be organized into behaviour that he can decide and choose. The value of the chosen end is confirmed and, reciprocally, the genuineness of the choice is manifested concretely through patience, courage, and fidelity. If I leave behind an act which I have accomplished, it becomes a thing by falling into the past. It is no longer anything but a stupid and opaque fact. In order to prevent this metamorphosis, I must ceaselessly return to it and justify it in the unity of the project in which I am engaged. Setting up the movement of my transcendence requires that I never let it uselessly fall back upon itself, that I prolong it indefinitely. Thus I can not genuinely desire an end today without desiring it through my whole existence, insofar as it is the future of this present moment and insofar as it is the surpassed past of days to come. To will is to engage myself to persevere in my will. This does not mean that I ought not aim at any limited end. I may desire absolutely and forever a revelation of a moment. This means that the value of this provisional end will be confirmed indefinitely. But this living confirmation can not be merely contemplative and verbal. It is carried out in an act. The goal toward which I surpass myself must appear to me as a point of departure toward a new act of surpassing. Thus, a creative freedom develops happily without ever congealing into unjustified facticity. The creator leans upon anterior creations in order to create the possibility of new creations. His present project embraces the past and places confidence in the freedom to come, a confidence which is never disappointed. It discloses being at the end of a further disclosure. At each moment freedom is confirmed through all creation.

However, man does not create the world. He succeeds in disclosing it only through the resistance which the world opposes to him. The will is defined only by raising obstacles, and by the contingency of facticity certain obstacles let themselves be conquered, and others do not. This is what Descartes expressed when he said that the freedom of man is infinite, but his power is limited. How can the presence of these limits be reconciled with the idea of a freedom confirming itself as a unity and an indefinite movement?

In the face of an obstacle which it is impossible to overcome, stubbornness is stupid. If I persist in beating my fist against a stone wall, my freedom exhausts itself in this useless gesture without succeeding in giving itself a content. It debases itself in a vain contingency. Yet, there is hardly a sadder virtue than resignation. It transforms into phantoms and contingent reveries projects which had at the beginning been set up as will and freedom. A young man has hoped for a happy or useful or glorious life. If the man he has become looks upon these miscarried attempts of his adolescence with disillusioned indifference, there they are, forever frozen in the dead past. When an effort fails, one declares bitterly that he has lost time and wasted his powers. The failure condemns that whole part of ourselves which we had engaged in the effort. It was to escape this dilemma that the Stoics preached indifference. We could indeed assert our freedom against all constraint if we agreed to renounce the particularity of our projects. If a door refuses to open, let us accept not opening it and there we are free. But by doing that, one manages only to save an abstract notion of freedom. It is emptied of all content and all truth. The power of man ceases to be limited because it is annulled. It is the particularity of the project which determines the limitation of the power, but it is also what gives the project its content and permits it to be set up. There are people who are filled with such horror at the idea of a defeat that they keep themselves from ever doing anything. But no one would dream of considering this gloomy passivity as the triumph of freedom.

The truth is that in order for my freedom not to risk coming to grief against the obstacle which its very engagement has raised, in order that it might still pursue its movement in the face of the failure, it must, by giving itself a particular content, aim by means of it at an end which is nothing else but precisely the free movement of existence. Popular opinion is quite right in admiring a man who, having been ruined or having suffered an accident, knows how to gain the upper hand, that is, renew his engagement in the world, thereby strongly asserting the independence of freedom in relation to thing. Thus, when the sick Van Gogh calmly accepted the prospect of a future in which he would be unable to paint any more, there was no sterile resignation. For him painting was a personal way of life and of communication with others which in another form could be continued even in an asylum. The past will be integrated and freedom will be confirmed in a renunciation of this kind. It will be lived in both heartbreak and joy. In heartbreak, because the project is then robbed of its particularity—it sacrifices its flesh and blood. But in joy, since at the moment one releases his hold, he again finds his hands free and ready to stretch out toward a new future. But this act of passing beyond is conceivable only if what the content has in view is not to bar up the future, but, on the contrary, to plan new possibilities. This brings us back by another route to what we had already indicated. My freedom must not seek to trap being but to disclose it. The disclosure is the transition from being to existence. The goal which my freedom aims at is conquering existence across the always inadequate density of being.

However, such salvation is only possible if, despite obstacles and failures, a man preserves the disposal of his future, if the situation opens up more possibilities to him. In case his transcendence is cut off from his goal or there is no longer any hold on objects which might give it a valid content, his spontaneity is dissipated without founding anything. Then he may not justify his existence positively and he feels its contingency with wretched disgust. There is no more obnoxious way to punish a man than to force him to perform acts which make no sense to him, as when one empties and fills the same ditch indefinitely, when one makes soldiers who are being punished march up and down, or when one forces a schoolboy to copy lines. Revolts broke out in Italy in September 1946 because the unemployed were set to breaking pebbles which served no purpose whatever. As is well known, this was also the weakness which ruined the national workshops in 1848. This mystification of useless effort is more intolerable than fatigue. Life imprisonment is the most horrible of punishments because it preserves existence in its pure facticity but forbids it all legitimation. A freedom can not will itself without willing itself as an indefinite movement. It must absolutely reject the constraints which arrest its drive toward itself. This rejection takes on a positive aspect when the constraint is natural. One rejects the illness by curing it. But it again assumes the negative aspect of revolt when the oppressor is a human freedom. One can not deny being: the in-itself is, and negation has no hold over this being, this pure positivity; one does not escape this fullness: a destroyed house *is* a ruin; a broken chain *is* scrap iron: one attains only signification and, through it, the for-itself which is projected there; the for-itself carries nothingness in its heart and can be annihilated, whether in the very upsurge of its existence or through the world in which it exists. The prison is repudiated as such when the prisoner escapes. But revolt, insofar as it is pure negative movement, remains abstract. It is fulfilled as freedom only by returning to the positive, that is, by giving itself a content through action, escape, political struggle, revolution. Human transcendence then seeks, with the destruction of the given situation, the whole future which will flow from its victory. It resumes its indefinite rapport with itself. There are limited situations where this return to the positive is impossible, where the future is radically blocked off. Revolt can then be achieved only in the definitive rejection of the imposed situation, in suicide.

It can be seen that, on the one hand, freedom can always save itself, for it is realized as a disclosure of existence through its very failures, and it can again confirm itself by a death freely chosen. But, on the other hand, the situations which it discloses through its project toward itself do not appear as equivalents. It regards as privileged situations those which permit it to realize itself as indefinite movement; that is, it wishes to pass beyond everything which limits its power; and yet, this power is always limited. Thus, just as life is identified with the will-to-live, freedom always appears as a movement of liberation. It is only by prolonging itself through the freedom of others that it manages to surpass death itself and to realize itself as an indefinite unity. Later on we shall see what problems such a relationship raises. For the time being it is enough for us to have established the fact that the words "to will oneself free" have a positive and concrete meaning. If man wishes to save his existence, as only he himself can do, his original spontaneity must be raised to the height of moral freedom by taking itself as an end through the disclosure of a particular content.

But a new question is immediately raised. If man has one and only one way to save his existence, how can he choose not to choose it in all cases? How is a bad willing possible? We meet with this problem in all ethics, since it is precisely the possibility of a perverted willing which gives a meaning to the idea of virtue. We know the answer of Socrates, of Plato, of Spinoza: "No one is willfully bad." And if Good is a transcendent thing which is more or less foreign to man, one imagines that the mistake can be explained by error. But if one grants that the moral world is the world genuinely willed by man, all possibility of error is eliminated. Moreover, in Kantian ethics, which is at the origin of all ethics of autonomy, it is very difficult to account for an evil will. As the choice of his character which the subject makes is achieved in the intelligible world by a purely rational will, one can not understand how the latter expressly rejects the law which it gives to itself. But this is because Kantism defined man as a pure positivity, and it therefore recognized no other possibility in him than coincidence with himself. We, too, define morality by this adhesion to the self; and this is why we say that man can not positively decide between the negation and the assumption of his freedom, for as soon as he decides, he assumes it. He can not positively will not to be free for such a willing would be self-destructive. Only, unlike Kant, we do not see man as being essentially a positive will. On the contrary, he is first defined as a negativity. He is first at a distance from himself. He can coincide with himself only by agreeing never to rejoin himself. There is within him a perpetual playing with the negative, and he thereby escapes himself, he escapes his freedom. And it is precisely because an evil will is here possible that the words "to will oneself free" have a meaning. Therefore, not only do we assert that the existentialist doctrine permits the elaboration of an ethics, but it even appears to us as the only philosophy in which an ethics has its place. For, in a metaphysics of transcendence, in the classical sense of the term, evil is reduced to error; and in humanistic philosophies it is impossible to account for it, man being defined as complete in a complete world. Existentialism alone gives —like religions—a real role to evil, and it is this, perhaps, which make its judgments so gloomy. Men do not like to feel themselves in danger. Yet, it is because there are real dangers, real failures and real earthly damnation that words like victory, wisdom, or joy have meaning. Nothing is decided in advance, and it is because man has something to lose and because he can lose that he can also win.

Therefore, in the very condition of man there enters the possibility of not fulfilling this condition. In order to fulfill it he must assume himself as a being who "makes himself a lack of being so that there might be being." But the trick of dishonesty permits stopping at any moment whatsoever. One may hesitate to make oneself a lack of being, one may withdraw before existence, or one may falsely assert oneself as being, or assert oneself as nothingness. One may realize his freedom only as an abstract independence, or, on the contrary, reject with despair the distance which separates us from being. All errors are possible since man is a negativity, and they are motivated by the anguish he feels in the face of his freedom. . . .

Is this kind of ethics individualistic or not? Yes, if one means by that that it accords to the individual an absolute value and that it recognizes in him alone the power of laying the foundations of his own existence. It is individualism in the sense in which the wisdom of the ancients, the Christian ethics of salvation, and the Kantian ideal of virtue also merit this name; it is opposed to the totalitarian doctrines which raise up beyond man the mirage of Mankind. But it is not solipsistic, since the individual is defined only by his relationship to the world and to other individuals; he exists only by transcending himself, and his freedom can be achieved only through the freedom of others. He justifies his existence by a movement which, like freedom, springs from his heart but which leads outside of him.

This individualism does not lead to the anarchy of personal whim. Man is free; but he finds his law in his very freedom. First, he must assume his freedom and not flee it; he assumes it by a constructive movement: one does not exist without doing something; and also by a negative movement which rejects oppression for oneself and others. In construction, as in rejection, it is a matter of reconquering freedom on the contingent facticity of existence, that is, of taking the given, which, at the start, *is there* without any reason, as something willed by man. A conquest of this kind is never finished; the contingency remains, and, so that he may assert his will, man is even obliged to stir up in the world the outrage he does not want. But this element of failure is a very condition of his life; one can never dream of eliminating it without immediately dreaming of death. This does not mean that one should consent to failure, but rather one must consent to struggle against it without respite. . . .

Suggested Readings

Augustine, St., *The Problem of Free Choice*, tr. M. Pontifex, Newman Press, Westminster, 1955.

Berofsky, Bernard, ed., *Free Will and Determinism*, Harper & Row, New York, 1966.

Cranston, Maurice, *Freedom: A New Analysis*, Longmans, Green and Co., London, 1953.

Edwards, Jonathan, *Freedom of the Will*, ed. P. Ramsey, Yale University, New Haven, 1957.

Enteman, Willard F., ed., *The Problem of Free Will*, Charles Scribner's Sons, New York, 1967.

Hampshire, Stuart, *Freedom of the Individual*, Harper & Row, New York, 1965.

Hook, Sidney, ed., *Determinism and Freedom in the Age of Modern Science*, New York University Press, New York, 1958.

Hume, D., *A Treatise of Human Nature*, Book II, Part III, Clarendon Press, Oxford, 1928.

Nowell-Smith, P. H., *Ethics*, Chapters 19–20, Pelican Books, Baltimore, 1954.

Relativism

❀ INTRODUCTION

It is a commonplace of our everyday discussions to assert that "Everything is relative." Uttered with the proper degree of finality and solemnity, this pronouncement is supposed to end all trivial debate about the truth or falsity of an issue. For apparently if everything is relative, the distinction between "truth" and "falsity" evaporates, and one position is no more credible or defensible than another. Hence it appears that everyone is equally right (and wrong), and all further discussion is idle.

The assertion that everything is relative is seldom used more often or more indiscriminately than in discussions concerning morals. Who has not been involved in a debate about the correctness or legitimacy of some course of action without being confounded by the claim of the relativist that there are no objective moral principles and that "Everything is relative"? This contention seems to strike at the very heart of every attempt to propound and defend a system of morality. It makes the would-be moralist appear to be purely arbitrary and presumptuous in seeking to impose his own appraisals on others, and it leaves him helpless in the face of the wrong which he wishes to identify and disallow.

At first glance one might suppose that the question concerning the relativity of morals could be easily answered. But a more careful study of this issue soon reveals that it is somewhat more complicated than it initially appears. In the essay entitled "Ethical Relativism and Ethical Absolutism Defined," Stace clearly distinguishes the questions of fact and questions of principle that so often are confused in treating this problem, and he defines two widely divergent positions that philosophers have maintained in this debate. Next, both Sumner and Kluckhohn present a wealth of sociological and anthropological material in support of their contrasting views. Sumner presents the case for ethical relativism while Kluckhohn contends that a cross-cultural study provides evidence for the view that there are some universal human values. Finally, the selections from the writings of Abraham Maslow and from the United Nations Charter illustrate attempts to formulate a number of fundamental moral principles that might be endorsed and promoted by people in all the countries of the world.

✿ W. T. STACE

30. *Ethical Relativism and Ethical Absolutism Defined*

Walter Terence Stace (1886–   ) was born in London and educated at
Edinburgh and Trinity College. He taught philosophy at Princeton
University from 1932 until his retirement in 1955. In 1949 he served as
President of the American Philosophical Association. Some of his majoı
works are: *A Critical History of Greek Philosophy* (1920), *The Concept
of Morals* (1937), *Religion and the Modern Mind* (1952), and *Mysticism
and Philosophy* (1960).

There is an opinion widely current nowadays in philosophical
circles which passes under the name of "ethical relativity." Exactly what
this phrase means or implies is certainly far from clear. But unquestionably
it stands as a label for the opinions of a group of ethical philosophers whose
position is roughly on the extreme left wing among the moral theorizers
of the day. And perhaps one may best understand it by placing it in contrast
with the opposite kind of extreme view against which, undoubtedly, it has
arisen as a protest. For among moral philosophers one may clearly distinguish a left and a right wing. Those of the left wing are the ethical
relativists. They are the revolutionaries, the clever young men, the up to
date. Those of the right wing we may call the ethical absolutists. They
are the conservatives and the old-fashioned.

According to the absolutists there is but one eternally true and
valid moral code. This moral code applies with rigid impartiality to all
men. What is a duty for me must likewise be a duty for you. And this will
be true whether you are an Englishman. a Chinaman, or a Hottentot. If
cannibalism is an abomination in England or America, it is an abomination
in central Africa, notwithstanding that the African may think otherwise.
The fact that he sees nothing wrong in his cannibal practices does not make
them for him morally right. They are as much contrary to morality for him
as they are for us. The only difference is that he is an ignorant savage who
does not know this. There is not one law for one man or race of men,
another for another. There is not one moral standard for Europeans, another for Indians, another for Chinese. There is but one law, one standard,
one morality, for all men. And this standard, this law, is absolute and
unvarying.

Moreover, as the one moral law extends its dominion over all the
corners of the earth, so too it is not limited in its application by any considerations of time or period. That which is right now was right in the

centuries of Greece and Rome, nay, in the very ages of the cave man. That which is evil now was evil then. If slavery is morally wicked today, it was morally wicked among the ancient Athenians, notwithstanding that their greatest men accepted it as a necessary condition of human society. Their opinion did not make slavery a moral good for them. It only showed that they were, in spite of their otherwise noble conceptions, ignorant of what is truly right and good in this matter.

The ethical absolutists recognizes as a fact that moral customs and moral ideas differ from country to country and from age to age. This indeed seems manifest and not to be disputed. We think slavery morally wrong, the Greeks thought it morally unobjectionable. The inhabitants of New Guinea certainly have very different moral ideas from ours. But the fact that the Greeks or the inhabitants of New Guinea think something right does not make it right, even for them. Nor does the fact that we think the same things wrong make them wrong. They are *in themselves* either right or wrong. What we have to do is to discover which they are. What anyone thinks makes no difference. It is here just as it is in matters of physical science. We believe the earth to be a globe. Our ancestors may have thought it flat. This does not show that it *was* flat, and is *now* a globe. What it shows is that men having in other ages been ignorant about the shape of the earth have now learned the truth. So if the Greeks thought slavery morally legitimate, this does not indicate that is was for them and in that age morally legitimate, but rather that they were ignorant of the truth of the matter.

The ethical absolutist is not indeed committed to the opinion that this own, or our own, moral code is the true one. Theoretically at least he might hold that slavery is ethically justifiable, that the Greeks knew better than we do about this, that ignorance of the true morality lies with us and not with them. All that he is actually committed to is the opinion that, whatever the true moral code may be, it is always the same for all men in all ages. His view is not at all inconsistent with the belief that humanity has still much to learn in moral matters. If anyone were to assert that in five hundred years the moral conceptions of the present day will appear as barbarous to the people of that age as the moral conceptions of the middle ages appear to us now, he need not deny it. If anyone were to assert that the ethics of Christianity are by no means final, and will be superseded in future ages by vastly nobler moral ideals, he need not deny this either. For it is of the essence of his creed to believe that morality is in some sense objective, not man-made, not produced by human opinion; that its principles are real truths about which men have to learn—just as they have to learn about the shape of the world—about which they may have been ignorant in the past, and about which therefore they may well be ignorant now.

Thus although absolutism is conservative in the sense that it is regarded by the more daring spirits as an out of date opinion, it is not necessarily conservative in the sense of being committed to the blind support of existing moral ideas and institutions. If ethical absolutists are sometimes conservative in this sense too, that is their personal affair. Such conservativism is accidental, not essential to the absolutist's creed. There is no logical reason, in the nature of the case, why an absolutist should not be a communist, an anarchist, a surrealist, or an upholder of free love. The fact that he is usually none of these things may be accounted for in various ways. But it has nothing to do with the sheer logic of his ethical position. The sole opinion to which he is committed is that whatever is morally right (or wrong)—be it free love or monogamy or slavery or cannibalism or vegetarianism—is morally right (or wrong) for all men at all times.

Usually the absolutist goes further than this. He often maintains, not merely that the moral law is the same for all the men on this planet—which is, after all, a tiny speck in space—but that in some way or in some sense it has application everywhere in the universe. He may express himself by saying that it applies to all "rational beings"—which would apparently include angels and the men on Mars (if they are rational). He is apt to think that the moral law is a part of the fundamental structure of the universe. But with this aspect of absolutism we need not, at the moment, concern ourselves. At present we may think of it as being simply the opinion that there is a single moral standard for all human beings.

This brief and rough sketch of ethical absolutism is intended merely to form a background against which we may the more clearly indicate, by way of contrast, the theory of ethical relativity. Up to the present, therefore, I have not given any of the reasons which the absolutist can urge in favour of his case. It is sufficient for my purpose at the moment to state *what* he believes, without going into the question of *why* he believes it. But before proceeding to our next step—the explanation of ethical relativity—I think it will be helpful to indicate some of the historical causes (as distinguished from logical reasons) which have helped in the past to render absolutism a plausible interpretation of morality as understood by European peoples.

Our civilization is a Christian civilization. It has grown up, during nearly two thousand years, upon the soil of Christian monotheism. In this soil our whole outlook upon life, and consequently all our moral ideas, have their roots. They have been moulded by this influence. The wave of religious scepticism which, during the last half century, has swept over us, has altered this fact scarcely at all. The moral ideas even of those who most violently reject the dogmas of Christianity with their intellects are still Christian ideas. This will probably remain true for many centuries even if Christian theology, as a set of intellectual beliefs, comes to be wholly rejected by every educated person. It will probably remain true so long as our civilization lasts. A child cannot, by changing in later life his intellectual creed, strip himself of the early formative moral influences of his childhood, though he can no doubt modify their results in various minor ways. With the outlook on life which was instilled into him in his early days he, in large measure, lives and dies. So it is with a civilization. And our civilization, whatever religious or irreligious views it may come to hold or reject, can hardly escape within its lifetime the moulding influences of its Christian origin. Now ethical absolutism was, in its central ideas, the product of Christian theology.

The connection is not difficult to detect. For morality has been conceived, during the Christian dispensation, as issuing from the will of God. That indeed was its single and all-sufficient source. There would be no point, for the naïve believer in the faith, in the philosopher's questions regarding the foundations of morality and the basis of moral obligation. Even to ask such questions is a mark of incipient religious scepticism. For the true believer the author of the moral law is God. What pleases God, what God commands—that is the definition of right. What displeases God, what he forbids—that is the definition of wrong. Now there is, for the Christian monotheist, only one God ruling over the entire universe. And this God is rational, self-consistent. He does not act upon whims. Consequently his will and his commands must be the same everywhere. They will be unvarying for all peoples and in all ages. If the heathen have other moral ideas than ours—inferior ideas—that can only be because they live in ignorance of the true God. If they knew God and his commands, their ethical precepts would be the same as ours.

Polytheistic creeds may well tolerate a number of diverse moral codes. For the God of the western hemisphere might have different views from those entertained by the God of the eastern hemisphere. And the God of the north might issue to his worshippers commands at variance with the commands issued to other peoples by the God of the south. But a monotheistic religion implies a single universal and absolute morality.

This explains why ethical absolutism, until very recently, was not only believed by philosophers but *taken for granted without any argument.* The ideas of philosophers, like the ideas of everyone else, are largely moulded by the civilizations in which they live. Their philosophies are largely attempts to state in abstract terms and in self-consistent language the stock of ideas which they have breathed in from the atmosphere of their social environment. This accounts for the large number of so-called "unrecognized presuppositions" with which systems of philosophy always abound. These presuppositions are simply the ideas which the authors of the systems have breathed in with the intellectual atmospheres by which they happen to be surrounded—which they have taken over therefore as a matter of course, without argument, without criticism, without even a suspicion that they might be false.

It is not therefore at all surprising to find that Immanuel Kant, writing in the latter half of the eighteenth century, not only took the tenets of ethical absolutism for granted, but evidently considered that no instructed person would dispute them. It is a noticeable feature of his ethical philosophy that he gives no reasons whatever to support his belief in the existence of a universally valid moral law. He assumes as a matter of course that his readers will accept this view. And he proceeds at once to enquire what is the metaphysical foundation of the universal moral law. That alone is what interests him. *Assuming* that there does exist such a law, how, he asks, can this be the case, and what, in the way of transcendental truth, does it imply? It never occurs to him to reflect that any philosopher who should choose to question his fundamental assumption could outflank his whole ethical position; and that if this assumption should prove false his entire moral philosophy would fall to the ground like a pack of cards.

We can now turn to the consideration of ethical relativity. . . . The revolt of the relativists against absolutism is, I believe, part and parcel of the general revolutionary tendency of our times. In particular it is a result of the decay of belief in the dogmas of orthodox religion. Belief in absolutism was supported, as we have seen, by belief in Christian monotheism. And now that, in an age of widespread religious scepticism, that support is withdrawn, absolutism tends to collapse. Revolutionary movements are as a rule, at any rate in their first onset, purely negative. They attack and destroy. And ethical relativity is, in its essence, a purely negative creed. It is simply a denial of ethical absolutism. That is why the best way of explaining it is to begin by explaining ethical absolutism. If we understand that what the latter asserts the former denies, then we understand ethical relativity.

Any ethical position which denies that there is a single moral standard which is equally applicable to all men at all times may fairly be called a species of ethical relativity. There is not, the relativist asserts, merely one moral law, one code, one standard. There are many moral laws, codes, standards. What morality ordains in one place or age may be quite different from what morality ordains in another place or age. The moral code of Chinamen is quite different from that of Europeans, that of African savages quite different from both. Any morality, therefore, is relative to the age, the place, and the circumstances in which it is found. It is in no sense absolute.

This does not mean merely—as one might at first sight be inclined to suppose—that the very same kind of action which is *thought* right in one country and period may be *thought* wrong in another. This would be a mere platitude, the truth of which everyone would have to admit. Even the absolutist would admit this—would even wish to emphasize it—since he is well aware that different peoples have different sets of moral ideas, and his whole point is that some of these sets of ideas are false. What the relativist means to assert is, not this platitude, but that the very same kind of action which *is* right in one country and period may *be* wrong in another. And this, far from being a platitude, is a very startling assertion.

It is very important to grasp thoroughly the difference between the two ideas. For there is reason to think that many minds tend to find ethical relativity attractive because they fail to keep them clearly apart. It is so very obvious that moral ideas differ from country to country and from age to age. And it is so very easy, if you are mentally lazy, to suppose that to say this means the same as to say that no universal moral standard exists,— or in other words that it implies ethical relativity. We fail to see that the word "standard" is used in two different senses. It is perfectly true that, in one sense, there are many variable moral standards. We speak of judging a man by the standard of his time. And this implies that different times have different standards. And this, of course, is quite true. But when the word "standard" is used in this sense it means simply the set of moral ideas current during the period in question. It means what people *think* right, whether as a matter of fact it *is* right or not. On the other hand when the absolutist asserts that there exists a single universal moral "standard," he is not using the word in this sense at all. He means by "standard" what *is* right as distinct from what people merely think right. His point is that although what people think right varies in different countries and periods, yet what actually is right is everywhere and always the same. And it follows that when the ethical relativist disputes the position of the absolutist and denies that any universal moral standard exists he too means by "standard" what actually is right. But it is exceedingly easy, if we are not careful, to slip loosely from using the word in the first sense to using it in the second sense; and to suppose that the variability of moral beliefs is the same thing as the variability of what really is moral. And unless we keep the two senses of the word "standard" distinct, we are likely to think the creed of ethical relativity much more plausible than it actually is.

The genuine relativist, then, does not merely mean that Chinamen may think right what Frenchmen think wrong. He means that what *is* wrong for the Frenchman may *be* right for the Chinaman. And if one enquires how, in those circsmstances, one is to know what actually is right in China or in France, the answer comes quite glibly. What is right in China is the same as what people think right in China; and what is right in France is the same as what people think right in France. So that, if you want to know what is moral in any particular country or age all you have to do is to ascertain what are the moral ideas current in that age or country. Those ideas are, *for that age or country,* right. Thus what is morally right is identified with what is thought to be morally right, and the distinction which we made above between these two is simply denied. To put the same thing in another way, it is denied that there can be or ought to be any distinction between the two senses of the word "standard." There is only one kind of standard of right and wrong, namely, the moral ideas current in any particular age or country.

Moral right *means* what people think morally right. It has no other meaning. What Frenchmen think right is, therefore, right *for Frenchmen.* And evidently one must conclude—though I am not aware that relativists are anxious to draw one's attention to such unsavoury but yet absolutely necessary conclusions from their creed—that cannibalism is right for people who believe in it, that human sacrifice is right for those races which practice it, and that burning widows alive was right for Hindus until the British stepped in and compelled the Hindus to behave immorally by allowing their widows to remain alive.

When it is said that, according to the ethical relativist, what is thought right in any social group is right for that group, one must be careful not to misinterpret this. The relativist does not, of course, mean that there actually is an objective moral standard in France and a different objective standard in England, and that French and British opinions respectively give us correct information about these different standards. His point is rather that there are no objectively true moral standards at all. There is no single universal objective standard. Nor are there a variety of local objective standards. All standards are subjective. People's subjective feelings about morality are the only standards which exist.

To sum up. The ethical relativist consistently denies, it would seem, whatever the ethical absolutist asserts. For the absolutist there is a single universal moral standard. For the relativist there is no such standard. There are only local, ephemeral, and variable standards. For the absolutist there are two senses of the word "standard." Standards in the sense of sets of current moral ideas are relative and changeable. But the standard in the sense of what is actually morally right is absolute and unchanging. For the relativist no such distinction can be made. There is only one meaning of the word standard, namely, that which refers to local and variable sets of moral ideas. Or if it is insisted that the word must be allowed two meanings, then the relativist will say that there is at any rate no actual example of a standard in the absolute sense, and that the word as thus used is an empty name to which nothing in reality corresponds; so that the distinction between the two meanings becomes empty and useless. Finally—though this is merely saying the same thing in another way—the absolutist makes a distinction between what actually is right and what is thought right. The relativist rejects this distinction and identifies what is moral with what is thought moral by certain human beings or groups of human beings. . . .

❀ W. G. SUMNER

31. Cultural Relativity and Ethical Relativism

William Graham Sumner (1840–1910) graduated from Yale in 1863. After graduation he became an Episcopal minister. In 1872 he accepted a chair at Yale University as Professor of Political and Social Science. An important and original thinker in economics, sociology, anthropology, and political philosophy, he was also a proponent of laissez-faire capitalism. Some of his major works are: *What Social Classes Owe to Each Other* (1883), *Folkways* (1907), and *The Science of Society* (1927).

1. DEFINITION AND MODE OF ORIGIN OF THE FOLKWAYS

If we put together all that we have learned from anthropology and ethnography about primitive men and primitive society, we perceive that the first task of life is to live. Men begin with acts, not with thoughts. Every moment brings necessities which must be satisfied at once. Need was the first experience, and it was followed at once by a blundering effort to satisfy it. It is generally taken for granted that men inherited some guiding instincts from their beast ancestry, and it may be true, although it has never been proved. If there were such inheritances, they controlled and aided the first efforts to satisfy needs. Analogy makes it easy to assume that the ways of beasts had produced channels of habit and predisposition along which dexterities and other psychophysical activities would run easily. Experiments with newborn animals show that in the absence of any experience of the relation of means to ends, efforts to satisfy needs are clumsy and blundering. The method is that of trial and failure, which produces repeated pain, loss, and disappointments. Nevertheless, it is a method of rude experiment and selection. The earliest efforts of men were of this kind. Need was the impelling force. Pleasure and pain, on the one side and the other, were the rude constraints which defined the line on which efforts must proceed. The ability to distinguish between pleasure and pain is the only psychical power which is to be assumed. Thus ways of doing things were selected, which were expedient. They answered the purpose better than other ways, or with less toil and pain. Along the course on which efforts were compelled to go, habit, routine, and skill were developed. The struggle to maintain existence was carried on, not individually, but in groups. Each profited by the other's experience; hence there was concurrence towards that which proved to be most expedient. All at last adopted the same way for the same purpose; hence the ways turned into customs and became mass phenomena. Instincts were developed in connection with them. In this way folkways arise. The young learn them by tradition, imitation, and authority. The folkways, at a time, provide for all the needs of life then and there. They are uniform, universal in the group, imperative, and invariable. As time goes on, the folkways become more and more arbitrary, positive, and imperative. If asked why they act in a certain way in certain cases, primitive people always answer that it is because they and their ancestors always have done so. A sanction also arises from ghost fear. The ghosts of ancestors would be angry if the living should change the ancient folkways.

2. The Folkways Are a Societal Force

The operation by which folkways are produced consists in the frequent repetition of petty acts, often by great numbers acting in concert or, at least, acting in the same way when face to face with the same need. The immediate motive is interest. It produces habit in the individual and custom in the group. It is, therefore, in the highest degree original and primitive. By habit and custom it exerts a strain on every individual within its range; therefore it rises to a societal force to which great classes of societal phenomena are due. Its earliest stages, its course, and laws may be studied; also its influence on individuals and their reaction on it. It is our present purpose so to study it. We have to recognize it as one of the chief forces by which a society is made to be what it is. Out of the unconscious experiment which every repetition of the ways includes, there issues pleasure or pain, and then, so far as the men are capable of reflection, convictions that the ways are conducive to societal welfare. These two experiences are not the same. The most uncivilized men, both in the food quest and in war, do things which are painful, but which have been found to be expedient. Perhaps these cases teach the sense of social welfare better than those which are pleasurable and favorable to welfare. The former cases call for some intelligent reflection on experience. When this conviction as to the relation to welfare is added to the folkways they are converted into mores, and, by virtue of the philosophical and ethical element added to them, they win utility and importance and become the source of the science and the art of living.

3. FOLKWAYS ARE MADE UNCONSCIOUSLY

It is of the first importance to notice that, from the first acts by which men try to satisfy needs, each act stands by itself, and looks no further than the immediate satisfaction. From recurrent needs arise habits for the individual and customs for the group, but these results are consequences which were never conscious, and never foreseen or intended. They are not noticed until they have long existed, and it is still longer before they are appreciated. Another long time must pass, and a higher stage of mental development must be reached, before they can be used as a basis from which to deduce rules for meeting, in the future, problems whose pressure can be foreseen. The folkways, therefore, are not creations of human purpose and wit. They are like products of natural forces which men unconsciously set in operation, or they are like the instinctive ways of animals, which are developed out of experience, which reach a final form of maximum adaptation to an interest, which are handed down by tradition and admit of no exception or variation, yet change to meet new conditions, still within the same limited methods, and without rational reflection or purpose. From this it results that all the life of human beings, in all ages and stages of culture, is primarily controlled by a vast mass of folkways handed down from the earliest existence of the race, having the nature of the ways of other animals, only the topmost layers of which are subject to change and control, and have been somewhat modified by human philosophy, ethics, and religion, or by other acts of intelligent reflection. . . .

5. THE STRAIN OF IMPROVEMENT AND CONSISTENCY

The folkways, being ways of satisfying needs, have suceeded more or less well, and therefore have produced more or less pleasure or pain. Their quality always consisted in their adaptation to the purpose. If they were imperfectly adapted and unsuccessful, they produced pain, which drove men on to learn better. The folkways are, therefore, (1) subject to a strain of improvement towards better adaptation of means to ends, as long as the adaptation is so imperfect that pain is produced. They are also (2) subject to a strain of consistency with each other, because they all answer their several purposes with less friction and antagonism when they cooperate and support each other. The forms of industry, the forms of the family, the notions of property, the constructions of rights, and the types of religion show the strain of consistency with each other through the whole history of civilization. The two great cultural divisions of the human race are the oriental and the occidental. Each is consistent throughout; each has its own philosophy and spirit; they are separated from top to bottom by different mores, different standpoints, different ways, and different notions of what societal arrangements are advantageous. In their contrast they keep before our minds the possible range of divergence in the solution of the great problems of human life, and in the views of earthly existence by which life policy may be controlled. If two planets were joined in one, their inhabitants could not differ more widely as to what things are best worth seeking, or what ways are most expedient for well living. . . .

15. ETHNOCENTRISM

Is the technical name for this view of things in which one's own group is the center of everything, and all others are scaled and rated with reference to it. Folkways correspond to it to cover both the inner and the outer relation. Each group nourishes its own pride and vanity, boasts itself superior, exalts its own divinities, and looks with contempt on outsiders. Each group thinks its own folkways the only right ones, and if it observes that other groups have other folkways, these excite its scorn. Opporbrious epithets are derived from these differences. "Pig-eater," "cow-eater," "uncircumcised," "jabberers," are epithets of contempt and abomination. The Tupis called the Portuguese by a derisive epithet descriptive of birds which have feathers around their feet, on account of trousers. For our present purpose the most important fact is that ethnocentrism leads a people to exaggerate and intensify everything in their own folkways which is peculiar and which differentiates them from others. It therefore strengthens the folkways.

16. ILLUSTRATIONS OF ETHNOCENTRISM

The Papuans on New Guinea are broken up into village units which are kept separate by hostility, cannibalism, head hunting, and divergences of language and religion. Each village is integrated by its own language, religion, and interests. A group of villages is sometimes united into a limited unity by connubium. A wife taken inside of the group unit has full status; one taken outside of it has not. The petty group units are peace groups within and are hostile to all outsiders. The Mbayas of South America believed that their deity had bidden them live by making war on others, taking their wives and property, and killing their men.

17

When Caribs were asked whence they came, they answered, "We alone are people." The meaning of the name Kiowa is "real or principal people." The Lapps call themselves "men," or "human beings." The Greenland Eskimo think that Europeans have been sent to Greenland to learn virtue and good manners from the Greenlanders. Their highest form of praise for a European is that he is, or soon will be, as good as a Greenlander. The Tunguses call themselves "men." As a rule it is found that nature peoples call themselves "men." Others are something else—perhaps not defined—but not real men. In myths the origin of their own tribe is that of the real human race. They do not account for the others. The Ainos derive their name from that of the first man, whom they worship as a god. Evidently the name of the god is derived from the tribe name. When the tribal name has another sense, it is always boastful or proud. The Ovambo name is a corruption of the name of the tribe for themselves, which means "the wealthy." Amongst the most remarkable people in the world for ethnocentrism are the Seri of Lower California. They observe an attitude of suspicion and hostility to all outsiders, and strictly forbid marriage with outsiders.

18

The Jews divided all mankind into themselves and Gentiles. They were the "chosen people." The Greeks and Romans called all outsiders "barbarians." In Euripides' tragedy of *Iphigenia in Aulis* Iphigenia says that it is fitting that Greeks should rule over barbarians, but not contrariwise, because Greeks are free, and barbarians are slaves. The Arabs regarded themselves as the noblest nation and all others as more or less barbarous. In 1896, the Chinese minister of education and his counselors edited a manual in which this statement occurs: "How grand and glorious is the Empire of China, the middle kingdom! She is the largest and richest in the world. The grandest men in the world have all come from the middle empire." In all the literature of all the states equivalent statements occur, although they are not so naïvely expressed. In Russian books and newspapers the civilizing mission of Russia is talked about, just as, in the books and journals of France, Germany, and the United States, the civilizing mission of those countries is assumed and referred to as well understood. Each state now regards itself as the leader of civilization, the best, the freest, and the wisest, and all others as inferior. Within a few years our own man-on-the-curbstone has learned to class all foreigners of the Latin peoples as "dagos," and "dago" has become an epithet of contempt. These are all cases of ethnocentrism.

19. PATRIOTISM

Is a sentiment which belongs to modern states. It stands in antithesis to the mediæval notion of catholicity. Patriotism is loyalty to the civic group to which one belongs by birth or other group bond. It is a sentiment of fellowship and cooperation in all the hopes, work, and suffering of the group. Mediæval catholicity would have made all Christians an in-group and would have set them in hostility to all Mohammedans and other non-Christians. It never could be realized. When the great modern states took form and assumed control of societal interests, group sentiment was produced in connection with those states. Men responded willingly to a demand for support and help from an institution which could and did serve interests. The state drew to itself the loyalty which had been given to men (lords), and it became the object of that group vanity and antagonism which had been ethnocentric. For the modern man patriotism has become one of the first of duties and one of the noblest of sentiments. It is what he owes to the state for what the state does for him, and the state is, for the modern man, a cluster of civic institutions from which he draws security and conditions of welfare. The masses are always patriotic. For them the old ethnocentric jealousy, vanity, truculency, and ambition are the strongest elements in patriotism. Such sentiments are easily awakened in a crowd. They are sure to be popular. Wider knowledge always proves that they are not based on facts. That we are good and others are bad is never true. By history, literature, travel, and science men are made cosmopolitan. The selected classes of all states become associated; they intermarry. The differentiation by states loses importance. All states give the same security and conditions of welfare to all. The standards of civic institutions are the same, or tend to become such, and it is a matter of pride in each state to offer civic status and opportunities equal to the best. Every group of any kind whatsoever demands that each of its members shall help defend group interests. Every group stigmatizes any one who fails in zeal, labor, and sacrifices for group interests. Thus the sentiment of loyalty to the group, or the group head, which was so strong in the Middle Ages, is kept up, as far as possible, in regard to modern states and governments. The group force is also employed to enforce the obligations of devotion to group interests. It follows that judgments are precluded and criticism is silenced. . . .

31. The Folkways Are "Right;" Rights; Morals

The folkways are the "right" ways to satisfy all interests, because they are traditional, and exist in fact. They extend over the whole of life. There is a right way to catch game, to win a wife, to make one's self appear, to cure disease, to honor ghosts, to treat comrades or strangers, to behave when a child is born, on the warpath, in council, and so on in all cases which can arise. The ways are defined on the negative side, that is, by taboos. The "right" way is the way which the ancestors used and which has been handed down. The tradition is its own warrant. It is not held subject to verification by experience. The notion of right is in the folkways. It is not outside of them, of independent origin, and brought to them to test them. In the folkways, whatever is, is right. This is because they are traditional, and therefore contain in themselves the authority of the ancestral ghosts. When we come to the folkways we are at the end of our analysis. The notion of right and ought is the same in regard to all the folkways, but the degree of it varies with the importance of the interest at stake. The obligation of conformable and cooperative action is far greater under ghost fear and war than in other matters, and the social sanctions are severer, because group interests are supposed to be at stake. Some usages contain only a slight element of right and ought. It may well be believed that notions of right and duty, and of social welfare, were first developed in connection with ghost fear and other-worldliness, and therefore that, in that field also, folkways were first raised to mores. "Rights" are the rules of mutual give and take in the competition of life which are imposed on comrades in the in-group, in order that the peace may prevail there which is essential to the group strength. Therefore rights can never be "natural" or "God-given," or absolute in any sense. The morality of a group at a time is the sum of the taboos and prescriptions in the folkways by which right conduct is defined. Therefore morals can never be intuitive. They are historical, institutional, and empirical.

World philosophy, life policy, right, rights, and morality are all products of the folkways. They are reflections on, and generalizations from, the experience of pleasure and pain which is won in efforts to carry on the struggle for existence under actual life conditions. The generalizations are very crude and vague in their germinal forms. They are all embodied in folklore, and all our philosophy and science have been developed out of them.

32.   THE FOLKWAYS ARE "TRUE"

The folkways are necessarily "true" with respect to some world philosophy. Pain forced men to think. The ills of life imposed reflection and taught forethought. Mental processes were irksome and were not undertaken until painful experience made them unavoidable. With great unanimity all over the globe primitive men followed the same line of thought. The dead were believed to live on as ghosts in another world just like this one. The ghosts had just the same needs, tastes, passions, etc., as the living men had had. These transcendental notions were the beginning of the mental outfit of mankind. They are articles of faith, not rational convictions. The living had duties to the ghosts, and the ghosts had rights; they also had power to enforce their rights. It behooved the living therefore to learn how to deal with ghosts. Here we have a complete world philosophy and a life policy deduced from it. When pain, loss, and ill were experienced and the question was provoked, Who did this to us? the world philosophy furnished the answer. When the painful experience forced the question, Why are the ghosts angry and what must we do to appease them? the "right" answer was the one which fitted into the philosophy of ghost fear. All acts were therefore constrained and trained into the forms of the world philosophy by ghost fear, ancestral authority, taboos, and habit. The habits and customs created a practical philosophy of welfare, and they confirmed and developed the religious theories of goblinism.

33. Relation of World Philosophy and Folkways

It is quite impossible for us to disentangle the elements of philosophy and custom, so as to determine priority and the causative position of either. Our best judgment is that the mystic philosophy is regulative, not creative, in its relation to the folkways. They reacted upon each other. The faith in the world philosophy drew lines outside of which the folkways must not go. Crude and vague notions of societal welfare were formed from the notion of pleasing the ghosts, and from such notions of expediency as the opinion that, if there were not children enough, there would not be warriors enough, or that, if there were too many children, the food supply would not be adequate. The notion of welfare was an inference and resultant from these mystic and utilitarian generalizations.

34. Definition of the Mores

When the elements of truth and right are developed into doctrines of welfare, the folkways are raised to another plane. They then become capable of producing inferences, developing into new forms, and extending their constructive influence over men and society. Then we call them the mores. The mores are the folkways, including the philosophical and ethical generalizations as to societal welfare which are suggested by them, and inherent in them, as they grow. . . .

65. What Is Goodness or Badness of the Mores

It is most important to notice that, for the people of a time and place, their own mores are always good, or rather that for them there can be no question of the goodness or badness of their mores. The reason is because the standards of good and right are in the mores. If the life conditions change, the traditional folkways may produce pain and loss, or fail to produce the same good as formerly. Then the loss of comfort and ease brings doubt into the judgment of welfare (causing doubt of the pleasure of the gods, or of war power, or of health), and thus disturbs the unconscious philosophy of the mores. Then a later time will pass judgment on the mores. Another society may also pass judgment on the mores. In our literary and historical study of the mores we want to get from them their educational value, which consists in the stimulus or warning as to what is, in its effects, societally good or bad. This may lead us to reject or neglect a phenomenon like infanticide, slavery, or witchcraft, as an old "abuse" and "evil," or to pass by the crusades as a folly which cannot recur. Such a course would be a great error. Everything in the mores of a time and place must be regarded as justified with regard to that time and place. "Good" mores are those which are well adapted to the situation. "Bad" mores are those which are not so adapted. The mores are not so stereotyped and changeless as might appear, because they are forever moving towards more complete adaptation to conditions and interests, and also towards more complete adjustment to each other. People in mass have never made or kept up a custom in order to hurt their own interests. They have made innumerable errors as to what their interests were and how to satisfy them, but they have always aimed to serve their interests as well as they could. This gives the standpoint for the student of the mores. All things in them come before him on the same plane. They all bring instruction and warning. They all have the same relation to power and welfare. The mistakes in them are component parts of them. We do not study them in order to approve some of them and condemn others. They are all equally worthy of attention from the fact that they existed and were used. The chief object of study in them is their adjustment to interests, their relation to welfare, and their co-ordination in a harmonious system of life policy. For the men of the time there are no "bad" mores. What is traditional and current is the standard of what ought to be. The masses never raise any question about such things. If a few raise doubts and questions, this proves that the folkways have already begun to lose firmness and the regulative element in the mores has begun to lose authority. This indicates that the folkways are on their way to a new adjustment. The extreme of folly, wickedness, and absurdity in the mores is witch persecutions, but the best men of the seventeenth century had no doubt that witches existed, and that they ought to be burned. The religion, statecraft, jurisprudence, philosophy, and social system of that age all contributed to maintain that belief. It was rather a culmination than a contradiction of the current faiths and convictions, just as the dogma that all men are equal and that one ought to have as much political power in the state as another was the culmination of the political dogmatism and social philosophy of the nineteenth century. Hence our judgments of the good or evil consequences of folkways are to be kept separate from our study of the historical phenomena of them, and of their strength and the reasons for it. The judgments have their place in plans and doctrines for the future, not in a retrospect. . . .

232. MORES AND MORALS; SOCIAL CODE

For everyone the mores give the notion of what ought to be. This includes the notion of what ought to be done, for all should cooperate to bring to pass, in the order of life, what ought to be. All notions of propriety, decency, chastity, politeness, order, duty, right, rights, discipline, respect, reverence, cooperation, and fellowship, especially all things in regard to which good and ill depend entirely on the point at which the line is drawn, are in the mores. The mores can make things seem right and good to one group or one age which to another seem antagonistic to every instinct of human nature. The thirteenth century bred in every heart such a sentiment in regard to heretics that inquisitors had no more misgivings in their proceedings than men would have now if they should attempt to exterminate rattlesnakes. The sixteenth century gave to all such notions about witches that witch persecutors thought they were waging war on enemies of God and man. Of course the inquisitors and witch persecutors constantly developed the notions of heretics and witches. They exaggerated the notions and then gave them back again to the mores, in their expanded form, to inflame the hearts of men with terror and hate and to become, in the next stage, so much more fantastic and ferocious motives. Such is the reaction between the mores and the acts of the living generation. The world philosophy of the age is never anything but the reflection on the mental horizon, which is formed out of the mores, of the ruling ideas which are in the mores themselves. It is from a failure to recognize the to and fro in this reaction that the current notion arises that mores are produced by doctrines. The "morals" of an age are never anything but the consonance between what is done and what the mores of the age require. The whole revolves on itself, in the relation of the specific to the general, within the horizon formed by the mores. Every attempt to win an outside standpoint from which to reduce the whole to an absolute philosophy of truth and right, based on an unalterable principle, is a delusion. New elements are brought in only by new conquests of nature through science and art. The new conquests change the conditions of life and the interests of the members of the society. Then the mores change by adaptation to new conditions and interests. The philosophy and ethics then follow to account for and justify the changes in the mores; often, also, to claim that they have caused the changes. They never do anything but draw new lines of bearing between the parts of the mores and the horizon of thought within which they are inclosed, and which is a deduction from the mores. The horizon is widened by more knowledge, but for one age it is just as much a generalization from the mores as for another. It is always unreal. It is only a product of thought. The ethical philosophers select points on this horizon from which to take their bearings, and they think that they have won some authority for their systems when they travel back again from the generalization to the specific custom out of which it was deduced. The cases of the inquisitors and witch persecutors who toiled arduously and continually for their chosen ends, for little or no reward, show us the relation between mores on the one side and philosophy, ethics, and religion on the other. . . .

438. Specification of the Subject

The ethnographers write of a tribe that the "morality" in it, especially of the women, is low or high, etc. This is the technical use of morality, —as a thing pertaining to the sex relation only or especially, and the ethnographers make their propositions by applying our standards of sex behavior, and our form of the sex taboo, to judge the folkways of all people. All that they can properly say is that they find a great range and variety of usages, ideas, standards, and ideals, which differ greatly from ours. Some of them are far stricter than ours. Those we do not consider nobler than ours. We do not feel that we ought to adopt any ways because they are more strict than our traditional ones. We consider many to be excessive, silly, and harmful. A Roman senator was censured for impropriety because he kissed his wife in the presence of his daughter.

439. Meaning of "Immoral"

When, therefore, the ethnographers apply condemnatory or depreciatory adjectives to the people whom they study, they beg the most important question which we want to investigate; that is, What are standards, codes, and ideas of chastity, decency, propriety, modesty, etc., and whence do they arise? The ethnographical facts contain the answer to this question, but in order to reach it we want a colorless report of the facts. We shall find proof that "immoral" never means anything but contrary to the mores of the time and place. Therefore the mores and the morality may move together, and there is no permanent or universal standard by which right and truth in regard to these matters can be established and different folkways compared and criticised. Only experience produces judgments of the expediency of some usages. For instance, ancient peoples thought pederasty was harmless and trivial. It has been well proved to be corrupting both to individual and social vigor, and harmful to interests, both individual and collective. Cannibalism, polygamy, incest, harlotry, and other primitive customs have been discarded by a very wide and, in the case of some of them, unanimous judgment that they are harmful. On the other hand, in the *Avesta* spermatorrhea is a crime punished by stripes. The most civilized peoples also maintain, by virtue of their superior position in the arts of life, that they have attained to higher and better judgments and that they may judge the customs of others from their own standpoint. For three or four centuries they have called their own customs "Christian," and have thus claimed for them a religious authority and sanction which they do not possess by any connection with the principles of Christianity. Now, however, the adjective seems to be losing its force. The Japanese regard nudity with indifference, but they use dress to conceal the contour of the human form while we use it to enhance, in many ways, the attraction. "Christian" mores have been enforced by the best breechloaders and ironclads, but the Japanese now seem ready to bring superiority in those matters to support their mores. It is now a known and recognized fact that our missionaries have unintentionally and unwittingly done great harm to nature people by inducing them to wear clothes as one of the first details of civilized influence. In the usages of nature peoples there is no correlation at all between dress and sentiments of chastity, modesty, decency, and propriety....

494. Honor, Seemliness, Common Sense, Conscience

Honor, common sense, seemliness, and conscience seem to belong to the individual domain. They are reactions produced in the individual by the societal environment. Honor is the sentiment of what one owes to one's self. It is an individual prerogative, and an ultimate individual standard. Seemliness is conduct which befits one's character and standards. Common sense, in the current view, is a natural gift and universal outfit. As to honor and seemliness, the popular view seems to be that each one has a fountain of inspiration in himself to furnish him with guidance. Conscience might be added as another natural or supernatural "voice," intuition, and part of the original outfit of all human beings as such. If these notions could be verified, and if they proved true, no discussion of them would be in place here, but as to honor it is a well-known and undisputed fact that societies have set codes of honor and standards of it which were arbitrary, irrational, and both individually and socially inexpedient, as ample experiment has proved. These codes have been and are imperative, and they have been accepted and obeyed by great groups of men who, in their own judgment, did not believe them sound. Those codes came out of the folkways of the time and place. Then comes the question whether it is not always so. Is honor, in any case, anything but the code of one's duty to himself which he has accepted from the group in which he was educated? Family, class, religious sect, school, occupation, enter into the social environment. In every environment there is a standard of honor. When a man thinks that he is acting most independently, on his personal prerogative, he is at best only balancing against each other the different codes in which he has been educated, e.g., that of the trades union against that of the Sunday school, or of the school against that of the family. What we think "natural" and universal, and to which we attribute an objective reality, is the sum of traits whose origin is so remote, and which we share with so many, that we do not know when or how we took them up, and we can remember no rational selection by which we adopted them. The same is true of common sense. It is the stock of ways of looking at things which we acquired unconsciously by suggestion from the environment in which we grew up. Some have more common sense than others, because they are more docile to suggestion, or have been taught to make judgments by people who were strong and wise. Conscience also seems best explained as a sum of principles of action which have in one's character the most original, remote, undisputed, and authoritative position, and to which questions of doubt are habitually referred. If these views are accepted, we have in honor, common sense, and conscience other phenomena of the folkways, and notions of eternal truths of philosophy or ethics, derived from somewhere outside of men and their struggles to live well under the conditions of earth, must be abandoned as myths. . . .

503. The Great Variety in the Codes

All the topics which have been treated in this chapter are branches or outreachings of the social code. They show how deep is the interest of human beings in the sex taboo, and in the self-perpetuation of society. Men have always tried, and are trying still, to solve the problem of well living in this respect. The men, the women, the children, and the society have joint and several interests, and the complication is great. At the present time population, race, marriage, childbirth, and the education of children present us our greatest problems and most unfathomable mysteries. All the contradictory usages of chastity, decency, propriety, etc., have their sense in some assumed relation to the welfare of society. To some extent they have come out of caprice, but chiefly they have issued from experience of good and ill, and are due to efforts to live well. Thus we may discern in them policies and philosophies, but they never proceed to form any such generalities as do rationally adopted motives. There is logic in the folkways, but never rationality. Given the premises, in a notion of kin, for instance, and the deductions are made directly and generally correctly, but the premises could never be verified, and they were oftener false than true. Each group took its own way, making its own assumptions, and following its own logic. So there was great variety and discord in their policies and philosophies, but with the area of a custom, during its dominion, its authority is absolute; and hence, although the usages are infinitely various, directly contradictory, and mutually abominable, they are, within their area of dominion, of equal value and force, and they are the standards of what is true and right. The groups have often tried to convert each other by argument and reason. They have never succeeded. Each one's reasons are the tradition which it has received from its ancestors. That does not admit of argument. Each tries to convince the other by going outside of the tradition to some philosophic standard of truth. Then the tradition is left in full force. Shocking as it must be to any group to be told that there is no rational ground for any one of them to convert another group to its mores (because this seems to imply, although it does not, that their folkways are not better than those of other groups), yet this must be said, for it is true. . . .

❀ CLYDE KLUCKHOHN

32. *Ethical Relativity: Yes and No*

Clyde Kluckhohn (1905–1960) was Professor of Anthropology at Harvard University. He was interested in relating anthropological findings to contemporary problems in value theory. His major works are: *Mirror for Man* (1949), *Anthropology and the Classics* (1961), *Navaho Witchcraft* (1962), and *Culture and Behavior: Collected Essays* which was edited by Richard Kluckhohn and published in 1962.

Professor Edel[1] says, "Indeterminacy—the fact of no definite answers available or achievable—seems to be the heart of the relativist position in ethical theory." Professor Brandt[2] takes substantially the same position

Reprinted from "Ethical Relativity: Sic et Non" in the *Journal of Philosophy*, 52 (1956), 663–677. This paper was originally presented at the meeting of the American Philosophical Association, Eastern Division, December 28, 1955. Reprinted by permission of the Journal of Philosophy and the author's estate.

[1]Abraham Edel, *Ethical Judgment*, Glencoe, Illinois, 1955, p. 30.

[2]Richard Brandt, *Hopi Ethics*, Chicago, 1954, p. 11; cf. also pp. 87 ff.

when he remarks that "a necessary condition for the tenability of ethical relativism" is to hold in principle that two people may assert "contradictory ethical views without either being mistaken." The thesis of this paper will be that recent developments in the behavioral sciences have tended to narrow the areas of indeterminacy while still affirming the necessity of ethical relativity in certain contexts.

Few anthropologists[3] would today defend without important qualification Ruth Benedict's[4] famous statement: ". . . the coexisting and equally valid patterns of life which mankind has carved for itself from the raw materials of existence." In part, I think we must admit, the abandonment of the doctrine of untrammeled cultural relativity is a reaction to the observation of social consequences. If one follows out literally and logically the implications of Benedict's words, one is compelled to accept any cultural pattern as vindicated precisely by its cultural status: slavery, cannibalism, Naziism, or Communism may not be congenial to Christians or to contemporary Western societies, but moral criticism of the cultural patterns of other people is precluded. Emotionally and practically, this extreme position is hardly tolerable—even for scholars—in the contemporary world.

But actually the trend of strictly scientific enquiry had shifted before there was general awareness of the more immediate implications of extreme relativism. During the nineteenth century anthropologists had tended to stress the unity of mankind and the diversity of the inanimate environment. At about the turn of the century, however, this emphasis came largely to be reversed. This was due in considerable part to Franz Boas. He stated explicitly that anthropology was interested in historically created diversities, leaving to psychology the exploration of common human nature. For at least a generation American anthropology (and, to a considerable degree, anthropology in the world in general) concentrated its attention upon the differences between peoples, neglecting the similarities. Recently, the balance has been righted somewhat. This occurred, no doubt, under the influence of factors of the sort studied by sociologists of knowledge. This is not, however, the whole story. Also significant was the breakdown of the isolation of anthropology from psychology and sociology. Since the present anthropological stance on relativity can be grasped only in the light of the inter-disciplinary thinking that has flourished of late, I shall briefly review some of the most relevant facts and theories of psychology and sociology. I shall turn then to a more extended consideration of the field where I can speak with more competence.

THE PSYCHOLOGICAL CONTRIBUTION

During the phase of the predominance of radical behaviorism, most American psychologists eschewed the realm of values and everything immediately pertinent to ethics. By 1935, however, E. L. Thorndike gave his

---

[3]M. J. Herskovits is a partial exception; cf *Man and His Works*, New York, 1948, pp. 76–77.

[4]*Patterns of Culture*, New York, 1934, p. 278.

presidential address to the American Association for the Advancement of Science on Values.[5] In 1945 even Clark Hull published a paper on values.[6] And over the past fifteen years Allport, Ames, Cantril, Frenkel-Brunswik, Hastorf, Maslow, and Woodruff—to name only a few—have discussed at considerable length the implications of psychological findings about human nature to values and specifically to ethics.

To summarize quickly this considerable literature is impossible. I shall therefore limit myself to some representative points from the writings of academic and of medical psychologists. Maslow, for example, writes:[7]

> Once granted reliable knowledge of what man *can* be under "certain-conditions-which-we-have-learned-to-call-good," and granted that he is happy, serene, self-accepting, unguilty, and at peace with himself only when he is fulfilling himself and becoming what can be, then it is possible and reasonable to speak about good and right and bad and wrong and desirable and undesirable. . . . The key concepts in the newer dynamic psychology are spontaneity, release, naturalness, self-acceptance, impulse-awareness, gratification. They *used* to be control, inhibition, discipline, training, shaping, on the principle that the depths of human nature were dangerous, evil, predatory, and ravenous.

Frenkel-Brunswik[8] likewise asserts the significance of social science for valuation:

> . . . individuals and cultures do not, on the whole, differ widely with respect to what are considered the ultimate ethical goals, so that arbitrariness on preferences is more a matter of means . . . the knowledge accumulated in the social sciences may help us to make a choice between alternative value systems. In renouncing any metaphysical or absolute position, we do not need to go to the other extreme of utter relativism. Although the social scientist, as a scientist, cannot make the ultimate choice for mankind, his function is to throw as much light as possible on the implications involved in existing value systems, and to make explicit all the ramifications inherent in the options.

Brandt[9] uses psychological theory (and especially the theorems of utility and of reward) to explain Hopi ethical norms. Asch[10] presents a particularly cogent discussion:

> The insufficiencies of an absolutist psychological theory of ethical judgments are obvious. It has no means for dealing with cultural diversity (or, for that matter, with intra-individual diversity). On the other hand, although the observations to which relativism refers have greatly widened the horizon of the social sciences, the psychological interpretation they have received poses equally

[5]*Science*, Jan. 3, 1936. For a significant discussion of the psychological aspect from the philosophical side see: Karl Duncker, "Ethical Relativity? (An Enquiry into the Psychology of Ethics.)," *Mind*, vol. 48 (1939), pp. 39–57.

[6]"Moral Values, Behaviorism, and the World Crisis," *Transactions of the New York Academy of Sciences*, Section of Psychology, Series II, vol. 7, pp. 90–94.

[7]"Psychological Progress in Understanding Human Nature and a Scientific Ethics," *Main Currents*, vol. 10, 1954, pp. 75–81.

[8]"Social Research and the Problem of Values: a Reply," *Journal of Abnormal and Social Psychology*, vol. 49, 1954, pp. 466–471.

[9]*Op. cit.*

[10]*Social Psychology*, New York, 1952, pp. 375–378.

serious difficulties . . . requiredness is not a property that belongs to an action irrespective of its setting and relations. Every judgment of the value of an act takes into account the particular circumstances under which it occurs. There follows the important consequence that the *same* act may be evaluated as right because it is fitting under one set of conditions and as wrong because it violates the requirements of another set of conditions. . . . The essential proposition of ethical relativism states that one can connect to the identical situation different and even opposed valuations . . . the fact of cultural differences cannot be automatically converted into an argument for a relativism of values. . . . Cultural differences are compatible with identity in values.

The Gestalt notions of "intrinsic requiredness" or "intrinsic appropriateness" have also been considered in detail by many other psychologists.

The medical psychologists, and especially the British psychoanalysts, have likewise turned their attention increasingly to some of the problems of ethics and of universal needs and values. Again, I must stop with a few examples. Money-Kyrle[11] maintains that there are "three fundamental subjective principles of primary morality" and that:

The basis of morality is therefore neither a priori and universal as the metaphysicians have claimed, nor empirical and relative as critical philosophers and anthropologists maintain, but empirical and universal in the sense that it is a quality, like binocular vision or an articulated thumb, which is found to be common to all mankind.

Flugel[12] sketches a "psychology of moral progress": from egocentricity to sociality; from autism to realism, moral inhibition to spontaneous "goodness"; aggression to tolerance and love, fear to security, heteronomy to autonomy, oretic (moral) judgment to cognitive (psychological) judgment. Dicks[13] refers with approval to Money-Kyrle's concept of "natural morality" and adds:

In simplest, proto-mental ways the rudiments of love rooted in the social-biological dependence on protective, nourishing objects, are clearly present and capable of flowering and maturation in human beings.

Contemporary psychologists and psychiatrists differ, of course, in their views on many of the issues with which we are here concerned. Yet there appears to be a growing trend toward agreement on two fundamentals:

(1) an insistence that psychological fact and theory must be taken into account in dealing with ethical problems;

(2) there are pan-human universals as regards needs and capacities that shape, or could rightly shape, at least the broad outlines of a morality that transcends cultural difference.

---

[11]"A Psychoanalytical Contribution to Ethics," *British Journal of Medical Psychology*, vol. 20, 1944, pp. 105–118.

[12]*Man, Morals, and Society*, New York, 1945.

[13]"In Search of Our Proper Ethic," *British Jorunal of Medical Psychology*, vol. 23, 1950, pp. 1–14.

THE SOCIOLOGICAL CONTRIBUTION

The sociologists have similarly been placing greater emphasis upon the universals. Kolb[14] writes:

The basic field conditions for the emergence of the human psyche have been relatively the same since man has been man: society, culture, symbolic interaction, and the potentialities of the biological organism interacting in the basic process of socialization. All social psychologists recognize these universal conditions and processes. Yet, impressed by the facts of social and cultural differences among societies, they have failed to inquire into the qualities of the universal emergent: human nature. . . . Surely it is probable that psychic systems the world over have certain identical basic structures and functions organized around universal psychic needs.

The methodological arguments advanced against universal psychic needs attest only to the difficulty of determining their nature, not to their absence.

In American sociology at least as far back as Cooley there has been a current of stress upon universals that cut across all cultures. The fact that every human being, irrespective of culture, has had the experience of intimate association with "the primary group" upon whom he was emotionally and otherwise dependent has been held to lead to the so-called universal sentiments: love, jealousy, respect, need for respect, and the like. All moralities, if not built upon these sentiments, must at least take account of them. This total conception, although arising from a different perspective, comes out at about the same place as the psychoanalytic view. The universal sentiments leading to a "natural morality" have a biological basis but the resultant is sociological rather than biological.

Parsons and Shils,[15] in rejecting radical relativism, point to functional interdependencies and to the limitations of possibilities:

The exhaustive character of the classification of pattern variables has far-reaching implications for the analysis of systems of moral standards; it provides a determinate range of variability and it allows only a number of combinations of alternatives which—on this level of generality at least—is sufficiently small to permit analysis with the resources we possess at present. There has been a tendency, under the impact of insight into the wider range of differences among cultures, to think, implicitly at least, of a limitlessly pluralistic value-universe. In its extreme form, the proponents of this view have even asserted that every moral standard is necessarily unique. There is much aesthetic sensibility underlying and justifying this contention, but it is neither convincing logically not fruitful scientifically. If carried to its logical conclusions, it denies the possibility of systematic analysis of cultural values. In fact, of course, all patterns of moral standards are interdependent with all the other factors which operate in the determination of action.

Once again, although the language used and the data cited are different, there is marked congruence between certain recent sociological and psycho-

14"A Social-Psychological Conception of Human Freedom," *Ethics*, vol. 63, 1953, pp. 180–189.

15*Toward a General Theory of Action*, Cambridge, 1951, p. 171.

analytic views. Roheim (1950)[16] argues the limitation of possibilities in the light of the facts that human infants invariably are dependent, have two parents of opposite sex, face the emotional problems of being in competition with their siblings for the attention of these parents, and possess basically similar neurological mechanisms for defenses and otherwise dealing with their dilemmas. He (along with Rank, Abraham, Marie Bonaparte, and other psychoanalysts) mobilize evidence for psychic universals in myths and other culture forms. Roheim maintains that in addition to demonstrable universals there are many other "potential universals." Erich Fromm takes the same general line in many recent writings.

CULTURAL RELATIVITY

Edel[17] begins his discussion of this subject with a subhead, "The Vagueness of the Concept." Certainly it has been employed, by anthropologists and by others, in importantly different senses. Hartung[18] defines it along the lines of Benedict: "Cultural relativity . . . asserts that any set of customs and institutions, or way of life, is as valid as any other." But he leaves out what any anthropologist holding the relativity position would immediately add: "for a group living under certain circumstances and having had a particular history." Hartung's statement, as it stands, comes close to the popular vulgarization of the doctrine which suggests, for instance, that if pre-marital promiscuity is approved in a certain tribe this gives "validity" to such practices among any people.[19] No anthropologist would subscribe to this interpretation of cultural relativity. Quite the reverse, indeed, for the doctrine of cultural relativity demands, precisely, that one look within rather than without.

Macbeath, I believe, expresses the central and dominant anthropological view when he writes: ". . . the simplest self-contained unit of conduct, which can justify or render intelligible a final moral judgment, is a way of life as a whole, or at least a very substantial part of such a way of life."[20] To be sure, there are anthropological embroideries. Some anthropologists have stressed, and probably overstressed, the inherent dignity in each humanly created custom. Others have underlined the "functional" inter-connections between ethical standards and the specific nature of the economy[21] or environmental situation. A few have implicitly, and perhaps

---

[16]*Psychoanalysis and Anthropology,* New York. On p. 435 Roheim says firmly: ". . . the psychic unity of mankind is more than a working hypothesis, it is so obvious that it hardly requires proof." Cf. the statement by a French psychologist, O. Mannoni, Chapter VIII, "L'Unité Humaine," in *Psychologie de la Colonisation,* Paris, 1950.

[17]*Op. cit.,* p. 205.

[18]"Cultural Relativity and Moral Judgments," *Philosophy of Science,* vol. 21, 1954, p. 118.

[19]Actually, Hartung himself says: ". . . I could just as logically adopt the conventions of any other culture I chanced to learn about . . ." (p. 122).

[20]*Experiments in Living,* London, 1952.

[21]Cf. Walter Goldschmidt, "Ethics and the Structure of Society," *American Anthropologist,* vol. 53, 1951, pp. 506–524.

explicitly, advocated cultural relativity on the romantically tinged ground that the sheer variety of standards, including moral standards, added enormously to the richness and piquancy of the world. In some cases relativity is used to bolster a special kind of ethical absolutism.[22]

No anthropologist, however, doubts that the theory of cultural relativity is in some sense forced by the facts and meaningful. There is an exuberant variation in ethical codes, and surely a satisfactory interpretation of morality must be able to account for the moral judgments found in all cultures. Where anthropologists are not in full agreement is as to the extent to which this variation is basic or comparatively superficial. Is ethical *intent* very similar if not identical the world over? Are variations largely related to means rather than ends? Are means and some of the more proximate ends determined by historical accident and local circumstances? Is the whole picture needlessly confused by the local symbolisms for expressing ultimate goals and enforcing ultimate standards that are universal or near-universal?

Universals

From the anthropological viewpoint, the question as to whether there are ethical universals is a part of a larger question: Are these universals or near-universals of any sort that cut across cultural boundaries? There is good agreement that there are—in some form or other. In the 1911 edition of *The Mind of Primitive Man* Boas called Chapter VI "The Universality of Culture Traits." In the 1938 edition[23] he wrote:

The dynamic forces that mould social life are the same now as those that moulded life thousands of years ago. We can follow the intellectual and emotional drives that actuate man at present and that shape his actions and thoughts.

While Boas held, as do most psychologists and psychiatrists, that the needs of men and their "thought processes" are essentially the same throughout the world in time and space and hence give rise to similar cultural forms such as values, Wissler was almost the only one of his associates or students who devoted empirical attention to this question. In *Man and Culture*[24] Wissler wrote a chapter on "The Universal Culture Pattern" in which he showed that the "ground plan" of all cultures is very similar. More recently, Murdock,[25] Kluckhohn,[26] and Trimborn[27] have examined these issues both conceptually and empirically. And Leslie White,[28] Gordon Childe,[29] and

22Cf. Edel, *op. cit.*, p. 209.
23New York, p. 195.
24New York, 1923.
25"The Common Denominator of Cultures," in *The Science of Man in the World Crisis* (R. Linton, ed.), New York, 1945.
26"Universal Categories of Culture," in *Anthropology Today*, Chicago, 1953.
27*Das Menschliche ist Gleich im Urgrund aller Kulturen*, Braunschweig, 1949 (Beiträge zum Geschichtsunterricht, No. 9).
28See, for example, "Energy and the Evolution of Culture," *American Anthropologist*, vol. 45, 1943, pp. 335–356.
29See, for example, *Social Evolution*, London and New York, 1951.

Julian Steward[30] have looked specifically at environmental, technological, and economic "determination" of cultural similarities.

That music, graphic arts, dancing, parallels in linguistic structure, standards of personal excellence, kinship terminology, such categories as age grading and many other formal similarities exist in all known cultures no one questions. Nor, on the other hand, does anyone dispute that such resemblances as approach universality are broad likenesses rather than concrete identities. Argument centers on three questions: (1) How numerous are these similarities? (2) Are they just "empty frames" which do not enable us to escape from the impasse of complete cultural relativity? (3) Are they cultural or subcultural or the "conditions for culture"? On the first question not much can be said at present beyond the fact that not enough research has been done to give more than an impressionistic answer.

The next two questions can be considered together. Professor Kroeber writes:[31]

> ... such more or less recurrent near-regularities of form or process as have to date been formulated for culture are actually mainly subcultural in nature. They are limits set to culture by physical or organic factors. The so-called "cultural constants" of family, religion, war, communication, and the like appear to be biopsychological frames variably filled with cultural content. ...

Since cultures include organization as well as content, I myself would include these "frames" as part of culture. They are incorporated—admittedly with variable content in detail—into ways of life and socially transmitted as part of the total tradition. In any case whether these phenomena are cultural or subcultural is, for purposes of the present paper, an academic haggle.

What is significant is that such categories remove cultures from the status of completely isolated monads and make some valid comparisons possible. While scientific analysis commonly unites what the lay mind distinguishes and separates what "common sense" groups together, these broad similarities at very least provide a starting point for valid comparison. Here I stand with Levi-Strauss[32] in his reply to some earlier strictures of Kroeber's upon "fake universals":

> Indeed, if behind such broad categories as Sacrifice, or Gifts, or Suicide, there are not at least some characters which are common to all forms—among, of course, many others which are different—, and if this does not allow the use of those categories as starting points for the analysis, then sociology may as well abandon every pretention to become scientific, and the sociologist must be resigned to pile up descriptions of individual groups, without any hope that the pile shall ever become of any use, except, perhaps, to cultural history. ...

[30]See, for example, "Cultural Causality and Law," *American Anthropologist*, vol. 51, 1949, pp. 1–27.

[31]"The Concept of Culture in Science," *Journal of General Education*, vol. 35, 1949, p. 188.

[32]"French Sociology," in *Twentieth Century Sociology* (Gurvitch and Moore, eds.), New York, 1945, pp. 525–526.

When Durkheim studies division of labor, it is in order to reach such abstract, hidden categories as "organic solidarity" and "mechanical solidarity"; when he analyzes suicide, he formulates the notion of integration of individual to the group; when Mauss undertakes a comparison between the different types of gifts, it is to discover, behind the more diversified types, the fundamental idea of reciprocity; when he follows the transformation of the psychological conceptions of the "Ego," it is in order to establish a relation between social forms and the concept of personality. These categories may be good or bad; they may prove useful or be wrongly chosen but. . . . They do not resemble the categories of "long," "flat," or "round," but rather such categories as "dilation," "ondulation," or "viscosity," of which the physicist has precisely made his study.

Linton[33] is squarely in the mainstream of contemporary anthropological opinion when he says: "Behind the seemingly endless diversity of culture patterns there is a fundamental uniformity."

Ethical Universals

The first thing to note is the universality of moral standards in general. To the philosopher and social scientist this generalization may appear too commonplace to require comment. But the universality may not strike the general zoologist as so obvious. Not only is *human* social life inevitably a moral life in theory and to a large extent in practice, but ethical principles are the fundament of most of the rest of the culture. Fortes[34] remarks:

Every social system presupposes such basic moral axioms . . . these axioms are rooted in the direct experience of the inevitability of interdependence between men in society. . . . The focal field of kinship is also the focal field of moral experience.

Every culture has a concept of murder, distinguishing this from execution, killing in war, and other "justifiable homicides." The notions of incest and other regulations upon sexual behavior, of prohibitions upon untruth under defined circumstances, of restitution and reciprocity, of mutual obligations between parents and children—these and many other moral concepts are altogether universal. The philosopher James Feibleman[35] goes a bit further than most anthropologists would in saying:

. . . the context of ethical values, as of other values, changes constantly; but the values have a striking similarity and even, we strongly suspect, an identity.

Anthropologists are more comfortable with a treatment like Linton's,[36] which emphasizes that the likenesses are primarily conceptual and that variation rages rampant as to details of prescribed behavior, instrumentalities, and sanctions. This is important as is also the fact that universality

33"Universal Ethical Principles: An Anthropological View," in *Moral Principles of Action* (Ruth Anshen, ed.), New York, 1952, p. 646.

34*The Web of Kinship Among the Tallensi*, Oxford, 1949, p. 346.

35"Introduction to an Objective, Empirical Ethics," *Ethics*, vol. 55, 1955, p. 106.

36"The Problem of Universal Values," in *Method and Perspective in Anthropology* (R. F. Spencer, ed.), Minneapolis, 1954, pp. 150–152, 166.

as such is not transmutable into a categorical imperative. Pascal's suggestion that moral canons exist in spite of such empirical universals may be correct in certain instances.

Universality may be due, or largely due, to diffusion or other historical accident. Universality may reflect the general moral immaturity of the human species. That is, present agreements may in some instances indicate no more than that human cultures have thus far evolved only to a roughly similar moral stage. Near-universality in other cases may mean only that there are many "sick societies." Nor does the fact that the simple but basic wants of all men are similar lead us inevitably to sweetness and light. It has made and can continue to make for bitter struggles for scarce goods. Similarly, as everyone knows, some of the worst wars in history have been fought not over "final" goals but rather over "means." Nevertheless the universalities in wants[37] and the universals and near-universals in moral concepts do generate two fairly cheerful propositions:

First, the similarities in human needs and human response-potentialities across cultures do at any rate greatly heighten the possibilities of cross-cultural communication once these core likenesses have been somewhat disentangled from their cultural wrappings;

Second, while we must not glibly equate universals with absolutes, the existence of a universal certainly raises this question: If, in spite of biological variation and historical and environmental diversities, we find these congruences, is there not a presumptive likelihood that these moral principles somehow correspond to inevitabilities, given the nature of the human organism and of the human situation? They may at any rate lead us to "conditional absolutes" or "moving absolutes," not in the metaphysical but in the empirical sense.

Discussion

Psychology, psychiatry, sociology, and anthropology in different ways and on somewhat different evidence converge in attesting to similar human needs and psychic mechanisms.[38] These, plus the rough regularities in the human situation regardless of culture, give rise to widespread moral principles which are very much alike in concept—in "intent." These considerations make the position of radical cultural relativity untenable. Indeed this view when pressed to its logical extreme soon reaches absurdity. If one is to evaluate an act or a moral judgment *entirely* by its context, it is inescapable that no two contexts are literally identical. And yet the brute fact is that the members of all societies create and are influenced by principles of some generality, by moral abstractions. Human beings generalize as well as discriminate. The human parade has many floats, but, when one

---

[37]Cf. Feibleman, *op. cit.*, pp. 106, 110.

[38]It has often been noted that, while culturally patterned behavior varies regularly, responses to totally new and unfamiliar situations may be fundamentally the same (i.e., at "raw human" level) in societies of quite diverse type.

strips off the cultural symbolism, the ethical standards represented are akin. The ostensible self-effacement of the Zuni and the exhibitionism of the Kwakiutl affirm the same moral value: allegiance to the norms of one's culture.

To be sure, there must be room left for relativity as regards specific moral rules—for what Macbeath calls the "operative ideals" of each distinct culture. Zuni and Kwakiutl behavior manifest at least one generic value in common. The variations in ideal-typical behavior in the two cases also, of course, reflect certain other values distinctive of the two cultures. The indeterminacy here may well appreciably diminish as science spreads throughout the whole world. If there is any "pan" movement in the world today, sweeping behind both "curtains" and into the "uncommitted third," this is science. And, as Hocking has remarked, if there is to be a common science in the world there will also arise, to some extent, a common conscience. Event then, however, *both* within[39] and between cultures moral behavior in specific instances and in all its details must be judged within a wide context *but with reference to principles which are not relative.*[40] This combines what R. B. Perry and P. B. Rice have called virtuous relativism and virtuous absolutism, though I much prefer "virtuous relativity" because the word "relativism" seems to imply the utter incommensurability of the entities.

Meanwhile, are there any criteria which can aid us to choose between varying forms of the same moral principles, between those principles which are in fact different, between contrasting hierarchies of principles? I believe there are, while granting fully that each remains to be worked out more adequately. First, I am attracted by Northrop's idea that the primitive concepts and primitive postulates of moral systems must be concordant with natural science knowledge. This is no naive "social Darwinism" which identifies the "is" with the "ought," attempting to derive ethics directly from science. Rather, this view correctly insists that in the world of real experience there is never a complete divorce between cognitive and existential propositions, that in the chains of feeling and reasoning that actually occur these two categories link in interdependence. Therefore, a morality based upon a theory that human nature is innately evil or innately good ought to check its primary existential premise against the observations the child psychologist makes of newborn infants, their tendencies and propensities. Just as there are some "psychic necessities" that are to a large degree autonomous, comparatively independent of each specific culture, so also it is possible in principle to check the logical and cognitive underpinnings of ethics against facts

[39]Because each culture must allow for the differentiation of individuals, tolerating and indeed supporting psychological minorities as long as this pluralism does not violate universal morality.

[40]Cf. Macbeath, *op. cit.,* p. 17: "If, then, the principle of moral judgment is the same everywhere, any account of it which is to be satisfactory must show that it is consistent with this diversity of moral judgments, that indeed the different moral judgments are really expressions of the same principle having regard to the different conditions and beliefs and cultures of those who pass them."

that are independent of culture. I have cautiously chosen a restricted application of Northrop's general thesis on natural science. I believe, however, that
different cosmological standpoints are relevant to moral systems, though the
relation may be both more vague and more complicated than Northrop has
argued.

Second, although confessing to some scepticism as to whether this be
Kant's categorical imperative in thin anthropological disguise, I think there
is something worth careful consideration in Macbeath's[41] theorem:

Any way of life whose general structure or scale of value does not admit
of being extended to mankind as a whole, without denying the common humanity
of some men and their right to be treated as persons, must be regarded as
unsatisfactory; and the more remodelling it needs to make this extension possible,
the more unsatisfactory it is.

This I would provisionally accept, provided it not be taken to apply to those
"secondary" moral categories that correspond to "taste" and to the deter-
minations produced by unique history and situation. However, not all culturally created values are of equal validity.

Finally, I subscribe—at least as an eventuality—to Anatol Rapa-
port's[42] thesis that "objective relativism" can lead to the development of
truly explicit and truly universal moral canons:

. . . it is incorrect to say that the scientific outlook is simply a by-product of a
particular culture. It is rather the essence of a culture which has not yet been
established—a culture-studying culture. Ironically, the anthropologists who often
are most emphatic in stating that no non-cultural standards of evaluation exist
are among the most active builders of this new culture-studying culture, whose
standards transcend those of the cultures which the anthropologists study and
thus give them an opportunity to emancipate themselves from the limitations of
the local standards. . . .

The moral attitudes contained in the scientific outlook have a different
genesis from those contained in ordinary "unconscious" cultures. They are a result
of a "freer choice," because they involve a deeper insight into the consequences
of the choice.

"Objective relativity" will increasingly be a corrective to the ethnocentrism
of all cultures, loosening their rigidities, but does not necessarily—or logically—lead to nihilism. What is right for Hindus in 1955 may not be precisely the same as what is right for Americans in 1955 but it will be of the
same *kind*—which is only a rephrasing of Plato's argument in the *Republic*.
Relativity has an indispensable place in judging acts in all their concreteness
but must be balanced by universality as regards the broad issues of principle,
especially those at a higher level of generality. Some values are invariant.
Certain of these we know already. Others will be discovered[43] by a combination of further empirical research and sound analysis. "Residual indeter-

41*Op. cit.*, p. 436.
42*Science and the Goals of Man*, New York, 1950, pp. 232-233.
43Cf. Edel, *op. cit.*, p. 294.

minacy"[44] will thereby be decreased. Radical relativity exaggerated the significance of outward form and of the historically determined accidentals in human cultures. While the specific manifestations of human nature vary between cultures and between individuals in the same culture, human nature is universal. All value systems have to make some of the same concessions to the natural world of which human nature is a part. Some needs and motives are so deep and so generic that they are beyond the reach of argument: pan-human morality expresses and supports them. Hence there must be respect alike for individual and cultural differences and for the more embracing needs and norms which must be commonly met. Principles as well as contexts must be taken into account.

Man "is capable of satisfying his biologically and culturally derived needs in a variety of ways."[45] But this relativity of proximate means does not imply that some goals are not salient for mankind in general. Nor should tolerance of a variety of means suggest any rejection of a passionate and uncompromising affirmation of pan-human ends. And these ends may change through time in important particulars. As Steward[46] says:

> Evolutionism is distinguished from relativism by the fact that the former attributes qualitative distinctiveness to successive stages, regardless of the particular tradition, whereas the latter attributes it to the particular tradition rather than to the development stage.

I believe that further progress on this difficult question of ethical relativity will be achieved by a combination of hard-headed empirical research with a theoretical analysis which begs as few metaphysical questions as possible. The "oughts" in all cultures (and the sanctions attached thereto) are observable and formulable in "is" terms. The existence of empirical universals or near-universals should be known as fully as possible. Each exception to a general rule poses a specific problem but a problem of a somewhat different order. The traits of a zoological species are not the less objective or in a sense "universal" because of the occasional birth of "sports" or monstrosities.

The present position is that neither extreme relativism nor extreme absolutism is tenable as a guiding hypothesis for further empirical enquiry. The contribution of behavioral scientists has made essential the use both of the concepts of universality and of relativity in the investigation of human acts in their cross-cultural dimension. Much remains to be done. Especially we require operational techniques for controlling differences of meaning among apparently similar values and for validating similarities when the phenomena appear quite various to the eye of the naive observer. And the sheer demonstration of empirical universals does not, of course, settle any question of absolutes or right or wrong. It is a significant step and would seem to place the burden of proof upon those who would deprecate such

---

44*Ibid.*, p. 337.

45E. T. Hall and G. L. Trager, *The Analysis of Culture*, Washington, 1953, p. 2.

46"Evolution and Process," in *Anthropology Today* (A. L. Kroeber, ed.), Chicago, 1953, p. 314.

values. But, in the main, such proof of universals will merely pose further questions. We must move from description to the testing of hypotheses, from positions to defend to searching for facts that will verify or reject a position. Both extremes have had their chance to speculate, to reason, and to speak out. The proper formulation of the elements of truth in these two extremes, forged in the teeth of the stubborn and irreducible facts now available, will require the cooperation of philosophers and behavioral scientists to the end of carefully pointed empirical investigations that may gradually settle the issues.

❀ ABRAHAM H. MASLOW

33. A Psychologist's Suggestions Towards A Universal Ethic

Abraham H. Maslow (1908–1970) was a professor of psychology at Brandeis University. He was the author of numerous articles and books, including *Motivation and Personality* (1954), *Toward a Psychology of Being* (1962), *Religions, Values and Peak-Experiences* (1964), and *Psychology of Science* (1966).

Humanists for thousands of years have attempted to construct a naturalistic, psychological value system that could be derived from man's own nature, without the necessity of recourse to authority outside the human being himself. Many such theories have been offered throughout history. They have all failed for mass purposes exactly as all other value theories have failed. We have about as many scoundrels in the world today as we have ever had, and *many more* neurotic, probably, than we have ever had.

These inadequate theories, most of them, rested on psychological assumptions of one sort or another. Today practically all of these can be shown, in the light of recently acquired knowledge, to be false, inadequate, incomplete, or in some other way lacking. But it is my belief that developments in the science and art of psychology, in the last few decades, make it possible for us for the first time to feel confident that this age-old hope may be fulfilled if only we work hard enough. We know how to criticize the old theories, we know, even though dimly, the shape of the theories to come, and, most of all, we know where to look and what to do in order to fill in

Reprinted from *Toward a Psychology of Being*, 2nd edition, by Abraham H. Maslow, ⓒ 1968 Litton Educational Publishing, Inc. Reprinted by permission of Van Nostrand Reinhold Company.

Selected from an address presented at a conference of the Research Society for Creative Altruism on Oct. 4, 1957, at the Massachusetts Institute of Technology. This address has been published in *New Knowledge in Human Values*, Harper & Brothers, New York, 1959. Footnotes renumbered.

the gaps in knowledge, that will permit us to answer the age-old questions, "What is the good life? What is the good man? How can people be taught to desire and prefer the good life? How ought children to be brought up to be sound adults?, etc." That is, we think that a scientific ethic may be possible, and we think we know how to go about constructing it.

The following section will discuss briefly a few of the promising lines of evidence and of research, their relevance to past and future value theories, along with a discussion of the theoretical and factual advances we must make in the near future. Since my space is too short to assay the level of confidence of these various data, I think it safer to judge them all as more or less probable rather than as certain.

Free Choice Experiments: Homeostasis

Hundreds of experiments have been made that demonstrate a universal inborn ability in all sorts of animals to select a beneficial diet if enough alternatives are presented from among which they are permitted free choice. This wisdom of the body is often retained under less usual conditions, e.g., adrenalectomized animals can keep themselves alive by readjusting their self-chosen diet, pregnant animals will nicely adjust their diets to the needs of the growing embryo, etc.

We now know this is by no means a perfect wisdom. These appetites are less efficient, for instance, in reflecting body need for vitamins. Lower animals protect themselves against poisons more efficiently than higher animals and humans. Previously formed habits of preference may quite overshadow present metabolic needs.[1] And most of all, in the human being, and especially in the neurotic human being, all sorts of forces can contaminate this wisdom of the body, although it never seems to be lost altogether.

The general principle is true not only for selection of food but also for all sorts of other body needs, as the famous homeostasis experiments have shown.[2]

It seems quite clear that all organisms are more self-governing, self-regulating, and autonomous than we thought twenty-five years ago. The organism deserves a good deal of trust and we are learning steadily to rely on this internal wisdom of our babies with reference to choice of diet, time of weaning, amount of sleep, time of toilet training, need for activity, and a lot else.

But more recently we have been learning, especially from physically and mentally sick people, that there are good choosers and bad choosers. We have learned, especially from the psychoanalysts, much about the hidden causes of such behavior and have learned to respect these causes.

In this connection we have available a startling experiment,[3] which

[1]P. T. Young, "The Experimental Analysis of Appetite," Psychol. Bull., 1941, 38:129–164.

[2]W. B. Cannon, Wisdom of the Body, Norton, 1932.

[3]W. F. Dove, "A Study of Individuality in the Nutritive Instincts; of the Causes and Effects of Variation in the Selection of Food," Amer. Nat., 1935, 69:469–544.

we have been trying to repeat at Brandeis, that is pregnant with implications for value theory. It turns out that chickens allowed to choose their own diet vary widely in their ability to choose what is good for them. The good choosers become stronger, larger, more dominant than the poor choosers, which means that they get the best of everything. If then the diet chosen by the good choosers is forced upon the poor choosers, it is found that *they* now get stronger, bigger, healthier, and more dominant, although never reaching the level of the good choosers. That is, good choosers can choose better than bad choosers what is better for the bad choosers themselves. If similar findings are made in human beings, as I think they will be, we are in for a good deal of reconstruction of all sorts of theories. So far as human value theory is concerned, no theory will be adequate that rests simply on the statistical description of the choices of unselected human beings. To average the choices of good and bad choosers, of healthy and sick people is useless. Only the choices and tastes and judgments of healthy human beings will tell us much about what is good for the human species in the long run. The choices of neurotic people can tell us mostly what is good for keeping a neurosis stabilized, just as the choices of a brain-injured man are good for preventing a catastrophic breakdown, or as the choices of an adrenalectomized animal may keep *him* from dying but would kill a healthy animal.

I think that this is the main reef on which most hedonistic value theories and ethical theories have foundered. Pathological motivated pleasures cannot be averaged with healthily motivated pleasures.

Furthermore, any ethical code will have to deal with the fact of constitutional differences not only in chickens and rats but also in men, as Sheldon[4] and Morris[5] have shown. Some values are common to all (healthy) mankind, but also some other values will *not* be common to all mankind, but only to some types of people, or to specific individuals. What I have called the basic needs are probably common to all mankind and are therefore shared values. But idiosyncratic needs generate idiosyncratic values.

Constitutional differences in individuals generate preferences among ways of relating to self, and to culture and to the world, *i.e.*, generate values. These researches support and are supported by the universal experience of clinicians with individual differences. This is also true of the ethnological data that make sense of cultural diversity by postulating that each culture selects for exploitation, suppression, approval or disapproval, a small segment of the range of human constitutional possibilities. This is all in line with the biological data and theories and self-actualization theories which show that an organ system presses to express itself, in a word, to function. The muscular person likes to use his muscles, indeed, *has* to use them in order to self-actualize and to achieve the subjective feeling of harmonious,

[4] W. Sheldon, *The Varieties of Temperament*, Harper, 1942.
[5] C. Morris, *Varieties of Human Value*, University of Chicago Press, 1956.

uninhibited, satisfying functioning which is so important an aspect of psychological health. People with intelligence must use their intelligence, people with eyes must use their eyes, people with the capacity to love have the *impulse* to love and the *need* to love in order to feel healthy. Capacities clamor to be used, and cease their clamor only when they *are* used sufficiently. That is to say, capacities are needs, and therefore are intrinsic values as well. To the extent that capacities differ, so will values also differ.

Basic Needs and Their Hierarchical Arrangement

It has by now been sufficiently demonstrated that the human being has, as part of his intrinsic construction, not only physiological needs, but also truly psychological ones. They may be considered as deficiencies which must be optimally fulfilled by the environment to avoid sickness and to avoid subjective ill-being. They can be called basic, or biological, and likened to the need for salt, or calcium or vitamin D because:

1. The person yearns for their gratification persistently.
2. Their deprivation makes the person sicken and wither, or stunts his growth.
3. Gratifying them is therapeutic, curing the deficiency-illness.
4. Steady supplies forestall these illnesses.
5. Healthy people do not demonstrate these deficiencies.

But these needs or values are related to each other in a hierarchical and developmental way, in an order of strength and of priority. Safety is a more prepotent, or stronger, more pressing, earlier appearing, more vital need than love, for instance, and the need for food is usually stronger than either. Furthermore *all* these basic needs may be considered to be simply steps along the time path to general self-actualization, under which all basic needs can be subsumed.

By taking these data into account, we can solve many value problems that philosophers have struggled with ineffectually for centuries. For one thing, it looks as if *there were* a single ultimate value for mankind, a far goal toward which all men strive. This is called variously by different authors self-actualization, self-realization, integration, psychological health, individuation, autonomy, creativity, productivity, but they all agree that this amounts to realizing the potentialities of the person, that is to say, becoming fully human, everything that the person *can* become.

But it is also true that the person himself does not know this. We, the psychologists observing and studying, have constructed this concept in order to integrate and explain lots of diverse data. So far as the person himself is concerned, all *he* knows is that he is desperate for love, and thinks he will be forever happy and content if he gets it. He does not know in advance that he will strive on *after* this gratification has come, and that gratification of one basic need opens consciousness to domination by another, "higher" need. So far as he is concerned, *the* absolute, ultimate value, synonymous with life itself, is whichever need in the hierarchy he is dominated by during a particular period. These basic needs or basic values therefore may be treated *both* as ends and as steps toward a single end-goal. It is true that there is a single, ultimate value or end of life, and *also* it is just as true that we have a hierarchical and developmental system of values, complexly interrelated.

This also helps to solve the apparent paradox of contrast between Being and Becoming. It is true that human beings strive perpetually toward ultimate humanness, which itself is anyway a different kind of Becoming and growing. It's as if we were doomed forever to try to arrive at a state to which we could never attain. Fortunately we now know this not to be true, or at least it is not the only truth. There is another truth which integrates with it. We are again and again rewarded for good Becoming by transient states of absolute Being, which I have summarized as peak-experiences. Achieving basic-need gratifications gives us many peak-experiences, each of which are absolute delights, perfect in themselves, and needing no more than themselves to validate life. This is like rejecting the notion that a Heaven lies someplace beyond the end of the path of life. Heaven, so to speak, lies waiting for us throughout life, ready to step into for a time and to enjoy before we have to come back to our ordinary life of striving. And once we have been in it, we can remember it forever, and feed ourselves on this memory and be sustained in time of stress.[6]

Not only this, but the process of moment to moment growth is itself intrinsically rewarding and delightful in an absolute sense. If they are not mountain peak-experiences, at least they are foothill-experiences, little glimpses of absolute, self-validative delights, little moments of Being. Being and Becoming are *not* contradictory or mutually exclusive. Approaching and arriving are both in themselves rewarding.[7]

I should make it clear here that I want to differentiate the Heaven ahead (of growth and transcendence) from the "Heaven" behind (of regression). The "high Nirvana" is very different in important ways from the "low Nirvana" even though most clinicians confuse them because they are also similar in some ways.

SELF-ACTUALIZATION: GROWTH

I have published in another place a survey of all the evidence that forces us in the direction of a concept of healthy growth or of self-actualizing tendencies.[8] This is partly deductive evidence in the sense of pointing out that, unless we postulate such a concept, much of human behavior makes no sense. This is on the same scientific principle that led to the discovery of a hitherto unseen planet that *had* to be there in order to make sense of a lot of other observed data.

[6]A. H. Maslow, "Cognition of Being in the Peak Experiences," *Journal of Genetic Psychology*, 1959. In press.

[7]A. H. Maslow, "Defense and Growth," *Merrill-Palmer Quarterly*, 1956, 36–47.

[8]A. H. Maslow, *Motivation and Personality*, Harper, 1954.

There is also some direct evidence, or rather the beginnings of direct evidence which needs much more research, to get to the point of certainty. The only direct study of self-actualizing people I know is the one I made,[9] and it is a very shaky business to rest on just one study made by just one person when we take into account the known pitfalls of sampling error, of wish-fulfillment, of projection, etc. However, the conclusions of this study have been so strongly paralleled in the clinical and philosophical conclusions of Rogers, of Fromm, of Goldstein, of Angyal, of Murray, of C. Bühler, of Horney, Jung, Nuttin, and many others that I shall proceed under the assumption that more careful research will not contradict my findings radically. We can certainly now assert that at least a reasonable, theoretical, and empirical case has been made for the presence within the human being of a tendency toward, or need for, growing in a direction that can be summarized in general as self-actualization, or psychological health or maturation, and specifically as growth toward each and all of the sub-aspects of self-actualization. That is to say, the human being has within him a pressure (among other pressures) toward unity of personality, toward spontaneous expressiveness, toward full individuality and identity, toward seeing the truth rather than being blind, toward being creative, toward being good, and a lot else. That is, the human being is so constructed that he presses toward fuller and fuller being and this means pressing toward what most people would call good values, toward serenity, kindness, courage, knowledge, honesty, love, unselfishness, and goodness.

Few in number though they be, we can learn a great deal from the direct study of these highly evolved, most mature, psychologically healthiest individuals, and from the study of the peak moments of average individuals, moments in which they become transiently self-actualized. This is because they are in very real empirical and theoretical ways, *most fully human.* For instance, they are people who have retained and developed all their human capacities, especially those capacities which define the human being and differentiate him from let us say the monkey. (This accords with Hartman's[10] axiological approach to the same problem of defining the good human being as the one who has more of the characteristics which define the concept "human being.") From a developmental point of view, they are more fully evolved because not fixated at immature or incomplete levels of growth. This is no more mysterious, or *a priori,* or question-begging than the selection of a type specimen of butterfly by a taxonomist or the most physically healthy young man by the physician. They both look for the "perfect or mature or magnificent specimen" for the exemplar, and so have I. One procedure is as repeatable in principle as the other.

Full humanness can be defined not only in terms of the degree to which the definition of the concept "human" is fulfilled, *i.e.,* the species

[9] *Ibid.*
[10] R. S. Hartman, *The Structure of Value,* forthcoming.

norm. It also has a descriptive, cataloguing, measurable, psychological definition. We now have from a few research beginnings and from countless
clinical experiences some notion of the characteristics both of the fully
evolved human being and of the well-growing human being. These characteristics are not only neutrally describable; they are also subjectively
rewarding, and pleasurable and reinforcing.

Among the objectively describable and measurable characteristics
of the healthy human specimen are:

1. Clearer, more efficient perception of reality.
2. More openness to experience.
3. Increased integration, wholeness, and unity of the person.
4. Increased spontaneity, expressiveness; full functioning; aliveness.
5. A real self; a firm identity; autonomy; uniqueness.
6. Increased objectivity, detachment, transcendence of self.
7. Recovery of creativeness.
8. Ability to fuse concreteness and abstractness, primary and secondary process cognition, etc.
9. Democratic character structure.
10. Ability to love, etc.

These all need research confirmation and exploration but it is clear
that such researches are feasible.

In addition, there are subjective confirmations or reinforcements of
self-actualization or of good growth toward it. These are the feelings of zest
in living, of happiness or euphoria, of serenity, of joy, of calmness, of responsibility, of confidence in one's ability to handle stresses, anxieties, and problems. The subjective signs of self-betrayal, of fixation, of regression, and of
living by fear rather than by growth are such feelings as anxiety, despair,
bordom, inability to enjoy, intrinsic guilt, intrinsic shame, aimlessness,
feelings of emptiness, of lack of identity, etc.

These subjective reactions are also susceptible of research exploration. We have clinical techniques available for studying them.

It is the free choices of such self-actualizing people (in those situations where real choice is possible from among a variety of possibilities) that
I claim can be descriptively studied as a naturalistic value system with which
the hopes of the observer absolutely have nothing to do, *i.e.*, it is "scientific."
I do not say "He *ought* to choose this or that" but only "Healthy people,
permitted to choose, are *observed* to choose this or that." This is like asking
"What *are* the values of the best human beings" rather than "What *should*
be their values?" or "What *ought* they do?" (Compare this with Aristotle's
belief that "it is the things which are valuable and pleasant to a good man
that are really valuable and pleasant.")

Furthermore I think these findings can be generalized to most of
the human species because it looks to me (and to others) as if *all* or most
people tend toward self-actualization (this is seen most clearly in the experiences in psychotherapy, especially of the uncovering sort), and as if, in
principle at least, all people are capable of self-actualization. . . .

THE PROBLEM OF CONTROLS AND LIMITS

Another problem confronting the morals-from-within theorists is to account for the easy self-discipline which is customarily found in self-actualizing, authentic, genuine people and which is *not* found in average people.

In these healthy people we find duty and pleasure to be the same thing, as are also work and play, self-interest and altruism, individualism and selflessness. We know they *are* that way, but not how they *get* that way. I have the clear impression that such authentic, fully human persons are the actualization of what *any* human being could be. And yet we are confronted with the sad fact that so few people achieve this goal, perhaps only one in a hundred, or two hundred. We can be hopeful for mankind because in principle anyone *could* become a good and healthy man. But we must also feel sad because so few actually *do* become good men. If we wish to find out why some do and some don't, then the research problem presents itself of studying the life history of self-actualizing men to find out how they get that way.

We know already that the main prerequisite of healthy growth is gratification of the basic needs, especially in early life. (Neurosis is very often a deficiency disease, like avitaminosis.) But we have *also* learned that unbridled indulgence and gratification has its own dangerous consequences, *e.g.*, psychopathic personality, irresponsibility, inability to bear stress, spoiling, immaturity, certain character disorders. Research findings are rare, but there is now available a large store of clinical and educational experience which allows us to make a reasonable guess that the young child needs not only gratification; he needs also to learn the limitations that the physical world puts upon his gratifications, and he has to learn that other human beings seek for gratifications, too, even his mother and father, *i.e.*, they are not only means to his ends. This means control, delay, limits, renunciation, frustration-tolerance, and discipline. Only to the self-disciplined and responsible person can we say, "Do as you will, and it will probably be all right."

REGRESSIVE FORCES: PSYCHOPATHOLOGY

And now we must face the problem of what stands in the way of growth; that is to say, the problems of cessation of growth and evasion of growth, of fixation, regression, and defensiveness, in a word, the attractiveness of psychopathology, or, as other people would prefer to say, the problem of evil.

Why do so many people have no real identity, so little power to make their own decisions and choices?

1. These impulses and directional tendencies toward self-fulfillment, though instinctive, are very weak, so that, in contrast with all other animals who have strong instincts, these impulses are very easily drowned out by habit, by wrong cultural attitudes toward them, by traumatic episodes, by erroneous education. Therefore, the problem of choice and of responsibility is far, far more acute in humans than in any other species.

2. There has been a special tendency in Western culture, historically determined, to assume that these instinctoid needs of the human being, his so-called animal nature, are bad or evil. As a consequence, many cultural institutions are set up for the express purpose of controlling, inhibiting, suppressing and repressing this original nature of man.[11]

3. There are two sets of forces pulling at the individual, not just one.[12] In addition to the pressures forward toward health, there are also regressive pressures backward, toward sickness and weakness. We can either move forward toward a "high Nirvana," or backward to a "low Nirvana."

I think the main factual defect in the value theories and ethical theories of the past and present has been insufficient knowledge of psychopathology and psychotherapy. Throughout history, learned men have set out before mankind the rewards of virtue, the beauties of goodness, the intrinsic desirability of psychological health and self-fulfillment. It's all as plain as ABC, and yet most people perversely refuse to step into the happiness and self-respect that is offered them. Nothing is left to the teachers but irritation, impatience, disillusionment, alternations between scolding, exhortation, and hopelessness. A good many have thrown up their hands altogether and talked about original sin or intrinsic evil and concluded that man could be saved only by extrahuman forces.

Meanwhile there lies available the huge, rich, and illuminating literature of dynamic psychology and psychopathology, a great store of information on man's weaknesses, and fears.[13] We know much about *why* men do wrong things, *why* they bring about their own unhappiness and their self-destruction, *why* they are perverted and sick. And out of this has come the insight that human evil is largely human weakness, forgivable, understandable and also, in principle, curable.

I find it sometimes amusing, sometimes saddening that so many scholars and scientists, so many philosophers and theologians, who talk about human values, of good and evil, proceed in complete disregard of the plain fact that professional psychotherapists every day, as a matter of course, change and improve human nature, help people to become more strong, virtuous, creative, kind, loving altruistic, serene. These are only some of the consequences of improved self-knowledge and self-acceptance. There are many others as well that can come in greater or lesser degree.[14]

The subject is far too complex even to touch here. All I can do is draw a few conclusions for value theory.

1. Self-knowledge seems to be the major path of self-improvement, though not the only one.

2. Self-knowledge and self-improvement are very difficult for most people. They usually need great courage and long struggle.

[11]A. H. Maslow, *Motivation and Personality;* A. M. Montagu, *The Direction of Human Development,* Harper, 1955.

[12]A. H. Maslow, "Defense and Growth," 36–47.

[13]O. Fenichel, *The Psychoanalytic Theory of Neuroses,* Norton, 1945.

[14]C. Rogers, *Client-Centered Therapy,* Houghton Mifflin, 1951.

3. Though the help of a skilled professional therapist makes this process much easier, it is by no means the only way. Much that has been learned from therapy can be applied to education, to family life, and to the guidance of one's own life.

4. Only by such study of psychopathology and therapy can one learn a proper respect for and appreciation of the forces of fear, of regression, of defense, of safety. Respecting and understanding these forces makes it much more possible to help oneself and others to grow toward health. False optimism sooner or later means disillusionment, anger and hopelessness.

5. To sum up, we can never really understand human weakness without also understanding human health. Otherwise we make the mistake of pathologizing everything. But also we can never fully understand or help human strength without also understanding human weakness. Otherwise we fall into the errors of overoptimistic reliance on rationality alone.

If we wish to help humans to become more fully human, we must realize not only that they try to realize themselves but that they are also reluctant or afraid or unable to do so. Only by fully appreciating this dialectic between sickness and health can we help to tip the balance in favor of health.

❀ UNITED NATIONS CHARTER

34. *The Universal Declaration of Human Rights*

PREAMBLE

Whereas recognition of the inherent dignity and of the equal and inalienable rights of all members of the human family is the foundation of freedom, justice and peace in the world,

Whereas disregard and contempt for human rights have resulted in barbarous acts which have outraged the conscience of mankind, and the advent of a world in which human beings shall enjoy freedom of speech and belief and freedom from fear and want has been proclaimed as the highest aspiration of the common people,

Whereas it is essential, if man is not to be compelled to have recourse, as a last resort, to rebellion against tyranny and oppression, that human rights should be protected by the rule of law,

Whereas it is essential to promote the development of friendly relations between nations,

Complete text adopted on December 10, 1948, by the General Assembly of United Nations.

Whereas the people of the United Nations have in the Charter re-affirmed their faith in fundamental human rights, in the dignity and worth of the human person and in the equal rights of men and women and have determined to promote social progress and better standards of life in larger freedom,

Whereas Member States have pledged themselves to achieve, in co-operation with the United Nations, the promotion of universal respect for and observance of human rights and fundamental freedoms,

Whereas a common understanding of these rights and freedoms is of the greatest importance for the full realization of this pledge,

Now, Therefore,

The General Assembly Proclaims

This Universal Declaration of Human Rights as a common standard of achievement for all peoples and all nations, to the end that every individual and every organ of society, keeping this Declaration constantly in mind, shall strive by teaching and education to promote respect for these rights and freedoms and by progressive measures, national and international, to secure their universal and effective recognition and observance, both among the peoples of Member States themselves and among the peoples of territories under their jurisdiction.

Article 1   All human beings are born free and equal in dignity and rights. They are endowed with reason and conscience and should act towards one another in a spirit of brotherhood.

Article 2   Everyone is entitled to all the rights and freedoms set forth in this Declaration, without distinction of any kind, such as race, colour, sex, language, religion, political or other opinion, national or social origin, property, birth or other status.

Furthermore, no distinction shall be made on the basis of the political, jurisdictional or international status of the country or territory to which a person belongs, whether it be independent, trust, non-self-governing or under any other limitation of sovereignty.

Article 3   Everyone has the right to life, liberty and security of person.

Article 4   No one shall be held in slavery or servitude; slavery and the slave trade shall be prohibited in all their forms.

Article 5   No one shall be subjected to torture or to cruel, inhuman or degrading treatment or punishment.

Article 6   Everyone has the right to recognition everywhere as a person before the law.

Article 7   All are equal before the law and are entitled without any discrimination to equal protection of the law. All are entitled to equal protection against any discrimination in violation of this Declaration and against any incitement to such discrimination.

Article 8   Everyone has the right to an effective remedy by the competent national tribunals for acts violating the fundamental rights granted him by the constitution or by law.

Article 9   No one shall be subjected to arbitrary arrest, detention or exile.

Article 10   Everyone is entitled in full equality to a fair and public hearing by an independent and impartial tribunal, in the determination of his rights and obligations and of any criminal charge against him.

Article 11   (1) Everyone charged with a penal offence has the right to be presumed innocent until proved guilty according to law in a public trial at which he has had all the guarantees necessary for his defence.

(2)) No one shall be held guilty of any penal offence on account of any act or omission which did not constitute a penal offence, under national or international law, at the time when it was committed. Nor shall a heavier penalty be imposed than the one that was applicable at the time the penal offence was committed.

Article 12   No one shall be subjected to arbitrary interference with his privacy, family, home or correspondence, nor to attacks upon his honour and reputation. Everyone has the right to the protection of the law against such interference or attacks.

Article 13   (1) Everyone has the right to freedom of movement and residence within the borders of each state.

(2) Everyone has the right to leave any country, including his own, and to return to his country.

Article 14   (1) Everyone has the right to seek and to enjoy in other countries asylum from persecution.

(2) This right may not be invoked in the case of prosecutions genuinely arising from non-political crimes or from acts contrary to the purposes and principles of the United Nations.

Article 15   (1) Everyone has the right to a nationality.

(2) No one shall be arbitrarily deprived of his nationality nor denied the right to change his nationality.

Article 16   (1) Men and women of full age, without any limitation due to race, nationality or religion, have the right to marry and to found a family. They are entitled to equal rights as to marriage, during marriage and at its dissolution.

(2) Marriage shall be entered into only with the free and full consent of the intending spouses.

(3) The family is the natural and fundamental group unity of society and is entitled to protection by society and the State.

Article 17   (1) Everyone has the right to own property alone as well as in association with others.

(2) No one shall be arbitrarily deprived of his property.

Article 18   Everyone has the right to freedom of thought, conscience and religion; this right includes freedom to change his religion or belief, and freedom, either alone or in community with others and in public or private, to manifest his religion or belief in teaching, practice, worship and observance.

Article 19   Everyone has the right to freedom of opinion and expression; this right includes freedom to hold opinions without interference and to seek, receive and impart information and ideas through any media and regardless of frontiers.

Article 20   (1) Everyone has the right to freedom of peaceful assembly and association.

(2) No one may be compelled to belong to an association.

Article 21   (1) Everyone has the right to take part in the government of his country, directly or through freely chosen representatives.

(2) Everyone has the right of equal access to public service in his country.

(3) The will of the people shall be the basis of the authority of government; this will shall be expressed in periodic and genuine elections which shall be by universal and equal suffrage and shall be held by secret vote or by equivalent free voting procedures.

Article 22   Everyone, as a member of society, has the right to social security and is entitled to realization, through national effort and international co-operation and in accordance with the organization and resources of each State, of the economic, social and cultural rights indispensable for his dignity and the free development of his personality.

Article 23   (1) Everyone has the right to work, to free choice of employment, to just and favourable conditions of work and to protection against unemployment.

(2) Everyone, without any discrimination, has the right to equal pay for equal work.

(3) Everyone who works has the right to just and favourable remuneration ensuring for himself and his family an existence worthy of human dignity, and supplemented, if necessary, by other means of social protection.

(4) Everyone has the right to form and to join trade unions for the protection of his interests.

Article 24   Everyone has the right to rest and leisure, including reasonable limitation of working hours and periodic holidays with pay.

Article 25   (1) Everyone has the right to a standard of living adequate for the health and well-being of himself and of his family, including food, clothing, housing and medical care and necessary social services, and the right to security in the event of unemployment, sickness, disability, widowhood, old age or other lack of livelihood in circumstances beyond his control.

(2) Motherhood and childhood are entitled to special care and assistance. All children, whether born in or out of wedlock, shall enjoy the same social protection.

Article 26   (1) Everyone has the right to education. Education shall be free, at least in the elementary and fundamental stages. Elementary education shall be compulsory. Technical and professional education shall be made generally available and higher education shall be equally accessible to all on the basis of merit.

(2) Education shall be directed to the full development of the human personality and to the strengthening of respect for human rights and fundamental freedoms. It shall promote understanding, tolerance and friendship among all nations, racial or religious groups, and shall further the activities of the United Nations for the maintenance of peace.

(3) Parents have a prior right to choose the kind of education that shall be given to their children.

Article 27   (1) Everyone has the right freely to participate in the cultural life of the community, to enjoy the arts and to share in scientific advancement and its benefits.

(2) Everyone has the right to the protection of the moral and material interests resulting from any scientific, literary or artistic production of which he is the author.

Article 28   Everyone is entitled to a social and international order in which the rights and freedoms set forth in this Declaration can be fully realized.

Article 29   (1) Everyone has duties to the community in which alone the free and full development of his personality is possible.

(2) In the exercise of his rights and freedoms, everyone shall be subject only to such limitations as are determined by law solely for the purpose of securing due recognition and respect for the rights and freedoms of others and of meeting the just requirements of morality, public order and the general welfare in a democratic society.

(3) These rights and freedoms may in no case be exercised contrary to the purposes and principles of the United Nations.

Article 30   Nothing in this Declaration may be interpreted as implying for any State, group or person any right to engage in any activity or to perform any act aimed at the destruction of any of the rights and freedoms set forth herein.

Suggested Readings

Asch, S. E., *Social Psychology,* Chapter 13, Prentice-Hall, New York, 1952.

Benedict, Ruth, *Patterns of Culture,* Houghton-Mifflin, Boston, 1934.

Duncker, K., "Ethical Relativity," *Mind,* XLVII, pp. 39–57, 1939.

Herskovits, Melville J., *Cultural Relativism,* Random House, New York, 1973.

Rader, Melvin, *Ethics and Society,* Chapter 5, Holt, New York, 1950.

Savery, B., "Relativity Versus Absolutism in Value-Therapy," *The Journal of Philosophy,* Vol. 34, pp. 85–93.

Westermarck, Edward A., *Ethical Relativity,* Harcourt, New York, 1932.

Emotivism

✿ INTRODUCTION

Epistemological problems have been of primary interest to philosophers in the twentieth century. With an increased understanding of the methodologies of the mathematical and the empirical sciences, contemporary philosophers have turned their attention elsewhere; they have sought to establish the epistemological basis of subjects which ordinarily are thought to lie outside the boundaries of the sciences. One such subject, of course, is moral philosophy.

That values are different in some important respects from facts is usually conceded. But exactly what are these differences? Can the same techniques that may be used in determining the truth or falsehood of factual propositions be used in establishing judgments of moral value? If not, what methods can appropriately be used? Indeed, are there any reliable methods whatsoever for the determination of moral worth? Or are moral judgments groundless expressions of preference which have no cognitive status at all?

Contemporary philosophers have been in serious disagreement concerning the proper answers to these questions. Traditionally Western philosophers had sought to ground moral judgments upon reason or revelation. Reason was mainly emphasized within the Graeco-Roman traditions, whereas the Judaeo-Christian tradition placed primary emphasis upon revelation. Philosophers since the time of Hume and Kant, however, have grown more circumspect. Indeed, many now are unwilling to place any reliance upon conclusions that are derived from either revelation or pure reason. What then can be the source of our knowledge or morality? Or is moral knowledge impossible?

The philosophers whose views are included in the following selections present widely divergent positions in regard to these questions. Sidgwick distinguishes and defends intuition and conscience as sources of moral truth whereas Thomas maintains that revelation and reason together must be regarded as the proper basis for this kind of knowledge. Thus both of these authors state and defend positions that remain rather close to the main traditions of moral philosophy. Alternatively, Ayer rejects these traditional views and defends the meta-ethical theory known as Emotivism. This theory rejects the position that moral judgments can be properly validated by means of revelation, intuition, reason, or sense-experience. Hence it would appear that there is no adequate way in which the truth of these expressions can be certified.

The last two philosophers, Lewis and Feigl, develop positions that are somewhat opposed to Emotivism. Lewis defends a view that Ayer had taken great pains to refute, namely that moral evaluations can be properly considered to be factual propositions. If Lewis' theory is correct, then moral judgments have the same epistemic status as propositions which express empirical facts. But the statement and defense of this position raises additional problems, some of which are treated by Feigl in the final selection. Feigl introduces a number of distinctions which are important to maintain while thinking about the epistemological issues raised by Ayer and Lewis. In addition, he makes some interesting suggestions as to how their positions may be partially reconciled. Undoubtedly the last word on this puzzling topic has not yet been written. Nevertheless, many valuable observations are made and instructive insights developed in the following pages.

❀ HENRY SIDGWICK

35. *Intuition and Conscience in Ethics*

Henry Sidgwick (1838–1900), a British philosopher, was educated at Trinity College of Cambridge University, where he later served as professor of moral philosophy. Though his interests were mainly in the field of ethics, he was one of the founders of the Society for Psychical Research. His main writings were: *The Methods of Ethics* (1874), *Principles of Political Economy* (1883), *The Elements of Politics* (1891), *Practical Ethics* (1898), and *Lectures on Kant* (1905).

1. I have used the term "Intuitional" to denote the view of ethics which regards as the practically ultimate end of moral actions their conformity to certain rules or dictates of Duty unconditionally prescribed. There is, however, considerable ambiguity as to the exact antithesis implied by the terms "intuition," "intuitive," and their congeners, as currently used in ethical discussion, which we must now endeavour to remove. Writers who maintain that we have "intuitive knowledge" of the rightness of actions usually mean that this rightness is ascertained by simply "looking at" the actions themselves, without considering their ulterior consequences. This view, indeed, can hardly be extended to the whole range of duty; since no morality ever existed which did not consider ulterior consequences to some extent. Prudence or Forethought has commonly been reckoned a virtue: and all modern lists of Virtues have included Rational Benevolence, which aims at the happiness of other human beings generally, and therefore necessarily takes into consideration even remote effects of actions. It must be observed, too, that it is difficult to draw the line between an act and its consequences:

Reprinted from *The Method of Ethics*, seventh edition (London: The Macmillan Co., 1913). Some sections have been renumbered and some footnotes omitted.

as the effects consequent on each of our volitions form a continuous series of indefinite extension, and we seem to be conscious of causing all these effects, so far as at the moment of volition we foresee them to be probable. However, we find that in the common notions of different kinds of actions, a line is actually drawn between the results included in the notion and regarded as forming part of the act, and those considered as its consequences. For example, in speaking truth to a jury, I may possibly foresee that my words, operating along with other statements and indications, will unavoidably lead them to a wrong conclusion as to the guilt or innocence of the accused, as certainly as I foresee that they will produce a right impression as to the particular matter of fact to which I am testifying: still, we should commonly consider the latter foresight or intention to determine the nature of the act as an act of veracity, while the former merely relates to a consequence. We must understand then that the disregard of consequences, which the Intuitional view is here taken to imply, only relates to certain determinate classes of action (such as Truth-speaking) where common usage of terms adequately defines what events are to be included in the general notions of the acts, and what regarded as their consequences.

But again: we have to observe that men may and do judge remote as well as immediate results to be in themselves good, and such as we ought to seek to realise, without considering them in relation to the feelings of sentient beings. I have already assumed this to be the view of those who adopt the general Perfection, as distinct from the Happiness, of human society as their ultimate end; it would seem to be the view of many who concentrate their efforts on some more particular results, other than morality, such as the promotion of Art or Knowledge. Such a view, if expressly distinguished from Hedonism, might properly be classed as Intuitional, but in a sense wider than that defined in the preceding paragraph: i.e., it would be meant that the results in question are judged to be good *immediately,* and not by inference from experience of the pleasures which they produce. We have, therefore, to admit a wider use of "Intuition," as equivalent to "immediate judgment as to what ought to be done or aimed at." It should, however, be observed that the current contrast between "intuitive" or "*a priori*" and "inductive" or "*a posteriori*" morality commonly involves a certain confusion of thought. For what the "inductive" moralist professes to know by induction, is commonly not the same thing as what the "intuitive" moralist professes to know by intuition. In the former case it is the conduciveness to pleasure of certain kinds of action that is methodically ascertained: in the latter case, their rightness: there is therefore no proper opposition. If Hedonism claims to give authoritative guidance, this can only be in virtue of the principle that pleasure is the reasonable ultimate end of human action: and this principle cannot be known by induction from experience. Experience can at most tell us that all men always do seek pleasure as their ultimate end (that it does not support this conclusion I have already tried to show): it cannot tell us that any one ought so to seek it. If this latter proposition is legitimately

390 INTUITION AND CONSCIENCE IN ETHICS

affirmed in respect either of private or of general happiness, it must either be immediately known to be true,—and therefore, we may say, a moral intuition—or be inferred ultimately from premises which include at least one such moral intuition; hence either species of Hedonism, regarded from the point of view primarily taken in this treatise, might be legitimately said to be in a certain sense "intuitional." It seems, however, to be the prevailing opinion of ordinary moral persons, and most of the writers who have maintained the existence of moral intuitions, that certain kinds of actions are unconditionally prescribed without regard to ulterior consequences: and I have accordingly treated this doctrine as a distinguishing characteristic of the Intuitional method, during the main[1] part of the detailed examination of that method. . . .

2. Further; the common antithesis between "intuitive" and "inductive" morality is misleading in another way: since a moralist may hold the rightness of actions to be cognisable apart from the pleasure produced by them, while yet his method may be properly called Inductive. For he may hold that, just as the generalisations of physical science rest on particular observations, so in ethics general truths can only be reached by induction from judgments or perceptions relating to the rightness or wrongness of particular acts.

For example, when Socrates is said by Aristotle to have applied inductive reasoning to ethical questions, it is this kind of induction which is meant.[2] He discovered, as we are told, the latent ignorance of himself and other men: that is, that they used general terms confidently, without being able, when called upon, to explain the meaning of these terms. His plan for remedying this ignorance was to work towards the true definition of each term, by examining and comparing different instances of its application. Thus the definition of justice would be sought by comparing different actions commonly judged to be just, and framing a general proposition that would harmonise with all these particular judgments.

So again, in the popular view of Conscience it seems to be often implied that particular judgments are the most trustworthy. "Conscience" is the accepted popular term for the faculty of moral judgment, as applied to the acts and motives of the person judging; and we most commonly think of the dictates of conscience as relating to particular actions. Thus when a man is bidden, in any particular case, to "trust to his conscience," it commonly seems to be meant that he should exercise a faculty of judging morally this particular case without reference to general rules, and even in opposition to conclusions obtained by systematic deduction from such rules. And it is on this view of Conscience that the contempt often expressed for "Casuistry" may be most easily justified: for if the particular case can be

[1]The wider of the two meanings of 'Intuition' here distinguished is required in treating of Philosophical Intuitionism.

[2]It must, however, be remembered that Aristotle regarded the general proposition obtained by induction as really more certain (and in a higher sense knowledge) than the particulars through which the mind is led up to it.

satisfactorily settled by conscience without reference to general rules, "Casuistry," which consists in the application of general rules to particular cases, is at best superfluous. But then, on this view, we shall have no practical need of any such general rules, or of scientific Ethics at all. We may of course form general propositions by induction from these particular conscientious judgments, and arrange them systematically: but any interest which such a system may have will be purely speculative. And this accounts, perhaps, for the indifference or hostility to systematic morality shown by some conscientious persons. For they feel that they can at any rate do without it: and they fear that the cultivation of it may place the mind in a wrong attitude in relation to practice, and prove rather unfavourable than otherwise to the proper development of the practically important faculty manifested or exercised in particular moral judgments.

The view above described may be called, in a sense, "ultra-intuitional," since, in its most extreme form, it recognises simple immediate intuitions alone and discards as superfluous all modes of reasoning to moral conclusions: and we may find in it one phase or variety of the Intuitional method,—if we may extend the term "method" to include a procedure that is completed in a single judgment.

3. But though probably all moral agents have experience of such particular intuitions, and though they constitute a great part of the moral phenomena of most minds, comparatively few are so thoroughly satisfied with them, as not to feel a need of some further moral knowledge even from a strictly practical point of view. For these particular intuitions do not, to reflective persons, present themselves as quite indubitable and irrefragable: nor do they always find when they have put an ethical question to themselves with all sincerity, that they are conscious of clear immediate insight in respect of it. Again, when a man compares the utterances of his conscience at different times, he often finds it difficult to make them altogether consistent: the same conduct will wear a different moral aspect at one time from that which it wore at another, although our knowledge of its circumstances and conditions is not materially changed. Further, we become aware that the moral perceptions of different minds, to all appearance equally competent to judge, frequently conflict: one condemns what another approves. In this way serious doubts are aroused as to the validity of each man's particular moral judgments: and we are led to endeavour to set these doubts at rest by appealing to general rules, more firmly established on a basis of common consent.

And in fact, though the view of conscience above discussed is one which much popular language seems to suggest, it is not that which Christian and other moralists have usually given. They have rather represented the process of conscience as analogous to one of jural reasoning, such as is conducted in a Court of Law. Here we have always a system of universal rules given, and any particular action has to be brought under one of these rules before it can be pronounced lawful or unlawful. Now the rules of positive law are usually not discoverable by the individual's reason: this may teach him that law ought to be obeyed, but what law is must, in the main, be communicated to him from some external authority. And this is not unfrequently the case with the conscientious reasoning of ordinary persons when any dispute or difficulty forces them to reason: they have a genuine impulse to conform to the right rules of conduct, but they are not conscious, in difficult or doubtful cases, of seeing for themselves what these are: they have to inquire of their priest, or their sacred books, or perhaps the common opinion of the society to which they belong. In so far as this is the case we cannot strictly call their method Intuitional. They follow rules generally perceived, not intuitively apprehended. Other persons, however (or perhaps all to some extent), do seem to see for themselves the truth[3] and bindingness of all or most of these current rules. They may still put forward "common consent" as an argument for the validity of these rules: but only as supporting the individual's intuition, not as a substitute for it or as superseding it.

Here then we have a second Intuitional Method: of which the fundamental assumption is that we can discern certain general rules with really clear and finally valid intuition. It is held that such general rules are implicit in the moral reasoning of ordinary men, who apprehend them adequately for most practical purposes, and are able to enunciate them roughly; but that to state them with proper precision requires a special habit of contemplating clearly and steadily abstract moral notions. It is held that the moralist's function then is to perform this process of abstract contemplation, to arrange the results as systematically as possible, and by proper definitions and explanations to remove vagueness and prevent conflict. It is such a system as this which seems to be generally intended when Intuitive or *a priori* morality is mentioned. . . .

4. By philosophic minds, however, the "Morality of Common Sense" (as I have ventured to call it), even when made as precise and orderly as possible, is often found unsatisfactory as a system, although they have no disposition to question its general auhority. It is found difficult to accept as scientific first principles the moral generalities that we obtain by reflection on the ordinary thought of mankind, even though we share this thought. Even granting that these rules can be so defined as perfectly to fit together and cover the whole field of human conduct, without coming into conflict and without leaving any practical questions unanswered,— still the resulting code seems an accidental aggregate of precepts, which stands in need of some rational synthesis. In short, without being disposed to deny that conduct commonly judged to be right is so, we may yet require some deeper explanation *why* it is so. From this demand springs a third species or phase of Intuitionism, which, while accepting the morality of common sense as in the main sound, still attempts to find for it a philo-

---

[3]Strictly speaking, the attributes of truth and falsehood only belong formally to Rules when they are changed from the imperative mood ("Do X") into the indicative ("X ought to be done").

sophic basis which it does not itself offer: to get one or more principles more absolutely and undeniably true and evident, from which the current rules might be deduced, either just as they are commonly received or with slight modifications and rectifications.[4]

The three phases of Intuitionism just described may be treated as three stages in the formal development of Intuitive Morality: we may term them respectively Perceptional, Dogmatic, and Philosophical. The last-mentioned I have only defined in the vaguest way: in fact, as yet I have presented it only as a problem, of which it is impossible to foresee how many solutions may be attempted: but it does not seem desriable to investigate it further at present, as it will be more satisfactorily studied after examining in detail the Morality of Common Sense.

It must not be thought that these three phases are sharply distinguished in the moral reasoning of ordinary men: but then no more is Intuitionism of any sort sharply distinguished from either species of Hedonism. A loose combination or confusion of methods is the most common type of actual moral reasoning. Probably most moral men believe that their moral sense or instinct in any case will guide them fairly right, but also that there are general rules for determining right action in different departments of conduct: and that for these again it is possible to find a philosophical explanation, by which they may be deduced from a smaller number of fundamental principles. Still for systematic direction of conduct, we require to know on what judgments we are to rely as ultimately valid. . . .

5. But the question may be raised, whether it is legitimate to take for granted (as I have hiherto been doing) the existence of such intuitions? And, no doubt, there are persons who deliberately deny that reflection enables them to discover any such phenomenon in their conscious experience as the judgment or apparent perception that an act is in itself right or good, in any other sense than that of being the right or fit means to the attainment of some ulterior end. I think, however, that such denials are commonly recognised as paradoxical, and opposed to the common experience of civilised men:—at any rate if the psychological question, as to the *existence* of such moral judgments or apparent perceptions of moral qualities, is carefully distinguished from the ethical question as to their *validity,* and from what we may call the "psychogonical" question as to their *origin.* The first and second of these questions are sometimes confounded, owing to an ambiguity in the use of the term "intuition"; which has sometimes been understood to imply that the judgment or apparent perception so designated is *true.* (I wish therefore to say expressly, that by calling any affirmation as to the rightness or wrongness of actions "intuitive," I do not mean to prejudge the question as to its ultimate validity, when philosophically considered: I only mean that its truth is apparently known immediately, and

---

[4]It should be observed that such principles will not necessarily be "intuitional" in the narrower sense that excludes consequences; but only in the wider sense as being self-evident principles relating to 'what ought to be.'

not as the result of reasoning.) I admit the possibility that any such "intuition" may turn out to have an element of error, which subsequent reflection and comparison may enable us to correct; just as many apparent perceptions through the organ of vision are found to be partially illusory and misleading: indeed the sequel will show that I hold this to be to an important extent the case with moral intuitions commonly so called.

The question as to the validity of moral intuitions being thus separated from the simple question "whether they actually exist," it becomes obvious that the latter can only be decided for each person by direct introspection or reflection. It must not therefore be supposed that its decision is a simple matter, introspection being always infallible: on the contrary, experience leads me to regard men as often liable to confound with moral intuitions other states or acts of mind essentially different from them,— blind impulses to certain kinds of action or vague sentiments of preference for them, or conclusions from rapid and half-unconscious processes of reasoning, or current opinions to which familiarity has given an illusory air of self-evidence. But any errors of this kind, due to careless or superficial reflection, can only be cured by more careful reflection. This may indeed be much aided by communication with other minds; it may also be aided, in a subordinate way, by an inquiry into the antecedents of the apparent intuition, which may suggest to the reflective mind sources of error to which a superficial view of it is liable. Still the question whether a certain judgment presents itself to the reflective mind is intuitively known cannot be decided by any inquiry into its antecedents or causes.

It is, however, still possible to hold that an inquiry into the Origin of moral intuitions must be decisive in determining their Validity. And in fact it has been often assumed, both by Intuitionists and their opponents, that if our moral faculty can be shown to be "derived" or "developed" out of other pre-existent elements of mind or consciousness, a reason is thereby given for distrusting it; while if, on the other hand, it can be shown to have existed in the human mind from its origin, its trustworthiness is thereby established. Either assumption appears to me devoid of foundation. On the one hand, I can see no ground for supposing that a faculty thus derived, is, as such, more liable to error than if its existence in the individual possessing it had been differently caused:[5] to put it otherwise, I cannot see how the mere ascertainment that certain apparently self-evi-

[5]I cannot doubt that every one of our cognitive faculties,—in short the human mind as a whole,—has been derived and developed, through a gradual process of physical change, out of some lower life in which cognition, properly speaking, had no place. On this view, the distinction between "original" and "derived" reduces itself to that between "prior" and "posterior' in development: and the fact that the moral faculty appears somewhat later in the process of evolution than other faculties can hardly be regarded as an argument against the validity of moral intuition; especially since this process is commonly conceived to be homogeneous throughout. Indeed such a line of reasoning would be suicidal; as the cognition that the moral faculty is developed is certainly later in development than moral cognition, and would therefore, by this reasoning, be less trustworthy.

dent judgments have been caused in known and determinate ways, can be in itself a valid ground for distrusting this class of apparent cognitions. I cannot even admit that those who affirm the truth of such judgments are bound to show in their causes a tendency to make them true: indeed the acceptance of any such *onus probandi* would seem to me to render the attainment of philosophical certitude impossible. For the premises of the required demonstration must consist of caused beliefs, which as having been caused will equally stand in need of being proved true, and so on *ad infinitum*: unless it be held that we can find among the premises of our reasonings certain apparently self-evident judgments which have had no antecedent causes, and that these are therefore to be accepted as valid without proof. But such an assertion would be an extravagant paradox: and, if it be admitted that all beliefs are equally in the position of being effects of antecedent causes, it seems evident that this characteristic alone cannot serve to invalidate any of them.

I hold, therefore, that the *onus probandi* must be thrown the other way: those who dispute the validity of moral or other intuitions on the ground of their derivation must be required to show, not merely that they are the effects of certain causes, but that these causes are of a kind that tend to produce invalid beliefs. Now it is not, I conceive, possible to prove by any theory of the derivation of the moral faculty that the fundamental ethical conceptions "right" or "what ought to be done," "good" or "what it is reasonable to desire and seek," are invalid, and that consequently *all* propositions of the form "X is right" or "good" are untrustworthy: for such ethical propositions, relating as they do to matter fundamentally different from that with which physical science or psychology deals, cannot be inconsistent with any physical or psychological conclusions. They can only be shown to involve error by being shown to contradict each other: and such a demonstration cannot lead us cogently to the sweeping conclusion that all are false. It may, however, be possible to prove that some ethical beliefs have been caused in such a way as to make it probable that they are wholly or partially erroneous: and it will hereafter be important to consider how far any Ethical intuitions, which we find ourselves disposed to accept as valid, are open to attack on such psychological grounds. At present I am only concerned to maintain that no general demonstration of the derivedness or developedness of our moral faculty can supply an adequate reason for distrusting it.

On the other hand, if we have been once led to distrust our moral faculty on other grounds—as (*e.g.*) from the want of clearness and consistency in the moral judgments of the same individual, and the discrepancies between the judgments of different individuals—it seems to me equally clear that our confidence in such judgments cannot properly be re-established by a demonstration of their "originality." I see no reason to believe that the "original" element of our moral cognition can be ascertained; but if it could, I see no reason to hold that it would be especially free from error.

6. How then can we hope to eliminate error from our moral intu-

itions? One answer to this question was briefly suggested in a previous chapter where the different phases of the Intuitional Method were discussed. It was there said that in order to settle the doubts arising from the uncertainties and discrepancies that are found when we compare our judgments on particular cases, reflective persons naturally appeal to general rules or formulæ: and it is to such general formulæ that Intuitional Moralists commonly attribute ultimate certainty and validity. And certainly there are obvious sources of error in our judgments respecting concrete duty which seem to be absent when we consider the abstract notions of different kinds of conduct; since in any concrete case the complexity of circumstances necessarily increases the difficulty of judging, and our personal interests or habitual sympathies are liable to disturb the clearness of our moral discernment. Further, we must observe that most of us feel the need of such formulæ not only to correct, but also to supplement, our intuitions respecting particular concrete duties. Only exceptionally confident persons find that they always seem to see clearly what ought to be done in any case that comes before them. Most of us, however unhesitatingly we may affirm rightness and wrongness in ordinary matters of conduct, yet not unfrequently meet with cases where our unreasoned judgment fails us; and where we could no more decide the moral issue raised without appealing to some general formula, than we could decide a disputed legal claim without reference to the positive law that deals with the matter.

And such formulæ are not difficult to find: it only requires a little reflection and observation of men's moral discourse to make a collection of such general rules, as to the validity of which there would be apparent agreement at least among moral persons of our own age and civilisation, and which would cover with approximate completeness the whole of human conduct. Such a collection, regarded as a code imposed on an individual by the public opinion of the community to which he belongs, we have called the Positive Morality of the community: but when regarded as a body of moral truth, warranted to be such by the *consensus* of mankind,—or at least of that portion of mankind which combines adequate intellectual enlightenment with a serious concern for morality—it is more significantly termed the morality of Common Sense. . . .

✿ GEORGE F. THOMAS

36. Reason, Revelation and Moral Philosophy

George F. Thomas (1899–   ) is chairman of the Department of Religion at Princeton University. Among his major works are: *Poetry, Religion and the Spiritual Life* (1951), *Christian Ethics and Moral Philosophy* (1955), and *Religious Philosophies of the West* (1965).

MORAL PHILOSOPHY: ITS NATURE AND LIMITATIONS

Moral philosophy arises among those who have became dissatisfied with the moral judgments and practices imposed by their society. When they reach intellectual maturity and have sufficient leisure for independent thinking, they discover that many of the moral rules and virtues inculcated by their society are irrational and inconsistent with one another. They begin to analyze critically the accepted moral judgments and practices and to clarify the meanings of moral concepts such as courage and justice. This process can be studied by any careful reader of the Socratic dialogues of Plato. One can watch Socrates' mind at work as he subjects the moral *opinions* of his fellow-Athenians to searching criticism in the attempt to arrive at genuine *knowledge*.

But philosophers are not content merely to refine and clarify the morality of their group; their ultimate aim is to establish morality on a more solid basis of *general principles* which are consistent and comprehensive. They cannot be satisfied with a plurality of rules which are not based upon fundamental principles approved by reason, and, since reason is common to all men, these principles must be *universally valid*.

What are the *presuppositions* of the moral philosophy which results from this interest in universal principles of moral conduct? The first is the *autonomy of the reason*. In group morality, man's duties are imposed upon him by his society; in rational morality, they are determined by himself. There is no place for any moral authority but that of reason and the only moral obligations that are binding upon a man are those he imposes as a rational being upon himself. For example, a moral law may have originated in a religious "revelation" and may have been transmitted by the Church. But it is accepted by the philosopher, if at all, because it commends itself to his reason, not because it has been thought to be revealed. The dignity of man as a rational person requires him to lay down principles to determine his own conduct rather than let others prescribe his duties for him. This

Reprinted with the permission of Charles Scribner's Sons from *Christian Ethics and Moral Philosophy*, pages 367–381, by George F. Thomas. Copyright © 1955 George F. Thomas.

implies that reason has the *capacity* to discover ethical principles which are true and that the work of reason can be carried through without serious interference and distortion by the philosopher's social affiliation, moral defects, and other irrational factors. . . .

The *value* of moral philosophy is obvious. As a rational being, a man cannot be content to follow blindly the morality of his group. When he begins to think for himself and realizes that there is much arbitrariness and inconsistency in the accepted moral rules, he is bound to ask, "What is truly good and right?" The moral philosopher has analyzed the virtues which deliver men from impulsive and foolish acts by providing them with an armor of habits against the assaults of passion. He has shown up the vanity of many values prized by his fellows, pointing out that wealth and power and glory are not as noble as justice and truth. He has appealed to them not to conform to customary practices which are cruel or meaningless.

Is moral philosophy, then, an adequate basis for the good life? Many moral philosophers have thought so, especially in our secular age. But there are *limitations* of moral philosophy which have always prevented most men, even educated men, from regarding it as by itself sufficient. What are these limitations?

First, moral philosophers are concerned with the discovery of what is good for men and right for them to do, but they have seldom been able to awaken in men a love of the good or to stimulate their wills to do the right. This is the familiar problem of moral *incentive* or *motive*. It may be admitted, with Sidgwick, that there is a desire in man to do that which is right and reasonable. But that desire, by itself, is not strong enough in most men to overcome the natural passions and social forces which are opposed to the right and reasonable. It is not enough to appeal to the reason; the will and the affections must somehow be brought into line with the dictates of reason. Plato realized the importance of moral education through associating pleasure with the good and pain with the evil, and Aristotle emphasized the necessity of forming right habits. But philosophers have seldom probed this problem very deeply. They have tended to assume that if we know our true good we will seek it and if we know our duty we will do it. Therefore, they have thought that when they have defined the good and the right, their task is over. But man's will is divided and he cannot love his true good with all his heart. Again and again, he finds himself in the tragic situation of St. Paul: he knows what is good but he chooses the evil. He is powerless by himself to acquire the virtues or perform the duties which are required of him by moral philosophy. If he is to attain true goodness, he must be radically transformed. His desires must be redirected and his affections fixed firmly upon the good.

Second, man's effort to attain virtue by himself is often a source of *moral dangers*. Although the greatest moral philosophers insist upon a disinterested devotion to the good, the realization of higher values often leads to moral pride and complacency. Man's self-centeredness even perverts his virtues and turns them into means of furthering his own interests. Without faith and love, the attempt to attain virtue and do good works often leads to self-righteousness. Apart from this tendency of natural egoism to corrupt the achievements of the moral will, the excessive dependence upon moral striving is accompanied by serious dangers. It sometimes produces inner tension and anxiety concerning the success of one's efforts. Moralism in the sense of strenuous effort by the will to "live up to" high ethical ideals without the power to do so may be the cause of inner conflict and failure. The result may be psychological frustration or even breakdown. More often moralism leads to a stern, unlovely character with strength but without graciousness and spontaneity. Some of the finest moral qualities cannot be attained by conscious willing at all but must come from the unconscious influence of other persons and from participation in the life of a moral community.

Third, there is no *imaginative vision* in moral philosophy capable of inspiring spontaneous love and devotion. The principles of moral philosophy are expressed in concepts rather than images. This is necessary for the sake of clarity and precision; but it prevents most moral philosophers from moving the heart and stimulating the will. One of the reasons Bergson does not recognize the morality of philosophers as a third type of morality along with "closed" and "open" morality is that its concepts seem to him to have little power over the will.[1] His tendency to anti-intellectualism leads him to minimize unduly the function of reason in morality, for reason can survey the various ends sought by men and organize them into a unified ideal. But it is a timely warning against the opposite tendency to neglect the non-rational factors in the moral life. What is there in moral philosophy which can stimulate aspiration like the Christian vision of a universal community based upon love of God as Father and love of all men as brothers?

Fourth, the ideals of moral philosophers also lack the appeal that comes from the *incarnation* of a way of life in a living person and the inspiration that is derived from *imitation* of him. One of the greatest sources of appeal in Platonism, which is close to religious morality in many ways, is the embodiment of its ideal in Socrates. The power of Buddhist ethics is due largely to the fact that the followers of the Buddha are called upon to "take refuge" in *him* as well as in his *teachings.* Certainly, the reason Christian ethics has been able to transform the lives of men is to be found not only in the teachings of Christ but also in his life and in union with him. While a moral philosophy presents men with an *ideal* to be followed, it seldom offers them the *example* of one who has followed it. Nor is its ideal embodied in the way of life of a *community* or *church,* whose members strengthen and encourage one another in their efforts to realize it. Is this the reason why the greatest rival of Christian ethics in our time is not philosophical ethics but the secularized religious ethics of Communism, with its imaginative vision of a classless society embracing all men, the embodiment of its ideal in great

---

[1]Bergson, H., *The Two Sources of Morality and Religion*, New York, Holt, 1935, p. 57.

leaders like Lenin, and its dependence upon an organized party to make its vision come true?

While moral philosophy has undoubtedly been one of the major sources of the ethical tradition of the Western world, these limitations force us to raise the question whether the attempt of many modern philosophers to separate moral philosophy from Christian ethics is not a fatal mistake. Should not moral philosophy and Christian ethics be regarded as complementary rather than mutually exclusive? May not the limitations of moral philosophy be overcome and its insights made more effective by the acceptance of Christian faith and love? May not Christians be aided by the insights of moral philosophy to obey God and serve their neighbors more wisely? The purpose of this chapter is to suggest that these questions should be answered in the affirmative, and to indicate a way in which the breach between Christian ethics and moral philosophy can be overcome.

THE AUTHORITY OF REVELATION AND THE AUTONOMY OF REASON

In carrying out this purpose, however, we shall be confronted with *objections* from moral philosophers and Christian theologians. Some moral philosophers repudiate Christian ethics on the ground that it is based on revelation rather than reason and consequently is "authoritarian." Some Christian theologians refuse to accept any of the theories of moral philosophers on the ground that they are useless and unnecessary for men of faith. It is essential to deal with these two objections before we attempt to show how Christian ethics and moral philosophy should be related to each other. We shall begin with the objection of secular moral philosophers that Christian ethics is "authoritarian."

With respect to the source of authority, Christian ethics and moral philosophy seem at first sight to be in absolute opposition to one another. Christian ethics derives its principles from the revelation recorded in the Bible. Liberal as well as orthodox Christians insist upon the authority of this revelation. In contrast, secular moral philosophers seem to reject every authority but that of reason. Moral philosophy, they insist, must be "autonomous"; the moralist must depend upon no source of truth beyond reason. This raises several important questions: In what sense does Christian ethics rest upon the authority of revelation? Insofar as it does so, is it necessarily "authoritarian?" Again, what do moral philosophers mean by the "autonomy" of the reason? Is this autonomy absolute or limited? Finally, is it possible to accept the "authority" of revelation without sacrificing the legitimate "autonomy" of the reason?

First, in what sense does Christian ethics assert the *authority of revelation?* Christians differ in their answer to this question. In Protestantism, Christian ethics is based upon the authority not of the Church but of the Bible. Since the Bible is the record of a divine revelation in history, this means that Christian ethics is ultimately based upon the authority of that revelation. However, the revelation cannot be simply identified with the words of the Bible in which it is expressed; the "Word" of God is not the same as the words in Hebrew and Greek by which it is mediated to us. Moreover, as Temple has said, it does not consist of dogmas and commandments stated in propositional form. It is a revelation of God and His redemptive activity, not of dogmas about God; of new life in love, not rules of conduct. For it is a revelation in historical events as interpreted by prophets and apostles, and the full meaning of historical events can never be exhausted by the words of any of its interpreters.[2] If so, the responsibility for interpreting the meaning of the revelation belongs to the individual person as a member of the Christian community. Does not God address men in the Biblical revelation as beings who can listen, understand, raise questions, and judge for themselves?

When understood in this way, the authority of revelation is wholly inconsistent with religious "authoritarianism." Religious "authoritarianism" is usually based upon belief in a visible authority, e.g., Church or Bible, as the source of dogmas which must be believed and rules which must be obeyed. Moreover, the pronouncements of this authority are unquestioned. They are felt to be binding whether or not they are approved by the reason and conscience of the individual. The free acceptance of revelation, as we have described it, is incompatible with this authoritarianism. According to our view, the acceptance of the authority of revelation by a Christian not only permits but demands that he use his reason fully in determining its meaning and its implications for his life.

This brings us to the question, what is the meaning of *"autonomy"* in moral philosophy? Positively, it asserts that man should determine his moral conduct by laws or principles approved by his own reason. Negatively, it denies the dependence of the rational will upon any external authority such as a church or state. According to Kant, it is "the property of the will to be a law to itself,"[3] and "the will possesses this property because it belongs to the intelligible world, under laws which, being independent of nature, have their foundation not in experience but in reason alone."[4] This view of the "autonomy" of the reason seems to assert that the reason lays down moral laws in complete independence of moral experience. However, Kant argued that his fundamental ethical principle was only a precise formulation of what is presupposed in the common moral consciousness. In any case, the usual method of philosophical ethics is to develop its principles through an examination of the moral experience of men as reflected in their moral judgments. Thus, "autonomy" means only that reason should not passively submit to an external authority, but should derive its ethical principles from reflection upon moral experience. If "autonomy" is interpreted in this way, reason may and should take into account every kind of moral experience, including that of religious men, in formulating its ethical principles.

[2]Temple, William, *Nature, Man and God*, London, Macmillan, 1940, Lecture 12.
[3]Kant, I., *The Metaphysics of Morals*, tr. by T. K. Abbott in *Kant's Theory of Ethics*, London, Longmans, Green, 1909, p. 66.
[4]Ibid., p. 72.

When the "authority" of revelation and the "autonomy" of reason are interpreted in this way, the absolute opposition between Christian ethics and moral philosophy is seen to be unnecessary. On the one hand, the Biblical revelation of moral truth was not imparted to men whose minds and consciences were passive, but was mediated to them through their moral experience. Moreover, it continues to be accepted by Christians because it seems to be confirmed by their own moral experience. Thus, there is nothing arbitrary or irrational about it. On the other hand, the moral philosopher depends upon the facts of moral experience, and since the value of his conclusions is determined largely by the depth and breadth of the moral experience from which he derives them, it is reasonable for him to take seriously the moral experience recorded in the Bible.

In fact, however, there is a fundamental *difference* between Christian ethics and secular moral philosophy in their interpretation of moral experience. Christian ethics is inseparable from the Christian faith that God has revealed His will in Christ. A philosopher who does not share this faith cannot accept Christian ethics as a whole, although he may incorporate into his own thinking certain ideas derived from it. Consequently, he cannot give the moral experience recorded in the Bible a "privileged position" in his examination of the facts of the moral consciousness. He may acknowledge that important and valid ethical ideas originated in this moral experience, but he cannot acknowledge their primacy in his ethical thinking.

Thus, while there is no logical necessity for an absolute opposition between Christian ethics and moral philosophy *as such,* there is a radical difference between Christian ethics and a *secular* moral philosophy. However, the Christian moralist can do much to bridge the gap. Although the secular moral philosopher refuses to give primacy to ethical insights derived from the Christian moral experience, the Christian moralist should acknowledge the truth of some of the ethical insights of moral philosophers and adapt them for the use of Christians. We shall indicate later in this chapter why he should do so and how he can do so in the most fruitful way.

In addition, he can seek to remove a common misconception from the minds of moral philosophers which stands in the way of their acceptance of the Christian faith and ethic. This is the idea that, while Christian ethics is based upon the moral experience of a particular people in the past, moral philosophy is a product of universal reason reflecting impartially upon the moral experience of all humanity. Because of this supposed difference between them, the secular moral philosopher believes that his method and conclusions are superior to those of the Christian moralist. But is his examination of moral experience as all-inclusive and impartial as he thinks? Does he actually analyze the moral judgments of *all* peoples of every time and place? Does he analyze moral judgments from the perspective of an *impartial* reason unconditioned by his own time and place?

The moral philosopher is incapable of such an analysis. The limitations of his knowledge and the effect of his culture upon him cannot be overcome. In his analysis he usually limits himself to the moral judgments of his own people or civilization. Even when he deals with the moral judgments of other peoples and other times, he is naturally influenced more deeply by those of his own. The ethical theories of Plato and Aristotle would have been impossible in any country except ancient Greece, and Kant's ethics is clearly a product of the Age of Reason. Thus, the perspective of the moral philosopher is not that of universal reason reflecting impartially upon the *general* moral experience of mankind; it is that of his own reason conditioned by the *particular* moral experience of his time and place. In reality, he accords, a "privileged position" to the particular moral experience of ancient Greeks or modern Europeans, as the Christian moralist accords such a position to the experience of Hebrew prophets and Christian apostles.

If so, the moral philosopher should not claim superiority for his method. Like the Chritian moralist, he gives the "privileged position" to those whom he believes to have been the wisest and best; and if he is pressed for the reason why he believes them to be so, it will be seen that his belief really rests upon metaphyical and ethical assumptions which he cannot demonstrate but accepts by a kind of faith. In brief, there is no such thing as an ethic which has been developed by pure reason without the aid of presuppositions. The difference between Christian ethics and secular moral philosophy is not that the former has presuppositions while the latter is free from them; it is that they derive their presuppositions from different sources. Can the moral philosopher prove that his presuppositions or the sources from which he draws them are superior to those of the Christian moralist? If the test of ethical presuppositions is their fruitfulness in ethical theory and their value as a guide in moral decisions, Christian ethics had stood this test successfully during many centuries. Can more be said of the ethical presuppositions by any philosopher?

FAITH AND REASON

The preceding argument concerning the relation of Christian ethics to moral philosophy presupposes a certain view of the nature of the Christian faith and its relation to reason. We must now make this view more explicit. Some philosophers suppose that faith has no cognitive value but is a wholly irrational act which springs from the will or the feelings. Now, it is certainly true that faith is not only intellectual assent; it is also a response of the whole self, including the will and heart, to the reality of God. But this does not destroy its *cognitive value.* For faith involves an apprehension of the reality and goodness of God as He has revealed Himself. It is not a blind faith, but a response to God as He has confronted man in his experience. It differs from reason when the latter is conceived as the faculty of discursive thinking. Faith *affirms* the reality and goodness of God as He is experienced and it leads to a commitment to Him. Reason, on the other hand, critically *examines* a judgment to determine whether there are adequate grounds for asserting it and it frequently leads to a refusal of commitment. Thus, faith is more adventurous than reason, reason more cautious than faith. But while faith goes beyond reason, it need not contradict any knowledge which has been definitely established by reason. And reason, which has a constructive as well as a critical task, cannot complete its task unless it is willing to accept premises or presuppositions which it cannot demonstrate. Thus, while faith without reason is uncritical, reason without faith is uncreative.

Of course, reason can attain to knowledge of certain kinds without the aid of faith. In the form of common sense, it can enable men to cope with problems of everyday life. In the form of science, it can describe natural phenomena, make predictions about future events, and design machines for exploiting natural resources. But it cannot attain to wisdom about the world as a whole or the highest good of man without *presuppositions* derived from faith.

The mind can understand reality, says Niebuhr, "only by making faith the presupposition of its understanding."[5] This is the Augustinian view of the relation between faith and understanding. "Credo ut intelligam," I believe in order that I may understand." Since every world view rests upon presuppositions which cannot be rationally demonstrated, each of us must face the problem as to whether he is to start with presuppositions derived, at least in part, from the religious experience of God as transcendent Reality and Good. If we try to avoid the problem by denying the possibility of a world view and contenting ourselves with the description of relations between natural phenomena, as in Positivism, we refuse to heed the highest demand of reason and to meet the deepest need of life itself. If we try to find the meaning of the whole of reality in some aspect of nature, e.g., matter or life, we are merely explaining the whole by one of its finite parts to which we have arbitrarily accorded a privileged position over other finite parts. But if we have had a vital religious experience, we can never be satisfied with anything less than a religious world view based upon an affirmation of faith in God as transcendent Reality and Good.

Of course, in laying hold of God by faith, man's "reach exceeds his grasp." Though God has revealed Himself in religious experience, He remains hidden in His transcendent otherness. Nevertheless, faith ventures out beyond the world of finite and contingent things and affirms an infinite and supersensible Being as the Ground of its existence, its nature, and its value.

Thus faith is a *source of truth* about reality, not a subjective fancy. As such, it involves, not only an act of trust, but also an intellectual act, an act of insight. That is why it is the source not only of religion but also of any philosophy which does justice to the transcendent element in experience. Every world view, irreligious as well as religious, is based upon a principle of meaning, a vision of truth, which is accepted by a kind of faith as the key to reality as a whole. In the words of Bradley, "metaphysics is the finding of bad reasons for what we believe on instinct."[6] A religious world view differs

[5]Niebuhr, R., *The Nature and Destiny of Man*, New York, Scribners, 1941, I, p. 158.

[6]Bradley, F. H., *Appearance and Reality*, New York, Macmillan, 1893, p. XIV.

from naturalistic world views in that the principle of meaning upon which it rests is a transcendent principle, God. The fact that it is transcendent, however, does not mean that it is irrelevant to our understanding of the finite and contingent things of the world in which we live and to our life in that world. Indeed, finite and contingent things, especially the life and spirit of man, find their meaning and explanation only in relation to it and apart from it they become unintelligible.

This is not a mere dogmatic assertion of religion alone; it can be confirmed by reference to other spiritual activities and values also. Plato points out in the "Symposium" how the experience of beautiful faces and forms leads on to the experience of beautiful souls and finally to the experience of Beauty itself as the transcendent principle which is invisible but is present in all visible things of beauty and is the ultimate source of their beauty. One does not have to accept the Platonic theory of Ideas as universal Forms which subsist in a realm of their own to see that he is describing the experience of all those who love beauty as something more than the "aesthetic surface" of a physical object. The sense of frustration of every great artist because he cannot capture perfectly the vision that hovers before him points in the same direction. Similarly, all moral striving seems to presuppose an absolute and perfect goodness that is never fully realized in men's conduct but that haunts them and beckons them on. Thus, the aesthetic and moral experience of man, like his religious experience, points to a transcendent Reality and Good beyond the natural world. But since religious faith apprehends directly this Reality and Good, it is the source of the highest knowledge. Without faith, all knowledge of finite reality through common sense or science becomes distorted and loses its crown of wisdom.

This is the theoretical significance of faith; its *moral significance* is equally important. Without faith the will of man is directed towards values that are near and immediately accessible because they belong to the world of actuality. He finds it hard, if not impossible, to conceive of a life radically different from his own or values radically different from those of the society in which he lives. But the man of faith has caught a vision of possibilities that go far beyond anything in the world of actuality, of a new life and other values which are richer and more blessed than those he knows around him. Thus, it is faith in the Christian sense which envisages a universal, "open" community in the place of the exclusive, "closed" societies in which men actually live. It sees the possibility of a more perfect love than that of even the best of men. Moreover, it trusts in the mercy and power of God to bring into reality that universal community and that perfect love in the lives of men. In this way, faith transforms the moral will by setting before it higher and broader purposes than those of the self or the group and strengthening it in its efforts to realize those purposes. By subjecting the self to the will of God, faith rescues it from its self-centeredness and self-love. It frees the self from its fears and anxieties about itself and enables it to give itself in love to others. Thus, faith not only apprehends God as the transcendent Reality who gives meaning to all existence, but also awakens devotion to

Him as the absolute Good which is the source of all the higher values of the moral life.

Modern rationalism has denied the necessity of faith. It has divorced reason from faith in philosophy and has not hesitated to attack faith. As a result, there has been a sharp *reaction against reason* itself on the part of certain Christian theologians. These theologians argue that modern man rejects faith in the Biblical revelation at his peril. If God is transcendent and other than man, they say, why should man's finite and puny reason hope to demonstrate His existence or comprehend His nature? Some of these theologians go even further. They attack the effort to know God by reason as a sign of man's infidelity and pride. Man must set aside the pretensions of reason and depend upon the Word of God alone.

This is a serious error. It is true that intellectual pride is one of the most widespread manifestations of modern secular Humanism. But the source of this intellectual pride is not to be found in the "pretensions of reason"; it is to be found in the pretensions of man. Reason should not be regarded as an entity in itself, personified, and regarded as capable of making pretensions. Reason is simply a function of the human self. It is the function by which the self seeks to understand reality in all its aspects, opening itself to all of them impartially and letting each of them speak in its own way. If so, reason should not deny revelation or dispute the right of man to faith. It should seek to understand what has been revealed by God in the historical events recorded in the Bible, as it tries to understand the phenomena of the senses or the imperatives of conscience. It should open itself to reality as a whole and try to interpret every phase of experience without prejudice against any.

Only when this is recognized does the true relation of reason to faith becomes manifest. Reason should accept the evidence of religious experience and faith for God and then seek to *understand* faith as clearly as possible, to express its meaning in terms that are intelligible to others, and to draw out its implications for conduct. Reason purifies our thinking about faith of false ideas, superstitions, and inconsistencies. It relates it to our experience as a whole. In short, reason seeks to understand faith, to relate it to the world, and to apply it to life. Reason needs faith to enable it to affirm the transcendent; faith needs reason to interpret the meaning of its affirmation.

✿ A. J. AYER

37. *Emotivism: A Positivist Analysis of Moral Judgments*

Alfred Jules Ayer (1910–   ), an important contemporary British philosopher, has been Grote Professor of Philosophy at University College, London. In 1959 he became Wykeham professor of Logic at Oxford University. Ayer has distinguished himself as one of the clearest expositors of logical positivism, an important twentieth century movement in philosophy. His major works include: *Language, Truth and Logic* (1936), *The Foundations of Empirical Knowledge* (1940), *Philosophical Essays* (1954), *The Problem of Knowledge* (1956), and *The Concept of a Person* (1963).

"Most of us would agree," said F. P. Ramsey, addressing a society in Cambridge in 1925, "that the objectivity of good was a thing we had settled and dismissed with the existence of God. Theology and Absolute Ethics are two famous subjects which we have realized to have no real objects." There are many, however, who still think that these questions have not been settled; and in the meantime philosophers of Ramsey's persuasion have grown more circumspect. Theological and ethical statements are no longer stigmatized as false or meaningless. They are merely said to be different from scientific statements. They are differently related to their evidence; or rather, a different meaning is attached to "evidence" in their case. "Every kind of statement," we are told, "has its own kind of logic."

What this comes to, so far as moral philosophy is concerned, is that ethical statements are *sui generis*; and this may very well be true. Certainly, the view, which I still wish to hold,[1] that what are called ethical statements are not really statements at all, that they are not descriptive of anything, that they cannot be either true or false, is in an obvious sense incorrect. For, as the English language is currently used—and what else, it may be asked, is here in question?—it is by no means improper to refer to ethical utterances as statements; when someone characterizes an action by the use of an ethical predicate, it is quite good usage to say that he is thereby describing it; when someone wishes to assent to an ethical verdict, it is perfectly legitimate for him to say that it is true, or that it is a fact, just as, if he wished to dissent

From an essay that originally appeared in *Horizon*, XX, No. 117 (1949). It has since been reprinted in A.J. Ayer, *Philosophical Essays*, (New York: St. Martin's Press, 1954). Reprinted by permission of St. Martin's Press and Macmillan & Co., Ltd., London.

[1]Ayer first published his views in his *Language, Truth and Logic*, Victor Gollancz, Ltd., London, 1936. In that work he maintained that sentences which express moral evaluations do not assert facts and that there is, therefore, no way to determine their truth or falsehood. Instead, such utterances serve primarily to evince the emotions of the speaker. This position has become known as the Emotive Theory.—Editor

from it, it would be perfectly legitimate for him to say that it was false. We should know what he meant and we should not consider that he was using words in an unconventional way. What is unconventional, rather, is the usage of the philosopher who tells us that ethical statements are not really statements at all but something else, ejaculations perhaps or commands, and that they cannot be either true or false.

Now when a philosopher asserts that something "really" is not what it really is, or "really" is what it really is not, that we do not, for example, "really" see chairs and tables, whereas there is a perfectly good and familiar sense in which we really do, or that we cannot "really" step into the same river twice, whereas in fact we really can, it should not always be assumed that he is merely making a mistake. Very often what he is doing, although he may not know it, is to recommend a new way of speaking, not just for amusement, but because he thinks that the old, the socially correct, way of speaking is logically misleading, or that his own proposal brings out certain points more clearly. Thus, in the present instance, it is no doubt correct to say that the moralist does make statements, and, what is more, statements of fact, statements of ethical fact. It is correct in the sense that if a vote were taken on the point, those who objected to this way of speaking would probably be in the minority. But when one considers how these ethical statements are actually used, it may be found that they function so very differently from other types of statement that it is advisable to put them into a separate category altogether; either to say that they are not to be counted as statements at all, or, if this proves inconvenient, at least to say that they do not express propositions, and consequently that there are no ethical facts. This does not mean that all ethical statements are held to be false. It is merely a matter of laying down a usage of the words "proposition" and "fact," according to which only propositions express facts and ethical statements fall outside the class of propositions. This may seem to be an arbitrary procedure, but I hope to show that there are good reasons for adopting it. And once these reasons are admitted the purely verbal point is not of any great importance. If someone still wishes to say that ethical statements are statements of fact, only it is a queer sort of fact, he is welcome to do so. So long as he accepts our grounds for saying that they are not statements of fact, it is simply a question of how widely or loosely we want to use the word "fact." My own view is that it is preferable so to use it as to exclude ethical judgements, but it must not be inferred from this that I am treating them with disrespect. The only relevant consideration is that of clarity.

The distinctions that I wish to make can best be brought out by an example. Suppose that someone has committed a murder. Then part of the story consists of what we may call the police-court details; where and when and how the killing was effected; the identity of the murderer and of his victim; the relationship in which they stood to one another. Next there are the questions of motive: the murderer may have been suffering from jealousy, or he may have been anxious to obtain money; he may have been avenging a private injury, or pursuing some political end. These questions of motive are, on one level, a matter of the agent's reflections before the act; and these may very well take the form of moral judgements. Thus he may tell himself that his victim is a bad man and that the world would be better for his removal, or, in a different case, that it is his duty to rid his country of a tyrant, or, like Raskolnikov in *Crime and Punishment*, that he is a superior being who has in these circumstances the right to kill. A psycho-analyst who examines the case may, however, tell a different story. He may say that the political assassin is really revenging himself upon his father, or that the man who persuades himself that he is a social benefactor is really exhibiting a lust for power, or, in a case like that of Raskolnikov, that the murderer does not really believe that he has the right to kill.

All these are statements of fact; not indeed that the man has, or has not, the right to kill, but that this is what he tells himself. They are verified or confuted, as the case may be, by observation. It is a matter of fact, in my usage of the term, that the victim was killed at such and such a place and at such and such a time and in such and such a mannner. It is also a matter of fact that the murderer had certain conscious motives. To himself they are known primarily by introspection; to others by various features of his overt behaviour, including what he says. As regards his unconscious motives the only criterion is his overt behaviour. It can indeed plausibly be argued that to talk about the unconscious is always equivalent to talking about overt behaviour, though often in a very complicated way. Now there seems to me to be a very good sense in which to tell a story of this kind, that this is what the man did and that these were his reasons for doing it, is to give a complete description of the facts. Or rather, since one can never be in a position to say that any such description is complete, what will be missing from it will be further information of the same type; what we obtain when this information is added is a more elaborate account of the circumstances of the action, and of its antecedents and consequences. But now suppose that instead of developing the story in this circumstantial way, one applies an ethical predicate to it. Suppose that instead of asking what it was that really happened, or what the agent's motives really were, we ask whether he was justified in acting as he did. Did he have the right to kill? Is it true that he had the right? Is it a fact that he acted rightly? It does not matter in this connection what answer we give. The question for moral philosophy is not whether a certain action is right or wrong, but what is implied by saying that it is right, or saying that it is wrong. Suppose then that we say that the man acted rightly. The point that I wish to make is that in saying this we are not elaborating or modifying our description of the situation in the way that we should be elaborating it if we gave further police-court details, or in the way that we should be modifying it if we showed that the agent's motives were different from what they had been thought to be. To say that his motives were good, or that they were bad, is not to say what they were. To say that the man acted rightly, or that he acted wrongly, is not to say what he did. And when one has said what he did, when one has described the situation in the way that I have outlined, then to add that he was justified, or alternatively that he was not, is not to say any more about what he did; it does not add a further detail to the story. It is for this reason that these ethical predicates are not factual; they do not describe any features of the situation to which they are applied. But they do, someone may object, they describe its ethical features. But what are these ethical features? And how are they related to the other features of the situation, to what we may provisionally call its "natural" features? Let us consider this.

To begin with, it is, or should be, clear that the connection is not logical. Let us assume that two observers agree about all the circumstances of the case, including the agent's motives, but that they disagree in their evaluation of it. Then neither of them is contradicting himself. Otherwise the use of the ethical term would add nothing to the circumstantial description; it would serve merely as a repetition, or partial repetition, of it. But neither, as I hope to show, is the connection factual. There is nothing that counts as observing the *designata* of the ethical predicates, apart from observing the natural features of the situation. But what alternative is left? Certainly it can be said that the ethical features in some way depend upon the natural. We can and do give reasons for our moral judgements, just as we do for our aesthetic judgements, where the same argument applies. We fasten on motives, point to consequences, ask what would happen if everyone were to behave in such a way, and so forth. But the question is: In what way do these reasons support the judgements? Not in a logical sense. Ethical argument is not formal demonstration. And not in a scientific sense either. For then the goodness or badness of the situation, the rightness or wrongness of the action, would have to be something apart from the situation, something independently verifiable, for which the facts adduced as the reasons for the moral judgement were evidence. But in these moral cases the two coincide. There is no procedure of examining the value of the facts, as distinct from examining the facts themselves. We may say that we have evidence for our moral judgements, but we cannot distinguish between pointing to the evidence itself and pointing to that for which it is supposed to be evidence. Which means that in the scientific sense it is not evidence at all.

My own answer to this question is that what are accounted reasons for our moral judgements are reasons only in the sense that they determine attitudes. One attempts to influence another person morally by calling his attention to certain natural features of the situation, which are such as will be likely to evoke from him the desired response. Or again one may give reasons to oneself as a means of settling on an attitude or, more importantly, as a means of coming to some practical decision. Of course there are many cases in which one applies an ethical term. without there being any question of one's having to act oneself, or even to persuade others to act, in any present situation. Moral judgements passed upon the behaviour of historical or fictitious characters provide obvious examples. But an action or a situation is morally evaluated always as an action or a situation of a certain kind. What is approved or disapproved is something repeatable. In saying that Brutus or Raskolnikov acted rightly, I am giving myself and others leave to imitate them should similar circumstances arise. I show myself to be favourably disposed in either case towards actions of that type. Similarly, in saying that they acted wrongly, I express a resolution not to imitate them, and endeavour also to discourage others. It may be thought that the mere use of the dyslogistic word "wrongly" is not much of a discouragement, although it does have some emotive force. But that is where the reasons come in. I discourage others, or at any rate hope to discourage them, by telling them why I think the action wrong; and here the argument may take various forms. One method is to appeal to some moral principle, as, for example, that human life is sacred, and show that it applies to the given case. It is assumed that the principle is one that already has some influence upon those to whom the argument is addressed. Alternatively, one may try to establish certain facts, as, for example, that the act in question caused, or was such as would be likely to cause, a great deal of unhappiness; and here it is assumed that the consideration of these facts will modify the hearer's attitude. It is assumed that he regards the increase of human misery as something undesirable, something if possible to be avoided. As for the moral judgement itself, it may be regarded as expressing the attitude which the reasons given for it are calculated to evoke. To say, as I once did, that these moral judgements are merely expressive of certain feelings, feelings of approval or disapproval, is an oversimplification. The fact is rather that what may be described as moral attitudes consist in certain patterns of behaviour, and that the expression of a moral judgement is an element in the pattern. The moral judgement expresses the attitude in the sense that it contributes to defining it. Why people respond favourably to certain facts and unfavourably to others is a question for the sociologist, into which I do not here propose to enter. I should imagine that the utilitarians had gone some way towards answering this question, although theirs is almost certainly not the whole answer. But my concern at present is only to analyse the use of ethical terms, not scientifically to explain it.

At this point it may be objected that I have been excessively dogmatic. What about the people who claim that they do observe ethical properties, non-natural properties, as G. E. Moore once put it,[2] not indeed through their senses, but by means of intellectual intuition? What of those who claim that they have a moral sense, and mean by this not merely that they have feelings of approval and disapproval, or whatever else may go to define a moral attitude, but that they experience such things as goodness or beauty in a way somehow analogous to that in which they experience sounds or colours? What are we to say to them? I may not have any experiences of this sort myself, but that, it may be said, is just my shortcoming. I am surely not entitled to assume that all these honest and intelligent persons do not have the experiences that they say they do. It may be, indeed, that the differences between us lie not so much in the nature of our respective experiences as in our fashion of describing them. I do in fact suspect that the experiences which

[2]Vide his *Principia Ethica*, Chapter 1.

some philosophers want to describe as intuitions, or as quasi-sensory apprehensions, of good are not significantly different from those that I want to describe as feelings of approval. But whether this be so or not, it does not in any way affect my argument. For let it be granted that someone who contemplates some natural situation detects in it something which he describes as "goodness" or "beauty" or "fittingness" or "worthiness to be approved." How this experience of goodness, or whatever it may be, is supposed to be related to the experiences which reveal the natural features of the situation has not yet been made clear, but I take it that it is not regarded merely as their effect. Rather, the situation is supposed to look good, or fitting, in much the same way as a face may be said to look friendly. But then to say that this experience is an experience of good will be to say no more than that it is this type of experience. The word "good,' or whatever other value term may be used, simply comes to be descriptive of experiences of this type, and here it makes no difference whether they are regarded as intuitions or as moral sensations. In neither case does anything whatsoever follow as regards conduct. That a situation has this peculiar property, the property whose presence is established by people's having such experiences, does not entail that it is preferable to other situations, or that it is anyone's duty to bring it into existence. To say that such a situation ought to be created, or that it deserves to exist, will be to say something different from merely saying that it has this property. This point is obscured by the use of an ethical term to describe the property, just because the ethical term is tacitly understood to be normative. It continues to fulfil its function of prescribing the attitude that people are to take. But if the ethical term is understood to be normative, then it does not merely describe the alleged non-natural property, and if it does merely describe this property, then it is not normative and so no longer does the work that ethical terms are supposed to do.

This argument may become clearer if, instead of designating the supposed property from the outset as "good," we refer to it simply as "X." The question then arises whether X is identical with good. How is this question to be interpreted? If it is interpreted as merely asking whether X is of a certain quality, whether it exhibits the character for which the word "good" is being made to stand, then the answer may very well be that the two are identical; but all that this amounts to is that we have decided to use the word "good" to designate what is also designated by "X." And from this no normative conclusion follows. It does not follow that the situation characterized by X has any value, if its having value is understood as implying not merely that it answers to a certain description but that it has some claim upon us, that it is something that we ought to foster or desire. Having appropriated the word "good" to do duty for X, to serve as a mere description of a special tone or colouring of the situation, we shall need some other word to do the normative work that the word "good" did before. But if "good" is allowed to keep its normative sense, then goodness may indeed be attributed to X, but the two cannot be identified. For then to say that X is good is not just to say that "X" stands for a certain property. It is to say that whatever

has this property is to be valued, sought, approved of, brought into existence
in preference to other things, and so on. Those who talk of non-natural
qualities, moral intuitions, and all the rest of it, may be giving peculiar
descriptions of commonplace experiences, or they may be giving suggestive
descriptions of peculiar experiences; it does not matter which view we take.
In either case we are left with the further question whether what is so described is to be valued; and this is not simply equivalent to asking what
character it has, whether natural, or non-natural, whatever that may mean.
Thus even if an intuitionist does have experiences that others do not have,
it makes no difference to the argument. We are still entitled to say that it is
misleading for him to use a value-term to designate the content of such experiences; for in this way he contrives to smuggle a normative judgement
into what purports to be a statement of fact. A valuation is not a description
of something very peculiar; it is not a description at all. Consequently, the
familiar subjective-objective antithesis is out of place in moral philosophy.
The problem is not that the subjectivist denies that certain wild, or domes-
ticated, animals, "objective values," exist and the objectivist triumphantly
produces them; or that the objectivist returns like an explorer with tales
from the kingdom of values and the subjectivist says he is a liar. It does not
matter what the explorer finds or does not find. For talking about values is
not a matter of describing what may or may not be there, the problem being
whether it really is there. There is no such problem. The moral problem is:
What am I to do? What attitude am I to take? And moral judgements are
directives in this sense.

We can now see that the whole dispute about the objectivity of
values, as it is ordinarily conducted, is pointless and idle. I suppose that
what underlies it is the question: Are the things that I value really valuable,
and how can I know that they are? Then one party gives the answer: They
are really valuable if they reflect, or participate in, or are in some other
mysterious way related to an objective world of values; and you can know
that they are by inspecting this world. To which their opponents reply that
there is no such world, and can therefore be no such inspection. But this
sort of argument, setting aside the question whether it is even intelligible, is
nothing to the purpose. For suppose that someone did succeed in carrying
out such an inspection. Suppose that he had an experience which we allowed
him to describe in these terms. He can still raise the questions: Are these
values the real ones? Are the objects that I am inspecting themselves really
valuable, and how can I know that they are? And how are these questions
to be answered? They do not arise, it may be said. These objective values
carry the stamp of authenticity upon their faces. You have only to look at
them to know that they are genuine. But, in this sense, any natural situation
to which we attach value can carry the stamp of authenticity upon its face.
That is to say, the value which is attached to it may be something that it
does not occur to us to question. But in neither case is it inconceivable that
the value should be questioned. Thus, these alleged objective values perform
no function. The hypothesis of their existence does no work; or rather, it

does no work that is not equally well done without it. Its effect is to answer the question: Are the things that I value really valuable? by Yes, if you have a certain sort of experience in connection with them. Let us assume that these experiences can be identified and even that there is some method for deciding between them when they appear to yield contradictory results. Even so, that someone does or does not have them is itself a "natural" fact. Moreover, this answer merely lays down one of many possible standards. It is on a par with saying: "The things that you value are really valuable if they increase human happiness, or they are really valuable if certain persons, your pastors and masters, approve of them." Then either one accepts the standard, or one raises the question again. Why should I value human happiness? Why should I be swayed by my pastors and masters? Why should I attach such great importance just to these experiences? In the end there must come a point where one gets no further answer, but only a repetition of the injunction: Value this because it is valuable.

In conducting this argument, I have put the most favourable interpretation upon my opponents' claims; for I have assumed that what is described as the apprehension of objective values may be a different experience from the everyday experience of attaching value to some natural situation; but, in fact, I am fairly confident that what we have here are two different ways of describing the same experience. And in that case the answer that the "objectivists" give to the question: Are the things that I value really valuable? is the "subjective" answer that they are really valuable if you value them, or perhaps that they are really valuable if certain other people value them. What we are given is an injunction not to worry, which may or may not satisfy us. If it does not, perhaps something else will. But in any case there is nothing to be done about it, except look at the facts, look at them harder, look at more of them, and then come to a moral decision. Then, asking whether the attitude that one has adopted is the right attitude comes down to asking whether one is prepared to stand by it. There can be no guarantee of its correctuness, because nothing counts as a guarantee. Or rather, something may count for someone as a guarantee, but counting something as a guarantee is itself taking up a moral standpoint.

All this applies equally to "naturalistic" theories of ethics, like Utilitarianism. By defining "right," in the way that Bentham does, as "conducive to the greatest happiness of the greatest number," one does give it a descriptive meaning; but just for that reason one takes it out of the list of ethical terms. So long as the word "right" keeps its current emotive force, the implication remains that what is right ought to be done, but this by no means follows from Bentham's definition. Nevertheless, it is clearly intended that the definition should somehow carry this implication; otherwise it would not fulfil its purpose. For the point of such a definition, as Professor Stevenson has well brought out in his *Ethics and Language*, is not that it gives precision to the use of a word, but that it covertly lays down a standard of conduct. The moral judgement is that happiness is to be maximized, and that actions are to be evaluated, praised or blamed, imitated or avoided, in proportion as they militate for or against this end. Now this is not a statement of fact, but a recommendation; and in the ordinary way the sense of such a recommendation is contained in some ethical term. These ethical terms can also be given a descriptive meaning, but it is not *qua* descriptive that they are ethical. If, for example, the word "wrong" is simply equated with "not conducive to human happiness," some other term will be needed to carry the normative implication that conduct of this sort is to be avoided; and it is terms of this kind, which are not descriptive, that I am treating as distinctively ethical.

I hope that I have gone some way towards making clear what the theory which I am advocating is. Let me now say what it is not. In the first place, I am not saying that morals are trivial or unimportant, or that people ought not to bother with them. For this would itself be a judgement of value, which I have not made and do not wish to make. And even if I did wish to make it it would have no logical connection with my theory. For the theory is entirely on the level of analysis; it is an attempt to show what people are doing when they make moral judgements; it is not a set of suggestions as to what moral judgements they are to make. And this is true of all moral philosophy, as I understand it. All moral theories, intuitionist, naturalistic, objectivist, emotive, and the rest, in so far as they are philosophical theories, are neutral as regards actual conduct. To speak technically, they belong to the field of meta-ethics, not ethics proper. That is why it is silly, as well as presumptuous, for any one type of philosopher to pose as the champion of virtue. And it is also one reason why many people find moral philosophy an unsatisfying subject. For they mistakenly look to the moral philosopher for guidance.

Again, when I say that moral judgements are emotive rather than descriptive, that they are persuasive expressions of attitudes and not statements of fact, and consequently that they cannot be either true or false, or at least that it would make for clarity if the categories of truth and falsehood were not applied to them, I am not saying that nothing is good or bad, right or wrong, or that it does not matter what we do. For once more such a statement would itself be the expression of a moral attitude. This attitude is not entailed by the theory, nor do I in fact adopt it. It would indeed be a difficult position to maintain. It would exclude even egotism as a policy, for the decision to consult nothing but one's own pleasure is itself a value judgement. What it requires is that one should live without any policy at all. This may or may not be feasible. My point is simply that I am not recommending it. Neither, in expounding my meta-ethical theory, am I recommending the opposite. It is indeed to be expected that a moral philosopher, even in my sense of the term, will have his moral standards and that he will sometimes make moral judgements; but these moral judgements cannot be a logical consequence of his philosophy. To analyse moral judgements is not itself to moralize.

Finally, I am not saying that anything that anybody thinks right is right; that putting people into concentration camps is preferable to allowing them free speech if somebody happens to think so, and that the contrary is also preferable if somebody thinks that it is. If my theory did entail this, it would be contradictory; for two different courses of action cannot each be preferable to the other. But it does not entail anything of the sort. On my analysis, to say that something which somebody thinks right really is right is to range oneself on his side, to adhere to that particular standpoint, and certainly I do not adhere to every standpoint whatsoever. I adhere to some, and not to others, like evrybody else who has any moral views at all. It is, indeed, true that in a case where one person A approves of X, and another person B approves of not-X, A may correctly express his attitude towards X by saying that it is good, or right, and that B may correctly use the same term to express his attitude towards not-X. But there is no contradiction here. There would be a contradiction if from the fact that A was using words honestly and correctly when he said that X was good, and that B was using words honestly and correctly when he said that not-X was good, it followed that both X and not-X were good, or that X was both good and bad. But this not follow, inasmuch as the conclusion that X is good, or that not-X is good, itself expresses the attitude of a third party, the speaker, who is by no means bound to agree with both A and B. In this example, indeed, he cannot consistently agree with both, though he may disagree with both if he regards both X and not-X as ethically neutral, or as contraries rather than contradictories in respect of value. It is easy to miss this point, which is essential for the understanding of our position. To say that anything is right if someone thinks so is unobjectionable if it means no more than that anyone is entitled to use the word "right" to refer to something of which he morally approves. But this is not the way in which it is ordinarily taken. It is ordinarily taken as the enunciation of a moral principle. As a moral principle it does appear contradictory; it is at least doubtful whether to say of a man that he commits himself morally both to X and not-X is to describe a possible attitude. But it may perhaps be construed as a principle of universal moral tolerance. As such, it may appeal to some; it does not, in fact, to me. But the important point is that it is not entailed by the theory, which is neutral as regards all moral principles. And here I may repeat that in saying that it is neutral as regards all moral principles I am not saying that it recommends them all alike, nor that it condemns them all alike. It is not that sort of theory. No philosophical theory is.

But even if there is no logical connection between this meta-ethical theory and any particular type of conduct, may there not be a psychological connection? Does not the promulgation of such a theory encourage moral laxity? Has not its effect been to destroy people's confidence in accepted moral standards? And will not the result of this be that something mischievous will take their place? Such charges have, indeed, been made, but I do not know upon what evidence. The question how people's conduct is actually affected by their acceptance of a meta-ethical theory is one for empirical investigation; and in this case, so far as I know, no serious investigation has yet been carried out. My own observations, for what they are worth, do not suggest that those who accept the "positivist" analysis of moral judgements conduct themselves very differently as a class from those who reject it; and, indeed, I doubt if the study of moral philosophy does, in general, have any very marked effect upon people's conduct. The way to test the point would be to convert a sufficiently large number of people from one meta-ethical view to another and make careful observations of their behaviour before and after their conversions. Assuming that their behaviour changed in some significant way, it would then have to be decided by further experiment whether this was due to the change in their philosophical beliefs or to some other factor. If it could be shown, as I believe it could not, that the general acceptance of the sort of analysis of moral judgements that I have been putting forward would have unhappy social consequences, the conclusion drawn by illiberal persons might be that the doctrine ought to be kept secret. For my part I think that I should dispute this conclusion on moral grounds, but this is a question which I am not now concerned to argue. What I have tried to show is not that the theory I am defending is expedient, but that it is true.

❀ C. I. LEWIS

38. *Knowing, Doing, and Valuing: A Pragmatist's View*

Clarence Irving Lewis (1883–1964), a distinguished American philosopher, was born in Stoneham, Massachusetts and educated at Harvard University. He taught philosophy at the University of California from 1911–1920 and at Harvard University from 1920 until his retirement in 1953. His main works were: *Mind and the World Order* (1929), *Symbolic Logic* (1932), *An Analysis of Knowledge and Valuation* (1946), *The Ground and Nature of the Right* (1955), and *Our Social Inheritance* (1957).

1. Evaluations are a form of empirical knowledge, not fundamentally different in what determines their truth or falsity, and what determines their validity or justification, from other kinds of empirical knowledge.

This fact has often been obscured by failure to distinguish mere apprehensions of good or ill in experience from predictions of the possible realizations of these qualities in particular empirical contexts, and from ap-

From Chapter 12 of *An Analysis of Knowledge and Valuation* (LaSalle, Ill.: The Open Court Publishing Co. 1946). Reprinted by permission of The Open Court Publishing Co. One section (no. 7) has been renumbered.

praisals of the objective value-quality resident in existent things. The first of these—direct findings of value-quality in what is presented—are not judgments; and unless or until they become the basis of some further prediction, they are not cognitive. But predictions of a goodness or badness which will be disclosed in experience under certain circumstances and on particular occasions, are either true or false, and are capable of verification in the same manner as other terminating judgments, which predict accrual of other qualities than value. This kind of foresight represents one of the most essential of cognitive capacities: indeed, we might say it is the root of all practical wisdom. And evaluations of things; appraisals of their potentialities for good or ill; are likewise true or false, and must be justified as well as confirmed by reference to experience. The manner of their validation, and of their confirmation, does not differ, in general, from that of attributions of other properties to objects.

The contrary conception has, of course, been frequent. It has been held that value-apprehensions are subjective or relative in a sense which is incompatible with their genuinely cognitive significance. Or it has been maintained that value-predications are not matter of fact statements at all, being merely expressions of emotion and hence neither true nor false.

But this is one of the strangest aberrations ever to visit the mind of man. The denial to value-apprehensions in general of the character of truth or falsity and of knowledge, would imply both moral and practical cynicism. It would invalidate all action; because action becomes pointless unless there can be some measure of assurance of a valuable result which it may realize. And this negation, if it be carried out consistently, likewise invalidates all knowledge; both because believing is itself an active attitude which would have no point if it were not better to be right than wrong in what one believes, and because knowledge in general is for the sake of action. If action in general is pointless, then knowledge also is futile, and one belief is as good as another.

2. This relation of action and evaluation is as obvious as it is important. But it is sometimes clouded by the fact that action is considered merely as "behavior," and value-judgments are so thought of as to be divested of both their cognitive and their imperative significance at one and the same time. We shall intend here to limit ourselves to what is plainly open to common sense; but it will be necessary to speak in terms which have been cleared a little of their common ambiguities. Such relatively verbal questions are tiresome—particularly so when they relate to matters of importance—but we must endure them, for the sake of clarity.

Action is behavior which is deliberate or decided upon; which is subject to critique and could at least be altered on reflection. Behavior which it is beyond the subject's power to control is not action. That is; we shall, in this context, limit "act" and "action" to the sense of "conduct."

Action—at least action of the sort called rational and sensible—is for the sake of realizing something to which positive value is ascribed, or of avoiding something to which disvalue is ascribed. In order not to tread on the toes of any for whom "rational' has other connotations, let us choose the more colorless term "sensible" here, and say that an action is *sensible* if and only if something to which comparative value is ascribed is expected to be realized as a result of it—where "comparative" refers to some contemplated alternative or alternatives.

This expectation of a result in the light of which an action is adopted, is its *intent;* the intent of the act, and the intent of the doer in adopting it.

All acts have in common the character of being intended or willed. But one act is distinguishable from another by the content of it, the expected result of it, which is here spoken of as its intent. There is no obvious way in which we can say what act it is which is thought of or is done except by specifying this intent of it. . . .

We shall include under "intent" the *whole* expected result of the act. Oftentimes such result would be complex, and have parts which would be differently valued. *That part* of the intent of an act for the sake of which it is adopted, we shall call its *purpose*. Sometimes the word "motive" is used in the sense here given to "purpose." And "motive" might come nearer to what is meant than "purpose" does in one respect: "motive" is generally applied only when some specific act is done or contemplated; whereas "purpose" is sometimes used to name what is desired (and viewed as possible) even though no specific mode of attaining this desired result should be in mind. There could be, thus, purposes which are not the purposes of any particular act, done or contemplated. Still "purpose of an act" remains unambiguous. Also, the word "motive" would not do so well here, being frequently used to indicate an underlying general principle, sentiment, or continuing attitude, rather than any expected consequence of a particular action.

"Purpose" and "intent," or "intention," are often taken to be synonymous, though common usage will hardly bear that out. In particular instances the purpose and the whole intent may coincide. More often, however, there will be some part of the expected result of action to which the doer is indifferent. And it happens rather frequently that an action is adopted for the sake of some consequence, A, though it is expected to have also the consequence B, and the doer would regard B, by itself, as undesirable. In cases of this last sort, if it be inquired concerning B, "Did you do that intentionally?," the truthful answer would be such as, "Yes; but only because B was bound up with A."

It will appropriate to extend the designation "sensible" to purposes as well as intentions; and to say that the purpose of an act is sensible only if what is purposed is something to which comparative value is ascribed. But it is to be observed that purpose of an act may be sensible when the intent of it, and the act itself, are not: the doer may adopt an action for the sake of some value included in the anticipated result, although he would judge this result as a whole to be disvaluable. We may also remark that, while it is plausible to suppose that there are actions the intent of which as a whole is not sensible, it is definitely less plausible that there is any act the purpose of which is not sensible; that anything is done *for the sake of* that which the doer recognizes as disvaluable. For example, one who yields to the solicitations of a present gratification, and in so doing, wittingly prejudices his own further interests, nevertheless does so *for the sake of* this gratification which he values: thus his purpose is still sensible, though his act and the intent of it are not. Even perverse acts would hardly be done except, paradoxically, for the sake of the satisfaction—which one values—in being thus perverse. In any case, it would be anomolous to call an act done for the sake of the recognizedly disvaluable, a *successful* act, whatever the outcome of it. Let us say, therefore, that an action is successful if and only if it is adopted for the sake of some anticipated consequence to which comparative value is ascribed, and this expectation is borne out by the result of performing the act.

This anticipated result will, in some cases, be decisively and finally verifiable; an enjoyable experience, for example. But in other cases, it will be something not thus completely verifiable at any given time, e.g., if the purpose is to make the world safe for democracy, or to bring about some other state of affairs, or create some object, whose value-consequences are expected to continue for an indefinite length of time. Since the success of an act whose purpose puts it in this latter class will never be fully verified, and since there is a tendency (included in the meaning) to withhold ascription of success or failure until it is demonstrated, it will be well to say that an act is to be called successful *so far as* the purpose of it is verifiably achieved. (With other characters, predication is regarded as true if the ascription is positively verifi*able*. The point of difference here is that "success" and "failure" have a temporal significance: an act succeeds only *when* the purpose of it is achieved; though a thing is as truly round, for example, before its roundness is verified as after.) The locution "so far successful" will also be appropriate to the fact that in some cases an ascribed value may be realized in the result of action but realized in some part only or not in the degree in which it was anticipated. . . .

3. Success is the desideratum of all action: that statement is a tautology. Nevertheless for the appraisal of an act as ascribable to the doer —for "judgment of an act" in the most frequent sense—the success of it is less important than another character which we may call its *practical justification*. This character is the character is the character of being guided by anticipation of something of comparative value, which prediction, whether true or not, is at the time when the action is contemplated and for him who contemplates it, valid as probable knowledge. That is to say; the character in question belongs to an act if and only if the intent of it is an expectation which is a *warranted empirical belief*.

This character of being practically justified (or unjustified) is more important to assess than is the success of action, for two reasons. First, because such justification is as near as we can come, at the time of decision, to assuring success: the rest is on the knees of the gods. And second, because the capacity to make decisions which are thus justified, or the liability to those which are unjustified, is a more important attribute of persons than is their success in particular actions. It is so, whether the person in question be one-self or another, because the practically justified character of his acts in general is the only rational basis for prediction of any individual's *future* success or failure. In so far as one's success in general does not correlate with the practically justified character of decisions in general, that lack of accord will be merely a matter of good or ill fortune, beyond one's power to affect.

We must note, of course, that such practical justification is not the same thing as moral justification—unless on some special theory of morals. If there can be stupidity in assessing empirical beliefs, for which stupidity the person in question is not responsible, then an act may be morally justified without being practically justified. And if there can be moral obliquity in a decision to act upon a sensible intention whose probability as an empirical eventuality is correctly assessed, then an act may be practically justified without being morally justified.

4. So much punctilio in the use of words is irksome, particularly where the matters in question are the familiar and continuing concerns of daily life. But if we have now succeeded in obviating ambiguities in the language commonly used of actions, while still remaining true to the important interests which such language connotes, then it becomes clear that, as was claimed at the outset, *no intention or purpose could be serious, and no action could be practically justifiable or attain success, if it were not that there are value-predications which represent empirical cognitions, and are predictive and hence capable of confirmation or disconfirmation.* On that point, these commonplace considerations would seem to be quite decisive.

Where ability to make correct judgments of value is concerned, we more typically speak of wisdom, perhaps, than of knowledge. And "wisdom" connotes one character which is not knowledge at all, though it is a quality inculcated by experience; the temper, namely, which avoids perversity in intentions, and the insufficiently considered in actions. But for the rest, wisdom and knowledge are distinct merely because there is so much knowledge which, for any given individual or under the circumstances which obtain, is relatively inessential to judgment of values and to success in action. Thus a man may be pop-eyed with correct information and still lack wisdom, because his information has little bearing on those judgments of relative value which he is called upon to make, or because he lacks capacity to discriminate the practically important from the unimportant, or to apply his information to concrete problems of action. And men of humble attainments so far as breadth of information goes, may still be wise by their correct apprehension of such values as lie open to them and of the roads to these. But surely wisdom is a type of knowledge; that type which is oriented upon the important and the valuable. The wise man is he who knows where good lies, and knows how to act so that it may be attained.

Even to "know what one likes" is a form of knowledge. Whether knowing what one likes is veridical knowledge of objective values or not, is a matter calling for further consideration. But without prejudice to that question, it may be observed that one who knows what he likes possesses that kind of knowledge which consists in ability to predict the accrual or non-accrual, under given conditions, of value-quality in his own experience. One who knows, for example, that he likes Bach and dislikes Stravinsky, may be as great a musical ignoramus as anyone chooses to allege, but when he looks at the concert program he knows what to expect. His value-predication has a verifiable content and possesses genuinely cognitive significance. Indeed, this kind of knowledge is perhaps the most important of all; not only personally but socially. At least half of the world's avoidable troubles are created by those who do not know what they want and pursue what would not satisfy them if they had it. And "we could deal with the villains if it weren't for the fools."

The enterprise of human living can prosper only if there are value-judgments which are true; judgments which predict the accrual of value-quality as a consequence of action, and which are positively verifiable by adoption of the mode of action in question. Only on this condition could any action have that kind of rightness or correctness which all sensible action aims to have; and only on this condition has any knowledge that import of usefulness for the guidance of action which constitutes the eventual significance of all attempts to know. These things being so, those who would deny the character of cognition and the possibility of truth to value-apprehensions, must find themselves, ultimately, in the position of Epimenides the Cretan who said that all Cretans are liars. Either their thesis must be false or it is not worth believing or discussing; because if it should be true, then *nothing* would be worth believing or discussing. And however much of logical ingenuity may be required for untangling paradoxes of this type, the point remains clear that whoever says what is incompatible with his own presumptive attitude in saying it must either be joking or he reduces himself to absurdity.

5. Recognition of this fact that judgments of value represent an essential and basic form of knowledge has been impeded in a number of different ways. But particularly in two; by the failure to distinguish between fundamentally different types of value-predication, and by the attempt to define the goodness of all kinds of goods so as to secure the point that nothing can be genuine and "objective" good which is to be attained through immoral action. In fact, the whole discussion of the validity of evaluations has often been characterized by a thorough entanglement of three matters which are, in their intrinsic nature, quite distinct: (1) the nature of ultimate or basic value; that kind of value from which the value of everything else correctly called valuable is derivative; (2) the question of the first-personality ("relativity," "subjectivity") or the impersonality ("community," "objectivity") of value-ascriptions; and (3) the question whether, and if so why, the possible realization of or possession of the valuable by other persons, legitimately lays claim to respect on one's own decisions of action.

The first of these is, of course, a fundamental question about evaluations. The second is itself a complex matter, but the root of it lies in considerations which are merely logical or have to do with our customary modes of speech. The third is a distinctive—perhaps *the* distinctive—question of ethics. The first two will demand of us lengthy consideration. The last is a separate topic outside the province of this book; though we shall make certain comments bearing on it.

We cannot make even a good beginning in the consideration of evaluations in general until we untangle the question what basic good is and what goods are derivative, from question of the subjectivity or objectivity of value-predications. And a first step here is to observe that there are three main types of value-predication, corresponding to the three main types of empirical statements in general.

First, there is expressive statement of a value-quality found in the directly experienced. One who says at the concert, "This is good," or who makes a similar remark at table, is presumably reporting a directly experienced character of the sensuously presented as such. He might, of course, have a quite different intention; he might be meaning to assert that the selection being played has a verifiably satisfactory character best attested by those endowed with musical discrimination and having long experience and training in music; or that the food verifiably meets all dietic standards in high degree. In that case, the immediately experienced goodness would, presumably, provide the empirical cue to his judgment, but what is *judged* would be no more than partially verified in this directly apprehended quality of the given—which itself requires no judgment. Such judged and verifiable goodness of the musical selection or the viands, is an objective property, comparable to the objective roundness of a plate, or the objective frequency of vibrations in the surrounding atmosphere.

Directly experienced goodness or badness, like seen redness or felt hardness, may become, when attended, the matter of a formulation or report which intends nothing more than this apparent quality of what appears. There are any number of questions about value-qaulity as thus immediate, which will have to be discussed in the next chapter. But it will hardly be denied that there is what may be called "apparent value" or "felt goodness," as there is seen redness or heard shrillness. And while the intent to formulate just this apparent value-quality of what is given, without implication of anything further, encounters linguistic difficulties, surely it will not be denied that there are such immediate experiences of good and bad to be formulated. We shall probably agree also that without such direct value-apprehensions, there could be no determination of values, or of what is valuable, in any *other* sense, or any significance for value-terms at all. Without the experience of felt value and disvalue, evaluations in general would have no meaning.

Any such formulation or report of apparent value, taken by itself and divested of all further implication, is an expressive statement; self-verifying (for him who makes it) in the only sense in which it could be called verifiable, and subject to no possible error, unless merely linguistic error in the words chosen to express it. Such a statement is true or false, since we could tell lies about the quality of immediate experience; but the apprehension expressed is not a judgment, and is not to be classed as knowledge, in the sense in which we have used that word.

Second, there are evaluations which are terminating judgments; the prediction, in the circumstances as apprehended, or in other and similarly apprehensible circumstances, of the possible accrual of value-quality in experience—for example, of enjoyment or of pain—conditional upon adoption of a particular mode of action. If I taste what is before me, I shall enjoy it; if I touch this red-glowing metal, I shall feel pain. Such judgments may be put to the test by acting on them, and are then decisively and completely verified or found false. Being predictive—verifiable but not verified—and subject to possible error, they represent a form of knowledge.

Third, there is that most important and most frequent type of evaluation which is the ascription of the objective property of being valuable to an existent or possible existent; to an object, a situation, a state of affairs, or to some *kind* of such thing. Such objective judgments of value are, as we shall find, considerably more complex than objective judgments of other characters than value. There is also much diversity amongst them: "X is valuable," in this objective sense, is a form of statement covering a great variety of meanings, and subject to troublesome ambiguities by reason of the difficulty of distinguishing these. But they all possess the common character of being what we have called non-terminating judgments. They are not, at any given time, decisively and completely verified, but always retain a significance for further possible experience and are capable of further confirmation. Like other judgments of objective fact or of any objective property, determination of their truth or falsity can never be completed, and they are, theoretically, never more than a probable, though often probable in the degree called "practically certain." Any particular confirmation of such a judgment comes by way of finding true some terminating judgment which is a consequence of it. And while there is no limit to the number of such terminating judgments, truth of which follows from the objective judgment of value, still there is nothing contained in the meaning of it which is not expressible by some terminating judgment or other. If, beyond what is thus expressible as some possible confirmation of it, the objective value-judgment should be supposed to have a further and different component of its significance, we should be unable to say or even to think to ourselves what this further component signified, or what conceivable difference the holding or not holding of it in fact would make to anybody under any thinkable circumstances.

Typically we should think of any such confirmation of the objective value of something as realization of some value-experience in connection with it. And there is question here—the question suggested, for example, by Mill's assertion that the only proof that a thing is desirable is its being desired[1]—whether objective value-judgments are not relative *exclusively* to the possibility of direct *value*-experience.

But a very little reflection reveals that such a conception would be unguarded: one may easily find evidence that a thing is valuable otherwise than through experiences of positive value. Just as one may find evidence that a thing is round or is hard in other ways than by seeing it round or feeling it hard, so too the objective value of a thing may be confirmed "indirectly" in other ways than by what would be called "experiencing the value of it."

For instance, judgment that my neighbor is a good musician may be confirmed by his rendition of difficult passages, though the selection he is presently at work on is one that leaves me cold, or even if I find his persistent exhibition of virtuosity an interruption to my train of thought and highly irritating. Or I may find evidence that my chisel is sharp, as a good chisel ought to be, through painfully cutting myself with it. We may still feel that in determination of any objective value, value-experiences occupy a privileged or peculiarly decisive place; but if so, this sense of their peculiar importance is elusive and will require to be probed. At least the conclusion would be ill-drawn, that a belief in objective value can be confirmed *only* through direct experiences of value.

Many of the puzzles which beset us about evaluation may be resolved or materially advanced by determining in which of these three senses the predication of value which is in question is to be taken. Does the statement made concern a value immediately found in experience? Then the matter lies outside any reasonable dispute: the finding of the subject of this experience is final; and concerning it there is no mistake that he can make. Any question about it concerns its evidential character as basis for some *different* evaluation; for judgment of *further* value-experiences derivable from the same thing, or judgment of some *objective* value-property of it; or else the question concerns merely the appropriateness of the language he uses for expressing what he finds in his experience.

Or is the value-predication in question intended to assert that under certain circumstances and by a certain procedure experience of a certain value-quality would accrue? It is then a terminating judgment; predictive, and verifiable or falsifiable. But it is *decisively* verifiable or falsifiable (in whatever sense the conditions of verification should be possible) by being put to the test. If or when it should be so tested, its truth or falsity will be absolutely determined, beyond any question or debate. But prior to such verification, at any time when, for example, it functions as a judgment of the desirability or undesirability of certain ways of acting, its believability

---

[1]"The only proof capable of being given that a thing is visible, is that people actually see it. The only proof that a thing is audible, is that people hear it: and so of the other sources of our experience. In like manner, I apprehend, the sole evidence it is possible to produce that anything is desirable, is that people do actually desire it." *Utilitarianism,* Chapter IV, 3rd paragraph.

rests upon inductive evidence drawn from past experience; and our assurance of it can be, theoretically, no better than probable.

Or does the value-predication signify the objective property of value or disvalue in some kind of existent? Its meaning is then translatable into some multiplicity of terminating judgments, each by itself decisively verifiable or falsifiable, and each representing some possible confirmation of this objective judgment. Such an affirmation of objective value will have some probability or improbability on antecedent grounds, and this probability may be indefinitely increased or diminished by the test of its confirmations; though always it will retain a further and as yet untested significance, because the number of such possible confirmations of it will not be finitely exhaustible. Also the evidence which we have or may obtain for it need not be confined to direct disclosures of value or disvalue in the thing in question, but may include other and indirect confirmations of its objective value.

6. All three of the types of value-predication mentioned above are forms of empirical statement. And any one, or all, of these could be confused with a quite different kind of statement about the valuable, which is neither a formulation of value as found nor a judgment which experience could verify or confirm. For example, the declaration that pleasure is the good; or that a thing is constituted good by being the object of an interest; or that goodness is a simple, unanalyzable quality; or that nothing is unqualifiedly good but a good will. Such are not empirical statements at all, but are analytic and knowable *a priori* or else false. They are judgments; but judgments in the same sense as "Hardness is impenetrability," "Hardness is determined by resistance to sudden impact," "Hardness is a simple, unanalyzable quality," or "Nothing is unqualifiedly hard but a hard heart." Such statements, if true at all, can be certified by some analysis of meaning; their truth is determinable by reflection, without other evidence than that of logic and of what would be formulated in definitions. . . .

7. There are many other questions concerning value in things which have been omitted here and must later be taken up in some detail. As has been mentioned, the modes of value-predication are more various and complex than are the modes in which other properties are perdicated to things; and objective value-predications are peculiarly liable to ambiguity on that account. We attempt here only to indicate the generic significance of "X has value," and the major and proximate subdivisions subordinate to that generic meaning. However, it may be best to mention briefly certain points which will have occurred to the reader already, in order to avoid misunderstanding of what has been said.

The word "value" is here used exclusively in the sense of a value-quality, value-character or value-property of something, or of a *kind* of value-quality, character or property. And we use the plural "values" in the same idiom in which "utilities" or "economic values" would commonly be used; that is, to refer not only to kinds of value but also to instances of value in things. As will appear from the whole discussion, the question whether values exist or subsist, apart from any entity which they characterize, is one which is completely empty, when questions which are essentially verbal have been cleared away.

We have been at no great pains to avoid the common ambiguity of "value" and "value-predication" as between (1) what has to do with positive value only, and (2) what has to do with value or disvalue, either one. This is so frequent a usage that it hardly needs special comment. Evaluations of course include ascriptions of negative as well as of positive value; and if one speaks of positive value only, the corresponding statement concerning disvalue or the disvaluable will usually go without saying.

It is a slightly more troublesome point that in predicting value to an existent, one often intends to weigh together *all* its potentialities for good and ill both, and strike a balance. But if this is the more frequent usage, still we cannot overlook the numerous modes of speech in which value-predications are relative, or restricted to a particular context, and predications of utility refer only to a particular use or a specific kind of utility. In calling a thing a good rifle, for example, one does not mean to decide the quyestion whether rifles in general, or this rifle in particular, possesses greater potentialities for realized good or for ill. One speaks of it in relation only to a specific class of purposes, connoted by the name "rifle" by which the object is called. Perhaps predication, in this case, falls in the class of judgments of putative use. But even .if we confine ourselves strictly to predications of genuine extrinsic value, we should still find that the varieties and complexities of such value-ascriptions exceed what might at first appear. Examination of these, however, is postponed.

It is another and more obvious ambiguity of value-predications that sometimes they intend ascription to a thing of first-personal value; though more often they intend to ascirbe value from the point of view of all who may be affected by existence of the thing in question. And here it is important to separate matters which are mainly linguistic and concern merely the characteristic intent with which statements in a certain mode are made, from any further question of ethical right or of any other kind of validity. It is a question of the most serious importance whether value, in a sense which carries an ethically valid imperative for action, may be ascribed from the first-personal point of view, or whether only that which conduces to the good of others also, or to the good of the greatest number, is validly good in the ethical sense. But that is a quite separate matter from the question what a statement attribuiing a value means to assert. There is no implication of ethical egoism in recognizing that sometimes people say "This is good" meaning no more than what could also be expressed by "I like it" or "I enjoy it." Nor is there acknowledgment of a moral obligation to consider others equally with oneself in recognizing that ordinarily ascriptions of value to things are dominated by our social sense. Up to this point at least, we have said nothing which bears upon that fundamental question of ethics, one way or the other.

Nor have we meant to touch upon the question of the "subjectivity" of values, or their "relativity" to individuals, beyond what is implied in saying that value in an existent consists in its potentialities for the realization of directly findable value-qualities in experience. If one suppose that statement to constitute a theory of value which is relativistic or subjectivistic, then it will be important to recognize the sense in which it *does* imply a relativity to persons of the quality ascribed by "This existent thing is good," where what is ascribed by the statement, "This existent thing is round" does *not* imply such relativity; and to separate *this* kind of relativity which is here affirmed from a different sense of relativity, with respect to which—as we conceive it—"This is good" and "This is round" are entirely comparable.

Between "This object is good" and "This object is round," there is that difference which follows from the fact that values are either intrinsic or extrinsic, and values in objects are extrinsic only; whereas this distinction has no application to roundness or other non-value properties. We may anticipate later discussion by saying that the final end by reference to which all values are to be appraised, is the end of some possible good life: that the goodness ascribable to objects is, therefore, some possible contribution of them to a life which would be found good in the living of it. And this implies that values in objects are extrinsic only. But we may also admit in advance that we take this conception of final good to be one which will be universally accepted if the intention of it is understood; and if there be anything in this later discussion which will convince them of error.

As has been pointed out, this fact that values in objects, and values ascribable to objective properties of them, are extrinsic only, is correlative with a certain dependence of "This presented object is good," in the objective sense of the word "good," upon the truth of "This is good"—or "*would be* found immediately good under certain circumstances"—in the expressive sense of "good." But for the rest, it implies no peculiar relativity of value-predications which would not characterize predications of properties in general to objects. Demonstrable truth of all such predications is eventually relative to their possible verification or confirmation in experience: they are meaningful only if they may be confirmed or disconfirmed, and true only if such test of them would have a psoitive result. But this does *not* imply that what is valuable is dependent on being actually experienced as valuable, or in fact upon its being actually experienced at all. If there be those who find this conception subjectivistic or relativistic, then at least this issue does not concern anything peculiarly at stake in the conception of values. Just because we draw a line between value or good in the expressive sense of what is immediately *found* good or valuable, and the potentiality of objects for inducing this quality in experience, value in objects, as here interpreted, is as much and as little subjective or relative as is redness or roundness or any other non-value property. This potentiality for experienced goodness which may reside in a thing does not depend on the question whether any particular person *does* find the thing good, any more than the roundness of a round object depends on the question whether a particular subject "sees it round" or actually finds it round as a result of a measurement with calipers. The thing "is what it is regardless of what anybody thinks or feels about it," as truly in the case of value as in the case of any other objective character. It is for this reason that evaluations represent a form of knowledge, and are liable to error. We *judge* such potentialities of things for contributing to a good life, and sometimes we misjudge them; and this kind of mistake is the most grievous of all possible errors, because of the peculiarly direct connection between value-judgments and our sensibly taken actions and our personal fortunes or misfortunes. . . .

❀ HERBERT FEIGL

39. *Validation and Vindication: An Analysis of the Nature and Limits of Ethical Arguments*

Herbert Feigl has taught philosophy at the University of Minnesota for a number of years. An important philosopher of science, he has written and edited numerous articles and books. Among these are: *Readings in Philosophical Analysis* (with Wilfrid Sellars), 1949, *Readings in the Philosophy of Science* (with May Brodbeck), 1953, *Current Issues in the Philosophy of Science* (with Grover Maxwell), 1961, and *Mental and the Physical: The Essay and a Postscript*, 1967.

The following schematic dialogue was constructed with the intention of illustrating some of the typical turns and twists which occur almost invaraiably when argument in moral issues is pursued through successive levels of critical reflection. A more systematic formulation of the philosophical conclusions that may be derived from a study of such justificatory arguments will be presented in the second part of this essay.

I. A Dialogue

A.: Under what conditions can war be morally justified?
B.: Under no conditions. I am a convinced pacifist and conscientious objector. There is no greater evil than war and deliberate killing.
A.: Would you rather be killed or enslaved than do any killing? Are there

From *Readings in Ethical Theory*, selected and edited by Wilfrid Sellars and John Hospers. Copyright, 1952, by Meredith Corporation. Reprinted by permission of Appleton-Century-Crofts and the author.

no circumstances, such as a need for self-defense that would justify killing?

B.: There are none.

A.: If you were saying that wanton killing and cruelty are to be condemned, I should heartily agree with you. But there are occasions in which killing is the only choice: a necessary evil, surely, but justifiable because it may be the lesser evil in the given circumstances.

      The point of view of the radical pacifist is unreasonable. More lives might ultimately be saved, and greater happiness for a larger number of people might result if the innocent victims of aggression were to wage a victorious war upon the aggressor. This is essentially the same reasoning that I would apply to the situation in which, for example, a robber threatened my own life or that of a friend.

B.: I admit that all these are very unfortunate situations. My sincerest efforts would be devoted to prevent their very occurrence (by whatever suitable means: education, reform, arbitration, compromise, reconciliation, etc.). But once such a situation arises I still believe that one should not kill.

A.: How do you justify this position?

B.: How does one justify *any* moral judgment? Obviously by deriving it from the basic moral laws. Respect for the life, the rights, the happiness of others is surely such a basic norm, is it not?

A.: I shall be curious to find out how such basic moral laws are proved or established. But before we enter into this deep question, tell me how you defend such a rigid adherence to non-violence, even if you yourself may easily become the victim of aggression or war.

B.: I shall not invoke religious principles here. Perhaps I can convince you if I make you aware of the consequences of the pacifist attitude. Once practiced by many it would tend to spread by way of emulation and thus sooner or later eradicate the evil of killing altogether.

A.: This is an optimistic assertion concerning the probability of certain consequences. In any case it is a question of fact which is not easily decided. However, your disagreement with me seems to go beyond whatever we may think about the facts, namely the conditions and consequences of attitudes. True enough, in your last remark you have tried to establish a common basis of evaluation. You appealed to a humanitarian principle which I do share with you. Still, I think that to kill is morally better than to be enslaved. Since you disagree with me on this, it is obvious that we diverge in *some* of our basic norms. This divergence in attitude can apparently not be removed by considerations of fact.

B.: Are ethical principles then a matter of personal whim and caprice?

A.: I did not mean to imply this at all. As our own cases show, we tend to have very strong and serious convictions in these matters. Far from being chosen arbitrarily, our moral attitudes are a result of the culture and the subculture in which our personalities are formed.

B.: We are not necessarily conforming to the prevailing patterns. I for one, am certainly not. I arrived at my views by independent and serious reflection.

A.: I don't wish to dispute it. And yet your attitudes are a causal consequence of many factors: heredity, environment (physical, and especially social; the influence of parents, friends, teachers, attractive and abhorrent examples, crucial experiences, etc.) and, yes, your (more or less) intelligent reflection upon the facts as they impress *you-as-you are*.

B.: If you are right, there are limits beyond which rational (i.e., logical and/or factual) argument cannot be extended. Intelligent reflection concerning means and ends, conditions and consequences operates within the frame of basic evaluations. Beyond those limits there could be only conversion by persuasion (rhetoric, propaganda, suggestion, promises, threats, re-education, psycho-therapy, etc.). There are also techniques of settlement of disagreements by way of compromise, segregation (separation, divorce) or higher synthesis. By "higher synthesis" I mean, for example, the abandonment or severe restriction of the sovereignty of individual nations and a transfer of all sentiments of loyalty to a world government. Only if none of these techniques succeeds, the indeed coercion by violence, alas, seems inevitable.— (Universal pacificism is the only solution! But that's not my point at the moment.)

A.: You have expressed my point of view very well. But you are obviously unwilling to agree to it.

B.: Indeed not. Everything in me cries out for a belief in objectively and universally valid standards of moral evaluation.

A.: You will not get very far if you assume some theological or metaphysical absolutes. Any reference to the revealed commands of a divine authority is futile. For you would have to tell how you can know those imperatives as divine; and even if you were to know them as such you would have to state a reason as to why anybody should obey them. The same criticisms apply to any alleged metaphysical insight into what man ought to be. And if you dismiss theological and metaphysical foundations for morality you will find it difficult to argue for standards that are independent of human needs and interests.

B.: It's precisely human needs and interests that provide a solid foundation for moral standards. In all cultures that we call 'civilized' there are essentially the same ideals of cooperation (as opposed to conflict), of helpfulness (as opposed to harmfulness), of love (as opposed to hatred), of justice (as opposed to inequity), and of perfection and growth (as opposed to stagnation and decay). Cultural relativity and the variability of human nature have been exaggerated. There is a significant core of essential features shared by all human beings. Human nature as it is constituted biologically and psychologically, and as it finds its existence in a context of interdependence with other human beings, could scarcely fail to develop just those ideals of morality. I admit that these ideals are only rarely fulfilled or even approximated in actual conduct. But they are *the* standards of ethical evaluation. It is with reference to this frame that we make our judgments of "good" and "bad," "right" and "wrong."

A.: Much as I share your ideals, I can't refrain from calling your attention to the fact that there are notable exceptions that restrict severely not only the universality of certain types of conduct (this is what you admitted), but also the universality of the very standards or ideals of morality. To many an ancient or oriental culture the idea of perfection or progress remained completely strange. The prevailing ideologies of capitalism and nationalism basically extol the ideals of competition over those of cooperation. Only superficially and often hypocritically do they pay lip service to humanitarian or Christian ideals. And the very principle of justice (in the sense of equal rights for all) has been flouted not only by tyrants, aristocrats and fascists but also by such eminent philosophers as Plato and Nietzsche. Our own divergence on the issue of radical pacificism is equally a case in point. There are countless further, possibly secondary and yet radical divergencies as regards attitudes toward civil liberties, sex and marriage, birth control, euthanasia, the role of religion (church and state), animals (vegetarianism, vivisection), etc., etc.

B.: Disregarding the secondary divergencies, I must say that the deviations from the more fundamental and true moral ideals are simply perversions and corruptions. Whoever denies the principles of justice and neighborliness is immoral. Kant was essentially right and convincingly logical in defining moral conduct by his categorical imperative. Only a principle that is binding for all and excludes any sort of arbitrary privilege and partiality can justifiably be called ethical. The ideals that I enumerated are the very essence of what is meant by "morality." To be moral consists precisely in placing oneself in the service of interests and ideals that transcend purely selfish purposes.

A.: This is what *you* mean by "morality." (And, of course, it is in keeping with traditional morality). But Neitzsche, for example, explicitly proposed a revolution in all traditional morality. Clearly, he considered his own value-system as the "true ethics." Are you not aware that you are begging the very question at issue? You speak of "true moral ideals"; you call certain views "immoral," "perverse," "corrupt"; you say that only certain types of principles can "justifiably be called ethical." You are using persuasive definitions[1] here. You call "moral" or "ethical" only

[1]This useful phrase was coined by C.L. Stevenson. In his book *Ethics and Language* (Yale University Press, 1944), p. 210 he explains it as follows:

"In any 'persuasive definition' the term defined is a familiar one, whose meaning is both descriptive and strongly emotive. The purport of the definition is to alter the descriptive meaning of the term, usually by giving it greater precision within the boundaries of its customary vagueness; but the definition does *not* make any substantial change

such doctrines or principles as agree with your own convictions about what is *right*. The fascination with the *"logicality"* of Kant's categorical imperative may in part lie in its implicit appeal to some version of the principle of sufficient reason: If there is no reason to discriminate (as regards rights and obligations) between two persons then such discrimination is willful, arbitrary, unjust. But far from involving strictly logical contradictions such "unjustifiable" discriminatons would merely violate *one* (not as you would say *"the"*) definition of justice. A reason for discrimination could always be found. That it may not be accepted as a "good," "relevant" or "sufficient" reason is but a consequence of the ethical principles or fundamental evaluations of some alternative system. Let me assure you again that I share your moral attitudes. But strongly as I feel about them, I see no need for, and no profit in defending them with bad logic. You cannot by some verbal magic establish justifications for ideals which obviously are neither logically nor empirically unique. These ideals compete with genuine alternatives.

B.: I can't believe this. The ideals that I have listed are the ones that will benefit humanity in the long run. Not just a particular group, but all of mankind.

Moreover these ideals are comprised by the essence of *rationality*. Man, the rational animal, is by his very nature not only characterized by his capacity for adequate deductive and inductive thinking, but also by his sense of justice and his abhorrence of violence as a method for the settlement of disputes.

A.: You are still begging the question. Those who do not accept the principle of equality are not interested in *all* of mankind. Furthermore, your time-honored conception of human nature is clearly not an account of actual fact, but of an ideal (by no means universally shared) which you utilize for a persuasive definition of MAN. You won't convince any serious opponents by mere *definitions*. But you might try to entice, persuade, educate or reform them in other ways. You may also hope that the increasing interdependence of all of mankind on this planet will eventually generate a fundamental uniformity in the principles of moral evaluation.

B.: You underestimate the rôle of experience in the settlement of moral conflicts and disputes. Those who have had an opportunity to experience different ways of life soon learn to discriminate between the better and the worse. Experience in the context of needs and interests, of claims and counter-claims, of existing and emerging rights and obligations in the social milieu soon enough mould the moral conscience of man. We do not live in a vacuum. The constant encouragements and discouragements of our actions and their underlying attitudes form the

---

in the term's emotive meaning. And the definition is used, consciously or unconsciously, in an effort to secure, by this interplay between emotive and descriptive meaning, a redirection of people's attitudes."

very atmosphere of the life in the family, the workshop, the market place, the tribunal, etc. Add to that the basic sympathy human beings feel for each other and you will have to admit that there is a large mass of empirical factors that operate in the direction of a common standard of social morality.

A.: If I may use a parallel drawn from the field of aesthetics, there are a great many people who prefer pulp-magazine stories to "good" literature; or swing (jazz, jive or whatever is the fashion) to "great" music. Similarly, there are plenty of people who have had an opportunity to experience both the ruthless and the kindly way of life and yet subscribe to the principles of the former. Kropotkin rightly, though somewhat sentimentally, pointed out that despite the cruel struggle for existence in the animal kingdom there is also a good deal of mutual help and self-sacrifice. If human sympathy were as fundamntal as (he and) you claim it is, there could hardly be such views as those of Nietzsche, Hitler, and Mussolini on the "greatness" of war. Only by endorsing one norm against other possible alternatives can you avail yourself of the premises by which to validate the special moral precepts which are dear to your heart.

B.: You still have failed to give me a single good reason why I or you or anyone should adhere to even those moral principles which we happen to share. Your position is a skepticism that could easily lead to moral indifference and cynicism.

A.: And what sort of a reason do you expect me to give you? If I provided you with premises from which you could *deduce* our moral standards, you would ask me for a justification of those premises. And you surely don't want a reason in the sense of a motive. You are motivated already. You do not seriously entertain doubt as long as this motivation prevails. And nothing that I've said was intended to undermine it. The aim of my remarks was clarification; not education, fortification or edification. Too many philosophers have sold their birthright for a pot of message.

II. Analysis and Conclusions

The foregoing argument illustrates among other things the ever-present pitfalls of the *petitio principii* in the procedures of justification. If the radical pacifist is accused of an exaggerated value-fixation upon "reverence for life" he is free to retort that his opponent has a hypertrophied value fixation upon liberty or upon the survival of the greater number of persons. In order to condemn some value-fixations as inhumane,, immoral or perverse, it is necessary to invoke some ideals or standards of humaneness, morality or normality. It is only with reference to such ideals or standards that we can justify the *approval* of thrift, honesty, friendship, the devotion to science or art, etc., and the *disapproval* of avarice, hypocrisy, elligerence, sexual aberrations, etc. From a purely factual psychological or socio-psychological point of view *all* value-fixations may be explained in terms of some causal-genetical principles, such as Wundt's "Heterogony of Purposes," Allport's "Functional Autonomy," or some other laws of motivation as formulated in psychoanalytic or behavioristic theories.

Let us suppose that socio-historical and anthropological research could show that there are basic invariant moral ideals embodied in otherwise diverse cultures. Even then it cannot be denied that the rank-order of the normative force of these ideals has varied with time, clime, and cultural conditions. Wise moral philosophers along with the great dramatists and novelists of the ages have always known that moral problems in their most poignant and irresoluble form consist in the conflict of good with good or right with right. The understandable hope for the demonstration of one unique set of standards in terms of which an objective and universally binding adjudication of all moral issues could be achieved, may well turn out to be chimerical. Only if certain basic—and to many people all-too-obvious-valuational premises are taken for granted, can we obtain the semblance of objective deducibility of more special moral rules. If, for example, we take for granted that the life of the species *homo sapiens* is to be preserved, that conflict and violence is to be minimized, then a great number of special precepts are derivable from these premises taken together with special facts and laws concerning human conditions and behavior. The truth implied in the critique of the "naturalistic fallacy" reduces to the truism that factual statements alone cannot possibly entail normative conclusions. Some normative premises are indispensable.

If rational argument, criticism or justification is to be distinguished from persuasion by means of the emotional and motivational expressions and appeals of language, what are the forms of such reasoning and what are its criteria of validity?

The classical doctrine of self-evidence as a criterion of validity or truth still exerts its powerful influence. Brentano, Husserl and the phenomenologists; G. E. Moore, C. D. Broad, W. D. Ross, A. C. Ewing and other recent English intuitionists have revitalized this ancient (and Cartesian) tradition. There is scarcely any space here even to remind the reader that this philosophical point of view is open to the most serious objections. Its relevance to the truth of the axioms of geometry have become suspect since the developments of the non-euclidean geometries and their application in modern physics and astronomy. More fundamentally, the recent developments in the philosophical foundations of logic and mathematics have shown that self-evidence is neither a necessary nor a sufficient condition for truth or validity. The better intentions of the intuitionists to the contrary notwithstanding, the doctrine of self-evidence is at fault precisely because it is psychologistic. The accent of self-evidence is a result of habituation. Basic principles or presuppositions which delimit a certain universe of discourse or specify a certain field of validating procedures acquire the appearance of absolute cogency and uniqueness, because they form the indispensable (and hence within this context unquestioned) *conditiones sine qua non* of the very enterprise which they make possible and for which they legislate. Finally, intuitive self-evidence cannot possibly be claimed to yield absolutely unique or indubitable knowledge. Notoriously and especially in regard to moral judgments (not to mention aesthetic evaluations) there is no unanimity on just *which* principles are self-evident. It requires some arrogance to claim one's own intuitions infallible, and the disagreeing intuitions of others as in need of revision (by "deeper reflection," "re-education," "enlightenment," etc.).

At this point one of the most crucial questions in all philosophy arises: Are the justifying principles of knowledge, i.e. the principles of deductive and inductive logic, as undemonstrable and as much lacking uniqueness as are the norms of moral judgments? If intuitive cogency is to be abandoned as a criterion of truth, are we not faced with an analogous plurality or relativity in regard to basic presuppositions in the field of cognition?

Only a few suggestions can here be made as regards these burdensome scruples.[2] Firstly, the validity of deductive or inductive inference is presupposed in ethical argument. But no distinctly ethical norms are required for the validation of knowledge-claims. Reasoning in matters of morality utilizes, as any reasoning must, principles of deductive inference when special cases are subsumed under general (in this case, moral) rules. And in any practical issue of moral choice, inductive inference is indispensable for the determination of the most likely consequences of actions. There is no question then, that in the context of validation, the principles of cognition are more fundamental than the norms of morality. I this sense we may safely claim the "primacy of *pure* reason." Secondly, despite the fashionable notions about "alternative logics" it can be shown that at least the rules of deductive inference possess a uniqueness which, even if not present in the same degree, is also characteristic of the rules of inductive inference.

In order to grasp this situation clearly, a fundamental distinction, often badly neglected or blurred beyond recognition, must now be drawn: When we speak of "justification" we may have reference to the legitimizing of a knowledge-claim; or else we may have in mind the justification of an action. The first case may be called *"justificatio cognitionis"* (validation) the second, *"justificatio actionis"* (vindication). The rules of deductive and inductive inference serve as the justifying principles in validation; purposes together with (inductively confirmed or at least confirmable) empirical knowledge concerning means-ends relations, or in the extreme, degenerate case with purely logical truths, serve as the basis of vindication (pragmatic justification). Only ends can justify means, even if in accordance with the well known slogan it will be admitted that a given end may not justify the utilization of every means for its attainment.

The word "reason" displays ambiguities similar to the word "justi-

---

[2]For a fuller discussion, cf. "De Principiis non disputandum . . . ? ," included in *Philosophical Analysis,* edited by Max Black, Cornell University Press, Ithica, N.Y., 1950.

fication." Besides naming a capacity of the human mind (part of which is the ability to state reasons) it is used in referring to causes and purposes, as well as to grounds of validation. Aristotle, Schopenhauer, and many thinkers between and after, have struggled to disentangle these and other meanings of "reason." Kant's distinction between the questions "*quid facti*" and "*quid juris*" has shed a flood of light on the basic issues of philosophy and has since become indispensable for the analysis of the problems of epistemology and ethical theory.

The justifying principles (*justificantia*) for the establishment of knowledge-claims have been retraced to their ultimate foundations in the rules of inference and substitution in deductive logic. We cannot without vicious circularity disclose any more ultimate grounds of validation here. Similarly the rules of maximal probability in inductive inference form the ultimate validating basis of all empirical reasoning. Correspondingly the supreme norms of a given ethical system provide the ultimate ground for the validation of moral judgments. No matter how long or short the chain of validating inferences, the final court of appeal will consist in one or the other type of justifying principles. Rational argument presupposes reference to a set of such principles at least implicitly agreed upon. Disagreement with respect to basic principles can thus only be removed if the very frame of validation is changed.[3] This can occur either through the disclosure and explication of a hitherto unrecognized common set of standards, i.e., still more fundamental validating principles to which implicit appeal is made in argument, or it can be achieved through the pragmatic justification of the adoption of an alternative frame, or finally, through sheer persuasion by means of emotive appeals.

Validation terminates with the exhibition of the norms that govern the realm of argument concerned. If any further question can be raised at all, it must be the question concerning the pragmatic justification (vindication) of the (act of) adoption of the validating principles. But this is a question of an entirely different kind. The answers we can give to this sort of question are apt to appear trivial, but for the sake of philosophical clarification they are nevertheless indispensable and illuminating. If the logical reconstruction of justification is pursued as here suggested, then even an obvious, not to say utterly trivial, vindication will at least make fully clear which aims are attained by means of the adoption of some specified validating principles. Thus it is quite plain that the adoption of the rules of deductive inference is pragmatically justifiable in that only reasoning which accords with them can insure the transition from true propositions to other true propositions. No vicious circularity is involved here. We are not attempting the (impossible) validation of ultimate validating principles. We can afford, and could not possibly refrain from, using

---

[3]For an extremely important and clarifying discussion of the distinction between questions within a presupposed frame and questions concerning the frame itself (in connection with closely related issues) cf. R. Carnap: "Empiricism, Semantics and Ontology," *Revue Internationale de Philosophie* 11, Jan. 1950.

logic in a vindicating argument, precisely because we are here concerned with arguments about means-ends relations. There is a similar vindication, formulated by H. Reichenbach[4] for the adoption of the principle of induction. The reasoning in both cases is purely deductive because of the extreme (degenerate) nature of the question at issue. In regard to induction the following holds: If there is an order of nature at all (and we don't know that there is and we don't know that there isn't—beyond the scope of actual observations) then the method of simplest generalization is the only method of which it can be demonstrated (deductively) that (1) it *can* (but of course need not) succeed in disclosing that order and (2) that it is self-corrective. This obvious, simple tautology provides a pragmatic justification of the adoption of the rule of induction for anyone who wishes to attain the two mentioned aims, namely to make true inductive inferences (e.g., predictions) and to be able to keep such inferences adaptable to the accumulating evidence.

It may be charged that our analysis is outrageously artificial; that we never have occasion to "choose" a basis of validation; that in real-life-situations we find validating and vindicating arguments so intimately fused, that their separation distorts severely the dialectics of both cognitive and valuative arguments. My reply is, firstly, that all logical analysis from Aristotle through Descartes down to our time necessarily consists of an artificial and schematic reconstruction[5] and its illuminating character depends precisely upon the disentanglement of factors or aspects which, though admittedly *fused* in ordinary argument are in danger of being *confused* in philosophical reflection. Secondly, I would say that those who make the charge under discussion, characteristically resolve the problems of justification simply by a *fiat* of definition. Induction, for example, is said to need no justification because the rule of induction defines (at least in part) *what we mean by "justifiable inference."* Similarly, as we have remarked already, such moral principles as those of justice or benevolence may be claimed to constitute (at least in part) *what we mean* by a *"(rational) morality."* If this sort of analysis results in a clear explication of the legislative principles of a given domain of validation, I should gladly admit that it is a helpful step in the clarification of philosophical perplexities. But it should be equally clear that this procedure is apt to rest its case simply with a persuasive definition of certain key-terms such as "rational," "valid," "probable," "morally right," etc. Once aware of the persuasive character of these definitions one should wish, in all candor, to state why one finds them persuasive. And the answer to this question must clearly refer to one's interests, purposes or ideals. Thus, while vindication can never prove

[4]*Experience and Prediction*, University of Chicago Press, 1938; §§ 38, 39; also: "On the Justification of Induction." *Journal of Phil.* 37, 1940, reprinted in Feigl and Sellars, *Readings in Philosophical Analysis*, Appleton-Century-Crofts, N.Y., 1949; and *The Theory of Probability*, University of California Press, 1949.

[5]See my article "Logical Reconstruction, Realism and Pure Semiotic," *Philosophy of Science*, 17, 1950, pp. 186-195.

(validate) any principles of validation, it can clarify their role in the context of human thought and action.

The validating principles of deductive and inductive logic do not seem at all to have any plausible alternatives or competitors. This is so, very likely because in this age of science our conception of the criteria of valid and reliable knowledge have already been so sharply focussed and so severely purged of pre-scientific (non-scientific and unscientific) elements. The purposes of the cognitive enterprise are today so clearly delimited that its basic criteria (but of course not its special methods and techniques) have attained practically universal consent.

It is only too tempting to hope for a similarly universal code of morals. But in view not only of the stark realities of group and culture-centered ethical standards, but also because of the ever present quandaries regarding the priority between the several supreme standards ("prima facie obligation," i.e., the validating principles of moral judgments) within a given group or culture we can scarcely expect a universal unanimity of purposes which would vindicate a set of unique standards and a rigid order of priority among them for any and all questions of moral decision. At this point, I must concede, that the relativism implicit in the emotivist analyses (of Stevenson, for example) may prove insuperable. But beyond this important concession I would stress that the emotivist assimilation of moral issues to questions of personal taste and preference does not even begin to do justice to the nature of argument and justification in the moral realm of discourse. There is a great deal of validation in ethical arguments which is only too easily lost sight of, if attention is primarily fixed upon persuasion or vindication.

In analogy to the analysis of justification in the cognitive domain I suggest that moral judgments are to be reconstructed as knowledge-claims and as subject to validation (or invalidation) by virtue of their accordance (or non-accordance) with the supreme norms of a given ethical system. In order to carry out this reconstruction, judgments of right and wrong, and likewise statements of obligation and of rights, must be construed as empirical propositions. This is possible only after these typically normative terms (and other relatives and derivatives "good," "evil," "desirable," "condemnable," etc.) have been given a factual reference in addition to their positive or negative emotive appeals. This means that we make, in this context deliberately a legitimate device of what in other contexts must indeed be repudiated as the "naturalistic fallacy."[6] This amounts to construing moral norms in the logical form of general laws. But in contradistinction to the general laws of the empirical sciences the moral laws are not

---

[6]This fallacy was most infelicitously labeled by G.E. Moore. As I view the matter, Moore's criticism should have been directed against the confusion of motivative appeals with factual meaning; or more closely in keeping with Moore's intentions, against the confusion of the phenomenological "oughtness" (its relatives and opposites) with the empirical characteristics of conduct with which these intuitively given (and indeed phenomenologically unanalyzable) qualities of moral awareness are associated.

subject to confirmation or disconfirmation by empirical evidence—at least and certainly not in the same sense. Their logical character is rather that of basic definitions or conventions for the use of normative terms with reference to empirical aspects of conduct, intentions, attitudes, personality traits and social objectives. In regard to the factual content as well as in their critical function, normative moral terms are quite similar to such terms of medicine as "healthy," "diseased," "normal," abnormal," "well-functioning," "mal-functioning," etc. Just as in questions regarding normality or abnormality in medicine we require a factual content (in addition to the emotive appeals) of these terms, in ethics. We need likewise factual reference in order to break through the circle of formal tautologies (such as "the good is that which it is right to accomplish") and to attach these formal-and-emotive terms to empirical aspects of the facts of individual and social life.

Only with a reconstruction of this sort can we escape the sterility of formalism in ethics. If we wish to know for example whether killing in self-defense is morally right, we cannot get an answer unless definite and empirically specified moral rules (including priority-rules as between standards) are provided as *justificantia cognitionis* of the *correctness* of the moral judgment at issue. Obviously the same considerations apply to questions of distributive and retributive justice, to the evaluation of the various virtues, of measures of social, legal, political reform, etc.

It is a simple consequence of the proposed analysis and reconstruction that it is futile to criticize one system of norms in terms of another which is logically incompatible with it. Validation of moral judgments always requires a set of given norms to which we must hold fast, at least temporarily, in order to examine the validity of more special moral judgments. As in the case of the justification of cognition, so here in the domain of ethics, the only further step concerns vindication. The purposes which may be adduced in vindicating arguments for a whole system of moral norms are embodied in the individual interests and social ideals which we have come to form in response to life experience. The principle of justice (the golden rule) or other implicit definitions of "right actions" may, for example, be vindicated by reference to the ideal of a peaceful, harmonious and coöperative society. Or the principle of benevolence may be vindicated by reference to the ideal of the greatest happiness of the greatest number. We see then that the perennial dispute between deontological and teleological theories in ethics may perhaps be settled by the recognition that the former are concerned with validation, the latter with vindication.

The present approach differs from both the intuitionistic and the emotivist point of view (and is in more than one way closer to the Kantian) in that the great variety of self-evident prima facie obligations countenanced by the intuitionists and the corresponding equally great variety of interest-fixations allowed for by the emotivists are supplanted by a relatively small number of basic norms and priority rules. Naturally, the task of demonstrating that this is an adequate and feasible reconstruction is enormous and has here been barely suggested. In contradistinction to the Kantian metaphysics of morals a plurality of alternative ethical systems is here envisaged as a matter of historical and contemporary fact. As long as there are changing and divergent terminal purposes and ideals there will be different systems of moral validation. The moral approval of a given ideal is of course trivially validated by the system which that ideal vindicates; and, contrariwise, trivially invalidated by an alternative incompatible system.—But enough has been said about the dangers of the petitio principii.

One final question: Does the pluralism and relativism implied in the preceding remarks rule out *objectivity* in ethics? As may be expected by now, the answer depends upon the precise meaning which one is going to connect with the term "objectivity."

The objectivity of the truths of arithmetic lies in their logical necessity. Anyone who understands the postulates and definitions of arithmetic and complies with the rules of deductive logic will concede the universal validity of arithmetical truth. The objectivity of propositions of factual knowledge means something different: the intersensual and intersubjective confirmation of knowledge-claims,—and everything that these phrases imply, especially the principles of confirmation. "Objectivity" in the moral domain may mean a variety of aspects: (1) The logical necessity inherent in validation. (2) The logical consistency of the norms of one system. (3) The factual objectivity of the characterization of the empirical features of attitudes, conduct, etc. which are the subject of moral appraisal. (4) The factual objectivity of statements regarding conditions-consequences and means-ends relations. (5) The factual objectivity of statements concerning human needs, interests and ideals as they arise in the social context. (6) The conformity of the norms with the basic bio-psycho-social nature of man, especially as regards the preservation of existence, the satisfaction of needs, and the facts of growth, development and evolution.[7] (7) The degree of universality with which certain moral norms are actually or potentially embodied in the conscience of man within given cultural groups or perhaps even in cultural groups of all times and climes. (8) The equality of all individual persons before the moral laws—as conceived in the universal applicability of these laws.

Crucial questions arise only in regard to the factual truth of the seventh point and the significance of the eighth. The actuality of universally common standards, as we have pointed out, is problematic. Only at the price of a precarious attenuation of meaning, if not of the risk of tautological vacuity, could one defend this claim. As to the potential convergence towards common standards we may allow for a cautious optimism. Finally, and perhaps most critically, there remains the question whether we shall mean by an "ethical norm" one which embodies a thorough-going impartiality. If so, then we have by definitional fiat implied the essence of the

[7]This elementary but important point stressed in naturalistic ethics from Aristotle down to the philosophizing biologists of our time, is apt to be neglected by purely analytical philosophers.

principle of justice the very conception of "moral law." But when we speak of the "ethics" of feudalism, or even of the "ethics" of Nazism, along with the "ethics" of christianity, or the "ethics" of democracy, we obviously utilize a different definition covering much more ground. Of course, we are free to declare that "fascist ethics" is a contradiction in terms; i.e. we may decide that a code of norms for the appraisal of conduct is to be called "ethics" only if it embodies at least the principles of benevolence and impartiality. But must we then not conclude that the word "ethics" itself is subject to persuasive definition?

Suggested Readings

Baier, K., *The Moral Point of View,* Cornell University Press, Ithaca, 1958.

Schlick, M., *Problems of Ethics,* tr. D. Rynin, Prentice-Hall, New York, 1939.

Stevenson, C. L., "The Emotive Meaning of Ethical Terms," *Mind,* XLVI, 1937.

Stevenson, C. L., "The Emotive Conception of Ethics and Its Cognitive Implications," *Philosophical Review,* LIX, 1950.

Toulmin, Stephen E., *An Examination of the Place of Reason in Ethics,* Cambridge University Press, New York, 1950.

LIBRARY OF DAVIDSON COLLEGE

on regular loan may be checked out for **two weeks.** Books
rculation Desk in order to be renewed.

regulations at the discretion of